The Internationalization of Government Procurement Regulation

AF889106

The Internationalization of Government Procurement Regulation

Edited by
Aris Georgopoulos
Bernard Hoekman
Petros C. Mavroidis

OXFORD
UNIVERSITY PRESS

OXFORD
UNIVERSITY PRESS

Great Clarendon Street, Oxford, OX2 6DP,
United Kingdom

Oxford University Press is a department of the University of Oxford.
It furthers the University's objective of excellence in research, scholarship,
and education by publishing worldwide. Oxford is a registered trade mark of
Oxford University Press in the UK and in certain other countries

© the various contributors 2017

The moral rights of the authors have been asserted

First Edition published in 2017

Impression: 1

All rights reserved. No part of this publication may be reproduced, stored in
a retrieval system, or transmitted, in any form or by any means, without the
prior permission in writing of Oxford University Press, or as expressly permitted
by law, by licence or under terms agreed with the appropriate reprographics
rights organization. Enquiries concerning reproduction outside the scope of the
above should be sent to the Rights Department, Oxford University Press, at the
address above

You must not circulate this work in any other form
and you must impose this same condition on any acquirer

Published in the United States of America by Oxford University Press
198 Madison Avenue, New York, NY 10016, United States of America

British Library Cataloguing in Publication Data
Data available

Library of Congress Control Number: 2016946044

ISBN 978–0–19–879674–9 (hbk.)
ISBN 978–0–19–879675–6 (pbk.)

Printed in Great Britain by
Clays Ltd, St Ives plc

Links to third party websites are provided by Oxford in good faith and
for information only. Oxford disclaims any responsibility for the materials
contained in any third party website referenced in this work.

TABLE OF CONTENTS

LIST OF FIGURES

LIST OF TABLES

LIST OF BOXES

LIST OF CONTRIBUTORS

Servet Alyanak is a judge seconded to the Turkish Ombudsman Institution, in Ankara, Turkey, He was previously affiliated to the Turkish Public Procurement Authority.

Robert D. Anderson is Counsellor and Team Leader for Government Procurement and Competition Policy in the Intellectual Property, Government Procurement and Competition Policy Division (IPD) of the World Trade Organization (WTO) Secretariat. He is a member of the World Bank's International Advisory Group on Procurement, an Honorary Professor, School of Law, University of Nottingham; and Part-time Faculty Member, World Trade Institute, University of Bern. Prior to joining the WTO in 1997, he held positions in the Canadian Competition Bureau, the Department of Finance of the Canadian Province of Saskatchewan and the Economic Council of Canada.

Malcolm Bosworth is Visiting Senior Research Fellow at the Asia Pacific School of Economics & Government, Australian National University in Canberra. A trade economist and world trade specialist, he has worked at the Productivity Commission (and its predecessors) for over twenty years as an economist and policy adviser to the Australian government on trade and industry policy. He has had a long association with the WTO, having worked for six years in the GATT Secretariat in Geneva. He is a frequent consultant for the WTO, World Bank, Asian Development Bank and the ASEAN and APEC secretariats.

Carlo Maria Cantore is an associate in the Brussels office of van Bael & Bellis. Prior to joining the firm he worked as a trainee at the Legal Service of the European Commission (Trade Policy and WTO) and interned at the Trade in Services Division of the WTO. He holds a PhD in International Trade Law from the European University Institute of Florence.

Lucian Cernat is the Chief Trade Economist of the European Commission. Until 2008, he held various positions at the United Nations in Geneva dealing with trade and development issues. He has authored numerous publications on the development impact of trade policies, WTO negotiations, EU preferential market access, regional trade agreements, competition policy, and corporate governance. Prior to his UN experience, he was a trade diplomat with the Romanian Ministry of Foreign Affairs, and part of the team negotiating bilateral trade agreements with the EuroMed area and Baltic countries, prior to Romania's accession to the EU. He obtained a PhD from University of Manchester and has a postgraduate diploma from Oxford University.

Arwel Davies is Associate Professor at the School of Law of the University of Swansea. His PhD on international public procurement regulation was completed at the University of Nottingham. His research interests are in the area of international economic law and he is a co-author of *World Trade Law: Text Materials and Commentary.*

Kamala Dawar is an international trade and competition law specialist at the University of Sussex. She conducts research, policy analysis and training for academic, inter-governmental and non-governmental organizations, including the WTO, World Bank, the European Commission, and public interest organizations. She has published articles on issues including WTO law and governance, public procurement, competition and consumer policy, preferential trading arrangements, and development issues.

Memory Dube is a senior trade officer at the African Development Bank. Before joining the bank she was a senior researcher in the Economic Diplomacy Programme at the South African Institute for International Affairs. Her areas of research interest include trade policy reform, WTO policy, regional economic integration, as well as trade and sustainable development. She holds an LLB (cum laude) from the University of Fort Hare, an LLM from Rhodes University and an LLM (cum laude) in International Trade and Investment Law from the University of Pretoria.

Zhou Fen is a PhD candidate, Central University of Finance and Economics, Beijing, China and the University of Turin (Italy) and a research assistant at China Institute for Public Procurement studies, Central University of Finance and Economics, China.

Cao Fuguo is Professor of Law at the Law School and Director, China Institute for Public Procurement Studies, of the Central University of Finance and Economics (CUFE), Beijing, China. He also directs the International Research Centre for Law and Economics and the China Procurement Research Group. Professor Cao is expert group member and a Chinese delegate to the working group on revision of the UNCITRAL Model Law on Public Procurement and also advises the World Bank on Chinese procurement law reforms. He was a Fulbright Scholar at George Washington University Law School in 2012–13.

Aris Georgopoulos is Assistant Professor in European and Public Law at the School of Law of the University of Nottingham and Head of the Research Unit for Strategic and Defence Procurement of the Public Procurement Research Group. He has been Research Fellow in the *Global Economics* research area of the Global Governance Programme, EUI and a Grotius Fellow at the Law School of the University of Michigan. He has taught at Universities in the United States, China, Turkey, Malaysia and Colombia, and is a member of the editorial board of the Public Procurement Law Review. He holds a PhD from the University of Nottingham Law School.

Bernard Hoekman is Professor in the Robert Schuman Centre for Advanced Studies at the European University Institute in Florence, Italy. He has held various senior positions at the World Bank, including Director of the International Trade Department and Research Manager in the Development Research Group, and worked as an economist in the GATT Secretariat. He obtained his PhD in economics from the University of Michigan and is a Research Fellow of the Centre for Economic Policy Research and a Senior Associate of the Cairo-based Economic Research Forum for the Arab Countries, Turkey, and Iran.

Gary Hufbauer is Reginald Jones Senior Fellow at the Peterson Institute for International Economics in Washington DC. He was formerly the Maurice Greenberg Chair and Director of Studies at the Council on Foreign Relations (1996–8), the Marcus Wallenberg Professor of

International Finance Diplomacy at Georgetown University (1985–92), deputy director of the International Law Institute at Georgetown University (1979–81), deputy assistant secretary for international trade and investment policy of the US Treasury (1977–9), and director of the international tax staff at the Treasury (1974–6). He has written extensively on international trade, investment, and tax issues.

Liezemarie Johannes is the Head of Research at Corruption Watch, South Africa.

Zornitsa Kutlina-Dimitrova is an economist in the Chief Economist and Trade Analysis Unit of DG Trade of the European Commission.

Paul M. Lalonde is Partner at Dentons Canada LLP's Toronto office. He focuses on government contracting law, international trade, anti-corruption, and international arbitration. He is one of Canada's pre-eminent lawyers in the procurement law field. Since 2010, he has been an advisor for the Government Procurement Agreement (GPA) project of the Taiwan External Trade Development Council and serves as a guest professor in international trade law at the University of Ottawa. He has held numerous leadership positions in the Bar, including as Co-chair of the International Bar Association North American Forum and Chair of the International Procurement Committee of the American Bar Association International Law Section and serves as Chair of the Legal Committee of Transparency International—Canada.

David Lewis is Executive Director, Corruption Watch, South Africa. He chaired the South African Competition Tribunal for a decade from its founding in 1999. Between 1975 and 1990 he worked in the trade union movement, serving as general secretary of the General Workers Union and national organizer of the Transport and General Workers Union, after which he directed University of Capetown's Development Policy Research Unit. He is a founder member of the International Competition Network, serving in its Steering Group from 2001 to 2008 and he was its chairman in 2008–9. Lewis was deputy chairman of the Industrial Development Corporation's board from 2002 to 2008, was appointed an extraordinary professor at the Gordon Institute of Business Science in 2009 and awarded an honorary doctorate in economics by UCT in 2010.

Petros C. Mavroidis is Edwin B. Parker Professor of Law at Columbia Law School, New York and also teaches at the University of Neuchatel, Switzerland. During 2011–16 he was on leave at the European University Institute. He was the American Law Institute chief reporter for the project on "Principles of International Trade Law: the WTO" that was completed in 2012 and holds a Dr iuris from the University of Heidelberg. His most recent publication is *The Regulation of International Trade*.

Patrick Messerlin is Chairman of the Steering Committee and Advisory Board of the European Centre for International Political Economy, Brussels, Professor emeritus of economics at Sciences Po Paris, and Director of Groupe d'Economie Mondiale (GEM) at Sciences Po since its creation in 1997. He has served as a special advisor to Mike Moore, the WTO Director General (2001–2), Co-chair (with Ernesto Zedillo) of the UN Millennium Development Goals Task Force on "Trade for Development," and has been a member of the World Economic Forum's Global Trade Council, which he chaired in 2010–11.

Tyler Moran is a research analyst at the Peterson Institute for International Economics.

Anna Caroline Müller is a Legal Affairs Officer in the Intellectual Property, Government Procurement and Competition Policy Division (IPD) of the WTO Secretariat, Geneva.

Caroline Nicholas is a lawyer with the International Trade Law Division of the United Nations Office of Legal Affairs (the Secretariat of the United Nations Commission on International Trade Law (UNCITRAL). She serves as the Secretary to the UNCITRAL Working Group on Procurement and is a member of the Editorial Board of the Public Procurement Law Review. Prior to joining UNCITRAL she advised on claims of the Kuwaiti Government arising from Iraq's 1990 invasion and occupation of Kuwait at the United Nations Compensation Commission, worked as an internal fraud investigator in the United Nations, and practiced in the private sector in the City of London and in Hong Kong, specializing in banking and insolvency litigation.

Eliza Niewiadomska is a counsel in charge of the public procurement sector at the Legal Transition Programme of the European Bank for Reconstruction and Development in London. She received her Master's in Law from Warsaw University, before obtaining a MSc. in Project and Enterprise Management at University College London. She has worked as a general counsel for public and private sector entities and a director of procurement and infrastructure projects in the utilities sector in Poland, was in charge of the legal teams of the Public Procurement Office of Poland and ComputerLand SA, a leading ICT company in Poland, and worked for PGE Polska Grupa Energetyczna SA in Warsaw.

Philippe Pelletier is a Legal Affairs Officer in the Intellectual Property, Government Procurement and Competition Policy Division (IPD) of the WTO Secretariat, Geneva.

Cesar Pereira is Partner at Justen, Pereira, Oliveira and Talamini Law firm. He practices in public procurement, infrastructure projects, commercial law, regulated industries, and arbitration. He was a Professor of Administrative Law at UniCuritiba, Brazil between 2002 and 2006. He is a Fellow of the Chartered Institute of Arbitrators (FCIArb) and President of CAM-FIEP, an arbitration center in Curitiba, Brazil. He has published widely on public procurement and arbitration.

Eduardo Pérez Motta is Partner, Agon. Economics, Law & Strategy, in Mexico City. He was President of the Federal Competition Commission from 2004 to 2013. In 2012 he served as the President of the International Competition Network. Between 2001 and 2004, he was Mexico's Ambassador to the WTO. Other former positions include head of the team that negotiated the free trade agreement between Mexico and the European Union; chief of staff to the Minister of Trade and Industry; Director General of Industrial Policy; and chief of staff of the Vice Minister for Revenue at the Finance Ministry. He holds a BS in economics from the Insituto Tecnológico Autónomo de México and has undertaken doctoral studies at UCLA. He is a member of the editorial board of Competition Policy International and the American Antitrust Institute's advisory board.

Arie Reich is Jean Monnet Professor of EU Law & Institutions at Bar Ilan University, Israel, where he has served as a former Dean of the Faculty of Law. He earned his Master and Doctorate in Law from the University of Toronto, and specializes in International Economic Law and EU Law. Until his appointment as Dean of the Faculty in 2008, he served as the President of the

Israeli Association for the Study of European Integration. He is a member of the Executive of the International Academy of Commercial and Consumer Law and is a National Correspondent for Israel to the UN Commission on International Trade Law (UNCITRAL). He has served as the Chairman of Israel's Anti-Dumping and Countervailing Duty Tribunal and been a Member of a three WTO dispute settlement panels.

Rafael Wallbach Schwind is an associate at the Justen, Pereira, Oliveira & Talamini Law firm in Brazil. He holds a Bachelor's degree from the Federal University of Parana, a Master's degree (LLM) from the University of Sao Paulo, and a doctorate (PhD) from the same University.

Anirudh Shingal is a Jean Monnet Fellow at the European University Institute. He has served as a Senior Research Fellow at the World Trade Institute in Bern, is a cluster-leader of a Swiss National Science Foundation funded work programme on trade impact assessments, and a faculty member of the Masters in International Law & Economics (MILE) program. He has a PhD in Economics from the University of Sussex. He is affiliated with the Centre for the Analysis of Regional Integration at Sussex (CARIS) and has worked with the World Bank and WTO.

Astghik Solomonyan is a graduate of Yerevan State University's Faculty of Law and studied for her LLM degree in International Economic and Business Law at the University of Groningen. She has worked for the OECD's Sigma project as a consultant, as a private sector lawyer, and as a contracts assistant for the World Vision International Beneficent Organization. She is currently the local legal expert on an EBRD procurement project in Armenia project while simultaneously studying for her PhD at the University of Zurich.

Bedri Kamil Onur Taş is Associate Professor of Economics at the Faculty of Economics and Administrative Sciences of Tobb University.

Sübidey Togan is a Professor of Economics at Bilkent University, Ankara and a Research Fellow with the Cairo-based Economic Research Forum for the Arab Countries, Turkey, and Iran. He received his PhD in Economics from the Johns Hopkins University in Baltimore. Prior to joining Bilkent University he taught at Texas A&M University, Clarkson University, and Middle East Technical University. He has published widely on Turkey's foreign trade regime, the Turkish economy, and on matters related to Turkish accession to the EU.

Paulina Valladares is a Consultant at Agon, Economics, Law and Strategy, Mexico City. Before joining Agon she was a Regional and International Affairs officer at the Mexican Competition Authority.

Christopher R. Yukins is a Professor at George Washington University Law School in Washington DC. He was for several years an attorney with the US Department of Justice, where he handled trials and appeals involving bid protests and contract claims against the US Government. He is also of counsel to the firm of Arnold & Porter LLP, serves on the steering committee to the International Procurement Committee of the American Bar Association International Law Section, and is an advisor to the US delegation to the working group on reform of the UNCITRAL Model Procurement Law.

Introduction and Overview

Aris Georgopoulos, Bernard Hoekman, and Petros C. Mavroidis

0.1 The Aims of the Book

The regulation of government procurement is anything but a new phenomenon. Regulation of the process governing the purchase of goods and services by state bodies using public funds has been linked since time immemorial with the idea of accountability in public office, and more generally with the notion of "good governance."[1] Although the regulation of government procurement within the legal order of a specific polity has a long history, at least in some parts of the world, regulation in this area of economic activity at the international level is a much more recent phenomenon. Early efforts to agree to international disciplines on government procurement practices only date back to the late 1960s and early 1970s, with the first generation of EU Directives and the first incarnation of the Agreement on Government Procurement (GPA), negotiated under the auspices of the General Agreement on Tariffs and Trade (GATT) during the Tokyo Round (1973–9). The Tokyo Round GPA was a "code," that is, an agreement where participation was optional, and de facto limited to members of the Organisation for Economic Co-operation and Development (OECD) (Hoekman and Mavroidis, 1997).

The GPA has since been renegotiated twice. During the Uruguay Round, it became a so-called Plurilateral Agreement, denoting that, as in the Tokyo Round code regime, participation was optional. In fact, the Uruguay Round GPA was one of the very few exceptions to the decision to multilateralize the various Tokyo Round codes during the negotiations between 1986 and 1994 that led to the establishment of the World Trade Organization (WTO). The so-called "Revised GPA" is the new GPA that is currently in place, the product of successful renegotiation of the Uruguay Round agreement during the Doha Round.

The WTO GPA is not the only agreement on procurement at the international level. Important parallel efforts include the work by the United Nations Commission on

[1] For example, the marble stele for the *Arsenal of Philo* in Piraeus (fourth century BC) contains detailed specifications (*syngraphai*) that were to be followed (von Hesberg, 2015: 140 ff.; Coulton, 1994: 80–2). In more modern times, the origins of the French *Code des marchés publics* can be traced back to Article 12 of the *Loi des Finances* of January 31, 1833 (De Cormenin, 1840: 420 ff.).

International Trade Law (UNCITRAL) to draft a Model Law on Procurement of Goods, Construction and Services, and the adoption of regulatory disciplines for procurement in regional trade arrangements (RTAs).[2] The latter have proliferated in recent times, resulting in a growing constellation of trade agreements that include chapters on government procurement.

What drives international negotiations? A major driver for international efforts to agree to rules of the road for procurement processes is that governments are major buyers of goods and services. In 2015 US government spending amounted to some US$6.5 trillion, while EU governments spent €6.7 trillion. In both cases, as is true for other countries, much of this expenditure is on social protection and other transfers, but a significant share is directed towards purchases of goods and services (OECD, 2015: 136).

The dynamic international regulatory landscape pertaining to this important area of economic policy is the subject of this book. An overarching aim of the volume is to examine whether the mix of plurilateral, bilateral, regional, and other forms of international cooperation is moving in a common direction, is coherent in the sense of pursuing equivalent objectives and approaches, and is leading to similar outcomes. Of specific interest is whether and to what extent international norms on public procurement have influenced government purchasing processes at the national level. To be able to answer this question, the book includes a number of country case studies. The selection of countries includes both advanced, high-income economies and a number of emerging economies. Some of these are members of the WTO GPA, others are not. The goal was to identify common elements and trends as regards what is considered to be good regulatory practice as embodied in international instruments, not to provide an exhaustive comparative analysis of national procurement systems and practices. The country cases span:

a. several high-income, advanced economies that are parties to plurilateral, regional, and/or bilateral instruments (Australia,[3] Canada, the EU, Israel,[4] New Zealand, and the USA);
b. a number of large developing countries that have significant domestic procurement markets as well as export industries that can bid on foreign procurement opportunities (Brazil, China, India, Mexico, Turkey, and South Africa); and

[2] For example, chapter 10 of the North American Free Trade Agreement (NAFTA) and the EU "third generation" Public Procurement Directives (see Chapter 5, this book).

[3] As discussed by Malcolm Bosworth in Chapter 17, Australia has concluded several PTAs that include procurement but only launched a bid to join the GPA on June 3, 2015.

[4] Israel is considered a developed country here, although under the UN Development Policy and Analysis Division (DESA) country classification it is still developing (United Nations, 2016: 160). Israel has been a signatory of the GPA from the very beginning, starting with the Tokyo Round procurement code.

c. one small economy in transition that is unique to date in having joined the GPA (Armenia).[5]

A key difference between the countries in the first two groups is that the first are all signatories to the GPA, whereas the second are not. Several of the developing economies in the second group have been discussing accession to the GPA, but to date none has done so. There is strong interest among incumbents to expand membership to include more developing countries, especially those with large markets, but most WTO members have preferred to stay out of the GPA. Among the questions that motivate this volume are why membership of the GPA remains limited. One hypothesis is that national procurement regimes and associated processes differ too much from what is required under the GPA; another is that preferential trade agreements (PTAs) are preferred substitutes for the GPA; a third is that the GPA may not be perceived to generate much in the way of economic benefits.[6]

The approach taken in addressing these and other questions is interdisciplinary. Our aim was to bring together a group of economists, political scientists, legal scholars, and practitioners with a solid understanding of both the extant international disciplines and national government procurement policies. The book is structured around a number of themes that relate to specific elements of prevailing international disciplines. The authors of each chapter were asked to consider the following issues:

a. the impact of the GPA as a set of applicable standards (for cases where countries are signatories) or as a regulatory reference point for case studies of countries that are not (yet) GPA members;
b. the degree to which industrial policy considerations feature in the relevant national (or regional) regulatory frameworks, or are (surreptitiously) accommodated in procurement practices;
c. the existence and use of enforcement mechanisms, with an emphasis on domestic challenge and review procedures that allow firms to contest the behavior of procuring entities;
d. the availability of data on procurement processes and outcomes; and
e. an assessment of the utility of international disciplines from a trade (market access) and good regulatory practice (governance) point of view.

[5] Note that Montenegro acceded to the GPA in July 2015 and Ukraine joined in May 2016. The former was not included in the case studies because the country is in the process of implementing the procurement regulations of EU. The Ukraine accession post-dated the completion of this book project.

[6] For example, small countries with little capacity to contest foreign procurement markets and with policy regimes that are largely consistent with good international practice have little incentive to join the GPA.

The extent to which these questions are addressed across the chapters varies, in part due to data availability constraints. The structured analyses in the chapters allow comparisons to be made as well as the state of play across countries to be assessed. Some of the emerging economies are much closer to international good practice than others, and some do a better job of data collection and reporting than some OECD countries (e.g., Turkey). At the same time, the authors were not constrained from highlighting issues that they perceived as deserving of particular mention, as we did not want our desire to address common themes to become a straitjacket that would thwart possibilities for underscoring idiosyncratic elements that could provide insights into the dynamics of the regulation of government procurement. What follows provides our take on the thematic questions and the extent to which internationalization of procurement processes is observed.

0.2 **Diffusion of International Norms and Disciplines**

As mentioned, there are several sources of international norms in the area of procurement practice and processes—most notably UNCITRAL and the GPA.

0.2.1 GPA AND VARIABLE GEOMETRY IN THE WTO

The GPA is the main plurilateral agreement included in the WTO edifice.[7] It has worked well in the sense that its members have successfully concluded a number of renegotiations that have extended its coverage and adapted the rules of the game. One reason for studying the GPA has nothing to do with procurement, as it is precisely its plurilateral character that is worth investigating. Following the demise of the Doha Round in 2015, WTO members may want to conclude additional plurilateral agreements under WTO auspices, and thus understanding how the GPA has worked and has impacted signatories as well non-parties is important from that perspective.

Few countries have voluntarily joined the GPA since it was first established. Many of those that have joined since 2005 did so because they acceded to the EU, which is a GPA signatory. Many GPA members—and the WTO Secretariat—are of the view that this is unfortunate and have sought to expand membership, both through a process of engagement and advocacy, and by relaxing some of the disciplines that were part of the rules of

[7] The only other WTO plurilateral agreement is the Agreement on Civil Aircraft, which largely became redundant following the inclusion of subsidy disciplines in the WTO (see Hoekman and Mavroidis, 2015).

the game in earlier vintages of the GPA (e.g., making transparency and notification requirements less onerous) and clarifying others (e.g., rules pertaining to the ability to use procurement for industrial policy purposes).

It may appear obvious that existing signatories would want to see more countries join the GPA, but the rationale for allowing for plurilateral agreements in the WTO is that governments are left free to decide for themselves whether to join, and those who are part of the club decide on a set of rules they perceive to be in their joint interest. If the club rules do not attract new members—or only a few over time—it is not clear why this is a problem. The "real world" driver for expansion is that many of the countries that remain outside the GPA offer large markets. This creates a tension for GPA members, who must balance what they collectively agree are good rules and make for good (welfare-enhancing) policy practice against their mercantilist export interests. It is an open question whether, from a good policy/national welfare perspective, relaxing rules to allow less transparency or more scope to allocate contracts to domestic firms is worth it in return for improved access to the procurement markets of potential new GPA members.[8]

0.2.2 MARKET ACCESS AND PROCEDURAL RULES

This tension between market access and rules plays out in any assessment of the impact of the GPA on procurement processes and outcomes at the national level. The GPA has two elements: a complex set of (bilaterally) negotiated market access concessions (commitments to open up procurement in a sector or by specific entities to competition from other GPA members), and a set of specific disciplines that apply to the procurement process with a number of provisions that are aimed to facilitate monitoring of whether these are implemented. On market access, the country chapters suggest that the effects of the GPA in terms of opening markets to foreign competition may be limited—members don't see much increase in foreign market share over time. One reason is that large parts of the procurement market are effectively excluded because the magnitude of contracts is too small, or because criteria for contract awards are such that a local presence is required for the eligibility or competitiveness of foreign bids. It is not at all straightforward to assess market access dynamics; as illustrated by the chapters in this book, data collection and reporting varies enormously across countries.

With regards to the rules themselves, it is also not clear how much of a difference they have made in GPA members. In fact, views—and evidence—differ on whether for

[8] Market access incentives matter: a key driver for new countries to join the GPA is the prospect of accession by China. Reportedly one reason why New Zealand recently decided to sign the GPA—which it had refused to do for decades because of its view that it would have very little benefits—was because of the prospect that China might join. Anderson et al. (2011) assess the value of expanding the country coverage of the GPA.

example the default requirement for open competitive bidding for above threshold contracts enhances value for money, or is in fact the most efficient procurement method. An example is the USA, which relies extensively on competitive negotiations and dialogue between procuring entities and bidders. While the US model may be more efficient and effective in obtaining value for money, necessary conditions for it to be feasible are effective control of corruption and accountability of procuring entities for performance, which are not satisfied in many countries. Another example is that the GPA has outlawed price preferences and offsets—specific measures aimed at giving local firms a better chance of getting contracts and forcing foreign firms to work with domestic companies if they are awarded a contract. As discussed in Section 0.3, a number of the country chapters note that the result of this may be that governments shift to alternative, often less transparent, mechanisms to achieve the same objectives. This trend is also observed in non-members of the GPA, suggesting that there is more at work than a simple dynamic in moving governments to adopt practices that will not fall foul of the GPA standards. This conclusion is bolstered by the fact that many non-GPA members employ procurement practices and procedures that are not that dissimilar to those applied by GPA members, which is due in part to the parallel efforts by international bodies such as UNCITRAL (Arrowsmith, 2009), the OECD, and other international organizations such as the World Bank to promote good regulatory practices in this area.

Whatever the case may be, an implication is that more attention must be devoted to internalizing the political economy dynamics when designing international disciplines. One (minimal) element of doing so is to ensure transparency. If the aim is in part to discipline discrimination, it is important to know that price preferences, or local content and offset policies, are not replaced with other policies that result in similar outcomes, but are less transparent. In countries with weak economic governance, less transparency can easily translate into corruption. However, the dynamics in the GPA seem to move toward a slight weakening of transparency disciplines—the most recent revision of the GPA requires less of signatories in terms of reporting than did earlier versions.

0.2.3 INDUSTRIAL POLICIES AND SMALL AND MEDIUM-SIZED ENTERPRISES

A common concern that underlies efforts to negotiate procurement rules in trade agreements is controlling the extent to which governments support local firms by discriminating against foreign suppliers. National legislation often requires procuring entities to promote the development of domestic industry or technology, to support particular types of firms such as small and medium-sized enterprises (SMEs), or to assist certain groups or regions within a country. By and large, the pursuit of such objectives involves discriminating against foreign suppliers. Examples include outright prohibitions on foreign sourcing (e.g., national civil servants must fly national airlines), threshold criteria for foreign sourcing to be permitted (a minimum cost or price differentials compared to local suppliers), offset mechanisms, technology transfer, and local content requirements.

The existence of such objectives implies that government procurement policies are often an exercise in "constrained cost minimization." The basic goal is value for money, subject to the other policy goals that need to be taken into account. In practice, these other goals often imply that, for all or part of any contract, the scope of competition is reduced to the set of firms that meet specific criteria laid out in legislation or procurement regulations.

The pursuit of industrial development or social equity objectives by governments (on the latter, see, for example, McCrudden, 2007) can have very different impacts on economic efficiency, depending on the instrument that is used. In general, the extent of efficiency losses will be minimized if instruments target directly the source of problem at hand (lack of economic opportunities for minority groups, regional economic wealth differentials, etc.).

Governments may want to promote SMEs by awarding these firms state contracts even though larger firms that are more efficient submit lower bids. A different course of action would have the government identify the impediments faced by SMEs and take measures that directly remedy them. If a critical impediment to the growth of small firms is access to credit, for example, policies are better directed toward bolstering the supply of credit to small firms, rather than using indirect means such as increasing the sales of small firms through government contracts that can then be used to obtain credit lines from banks.

A recent study that analyzed selected country experiences in promoting the participation of SMEs and firms owned by or employing disadvantaged groups concludes that it is difficult to evaluate how effective or efficient procurement policies are in assisting such groups, because most countries do not have a system for evaluating costs and benefits and, thus, their impact (or costs) (GHK, 2010). Available audit information demonstrates high potential for fraud and corruption and high compliance costs for such programs (an issue discussed in Chapter 16 and Chapter 17). Matters are compounded by evidence of "creep" as political pressure results in more and more groups becoming eligible for preferences. In practice, other instruments are likely to be more effective and less costly in achieving social goals (Horowitz, 2012). These considerations have direct relevance for the design of government procurement policies. Governments may be more inclined to eliminate a procurement scheme that favors a certain industry if they know that other forms of state intervention can better attain this objective. Furthermore, if the chosen form of state intervention directly tackles the constraints confronting the favored industry's or group's performance, then economic efficiency can be improved also (Evenett and Hoekman, 2005).

In many countries there appears to be a trend to move away from price preferences and similar "traditional" instruments to give domestic firms a better chance of getting contracts toward criteria-based systems in which weighting schemes are used to give additional "points" for SME content, but that do not explicitly discriminate against foreign bidders on the basis of nationality. Thus, if foreign bidders use a significant amount of local SME-provided inputs, they may be (more) competitive and win contracts. Many of the country papers suggest that procurement is used as an element of industrial/regional development policy without explicitly discriminating against foreign companies. What the policies do is to bolster incentives for foreign firms to invest locally, that is, procurement becomes an indirect investment incentive that may well complement direct investment promotion activities and investment incentives, fiscal or otherwise, that all states offer.

The bottom line is that policy is aimed at increasing employment and turnover locally, but is not tied to ultimate ownership of winning bidders. This raises the question of whether these policies result in distortions and how large these are, an issue that is explored in several chapters but one that clearly requires much more in-depth research.

0.2.4 ENFORCEMENT DYNAMICS: REVIEW AND CHALLENGE PROCEDURES

A feature of the GPA and the UNCITRAL Model Law, as well as of some PTAs, is the provision of domestic review mechanisms—also called bid-protest or challenge procedures—through which firms can contest the procurement practices applied by government entities. Variants of such mechanisms exist, at least on paper, in most of the countries covered in this book. The inclusion of domestic review procedures in the GPA is an important feature that distinguishes the plurilateral GPA from the other multilateral and plurilateral WTO agreements, which only provide for state-to-state dispute settlement. Many of the PTAs with procurement chapters also include provisions for dispute resolution mechanisms between signatories, but go beyond the WTO by including the possibility of direct challenges by economic operators.

Without formally endorsing "direct effect" (or "self-executing" in US parlance) of WTO law, the challenge procedures embedded in Article XX of the GPA provide private parties with the right to invoke WTO law before domestic courts. Thus, this mechanism comports two novelties: first, it is private parties that can invoke WTO law; and second, they can do so before domestic courts. The latter entails the need for coordination, as different national courts might interpret the GPA requirements in different ways, but this is not addressed by the GPA.

The chapters reveal that domestic review procedures are used intensively in some countries—including non-GPA members—but are not used, or are used with a debatable degree of effectiveness, in others. The GPA does not appear to monitor what goes on in this area. Arguably, this undermines claims regarding the centrality of transparency in the GPA, a view that is bolstered by the observation that GPA disciplines on this front have been weakened in the most recent revision of the agreement.[9] In principle, domestic review procedures should greatly reduce the need for "standard" transparency mechanisms that revolve around policy monitoring, surveillance, and notification—firms are at the coalface and therefore can contest non-compliant measures in real time. There is no need to go through a process of monitoring policy developments and indirectly assessing whether governments are implementing their commitments *if* firms have access to effective domestic review procedures.

Therefore, a first-order question is whether bid protest is doing the job, and if not, why not. Given an understanding of that question, one can ask what the GPA could do to improve matters.

This insight motivates the focus in the country chapters on the operation of bid-protest/domestic review processes. As we have both GPA and non-GPA members, we are interested in assessing whether there are systematic differences between the two sets of countries, and specifically, if a lack of transparency is addressed for GPA members through domestic review processes. Questions that are of interest here include the "participation rate" of foreign companies in bid challenge and review procedures and the types of issues that are raised. A better understanding of domestic review mechanisms is needed to determine, for example, how the WTO Secretariat might best work toward enhancing transparency by complementing or addressing identified weaknesses of domestic review procedures.

Unfortunately, the use of domestic review remains too much of a black box in many countries. In part, this reflects the difficulty of determining the "nationality" of firms—who owns the firms that contest procurement auctions is often not obvious from publically available information, and is one of the areas for more intensive data collection looking forward.

0.2.5 TRANSPARENCY: THE DATA CHASE

Transparency and dispute settlement and enforcement are complements. By throwing light on an issue, problems might disappear—in the inimitable characterization of US Supreme Court Justice Brandeis, light is the most effective disinfectant. Transparency is critical for both efficient procurement practices and for international cooperation

[9] See, for example, Reich (2009). Several of the chapters on this book delve deeper into this question.

(disciplines) to be effective. The GPA system cannot function absent knowledge about what, when, and how goods and services are procured.

The most famous litigation under the Tokyo Round GPA—the dispute between the US and Norway regarding the toll ring system of the city of Trondheim—was for all practical purposes the necessary consequence of the absence of transparency.[10] In fact, this dispute showed that effective remedies might be disproportionate precisely because of the absence of transparency. It would have been unreasonable for the GATT panel to recommend that Norway undo the ring system that had been built and re-open the bid. Additionally, who is the injured party here? In the counterfactual world in which Norway had been transparent, any company specializing in the construction of toll ring systems originating in any GPA signatory could, in principle at least, have won the bid. All this to state that transparency is a key provision in the GPA regime.

The Revised GPA relies on members to provide information through a notification process. As was illustrated by the 2008 financial crisis, and more generally by the very partial compliance of WTO members with the many notification requirements that are included in WTO agreements, countries have weak incentives to self-notify. WTO statistics on the use of some trade policies are very patchy and incomplete. With this in mind, the contributors to this book were asked to reflect on what aspect of transparency needs to be strengthened—both in the context of the GPA and more generally.

0.3 **Overview of the Chapters**

The chapters are divided into three parts that reflect different dimensions of the internationalization of procurement regulation and governance. Part I examines the process of internationalization of procurement regulation, by looking at the main instruments and processes that carry it forward. Part II contains the country case studies. Part III focuses on issues related to transparency and the design of international cooperation in the procurement area.

0.3.1 PART I: INTERNATIONAL FOCAL POINTS FOR PROCUREMENT DISCIPLINES

The starting point from an internationalization perspective is the only enforceable international instrument regulating government procurement behavior—the GPA. Part I therefore starts with a chapter on the GPA. But other international instruments

[10] Mavroidis (1993) discusses this dispute in detail.

have also been developed and used, including RTAs and the UNCITRAL Model Law on Public Procurement.

In Chapter 1, Arwel Davies analyzes the GPA's development over time and the interplay between national procurement regulation and other international regulatory instruments. Davies explores the GPA's achievements as well as the deficiencies that have been revealed since its establishment, and provides a commentary on the Work Programme that was agreed in conjunction with the latest renegotiation of the agreement. This includes a focus on enhancing the participation of SMEs.

In Chapter 2, Robert Anderson, Anna Caroline Müller, and Philippe Pelletier examine the interplay between the GPA and the many RTAs concluded between GPA parties and non-GPA parties,[11] including the final text of the Trans-Pacific Partnership (TPP). The authors argue that disciplines on government procurement in RTAs broadly track those of the GPA. This helps to minimize conflicts with the GPA, while helping non-GPA countries that are members of RTAs that include procurement disciplines to familiarize themselves with what is entailed, potentially facilitating future accession to the GPA. The view is defended that in the long run, RTAs may prove to be "building blocks" that enhance, as opposed to undermine, the growth of GPA membership This leads the authors to conclude that the GPA is likely to remain at the center of WTO members' efforts to liberalize trade and promote efficient procurement practices and good governance in this policy area.

Chapter 3 by Caroline Nicholas explores lessons learned from the experience of the UNCITRAL Model Law on Public Procurement, which is designed to promote the harmonization of domestic laws in the field of public procurement. Nicolas describes and examines UNCITRAL processes and the Model Law, both as they were conceived and how they work in practice. She considers, in particular, how and the extent to which the process of international law-making contributes to the internationalization of procurement regulation. She discusses the benefits of the consensus-based UNCITRAL approach—which differs importantly in this respect from the exclusive nature of deliberations in the GPA and RTA settings—and the implications of success being contingent upon broad, representative, and effective participation. However, she also notes that politicization of the process may prevent the emergence of both good technical solutions as well as consensus, and concludes that securing sufficient participation remains an ongoing challenge (helping to explain the revealed preference for international clubs in this policy area).

Part I concludes with Chapter 4 by Kamala Dawar, which examines the nature and application of the most-favored nation (MFN) principle under the GPA and the General Agreement on Trade in Services (GATS), with specific reference to RTAs with

[11] The terms PTAs and RTAs are used interchangeably in this volume by the authors.

procurement market access commitments. Dawar argues that under the GPA, the MFN principle is based on strict reciprocity and a conditional MFN requirement. Furthermore, any access to procurement markets for services is conditioned and constrained not only by the GATS schedules, but also by the application of the MFN principle operating within the GATS. She questions whether the WTO legal framework and method of negotiating procurement provisions works against the wider objectives of the WTO. She also tests this hypothesis by examining the procurement commitments set out in selected RTAs signed between GPA parties, between a GPA party and non-GPA party, and those signed between non-GPA parties.

0.3.2 PART II: COUNTRY STUDIES

The country case studies examine the extent to which the internationalization of regulation in the area of government procurement has influenced government purchasing rules, policies, and practices at the national level. Part II starts with a short chapter on the European Union (EU), which is not a country but an economic integration arrangement. However, because of the Common Commercial Policy, the EU acts and negotiates by and large as a single actor on trade policy matters. As the regulatory regime that governs the EU internal market also spans public procurement and has been the subject of close study elsewhere (e.g., Arrowsmith, 2014), Chapter 5 by Carlo-Maria Cantore and Sübidey Togan is limited to a short overview of developments in EU procurement law and regulation, with a specific focus on the questions of interest to this volume, including the use and efficacy of domestic review mechanisms. Several other chapters focus on specific dimensions of the EU procurement regime—including transparency and efforts to enhance access to foreign procurement markets.

The following chapters focus on three countries in the EU's "neighborhood." Chapter 6 by Eliza Niewiadomska and Astghik Solomonyan examines Armenia's regulation of public procurement. They discuss a European Bank of Reconstruction and Development (EBRD)-UNCITRAL technical cooperation initiative and how the 2011 UNCITRAL Model Law was used as a reference point and tool to bridge gaps between the public procurement commitments arising from Armenia's membership of the Eurasian Economic Union (EEU) and those arising as a result of Armenia's participation in the GPA. Armenia was the first developing/transition country to accede to the GPA, influenced in part by a desire to adopt best practices in procurement regulation and to move toward a market economy. The eventual decision by Armenia to join the EEU, as opposed to implementing a Deep and Comprehensive Free Trade Area (DCFTA) with the EU, implied that three sets of procurement standards were on the table—those of the EU, of the GPA, and of the EEU. The extent to which these are compatible or otherwise makes the Armenian case of particular interest, as it provides valuable information on the degree to which these different regimes are compatible—or can be made compatible.

Chapter 7 by Sübidey Togan, Bedri Kamil Onur Taş, and Servet Alyanak examines the procurement regime in Turkey, an EU accession candidate. They argue that although the adoption of the Public Procurement Law of 2002 was inspired by, and took into account, the then prevailing EU public procurement regime, as well as the 1994 GPA and the UNCITRAL Model Law, procurement practices in Turkey have not converged toward these high international standards. Instead, there has been increasing divergence. Turkish procurement regulation does not cover utilities, many important agencies (such as the Mass Housing Administration), or build-operate-transfer (BOT) projects. The law does not have a defined list of covered entities and, in practice, transparency provisions are often not adhered to. Thus, significant areas of procurement are in effect not contestable for foreign suppliers. Although Turkey's procurement regime is better than many others in some respects—for example, when it comes to compiling and reporting statistics—the authors argue that major reforms are needed to ensure implementation of the law and to expand its coverage.

Chapter 8 by Arie Reich discusses the procurement regime in Israel and the ways in which international commitments are implemented. Reich explains the central role played by the judiciary, first in establishing the principles that govern public procurement in Israel before the enactment of a specific legislative instrument in the area, and second in applying and enforcing the bid-challenge system. The chapter also explores Israel's system of domestic preferences, offset policies, and exemptions, and how these are integrated in a regulatory regime that is informed by the GPA as well as international guidelines on procurement. Reich concludes by arguing that the history of Israel's regulatory experience in public procurement may provide useful lessons to other economies that are considering the adoption of international disciplines in this area.

Chapter 9 by Christopher Yukins examines the US federal procurement market and discusses how US federal procurement laws and regulations, typically created without reference to international best practices or the potential impact on trade, create a number of direct and indirect barriers to trade, and explains why mechanisms such as transparency obligations, electronic procurement, and bid-challenge procedures have not managed so far to address these barriers. Yukins stresses the importance of channels of communications between those who draft procurement rules in the USA and their counterparts in other countries and trade blocs. He argues that such communications could take a bilateral form—as will be the case of the Transatlantic Trade and Investment Partnership (TTIP) if and when this is concluded—but ultimately, it is desirable that such engagement is accommodated within the WTO and other international bodies.

Chapter 10 by Gary Hufbauer and Tyler Moran complements Chapter 9 by providing a succinct discussion of the commitments on government procurement matters that the USA has sought from its trading partners, and the commitments that the USA has made in turn, with a particular focus on how these have evolved over time. The authors make a number of specific suggestions as to how US procurement at the state level—as opposed to federal level procurement—may be included in both PTAs and at the international level.

Chapter 11 by Paul Lalonde reviews recent developments in Canadian public procurement law and practice, with a particular focus on the implementation of international agreements by Canada, including the Comprehensive Economic and Trade Agreement (CETA) that was concluded with the EU. Lalonde identifies certain deficiencies in Canada's public procurement practices as compared to the obligations embedded in the agreements and basic standards of transparency and fairness in procurement. He identifies persistent challenges in obtaining statistics on public procurement processes and outcomes, and makes suggestions for improving the collection and dissemination of procurement-related data. The chapter also provides reflections on the impact of international trade agreements on procurement law and practice in Canada, including how these have affected the treatment of foreign bidders in the procurement process.

Chapter 12 by Eduardo Pérez Motta and Paulina Valladares examines the government procurement system in Mexico, summarizing the applicable legal framework, the role of competitive tendering, and complementary measures aimed at reducing the scope for corruption and collusion. The chapter pays particular attention to the role of competition policy and recent actions by the Mexican government to implement best practices to ensure the integrity of procurement processes.

Chapter 13 by Cesar Pereira and Rafael Schwind explores the current status of the Brazilian public procurement regulatory landscape and considers perspectives for greater internationalization in the future. The authors discuss the level of market access given to foreign bidders, the applicability of international government procurement rules and practices, and the level of coordination between Brazilian domestic government procurement laws and international models. The chapter concludes with an examination of the effects of the current level of internationalization of Brazilian public procurement, especially regarding the use of offsets and similar policies.

Chapter 14 by Cao Fuguo and Zhou Fen discusses the Chinese public procurement system, reviews its main attributes and effectiveness, and identifies the areas where international norms are most, less, or not very relevant. The authors also discuss procurement issues in the PTAs to which China is a party and China's engagement in seeking accession to the GPA, and more generally, China's current stance toward procurement law internationalization. They conclude by arguing that a pragmatic approach should be considered by GPA members to facilitate China's membership. This could span a willingness to consider less in the way of market access commitments and an acceptance that the internationalization of Chinese procurement law will be an incremental and gradual process.

In Chapter 15, Anirudh Shingal analyzes India's procurement policy, arguing that by and large the rules that govern public purchasing at the federal and sub-federal levels in

India follow international regulatory models, but that their implementation falls short in providing transparency, accountability, efficiency, and professionalism in the award of public contracts. He discusses the implementation of the mandatory use of e-procurement for federal, sub-federal, and public-sector enterprise contracts, as well as other elements of the 2012 Public Procurement Bill, which provides for an independent dispute resolution mechanism and integration of Indian states within a national procurement policy. Shingal concludes that recent reforms will do much to ensure the compatibility of the Indian regulatory system with international disciplines such as the GPA. As a result, a decision to join the GPA would mainly involve an assessment of the extent to which this will improve access to the procurement markets of other GPA parties.

Chapter 16 by Memory Dube, Lizemarie Johannes, and David Lewis analyzes the South African government's procurement regime. Their focus is on an overarching question that is pertinent for many developing countries—whether adherence to international trading instruments and rules such as the GPA would, and should, permit the implementation of national policies and related criteria that will promote industrial development, whilst simultaneously helping to capture the efficiency gains that come with trade liberalization. The authors also examine the likely impact that adherence to international disciplines, such as those embedded in the GPA, could have in reducing the procurement system's vulnerability to corruption.

Part II concludes with Chapter 17 by Malcolm Bosworth, who analyzes developments in government procurement arrangements across the Tasman and assesses the extent to which recent Australian and New Zealand trade agreements containing government procurement commitments have contributed to domestic reforms of these policies. Bosworth concludes that the PTAs have had little or no reform impact. He argues in particular that in the case of Australia, PTA commitments have not prevented procurement processes—especially at the sub-federal level—from becoming less open and competitive. Transparent, relatively straightforward price preferences favoring local content have largely been replaced by hidden, and more costly, discretionary discriminatory measures. Australia's PTA commitments on government procurement essentially accommodated these trends by adopting wide-ranging exemptions to exclude measures favoring localization, including programs for regional development and support for SMEs and indigenous enterprises. Moreover, PTA commitments apply on a conditional MFN basis and hence automatically entail discrimination between trading partners.

Bosworth argues that Australia has missed an opportunity to use PTA negotiations to improve the level of liberalization of its procurement regime, and that these negotiations might have distracted government efforts in this area. He observes that in contrast to Australia's extensive use of government procurement policies to achieve industrial policy goals, New Zealand has maintained a relatively open and non-discriminatory government procurement regime based not on commitments in trade agreements, but rather on unilateral reforms that are applied on a non-discriminatory basis. In conclusion,

Bosworth echoes Yukins by arguing that instruments such as the GPA may look good on paper but preserve major import-restrictive measures. This again points to the need for more transparency in trade negotiations. The central policy message is that trade agreements cannot substitute for unilateral reforms.

0.3.3 PART III: TAKING STOCK AND LOOKING FORWARD

The final part of the volume contains three chapters that examine, from different angles, the issue of transparency and the importance of an evidence-based scrutiny as a sine qua non element for a meaningful evaluation of the utility of international disciplines in government procurement.

In Chapter 18, Lucian Cernat and Zornitsa Kutlina-Dimitrova argue that figures derived from traditional national accounts statistics fail to capture the international dimension of public procurement, which is necessary for trade negotiations in this field. They observe that the absence of hard data and clear indicators that measure international procurement flows and the extent of "home bias" may hamper progress in agreeing to more liberal procurement rules, as well as monitoring the implementation of existing procurement provisions in trade agreements. The authors propose a basic conceptual framework for data collection and suggest that this framework should be the basis of an agreed data collection methodology that all WTO members would be ready to apply in their domestic procurement legislation. Such a methodology could be tested and fine-tuned based for some pilot cases, covering countries with different legal systems and levels of development. The authors also propose that the required data collection process in developing countries be supported by donor agencies and other relevant international organizations (such as the OECD, the IMF, the World Bank, and UN agencies).

Chapter 19 by Patrick Messerlin uses different sources of data to assess the relative level of openness of the public procurement markets of major trading nations, with a specific focus on the EU. He argues that these data reveal a picture that is different from what is commonly argued to be the case by policymakers in the EU, in that the Union is less open and other countries are less closed. The extent of the divergence between the discourse and what the data suggest is difficult to assess given the absence of appropriate data on government sourcing patterns, suggesting that greater effort is needed to compile more accurate statistics, but also a need to take into account more basic economic factors such as the size of economies. Messerlin argues that the lack of good information on the state of play as regards market access makes the European Commission's proposals to adopt a regulation that requires reciprocity in granting access to EU procurement markets (European Commission, 2012) a bad idea.

Part III and the volume concludes with Chapter 20 by Bernard Hoekman. He reviews the empirical evidence regarding the impacts of reciprocally negotiated market access commitments on sourcing patterns and concludes that these do not appear to have been effective in inducing governments to buy more from foreign suppliers. Hoekman observes that foreign sourcing by governments has been rising for most countries, independently of whether states have made international commitments to this effect, although there is some evidence that this trend was reversed post-2008 in several countries that had the freedom to do so. In this respect Hoekman suggests that procurement agreements may play a role as a lock-in mechanism that constrains a shift away from efficient public purchasing in times of economic pressure. He suggests that assessments of the effects of trade agreements on procurement outcomes must go beyond a narrow consideration of whether and how procurement per se is included, and center more on the extent to which trade agreements more generally promote a pro-competitive environment. This may require some reconsideration of the design of international cooperation on procurement regulation, with less emphasis on specific market access reciprocity and greater focus on good procurement practices and principles, efforts to boost transparency, and pursuit of pro-competitive policies.

0.4 **Concluding Remarks**

To what extent are countries influenced by international norms and knowledge regarding "good practices"? How much more is achieved by making binding international commitments that are embedded in trade agreements? Answers to these questions are central to determining the utility of extant international trade disciplines and norms, and the design of such disciplines from the perspective of improving procurement processes and outcomes.

The analyses in the chapters in this volume demonstrate that despite the surge of PTAs that include comprehensive procurement chapters, the GPA remains the central point of reference in the "solar system" of international procurement disciplines. While the GPA has found it difficult to attract "new planets" to its orbit, PTAs may make this more likely. However, to date no PTAs with large emerging economies have been concluded that include procurement. China joining the GPA could be a game changer, but it is uncertain if and when this will occur.

Although its importance as an international regulatory standard must be recognized, it is debatable whether the GPA has done much to expunge governments' desires to discriminate against foreign suppliers in public purchases. These desires were the major reason that government procurement was excluded from the original GATT in 1947. The same doubt can be expressed when it comes to PTAs—the EU of course being the major exception. As discussed in the chapter by Hoekman, there is little evidence that trade agreements have a significant economic impact on procurement patterns. Clearly much depends on how ambitious a PTA is—many of the extant PTAs are not very far-reaching, although this may be changing. The recent Comprehensive Economic and Trade Agreement (CETA) between Canada and the EU is an example of a PTA that is likely to have a major impact on the opening up of Canadian procurement markets to EU firms.[12]

The latest revision of the GPA led to a number of changes aimed at making membership more attractive to developing countries. This may be a double-edged sword. It should not be forgotten that the raison d'être of the GPA is to increase cross-border trade amongst signatories. The re-orientation of the GPA to span other policy areas and directions that are being considered in GPA work programs runs the risk of being misinterpreted as an attempt by the GPA to reinvent its raison d'être and as a sign of weakness, not of success.[13] In particular, there is the concern that in an attempt to attract more developing country membership, GPA incumbents may divert its focus away from what is considered to be its primary aim. Efforts to make the agreement more attractive for developing countries are welcome in principle, but may give rise to a temptation to over-concentrate resources and energy on this purpose, rather than on tackling important issues that prevent the agreement from reaching its full potential as a driver for increasing cross-border trade in government procurement. The temptation might be stronger if the WTO Secretariat feels that this might be a less controversial way to strengthen its role, particularly if there is the perception that its traditional role and mission has reached a stalemate.

This suggests that strengthening the mechanisms for transparency in data collection and reporting remains a key aspect for achieving the aims of the GPA and supporting what could be loosely termed the "brand of the club." The GPA "brand" is important because it provides not only access to sizeable market opportunities, but also a "badge" showing that members abide by a set of rules of good governance and accountability. This is an important consideration that could attract developing countries and economies in transition that would like to confirm their commitments in this regard. Without accurate and timely data on what is procured from foreign companies, there will be concerns over the usefulness and relevance of the GPA as a whole. It is for this reason that agreement on a methodology for data collection and allocation of the resources needed to compile and analyze procurement processes should be a key priority for GPA members.

[12] As discussed in Chapter 11, CETA may open markets to the EU to a greater extent than is the case for Canadian firms that are located in different Canadian provinces. Canada is also interesting in that it incorporates international procurement disciplines into domestic law, thus allowing private agents to invoke these provisions before national courts.

[13] The revised GPA includes a number of work programs that are intended to improve the implementation and administration of the revised agreement and that may inform the direction that future renegotiation of the Agreement may take—see Chapter 2 and Chapter 20.

The role of the WTO Secretariat needs to be strengthened in order to ensure compliance with the GPA commitments undertaken by the parties, particularly with regards to the proper and timely reporting of data. This could involve a joint venture with other organizations such as the OECD and UNCTAD. There are limits that the nature of the WTO imposes on the role of the Secretariat, but it is important that a stronger system of accountability be put in place including, for example, "peer pressure" and "naming and shaming mechanisms" through the publication of procurement performance. GPA signatories, particularly the big players like the US and the EU, have sufficient incentives to agree on such a mechanism that evidences their commitment to the GPA objectives at a time when they are trying to convince third countries with big markets to join these disciplines.

REFERENCES

Anderson, R., Pelletier, P., Osei-lah, K., and Muller, A. 2011. "Assessing the Value of Future Accessions to the WTO Agreement on Public Procurement: Some New Data Sources, Provisional Estimates, and an Evaluative Framework for Individual WTO Members Considering Accession." WTO Staff Working Paper ERSD 2011–15, Washington, DC.

Arrowsmith, S. (ed.) 2009. *Reform of the UNCITRAL Model Law on Procurement: Procurement Regulation for the 21st Century*. Eagan, MN: West.

Arrowsmith, S. 2014. *The Law of Public and Utilities Procurement*, vol. 1, 3rd edition. London: Sweet & Maxwell.

Coulton, J. 1994. "Cities and Architecture." In J. Boardman (ed.), *The Cambridge Ancient History: Plates to Volumes V and VI*. Cambridge: Cambridge University Press, 55–84.

De Cormenin, M. 1840. *Droit Administratif*, vol. 2. 5th edition. France: Pagnere.

European Commission. 2012. "Proposal for a Regulation of the European Parliament and the Council on access of Third-Country Goods and Services to the Union's Internal Market in Procurement and Procedures Supporting Negotiations on Access of Union goods and Services to the Public Procurement Markets of Third Countries." COM (2012) 124 final, Brussels, March 21.

Evenett, S. and Hoekman, B. 2005. "Government Procurement: Market Access, Transparency, and Multilateral Trade Rules." *European Journal of Political Economy* 21(1): 163–83.

GHK 2010. "Evaluation of SME Access to Public Procurement Markets in the EU." Report for DG Enterprise and Industry, Brussels, September.

Hoekman, B. and Mavroidis, P. C. (ed.) 1997. *Law and Policy in Public Purchasing*. Ann Arbor: University of Michigan Press.

Hoekman, B. and Mavroidis, P. C. 2015. "Embracing Diversity: Plurilateral Agreements and the Trading System." *World Trade Review* 14(1): 101–16.

Horowitz, D. 2012. "Achieving Social Diversity through the Use of Supplier Preferences in the Procurement Process," World Bank, Washington, DC (available at: <https://consultations.worldbank.org/Data/hub/files/meetings/Procurement_Policies/BP-DIVERSITY-THROUGHSUPPLIERPREFERENCES.pdf>> (accessed July 19, 2016)).

McCrudden, C. 2007. *Buying Social Justice: Equality, Government Procurement and Legal Change*. Oxford: Oxford University Press.

Mavroidis, P. C. 1993. "Government Procurement Agreement, the Trondheim Case: The Remedies Issue." *Aussenwirtschaft* 48: 77–94.

OECD. 2015. *Government at a Glance 2015*. Paris: OECD Publishing (available at: <http://dx.doi.org/10.1787/gov_glance-2015-42-en> (accessed July 19, 2016)).

Reich, A. 2009. "The New Text of the Agreement on Government Procurement: An Analysis and Assessment." *Journal of International Economic Law* 12(4): 989–1022.

United Nations. 2016. *World Economic Situation and Prospects 2016*. New York: UN.

Von Hesberg, H. 2015. "Greek and Roman Architects." In C. Marconi (ed.), *The Oxford Handbook of Greek and Roman Art and Architecture*. Oxford: Oxford University Press, 136–51.

Part I

International Focal Points for Procurement Disciplines

1 The Evolving GPA

Lessons of Experience and Prospects for the Future

Arwel Davies

1.1 Introduction

The World Trade Organization (WTO) Agreement on Government Procurement (GPA) occupies a central position as the most significant international instrument of procurement market liberalization today. Its primary focus is the elimination of discriminatory laws and practices resulting in compartmentalized procurement markets and impermissible distinctions between domestic and foreign goods, services, and suppliers based solely on origin and nationality. Procurement at the WTO is therefore first and foremost an issue of trade liberalization, market access, and the avoidance of protectionism.[1]

The WTO's web-based information on the GPA indicates that procurement markets open to competition among suppliers of the GPA parties are "currently valued at up to US$1.7 trillion dollars annually,"[2] with around 75 percent of this value attributable to the European Union (EU) and the USA (Anderson et al., 2011b: p. 18). Beyond this, a wealth of introductory information is provided on the GPA's expanding membership and contract/procuring entity coverage, as well as its development from the 1979 Tokyo Round Code on Government Procurement to the entry into force of the revised GPA in April 2014. The picture presented is justifiably of a success story. While procurement market liberalization remains firmly rooted to the optional/plurilateral model, there have been significant gains. Market access under the revised GPA is estimated to have increased by between $80 billion and $100 billion annually. According to Anderson

[1] This is clear from the opening paragraphs of the GPA's preamble:

Recognizing the need for an effective multilateral framework for government procurement, with a view to achieving greater liberalization and expansion of, and improving the framework for, the conduct of international trade; *Recognizing* that measures regarding government procurement should not be prepared, adopted or applied so as to afford protection to domestic suppliers, goods or services, or to discriminate among foreign suppliers, goods or services.

[2] Available at: <http://www.wto.org/english/tratop_e/gproc_e/gp_gpa_e.htm> (accessed November 2014); see also Anderson et al. (2011b).

(2014), this results from coverage of 400–500 additional procuring entities, coverage by three major parties of build-operate-transfer arrangements, generally expanded coverage of services procurement (especially telecommunications), and coverage by all parties of the full range of construction services.[3] Information on coverage commitments will become easier to access with the launch of the e-GPA portal, which provides a single point of access to the market access information.[4] The revised GPA itself, with which national procurement regimes must comply, has a more logical structure and is improved in its content especially in its recognition of electronic forms of communication and procurement.

However, membership, while expanded, remains limited. With the recent accessions of New Zealand and Montenegro, the GPA now covers 45 of the WTO's 162 members, a figure which includes the 28 EU member states. The membership is also imbalanced toward developed countries, albeit there is at least the possibility for this position to gradually change. Article V of the revised GPA contains strengthened transitional arrangements for developing and least developed WTO members. Furthermore, some WTO members that have started the process of accession to the GPA are, according to World Bank criteria,[5] lower-middle-income countries (Moldova, Kyrgyz Republic, Ukraine). Mongolia and Tajikistan, which have provisions on GPA accession in their protocols of accession to the WTO, are respectively lower-middle-income and low-income countries. Future accessions—in particular by China, which submitted its first coverage offer in 2007—could prompt other states toward membership. Suppliers from other (Brazil, Russia, India, China) BRICS countries may petition their governments for the same access to overseas procurement markets as that enjoyed by China's suppliers by reason of GPA membership. It is therefore possible that we are on the brink of a period of intense activity toward an expansion in the level and diversity of membership.

Going forward, a total of five work programs are in place which aim to progress negotiating issues which could not be fully resolved in the GPA renegotiation.[6] These relate to supporting the participation of small and medium-sized enterprises (SMEs) in procurement, improving the collection and reporting of statistical data relating to the GPA, promoting the use of sustainable procurement practices consistently with the

[3] It is difficult to comment on the extent of the achievement with regard to the market access dimension. This rather depends on whether the aspirations and expectations of negotiators were met. The gain in market access opportunities seems to be of the order of 5–10 percent. It therefore seems clear that substantial future gains will come more from accessions than from further commitments from existing GPA parties. It has been estimated, for example, that the accession of China alone will yield market access gains in the range of $113–$289 billion (Anderson et al., 2011b: p. 13).

[4] Available at: <https://e-gpa.wto.org/> (accessed July 20, 2016).

[5] Available at: <http://data.worldbank.org/country>(accessed July 20, 2016).

[6] The work programs are referred to in Appendix 2 of Adoption of the Results of the Negotiations under Article XXIV:7 of the Agreement on Government Procurement, Following Their Verification and Review, as Required by the Ministerial Decision of December 15, 2011 (GPA/112), para. 5, GPA/113, April 2, 2012.

GPA, addressing restriction and exclusions in coverage commitments, and safety standards in international procurement.

This chapter is divided into seven sections. Section 1.2 discusses the GPA's objectives. These can be better understood by locating the GPA within the overall tapestry of procurement regulation comprising national regulation and other international instruments. Section 1.3 discusses domestic review procedures. The role and value of these procedures is covered and some questions which may have slipped under the radar are posed. Do the rulings of the bodies reviewing supplier complaints have to be binding on the procuring entity? Must it be possible for the review to eventually come before a court? If not, is this position consistent with the United Nations Conference Against Corruption (UNCAC)?[7] Section 1.4 turns to the new work program on supporting SME participation. The economic and social justice rationales for supporting SMEs and, more broadly, enterprises in which historically disadvantaged individuals (HDIs) have a strong stake are covered. As the work program seems to be focused on removing discrimination in this area, the extent to which this can be realistically achieved is considered. Section 1.5 highlights a possible deficiency in the revised GPA in the required scope of statistical reporting. It is arguably at odds with the GPA's trade liberalization remit that there is no express obligation to report on the extent to which foreign suppliers are winning contracts, or on the origin of goods and services purchased. Section 1.6 considers a doctrinal development arising from the *Canada—Renewable Energy* case.[8] The question is whether procurement and buy national policies are carved out of multilateral coverage under the General Agreement on Tariffs and Trade (GATT) to the extent that has been commonly understood. Section 1.7 concludes.

1.2 The GPA's Objective/s: Trade Liberalization, Non-Discrimination, Good Governance, Integrity, Efficiency

What is the GPA for? What are its direct objectives and can GPA membership indirectly or incidentally contribute toward the achievement of other objectives? Where and how should the boundary between direct objectives and incidental benefits be drawn? As

[7] United Nations, Treaty Series, vol. 2349. The Convention was adopted by the United Nations General Assembly by its resolution 58/4. In accordance with article 68(1) of the Convention, the Convention entered into force on December 14, 2005. The text of the Convention is also available at: <https://www.unodc.org/unodc/en/treaties/CAC/> (accessed November 2014).

[8] WT/DS412/AB/R, *Canada—Certain Measures Affecting the Renewable Energy Generation Sector*; WT/DS426/AB/R, *Canada—Measures Relating to the Feed-In Tariff Programme.*

discussed in this section, the answers to these questions emerge not so much from considering the GPA in isolation, but rather from the GPA's relationship with both national procurement regimes, and other international procurement instruments.

As noted, procurement at the WTO is first and foremost an issue of trade liberalization, market access, and the avoidance of protectionism. The GPA's primary General Principle in Article IV is non-discrimination while the more specific rules which require transparent procurement procedures are primarily directed towards making discrimination more difficult or easier to monitor and detect (Anderson and Arrowsmith, 2011: p. 15). For several reasons, however, it is appropriate for the GPA to refer to other values and objectives, such as integrity and efficiency. This is to some extent inevitable because the very same general principles and specific transparency-based rules which make discrimination more difficult can also safeguard against corruption and contribute toward achievement of value for money. The GPA's preamble recognizes this connection. While the opening preamble recitals are devoted to trade liberalization and the avoidance of protectionism, it is further provided in the third recital that:

> the integrity and predictability of government procurement systems are integral to the efficient and effective management of public resources, the performance of the Parties' economies and the functioning of the multilateral trading system.

In a limited sense, it can be argued that the GPA now pursues the objective of value for money, which is clearly related to "the efficient and effective management of public resources." However, it is probably more accurate to view the recital above as reflecting the potential benefits which GPA membership can bring toward achieving value for money, with the content of this imprecise concept, and exactly how to achieve it, remaining within the domain of national policy-makers.

It is possible here to use the analogy of passing the baton in a relay race. Non-discrimination is not an end in itself in the trade context unless we attach moral opprobrium to treating foreign suppliers differently merely because of their nationality. Rather, non-discrimination is a device to facilitate the materialization of the benefits of competition in the marketplace. Non-discrimination is a useful device in this regard, but it is not sufficient in itself. The benefits will only materialize to the extent that there is some conception of the efficient use of public resources at the national level. An admittedly improbable scenario can be used to illustrate this point. Suppose that a procuring entity does not discriminate. Indeed, it places all its contracts with foreign suppliers and consistently purchases the most expensive and poorest quality goods and services available in the market place. The discrimination norm here, while observed, has not contributed toward its ultimate end because the procuring entity has no conception of the efficient use of public resources. The question raised is the extent to which international rules need to address the achievement of value for money. In terms of regulating this matter, the baton should be passed at an early stage, partly because all states have some conception of the efficient use of public resources, and partly because there are legitimate and wide differences in what this means—especially in the extent to which procurement is used to achieve horizontal policies, such as the advancement of previously disadvantaged groups and support for SMEs. As such, references to efficiency can appropriately feature in preamble recitals, but caution should be exercised before developing such statements into enforceable specific obligations. Non-discrimination is the GPA's main enforceable obligation, while value for money is among the benefits which GPA membership can contribute toward achieving.

Moving to the GPA's relationship with other international procurement instruments, many of these instruments both replicate the GPA's rules and share the GPA's primary concern with trade liberalization. This applies most strongly to bilateral/regional trade agreements with procurement chapters.[9] On the other hand, other instruments with broadly similar rules to the GPA may *not* share its primary concern with non-discrimination and trade liberalization, or at least may approach these concepts from a different perspective.

Under the GPA, the main barrier to international trade is discrimination itself, which is generally prohibited for covered procurement. In contrast, the barriers to international trade with which the UNCITRAL Model Law on Public Procurement is arguably more directly concerned are in the form of regulatory voids, deficiencies, or divergences.[10] These problems can generate a "chilling" effect on international trade. As the Model Law's Guide to Enactment notes, "the ability and willingness of suppliers and contractors to sell to foreign governments is hampered by the inadequate or divergent state of national procurement legislation in many countries."[11] Expressed in an exaggerated manner, markedly divergent national laws could all be non-discriminatory and therefore

[9] See Chapter 2. One of the questions raised in the conference was why developing countries enter into bilateral/regional trade agreements containing procurement chapters with developed countries who are GPA members as opposed to joining the GPA. Perhaps part of the explanation lies in the nature of the choice. Were the choice to be between contemporaneously entering into multiple separate agreements with all GPA members, or joining the GPA itself, the latter option would be a strong contender. However, the choice is rather between joining the GPA or entering into trade agreements with GPA members on an individual basis over a period of time. The more advanced this process, the more it can be said that the state in question might just as well become a GPA member. However, based on data presented in 2011, Chile is the most advanced in terms of entering into trade agreements with GPA members as opposed to joining the GPA itself. While it has trade agreements with the EU, the US, Japan, and the EFTA countries (Iceland, Liechtenstein, Norway, and Switzerland), it does not have trade agreements with government procurement provisions with the remaining GPA members (Canada, Hong Kong, China, Israel, Armenia, Korea, Singapore, Aruba, and Chinese Taipei). The data are presented in Anderson et al. (2011a).

[10] The full text of the Model Law 2011 and its Guide to Enactment are available at <http://www.uncitral.org/uncitral/uncitral_texts/procurement_infrastructure.html> (accessed November 2014); see Nicholas (2011, 2012).

[11] Guide to Enactment (2012, henceforth "the Guide"), p. 2, para. 2.

of limited direct concern under the GPA.[12] However, this divergence generates the chilling effect on international trade of greater concern under the Model Law.

The idea that the Model Law is not as directly concerned with discrimination as the GPA is reinforced by its coverage. It is designed to be applicable to all procurement within enacting states,[13] some of which will inevitably involve discriminatory laws and policies[14] which could violate the GPA for covered procurement. The somewhat different perspectives of the Model Law and the GPA are arguably appropriate and intuitive. More than the GPA, the Model Law is an instrument of particular value to states which are developing procurement rules for the first time or are improving and modernizing their existing rules.[15] It is understandable that these states are primarily concerned with the integrity of the procurement process and the avoidance of abuse with a view to enhancing value for money.[16] States can go a considerable way toward enhancing integrity and at least some way toward enhancing value for money without opening their procurement markets to international competition. Undoubtedly, "external liberalization" will tend to produce competition among a deeper pool of suppliers, thereby further enhancing value for money. International liberalization also brings the possibility of other benefits such as access to technology that is not available in the home market.[17] However, it may be that many states view these benefits as accruing from a potential second phase of procurement liberalization, the first phase being devoted to enhanced integrity and value for money through internal competition.[18]

[12] GPA membership can of course promote convergence in national procurement systems and thereby reduce the extent to which regulatory divergence is itself a barrier to trade. Indeed, this is implicit in the GPA's first preamble recital: "Recognizing the need for an effective multilateral framework for government procurement, with a view to achieving greater liberalization and expansion of, and improving the framework for, the conduct of international trade." For a discussion of the value of harmonization and related themes, see Yukins and Schooner (2007).

[13] Article I of the Model Law declares, "[t]his Law applies to all public procurement."

[14] This is recognized in the following Model Law provisions:

Article 8. Participation by suppliers or contractors

1. Suppliers or contractors shall be permitted to participate in procurement proceedings without regard to nationality, except where the procuring entity decides to limit participation in procurement proceedings on the basis of nationality on grounds specified in the procurement regulations or other provisions of law of this State.

[15] The Guide: p. 2, para. 5.

[16] The Guide (p. 3, para. 8) refers to "value for money and the avoidance of abuse in public procurement" as the "overarching aims of the Model Law," without also referring to non-discrimination in this immediate context.

[17] The benefits of "external liberalization" is among the themes explored in Anderson, Kovacic, and Müller (2011).

[18] This suggestion is corroborated by Anderson (2011b: pp. 24–5). The authors comment that countries often note in technical assistance seminars that enhanced competition and good governance can be achieved without GPA membership. The authors suggest that "The real question is whether the GPA accession process, and continuing participation in the Agreement, can stimulate or reinforce the necessary domestic reforms, and introduce a degree of ongoing monitoring that helps in maintaining a 'clean' and competitive procurement system."

Even though instruments such as the Model Law and the GPA may have a different focus or primary rationale, there is every reason for these instruments to co-exist in a mutually reinforcing manner. This is clearly recognized in the Model Law's Guide to Enactment, which refers to ensuring the widest possible use of the Model Law and the consequent need for harmony, in particular, with the GPA.[19] While the GPA does not refer to the Model Law, it is interesting to note that the Appellate Body referred to it in *Canada—Renewable Energy*. In probing the meaning of the term "procurement" in the GATT Article III:8 derogation, it referred not to perhaps the most obvious source of inspiration, the GPA, but rather to the 2011 Model Law. It was noted that the formal procedures under which governments acquire products "typically express principles, such as efficiency or transparency."[20]

Perhaps more significantly, the GPA and the Model Law are brought into a mutually reinforcing relationship via the reference in both instruments to the UNCAC.[21] Article 9.1 of UNCAC requires that procurement is "based on transparency, competition and objective criteria in decision-making, that are effective, *inter alia*, in preventing corruption." Article 9.1(d) was of particular relevance to the strengthening of the domestic review procedures in Chapter VIII of the Model Law. The Model Law now gives effect to the UNCAC requirement for an "effective system of domestic review, including an effective system of appeal." As such, the Model Law 2011 and the GPA are now more closely aligned in this respect. A new general principle has also been added to the revised GPA under which procurement should be conducted in a "transparent and impartial manner that . . . avoids conflicts of interest and prevents corrupt practices."[22] This provision reflects the realization that GPA membership has always had the potential to promote good governance through channels such as ready access to applicable procurement rules and contract opportunities, limiting the discretion of procurement officers and independent review of compliance with procedural rules.

As for the enforceability of the new provisions, it is difficult to accept that panels and the Appellate Body will be prepared to engage directly with whether it has been breached. Conflicts of interests and (even more so) corruption are sensitive matters. The Appellate Body does not engage directly with another sensitive (but less sensitive)

[19] Guide: pp. 11–12, Section 6. Article 3 of the Model Law provides that treaty obligations prevail when in conflict with the Model Law.

[20] WT/DS412/AB/R, *Canada—Certain Measures Affecting the Renewable Energy Generation Sector*; WT/DS426/AB/R, *Canada—Measures Relating to the Feed-In Tariff Programme*, para. 5.59.

[21] GPA preamble: "*Recognizing* the importance of transparent measures regarding government procurement, of carrying out procurements in a transparent and impartial manner and of avoiding conflicts of interest and corrupt practices, in accordance with applicable international instruments, such as the United Nations Convention Against Corruption."
While the Model Law does not itself refer to UNCAC, there are several references to it in the Guide (p. 3, para. 8; p. 306, para. 1).

[22] Revised GPA Article IV(4).

matter—that of whether a measure is "applied so as to afford protection to domestic production." While it is clear that this is an independent legal test which must be considered separately under GATT Article III:2 second sentence, no attempt needs to be made to ascertain the subjective intent of individual policy-makers. The matter is desensitized by considering whether protective application can be ascertained from the "design, the architecture, and the revealing structure of a measure."[23] Panels are therefore likely to distance themselves from direct engagement with alleged conflicts of interest and corruption, choosing instead to view the new provision as providing interpretive context for other more specific provisions. As such, the main impact of the new provision is likely to be to inform the future development of the specific transparency-based rules.

In sum, the GPA remains first and foremost an instrument of trade liberalization. Undoubtedly, this liberalization can also enhance the achievement of value for money through increased competition, even though the meaning of this concept and how to achieve it are matters for national regulation. When trade liberalization means that contracts are placed with foreign suppliers, this is not at all necessarily at the expense of domestic suppliers. The local capacity to perform large contracts might not exist, but existing small firms could benefit from sub-contracting and technology transfer.[24] Trade liberalization in the procurement context should not have any pejorative connotation. There is also growing understanding of the ways in which GPA membership can contribute toward good governance. Of particular note here is the idea of GPA membership enabling states to "lock-in" reforms directed toward increasing transparency and integrity which might otherwise be more susceptible to erosion.[25] It is also increasingly possible to think about international procurement instruments which may have somewhat different primary rationales as each contributing toward a coherent whole. To some extent, the GPA takes over the baton from the Model Law.

1.3 Enforcement and Remedies under the GPA

The country studies focus in part on the national implementation of the GPA requirements on enforcement and remedies. This section provides an account of these requirements.

When suppliers consider that the GPA has not been properly implemented, or that it has been breached in the context of a particular award procedure, they can take advantage of the requirement to provide for domestic review procedures. Significantly,

[23] WT/DS8,10, 11/AB/R, *Japan—Taxes on Alcoholic Beverages* adopted November 1, 1996, p. 29.
[24] These are among the themes developed by Anderson et al. (2011b).
[25] This term was used by Niewiadomska (2014).

suppliers can resort to these procedures independently of their governments, so that this form of enforcement is fundamentally different to intergovernmental dispute settlement under the Dispute Settlement Understanding (DSU).

The rationale for the obligation in international instruments to provide for domestic review procedures is referred to in the Model Law 2011 Guide to Enactment:

> An effective challenge mechanism helps to make the Model Law to an important degree self-policing and self-enforcing, since it provides an avenue for suppliers and contractors that have a natural interest in monitoring procuring entities' compliance with the provisions of the Model Law in each procurement procedure. It also helps foster public confidence in the procurement system as a whole. An additional function of a challenge mechanism is to act as a deterrent: its existence is designed to discourage actions or decisions knowingly in breach of the law. For these reasons, a challenge mechanism is an essential element of ensuring the proper functioning of the procurement system and can promote confidence in that system.[26]

In the revised GPA, the minimum requirements for domestic review procedures are set out in Article XVIII (see Box 1.1).

The GPA 1994 did not contain the above-mentioned paragraph (b), so that suppliers apparently had to be given the opportunity to challenge "a breach of the Agreement." Some commentators interpreted this language as indicating that the GPA was intended to have direct effect in the legal systems of all its parties (Cottier, 2002). Had this been correct, national review bodies would be required to apply the GPA itself, rather than national implementing measures in the event of a conflict. It is now clear from the inclusion of paragraph (b) that direct effect is a matter for individual parties.[27] Therefore,

BOX 1.1 GPA ARTICLE XVIII:1 DOMESTIC REVIEW PROCEDURES

Article XVIII:1 Domestic Review Procedures

1. Each Party shall provide a timely, effective, transparent, and non-discriminatory administrative or judicial review procedure through which a supplier may challenge:
   (a) a breach of the Agreement; or
   (b) where the supplier does not have a right to challenge directly a breach of the Agreement under the domestic law of a Party, a failure to comply with a Party's measures implementing this Agreement,

arising in the context of a covered procurement, in which it has, or has had, an interest. The procedural rules for all challenges shall be in writing and made generally available.

[26] The Guide: p. 228, para. 2.

[27] It is interesting to note that, in Canada, it is possible for suppliers to base their claim on an alleged breach of the GPA itself, as well as all other applicable international agreements. The Canadian International Trade Tribunal Procurement Inquiry Regulations (SOR/93-602) provide: "11. If the Tribunal conducts an inquiry into a complaint, it shall determine whether the procurement was conducted in accordance with the requirements set out in whichever of NAFTA, the Agreement on Internal Trade, the Agreement on

when the supplier's complaint is that the GPA has not been properly implemented by a state which does not recognize the direct effect of the WTO agreements, the appropriate course of action would be for the supplier to petition its government to institute intergovernmental proceedings under the DSU.

In contrast, when the GPA has been properly implemented but when the relevant national rules have not been followed by an entity in a specific procurement, suppliers can usefully have recourse to domestic review procedures. Indeed, the requirement for parties to provide for these procedures stems from the inadequacy of the DSU in providing a meaningful solution where the complaint relates to a specific procurement. The timetable for resolving disputes under the DSU is understandably protracted and there is no provision for interim remedies, such as the suspension of the award procedure, at the start of the dispute.[28] Indeed, there would be little point in providing for suspension, unless a panel could order the recommencement of the procedure in the event of a breach being confirmed. It is generally understood, however, that the standard recommendation under DSU Article 19 has only prospective effect. The requirement to "bring the [inconsistent] measure into conformity" is a forward-looking remedy which does not entail reparations for injury caused by WTO violations (see Davies, 2006).

In the procurement context, the *Trondheim* case,[29] decided under the Tokyo Round GPA, confirms that remedies following intergovernmental proceedings at the WTO cannot have an impact on past conduct. The case involved the Norwegian Public Roads Administration, which awarded a contract relating to electronic toll collection equipment for a toll system around the city of Trondheim to a Norwegian company, Micro Design. As limited tendering was used (then referred to as "single tendering"), the award was not preceded by any competitive tendering procedure. This was challenged by the United States on the basis that the use of limited tendering had excluded "viable and eager competition from a capable United States supplier." The panel first found that the use of limited tendering was not justified under the governing provisions in effect at that time.[30] Therefore the national treatment provision then contained in Article II:1

Government Procurement, the CCFTA, the CPFTA, the CCOFTA, the CPAFTA, the CHFTA or the CKFTA applies." The suppliers' complaints can be viewed at <http://www.citt.gc.ca/en/procurement?field_case_year_value%5Bvalue%5D%5Byear%5D=2013> (accessed July 20, 2016).

[28] The GPA 1994 Article XXII:6 had provided that "[e]very effort should be made to accelerate the proceedings to the greatest possible extent" and then went on to recommend specific reduced deadlines. Interestingly, this provision has been jettisoned from the revised GPA, which probably reflects the view that breaches of the GPA in the context of specific procurements can only realistically be challenged at the national level.

[29] *Norway—Procurement of Toll Collection Equipment for the City of Trondheim*, panel report adopted by the Committee on Government Procurement May 13, 1992, BISD 40S/319.

[30] Article V:15(e) of the Tokyo Round GPA.

(now Article IV:1) was found to have been breached. The panel then considered the remedies which the United States had requested:

> Para. 4.17: the Panel noted that all the acts of non-compliance alleged by the United States were acts that had taken place in the past. The only way mentioned during the Panel's proceedings that Norway could bring the Trondheim procurement into line with its obligations under the Agreement would be by annulling the contract and recommencing the procurement process. The Panel did not consider it appropriate to make such a recommendation. Recommendations of this nature had not been within customary practice in dispute settlement under the GATT system and the drafters of the Agreement on Government Procurement had not made specific provision that such recommendations be within the task assigned to panels under standard terms of reference. Moreover, the Panel considered that in the case under examination such a recommendation might be disproportionate, involving waste of resources and possible damage to the interests of third parties.

The panel also noted that proposals had been made in relation to revising the Tokyo Round GPA which were intended to "address the difficulty felt to exist in obtaining effective redress in respect of complaints about specific procurements."[31] The negotiations resulted in revisions to the Uruguay Round GPA which are now found in Article XVIII of the revised GPA. This provision advises that "the Party of the procuring entity conducting the procurement shall encourage the entity and the supplier to seek resolution of the complaint through consultations."[32] It then sets out requirements on the identity and attributes of the review body, and the remedies which it should have at its disposal.

1.3.1 THE IDENTITY AND ATTRIBUTES OF THE REVIEW BODY

Article XVIII:4 provides that "[e]ach Party shall establish or designate at least one impartial administrative or judicial authority that is independent of its procuring entities to receive and review a challenge by a supplier arising in the context of a covered procurement." Paragraph 5 goes on to provide that "a body other than an authority referred to in paragraph 4 can initially review a challenge." It may therefore be permissible for the procuring entity complained of to initially review the challenge, although this could be regarded as an unnecessary procedural formality if the formal complaint was preceded by consultations between the aggrieved supplier and the procuring entity. An alternative could therefore be for challenges to be initially reviewed by the government entity with oversight of the entity complained of.

[31] Para. 4.27. [32] Revised GPA Article XVIII:2.

Where there is an initial review by a non-independent authority, parties must provide for an appeal against the initial decision to an impartial administrative or judicial authority. Paragraph 6 provides that where this review body is not a court, it must either be subject to judicial review or operate with what might be described as "court-like" procedures. Participants must, for example, have the right to be heard prior to a decision and have access to all proceedings.

It is not expressly provided that entities must follow review body recommendations, although this is arguably implicit in the need to provide for access to courts or court-like procedures. Some international rules are not as strict in this respect. For example, the North America Free Trade Agreement states that entities should "normally" follow the recommendations of the review body.[33] It is unclear whether this position would be acceptable as an implementation of the GPA. This is because reference is made to the review body making "decisions or recommendations."[34] The use of "recommendations" can be interpreted as indicating that the entire content of the review body report can be non-binding. However, this interpretation is difficult to accept bearing in mind that review procedures must be "effective." A possible intermediate interpretation would be that the decision on whether the rules have been breached must be binding, while recommendations on how to remedy the situation can be non-binding. However, this interpretation would make the GPA less strict than the 2011 Model Law, whose Article 67.9 refers to "decisions" as opposed to recommendations, and gives a strong impression that the content of these decisions is binding through use of language such as "prohibit," "require," and "overturn."

For a couple of reasons, the minimum requirements described above arguably provide less protection to aggrieved suppliers than the equivalent rules in the previous text. The GPA 1994 did not envisage the possibility of initial review of a challenge by a body other than an impartial administrative or judicial authority.[35] This initial review could be viewed by suppliers as either an unwanted hurdle, or as an opportunity to "nip the matter in the bud."[36] A second aspect which arguably reduces the level of protection relates to the attributes of the review body. As noted, the revised GPA requires parties to "designate at least one impartial administrative or judicial authority that is independent of its procuring entities." The previous text was more fulsome in requiring that

[33] NAFTA Article 1017:1(l). [34] Revised GPA, Article XVIII:6(f).

[35] The Model Law Guide indicates that there are different state practices in this area: "Some States are more flexible by not requiring the supplier or contractor to exhaust the challenge mechanism at the procuring entity before filing an application before the independent body or the court" (p. 237, para. 7).

[36] The Guide elaborates on both possible perceptions. Review by the procuring entity itself may, "facilitate a swift, simple and relatively low-cost procedure, which can avoid unnecessarily burdening other forums with applications and appeals that might have been resolved by the parties at an earlier, less disruptive stage, and with lower costs." On the other hand, it is also noted that, "procuring entities [sometimes] simply ignore the request, and submitting one operates in practice merely to delay a formal application in another forum" (p. 230, para. 11).

challenges "be heard by a court or by an impartial and independent review body with no interest in the outcome of the procurement and the members of which are secure from external influence during the term of appointment."[37] On this change, Arie Reich comments that "[n]ot only is the exact nature of such independence not elaborated in the Revised Text but it also ignores the need to ensure that the body's members are secure from other external influence, such as influence from competing suppliers" (Reich, 2009: p. 1015). This may slightly overstate the problem, as a review body whose members could be subject to influence by competing suppliers would not be impartial. However, I am inclined to agree that there was no need to streamline the old language.

A final observation here is that it remains permissible under a minimal GPA implementation to keep review out of the courts. It is permissible under the GPA for the appeal to be to an impartial administrative authority operating under what might be described as "court-like" procedures. The question raised is whether this is consistent with the UNCAC, which requires an "effective system of domestic review, including an effective system of appeal." It is submitted that the possibility of appeal to the courts is not required. The Guide to Enactment to the Model Law 2011 gives the impression that this would be inconsistent with the legal traditions of states with established systems of review in non-judicial independent bodies.[38] In such states, the effective system of appeal could be from the procuring entity itself to the independent body, or within the independent body. However, this matter is not free from doubt as indicated by the following statement from the 2013 UNCITRAL Guidance on Procurement Regulations:

> the procurement regulations must be compliant with the international obligations of the enacting State, including under the United Nations Convention against Corruption (New York, 31 October 2003) and the WTO GPA, which may require them to ensure effective appeal to an independent body and that decisions of any review body that is not a court be open to judicial review.[39]

1.3.2 REMEDIES

The rationale for rapid interim measures is that if the procurement process is permitted to continue during the challenge procedures, the final remedy is unlikely to be very helpful in terms of encouraging suppliers to complain and deterring breaches. This is because a contract might be concluded or even performed during the review procedure. Should these events be permitted to occur, any remedy other than a declaration that a breach has occurred becomes unlikely because of prejudice to the successful supplier and

[37] GPA 1994, Article XX:6. [38] The Guide: p. 299, para. 15.
[39] Guidance on Procurement Regulations (2013: p. 61, para. 4).

BOX 1.2 GPA ARTICLE XVIII:7

Article XVIII:7 Each Party shall adopt or maintain procedures that provide for:

(a) rapid interim measures to preserve the supplier's opportunity to participate in the procurement. Such interim measures may result in suspension of the procurement process. The procedures may provide that overriding adverse consequences for the interests concerned, including the public interest, may be taken into account when deciding whether such measures should be applied. Just cause for not acting shall be provided in writing; and
(b) where a review body has determined that there has been a breach or a failure as referred to in paragraph 1, corrective action or compensation for the loss or damages suffered, which may be limited to either the costs for the preparation of the tender or the costs relating to the challenge, or both.

the public interest in the prompt delivery of government functions. In contrast, if the procurement process can be suspended at an early stage, the possibility of re-commencement being ordered is preserved.

The language in Article XVIII:7 paragraph (a) (see Box 1.2) could be more prescriptive without clashing with prevailing legal traditions. In particular, the language could indicate that review bodies must have the power to suspend the procurement process at any point until the conclusion of a procurement contract, subject to taking account of the "overriding adverse consequences" referred to. However, it would probably be a step too far to require that review bodies be empowered to suspend the performance of a contract. This is envisaged only as a possible option in the Model Law 2011.[40]

As regards the final remedies envisaged by paragraph (b), it is reasonably clear that review bodies must have both remedies (correction and compensation) at their disposal, again, on the basis that "effective" challenge procedures are required. Of these two remedies, corrective action will generally be by far the most important, given that the compensation remedy can permissibly be a limited one.[41] Corrective action might involve preventing the procuring entity from following a non-compliant procedure and requiring it to proceed in a compliant manner. It could also extend to overturning the award of a wrongfully awarded contract when this possibility is recognized in the jurisdiction in question.

The GPA's minimum requirements for domestic review procedures have been criticized as insufficiently strong and prescriptive. However, they are minimum requirements and there is nothing to prevent states from applying more robust procedures. Also, the GPA has to be a reasonably good fit for many jurisdictions. Prescriptive

[40] Article 67.3.

[41] It notable that the Israel–Mexico FTA provides that compensation "shall [rather than may] be limited to costs for tender preparation or protest" (Article 6.17.7(c)). The Model Law 2011 also envisages this formulation as a possible implementation of its Article 67.9(i).

language could make it difficult for some states to comply even when they provide for an overall system which is effective.

1.4 **Supporting the Participation of SMEs in Procurement**

Taking a step back from the new work program on SMEs, it is worth sketching the different perceptions on the nature of the problems and challenges in this area. The different perceptions have a common origin. National policies to support SMEs and, more broadly, enterprises owned by historically disadvantaged individuals (HDIs) tend to be discriminatory. From here, perceptions split off in two directions. In one view, the discrimination is problematic and the challenge is to remove it. The opposing perception views the discrimination as an intractable, necessary, and justifiable aspect of the social policy. The challenge is not to remove the discrimination, but rather to assess how the GPA can better accommodate these policies with a view to expanding its membership. The SME work program appears to be focused on the former perception.

The intention is to consider "best practice with respect to measures and policies that the parties use to support the participation of SMEs in government procurement."[42] Glancing at the relevant Decision,[43] it is immediately apparent that the work program views policies which discriminate in favor of domestic SMEs as undesirable, thereby reinforcing the GPA's primary rationale. The second paragraph provides:

> Avoidance of Discriminatory SME Measures: The Parties shall avoid introducing discriminatory measures that favour only domestic SMEs and shall discourage the introduction of such measures and policies by acceding Parties.

Reference is later made to an SME survey and to the implementation of the outcome of this survey. However, the wording implies that SME policies which favor only domestic SMEs cannot qualify as best practice:

> 4.2 Implementation of the Outcome of the SME Survey
>
> (a) The Parties shall promote the adoption of the best practices identified in the assessment of the survey to encourage and facilitate participation of SMEs of the Parties in government procurement.

[42] <http://www.wto.org/english/tratop_e/gproc_e/gpa_wk_prog_e.htm> (accessed November 2014).

[43] Appendix 2, Annex C of Adoption of the Results of the Negotiations under Article XXIV:7 of the Agreement on Government Procurement, Following Their Verification and Review, as Required by the Ministerial Decision of December 15, 2011 (GPA/112), para. 5, GPA/113, April 2, 2012.

(b) With respect to other measures, the Committee shall encourage the Parties that maintain such measures to review them with a view to eliminating them *or applying them to the SMEs of the other Parties*. These Parties shall inform the Committee about the outcome of the review (emphasis added).

Accepting that the work program is about fostering SME participation while also removing discrimination, there are a number of related queries. The first relates to its narrowness or breadth, since states can have different perceptions of what is meant by SME participation. A second query is whether there are plausible rationales for promoting SME participation. Why, if at all, is this important? A third query is whether it is realistic to expect much progress in removing or reducing the discriminatory content of SME policies.

On the first query, some states pursue SME participation in a direct and literal sense based on measurements broadly related to the size of enterprises.[44] States also pursue SME participation indirectly or incidentally. Policies which support enterprises based on their ownership and management by HDIs are perhaps more likely to support small enterprises than large ones. While the work program refers only to SMEs, the possibility of a broad remit should not be excluded at this early stage. In the envisaged survey, parties will be required to indicate how they define SMEs, and what "economic, social, and other goals" are pursued. It is possible that some GPA parties—the US in particular—will highlight that some of its policies are directed toward minority-owned enterprises. Perhaps the likelihood, however, is that the work program will be restricted to national policies which define SMEs with reference to size as opposed to ownership parameters. This is because the work program applies to current GPA parties, among whom SME participation in the direct and literal sense is more prevalent than policies supporting companies owned by HDIs. This tends to be more closely associated with states which are not yet GPA parties, such as South Africa and Malaysia (which has observer status). It may be that the focus on SME participation in the narrow sense is a sensible starting point before consideration of social policies more broadly. There is more potential for agreement on what an SME is when only size parameters are considered. Also, there may be more scope for removing discrimination when SME participation is understood in the narrow sense (as discussed further later in this section).

What are the rationales for promoting SME participation? As Linarelli (2011) asks:

> Why should law and public policy allocate scarce resources to SMEs? Why not let the capital markets decide which businesses should succeed and which not? Why is government intervention beyond that of supporting efficient capital markets necessary to support SMEs? (p. 447).

44 For a discussion of the various methods for defining small businesses and SMEs in the EU and US, see Kidalov (2011).

Based on a review of the literature, Linarelli identifies a number of possible economic arguments in favor of policies to assist SMEs in general. Competition and entrepreneurship can be enhanced with benefits for economy-wide efficiency, innovation, and aggregate productivity. The industrial base can be broadened, thereby countering monopolistic practices. SMEs may also be more productive than larger enterprises and more labor intensive, with greater potential to alleviate poverty. Suffice it to say that these are not uncontested arguments. Linarelli proceeds to review the studies of SME preference policies in procurement, finding some evidence that they can enhance competition by encouraging other firms to bid more aggressively in order to overcome preferences and win contracts. Of course, the possibility of enhanced competition is more strongly associated with SME preferences than set-asides.

While there may be commercial rationales for SME preferences (they may enhance value of money), the stronger tenet of Linarelli's work is to argue that there are more important social justice and human rights rationales, especially in the context of enterprises owned by HDIs:

> Distributive justice and economic efficiency may work at cross-purposes. A social arrangement may be efficient and yet fundamentally unjust. Let us assume that governments only focus their attention on transaction costs and reducing barriers to entry in government procurement. Facilitating the operation of markets in government procurement does not "guarantee" fair participation in those markets by SMEs and HDIs. It might be efficient to only have large multinational enterprises, which have the benefits of economies of scale and low-cost global supply chains, providing bundled goods and services to government, regardless of the national origins of these goods and services, and regardless of the working conditions or wages paid for these goods and services to labour, and regardless of ownership of these firms, and so on. Governments, however, have duties that go beyond efficiency in procurement. They have duties of justice. While all social institutions are required to meet the demands of justice, a government as a buyer is a special role to promote justice; it is now well accepted that governments can and do use procurement as a social policy tool (p. 452).

In sum, SME participation can, at the same time, promote strictly economic goals and broader social justice goals. However, there is a compelling argument that social justice goals stand alone and can be legitimately pursued independently of economic goals.

The third query is whether it is realistic to expect much progress in removing the discriminatory content of SME policies. Do states wish to continue pursuing discriminatory SME policies outside of GPA coverage by way of negotiated derogations, or do they perceive that the benefits of these policies can be achieved even when the discrimination is removed?

Preferences and set-asides in favor of domestic SMEs are *de jure* discriminatory and contrary to the national treatment principle in Article V:1 of the GPA. This is because the nationality-based discrimination is indisputable from the face of the measure. All foreign firms are ineligible, while some domestic firms are eligible. This discrimination could be removed by extending eligibility to all SMEs of the GPA Parties. A common definition of an SME would help in aiding understanding of eligibility, but this is not strictly necessary in order to remove discrimination. Eligibility of all enterprises of the GPA parties meeting national criteria would be *de jure* non-discriminatory and probably also *de facto* non-discriminatory. The extended eligibility removes the explicit differentiation between domestic and foreign suppliers. On *de facto* discrimination, foreign suppliers as a group (foreign SMEs and non-SMEs) are treated no less favorably than domestic suppliers as a group (domestic SMEs and non-SMEs).[45] An additional observation is that the point made earlier when contrasting the GPA and the Model Law applies here. Divergent national rules on the definition of an SME can all be non-discriminatory and, therefore, of limited direct concern under the GPA. However, divergent definitions could still have a chilling effect on international trade of more direct concern under the Model Law.

Of course, any discussion of what steps would remove discrimination must consider the practicalities and political considerations. Reaching a common definition of an SME among GPA parties is probably unrealistic by reason of the volume of variables. Individual states may have different definitions for different types of industries and procurement contracts,[46] and it might be regarded as incomplete to consider the positions of only existing parties as opposed to also future accessions. Furthermore, the formulation and enforcement of SME recognition rules even at the national level can be a formidable challenge.[47] Perhaps the most that can be achieved here is a soft mutual recognition principle, along the lines of Article 2.7 of the TBT Agreement, under which a GPA party would give positive consideration to recognizing a supplier as an SME when that supplier is so recognized by any other party. The alternative of allowing foreign suppliers to apply for SME status under national rules may not be any more realistic. SME preferences and set-asides respond to the difficulties encountered in accessing national procurement markets. Suppliers can reasonably be expected to apply for recognition under their national rules, but they are unlikely to have the resources to apply for recognition under the rules of many other GPA parties.

Apart from these practical difficulties, the question is whether it is politically realistic to expect states to extend domestic SME preferences and set-asides to foreign suppliers. The perception might be that the achievement of the policy is undermined every time a contract is awarded to a foreign SME. This need not be the perception if the policy is intended to gradually improve the competitiveness of domestic SMEs. Extending the

[45] In WTO law, it is now firmly established that a group comparison applies as opposed to an approach which has been variously termed individual or diagonal comparison or best treatment. Under this (discredited) approach, there could be *de facto* discrimination on the basis that there is a foreign non-SME which is treated less favorably than a domestic SME (see Davies, 2015).

[46] See Kidalov (2011: pp. 461–5). Of the US position, the author notes that a "business concern may be small in one industry category and yet large in another" (p. 463).

[47] On the development of this process in China, see Cao (2013).

SME preference or set-asides to SMEs of all GPA parties would deepen and intensify competition among similarly situated enterprises. However, this raises another barrier. States may wish to shelter their SMEs from competition not only from larger domestic and foreign enterprises, but also from foreign SMEs.

When we move beyond SMEs per se toward enterprises owned by defined national HDIs, the desire to reserve the policy's benefit for the defined enterprises may be overwhelming. Bolton and Quinot (2011) note that, in South Africa, an HDI is defined in regulations "to refer to those individuals disenfranchised under apartheid, women and the disabled, but in all instances restricted to South African citizens" (p. 463). In describing the regulations adopted under the relevant enactment,[48] the authors note the possibility of preference points "for being an HDI and/or contracting with an HDI."[49] They also note that, under the regulations, "preference points . . . must include preference points for equity ownership by HDIs."[50] While these preferences may not be *de jure* discriminatory, because some foreign firms could be eligible, they are probably *de facto* discriminatory on the basis that the preferences will disproportionately benefit domestic suppliers.

Subsequent to the Bolton and Quinot contribution, revised regulations entered into force in 2011.[51] The new regime is less trade restrictive and less overtly discriminatory than the previous regime, and therefore enhances competitive opportunities for foreign firms. The primacy afforded to domestic HDI ownership at the award stage has been reduced. Indeed, the terminology has changed from HDI to Broad-Based Black Economic Empowerment (B-BBEE). For contracts up to a value of one million rand, a maximum of eighty points can be awarded for price, and a maximum of twenty points for the level of attainment of B-BBEE status. Within this twenty points, there are a number of elements with different weightings, as shown in Table 1.1.[52]

While the first two elements will tend to heavily favor domestic suppliers, the others are more neutral in terms of the capacity of domestic and foreign suppliers to score

Table 1.1 B-BBEE elements and weightings

Ownership	25 points
Management Control	15 points
Skills Development	20 points
Enterprise and Supplier Development	40 points
Socio-economic Development	5 points

[48] Preferential Procurement Policy Framework Act 2000 (Act No. 5 of 2000).
[49] Preferential Procurement Regulations 2001, regulation 4(2).
[50] Preferential Procurement Regulations 2001, regulation 13(1).
[51] Preferential Procurement Regulations 2011, which must be read with the Broad Based Black Economic Empowerment Act (53/2003) Codes of Good Practice, Gazette No. 36928, October 11, 2013.
[52] Codes of Good Practice, Statement 000-8.1.

highly. As an example, the most important component of the Enterprise and Supplier Development element is Preferential Procurement, on which foreign suppliers could score highly by sub-contracting to high level B-BBEE suppliers.

More than the outgoing regime, the new regime recognizes that pursuing the social policies at issue is not necessarily incompatible with awarding contracts to foreign firms. However, the revised regime at least could amount to *de facto* discrimination on the basis that certain elements (Ownership and Management Control) are likely in practice to favor domestic suppliers.

Based on these observations, I am skeptical of the prospects for completely removing the discriminatory nature of SME policies, especially when there is an HDI dimension. Having said this, it is a worthwhile endeavor to at least explore these prospects. The GPA is an instrument of trade liberalization whose central principle is non-discrimination for covered procurement. It arguably does not need to shift toward a different role served very well by other instruments such as the Model Law which, as noted, applies in principle to all procurement and is not so focused on removing discrimination.[53] On the other hand, it is also possible to argue that the work program does not respond to the GPA's biggest challenge—that of expanding its membership. A recalibrated work program would acknowledge that SME policies are understandably discriminatory and focus on how such policies can be better accommodated, in particular for possible future members. The focus would then need to be on matters such as the asymmetry in the capacity of large and small economies to negotiate for derogations, and the possibility of allowing GPA parties to justify discriminatory policies on any legitimate public policy ground as opposed to the closed list of exceptions in Article III:2.

1.5 **Collection and Reporting of Statistical Data Relating to the GPA**

In common with the GPA 1994, the revised GPA contains obligations on the collection and reporting of statistics. The content of these obligations have been reduced. For example, under the GPA 1994, the annual reporting requirement for Annex 1 entities

[53] It is clear that the Model Law is designed to accommodate the pursuit of socio-economic policies with discriminatory impact. This subject area is discussed in the Guide (pp. 4–6). It is noted that through measures envisaged in the Model Law's substantive provisions, "procurement may be set aside for particular groups or sectors of the economy, or those sectors or groups may receive a preferential treatment in the procurement procedure concerned" (p. 4, para. 13). At the same time, the Guide strikes several notes of caution. It highlights, for example, that preferences tend to be more beneficial than set asides in terms of fostering the development of protected enterprises. Socio-economic policies are described as "exceptional measures" because they depart from "full and open competition." The danger of suppliers artificially remaining as SMEs is mentioned, as is the importance of remaining in conformity with international obligations including the GPA.

applied to "statistics on the estimated value of contracts awarded, both above and below the threshold value, on a global basis and broken down by entities."[54] The equivalent obligation in the revised GPA applies only to "contracts covered by this Agreement," thereby excluding below-threshold procurements.[55] The obligations for Annexes 2 and 3 entities have been reduced to a greater extent. The GPA 1994 extended to "statistics on the estimated value of contracts awarded above the threshold value broken down by categories of entities and categories of products and services," as well as "statistics on the total value of contracts awarded above the threshold value under each of the cases of Article XV [limited tendering]."[56] Under the revised GPA, for Annexes 2 and 3 entities, the required statistics need only cover "the number and total value of contracts covered by this Agreement awarded by all such entities, broken down by Annex."[57] Therefore, the statistical breakdown no longer needs to be by "categories of products and services," and no longer needs to refer to the total value of above-threshold contracts awarded via limited tendering.

A possible response to the comparisons above is that, while the content of the obligations has been reduced in terms of the amount of information which must be provided, the required accuracy of the more limited information which must now be provided has been increased. In other words, less information of higher accuracy must now be provided. This is because the GPA 1994 refers on two occasions to "statistics on the estimated value,"[58] whereas the revised GPA, at least initially, does not refer to estimates. This argument has little weight. The GPA 1994 refers to "statistics" without qualification more often than it refers to estimates. More importantly, the revised GPA ultimately permits estimates even for the more limited information that must be provided.[59]

The impression that the revised GPA has taken a backward step is reinforced by another aspect of the need to provide statistical information. As the GPA is an instrument of trade liberalization, it would be informative for GPA members and non-members to be able to access information on such matters as the level of participation and success of foreign suppliers, the level of foreign ownership of successful domestic suppliers, and the origin of goods and services purchased.

The GPA 1994 contained a soft obligation in this respect. Article XIX:5 concluded with the following statement:

> To the extent that such information is available, each Party shall provide statistics on the country of origin of products and services purchased by its entities. With a view to ensuring that such statistics are comparable, the Committee shall provide guidance on methods to be used.

54 GPA 1994, Article XI:5(a).
55 Revised GPA, Article XVI:4(a).
56 GPA 1994, Article XIX:5(b) and (c).
57 Revised GPA, Article XVI:4(b).
58 GPA 1994, Article XI:5(a).
59 Revised GPA, Article XVI:4(c) refers to "estimates for the data required . . . with an explanation of the methodology used to develop the estimates, where it is not feasible to provide the data."

While it might reasonably have been thought that this obligation would have been strengthened in the revised GPA, it has instead been jettisoned.

As for why the statistical reporting requirements have become less onerous, there are two explanations. The level of compliance with the statistical reporting requirements in terms of how comprehensive and timely the reports are has been variable. For example, information on the origin of products and services purchased features strongly in the reports of Hong Kong, China,[60] while being absent from EU reports.[61] It is therefore plausible that the reporting obligations have been reduced in order to increase the correspondence between what should be submitted and the actual content of reports. Another explanation is to raise the prospects for increased membership. There is something of a paradox here. Prospective members may find it marginally easier to accede to an instrument with reduced statistical reporting obligations. On the other hand, the availability of detailed information from existing members can enable prospective members to make informed decisions. This point is recognized in the work program on the Collection and Reporting of Statistical Data:

> Considering that statistical data that illustrate the extent to which the Parties procure goods and services covered by the Agreement from other Parties to the Agreement could be an important tool in encouraging other WTO Members to accede to the Agreement.

In light of this work program, the less onerous obligations in the revised GPA can be regarded as an experimental and short-term strategy to marginally increase the prospects of membership expansion. This is perhaps a case of one step backward, to be followed by two steps forward in the event of the work program generating positive outcomes.

1.6 Procurement May Not Be Carved Out of Multilateral Rules Such as GATT Article III to the Extent That Has Been Commonly Thought

The questions of whether and how government procurement should be regulated are among the most challenging that GATT and WTO negotiators have faced. The sensitivity of the area became clear at a very early point in the history of international

[60] See, for example, GPA/123/Add.2, Statistics for 2013 Reported Under Article XIX:5 of the Agreement (1994), October 9, 2014 (available at: <https://docs.wto.org/dol2fe/Pages/FE_Browse/FE_B_009.aspx?TopLevel=3971#/> (accessed July 20, 2016)).

[61] On the related matter of supplier and service provider nationality, the EU reports refer to the lack of "a consistent method to trace contracts awarded to companies from other GPA Parties as a large number of contracts were awarded to suppliers that are subsidiaries of foreign companies or agents for foreign suppliers," GPA/108/Add.7, Statistics for 2010 Reported Under Article XIX:5 of the Agreement (1994), October 22, 2014.

procurement regulation. It is striking that the Suggested Charter for an International Trade Organisation, drafted by the United States and published in September 1946, originally proposed that government procurement should be subject to the general national treatment obligation.[62] However, it quickly became apparent that this would not be possible because of the prevalence of discriminatory laws and practices involving preferences for domestic suppliers. Indeed the Charter's initial inclusion of procurement was substituted with a derogation which survives to this day:[63]

> GATT Article III:8(a)
> The provisions of this Article shall not apply to laws, regulations or requirements governing the procurement by governmental agencies of products purchased for governmental purposes and not with a view to commercial resale or with a view to use in the production of goods for commercial sale.

This derogation may not be as broad as has generally been thought. The Appellate Body's message in *Canada—Renewable Energy* is that it will not serve to shelter challenged measures from the disciplines of Article III on a blanket or "self-judging" basis. [64] Japan and the EU complained of domestic content requirements applicable in the construction of solar and wind power generation facilities in the Feed-in Tariff (FIT) program established by the Ontario Power Authority.[65] Under the FIT program, generators of electricity via renewable sources delivered into the Ontarian system were paid a guaranteed price under twenty-year or forty-year contracts. The meeting of minimum domestic content levels was among the conditions for being offered a contract. Both Japan and the EU argued that the domestic content requirements infringed the GATT Article III:4 national treatment obligation on the basis that their energy generation equipment was being treated less favorably than like products of Ontarian origin.[66,67]

[62] Article 9(1) covered "laws and regulations governing the procurement by governmental agencies of supplies for public use other than by or for the military establishment", (available at: <http://www.worldtradelaw.net/document.php?id=misc/Suggested%20Charter.pdf> (accessed November 2014)).

[63] The derogation first appeared in Article 2(5) of the Tentative and Non-Committal Draft Suggested by the Delegation of the United States of February 7, 1947, E/PC/T/C.6/W.53 (available at: <http://www.worldtradelaw.net/document.php?id=misc/Draft%202.pdf> (accessed July 20, 2016)).

[64] WT/DS412/AB/R, *Canada—Certain Measures Affecting the Renewable Energy Generation Sector*; WT/DS426/AB/R, *Canada—Measures Relating to the Feed-In Tariff Programme*, adopted May 24, 2013. On the subsidy dimension of this case, see Rubini (2012), Cosbey and Mavroidis (2014), and Pal (2014).

[65] This body was established under Ontario's Electricity Restructuring Act of 2004 as a government agency responsible for managing Ontario's electricity supply.

[66] GATT Article III:4 provides in the relevant part: "The products of the territory of any contracting party imported into the territory of any other contracting party shall be accorded treatment no less favourable than that accorded to like products of national origin in respect of all laws, regulations and requirements affecting their internal sale, offering for sale, purchase, transportation, distribution or use."

[67] Both complainants argued that there was a "stand-alone" GATT Article III:4 violation (see panel report, paras 3.1–4.3). The complainants also supplemented this claim with an alleged violation of Article 2.1 of the TRIMs Agreement. The Appellate Body confirmed that the GATT Article III:8(a) procurement

Canada countered that the above derogation applied. For Canada, the FIT program constituted "laws and requirements that govern the procurement of renewable electricity for the governmental purpose of securing an electricity supply for Ontario from clean sources, and 'not with a view to commercial resale or with a view to use in the production of goods for commercial sale'."[68] No complaint was brought under the GPA. This would not have been possible, partly because the Ontario Power Authority was not a covered entity under the Uruguay Round GPA.[69]

The panel ultimately found that the derogation was not available because the electricity was purchased "with a view to commercial resale" by reason of the profit made by the Government of Ontario from resale of FIT program electricity to consumers, and because the resales were made in competition with licensed electricity retailers.[70] As the derogation was ultimately not available, the domestic content requirement was confirmed as a GATT Article III:4 violation.[71] Of greater significance for this article are the panel's earlier findings, which were favorable towards the availability of the derogation and which were overruled by the Appellate Body. The issue, according to the panel, was whether the challenged measures could be characterized as "laws regulations or requirements *governing* procurement."[72] In terms of the identity of the challenged measures, the panel focused on the domestic content requirements, emphasizing that this measure compelled the purchase and use of equipment sourced in Ontario "as a necessary prerequisite for the alleged procurement . . . to take place."[73] As there could not be any procurement of electricity without meeting the domestic content requirement, this requirement governed procurement for the purposes of the derogation.

derogation applies to measures "that fall within the scope of Article 2.2 of the TRIMs Agreement and the Illustrative List annexed thereto" (Appellate Body report, para. 5.33). Therefore, if GATT Article III:4 does not apply to a measure by reason of the Article III:8(a) procurement derogation, then Article 2.1 of the TRIMs Agreement also does not apply to this measure.

[68] Appellate Body report, para. 1.10.

[69] Canada's commitments under the Uruguay Round GPA and the Revised GPA at the sub-central (Annex 2) level can be viewed at <http://www.wto.org/english/tratop_e/gproc_e/gp_app_agree_e.htm>. Notably, a new entity known as the Integrated Electricity System Operator (IESO) has absorbed the old Ontario Power Authority as of January 2015. The IESO falls under the Ontario Ministry of Energy. The revised GPA covers "all Ministries of the Province" of Ontario. Therefore, it is reasonably clear that the IESO is now a covered entity. This does not in itself mean that FIT contracts are now covered by the GPA. This is because goods or services "procured with a view to commercial sale or resale" are not covered (revised GPA, Article II:2).

[70] However, the panel also noted that "commercial resale" would not always necessarily involve profit, noting that "loss-making sales can be, and often are, a part of ordinary commercial activity" (para. 7.151). The Appellate Body seemed to broadly agree with this understanding in elaborating its own view of the "not with a view to commercial resale" language in para. 5.71. However, it did not apply this aspect of the derogation to the facts. As explained in the main text, the Appellate Body considered the derogation to be unavailable independently of the "commercial resale" test.

[71] Panel report, para. 7.167.

[72] *Canada—Renewable Energy*, panel report, para. 7.122.

[73] *Canada—Renewable Energy*, panel report, para. 7.124.

The crucial insight here is that there need not be any connection between the products discriminated against and the products procured in order for the derogation to apply. The products need not be in a competitive relationship, and it is also irrelevant that the products might otherwise be in a close relationship in the sense that electricity cannot be generated and then procured without electricity-generating equipment. To illustrate this point using an example not used by the panel, requirements to buy buffalo meat sourced in Ontario as a prerequisite for gaining an electricity supply contract would still have governed the procurement of electricity. The panel therefore proceeded to dismiss the EU's alternative understanding under which the derogation should be understood as referring only to measures that directly affect a product identical to the product allegedly procured.[74] This position is the opposite extreme to that preferred by the panel. While rejecting this understanding, and indeed the need for any degree of similarity between the products at issue, the panel nevertheless noted a "close relationship" between the products subject to the domestic content requirements (generating equipment) and the product allegedly procured (electricity).[75] In sum, for the panel, the domestic content requirements were laws "governing" procurement indicating the availability of the Article III:8(a) derogation.

In contrast to the panel, the Appellate Body paid particular attention to the phrase "products purchased" when deciding whether the domestic content requirements governed the procurement. The core idea here was that the derogation had to be understood in relation to the obligations of Article III. The derogation "becomes relevant only if there is discriminatory treatment of foreign products that are covered by the obligations in Article III, and this discriminatory treatment results from laws, regulations, or requirements governing procurement by governmental agencies of products purchased."[76] The "same discriminatory treatment" had to be considered both under Article III and the derogation. It followed that the term "products purchased" in the derogation was tied to the scope of the "products" covered by Article III. This resulted in the crucial insight that, for the derogation to apply, "the product of foreign origin [electricity generating equipment] must be in a competitive relationship with the product purchased

[74] *Canada—Renewable Energy*, panel report, para. 7.126.

[75] *Canada—Renewable Energy*, panel report, para. 7.127. The panel's interpretation has sometimes been misunderstood as being dependent upon the noted "close relationship." However, it is reasonably clear that the panel considered that the measure governed procurement independently of this close relationship between electricity and generating equipment. The panel commenced para. 7.127 by noting that "the 'Minimum Required Domestic Content Level' is a necessary prerequisite for the alleged procurement by the Government of Ontario to take place, and to this extent, we are of the view that such requirements 'govern' the alleged procurement." The subsequent reference to the "close relationship" is therefore an *obiter dictum*, rather than a condition for the derogation to apply. Hence, it is submitted that the reference to buffalo meat is a correct example of the panel's understanding of the derogation.

[76] *Canada—Renewable Energy*, Appellate Body report, para. 5.63.

[electricity]."[77] The competitive relationship encompassed products which were either identical or like, or directly competitive or substitutable.[78] As there was no competitive relationship, the domestic content requirements were not "laws, regulations or requirements governing the procurement by governmental agencies" of electricity within the meaning of Article III:8(a).[79] As such, the discrimination relating to generating equipment in the FIT contracts was not covered by the derogation.

How do these different interpretations apply in the type of situation into which, it can reasonably be supposed, the procurement derogation was incorporated in order to cover? Buy national policies involving discriminatory preferences and set-asides in favor of domestic goods have been under the spotlight in recent years following the economic downturn of 2008–9 and the increased emphasis on public infrastructure spending. The American Recovery and Reinvestment Act of 2009 was among the most prominent instruments.[80] The Act was passed with a provision stipulating that the new Buy American requirements "shall be applied in a manner consistent with United States obligations under international agreements."[81] Commentators have assessed whether the Recovery Act and its implementing federal regulations breach the WTO commitments of the US (Linarelli, 2011). Understandably, the primary focus has been on whether the Recovery Act breaches the GPA. It is generally thought that a breach is unlikely. When the contracts are not covered by the GPA, the Buy American requirements can be applied while covered contracts are exempt from Buy American treatment. With regard to GATT Article III, commentators tend to cite the paragraph 8 derogation as exempting government procurement from national treatment. However, as a result of *Canada—Renewable Energy*, it must also be asked whether buy national requirements are covered by GATT Article III:4.

Take the example of a buy national requirement under which steel used in the construction of a highway must be of US origin. Such a requirement clearly falls under Article III:4 to the extent that it applies since imported steel is treated less favorably than like domestic steel. Arguably, Article III:4 does now apply because the Article III:8(a) derogation may not be available. Based on the Appellate Body's interpretation, the subject matter of the contract is a highway, which is not in a competitive relationship with the steel being discriminated against under Article III:4. In contrast, the panel's approach has the potential of extending the derogation to this situation. As the highway construction contract requires the use of domestic steel, this requirement governs the procurement. There is also a reasonably strong connection between the

[77] *Canada—Renewable Energy*, Appellate Body report, para. 5.74.
[78] *Canada—Renewable Energy*, Appellate Body report, para. 5.63.
[79] *Canada—Renewable Energy*, Appellate Body report, para. 5.79.
[80] Public Law No. 111-5, 123 Stat, 115 of February 17, 2009 (the "Recovery Act").
[81] Recovery Act Section 1605(d).

steel discriminated against under Article III and the highway construction project, which cannot be completed without steel. Continuing with the other main element of the derogation, the purchase of the highway would not be "with a view to commercial resale" so that, under the panel's analysis, the buy national requirement in relation to the steel would fall under the derogation. Article III:4 would be inapplicable.

Of course, it would be extraordinary if Article III:4 were to apply in the aforementioned situation. The original Buy American Act was passed in 1933 and it is reasonable to suppose that GATT Article III:8(a) was incorporated in order to shelter this instrument, and comparable instruments maintained by other states, from review under Article III. The question is therefore how the Appellate Body's approach would be applied or refined in this situation.

A possible refinement is that the Appellate Body's interpretation will only potentially result in the non-availability of the derogation when the goods subject to discrimination (electricity-generating equipment) are not a physical input of the product being procured (electricity). In this situation, there is a workable distinction between the two products, and the availability of the derogation depends in part on whether the separate products are in a competitive relationship. If they are not, the derogation will not be available to shelter the discrimination from a GATT Article III:4 claim. In contrast, the steel is a physical input and consumed in the construction of a highway. As such, it is arguable that the product subject to discrimination (steel) and the product being procured (steel) are one and the same, and therefore self-evidently in a competitive relationship. However, this argument is not wholly convincing. It requires a formalistic view of what is being procured that is removed from commercial reality. While the steel is a consumed physical input and the electricity-generating equipment is not, the price of the electricity will, over time, involve recouping the cost of the generating equipment, just as the price of the highway involves recouping the cost of the steel. It is also arguably artificial to concede that steel is being procured in the context of highway construction. One of Canada's statements in a NAFTA Chapter 11 claim, *Mesa Power v Canada*,[82] is particularly striking. It notes that, in *ADF v United States*,[83] "the state of Virginia was not procuring steel, and it certainly was not procuring the process by which steel was manufactured; it was procuring the construction of a highway interchange."[84] If this is accepted, the GATT Article III:8(a) derogation would not shelter a buy national requirement in relation to steel from review under Article GATT Article III:4. There is no competitive relationship between a highway and steel.

[82] The submissions are available at: <http://www.international.gc.ca/trade-agreements-accords-commerciaux/topics-domaines/disp-diff/mesa.aspx?lang=eng> (accessed July 20, 2016).

[83] ICSID ARB(AF)/00/1, Award January 9, 2003.

[84] *Mesa Power v Canada*, Government of Canada, Rejoinder on the Merits, July 2, 2014, para. 77.

It is possible that the Appellate Body was aware that its test could produce odd results in a situation different from that before it:

> What constitutes a competitive relationship between products may require consideration of inputs and processes of production used to produce the product. In its rebuttal of Canada's claim under Article III:8(a), the European Union acknowledges that the cover of Article III:8 (a) may also extend to discrimination relating to inputs and processes of production used in respect of products purchased by way of procurement. Whether the derogation in Article III:8(a) can extend also to discrimination of the kind referred to by the European Union is a matter we do not decide in this case.[85]

This passage commences as an elaboration of the nature of the required "competitive relationship between products." It is clear, of course, that the test for "like" products under Article III can involve considering inputs. The Appellate noted in *Japan—Alcoholic Beverages* that "the product's properties, nature and quality" are among the criteria for determining likeness under GATT Article III:2 first sentence.[86] Partly on this basis, vodka and shochu were found to be like products. However, it is difficult to see how this understanding applies in the present context. Steel as a material and a highway which contains steel as an input share a physical characteristic, but this does not place them in a competitive relationship. In the passage, the Appellate Body proceeds to note the European Union's acknowledgement. It is perhaps notable that the reference to "competitive relationship" is not repeated here. Perhaps the Appellate Body is signaling that the derogation might apply to discrimination in relation to steel used in a highway procurement notwithstanding the absence of any competitive relationship. Some support for this position can be found in a subsequent statement in which the meaning of "governmental purposes" within the derogation was discussed:

> An obvious example is where a governmental agency purchases a good, uses it to discharge its governmental functions, and the good is totally consumed in the process. None of the participants disputes that this would constitute an example of a good purchased for governmental purposes.[87]

The meaning of "governmental purposes" is, however, a separate matter from the earlier issue of whether the measure governs the procurement—the matter for which the Appellate Body requires a competitive relationship. Therefore, this passage does not establish that this relationship is established, or that it is waived, when the good is consumed.

[85] *Canada—Renewable Energy*, Appellate Body report, para. 5.63 (notes omitted). A very similar statement was provided in note 523, para. 5.74.

[86] WT/DS8,10,11/AB/R, p. 20, *Japan—Taxes on Alcoholic Beverages*, adopted November 1, 1996.

[87] *Canada-Renewable Energy*, Appellate Body report, para. 5.68.

The analysis can now be summarized:

1. If the product discriminated against (generating equipment) is not a physical input of the product procured (electricity), the derogation is only potentially available if the two products are in a competitive relationship.
2. If the product discriminated against (steel) is a physical input of the product procured (highway), it can be said that steel has been procured. This would satisfy the need for a competitive relationship.
3. While a physical input test provides a workable distinction, it does not correspond with commercial reality since the cost of electricity depends on the cost of the generating equipment, just as the cost of highways depends of the cost of the steel.
4. If it is acknowledged that the highway procurement is not directly a procurement of steel, the competitive relationship test is not satisfied. The derogation can then only apply if the need for a competitive relationship is jettisoned when the product discriminated against is a physical input of the product procured. It might be enough, using the panel's interpretation, that the domestic content requirements govern the procurement in the sense that the award of a highway contract depends on using domestic steel.

Thus, when the Appellate Body's approach is applied in a different and paradigm situation, it can only produce what must surely be the correct result (derogation available) either by using reasoning at odds with commercial reality, or, if we are to acknowledge commercial reality, by jettisoning the need for any competitive relationship and using an alternative test such as that developed by the panel.

As indicated, procurement derogations have been interpreted in NAFTA Chapter 11 investor state dispute settlement cases. The tribunal in *ADF v United States* confirmed that a highway construction project in which Buy American requirements were applied in relation to steel was covered by a derogation.[88] However, the reasoning and outcome here cannot be automatically applied in the GATT/WTO context because both the substantive obligations and the derogation are drafted in different terms. NAFTA Article 1108(7) and (8) provides that several substantive obligations such as National Treatment, Most-Favored-Nation Treatment, and Performance Requirements "do not apply to procurement by a Party or a state enterprise." The very brevity of this derogation means that there are fewer express elements which must be satisfied compared to GATT Article III:8. It does not, for example, expressly provide that the products purchased must be for the benefit or use of government, although it is arguable that this concept is inherent to the ordinary meaning of "procurement." It may therefore be that the NAFTA

[88] ICSID ARB(AF)/00/1, Award January 9, 2003, paras. 159–74.

derogation can shelter a measure from review under Chapter 11, when the same measure would not be sheltered from review in WTO proceedings under GATT Article III.

It is possible that the scope of the NAFTA procurement derogation will be considered in *Mesa Power v Canada,* in which an American investor is challenging the measures at issue in *Canada—Renewable Energy.* The claimant in *Mesa* contends that the WTO Appellate Body's reasoning should be carried over to the NAFTA Chapter 11 procurement derogation. It therefore considers that the NAFTA derogation can only apply when the goods being procured are identical to the goods subject to domestic content provisions.[89] Of course, this is was not the test established by the Appellate Body, since it is well established that non-identical products can be in a competitive relationship. Canada's position is that the plain language of the NAFTA derogation does not envisage so tight a nexus between the product discriminated against and the product purchased.[90] Indeed, Canada goes so far as to argue that the derogation could not possibly be interpreted as not applying to domestic content requirements. Given that "the majority of the world's nations discriminate in their government procurement," had the NAFTA parties intended for the Chapter 11 investment obligations to cover domestic content requirements in government procurement, they would have expressly so provided.[91]

It will be interesting to see what the *Mesa* tribunal makes of these arguments. One point is reasonably certain—if the tribunal follows the methodology of many previous NAFTA Chapter 11 tribunals, it will at least engage with the WTO law position. The Award ought therefore to further elucidate on the relationship between the trade law and investment law regimes.

To conclude this section, the Appellate Body's interpretation of GATT Article III:8(a) in *Canada—Renewable Energy* has the potential to bring swathes of discriminatory domestic content requirements, many of which may be excluded from the GPA's coverage, within the scope of GATT Article III. As this was surely not the Appellate Body's intention, the challenge is to suggest how the competitive relationship test should be applied in paradigm situations in order to ensure that the derogation is available. The test can only survive if an unconvincing distinction is drawn between situations when goods discriminated against are incorporated into other goods, and situations in which there is no incorporation. It is therefore difficult to accept that the Appellate Body's view of when a measure governs procurement is correct. In contrast, the panel's test is generally applicable, easier to understand, and corresponds with commercial reality. It also does not seem to be at odds with the treaty language to find that a measure governs procurement when the contract cannot be awarded unless certain conditions are fulfilled, or when contract performance requires that conditions are fulfilled. This establishes a close connection between the measure and the procurement even if there is no

[89] *Mesa Power,* Claimant's Reply Memorial, para. 205.

[90] *Mesa Power,* Canada—Rejoinder, para. 78.

[91] *Mesa Power,* Canada—Rejoinder, para. 78.

competitive relationship between the products discriminated against under the measure and the procured products. While the panel's interpretation expands the scope of the derogation, its availability does not depend solely on whether the measure governs procurement. Furthermore, when the derogation applies, the discrimination does not fall into a legal vacuum. While GATT Article III will not apply, the GPA may apply depending on contract coverage; a matter which is the subject of hard fought concessions.

1.7 **Conclusion**

The idea of a "global revolution" in international procurement regulation may never have been more apt. The revised GPA, with its increased contract coverage, has finally entered into force. During the same time frame another major international instrument, the UNCITRAL Model Law, has been revised. At the preferential trade agreement level, the negotiations toward a Transatlantic Trade and Investment Partnership between the EU and US are ongoing. In this context, reference has been made to both coverage commitments and new disciplines going beyond the GPA (Craven, 2014).

Within this ongoing process, the GPA's distinctive features are that it concentrates on trade liberalization and market access as between a significant and growing body of parties with enforcement and remedies primarily via domestic challenge procedures. Going forward, the most significant challenge is likely to be to maintain and enhance the GPA's relevance for an increasingly diverse membership. While there will continue to be difficult tensions to reconcile, there is every reason for optimism in light of recent developments and a sense of significant momentum.

REFERENCES

Anderson, R. D. 2014. "The Coming into Force of the Revised WTO Agreement on Government Procurement, and Related Developments."*Public Procurement Law Review* NA160–3.

Anderson, R. D. and Arrowsmith, S. 2011. "The WTO Regime on Government Procurement: Past, Present and Future." In S. Arrowsmith and R. D. Anderson (eds), *The WTO Regime on Government Procurement: Challenge and Reform*. Cambridge: Cambridge University Press, 3–58.

Anderson, R. D., Kovacic, W. E., and Müller, A. C. 2011. "Ensuring Integrity and Competition in Public Procurement Markets: A Dual Challenge for Good Governance." In S. Arrowsmith and R. D. Anderson (eds), *The WTO Regime on Government Procurement: Challenge and Reform*. Cambridge: Cambridge University Press, 681–718.

Anderson, R. D., Müller, A. C., Osei-Lah, K., Pardo De Leon, J., and Pelletier, P. 2011a. "Government Procurement Provisions In Regional Trade Agreements: A Stepping Stone to

GPA Accession." In S. Arrowsmith and R. D. Anderson (eds), *The WTO Regime on Government Procurement: Challenge and Reform*. Cambridge: Cambridge University Press, 561–656.

Anderson, R. D., Pelletier, P., Osei-Lah, K., and Müller, A. C. 2011b. "Assessing the Value of Future Accessions to the WTO Agreement on Government Procurement (GPA): Some New Data Sources, Provisional Estimates, and an Evaluative Framework for Individual WTO Members Seeking Accession." WTO Staff Working Paper ERSD-2011-15, Geneva (available at: <http://www.wto.org/english/res_e/reser_e/ersd201115_e.pdf> (accessed July 20, 2016).

Bolton, P. and Quinot, G. 2011. "Social Policies in Procurement and the Agreement on Government Procurement." In S. Arrowsmith and R. D. Anderson (eds), *The WTO Regime on Government Procurement: Challenge and Reform*. Cambridge: Cambridge University Press, 459–80.

Cao, F. 2013. "Building Up SME Programmes in Government Procurement in China: Legal Structure, Recent Developments and the Way Forward towards the WTO-GPA." *Public Procurement Law Review* 6: 211–24.

Cosbey, A. and Mavroidis, P. C. 2014. "A Turquoise Mess: Green Subsidies, Blue Industrial Policy and Renewable Energy: The Case for Redrafting the Subsidies Agreement of the WTO."*Journal of International Economic Law* 11: 11–47.

Cottier, T. 2002. "A Theory of Direct Effect in Global Law." In A. Von Bogandy, P. C. Mavroidis, and Y. Mény, (eds), *European Integration and International Co-ordination*. The Hague: Kluwer Law International, 99–122.

Craven, R. 2014. "EU-US Transatlantic Trade and Investment Partnership Agreement: The European Commission's Negotiating Position on Public Procurement." *Public Procurement Law Review* NA65–76.

Davies, A. 2006. "Reviewing Dispute Settlement at the World Trade Organization: A Time to Reconsider the Role/s of Compensation." *World Trade Review* 5(1): 31–67.

Davies, A. 2015. "Group Comparison Versus Best Treatment in International Economic Law Non-Discrimination Analysis" (available at: SSRN: <http://papers.ssrn.com/sol3/papers.cfm?abstract_id=2564609>(accessed July 20, 2016).

Kidalov, M. K. 2011. "Small Business Contracting in the United States and Europe: A Comparative Assessment." *Public Contract Law Journal* 40(2): 443–510.

Linarelli, J. 2011. "The Limited Case for Permitting SME Procurement Preferences in the Agreement on Government Procurement." In S. Arrowsmith and R. D. Anderson (eds), *The WTO Regime on Government Procurement: Challenge and Reform*. Cambridge: Cambridge University Press, 444–58.

Nicholas, C. 2011. "Work of UNCITRAL on Government Procurement: Purpose, Objectives and Complementarity with the Work of the WTO." In S. Arrowsmith and R. D. Anderson (eds), *The WTO Regime on Government Procurement: Challenge and Reform*. Cambridge: Cambridge University Press, 746–72.

Nicholas, C. 2012. "The 2011 UNCITRAL Model Law on Public Procurement." *Public Procurement Law Review* NA111–23.

Niewiadomska, E. 2014. "EBRD UNCITRAL Initiative: Lessons Learned in Armenia." Paper presented at "The Internationalisation of Government Procurement" conference, EUI, Florence, December 15–16.

Pal, R. 2014. "Has the Appellate Body's Decision in Canada—Renewable Energy / Canada—Feed-in Tariff Program Opened the Door for Production Subsidies?" *Journal of International Economic Law* 17(1): 125–37.

Reich, A. 2009. "The New Text of the Agreement on Government Procurement: An Analysis and Assessment." *Journal of International Economic Law* 12(4): 989–1022.

Rubini, L. 2012. "Ain't Wastin' Time No More: Subsidies for Renewable Energy, The SCM Agreement, Policy Space, and Law Reform." *Journal of International Economic Law* 15(2): 525–79.

Yukins, C. and Schooner, S. 2007."Incrementalism: Eroding the Impediments to a Global Public Procurement Market." *Georgetown Journal of International Law* 38: 529–76.

2 Regional Trade Agreements and Procurement Rules

Facilitators or Hindrances?

Robert D. Anderson, Anna Caroline Müller, and Philippe Pelletier

2.1 Introduction

Government procurement is of considerable importance as an element of economic activity, accounting for more than 15 percent of gross domestic product (GDP), on average, in both developed and developing economies (OECD, 2002; see also Anderson et al., 2012). Government procurement is, furthermore, an essential input to the delivery of broader public services and functions of government, such as investment in transportation, telecommunications, energy, and other vital public and business infrastructure; the provision of public services such as the construction and maintenance of schools, hospitals, and public sanitation systems; and the efficient delivery of medicines and other aspects of health care.[1] As a result, the efficiency and effectiveness of government procurement systems can have a far-reaching impact on developmental processes. Moreover, apart from their impact on these specific functions of government, well-designed procurement systems can have positive spillovers to the state of governance systems generally, thereby strengthening public confidence in government (see also Anderson, Kovacic, and Mueller, 2011). As such, government procurement has a developmental significance that transcends its magnitude as an aspect of economic activity (Anderson et al., 2012; Niggli and Osei-Lah, 2014).

Binding international agreements relating to government procurement can help countries to optimize their procurement systems and promote growth and development in at least three distinct ways (for a useful related discussion, see Evenett and Hoekman, 2005). First, to the extent that they open up procurement markets to increased competition, including through international trade, they can help governments procure the best

[1] For an analysis of the importance of sound government procurement and competition policies in order to foster innovation and access to medical technology, see World Health Organization (WHO), World Intellectual Property Organization (WIPO), and World Trade Organization (WTO) (2013), various sections.

internationally available goods and services at an optimal price, that is, they can help achieve best value for money in the provision of essential public goods and services. Second, the market access achieved through reciprocal international trade liberalization in the government procurement sector can provide for significant economic opportunities for the private sector and can thus stimulate economic growth. Third, to the extent that international agreements entrench and promote principles of non-discrimination, transparency, and procedural fairness, such agreements can guide countries toward increased integrity and good governance. The benefits of this may spill beyond procurement systems per se. Related to these, putting in place transparent and fair procurement systems may also encourage beneficial in-bound foreign direct investment. In fact, all these effects tend to be mutually reinforcing (Anderson et al., 2012; for an important application to Africa, see also Niggli and Osei-Lah, 2014).

In the past, government procurement has been effectively carved out of the main multilateral rules of the WTO system. Broad exceptions limit the application of the GATT's and the GATS' most-favored nation (MFN) obligations and related market access and national treatment commitments in this area. This is despite the fact that government procurement accounts for, or potentially accounts for, a very significant proportion of goods and services trade.[2] For example, it has been estimated that in some sectors, the procurement of services by governments could represent as much as 30 percent of overall services trade (Hoekman and Primo Braga, 1997; Anderson and Mueller, 2009). As such, access to procurement markets can also have an important bearing on the scale of operations and the resulting overall competitiveness of individual suppliers. This is to say nothing of the broader benefits of trade liberalization in this sector, which have already been noted.

The resulting gap in the international trading system is filled, at least to an extent, by the plurilateral WTO Agreement on Government Procurement ("GPA" or "the Agreement") and by regional trade agreements (RTAs) embodying related disciplines.[3] Such rules represent an important complement to general trade rules on market access. In general, to participate meaningfully in public tenders and related processes, foreign suppliers not only need the formal right to participate in such processes on a non-discriminatory basis, but also more general rights of market access and establishment. Conversely, the right to participate in government procurement activities can reinforce

[2] The share of government procurement markets that is potentially internationally contestable (i.e., that could be opened to international trade) has been conservatively estimated as between 5.1 percent and 7.57 percent of GDP in most countries (OECD, 2002). It should be noted that these estimates treat all defense-related expenditure as non-tradable. As a result, they arguably underestimate the true extent of potentially contestable procurement, as several countries have in fact opened their non-sensitive defense-related procurement sectors to international competition (Pelletier, 2015).

[3] The term "RTA" is used in this chapter to describe any reciprocal trade agreement between two or more partners.

the value of more general market access rights to an important extent (for an elaboration of this core element of our analysis, see Section 2.2.2).

To be sure, the GPA currently covers only forty-seven of the WTO's 164 member governments; and only a part of the procurement of each participating government. As such, the gap identified in the international trading system is only partially filled. There are, nonetheless, reasons for optimism regarding both the progressive expansion of the Agreement's membership and, over time, the coverage of individual parties (see Section 2.5).

With regard to RTAs, the majority of such agreements that have been notified to the WTO in recent years contain provisions on government procurement, whether of a detailed or a limited nature. Altogether, around eighty WTO Members have undertaken, on at least one occasion, trade liberalization in the area of government procurement, either via the GPA or an RTA (see Table 2.1). This represents approximately 50 percent of the WTO's membership. These figures are likely to grow in the coming years in light of the ongoing GPA accessions (including, for example, that of China) and other RTAs currently under negotiation/still to be ratified (e.g., the Trans-Pacific Partnership, or TPP).

Table 2.1 WTO members having undertaken GPA-style commitments on government procurement, either via the GPA itself and/or in RTAs

No GPA parties	WTO Member
1.	Armenia
2.	Canada
3.	the EU
31.	and its 28 member states
32.	Hong Kong, China
33.	Iceland
34.	Israel
35.	Japan
36.	Korea
37.	Liechtenstein
38.	Montenegro
39.	the Netherlands with respect to Aruba
40.	New Zealand
41.	Norway
42.	Singapore
43.	Switzerland
44.	Chinese Taipei
45.	United States

Other WTO Members with GP-related commitments in RTAs	
46.	Antigua and Barbuda
47.	Australia
48.	Bahrain
49.	Barbados
50.	Belize
51.	Brunei
52.	Chile
53.	Costa Rica
54.	Colombia
55.	Dominica
56.	Dominican Republic
57.	El Salvador
58.	Georgia
59.	Guatemala
60.	Grenada
61.	Guyana
62.	Haiti
63.	Honduras
64.	Jamaica
65.	Kuwait
66.	Mexico
67.	Moldova
68.	Morocco
69.	Nicaragua
70.	Oman
71.	Panama
72.	Peru
73.	Saint-Kitts and Nevis
74.	Saint Lucia
75.	Saint Vincent and the Grenadines
76.	Saudi Arabia
77.	Suriname
78.	Trinidad and Tobago
79.	Ukraine
80.	United Arab Emirates
81.	Qatar

Provisions on government procurement liberalization in RTAs are of interest for a number of reasons, some specific to the field of government procurement and some general or systemic. First, such provisions can already provide, at least to an extent, the benefits of broader liberalization, including enhanced competition in domestic procurement activities and access to foreign markets. Second, RTAs provide an important point of comparison with the GPA. Third, to the extent that the rules embodied in RTAs replicate those of the GPA, they may facilitate future GPA accessions, by acclimatizing procurement officials to relevant procedures and catalyzing related legislative and policy reforms. Indeed, the overall viewpoint of this chapter is that, in the area of government procurement, RTAs generally introduce relatively little in the way of "spaghetti-bowl" effects and, overall, are favorable to the proliferation of procurement reforms and common rules. On the other hand, to the extent that RTAs already provide the access to foreign procurement markets that governments seek, they may, in some cases, limit part of the remaining incentive for GPA accession.

There is, to be sure, a wider issue concerning the significance of RTAs and even a plurilateral agreement such as the GPA for global welfare. This is the long-standing issue of trade diversion versus trade creation (Arrowsmith, 2003; Anderson et al., 2011). This concern is not, however, the focus of the current chapter. Rather, the analysis in this chapter assumes, as a point of departure, that the GPA is both net trade-creating and global welfare-enhancing. It then considers the significance of government procurement chapters in RTAs both in their own right and vis-a-vis the GPA. This approach is based, in part, on a recognition that the effects of the GPA and procurement provisions in RTAs go beyond trade creation among the participating countries and include also: (i) important efficiencies in the national procurement systems of the individual participants, to some extent independent of the actual amount of trade that is created;[4] and (ii) demonstration and learning effects regarding good procurement practices that spill beyond the bounds of any individual RTA and even the GPA itself. In addition, as the prospects appear good for a significant expansion of the GPA's membership in the coming years, this could alleviate the potential risk of trade diversion, over time.

The remainder of the chapter begins with an overview of the GPA and the relationship between general goods and services and government procurement disciplines in international trade agreements (Section 2.2). Section 2.3 of the chapter delves into essential aspects of government procurement provisions in RTAs that underpin the rest of the analysis. Thereafter, Section 2.4 provides information on the market access dimensions of government procurement in recent RTAs, in comparison with the revised GPA. Some other respects in which the GPA and RTAs may have differential effects are also noted.

[4] There is a solid basis for this assumption. See, for example, the discussion of Korea's accession to the GPA in Choi (2003). Choi finds that "Korea's accession to the GPA has brought [about] improvement in the competitive nature and efficiency of the government procurement market, [even though it has] has not resulted in any significant increase in import penetration."

Section 2.5 highlights some additional reasons why we expect that, in the long run, countries will gravitate toward GPA participation even where they already enjoy significant trade benefits via RTAs. Section 2.6 provides concluding remarks.

2.2 The WTO's Government Procurement Agreement and Its Complementarity with General Trade Rules: An Overview

2.2.1 THE WTO'S AGREEMENT ON GOVERNMENT PROCUREMENT (GPA)

The GPA is, to date, the only legally binding agreement in the WTO focusing on the subject of government procurement. It is a plurilateral agreement, meaning that it comprises only a subset of the full membership of the WTO. Currently, the Agreement binds forty-seven of the WTO's Members.[5] The latest WTO Members that have joined the Agreement, Ukraine and Moldova, concluded their negotiations for accession to the GPA in the second half of 2015, and became full GPA parties on May 18 and July 14, 2016 respectively. Fifteen other WTO Members, including Australia, China, Russia, Saudi Arabia, and Kazakhstan, either have formally initiated the process of accession to the Agreement or have related commitments in their WTO accession protocols.[6] Currently, the accession processes of Australia, China, the Kyrgyz Republic, and Tajikistan are under active consideration by the Committee on Government Procurement.

The original WTO Agreement on Government Procurement, the "GPA 1994" was negotiated in parallel with the Uruguay Round and entered into force on January 1, 1996. On December 15, 2011, in parallel with the Eighth WTO Ministerial Conference, the parties to the GPA reached political agreement on the conclusion of the renegotiation of the Agreement that they had conducted over more than a decade.[7] The results of the

[5] These comprise: Armenia, Canada, the European Union, with its twenty-eight member states, Hong Kong, China, Iceland, Israel, Japan, Korea, Liechtenstein, Montenegro, Moldova, the Kingdom of the Netherlands with respect to Aruba, New Zealand, Norway, Singapore, Switzerland, Chinese Taipei, and the United States. For a review of the evolution of the GPA from its inception until recent times, see Anderson and Arrowsmith (2011).

[6] Overall, eight WTO Members are in the process of negotiating their accessions to the Agreement: Australia, Albania, China, Georgia, Jordan, the Kyrgyz Republic, Oman, and Tajikistan. A further seven WTO Members have provisions regarding accession to the Agreement in their respective Protocols of Accession to the WTO: Afghanistan, Kazakhstan, the former Yugoslav Republic of Macedonia, Mongolia, the Russian Federation, Saudi Arabia, and Seychelles.

[7] The basis for the renegotiation was provided in Article XXIV:7(b) and (c) of the GPA 1994, which called for the parties to undertake negotiations with a view to improving the Agreement and achieving the greatest possible extension of its coverage among all parties, and eliminating any remaining discriminatory measures and practices. The negotiations commenced in 1997. For related background, see Anderson and Osei-Lah (2011a).

renegotiation comprised: (i) the revised text of the Agreement;[8] (ii) a significant expansion of the parties' market access commitments, valued at US$80–100 billion annually (see Box 2.1);[9] and (iii) a set of agreed work programs relating to the administration

BOX 2.1 THE EXPANSION OF MARKET ACCESS COMMITMENTS ACHIEVED IN THE GPA RENEGOTIATION

The conclusion of the GPA renegotiation is important for multiple reasons. Inter alia, it has added an estimated $80–100 billion annually to the value of the market access commitments by the parties under the Agreement.[10] This derives from:

- coverage by the Parties of (at a minimum) more than 500 additional central, local and other government agencies under the Agreement. This includes, as just one party's (Canada's) contribution, the coverage under the Agreement, for the first time, of its sub-central level of government (i.e., all of its provinces and territories)—already a contribution that has been valued in the tens of billions of dollars;
- some improvements in the coverage of goods;
- downward adjustments in the thresholds applied under the Agreement by a few parties, notably Israel, Japan, Korea, and the Netherlands with respect to Aruba;
- significant coverage of new services sectors by the following GPA parties: the European Union, Hong Kong, China, Iceland, Israel, Japan, Korea, Liechtenstein, the Netherlands with respect to Aruba, Norway, Singapore, Switzerland, and the United States. In all, fifty new services or sub-categories of particular services have been added to coverage. The coverage of telecommunications services, in particular, has been increased by the following eight parties: the European Union, Hong Kong, China, Iceland, Liechtenstein, the Netherlands with respect to Aruba, Norway, Switzerland, and the United States. As a result, nine parties are now covering telecommunication services in full;

(*continued*)

[8] The revised GPA improves on the existing text of the Agreement in various significant ways. For example, the revised text entails a complete revision of the wording of the various provisions of the Agreement to streamline them and make the text easier to understand. It updates the Agreement to take into account developments in current government procurement practice, notably the use of electronic tools. The revised text also sets out related requirements regarding the general availability and interoperability of the information technology systems and software used; the availability of mechanisms to ensure the integrity of requests for participation and tenders; and maintenance of data to ensure the traceability of the conduct of covered procurement by electronic means. It incorporates additional flexibility for parties' procurement authorities, for example in the form of shorter notice periods when electronic tools are used. Shorter time periods have also been allowed for procuring goods and services of types that are available on the commercial marketplace (see also Anderson, 2012). For further information on the new transitional measures available under the revised text, see Box 2.6.

[9] It should be noted that not all of the additional coverage provided is necessarily available to each of the Parties, due to country-specific derogations that may apply. For further details, see Box 2.1.

[10] This brings the total coverage of the Agreement to an estimated $1.7 trillion in procurements by the parties annually. It should be noted that each party to the GPA will not necessarily benefit individually from all the extended coverage of the Agreement inasmuch as each party may apply special derogations in certain cases. For relevant details, see WTO Committee on Government Procurement (2012b) and Pelletier (2015).

BOX 2.1 (CONTINUED)

- full coverage by all parties of construction services (CPC 51); and
- for the first time, explicit coverage of build-operate-transfer contracts (BOTs)/public works concessions or other forms of public–private partnerships by three parties (the European Union, Japan, and Korea). This, in itself, is a very significant addition to coverage.

and expected further evolution of the Agreement,[11] to be conducted by the WTO Committee on Government Procurement.[12] Subsequently, on March 30, 2012, after the timely completion of a legal review and verification process, parties formally adopted the results of the renegotiation (WTO Committee on Government Procurement, 2012a). The revised Agreement came into effect on April 6, 2014, thirty days after the submission of formal acceptances of the "Protocol of Amendment" by two-thirds of the parties to the Agreement.[13]

2.2.2 THE COMPLEMENTARITY OF GENERAL TRADE RULES AND GOVERNMENT PROCUREMENT DISCIPLINES

As pointed out in the introduction to this chapter, despite its potential significance for both goods and services trade, government procurement has been effectively carved out of the main WTO multilateral trade rules. In particular, the application, to government procurement, of the GATT's and GATS' MFN obligation as well as market access and national treatment commitments have been suspended. The gap left by the absence of multilateral disciplines on government procurement trade is partially filled, at the international level, by the WTO Agreement on Government Procurement. But how large is the remaining gap, and why is it of relevance? Can RTAs usefully fill that gap?

[11] These comprise: (i) a work program to consider best practices with respect to measures and policies that the Parties use to support the participation of small and medium-size enterprises (SMEs) in government procurement; (ii) a work program to enable parties to improve procedures followed in the collection and reporting of statistical data relating to the Agreement; (iii) a work program to promote the use of sustainable procurement practices, consistent with the Agreement; (iv) a work program to address restrictions and exclusions in parties' coverage commitments under the Agreement; and (v) a work program on safety standards in international procurement.

[12] For additional details, see WTO Committee on Government Procurement (2012b), paragraphs 7–10.

[13] The parties to the GPA 1994 that have, to date, submitted their instruments of acceptance and for which the revised Agreement has entered into force are Armenia, Canada, the European Union with its twenty-eight member States, Hong Kong, China, Iceland, Israel, Japan, Korea, Liechtenstein, the Netherlands with respect to Aruba, Norway, Singapore, Chinese Taipei, and the United States. Switzerland is yet to submit its instrument of acceptance.

First of all, the GPA is a plurilateral agreement, meaning that not all WTO Members are party to it. Overall, therefore, the situation remains that the wider WTO membership has not signed up to international trade rules opening procurement markets internationally in the framework of the WTO.[14] Second, RTAs are, by nature, fragmented agreements among a subset of countries only. Therefore, important potential for the expansion of disciplines relating to government procurement continues to exist.

Why is this of relevance? First of all, as pointed out in the introduction, procurement markets are an important part of economic activity in most countries, in their own right. Furthermore, general market access commitments on trade in goods and services, on the one hand, and commitments on government procurement of goods and services, on the other hand, are likely to bear importantly on the effectiveness of each other. The reason is that commitments on government procurement generally deal only with the right to participate in procurement activities (bidding and related processes) as such, whereas the ability to bid competitively will also depend on more general conditions of market access (e.g., tariffs or the rights of establishment of service suppliers).

The relationship between coverage of commitments under the GATS and the GPA illustrates this point. Possible interactions are summarized in Table 2.2. Overall, market access provided under the GATS has a very important impact on suppliers' ability to compete in government procurement markets if, and to the extent that, the services supplied to the government are sourced internationally. For example, rights of establishment or of cross-border supply granted to foreign service suppliers in a given services

Table 2.2 Complementarity of GPA and GATS commitments

GPA service commitments?	GATS commitments?	Commercial result
Yes	Modes 1 and 2 only; modes 3 and 4 "unbound" or partially restricted	Limited ability to compete in procurement markets, notwithstanding that relevant service is covered.
Yes	Modes 1 to 4 fully committed ("none")	Full ability to compete in procurement markets of interest.
No	Modes 1 and 2 only; modes 3 and 4 "unbound" or partially restricted	Negative effects of exclusion from procurement markets are reinforced by limited GATS commitments.
No	Modes 1 to 4 fully committed ("none")	Notwithstanding GATS rights in respect to modes 1 to 4, commercial utility may be affected by exclusion from procurement markets.

[14] See also Arrowsmith (2003, p. 30). This is despite the fact that there is a growing number of bilateral or regional trade agreements, including agreements by GPA parties with non-GPA parties or among non-GPA parties, with chapters on government procurement. See Anderson et al. (2011) and Anderson et al. (2014).

sector under the GATS can have an important bearing on the latter's ability to compete effectively for such contracts under the GPA. Similarly, whether or not a procurement contract can be fulfilled by a foreign supplier through the presence of natural persons can have an important bearing on that supplier's competitiveness in areas such as business services and construction and related services. At the limit, GPA commitments may be relatively meaningless without some degree of corresponding GATS market access/ national treatment commitments.

Access to procurement markets (governed by the GPA) can also have an important bearing on the scale of operations and therefore the competitiveness of individual suppliers generally. Often, in fact, the largest contracts of individual suppliers will be with government entities (Hoekman and Primo Braga, 1997). If a foreign supplier is excluded from these, this will affect its commercial presence in the market independent of market access rights under general trade agreements. GPA coverage thus adds commercial value and viability to commitments in the multilateral trade agreements, and vice versa. This economic, rather than legal, interrelationship also exists in the context of government procurement and services liberalization in RTAs.

Clearly, the fact of the GPA's limited membership as compared to the multilateral agreements means that many WTO Members do not benefit from the synergies that are possible between these two fields of trade regulation. The following sections discuss the level of liberalization achieved through RTAs in order to assess to what extent they contribute to "filling the gap" left by the WTO Agreements and to what extent an economic incentive remains to expand the GPA's membership.

2.3 Trends in Recent RTAs: Growing Inclusion of Dedicated Chapters on Government Procurement and Resulting Issues for Reflection

Separately from the modernization of the GPA and the augmentation of related market access commitments, government procurement has increasingly been made subject to disciplines negotiated in the context of RTAs.[15] As noted in the introduction to this chapter, government procurement chapters in regional trade agreements are of interest for a number of reasons, some specific to the field of government procurement and some general or systemic. To begin with, in many jurisdictions, government procurement provisions in RTAs go a long way to establish the prevailing conditions of trade and

[15] This section draws on Anderson et al. (2014); Anderson et al. (2011); and Anderson and Mueller (2009).

competition in public procurement markets.[16] This impact may be manifested through both behavioral rules that regulate procurement procedures and through coverage schedules that subject specific procurements to international competition. As such, government procurement provisions in RTAs can directly affect performance in a key economic sector with implications for economy-wide development and growth.

Second, provisions on government procurement in RTAs provide an important point of comparison with the GPA. In broad terms, both the GPA and government procurement provisions in RTAs address the same subject matter—that is, the application of non-discrimination principles, rules for the conduct of procurement, and so on.

Additionally, provisions on government procurement in RTAs that broadly track those of the GPA can facilitate accessions to the Agreement. The process of GPA accession has two main aspects: first, verification of the consistency of the acceding party's national legislation with the norms and requirements of the GPA; and second, negotiations on coverage issues (in particular, on the "Appendix I Offer" of the acceding party, which sets out the entities to be covered and other aspects of coverage). Where a WTO Member acceding to the GPA has already adopted, or committed itself to adopting, legislation consistent with RTA provisions modeled on the GPA, it is likely to be well ahead in regard to the first aspect. It may also have an advantage in regard to the second aspect, to the extent that the RTA(s) in question also involve coverage commitments similar to the GPA (this aspect will be discussed in Section 2.4). Overall, it is our belief that this benign or positive impact of RTAs, in this sector, is likely to predominate (see also Anderson et al., 2011; Ueno, 2013; and Anderson et al., 2014).

These benign (in our view) features of RTAs in the government procurement sector are well-manifested by the treatment of government procurement in the recent Trans-Pacific Partnership Agreement (TPP) (see Box 2.2). The Agreement, which is still to come in force, contains a detailed chapter (chapter 15) on government procurement that tracks and extends the reach of the core rules of the WTO GPA in multiple ways,[17] potentially also illustrating possibilities for the future evolution of the GPA itself. In particular, and as amplified in Box 2.2, the text of chapter 15 is based on the same principles as the GPA (non-discrimination, transparency, and procedural fairness) and, in most of its provisions, tracks closely the actual language used in the revised version of the GPA that came into force in 2014. In specific instances, the TPP text has "tweaked" the GPA's rules in ways that could, if of interest to other parties, even be picked up in future versions of the

[16] Obviously, this may be particularly true for parties to RTAs that are not also parties to the WTO GPA. In fact, however, in the clear majority of cases, provisions on government procurement in RTAs incorporate, whether by reference or explicitly, elements of the GPA. This is the case even for WTO Members that are not parties to the Agreement. Hence, the actual conditions of trade and competition in public procurement markets often depend on a complex interaction between RTAs and the GPA, and the impact and influence of the GPA extends beyond those WTO Members that are formally parties to it.

[17] See USTR website (n.d.).

BOX 2.2 GOVERNMENT PROCUREMENT IN THE TRANS-PACIFIC PARTNERSHIP: COMPLEMENTARY RELATIONSHIP WITH THE REVISED WTO AGREEMENT ON GOVERNMENT PROCUREMENT (GPA)

The TPP, when it is implemented, will substantially reduce barriers to trade among the 12 participating Pacific Rim countries. The Agreement contains a detailed chapter (chapter 15) on government procurement that tracks and extends the reach of the core rules of the WTO GPA in multiple ways, potentially also illustrating possibilities for the future evolution of the GPA itself:

- The text of the TPP's government procurement chapter is based on the same principles as the GPA (non-discrimination, transparency and procedural fairness) and, in most of its provisions, tracks closely the actual language used in the revised version of the GPA that came into force in 2014. The text carries over a number of improvements embodied in the revised GPA (as compared with the 1994 Agreement), for example, regarding the use of electronic tools and, very significantly, the revised GPA's new provisions on special and differential treatment for developing countries.
- In specific instances, the TPP text has "tweaked" the GPA's rules—for example, it clarifies that conditions for participation can be designed to promote compliance with international labor rights, and that the general exception allowing Parties to adopt or maintain measures necessary to protect human, animal, or plant life or health includes environmental measures. The TPP text on government procurement also:
  - Expands on the precedent-setting provision of the revised GPA regarding integrity in procurement practices, requiring that "Each Party shall ensure that criminal or administrative measures exist to address corruption in its government procurement." Each Party must also ensure that it has in place policies and procedures to eliminate or manage potential conflicts of interest in its procurement system; and
  - Goes further than the revised GPA in emphasizing the importance of participation by small and medium-sized enterprises (SMEs) in government procurement, requiring transparency with respect to related measures.
- The coverage (market access) commitments of the TPP government procurement chapter are of much interest. The structure of such commitments in the TPP tracks very closely that of the GPA "schedules." Build-operate-transfer contracts (BOTs)/public works concessions are covered by some parties under both agreements, with the difference that the TPP includes a definition of build-operate-transfer contracts (BOTs)/ public works concessions in its text.
- The comparative breadth of the TPP parties' coverage commitments reveals an important further interaction with the GPA:
  - Typically, TPP parties that are also GPA parties (i.e., Canada, Japan, New Zealand, Singapore, and the United States) follow or stay behind their GPA commitments (for example, the US and New Zealand do not cover sub-central government entities under the TPP, as they do under the GPA, and Japan, New Zealand and the US offer less coverage at the "other entity" level as compared to the GPA);
  - TPP parties that are not parties to the GPA but have significant experience with liberalized government procurement markets under other agreements (i.e., Australia, Chile, Mexico, and Peru) have taken substantial coverage commitments;
  - TPP parties that are not parties to the GPA and have limited or no experience with liberalization in this sector (i.e., Malaysia, Vietnam, and Brunei) have taken commitments that are not as comprehensive as that of the other TPP parties and are subject to transitional measures;

(*continued*)

BOX 2.2 (CONTINUED)

- ○ As such, the TPP preserves an incentive for parties seeking broader access to markets in this sector to eventually join the GPA.[18]
- Three side letters to the TPP's government procurement chapter further contribute to global convergence and harmonization in the area of international procurement rules. A first letter, between Canada, Mexico, and the United States, contains an agreement that the TPP rules will replace NAFTA's government procurement rules. Another NAFTA-related side letter between Canada and the United States will align the two countries' NAFTA thresholds with the TPP (and the GPA). A third letter between Australia and the US will similarly align those two countries' thresholds at the central government level in the Australia–US RTA with that of the TPP (and the GPA).

Sources: USTR Website (n.d.) and Grier (2016).

GPA. For example, it clarifies that conditions for participation can be designed to promote compliance with international labor rights, and that the general exception allowing Parties to adopt or maintain measures necessary to protect human, animal or plant life or health also includes authority for appropriate environmental protection measures.

The structure of the market access commitments in chapter 15 (TPP) also tracks very closely that of the GPA "schedules." Perhaps most significantly, the TPP chapter preserves an incentive for parties seeking broader access to markets in this sector to eventually join the GPA, in that the TPP parties that are also GPA parties (i.e., Canada, Japan, New Zealand, Singapore, and the United States) follow or stay behind their commitments in the GPA. As explained in Box 2.2, three side letters to the TPP's government procurement chapter further contribute to global convergence and harmonization in the area of international procurement rules.[19]

Anderson et al. (2014) analyzed a total of 250 agreements, allocated into three broad categories: (i) agreements between GPA parties; (ii) agreements between a GPA party and a non-GPA party; and (iii) agreements between non-GPA parties (these distinctions are also retained in the current chapter).[20] Within each category, a further distinction was made between: (a) RTAs having no provisions on government procurement; (b) RTAs having only a single or a few government procurement provisions; and (c) RTAs having detailed provisions on government procurement and related market access commitments.

A few observations on each of these categories are as follows. First, around 45 percent, or 110, of the agreements considered have no provisions on government procurement

[18] Australia's recent application for accession to the GPA may be considered as an example in this regard.
[19] See also Grier (2016).
[20] The TPP was not included in this set of agreements, as the agreement had not yet been publicly released.

(no market access commitments). These agreements include several plurilateral regional economic integration agreements.[21] This category of agreements also includes a good number of RTAs signed between members of the Commonwealth of Independent States (CIS) (around thirty-five RTAs).[22] The majority of the agreements without government procurement provisions are concluded between non-GPA parties, which are more likely to not have internal government procurement regimes compliant to international standards in place than countries which are already party to an international agreement including government procurement provisions, such as the GPA and/or NAFTA.[23] Finally, this category includes some of the oldest RTAs notified to the WTO—around fifty of these agreements entered into force more than fifteen years ago and, in some cases, even before the creation of the WTO in 1995. Hence, this category of agreements is not necessarily indicative of current trends.

Second, sixty-seven of the agreements (around 27 percent) considered incorporate a single or (in a some cases) two or three basic provisions on government procurement, often identifying government procurement liberalization as an objective, and sometimes establishing non-discrimination principles without translating these goals into more tangible procedural and coverage commitments.[24] The common denominator of these

[21] For example, the EU treaty + EU enlargements (3); the Central American Common Market (CACM); the ASEAN Free Trade Area (AFTA); the Asia-Pacific Trade Agreement (APTA); the Central American Common Market (CACM); the South Asian Association for Regional Cooperation Preferential Trading Arrangement (SAPTA); the Common Market for Eastern and Southern Africa (COMESA); the Economic Community of West African States (ECOWAS); the Economic and Monetary Community of Central Africa (CEMAC), the South Asian Free Trade Agreement (SAFTA); the Southern African Customs Union (SACU); the South Asian Preferential Trade Arrangement (SAPTA); and the West African Economic and Monetary Union (WAEMU). This might be seen as an indication that negotiation of government procurement provisions is (perceived as) difficult where a larger number of parties takes part in the negotiations. The assessment of coverage offers, for example, requires insights into the internal structure of government and purchasing entities of participating countries. On the other hand, in some cases, regional integration leads to the regulation of government procurement at the regional level without necessarily addressing the topic in the regional integration agreement itself. See, for example, relevant Directives of the European Union.

[22] In that regard, it is worth noting that the more recently created Eurasian Economic Union does contain detailed provisions on government procurement, thus signalling a policy shift.

[23] Some of these non-GPA parties seem to have taken a deliberate policy choice not to include government procurement disciplines in RTAs (e.g., India and China). It will be interesting to see whether China's accession to the GPA—negotiations are ongoing—will engender a change in policy in regard to RTAs.

[24] These provisions tend to be "future oriented" in that they favor soft commitments to future negotiations and developments over binding obligations. This approach is predominant in agreements concluded by the EU and EFTA in their relations with North African and Middle Eastern countries. It is also often found in the agreements of Turkey with Eastern European and Middle Eastern countries, and Japan has introduced a comparable approach in RTAs with Asian countries. Mexico and other Latin American/ Caribbean countries have used, in a few cases, future-oriented provisions in RTAs mostly in view of future negotiations. Furthermore, this category of agreements includes several plurilateral regional economic integration agreements (e.g., the Caribbean Community (CARICOM); the Central European Free Trade Agreement (CEFTA); the Commonwealth of Independent States (CIS); the East African Community (EAC); MERCOSUR; and the Pacific Island Countries Trade Agreement (PICTA)).

agreements is that the parties to these agreements clearly recognize the relevance of government procurement to international trade and consider the liberalization of their respective public procurement markets as an objective of the RTA in question. This category of agreements can thus be seen as a useful initial step toward further development of government procurement rules and related liberalization.

The third major approach (embodied in seventy-three, or around 27 percent, of the agreements examined in Anderson et al. (2014)) contains more detailed provisions on government procurement than those found in the second category and, very importantly, includes market access commitments. These comprise twelve RTAs between GPA Parties, thirty-six agreements between GPA parties and non-GPA parties, and twenty RTAs between non-GPA parties. Altogether, these RTAs cover around seventy-five WTO Members, mainly originating from the following geographical regions: Latin America (South, Central and the Caribbean), North America, Europe, and a number from Asia (e.g., Australia, Japan, Korea, New Zealand, and Singapore). It also comprises one member from Africa (Morocco), one from the Commonwealth of Independent States (CIS) (Ukraine) and two countries from the Middle East (Oman and Bahrain).[25] *A salient finding regarding RTAs in this category is that the relevant provisions tend to track very closely the provisions of the GPA itself (whether the 1994* or *the 2012 Agreement).*

Provisions on government procurement in the RTAs notified to the WTO—both those that deal with procurement in one or two basic provisions and those that address it in a more detailed fashion—are linked to the GPA in important ways. To begin with, often at least one party to the agreement is a GPA party. Moreover, a considerable number of the agreements containing less detailed provisions on government procurement incorporate one of two types of references to broader international rules on government procurement. In the first case, a joint committee or similar body is mandated to consider further opening of procurement markets especially in the light of international regulations. In the second, parties make an explicit commitment, albeit in a soft or non-binding fashion, to accede to the GPA. These agreements therefore clearly aim at preparing the parties for a further development of regulations on government procurement, or even possible GPA accession.

Most importantly, though, we find that in the case of agreements containing detailed provisions on government procurement, the 1994 GPA text (and more recently the revised GPA text) has clearly served, with only occasional and sporadic exceptions, as the

[25] For an updated list of WTO Members with relevant commitments, see Table 2.1. The fact that these numbers have gone up since the publication of Anderson et al. (2014) and now include over eighty WTO Members, including two new countries from Central and Eastern Europe (Georgia and Ukraine) and three new countries from the Middle East (Saudi Arabia, the United Arab Emirates, and Qatar) clearly shows a growing trend toward inclusion of detailed government procurement chapters in RTAs among an increasingly diverse set of WTO Members.

model for the relevant chapters. This is true both for agreements of this nature between non-GPA parties and for agreements involving GPA parties. This is an important finding in its own right—it implies that a significant number of countries, including, for example, major Latin American developing countries that are currently outside the GPA, have in fact committed themselves to implement GPA-style disciplines via RTAs.

A further observation is that GPA parties participating in RTAs containing provisions on government procurement appear to be mindful of the linkages between the bilateral and the plurilateral levels and have made efforts to avoid overlapping, incompatible obligations. This is achieved through various means. First, obligations are modeled on the GPA. Alternatively, GPA provisions are imported by reference, ensuring a harmonized approach. Furthermore, MFN obligations are generally avoided so that obligations under RTAs and the GPA can be kept separate.

Overall, we find that the co-existence of the GPA with the government procurement provisions of RTAs seems to involve relatively little in the way of the negative or "spaghetti-bowl" effects to which reference is often made in the context, for example, of diverging tariff bindings relating to trade in goods at the bilateral/regional versus the multilateral level. This is important since international government procurement commitments involve procedural and behavioral rules regarding which disharmony could entail significant costs. Most significantly, the fact that government procurement provisions in RTAs broadly track those of the GPA also makes feasible a significant further broadening of the GPA's membership (if WTO Members choose to pursue this), to the extent that it has already brought participating WTO Members' procurement legislation and practices broadly in line with GPA norms.

This raises an important question for reflection: Why have non-GPA parties been willing to adopt GPA-style procurement regimes and undertake government procurement trade liberalization in RTAs, but have not been willing to join the GPA? Section 2.4 analyzes the levels of liberalization in terms of market access achieved in RTAs as compared to the GPA, in order to be able to draw further conclusions as to whether participation in RTAs is likely to facilitate GPA accession.

2.4 The GPA versus RTAs: Comparative Impact on Market Access and Other Considerations

This section examines the comparative effectiveness of the GPA and RTAs as vehicles for liberalization in the government procurement sector. As a preliminary consideration, it is important to emphasize that neither the GPA nor RTAs with procurement chapters provide for all-encompassing, complete coverage commitments. With regard to the GPA, the Agreement does not apply to the entire government procurement market of

BOX 2.3 THE STRUCTURE OF GPA MARKET ACCESS/COVERAGE SCHEDULES (APPENDIX I OF THE AGREEMENT)

For each GPA party, Appendix I is divided into seven Annexes which deal, respectively, with (i) central government entities covered by the Agreement; (ii) covered sub-central government entities; (iii) "other" covered entities (e.g., utilities and SOEs); (iv) coverage of goods; (v) services coverage; (vi) coverage of construction services; and (vii) any general notes.

Annex 1 Central Government Entities
Annex 2 Sub-Central Government Entities
Annex 3 Other Entities
Annex 4 Goods
Annex 5 Services
Annex 6 Construction Services
Annex 7 General Notes

The Annexes also specify the threshold values above which individual procurements are subject to the GPA disciplines. In addition, the Annexes of most parties contain notes that qualify the application of the Agreement. In principle, all goods are covered if procured by a covered entity and not excluded specifically.

parties.[26] On the contrary, the obligations under the Agreement only apply to procurement: (i) by the procuring entities that each party has listed in Annexes 1–3 of Appendix I, relating respectively to central government entities, sub-central government entities, and other entities such as utilities; (ii) of goods; and (iii) of services and construction services that are specified in lists, found respectively in Annexes 4–6 of Appendix I. Furthermore, the GPA only applies to procurement contracts of an estimated value not less than certain thresholds, which are specified in each party's Appendix I Annexes (see Box 2.3). These three different dimensions of coverage with regard to entities, goods, and services (including construction services), and threshold levels all have to be taken into account in a cumulative manner when determining coverage under the GPA. In other words, a specific procurement only falls within the ambit of the GPA's rules if the procuring entity is covered, if the service or good procured is included in the relevant party's commitments, and if the value of the procurement in question is above the threshold levels indicated in the relevant party's schedules.

Furthermore, the general notes at the end of most parties' schedules, provide for a number of exceptions.[27]

[26] For fuller analysis of the GPA parties' market access commitments under the revised GPA, see Pelletier (2015).

[27] It should be noted that exceptions from the obligations of the Agreement are also allowed for developing countries in certain situations (see Article V of the revised GPA, and Box 2.6) and for non-economic reasons, for example to protect national security interests, public morals, order or safety, human, animal, or plant life or health or intellectual property, and so on.

As highlighted in our previous analyses of this issue (Anderson and Mueller, 2009; Anderson et al., 2011, 2014), the structure of government procurement coverage commitments in RTAs closely follows the structure of the GPA market access schedules, as described above.[28] The GPA therefore provides for a framework in which a direct comparison is possible.

Looking at liberalization commitments made under the GPA and in RTAs, we reach the overall conclusion that if and when WTO Members decide to liberalize procurement markets via the GPA, they often are willing/able to offer greater market access under the GPA than in RTAs. While some RTAs provide for procurement commitments that are deeper than those of the GPA in particular respects (e.g., additional services sectors or coverage of build-operate-transfer arrangements), this is by no means true generally with regard to all dimensions of coverage. Indeed, a number of inter-linked elements have to be taken into account in estimating the overall value of commitments (e.g., the thresholds and the entities covered) with regard to government procurement markets.[29] Overall, the market access opportunities created by government procurement chapters in RTAs are significantly less than those available under the revised GPA. The main arguable exceptions concern some RTAs between GPA parties that "top up" existing GPA commitments in limited ways and a few agreements in Latin America which liberalize regional procurement markets beyond the level generally achieved in the GPA in a geographically limited context.

To address one set of examples, US RTAs with non-GPA parties typically involve less extensive entity coverage on the part of the US than do agreements with GPA parties. Second, among the three US FTAs with GPA parties, only one—the RTA with Korea—provides greater coverage of entities for the US (though only at the central government level) than the GPA itself. In that case, however, the market access commitments achieved explicitly affirm and build directly on the two parties' GPA commitments, suggesting (importantly) that they were possible only on that basis (Table 2.3).

Further to these, among the agreements in the first category (i.e., RTAs between the US and another GPA party), the recent Korea–US RTA is sometimes cited as the "state of the art" and represents a possible paradigm for other US trade initiatives (Schott and Cimino, 2013). As an RTA concluded between two existing GPA parties, it adds on to the coverage commitments made under the GPA. However, its applicability as a paradigm for a US chapter on government procurement with a *non-GPA party* is doubtful, in that *it builds directly and explicitly on the GPA commitments of the two countries (US and*

[28] With the exception of some RTAs, such as the EFTA Convention, which covers specific sectors.

[29] Further elements relevant to determining coverage under RTAs and/or the GPA are thresholds, goods, services and construction services coverage, and exceptions to coverage. A full analysis of all those aspects goes beyond the scope of this chapter.

Table 2.3 Entity coverage commitments in US' RTAs as compared to the revised (2012) GPA

No	Agreement	Central government entities	Sub-central government entities	Other entities
I. The GPA				
All GPA Parties		More than 1,700 entities	More than 2,000 entities	More than 1,500 entities
The US' commitments under the revised GPA		**89 entities**	**37 states**	**10 entities**
II. RTAs between GPA parties				
1.	**US-Singapore**	As in their respective GPA schedules (by reference)	As in their respective GPA schedules (no entity coverage for Singapore)	As in their respective GPA schedules (by reference)
2.	**US–Israel**	As in their respective schedules of the GATT Tokyo Round GPA 1988 (by reference) **US**: 53 entities (36 less than the revised GPA): **Israel**: 1 entity for Israel (i.e., Ministry of Defense)	Not covered	
3.	**US–Korea**	**US**: 79 entities (10 less than the GPA); and **Korea**: 51 entities (9 more than the GPA).	Not covered	
III. RTAs between GPA Parties and Non-Parties				
4.	**NAFTA (Goods/ services)**[30]	**Canada**: 78 entities (as in the GPA); **Mexico**: 86 entities; **US**: 53 entities (36 less than the GPA)	Not covered	**Canada**: 10 entities (as in the GPA); **Mexico**: 48 entities; **US**: 6 entities (4 less than the GPA)
5.	**US–Australia**	**US**: 79 entities (10 less the GPA); **Australia**: similar positive list	**US**: 31 states, (6 less than the GPA); **Australia**: extensive list	**US**: 7 entities (3 less than the GPA); **Australia**: similar positive list
6.	**US–Bahrain**	**US**: 52 entities (37 less than the GPA); **Bahrain**: equivalent list	Not covered	**US**: 7 entities (3 less than the GPA); **Bahrain**: positive list (17 entities, including Bahrain Petroleum)

[30] See Section 2.2 and Box 2.2 for information on the side letters to the TPP that will align NAFTA's government procurement rules and thresholds with that of the TPP (and the GPA).

7.	US–Chile	**US**: 79 entities (10 less than the GPA);	**US**: 37 states covered, as in its GPA schedule;	**US**: 10 entities (like in GPA)
		Chile: 20 entities (19 ministries and the Office of the President of the Republic)	**Chile**: List of 51 entities, Gobernaciones in 13 different regions + list of 341 municipalities	**Chile**: 11 entities
8.	US–Colombia	**US**: 78 entities (11 less than the GPA);	**US**: 8 states + Puerto Rico (29 less than the GPA);	**US**: 7 entities (3 less than the GPA);
		Colombia: 28 entities	**Colombia**: 38 gobernaciones	**Colombia**: 22 entities
9.	US–DR-CAFTA	**US**: 79 entities (10 less than the GPA);	**US**: 22 states + Puerto Rico (15 less than the GPA) (and for Honduras 16 states + Puerto Rico);	**US**: 7 entities (3 less than the GPA);
		Others: more exceptions than under GPA	**Others**: extensive lists	**Others**: more or less extensive lists.
10.	US–Morocco	**US**: 79 entities (10 less than the GPA);	**US**: 23 states (14 less than the GPA);	**US**: 7 entities (3 less than the GPA);
		Morocco: 30 entities	**Morocco**: extensive list	**Morocco**: extensive list
11.	US–Oman	**US**: 50 entities (39 less than the GPA);	not covered	**US**: 7 entities (3 less than the GPA);
		Oman: equivalent list		**Oman**: positive list (17 entities, including Bahrain Petroleum)
12.	US–Panama	**US**: 78 entities (11 less than the GPA)	**US**: 8 states + Puerto Rico (29 less than the GPA)	**US**: 7 entities (3 less than the GPA);
		Panama: 16 entities	**Panama**: 12 provinces	**Panama**: 30 entities + the Authority of the Panama Canal
13.	US–Peru	**US**: 78 entities (11 less than the GPA);	**US**: 8 states + Puerto Rico covered (29 less than the GPA);	**US**: 7 entities (3 less than the GPA);
		Peru: extensive list (61 entities)	**Peru**: 25 entities	**Peru**: 23 entities

Korea). This and other relevant features of the government procurement chapter of this agreement are summarized in Box 2.4.

Concerning FTAs between the US and non-GPA parties, the government procurement chapter of the Colombia–US Agreement provides a pertinent example (see Box 2.5).

As shown in Box 2.5, the market access opportunities created by the Colombia–US Agreement—especially for Colombia—are significantly fewer than those potentially available under the GPA. More broadly, the record shows that the market access benefits that are created in the government procurement sector by US RTAs with non-GPA parties are almost always fewer than those available via GPA participation. An arguable exception is the US–Chile RTA, in which Chile achieved access to the US procurement sector which was comparable to that offered by the US to its partners under the 1994 GPA, in return for very significant market access concessions by Chile. The US–Chile Agreement does not, however, include the additional coverage at the central government

BOX 2.4 THE GOVERNMENT PROCUREMENT CHAPTER OF THE US–KOREA RTA (IN FORCE IN 2012): RELIANCE ON THE GPA

The US–Korea RTA is widely regarded as a state-of-the-art bilateral trade agreement. The government procurement chapter of the Agreement builds importantly (and explicitly) on the WTO GPA:

- it expressly re-affirms both parties' rights and obligations under the GPA;
- with regard to behavioral rules governing the operation of procurement markets, in most respects it incorporates by reference the relevant rules of the GPA;
- in a few cases, select rules (e.g., regarding electronic tools and conditions for participation) that have now been included in the revised 2012 GPA are carried over in the US–Korea RTA; and
- with regard to compliance mechanisms, it relies upon rather than displaces the core enforcement mechanisms of the GPA (robust domestic review or "bid challenge" systems and, ultimately, the WTO dispute settlement machinery).

level that the US subsequently granted to its GPA partners in the negotiation of the 2012 GPA.[31]

To summarize, US bilateral agreements with non-GPA parties consistently involve lower levels of market access commitments than do agreements with countries that have already joined the GPA. In this respect, it is fair to say that GPA accession is the key to higher levels of market access for both the US and its trade partners. Furthermore, while the above examples focus on the US as an example of a GPA party actively concluding RTAs with non-GPA parties, similar findings hold true with regard to other GPA parties as well.

Overall, participation in the GPA provides, therefore, a broader set of market access opportunities than mere participation in an RTA with a government procurement chapter. The question as why non-GPA parties have been willing to adopt GPA-style procurement regimes and undertake government procurement trade liberalization in RTAs, but have not been willing to join the GPA therefore remains. Similarly, the fact that RTAs only achieve fragmented and limited liberalization of government procurement markets means that a high, unused potential for a boost in international trade through the liberalization of untapped procurement markets remains (Anderson et al., 2014). To be sure, the relative extent of market access commitments is only one respect in which the GPA and RTAs embodying government procurement commitments can be compared. Other dimensions may include:

[31] This shows a potential further weakness of RTAs as compared to the GPA: the lack of an institutionalized forum makes it difficult to take into account developments that occur after the conclusion of the RTA. In comparison, the work of the GPA Committee ensures that the Agreement evolves over time.

BOX 2.5 AN EXAMPLE OF WHAT CAN BE ACHIEVED IN A GOVERNMENT PROCUREMENT CHAPTER IN AN RTA BETWEEN THE US AND A NON-GPA PARTY: THE COLOMBIA–US RTA (CONCLUDED IN 2006; BROUGHT INTO FORCE ONLY IN 2012)

- In general, the market access opportunities created by the GP chapter of the Colombia–US RTA *are substantially fewer* than those available as between the US and its GPA Partners:
- At the sub-central level, **the US** covers only eight states and Puerto Rico (as compared to thirty-seven states in the GPA); and in regard to central government entities (Annex 1) and all other entities (Annex 3), the US covers fewer entities than under the revised GPA.
- On the other hand, **Colombia** has offered significant coverage to the US under the agreement (e.g., a total of twenty-eight entities in the three branches of the central government (i.e., executive, legislative, and judicial); thirty-two Gobernaciones (comparable to US states) at the sub-central government level; and it also covers important state-owned enterprises.
- The GP Chapter of the Colombia–US RTA relies implicitly on the GPA in that it incorporates a version of the GPA procedural rules.
- With regard to compliance, government procurement commitments in the Colombia–US RTA are, of course, not enforceable via the WTO dispute settlement system. The transitional mechanisms of the revised GPA also do not apply.

Source: Pelletier (2015).

- the scope for rationalization/synergizing of commitments regarding government procurement per se and general market access commitments (such as those granted under GATT and GATS in the WTO framework), as highlighted in Section 2.2.2. Here, it seems at least arguable that the GPA has an advantage given its status (via Annex 4 of the Marrakesh Agreement) as an integral element of the WTO system;
- the relative institutional solidity of the GPA and relevant RTA disciplines, taking account of aspects such as the availability of the WTO dispute settlement system, the broader availability of technical assistance and capacity building to facilitate implementation of relevant commitments, and the institutional support provided by the Committee on Government Procurement;
- related to the foregoing points, the potentially greater positive spillovers with respect to governance systems emanating from commitments in the GPA as compared to RTAs due to their greater visibility, enforceability, and institutional solidity; and
- importantly, given the admittedly limited coverage of the present GPA as compared to the overall scope and size of government procurement markets worldwide, the scope for and likelihood of progressive deepening of market access commitments and updating of related procedural disciplines.

In light of these considerations, our overall view is that the GPA is at, and will remain at, the center of global efforts to promote liberalization/sound rules and broaden access to government procurement markets. As has been demonstrated, government procurement provisions in RTAs that address the issue substantively themselves rely on the GPA in diverse ways. Nonetheless, to the extent that government procurement chapters in RTAs themselves tend to track the GPA rather closely, such agreements can clearly facilitate eventual accession to the GPA. Thus, the possibility of the quasi-multilateralization of the GPA, over time, should not be ruled out. Section 2.5 sets out the characteristics of the revised GPA that, in our view, open the possibility for a significant broadening of the GPA's membership in the coming years.

2.5 The GPA as an Emerging Pillar of the Twenty-First-Century Global Economy

This section looks at the current status, future prospects, and inherent sources of strength of the GPA, as a further basis for reflection on its relative strengths and role as compared to RTAs. An obvious limitation of the GPA is that roughly two-thirds of the WTO's Members remain outside of it, and the majority of these have not shown an interest in joining the Agreement in the future.[32] The membership of the Agreement has, nonetheless, increased substantially since its first entry into force: whereas in 1996, only twenty-three WTO Members were covered by the Agreement,[33] forty-seven WTO Members are now covered. Moreover, a gradual broadening of the GPA's membership over time, together with a progressive deepening of market access commitments, is not at all unrealistic—already, eight additional WTO Members have started the process of accession to the Agreement;[34] a further seven have made similar commitments in connection with their WTO accession protocols.[35] A large number of other WTO Members, including members from Africa, Asia, Eastern Europe, the Middle East and Latin America, participate in bilateral agreements which potentially make GPA accession relatively easy by including very similar commitments in government procurement chapters. The resulting potential gains in the value of GPA-covered market access commitments are very substantial—they have been estimated in the range of US $439–1,123 billion annually (Anderson et al., 2012).

[32] See also Anderson and Osei-Lah (2011b).

[33] Canada, the EU, and its then fifteen member states, Israel, Japan, the Netherlands with respect to Aruba, Norway, Switzerland, and the United States. Hong Kong, China, Korea, Liechtenstein, and Singapore joined in 1997.

[34] See note 6.

[35] See note 6.

The recent conclusion of the GPA renegotiation and entry into force of the revised Agreement holds the potential to encourage and facilitate future GPA accessions in multiple ways. First, the conclusion of the renegotiation was made possible due to the possibility, under the GPA, to adapt coverage to the reciprocal commitments provided by each party to the Agreement, which GPA parties prefer to a strict MFN approach. Second, by increasing the sum of market access opportunities made available via the Agreement, the renegotiation has strengthened the incentive for outsiders to join the Agreement. Third, the GPA's provisions relating to developing countries ("special and differential treatment" (S&D) or "transitional measures") have been improved in order to facilitate future accessions, by offering an array of possible transitional measures that can be tailored to the needs of specific acceding parties, without eroding the principles of reciprocity. Fourth, the new flexibilities contained in the revised Agreement make it easier to implement for all Parties, including new ones. Lastly, the conclusion could have a psychological impact—it has undeniably raised the profile of the Agreement, and has also demonstrated the seriousness and the results orientation of the parties.

Elaborating on these aspects of the Agreement in turn, first, the more direct application of the reciprocity principle under the GPA than under some other WTO agreements provides parties with the opportunity to adapt their coverage commitments flexibly to what they get in return, thereby taking up an important success factor of RTAs. To explain this legally, the application of the GPA's MFN and national treatment principles are limited to "covered procurement." In the GPA context, this is interpreted as meaning that these provisions do not apply to questions of market access, thus permitting for country-specific derogations in coverage schedules. This approach differs significantly from that taken under GATT and GATS rules in that the GPA expressly permits negotiated exclusions from both national treatment and MFN through the coverage schedules without restrictions. While systemically this may make the GPA less ambitious, it also provides important "wiggle room" to find negotiated, tailor-made solutions.

Second, as an essential design feature of the Agreement and a safeguard against free riding, the (now augmented) market access benefits under the GPA are available only to parties to the Agreement. This follows from the fact that, in the GPA, the MFN principle only applies with regard to treatment accorded to goods, services, and suppliers of other parties to the Agreement. The GPA parties have implicitly decided not to "multilateralize" the GPA's liberalization benefits by making them freely available to other WTO Members, with no corresponding commitments on the part of those other WTO Members. Rather, accession to the Agreement is required and, again, reciprocity is maintained.

Third, as a key aspect of the recent textual revision, the GPA's S&D provisions have been made more specific and concrete. The resulting provisions embody important features that arguably respond to concerns that have been identified with respect to S&D in the WTO more generally (see Box 2.6).

BOX 2.6 NEW TRANSITIONAL MEASURES FOR DEVELOPING COUNTRIES IN THE REVISED GPA TEXT

In a key change, the transitional measures (or S&D) that are available to developing countries that accede to the Agreement have been clarified and improved. The transitional measures that are potentially available, subject to negotiations, include: price preferences; offsets; phased-in addition of specific entities and sectors; and thresholds that are initially set higher than their permanent level. The time periods during which these measures would apply are subject to negotiation, and not to arbitrary caps. Provision has also been made for delaying the application of any specific obligation contained in the Agreement, other than the requirement to provide equal treatment to the goods, services, and suppliers of all other parties to the Agreement, for a period of five years following accession to the Agreement for Least Developed Countries (LDCs) or up to three years for other developing countries. These periods can be extended by decision of the Committee on Government Procurement, on request by the country concerned (see Mueller, 2011; and, for a path-breaking application to Africa, Niggli and Osei-Lah, 2014).

The approach to S&D under the revised GPA differs from the traditional approach to S&D in the WTO in interesting respects. First, the transitional measures noted above are not available "as of right" but are to be awarded on the basis of the specific developmental needs of acceding parties, subject to negotiation with the other parties. Second, such S&D as may be awarded is clearly intended to be time-bound. Third, rather than providing for S&D on a "non-reciprocal" basis (i.e., without regard to the preservation of a balance of market access opportunities), the relevant provisions of the revised GPA stipulate that the market access opportunities that will be made available to acceding parties are "subject to any terms negotiated between [other parties] and the developing country in order to maintain an appropriate balance of opportunities under this Agreement"—thereby preserving (or at least creating the possibility of preserving) the principle of reciprocity. Arguably, this approach represents an alternative paradigm for S&D in the WTO that avoids some or all of the problems concerning past approaches that have been highlighted by academic critics (Anderson, 2014; building on Mueller, 2011).

With regard to the scope for and likelihood of further evolution of the Agreement/ progressive deepening of relevant commitments, this is deliberately built into the Agreement (as it was in the 1994 Agreement). Specifically, Article XXII:7 of the revised Agreement provides that:

> Not later than the end of three years from the date of entry into force of the Protocol Amending the Agreement on Government Procurement, adopted on 30 March 2012, and periodically thereafter, the Parties shall undertake further negotiations, with a view to improving this Agreement, progressively reducing and eliminating discriminatory measures, and achieving the greatest possible extension of its coverage among all Parties on the basis of mutual reciprocity, taking into consideration the needs of developing countries.

Further negotiations will also be facilitated by an agreed set of work programs that was negotiated as an integral outcome of the renegotiation of the 1994 Agreement. The following work programs are the subject of specific Committee Decisions that are annexed to the Ministerial Decision of December 15 and which, like the other agreed results of the negotiations, came into effect in April 2014:

- a work program to consider best practices with respect to measures and policies that the parties use to support the participation of small and medium-size enterprises (SMEs) in government procurement;[36]
- a work program to enable parties to improve procedures followed in the collection and reporting of statistical data relating to the Agreement;[37]
- a work program to promote the use of sustainable procurement practices, consistent with the Agreement;[38]
- a work program to address restrictions and exclusions in parties' coverage commitments under the Agreement;[39] and
- a work program on safety standards in international procurement.[40]

In addition to these work programs, a further attachment to the Ministerial Decision calls for the initiation of additional work programs, at a time to be determined, on the following subjects: (a) a review of the use, transparency, and the legal frameworks of public–private partnerships, and their relationship to covered procurement; (b) the advantages and disadvantages of developing common nomenclature for goods and services; and (c) the advantages and disadvantages of developing standardized notices.[41]

It will be evident that the foregoing work programs respond both to socio-political concerns shared by all parties and to continuing negotiating interests of at least some of the parties. For example, the issue of restrictions and exclusions in parties' coverage commitments under the Agreement is of direct significance for future negotiations under the Agreement. Similarly, most or possibly all parties are interested in promoting access to government procurement processes by SMEs; nonetheless, approaches to promoting such access differ and can also be a source of concern from a market access point of view. And, the work program on improvement of the collection and reporting of statistical data relating to the Agreement is an essential underpinning for related negotiations. To be sure, the foregoing work programs are exploratory in nature; they nonetheless hold the potential to contribute importantly to the future evolution of the Agreement and/or its administration. At the very

[36] See *Decision on the Outcomes of the Negotiations under Article XXIV:7 of the Agreement on Government Procurement*, GPA/113 of April 2, 2012, Annex 5.

[37] See *Decision on the Outcomes of the Negotiations under Article XXIV:7 of the Agreement on Government Procurement*, GPA/113 of April 2, 2012, Annex 6.

[38] See *Decision on the Outcomes of the Negotiations under Article XXIV:7 of the Agreement on Government Procurement*, GPA/113 of April 2, 2012, Annex 7.

[39] See *Decision on the Outcomes of the Negotiations under Article XXIV:7 of the Agreement on Government Procurement*, GPA/113 of April 2, 2012, Annex 8.

[40] See *Decision on the Outcomes of the Negotiations under Article XXIV:7 of the Agreement on Government Procurement*, GPA/113 of April 2, 2012, Annex 9.

[41] See *Decision on the Outcomes of the Negotiations under Article XXIV:7 of the Agreement on Government Procurement*, GPA/113 of April 2, 2012, Annex 4.

least, it should not be assumed that the revised Agreement is unlikely to evolve further, or that related market access commitments will not be progressively deepened.

2.6 **Concluding Remarks**

This chapter has discussed the relationship between general trade rules and commitments on government procurement with reference to both relevant WTO agreements and recent RTAs. Both economic and legal dimensions have been considered, and a number of insights have emerged. To begin with, and as noted in Section 2.2, a strong complementarity exists between general trade commitments (as under the GATT and the GATS) and government procurement commitments (as under the GPA). The complementarity of general trade commitments and government procurement commitments is first and foremost a matter of economics. The relationship between the GATS and the GPA illustrates this point. Typically, rights of establishment or of cross-border supply granted to foreign service-suppliers in a given service sector under the GATS will have an important bearing on their ability to compete effectively for such contracts under the GPA. This is because foreign suppliers not only have to secure the right to participate in tenders on a non-discriminatory basis, but also need to rely on general market access rights to be able to supply services to government. Conversely, access to procurement markets (governed by the GPA) can also have a significant bearing on the scale of operations and therefore the competitiveness of individual suppliers generally. The fact of the GPA's limited membership as compared to the multilateral agreements means that many WTO Members do not benefit from the synergies that are possible between these fields of trade regulation.

As developed in Section 2.3, government procurement chapters in RTAs typically are modeled substantially or entirely on the text of the GPA (in some cases, the 1994 version of the text, and in others, the revised version). As a consequence, the significance of the GPA as an instrument of international economic policy goes beyond its actual membership. The fact that government procurement disciplines in RTAs broadly track those of the GPA also makes easier a significant further broadening of the GPA's membership (if WTO Members choose to pursue this), to the extent that it has already brought participating WTO Members procurement legislation and practices broadly in line with GPA norms. From this standpoint at least, clearly, government procurement chapters in RTAs are more likely to facilitate than to hinder eventual accession to the GPA by relevant WTO Members.

With regard to the structure and extent of coverage commitments, as developed in Section 2.4, the approach used to schedule government procurement commitments in RTAs closely follows the structure of the GPA market access schedules. Additionally, while some RTAs provide for government procurement commitments that are deeper than those of the GPA in particular respects (e.g., additional services sectors or lower thresholds), this is by no means true generally when all dimensions of coverage are considered. Overall, the market access opportunities created by government procurement chapters in RTAs generally are significantly less than those available under the revised GPA. This preserves an important incentive for eventual GPA accession by relevant WTO Members.

Section 2.5 looked at the current status, inherent strengths and future prospects of the GPA, as a further basis for reflection on its role as compared to RTAs. To summarize, the successful renegotiation of the GPA has substantially raised the profile of the Agreement in the WTO and enhanced its contribution to market openness, good governance, and the effective management of public resources. Its growing membership, institutional strength, potential to evolve over time, and the new S&D provisions embodied in it make the revised GPA an attractive target for economies seeking to achieve economic growth and development through trade. For all these reasons, regional trade agreements embodying government procurement chapters are unlikely to eclipse its role. Indeed, the possibility of an eventual quasi-multilateralization of the Agreement through eventual further accessions to it by transition and developing economies, often building on their experience in relevant RTAs, should not be ruled out.

ACKNOWLEDGMENTS

Thanks are due to Aris Georgopoulos and Arie Reich for helpful comments on the conference version, and to Harsha Singh for collaboration on related work. Nivedita Sen helped with the checking of the chapter. The views expressed are the authors' and should not be attributed to the WTO or its Secretariat.

REFERENCES

Anderson, R. D. 2012. "The Conclusion of the Renegotiations of the World Trade Organization Agreement on Government Procurement: What It Means for the Agreement and for the World Economy." *Public Procurement Law Review* 21(3): 83–93.

Anderson, R. D. 2014. "Reflections on Bagwell and Staiger in Light of the Revised WTO Agreement on Government Procurement." In R. C. Freenstra and A. M. Taylor (eds), *Globalization in an Age of Crisis: Multilateral Economic Cooperation in the Twenty-First Century*. Chicago, IL: University of Chicago Press for the National Bureau of Economic Research, 124–130. Available at: http://www.nber.org/chapters/c12582.pdf.

Anderson, R. D. and Arrowsmith, S. 2011. "The WTO Regime on Government Procurement: Past, Present and Future." In S. Arrowsmith and R. D. Anderson (eds), *The WTO Regime on Government Procurement: Challenge and Reform*. Cambridge: Cambridge University Press, 3–58.

Anderson, R. D., Kovacic, W. E., and Müller, A. C. 2011. "Ensuring Integrity and Competition in Public Procurement Markets: A Dual Challenge for Good Governance." In S. Arrowsmith and

R. D. Anderson (eds), *The WTO Regime on Government Procurement: Challenge and Reform*. Cambridge: Cambridge University Press, 681–718.

Anderson, R. D., Locatelli, C., Mueller, A.C., and Pelletier, P. 2014. "The Relationship between Services Trade and Government Procurement Commitments: Insights from Relevant WTO Agreements and Recent RTAs." WTO Staff Working Paper ERSD-2014–21, Geneva (available at: <http://www.wto.org/english/res_e/reser_e/ersd201421_e.htm> (accessed July 21, 2016)).

Anderson, Robert D. and Mueller. (2009). "Market access for the government procurement of services: comparing recent PTAs with WTO achievements." In Juan A. Marchetti and Martin Roy (eds), *Opening Markets for Trade in Services*. Cambridge: Cambridge University Press, 435–74.

Anderson, R. D., Mueller, A. C., Osei-Lah, K., Pardo de Leon, J., and Pelletier, P. 2011. "Government Procurement Provisions in Regional Trade Agreements: A Stepping Stone to GPA Accession?" In S. Arrowsmith and R. D. Anderson (eds), *The WTO Regime on Government Procurement: Challenge and Reform*. Cambridge: Cambridge University Press, 561–656.

Anderson, R. D. and Osei-Lah, K. 2011a. "The Coverage Negotiations under the Agreement on Government Procurement: Context, Mandate, Process and Prospects." In S. Arrowsmith and R. D. Anderson (eds), *The WTO Regime on Government Procurement: Challenge and Reform*. Cambridge: Cambridge University Press, 149–74.

Anderson, R. D. and Osei-Lah, K. 2011b. "Forging a More Global Procurement Market: Issues Concerning Accessions to the Agreement on Government Procurement." In S. Arrowsmith and R. D. Anderson (eds), *The WTO Regime on Government Procurement: Challenge and Reform*. Cambridge: Cambridge University Press, 61–91.

Anderson, R. D., Pelletier, P., Osei-Lah, K., and Mueller, A. C. 2012. "Assessing the Value of Future Accessions to the WTO Agreement on Government Procurement (GPA): Some New Data Sources, Provisional Estimates, and an Evaluative Framework for Individual WTO Members Considering Accession." *Public Procurement Law Review* 21(4): 113–38 (early version circulated as WTO Staff Working Paper ERSD-2011–15, available at: <http://www.wto.org/english/res_e/reser_e/ersd201115_e.htm> (accessed July 21, 2016)).

Arrowsmith, S. 2003. *Government Procurement in the WTO*. The Hague: Kluwer Law

Choi, I. 2003. "The Long and Winding Road to the Government Procurement Agreement: Korea's Accession Experience." In W. Martin and M. Pangestu (eds), *Options for Global Trade Reform: A View from the Asia-Pacific*. Cambridge: Cambridge University Press, 249–69.

Evenett, S. and Hoekman, B. 2005. "Government Procurement: Market Access, Transparency and Multilateral Trade Rules." *European Journal of Political Economy* 1: 163–83.

Grier, J. 2016. "TPP Procurement: Harmonizing FTAs," *Perspectives on Trade*, January 12 (available at: <http://trade.djaghe.com/?p=2364>).

Hoekman, B. and Primo Braga, C. A. 1997. *Protection and Trade in Services: A Survey*. Washington, DC: The World Bank.

Müller, A. C. 2011. "Challenge and Reform Special and Differential Treatment and Other Special Measures for Developing Countries under the Agreement on Government Procurement: The Current Text and New Provisions." In S. Arrowsmith and R. D. Anderson (eds), *The WTO Regime on Government Procurement: Challenge and Reform*. Cambridge: Cambridge University Press, 339–76.

Niggli, N. C. and Osei-Lah, K. 2014. "Infrastructure Provision and Africa's Trade and Development Prospects: Potential Role and Relevance of The WTO Agreement on Government Procurement (GPA)." WTO Staff Working Paper ERSD-2014–20, Geneva (available at: <http://www.wto.org/english/res_e/reser_e/ersd201420_e.htm> (accessed July 21, 2016)).

OECD. 2002. "The Size of Government Procurement Markets, Paris" (available at: http://www.oecd-ilibrary.org/industry-and-services/the-size-of-government-procurement-markets_9789264196308-en (accessed July 21, 2016)).

Pelletier, P. 2015. "La révision de 2012 de l'Accord de l'OMC sur les marchés publics: son contexte et les dimensions de son champ d'application." In J. H. Currie and R. Provost (eds), *The Canadian Yearbook of International Law*, vol. 51. Toronto: University of British Columbia Press.

Schott, J. J. and Cimino, C. 2013. "Crafting a Transatlantic Trade and Investment Partnership: What Can Be Done?" Peterson Institute Policy Brief No. PB 13–8, Washington, DC.

Ueno, A. 2013. *Multilateralising Regionalism on Government Procurement*. Paris: OECD.

USTR (United States Trade Representative) (n.d.). "Text of the Trans-Pacific Partnership," Chapter on Government Procurement (chapter 15) (available at: <https://medium.com/the-trans-pacific-partnership/government-procurement-ac9def5bba92#.7zrccefkg> (accessed July 21, 2016)).

WTO Committee on Government Procurement. 2012a. "Adoption of the Results of the Negotiations under Article XXIV:7 of the Agreement on Government Procurement, Following Their Verification and Review, as required by the Ministerial Decision of 15 December 2011 (GPA/112)," Paragraph 5, GPA/113, April 2, 2012 (available at: <https://docs.wto.org/> (accessed July 21, 2016)).

WTO Committee on Government Procurement. 2012b. "Report of the Committee to the General Council," GPA/116 (available at: <https://docs.wto.org/> (accessed July 21, 2016)).

3 UNCITRAL and the Internationalization of Government Procurement Regulation

Caroline Nicholas

3.1 Introduction

The United Nations Commission on International Trade Law (UNCITRAL) was established in 1966. Its mandate, as stated in General Assembly Resolution 37/106, is "to further the progressive harmonization and unification of the law of international trade,"[1] by the issue of harmonized texts that seek to remove the types of barriers to cross-border trade that substantive rules can impose. It is thus one of the international rule-formulating agencies in the international trade sphere (together with Unidroit, the Institute for the Unification of Laws, and The Hague Conference on Private International Law). International trade law, in UNCITRAL terms, is the "body of rules governing commercial relationships of a private nature involving different countries."[2] Public procurement has been deemed to fall within that scope: UNCITRAL's mandate includes "international commercial relations on the level of private law entered into by governmental and other public bodies."[3]

The organizations most active in international and regional public procurement reform have different remits: the prevention of corruption, freeing up trade, ensuring equal treatment of suppliers in member states, and so on. In this context, the World

[1] "Origin, Mandate and Composition of UNCITRAL," available at: <http://www.uncitral.org/uncitral/en/about_us.html>. Unless otherwise indicated, UNCITRAL documents on public procurement are available at <http://www.uncitral.org/uncitral/en/commission/working_groups/1Procurement.html>. Websites were accessed on December 9, 2014.

[2] Report submitted by the Secretary-General to the General Assembly at its twenty-first session, 1966, United Nations Document A/6396, para. 10. See also Document A/6396/Add. 1 and 2, available at: <http://www.uncitral.org/uncitral/en/commission/sessions/pre.html>.

[3] Report submitted by the Secretary-General to the General Assembly at its twenty-first session, 1966, United Nations Document A/6396, para. 12.

Trade Organization (WTO), as a body that addresses state-to-state relations in international trade, has issued its Agreement on Government Procurement (GPA) as a (plurilateral) agreement between states that seeks to open up markets "to international competition by preventing States parties from discriminating against suppliers from other States parties, and applying rules of transparency and open competition in procurement" (Nicholas, 2011: p. 746).[4] By contrast, UNCITRAL's primary objective in its Model Law on Public Procurement (2011, the "Model Law")[5] is to provide a template for the design of national procurement systems, so "that the government purchaser will spend public funds with responsibility and accountability, and thus will obtain value for money."[6] In addition, though there is a heavy emphasis on unrestricted international participation (see, for example, Article 8 of the Model Law and commentary in the accompanying Guide to Enactment).

Fortunately, from the internationalization perspective, however, and as Arrowsmith has noted, "[i]n general, it can be seen that, to a great extent the formal rules on procurement procedures considered appropriate for opening international markets are similar to those often adopted to implement national objectives of value for money and probity. One consequence is that the parallel developments which have occurred in procurement regulation at the domestic level, on the one hand, and the international plane, on the other, have to a certain degree supported and reinforced each other" (Arrowsmith, 1998, cited in Arrowsmith and Wallace, 2000).[7] Parallel work in the WTO and UNCITRAL has sought to encourage greater cross-border procurement trade in practice through the harmonization or convergence of rules at the national level, both as regards preventing discrimination against overseas suppliers and through highly similar procedures. Both regimes address Arrowsmith's "structural restrictions" to cross-border procurement—as Yukins and Schooner (2006) put it, "when vendors run headlong into dense and alien procurement regimes."

[4] The United Nations Convention against Corruption (available at: <http://www.unodc.org/unodc/en/treaties/CAC/index.html>) requires public procurement systems to be based on "transparency, competition and objective criteria in decision-making," that are "effective, inter alia, in preventing corruption." The European Union's (EU) procurement rules seek to open up the public procurement market, and to ensure free movement of goods, construction and services, within the EU (available at: <http://eur-lex.europa.eu/legal-content/EN/TXT/?uri=celex:32014L0024>). The Asia-Pacific Economic Cooperation (APEC), the Free Trade Area of the Americas Agreement (FTAAA), the North American Free Trade Agreement (NAFTA), the Organization of American States (OAS), and COMESA Directive have regional instruments setting standards for national procurement systems, applying a non-discrimination approach similar to that of the GPA.

[5] The text of the Model Law and accompanying Guide to Enactment are available at: <http://www.uncitral.org/uncitral/uncitral_texts/procurement_infrastructure.html>.

[6] Guide to Enactment, Part II, commentary on the Preamble to the Model Law, Section A, para. 2 on p. 35.

[7] Arrowsmith, Linarelli and Wallace (2000: chapter 4, pp. 157–236, at p. 233), citing Arrowsmith (1998: p. 3 (*Public Procurement: Global Revolution*)); cited in Popowska (1997: pp. 23–31).

Thus the notion of internationalization that we shall consider refers to instruments such as UNCITRAL's for harmonizing the substantive rules applicable to public procurement (rather than the question, for example, of whether there is in fact more cross-border trade in public procurement).

3.2 **Harmonization of the Private Law Rules Governing International Trade**

Harmonization in this field is not new: it has been noted that the process itself started over a century ago and that, historically speaking, its main aim was to enhance legal certainty and predictability. More recently, harmonization is considered to have a positive role in reducing transaction costs and facilitating business worldwide (Faria, 2009). As early as 1966, when UNCITRAL was founded, the importance of the international community in designing international trade law was appreciated—the formulation of the rules of international trade by "international formulating agencies" such as UNCITRAL was recognized as the "outstanding characteristic of the modern development of international trade law."[8] Hence an analysis of the instruments produced by these agencies in public procurement regulation should provide an insight into whether or not public procurement rules are, in fact, internationalized.

Although the objective of the present edited collection is not to look backwards at the development of existing international instruments in public procurement, examining what the editors call the "drivers of the process" indeed requires a careful consideration of the process by which "international formulating agencies"—in this case, UNCITRAL—develop and issue their texts. In this case, we will place a particular focus on UNCITRAL's Model Law on Public Procurement. In short, does that process ensure that the international instruments it generates are coherent, reflect best international practice can be used in conjunction with other relevant international texts, and can be adapted to be used in a sufficiently wide range of legal traditions, cultures, and levels of development? In addition, can internationalization be assessed at the level of formal rules?

As the former Legal Counsel of the United Nations, Hans Corell, stated in 2000, UNCITRAL's achievements in achieving harmonization are "the result of two aspects of extraordinary cooperation...: the cooperation among States participating in the work of the Commission and the cooperation with interested international organisations of the public and private sectors."[9]

[8] Report submitted by the Secretary-General to the General Assembly at its twenty-first session, 1966, United Nations Document A/6396, para. 25.

[9] Opening Speech at UNCITRAL's thirty-third session, available at: <http://www.un.org/law/counsel/uncitral.htm>.

This chapter examines both elements of the process of international cooperation as it takes place in UNCITRAL, and will draw some conclusions about their impact on some key issues in public procurement regulation. In the same speech, Corell also voiced concerns about the process leading to a "multilaterally-funded dis-unification of law," which he considered to be a "particularly disturbing phenomenon, as it hits at the heart of UNCITRAL's mandate." He concluded that "[t]he resulting fragmentation and dispersion of efforts render the task of unifying and harmonizing the laws a daunting one." This chapter will also consider whether his conclusions may apply to the internationalization of public procurement regulation today, insofar as the UNCITRAL context indicates.

3.3 International Cooperation in the Negotiation of UNCITRAL Texts

3.3.1 UNCITRAL WORKING METHODS

An analysis of international cooperation in UNCITRAL must start with its working methods. In short, and following an intergovernmental negotiating process, UNCITRAL texts are adopted by its member states at its annual plenary session—called, by participants and the Secretariat alike, the "Commission session."[10] When those texts are adopted and with a view to seeing harmonization in practice, UNCITRAL also issues a request to all states to use and support its texts. For example, when adopting the UNCITRAL Model Law on Public Procurement, the Commission "*[r]ecommend[ed]* that all States use the UNCITRAL Model Law on Public Procurement in assessing their public procurement legal regime and give favourable consideration to the UNCITRAL Model Law on Public Procurement when they enact or revise their laws," and "*[r]equest[ed]* all States to support the promotion and implementation of the UNCITRAL Model Law on Public Procurement."

The goal of its working methods is to ensure that UNCITRAL instruments are capable of broad acceptability and use. Hence, UNCITRAL texts need to be negotiated with the involvement of "a variety of participants, including member States of UNCITRAL, which represent different legal traditions and levels of economic development; non-member States; intergovernmental organizations; and non-governmental organizations," so that they "are widely acceptable as offering solutions appropriate to different legal traditions and to countries at different stages of economic development" (United

[10] The Commission sessions are held in alternate years at the United Nations Headquarters in New York and at the Vienna International Centre at Vienna.

Nations, 2013). In this regard, as Kelly (2009) notes in an in-depth consideration of UNCITRAL's working methods, "UNCITRAL... prides itself on openness."

As an intergovernmental body, UNCITRAL operates through public meetings known as sessions.[11] Once a topic of work for UNCITRAL has been identified,[12] the development of a text on the topic normally takes place through one of UNCITRAL's six Working Groups, in accordance with the terms of a mandate given to the Working Group concerned by the Commission. The Working Groups also operate through "sessions," which typically last for one week and take place once or twice a year.[13]

UNCITRAL is structured to ensure that the various geographic regions and the principal economic and legal systems of the world are fairly represented at its sessions. UNCITRAL's *members* are sixty states elected from among the UN member states for terms of six years (and the terms of half the members expire every three years, so there is regular turnover).[14] Also eligible to take part (by invitation) in UNCITRAL's activities are *observers*—that is, all other UN member states and interested international observers. International observers are international organizations and non-governmental organizations (NGOs) that are international in remit and membership and that have specialist knowledge of the subject matter concerned.

Participation at Commission and Working Group sessions is open to all UNCITRAL members and observers (but not to individuals). All participants other than UNCITRAL members take part in sessions of the Commission and those of its Working Groups as observers. Observers are permitted to participate in discussions to the same extent as members (including the option to submit papers for consideration) (United Nations, 2008: para. 378),[15] though decisions of the Working Groups and Commission are taken by UNCITRAL member states alone. As those decisions are taken by consensus (i.e., without a vote),[16] the opportunity offered to observers to influence the

[11] These meetings are public meetings, as required by Rule 60 of the Rules of Procedure of the General Assembly. UNCITRAL itself has no official rules of procedure. At its first session, the Commission decided that it would be guided by the general principle that the rules of procedure of the General Assembly would apply *mutatis mutandis* to the Commission. These rules have been followed, subject to decisions by the Commission to alter specific rules. See Document A/CN.9/638, paras 4–12, A/CN.9/638/Add.1, paras 5–8, and, more generally, A/CN.9/638 and Adds 1–6, available at: <http://www.uncitral.org/uncitral/en/about/methods_documents.html>. After a review of its working methods, a record of the methods was set out in an Annex to the Commission's annual report to the General Assembly; see United Nations (2010), available at: <http://www.uncitral.org/uncitral/en/about/methods_documents.html>.

[12] See Section B.1, United Nations Document A/CN.9/752, available at: <http://www.uncitral.org/uncitral/commission/sessions/45th.html>

[13] Also alternating between New York and Vienna.

[14] See, further, "Origin, Mandate and Composition of UNCITRAL," available at: <http://www.uncitral.org/uncitral/en/about/origin.html>.

[15] Note, however, that one member state objected to this practice.

[16] There has been only one formal vote in UNCITRAL, regarding the move of the Secretariat from New York to Vienna in 1973—see, further A/CN.9/638/Add.4, paras 2–15.

consensus-building process through sharing relevant experience and expertise is one with real impact.

At the Working Group sessions, there can be and often is lively debate on policy issues and how they should be reflected in the ultimate text. Although member states are intended to lead the process, it is not designed as a political one, given UNCITRAL's own status as a non-political body (Cheng, 1988: p. 125). More generally, the importance of avoiding politicization of the process was noted as being key to UNCITRAL's success right from its inception—at its first session, the Commission had before it a report on the progressive development of the law of international trade in which it was noted that "harmonization is more easily achieved in technical branches of the law than in subjects closely connected with national traditions and basic principles of domestic law."[17] Thus UNCITRAL was steered away from politically sensitive topics towards the more technical ones, and in general terms this remains the case.

3.3.1.1 Transparency in UNCITRAL's Working Methods

In preparation for its Working Group sessions, the UNCITRAL Secretariat, with the assistance of outside experts, researches and submits papers on the issues arising in a particular topic. The papers analyze proposals and survey experience and commentary on the issues concerned and propose draft legislative provisions for a text on the topic at issue, for the Working Groups to consider. These documents, or "working papers," are made available on the UNCITRAL website in advance of the sessions of the Working Group and in all six official languages of the United Nations (Arabic, Chinese, English, French, Russian, and Spanish).[18] At the sessions of the Working Groups, the working papers are discussed and issues deliberated.

The Secretariat also drafts reports of the Working Groups, which summarize the deliberations at each session and record interim decisions. Each Working Group considers and adopts its report at the end of each session, and these reports are submitted to the Commission for its review (and also made available on the UNCITRAL website in all official languages). Although this system does not prevent issues from being reopened if there is a consensus in a subsequent Working Group session to do so, it is relatively uncommon for this to take place.

UNCITRAL's transparent, non-political approach is also designed to allow for informed debate outside the Working Group sessions so that participants can discuss issues at the sessions after wide consultation, as part of and support for the consensus-building

[17] Report submitted by the Secretary-General to the General Assembly at its twenty-first session, 1966, United Nations document A/6396, para. 203.

[18] All working papers produced during the development of the Model Law on public procurement are available at: <http://www.uncitral.org/uncitral/en/commission/working_groups/1Procurement.html>.

process, and to encourage participation at the sessions themselves. Indeed, a review of the bibliography on public procurement found on the UNCITRAL website shows that academic debate on the topics flourished during the period that the Model Law was being negotiated (2004–11).[19] As has been noted elsewhere, "not only did these discussions assist the technical rigour of the debate within UNCITRAL, but they also allowed areas of the reforms that were under consideration to be used by States reforming their public procurement laws at that time. For example, Mexico based its provisions on the then draft text for framework agreements" (Nicholas, 2013: p. 4).[20]

3.3.1.2 Decisions by Consensus

At the end of debates on particular issues and when deciding on the resulting provisions, the Working Groups recommend texts to the Commission and the Commission adopts them "by consensus," again underscoring their general acceptability. The UNCITRAL concept of "consensus" requires some explanation.[21] The Commission has described it thus: it "may reflect a complete agreement as to substance and a consequent absence of reservations. It may also be based on the substantially prevailing view, a flexible notion that does not embody a pre-defined mode of calculation and is characterized by a strong majority of opinions and the absence of formal objection and vote" (United Nations, 2009: para. 387).[22] Early reports of the Commission explicitly stated that decisions at the session were taken by consensus, and sometimes reference was made to actions taken by the Commission unanimously, probably to distinguish a high degree of agreement from cases in which a decision was reached by general agreement without strong objection, even though unresolved differences and concerns remained.[23] Later Commission records have ceased to identify the extent of agreement. As Kelly (2009) recalled from the Secretariat papers on the topic, a practice has evolved where "consensus [is] based upon what was sometimes described as the 'substantially prevailing view.'"[24]

As one delegation observed in 2007, "[m]ost states have welcomed the fact that UNCITRAL decisions have been made without the need for a formal vote. The General Assembly has repeatedly commended UNCITRAL for having reached its decisions by consensus. By seeking to find solutions that are generally acceptable, UNCITRAL has

[19] Available at: <http://www.uncitral.org/uncitral/en/publications/bibliography_consolidated.html>. Indeed, an entire book (Arrowsmith, 2009) was devoted to the UNCITRAL reforms.

[20] See also Dávila (2011), as cited in Nicholas (2013).

[21] For an in-depth consideration of "consensus" in the UNCITRAL context, see Document A/CN.9/638/Add.4.

[22] This description was not subsequently included in UNCITRAL's statement of its Rules of Procedure and Methods of Work, however.

[23] See Document A/CN.9/638/Add.4, paras 10–11 and 21.

[24] Kelly (2009: p. 7), citing Document A/CN.9/638/Add.4, para. 17.

avoided politicization and entrenched disagreement, remained technically focused, and established itself as an effective standard setting organization. This method of work has benefited countries in all economic stages, especially developing and emerging states."[25]

3.3.2 GENERAL APPLICABILITY AS A PRE-REQUISITE FOR INTERNATIONALIZATION

As the above description demonstrates, it is the combination of the process of consensus-building and the eventual result that allows for UNCITRAL texts to reach the desired level of acceptability. The Sixth Committee of the General Assembly (its legal committee, and the one to which UNCITRAL presents its annual report) has emphasized that UNCITRAL's approach allows "States with different social-economic systems, different levels of development and different legal systems and historical traditions, to base [UNCITRAL's] work on careful regard for proposals submitted and respect for mutual interests. In the opinion of these representatives, the consensus method [is] conducive to achieving a larger cooperation among countries having different legal, economic and social systems and [ensures] that the uniform rules derived from the work of the Commission [are] generally acceptable."[26]

This concept of general, or—as it is now expressed—universal applicability has also, naturally enough, been highlighted in the context of UNCITRAL's work on public procurement. The Guide to Enactment that accompanies the Model Law notes that the "potential of the Model Law as an instrument to support the harmonization of procurement regulation internationally can be fully realized only to the extent that it is used by all types of States."[27] The importance of the Model Law is that it is not "[a] text designed with any particular groups of countries or particular state of development in mind, and... it does not promote the experience in or approach of any one region."[28]

3.3.3 PARTICIPATION IN UNCITRAL'S WORK

UNCITRAL's objective of seeking to turn the theory of openness, inclusiveness, and multilingualism into a practice that genuinely results in universally applicable texts, and

[25] Document A/CN.9/639, para. 6, citing GA resolutions 43/166, 42/152, 41/77, 40/71, 39/82, 38/134, (available at: <http://www.uncitral.org/uncitral/en/commission/sessions/40th.html#second>).

[26] Document A/CN.9/638/Add.4, para. 7.

[27] Available at: <http://www.uncitral.org/uncitral/uncitral_texts/procurement_infrastructure.html>.

[28] See the Guide to Enactment, Part I, General Remarks, p. 2, para. 5 (available at: <http://www.uncitral.org/uncitral/uncitral_texts/procurement_infrastructure.html>).

particularly universally acceptable texts that are of the high standard traditionally generated by and so expected of UNCITRAL is not without challenge.[29] The most pressing such challenge is securing sufficiently wide and meaningful participation at UNCITRAL sessions to ensure that the process is sufficiently rigorous and balanced that transferable best practice can emerge.

UNCITRAL records that the delegations and observer delegations may comprise "government officials, academics, experts or private sector lawyers" (United Nations, 2013: para. 6), and ideally its Working Groups should comprise therefore a balance of individuals across delegations from all regions and (in the international organization and NGO context) from all sectors. In a recent study into participation in the UNCITRAL Working Group on Insolvency, it was stated that, "[f]or maximal impact, . . . a delegation qua delegation [footnote omitted] will combine (i) high and consecutive attendance of delegations; (ii) high and consecutive attendance of particular delegates; (iii) the conjunction of consistently attending delegates and delegations; (iv) occupationally diverse delegations; and (v) full or dense delegations" (Halliday, Pacewicz, and Block-Lieb, 2013: p. 285).

As UNCITRAL has itself noted, UNCITRAL is not alone in requesting the resources of national governments to engage in and support its work—it competes with other international policy-making bodies. "The international law scene has greatly changed since the establishment of UNCITRAL. The attention of policymakers is often drawn to other areas, such as environmental law or criminal law, and resources, particularly in developing countries, are seldom available for the consideration of international trade law texts. Moreover, international business law is often perceived as a highly technical matter, involving private sector interests and requiring long-term attention."[30]

UNCITRAL follows the policy of the General Assembly in not surveying participation in its sessions,[31] so assessing attendance is challenging. There are, however, anecdotal indications to the effect that there may be some decline in participation in some UNCITRAL areas of work and at Commission sessions, particularly as regards representation of delegations from capitals. In 2008, for example, a member state regretted "that during the last year several members of UNCITRAL were not represented at its sessions and working groups."[32]

A further UNCITRAL member state in 2007 had voiced concerns that there was a "perception that the working methods of the Commission and its working groups might

[29] See, for example, Sono (1984), Herrmann (1998), and, more recently, Guglya (2012).

[30] A comment made in the context of use of UNCITRAL texts, but, it is submitted, of general application; see Document A/CN.9/752, para. 42.

[31] Participation in UNCITRAL sessions is recorded in a List of Participants, which is made available to participants but not to the general public.

[32] Austria's delegate, speaking to the Sixth Committee (Legal) of the General Assembly in 2008; see <http://www.un.org/press/en/2008/gal3346.doc.htm>.

not sufficiently encourage effective participation in the creation of UNCITRAL standards or the subsequent enactment of those standards by a broad range of States."[33]

A significant issue is the cost of participation in UNCITRAL. Kelly (2009: p. 9) notes that UNCITRAL does not fund participation at its Working Group and Commission sessions. This is largely accurate, though UNCITRAL does have a UNCITRAL Trust Fund for Travel Assistance to assist delegates from developing countries to attend its Commission sessions in Vienna. When making the statement referred to in the previous paragraph, the member state continued with an appeal "for contributions to be made to the Commission's trust fund for travel assistance to developing countries that were Commission members. Austria had made a voluntary contribution to the fund this year." This type of appeal is repeated annually at the Commission session and by the Chairman of UNCITRAL and Legal Counsel to the Sixth Committee, but the fund remains very small.

However, it is not just traveling to sessions of the Working Group that involves significant cost for member states and observers—if participation is to be meaningful, preparation for the sessions is required, involving (for example) wide-ranging consultations within the countries concerned and/or among members of organizations. Such consultations may themselves require further translation of documents, the convening of meetings, the designing, conducting, and reviewing of surveys, statistical analysis, and so on—a process that requires detailed knowledge of the subject matter at issue.

A member state also voiced concerns that "private professional associations considered as NGOs play a major role because of the expertise they possess in the areas under discussion. Financial considerations also play a significant part: UNCITRAL has no funding available for these experts' travel and accommodation expenses. The result is that the experts most frequently present alongside the delegates of those States that can afford to send them are the representatives of these private associations."[34] That is, national delegations may be private representatives rather than government employees, with accordingly different experience and perhaps desired outcomes.

In the context of UNCITRAL's Working Group on Insolvency, it was suggested that developed countries were over-represented in the development of UNCITRAL's Model Law on Cross-Border Insolvency in terms of frequency of participation and activity in UNCITRAL meetings, and that NGOs from the developed world were also dominant (Halliday, Pacewicz, and Block-Lieb, 2013: p. 280). It should be added that commentary on UNCITRAL's texts does not indicate that the quality of its texts has been affected; indeed, in a recent letter to the *Financial Times* and in fact citing the successful precedent

[33] See Document A/62/17 (Part I), para. 234, available at: <http://www.uncitral.org/uncitral/en/commission/sessions/40th.html#second>.

[34] Document A/CN.9/635, para. 3.1, available at: <http://www.uncitral.org/uncitral/en/commission/sessions/40th.html>.

of UNCITRAL's Model Law on Cross-Border Insolvency itself, UNCITRAL's model law approach is recommended.[35] Without empirical studies into attendance at other UNCITRAL Working Groups and the Commission itself, it is not possible to assess this study's conclusions or whether they are of more general application, but that there are risks to UNCITRAL's aspirations for its texts is evident.

Following comments on concerns over UNCITRAL's working methods submitted to the Commission in 2007, these questions were debated during the following several sessions. It was also stated in this debate that, "[a]t its inception UNCITRAL [had] adopted a workable method (administered by the Secretariat in consultation with Member States) for identifying those non-state entities with particular knowledge, expertise, or experience in the subjects under consideration. . . . The Commission has repeatedly recognized that the participation of nongovernmental organizations with international expertise is critical to the quality of texts formulated by the Commission, as well as its program of work."[36] Kelly (2009: p. 18) has noted that the debate showed differing views about the importance of "the fact that some States may be in a better position to fund expert participation." It was also suggested that "means through which member States might increase their sense of ownership and responsibility in respect of UNCITRAL through stronger control over the standard-making activity of the Commission" could be considered.[37] After a careful review of its working methods, and recalling the need to encourage expert input and to balance the interests of member states with that need, UNCITRAL issued a statement of working methods, which clarified (as suggested) "to invited non-governmental organizations their role as contributors and not decision-makers."[38] It is submitted that this approach is the correct one—UNCITRAL's texts are generally directed at national legislators and policy-makers, and the national context as well as the expert one needs to be taken into account.

UNCITRAL has also taken steps to ensure that its Colloquia are open and transparent: a section of its website lists those meetings and the documents produced for them, and Colloquia reports are submitted to the Commission for its consideration.[39]

The delegation that opened the above debate was concerned, however, that "[t]echnical points are examined in greater detail by informal meetings, where a core of experts has the

[35] "Model law is the key to protecting 'unprotected' government debt," December 7, 2014 (available at: <http://www.ft.com/intl/cms/s/0/1e7f9980-7be6-11e4-a695-00144feabdc0.html?siteedition=intl#axzz3La8WgUTa>).

[36] Document A/CN.9/639, para. 13 (footnotes omitted), available at: <http://www.uncitral.org/uncitral/en/commission/sessions/40th.html#second>.

[37] Report of the Commission, A/62/17 (Part I), para. 234, available at: <http://www.uncitral.org/uncitral/en/commission/sessions/40th.html#second>.

[38] See UNCITRAL rules of procedure and methods of work, Annex III to the Commission Report A/65/17, available at: <http://www.uncitral.org/uncitral/en/commission/sessions/43rd.html>, and Document A/CN.9/639, para. 13(c).

[39] See <http://www.uncitral.org/uncitral/en/commission/colloquia.html>.

key role. These meetings, like the Colloquia, are usually convened by the Secretariat."[40] In this context, the Commission noted that the Secretariat "has sought the assistance of outside experts from different legal traditions in preparing materials for consideration by working groups. Those expert group meetings have enabled the Secretariat to prepare materials that are more thoroughly researched and developed than might otherwise be the case. More extensive use of such informal methods may save, or enable more effective use of, meeting time for both the Commission and the working groups." However, the Commission also took note of concerns about possible over-representation and excessive influence of some experts,[41] and has emphasized the importance of developing its texts through its Working Group sessions. For example, at its Commission session in 2013, it stated that "the development of UNCITRAL texts as a matter of course should be undertaken through the Working Group process. In that regard, the Commission recalled the link between that formal negotiation process and the universal applicability and hence acceptance of UNCITRAL texts, the importance of the transparency that that process conferred, and the need to continue the inclusive working methods of UNCITRAL. It was also agreed that the multilingualism of the working methods of UNCITRAL constituted key support for its work and, even though it was resource-hungry, should be continued."[42]

Even sufficiently wide and representative participation, however, will not alone guarantee success. Faria (2009) recalls that the process of developing international texts is known to leave much to be desired: "of necessity unification and harmonization proceed slowly, by small steps, with imperfect achievements. It is unrealistic to expect anything approaching perfection."[43] Furthermore, he notes, international texts "are inevitably and confessedly drafted as multi-cultural compromises between different schemes of law,"[44] and "[l]egal unification through binding instruments has also been criticised for producing 'sub-optimal,' vaguely drafted rules for the purpose of achieving political compromise."[45] Echoing the debate in UNCITRAL set out above, he refers to the risk of "private legislators' heavily influenced by lobbying groups seeking to promote their economic interests, and working in an environment of scant accountability" (though this is not a comment based on experience in UNCITRAL).[46] Kelly asserts that states may have an interest in the international norms because they will, "if widely adopted, ... affect their power" (Kelly, 2009: p. 19)—that is, norms that are closer to the

[40] Document A/CN.9/635, para 3.1.

[41] Document A/CN.752, para. 38.

[42] Document A/68/17, para. 300. Schwartz (2003), among others, has recognized the importance of linguistic barriers to internationalization.

[43] Faria (2009), quoting Farnsworth (1996).

[44] Faria (2009), quoting Hobhouse (1990).

[45] Walt (1999), as cited by Faria (2009: p. 10).

[46] Faria (2009), citing Stephan (1996: p. 681).

domestic position may confer political advantage, thus encouraging states to seek to promote their own approach. Although these commentators were speaking primarily of conventions and not about UNCITRAL experience itself, it is submitted that the points made indeed raise risks that can arise in any international negotiation.

So the imperative, then, is to ensure high-quality, transferable experience as the basis of international instruments. This requires that the various inevitable interests are balanced through a broad and representative participation in the rule-making body concerned. As austerity continues in many regions, developed countries may struggle to finance full participation in UNCITRAL. Recent consultations on the question of whether UNCITRAL should take up legislative development in public–private partnerships have yielded a common response from developing states to the effect that they would be keen users of an UNCITRAL text in this field, but that they are unwilling and/or unable to finance participation or to devote and divert their scarce resources to prepare for participation in the development of texts through a Working Group—a stance that may have wider application. Thus, meeting the participation challenge that UNCITRAL and its member states face may remain difficult, at least in the short term.

3.3.4 COOPERATION WITH INTERNATIONAL ORGANIZATIONS

Hans Corell noted that "[t]he first specific task given to [UNCITRAL] in pursuance of [its] mandate is to coordinate the work of organisations active in the field of international trade law and to encourage cooperation among them."[47] The potential for coordination among international and regional organizations (such as the regional development banks or regional trade liberalization bodies) to balance, for example, over- or under-representation of a region is clearly significant. Experience from UNCITRAL sessions, however, does not indicate this happens as a matter of routine.

Back in 2000, the fact that UNCITRAL was not sufficiently effective in securing this type of coordination was one of Corell's key concerns, as he set out in some detail: "Unfortunately, our efforts in establishing and maintaining cooperation have not been consistently successful. There is still a disturbing amount of overlapping or even outright conflicting initiatives being taken by various global and regional organizations, within and outside the United Nations system.... Insufficient coordination at the international rule-making level is sometimes worsened by lack of coordination in the implementation of multilateral or bilateral aid programs supporting domestic law reform in recipient

[47] Opening Speech at UNCITRAL's thirty-third session, available at: <http://www.un.org/law/counsel/uncitral.htm>.

countries, which on occasion fail to give adequate consideration to trade law texts prepared by international formulating agencies, such as UNCITRAL."[48]

There is an ever-increasing number of other organizations with which UNCITRAL might, or should, coordinate, as has been acknowledged and as is evident in UNCITRAL's reports.[49] As the annual Secretariat reports to the Commission note, and in accordance with its mandate, UNCITRAL seeks "to ensure coordination of the related activities of the different organizations, share information and expertise and avoid duplication of work and the resultant work products."[50] These activities, which are conducted largely as Secretariat-to-Secretariat activities, include identifying relevant activities of international organizations and participating in other bodies' own working groups, expert groups, and so on. The Secretariats of UNCITRAL and Unidroit and the Permanent Bureau of the Hague Conference, with the assistance of outside experts, have published "comparison and analysis of major features of international instruments relating to secured transactions."[51]

However, and as Faria has noted, "[a]ll organisations especially devoted to legal harmonization (Hague Conference, Unidroit, UNCITRAL) have in common a chronic lack of Secretariat resources, which severely limits the number of initiatives they are capable of handling at any given time." In the latest Secretariat report on coordination and similar activities to the Commission, it is noted that the UNCITRAL Secretariat contributes to procurement policy-making and technical assistance activities being carried out by the World Bank (on several projects), the Organisation for Economic Cooperation and Development (also on several projects), the European Bank for Reconstruction and Development, the United Nations Environment Programme, the United Nations Office on Drugs and Crime (UNODC), the WTO, and others—and that many of these bodies are considering overlapping issues.[52]

The UNCITRAL Secretariat has made cooperation with the above organizations and their Secretariats, a priority to ensure that "the Model Law may be used by States parties to [other international] texts and agreements without major amendment of their national procurement legislation."[53] Joint capacity-building activities (also in coordination with other donors) and exchange of information help both to ensure policy

[48] Opening Speech at UNCITRAL's thirty-third session, available at: <http://www.un.org/law/counsel/uncitral.htm>.

[49] UNCITRAL reports on Technical Assistance and Cooperation, and Coordination Activities are available on its website for each Commission session (see, for example, the 2014 session at <http://www.uncitral.org/uncitral/commission/sessions/47th.html>).

[50] Document A/CN.9/809, para. 3, available at: <http://www.uncitral.org/uncitral/commission/sessions/47th.html>. A similar report is made to the Commission each year.

[51] See Document A/CN.9/720, Basic Facts, para. 24.

[52] See "Coordination Activities," Document A/CN.9/809, and "Technical Cooperation and Assistance," Document A/CN.9/818, available at: <http://www.uncitral.org/uncitral/commission/sessions/47th.html>.

[53] Guide to Enactment, Part I, Section 6, "International Context of the Model Law and Promotion of International Participation in Procurement Proceedings," pp. 11–12, paras 38–9.

coherence and avoid duplication of effort. Representatives of the above organizations have been invited to and have attended UNCITRAL Working Group sessions and events. Consequently, users of policy documents, capacity-building materials and other reports from the organizations cited will find cross-references to the Model Law and Guide to Enactment, and vice versa. More formal cooperation, should resources allow, would no doubt further assist national reform efforts.

Consequently, it is clear that the resource-challenged Secretariats of the various organizations, including UNCITRAL, cannot ensure that the details of policies and rules are consistently developed. Furthermore, and if the indications of resource constraints in the UNCITRAL legislative development process are mirrored elsewhere, there is little likelihood of coordination within the different government departments that handle, for example, anti-corruption and governance, international law and trade liberalization, and coordination between states, to ensure that consistent positions are taken in these myriad organizations.

3.4 **Extent of Harmonization in International Instruments on Public Procurement: Now and in the Future**

3.4.1 KEY POLICY ISSUES DEBATED IN UNCITRAL

The process of negotiation in UNCITRAL gave rise to wide-ranging debate, often reflecting different organizations' perspectives on the extent of commercial discretion that should be afforded government officials. Particularly contentious issues (from the private law perspective, i.e. other than national preference and related policies) included: choice of and use of procurement methods, particularly for the procurement of complex and high-value items and services; the conditions for use of framework agreements (indeed, whether there should be any conditions at all); and the nature of the relief that should be made available in a remedies system (including the ability to overturn concluded contracts, award compensation for lost profits, and interim relief). Indeed, in the context of remedies systems, the widely varying national experiences ranged from those seeking to reduce a flood of arguably vexatious and frivolous litigation apparently seeking to enhance bidders' prospects, to those seeking to encourage challenges at all. The Guide to Enactment notes that an effective remedies system is a requirement of the UN Convention Against Corruption (which makes provision for procurement as part of its "Preventive Measures" Chapter).[54] While there is no definition or guidance of the

[54] See Article 9, "Public Procurement and the Management of Public Finances"; Article 9(1) addresses procurement, and Articles 9(2) and 9(3) address the management of public finances.

characteristics of an "effective" system from the custodians of the Convention, the Guide sets out UNCITRAL's interpretation. The UNCITRAL experience also indicated member states' concerns about interference in assessing the legality of government acts and upon the interaction of executive and the judicial branches of a particular state, an area not within UNCITRAL's mandate and unlikely in any event to lead to consensus. Accordingly, the Guide to Enactment notes that the Model Law provides significant flexibility as regards the manner in which its provisions might be implemented to suit local circumstances,[55] and so this is an example of an area in which how formal rules apply domestically may vary widely (and, consequently, it may prove difficult to include the topic in regional agreements concerning government procurement).

Nonetheless, and despite differences in views, the reports of the Working Groups do not show attempts to promote the national experience of individual member states, though it is clear that the influence of the recently issued European Union Public Procurement Directives and some other national and regional experience was not insignificant. Indeed, what is also evident from the Working Group reports is that reference to these systems was made because they offered sources of modern and good practice, and there was no assumption that such practice would necessarily transfer into good practice in the UNCITRAL context. Thus the Working Groups analyzed transferability; that is, as Schwartz (2003) notes, whether "developing nations and others with developing systems of government procurement law may derive important lessons from the evolution of procurement law regimes in developed nations such as the United States—or the European Union."

The Model Law contains a new public procurement method to allow for structured interactive procurement of complex and high-value projects (called "Request-for-proposals with dialogue").[56] The discussions on the proposal itself, the draft provisions, and accompanying guidance provide an interesting snapshot of some significant policy differences among the states and organizations active in the Working Group at that time. In the spring 2009 session, several delegations first proposed a new "competitive negotiations" procurement method,[57] which was based on the notion that "in practice requests for proposals were typically the solicitations used to launch competitive negotiations."[58] After several iterations (including a suggestion that this method should be

[55] Guide to Enactment, Part II, commentary to Chapter VIII, "Challenge Proceedings," starting at p. 268.

[56] Footnote 5, supra.

[57] See document A/CN.9/WG.I/XVI/CRP.2—Proposed Article 40: Competitive Negotiations Proposal submitted by Austria, the United Kingdom, and the United States, available at: <http://www.uncitral.org/uncitral/en/commission/working_groups/1Procurement.html>.

[58] See Document A/CN.9/WG.I/XVI/CRP.2—Proposed Article 40: Competitive Negotiations Proposal submitted by Austria, the United Kingdom, and the United States, para. 3, available at: <http://www.uncitral.org/uncitral/en/commission/working_groups/1Procurement.html>.

called "competitive dialogue" and should reflect its EU equivalent),[59] the final text of the "Request-for-proposals with dialogue" was agreed. The variations in the views of delegates expressed during this process included the extent to which evaluation criteria and descriptions (including specifications) could be modified during the procedure, the nature of the interaction between the dialogue-based methods and procurement planning (whether the method should follow detailed planning or whether it might include an "advisory multi-step process"), and how to provide guidance on the use of the method, as the Working Group "concluded that the Guide should stress that sufficient capacity to operate [this and similar] methods would be critical for their successful use."[60] The main issue involved was that the method "presupposed significant discretion on the part of procuring entities in decision-making, and therefore it raised higher risks of corruption and abuse than might be present in other less flexible procedures. However, it was reported that the value of this procurement method had resulted in benefits to the procuring entity in enabling it to obtain the best solution to its procurement needs, and thus that there would be advantages to developed and developing countries alike in its use. It was also stressed that the opportunity cost of not providing for such negotiations should be taken into account."[61]

The Guide to Enactment accordingly addresses these matters regarding "Request-for-proposals with dialogue": "[t]he capacity to engage in the type of dialogue envisaged, notably as regards the presentation and explanation of needs, the examination and evaluation of different technical solutions, and structures to avoid the possibility of abuse in favouring certain suppliers or contractors by providing different information to each of them during the dialogue."[62] In other words, while many international instruments may include a method similar to the "Request-for-proposals with dialogue" method, it may not in fact be widely enacted at the domestic level (and this position may also be the case for similar methods outside the EU). Indeed, while some studies presented to the Working Group had noted a move away from (open) tendering as the primary procurement method towards competitive negotiations and other interactive techniques in some systems, and despite the strongly expressed views in favor of a more flexible approach, the Working Group reaffirmed that open tendering would remain the procurement method of choice under the Model Law, as reflected in the commentary to Chapter III in the Guide to Enactment.[63] Particular concerns were also expressed about competitive negotiations (the relatively unstructured method provided

[59] See, for example, <http://www.uncitral.org/pdf/english/commissiondocs/a-cn9-XLII-crp-2-e.pdf> and <http://www.uncitral.org/pdf/english/workinggroups/wg_1/wp.71.add5-e.pdf>.

[60] See A/CN.9/WG.I/WP.71, paras 21–22, A/CN.9/WG.I/WP.71/Add.5, and A/CN.9/672, paras 14–30, available at: <http://www.uncitral.org/uncitral/en/commission/working_groups/1Procurement.html>.

[61] A/CN.9/672, para. 16.

[62] Guide to Enactment, p. 184, para. 10, discussing "Enactment: Policy Considerations" in the context of Chapter V, "Procurement Methods."

[63] Guide to Enactment, p. 130 onwards, Commentary to Chapter III, "Open Tendering."

for in Article 51 of the Model Law). The method, by comparison with other interactive methods (some request-for-proposals methods, two-stage tendering), is noted in the Guide to involve very flexible procedures, and consequently not to "provide the same levels of transparency, integrity and objectivity in the process as are present in other competitive procurement methods, and the method is therefore at greater risk of abuse and corruption."[64] Consequently, it is limited to "the exceptional circumstances set out in article 30 (4) (a)–(c): urgency, catastrophic events and the protection of essential security interests of the enacting State."[65]

In the light of these debates, some commentators have queried whether the Model Law operates as a mean or a even lowest-common denominator of procurement policy as a result of the process of negotiation. While it is correct that general applicability requires the most progressive and the most conservative to be accommodated, the approach of the Model Law is to permit options to reflect the maturity or sophistication of different enacting states—and, in particular with regard to the use of country systems by donors, to allow donor requirements to be accommodated. The Guide explains the UNCITRAL approach to the selection of procurement methods (on both enactment and usage) as follows: "Taking account of the differing stages of development of procurement systems in enacting States, this section of the Guide comments on features of certain procurement methods that are intended to permit more or less discretion on the part of the procuring entity, and the capacity and infrastructure needed to operate them effectively. The aim is to enable enacting States to decide whether or not each method is appropriate for their local circumstances, by reference also to the issues raised in the commentary on implementation and use in the following section."[66] Consequently, it would be illusory to conclude that any state that has enacted the Model Law will have the same suite of procurement methods, and the same approach to discretion on the part of government officials. Nonetheless, broadly equivalent levels of transparency are required in procurement methods other than those designed for urgent, emergency, or very low-value procurement.

Transparency considerations in the Model Law were afforded a high level of emphasis—rightly, it is submitted, as many of its users historically have been developing countries and those in transition. An example of the situation as regards socio-economic policies illustrates the point: all criteria that could be used to eliminate suppliers or their bids or to favor certain groups (such as SMEs, or products or services with "green" characteristics), and whether expressed as qualification criteria, responsiveness requirements or evaluation criteria, are subject to the same exacting transparency requirements.

[64] Guide to Enactment, p. 128, para. 2, discussing competitive negotiations.

[65] Guide to Enactment, para. 1.

[66] Guide to Enactment, p. 128, para. 2, discussing "Enactment: Policy Considerations" in the context of procurement methods and conditions for use.

All must be disclosed in the solicitation documents under Articles 39, 47, and 49—including as regards their manner of application. Thus socio-economic criteria are treated as any other criteria, a major development from the earlier opaque flexibility to take such criteria into account both in UNCITRAL and elsewhere. The Guide also notes the enormous potential of e-procurement to enhance transparency in practice—one of the reasons for updating the Model Law from its 1994 version—so while many of the rules may not appear to have changed significantly as regards transparency, the expectation is that users of the text will in fact operate with considerably greater transparency.[67]

3.4.2 HARMONIZATION IN THE MODERN CONTEXT

UNCITRAL's mandate refers to the "progressive harmonization" of international trade law, or as Block-Lieb and Halliday (2006: p. 498) put it, a "unification over time." Documents issued by UNCITRAL since its inception have provided an ever-more flexible notion of harmonization—along the lines of reducing divergences rather than promoting uniformity. UNCITRAL defines "harmonization" as the "process through which domestic laws may be modified to enhance predictability in cross-border commercial transactions" ("Unification," on the other hand, is "the adoption by States of a common legal standard governing particular aspects of international business transactions"). Its website now describes its mandate as the "the modernisation and harmonization of rules on international business."[68]

"Modernizing" rather than "harmonizing" raises more challenging issues for the negotiation of international instruments, as Block-Lieb and Halliday (2006) have noted. Traditional harmonization "may present only minimal intrusions upon national legislation, involving the identification of common approaches among existing domestic laws." Modernization, they continue, can arise either "where national law exists on a topic, but is viewed by the international community as out-of-date," or "where technical or market developments have outstripped existing law and the lack of suitable regulation is viewed by the international community to stall commercial development," where, for example, UNCITRAL might "create new law, and in so doing purport to speak authoritatively to national legislatures both about the need and the content of law."[69]

In 2003, when mandating a Working Group to revise the 1994 Model Law on Procurement of Goods, Construction and Services (the 1994 "Model Law"),[70] and

[67] Guide to Enactment, Part I, Section 3, p. 25 onwards, "Specific Issues Arising in the Implementation and Use of e-Procurement."

[68] <http://www.uncitral.org/uncitral/en/about_us.html>.

[69] <http://www.uncitral.org/uncitral/en/about_us.html>.

[70] The 1994 Model Law is available at: <http://www.uncitral.org/uncitral/uncitral_texts/procurement_infrastructure.html>.

while emphasizing that the 1994 Model Law's key provisions should not be amended,[71] the Commission noted that "novel issues and practices had arisen since its adoption, which might justify an effort to adjust its text."[72] UNCITRAL was therefore engaged in more than traditional "harmonization"; it was also "modernizing" the 1994 text. Indeed, the introduction of "Request-for-proposals with dialogue" could arguably be said to involve the more radical type of modernization described above. Perhaps unsurprisingly, the World Bank signaled to the Working Group that it was uncomfortable with allowing some of the features—notably, negotiations of a sort—involved in this method.[73]

As a result, the Guide to Enactment contains a statement that "enacting States may wish to take into account that, historically, the procurement rules of some multilateral development banks have not included procurement methods equivalent to request for proposals with dialogue or competitive negotiations as provided for in the [2011] Model Law. These multilateral donors have included methods with the features of the Model Law's request for proposals without negotiation and request for proposals with consecutive negotiations only for the procurement of consulting (e.g., advisory) services. Consequently, and in the light of possible developments, enacting State—potential borrowers from the multilateral development banks—should verify the public procurement policies of those donors at the relevant time that will be applicable to procurement projects financed by such donors."[74] This final caveat replaced an earlier suggestion that the Guide should alert potential Model Law users that "[s]ome multilateral development banks may not authorize the use of this method in projects financed by them."[75] This caveat echoed the World Bank's reservations expressed about the use of competitive negotiations when the 1994 Model Law was adopted—the then observer to UNCITRAL stated that the Bank would generally not recommend this method.[76]

At issue is whether this is a one-off difference of opinion, or whether it indicates more significant lack of international consensus on procurement's formal rules. Yukins and Schooner (2006: p. 531) state that "the world procurement market is evolving toward a unified, open model," and to "a common procurement market, based on common instruments," though it may be at least a generation away. Gordon (2013), however,

[71] Report of the UNCITRAL Commission on its thirty-sixth session, A/58/17, 2013, para. 226, available at: <http://www.uncitral.org/uncitral/en/commission/sessions/36th.html>.

[72] Report of the UNCITRAL Commission on its thirty-sixth session, A/58/17, 2013, para. 229.

[73] See also Document A/CN.9/718, para. 69.

[74] Guide to Enactment, p. 130, para. 9, discussing "Enactment: policy considerations" in the context of procurement methods and conditions for use.

[75] See also Document A/CN.9/718, para. 69.

[76] See United Nations Yearbook (United Nations, 1994: p. 361, para. 64): "64. In recent years, the World Bank . . . recommended the Model Law with some reservations. For example, it suggested that the method of competitive negotiation should not be applied, and once the draft was approved, the Bank would probably also recommend against application of article 16, paragraph 3(b) [in that iteration, the rules governing the use of the default method for the procurement of services]."

suggests that unification of procurement regulation is neither achievable nor desirable: he considers that harmonization is not "a trend toward uniformity" in which all countries have identical rules, but the emergence of systems based on the same principles so that the desired outcomes are highly similar. Examples of differences in national laws that he cites include minimum time periods for tender submission and whether past performance can be used as an evaluation criterion, as well as the extent to which negotiations and other discussions with potential suppliers are permitted during the tendering process—the issue raising widely divergent opinions in UNCITRAL as described above. Gordon's view is reflected in that, the laws considered are all accepted as compatible with the requirements of the GPA.

These comments are not contradictory to the extent that there is a certain degree of uniformity in terms of many of the formal rules in the international instruments, as Arrowsmith and Gordon state,[77] but that this uniformity is not (yet) reflected in domestic enactments. In this respect, and applying Block-Lieb and Halliday's comments to the procurement context, such international instruments will serve to internationalize public procurement regulation only "where national legislatures implement the [instruments'] provisions by adopting domestic legislation that closely tracks the [instruments themselves]." Indeed, as Yukins and Schooner note, harmonized international instruments indeed need to be "institutionalized" (i.e., enacted domestically). In other words, the legal certainty and predictability that UNCITRAL seeks to promote in public procurement law at the national level remains a work in progress, and one that arises because there is not yet an international consensus on the use of, among other things, negotiations in complex procurement.

Indeed, as the goal of harmonization—or internationalization—does not stop at the issue of laws or rules but requires consistent implementation and use,[78] the extent to which rule-formulating agencies are involved in implementing and using their texts is highly relevant. This question raises difficulties in the UNCITRAL context. States or other policy-makers and their advisers can simply download and use the Model Law, without reference to the UNCITRAL Secretariat. Indeed, unlike those implementing an international treaty or acceding to a convention, there is no requirement to notify UNCITRAL when using its soft law texts. UNCITRAL itself, in recent pronouncements at the Commission session, has not indicated that more resources should be devoted

[77] Gordon (2013) refers to transparency in the broad sense in regulations and bidding procedures, but also at some more detailed level in public bid opening, the use of non-price criteria, and "standstill" periods between decision to award and the final award of contracts.

[78] See, for example, Document A/CN.9/752, para. 41, in which it is said that, "[b]y focusing on the use and adoption of those texts, promotional activities give that legislative activity meaning and relevance. Without those activities, the legislative texts remain little more than reference tools...and UNCITRAL's goal of harmonization cannot be achieved."

to technical assistance activities supporting its texts.[79] It may indeed be accurate to say that the goal of a coherent set of international norms and standards remains a generation away.

3.5 Conclusions

This chapter has underscored the link between participation in the UNCITRAL process, its use of consensus, and the acceptability of UNCITRAL texts, and has raised some challenges that the process faces. The UNCITRAL experience has highlighted differences among policy-makers in public procurement, perhaps most notably on the question of risk tolerance and management, and that these differences arise both among states and in states as compared with some members of the donor community.[80] They may be most acute in the procurement of the more complex items, where greater discretion may be apparent, than more "standard" procurement, but a study of recent experience in Ghana indicates that elements of this issue are present even in open tendering, long considered the "gold standard of UNCITRAL" and, with minor variations, a method used worldwide (Borson, 2014).[81]

The debate in UNCITRAL over its working methods, as Kelly (2009: p. 18) observed, highlights tensions between control of member states and influence of observers and experts in international law-making. As novel issues continue to emerge in public procurement—sustainable procurement, to name just one—the manner in which the issues are debated and consequently reflected in international instruments in turn will frame domestic systems (and recalling that it is at this level that procurement in fact takes place).

[79] See, for example, the Report of the Commission's forty-seventh session in 2014, A/69/17, paras 261–6, considering "Support activities," in which the Commission stated that "there could be risks to achieving UNCITRAL's core mandate [legislative development] if the proportion of extra-budgetary funding was excessive as compared with UNCITRAL's regular budget resources."

[80] In *The World Bank and Public Procurement: An Independent Evaluation* (World Bank, 2015), the World Bank's Independent Evaluation Group considered the parallel systems concern. It said, "[l]ooking at the potential for greater use of client countries' own procurement systems, some country clients point out gains from alleviating the need to maintain parallel systems. However, private suppliers want the World Bank to retain its role to ensure a level playing field, greater transparency in selection, and perceptions of higher levels of recourse. There is scope for the Bank to move further toward using country systems, on an incremental basis, in line with the approach adopted by global partners, taking into account its own risk assessments, country counterpart views, agency capabilities, and the views of the private sector. There is a need to consider how assurance could be provided that there would be no change to the Bank's legal remedies and no change in existing rights and obligations concerning fraud and corruption." See, further, the documents available at: <http://ieg.worldbank.org/evaluations/world-bank-group-and-public-procurement>.

[81] Report of Working Group I (Procurement) on the Work of its Ninth Session, Document A/CN.9/595, para. 87.

As a result, it is submitted that attempts to reach truly harmonized or consistent international instruments in public procurement should not press forward faster than the pace at which international consensus on formal rules and procedures can emerge through international cooperation, such as in UNCITRAL. Trying to force the pace may tempt states to promote their national models, or organizations their own models, whether in the genuine belief that they represent the best solution or for political or other advantage. So doing could lead to "zero-sum bargaining" of the type that has been observed in attempts to reach agreement on a binding text (Block-Lieb and Halliday, 2006: p. 478). As has been noted in the context of developing conventions, such negotiation involves risks, including the "exclusion of issues on which delegates cannot reach consensus, or, worse still, . . . reliance on compromise language that leaves an issue either unresolved or muddier than before" (Block-Lieb and Halliday, 2006: p. 479), clearly not what internationalization of public procurement is intended to achieve. In this regard, ensuring broad, representative, and effective participation in the international formulating agencies, including UNCITRAL, remains a key challenge, as does ensuring that the focus of reform efforts continues to procedures in practice and not just as conceived on paper.

ACKNOWLEDGMENTS

The opinions expressed in this chapter are personal and are not to be viewed as representing official views of the United Nations.

REFERENCES

Arrowsmith, S. 1998. "National and International Perspectives on the Regulation of Public Procurement: Harmony or Conflict?" In H. Olszewskiego and B. Popowskiej (eds), *Gospodarka Admininstracja Samorzad*. Poznan: Wyd. Printer. Also published in S. Arrowsmith and A. Davies (eds), *Public Procurement Global Revolution*. London: Kluwer Law International, 3–26.

Arrowsmith, S. (ed.). 2009. *Reform of the UNCITRAL Model Law on Procurement: Procurement Regulation for the 21st Century*. Eagan, MN: West.

Arrowsmith, S., Linarelli, J., and Wallace, D. 2000. *Regulating Public Procurement: National and International Perspectives*. The Hague: Kluwer Law International.

Block-Lieb, S. and Halliday, T. 2006. "Harmonization and Modernization in UNCITRAL's Legislative Guide on Insolvency Law." *Texas International Law Journal* 42(3): 475.

Borson, F. 2014. "The Influence of External Procurement Rules on the Application of Procurement Regulation in Africa: A Case Study of Ghana" (available at: <http://www.nottingham.ac.uk/pprg/documentsarchive/phdconference2014/borson.pdf> (accessed July 21, 2016)).

Cheng, C.-J. 1988. *Clive M. Schmitthoff's Select Essays on International Trade Law*. Leiden: Brill.

Dávila, J. 2011. "CompraNet como herramienta de Modernización de las Compras Públicas. Caso de México" (available at: <http://ricg.org/vii-conferencia-anual-de-la-ricg/contenido/113/es/> (accessed July 21, 2016)).

Faria, J. A. E. 2009. "Future Directions of Legal Harmonisation and Law Reform: Stormy Seas or Prosperous Voyage." *Uniform Law Review* 14(1/2): 5–34.

Farnsworth, E. A. 1996. "Unification and Harmonization of Private Law." *Canadian Business Law Journal* 27.

Gordon, D. I. 2013. "Anti-Corruption Internationally: Challenges in Procurement Markets Abroad—Part II: The Path Forward for Using Procurement Law to Help with Development and the Fight Against Corruption." *West Government Contracts Year in Review Conference Covering 2012 Conference Briefs*. Thomson Reuters 1: 48–62.

Guglya, L. 2012. "Same Act–Different Scope: The International [Arbitration] Criterion in the Arbitration Laws of the Eurasian UNCITRAL Model Law–Compliant Jurisdictions." In *Quality of Legal Acts and Its Importance in Contemporary Legal Space*. Riga: University of Latvia Faculty of Law, 477–88.

Halliday, T. C., Pacewicz, J., and Block-Lieb, S. 2013. "Who Governs? Delegations and Delegates in Global Trade Lawmaking." *Regulation and Governance* 7(3): 279–98.

Herrmann, G. 1998. "UNCITRAL Arbitration Law: A Good Model of a Model Law." *Uniform Law Review*, 483–98.

Hobhouse, J. S. 1990. "International Conventions and Commercial Law: The Pursuit of Uniformity." *The Law Quarterly Review* 106: 530–5.

Kelly, C. 2009. "The Politics of International Economic Law: Legitimacy and the UNCITRAL Working Methods." Brooklyn Law School Legal Studies Paper No. 140 (available at: <http://papers.ssrn.com/sol3/papers.cfm?abstract_id=1371214>/> (accessed July 21, 2016)).

Nicholas, C. 2011. "Work of UNCITRAL on Government Procurement: Purpose, Objectives, and Complementarity with the Work of the WTO." In S. Arrowsmith and R. D. Anderson (eds), *The WTO Regime on Government Procurement: Challenge and Reform*. Cambridge: Cambridge University Press, 746–72.

Nicholas, C. 2013. "The 2011 UNCITRAL Model Law on Public Procurement and Its Guide to Enactment: A Challenging Opportunity." Paper presented at the Conference on Public Procurement: Global Revolution VI, Nottingham, June, 24–25.

Olszewski, H. and Popowska, B. (ed.) (1997). *Gospodarka Administracja Samorzad 9*, 23–31.

Schwartz, J. 2003. "On Globalization and Government Procurement." In S. Arrowsmith and M. Trybus (eds), *Public Procurement: The Continuing Revolution*. The Hague: Kluwer Law International.

Sono, K. 1984. "John O. Honnold." *University of Pennsylvania Law Review* 132.947: 947–49 (available at: <http://scholarship.law.upenn.edu/cgi/viewcontent.cgi?article=4599&context=penn_law_review> (accessed July 21, 2016)).

Stephan, P. B. 1996. "Accountability and International Lawmaking: Rules, Rents and Legitimacy." *Northwestern Journal of International Law and Business* 17: 681–735.

United Nations. 1994. *Yearbook of the United Nations 2014*. New York: UN (available at: <http://www.uncitral.org/pdf/english/yearbooks/yb-1994-e/yb_1994_e.pdf> (accessed July 21, 2016)).

United Nations. 2008. “Report of the United Nations Commission on International Trade Law, 41st Session (16 June–3 July 2008).” Document A/63/17 (available at: <http://www.uncitral.org/uncitral/en/commission/sessions/41st.html> (accessed July 21, 2016)).

United Nations. 2009. “Report of the United Nations Commission on International Trade Law, 42nd Session (29 June–17 July 2009).” Document A/64/17 (available at: <http://www.uncitral.org/uncitral/en/commission/sessions/42nd.html> (accessed July 21, 2016)).

United Nations. 2010. “Report of the United Nations Commission on International Trade Law, 44th Session (26 June–9 July 2010).” Document A/65/17 (available at: (http://www.uncitral.org/uncitral/commission/sessions/44th.html, accessed July 21, 2016)).

United Nations. 2013. “The UNCITRAL Guide: Basic Facts about the United Nations Commission on International Trade Law” (available at: <http://www.uncitral.org/uncitral/en/about_us.html> (accessed July 21, 2016)).

Walt, S. 1999. “Novelty and the Risks of Uniform Sales Law.” *Virginia Journal of International Law Association* 39: 671–705.

World Bank. 2015. *The World Bank Group and Public Procurement: An Independent Evaluation*. Independent Evaluation Group Studies. Washington, DC: World Bank Group (available at: <http://documents.worldbank.org/curated/en/2015/02/23994473/world-bank-group-public-procurement-independent-evaluation> (accessed July 21, 2016)).

Yukins, C. R. and Schooner, S. L. 2006. “Incrementalism: Eroding the Impediments to a Global Public Procurement Market.” *Georgetown Journal of International Law* 38: 529, at 558.

4 The Government Procurement Agreement, the Most-Favored Nation Principle, and Regional Trade Agreements

Kamala Dawar

4.1 Introduction

This chapter examines the application of the most-favored nation (MFN) principle under the WTO Agreement on Government Procurement (GPA) with reference to RTAs with substantive government procurement commitments. The chapter initially looks at the operation of the MFN principle among the parties of the GPA, pursuant to Article IV. It then examines the implications of the GATS Article II MFN principle with reference to the GPA parties' commitments in the procurement of services and construction services. The chapter finally turns to assessing the RTA market access commitments for the procurement of goods, services, and construction services, again with reference to the scope of the MFN principle operating under Article IV of the GPA. It undertakes this analysis for selected RTAs between GPA parties, RTAs signed between a GPA party and non-GPA party, and, further, those RTAs with procurement provisions signed between non-GPA parties.

The liberalization of government procurement markets under the GPA is based on strict reciprocity and a conditional MFN requirement. Under the GPA, the MFN requirement is frequently set aside with respect to the parties' market access commitments in goods, services and construction services. These exceptions are formally set out in the Annexes and General Notes, which are included in the Appendix to the Agreement and form an integral part of the Agreement. As such, bilaterally negotiated concessions continue to take precedence over a commitment to provide for liberalization through the principle of unconditional non-discrimination between the parties. This reflects the sensitivity of these negotiations. For the adherence to the strict reciprocity principle detracts from the widely accepted benefits that are attached to an open trading system.

Second, with regard to the coverage of procurement in services and construction services under the GPA, any access to procurement markets is conditioned and constrained by the GPA's "relationship of correspondence" (Blank and Marceau, 1996: p. 48) to the GATS schedules and, consequently, by the application of the MFN principle operating within the GATS. This is because even though government procurement is excluded from the core provisions of the GATS, the GPA itself deals only with government procurement policies; it cannot address measures such as trade restrictions that affect the ability of foreign enterprises to sell services to governments (Anderson and Müller, 2008).

One of the significant implications of this distinct relationship of correspondence is that GPA parties do not have the mandate to open up markets for services and contract services for the purposes of government procurement beyond that which has already been committed under their GATS schedules. This could be seen to provoke the need to use RTAs as an alternative and established vehicle from which to negotiate commitments that go beyond that provided under the GPA—so called "GPA+" commitments. This is both for those GPA parties seeking further access into the procurement markets of both other GPA parties, as well as with non-GPA parties.

Third and consequently, the negotiation of RTAs with GPA+ commitments set out in their schedules nevertheless raises questions about their *prima facie* legality under the GPA. For under this agreement, there is a noteworthy absence of a general legal provision to permit and condition exceptions to the MFN principle. This is in stark contrast to the GATT, pursuant to Article XXIV, and pursuant to Article V GATS. This presents a dilemma. It is of potential consequence for those RTAs signed by GPA parties that liberalize procurement markets for goods, services, or construction services markets beyond the GPA obligations and schedules. If it is accepted that GPA parties are dependent upon the existing services and construction services they have already negotiated under their GATS schedules, those parties wishing to open their procurement markets any further are presented with no option other than to ignore their obligation to provide MFN treatment under the GPA.

The chapter concludes that these overlapping, possibly conflictual, or even trade-restricting legal obligations and the methods of negotiating them work against the wider objectives of the WTO and the GPA. More desirable options would most likely involve WTO members moving away from promoting market liberalization based on strict reciprocity and conditional MFN. This could help to prevent the use of government procurement commitments to protect certain domestic producer interests, rather than to seek and maintain an open trading system.

4.2 Reciprocity and the Application of MFN under the GPA

The WTO system is designed to promote mutually agreed reductions of trade barriers—through the reciprocity principle, and non-discriminatory treatment among members—through the most-favored nation principle (MFN). The wedding of reciprocity and non-discrimination serves to remove the prisoner's dilemma attached to adverse terms-of-trade effects associated with unilateral tariff reductions. Together, they preserve the value of concessions that a member achieves in a current negotiation against erosion in a future negotiation to which it may not be a party.

Reciprocity and non-discrimination are thus cornerstone principles of the multilateral trading system. More specifically, reciprocity is the rule by which several parties manage to maintain a balance and symmetry of treatment by granting the same or equivalent rights and benefits to each other. Reciprocity is therefore *conditional* in that it is contingent on rewarding actions and, moreover, ceases when such actions cease; for while the act of giving is voluntary, the act of the recipient is obligatory.

There are two types of reciprocity of immediate interest to this chapter: open and restrictive reciprocity (Yanai, 2002). Open reciprocity does not demand any direct response to an antecedent action. It rather imposes on the receiving side a certain obligation for repayment in the future. Open reciprocity characterizes the negotiations followed under the GATT. Restrictive reciprocity, on the other hand, places much greater emphasis on a simultaneous exchange of strictly equivalent benefits and/or obligations. This restrictive approach characterizes the negotiations followed under the GPA.

The principle of MFN serves as a primary defense against trade discrimination. In the WTO, the MFN obligation is embodied in GATT Article I.1, which obligates parties to extend to all other parties, immediately and without discriminatory conditions, the most favorable trade market access concessions it has granted, or may grant, to any third party. The GATT's particular embodiment of MFN has been called "unconditional" MFN because this treatment is offered by members on a multilateral basis to all other members. That is, unconditional MFN requires non-discrimination even when reciprocity is violated; MFN treatment is offered to all members without regard to equal participation in the exchange of market access concessions that led to a particular MFN agreement. And as such, this unconditionality may even encourage countries to not reciprocate, thereby causing a free-rider problem. This free-rider problem may well have undermined incentives to expand on WTO multilateral agreements in other trade areas, such as procurement. As Schwartz and Sykes (1997: p. 62) point out:

> [T]he MFN obligation protects the value of concessions against future erosion through discrimination. If country A receives a concession from country B and is not entitled to MFN treatment from B, then the value of the concession can be undermined if country B later makes an even better concession to country C on the same goods (or close substitutes). Faced with this uncertainty, country A would offer less for the concession in the first place (as would country B for the reciprocal concession), and fewer valuable deals would be struck.

In other words, MFN clauses vary to serve different purposes at different times. Unlike the GATT MFN provision, within the WTO's plurilateral agreements the MFN principle requires only *conditional* treatment. From the outset, under the various plurilateral codes, including the Government Procurement Code, non-discriminatory treatment was made conditional on an explicitly strict reciprocal exchange of rights and obligations. This included market access concessions among parties to the agreement. From its inception, then, the plurilateral Government Procurement Code sought to address the free-rider problem. The Code was always an example of an agreement that places access concessions on a *strict* reciprocity and on a *conditional* MFN basis. This approach has become further entrenched under the GPA, and indeed led to the accusation that the Agreement:

> violates every possible notion of non-discriminatory multilateralism. It could quite accurately be described as an accumulation of preferential bilateral agreements between a limited number of parties somehow brought together under one shaky roof (Reich 1997: p. 127).

Despite the acknowledged limitations of liberalization and non-discrimination under conditional MFN obligations, it remains the case that in establishing a plurilateral agreement, the signatory parties still sought to promote the expansion of trade. This clearly would not otherwise have been negotiable under the GATT, due to its stress on non-reciprocal and unconditional non-discrimination requirements. Government procurement has traditionally been placed at the heart of national governance policy, and deployed to address a variety of sometimes incompatible objectives. Consequently, sovereignty issues will be more salient during negotiations to liberalize these traditionally protected markets to foreign competition.

4.2.1 APPENDIX 1 TO THE GPA

The strictness of the reciprocity principle and conditionality operating under the GPA MFN obligation is formally set out in an appendix and forms an integral part of the Agreement. The coverage of the Agreement is set out for each signatory party in Appendix I, which is divided into Annexes concerning the specific coverage of the obligations. The Annexes address: (1) central government entities covered by the Agreement; (2) covered sub-central government entities; (3) "other" covered entities (e.g., utilities); (4) goods; (5) services coverage; (6) coverage of construction services; and (7) General Notes.

The Annexes are negotiated along four basic parameters, consisting of: (i) the value of procurement—covering only contracts estimated to exceed a certain value threshold; (ii) the identity of the procuring entity—covering only those listed by each party in its annexes; (iii) the type of goods or services procured—consisting of all goods, apart from some expressly excluded by each party, and only services listed by each party in its annexes; and (iv) the origin of the goods or services—including only countries that are GPA parties. In addition to these schedules, the Annexes typically also contain

General Notes in Annex 7, which significantly further qualify the application of the Agreement. Box 4.1 highlights the bilateral nature of these commitments, indicating that Korea will specifically not extend some of the benefits it offers under the GPA to specified GPA parties—in this case, five individual member states of the EU and Canada.

GPA market access negotiations are therefore highly complex, constructed on a request-and-offer approach where an initial offer from all the parties is submitted to the GPA Committee. On the basis of those submissions, the parties start *bilateral* negotiations. The GPA follows the GATS negotiating approach but with added complexities. During the GATS negotiations, the issue concerns whether to include a service or not in the Schedule of Specific Commitments and to determine to what extent a party will commit to that inclusion. That is, whether or not to negotiate specific services with a full commitment, where MFN and national treatment apply; or with a partial commitment, where MFN and national treatment comments are subject to conditions; or lastly inclusion without commitments, which is unbound with only the MFN requirement. In the case of the GPA negotiations, not only must the parties decide which services and goods and construction are covered by the obligations, but they must also negotiate which contracting authorities or entities will be included in Annex I–III and then, additionally, the value of the thresholds that will trigger the scope of application of the agreement in each case and category of procurement.

It is significant that under the GATS, specific restrictions to the MFN principles are permitted under Article II:2 *only* if listed and subject to the conditions set out in the Annex on Article II exemptions. In contrast to this, parties to the GPA also commonly qualify the scope of the coverage of their obligations within Annex 7 General Notes (see Box 4.1). The 2014 WTO study of the application of reciprocity in regard to services under the GPA indicated that nine parties—including Canada, the EU, and the US—based their commitments on strict mutual reciprocity (Anderson et al., 2014).[1] These parties specified in the General Notes that the GPA applies only to the services listed in their commitments, in respect of a given party, and only to the extent that this party has given reciprocal access to the service concerned. For example, the US General Notes exclude Japan from the award of contracts by entities recorded in Annex 3 that are responsible for the generation and distribution of electricity; thereby excluding the MFN obligation for these types of procurement as regards Japan.

In sum, while the MFN principle remains at the core of the GPA, the focus on strict reciprocity has led to large bilateral exclusions and derogations within the Annexes. The parties to the Agreement are cautiously inching ahead with market access concessions on a *quid pro quo* basis, rather than displaying a wholehearted policy to

[1] The other six parties are Iceland, Korea, Liechtenstein, Switzerland, Norway, and Chinese Taipei.

BOX 4.1 REPUBLIC OF KOREA (WTO GPA GENERAL NOTES: 2015)[2]

GENERAL NOTES

1. Korea will not extend the benefits of this Agreement
   (a) as regards the award of contracts by the National Railroad Administration,
   (b) as regards procurement for airports by the entities listed in Annex 1,
   (c) as regards procurement for urban transportation (including subways) by the entities listed in Annexes 1 and 2
   to the suppliers and service providers of member states of the European Communities, Austria, Norway, Sweden, Finland, and Switzerland, until such time as Korea has accepted that those countries give comparable and effective access for Korean undertakings to their relevant markets.
2. For goods and services (including construction services) of Canada and suppliers of such goods and services, this Agreement does not apply to procurement by the entities listed in Annexes 2 and 3. Korea is prepared to amend this note at such time as coverage with respect to these Annexes can be resolved with Canada.
3. A service listed in Annex 4 is covered with respect to a particular party only to the extent that such party has included that service in its Annex 4.

harness the widely acknowledged benefits of internationally competitive procurement markets for good governance, consumers, and taxpayers (Hoekman and Mavroidis, 1996; Arrowsmith and Trybus, 2003; Anderson and Kovacic, 2009). The strictly reciprocal and conditional MFN nature of these market access commitments is amply evident within the GPA. If one party considers that another's commitments are insufficient, it may exclude it from one of the sectors included, or from contracting authorities covered. The OECD has estimated that if reciprocity were not taken into consideration—that is, if the commitments were applied on an unconditional MFN basis among GPA parties—the average level of commitments would be 16 percent higher than with reciprocity (Ueno, 2014). High impacts (more than 25 percentage points) are observed in space transport services and banking services, while there is relatively little impact in construction services.

4.2.2 THE US–CANADA AGREEMENT ON GOVERNMENT PROCUREMENT

The case of the US–Canada Agreement on Government Procurement (AGP) is an instructive example of both strict reciprocity and effective negotiating muscle by GPA parties outside of the venue of the WTO. As a policy response to the 2008 global financial

[2] Available at: <https://www.wto.org/english/tratop_e/gproc_e/appendices_e.htm#kor> (accessed July 21, 2016).

crisis, the US federal government enacted The Buy American Act in 2009. This seemingly discriminatory measure was made fully consistent with US obligations under the GPA because GPA parties were explicitly carved out from the Buy American Act requirements in a Savings Clause (ARRA Section 1605(d)).

However, despite being a party to the GPA, Canadian companies were still excluded from the US sub-national procurement opportunities funded by that legislation. To redress this under the subsequent 2010 US–Canada AGP, the US extended to Canada its 1994 GPA commitments on sub-national procurement, which cover thirty-seven US states. In exchange, Canada made an unprecedented market access concession to provide US companies with a degree of permanent access to procurement markets in all provinces and territories except Nunavut. Following the conclusion of the AGP, the US was the only GPA signatory country to which Canada's sub-national procurement commitments initially applied. It was not until negotiating the revised 2012 GPA and accompanying schedules that Canada subsequently expanded its market access commitments to reflect the US–Canada AGP outcome.

The fact that the US had previously opened its sub-national procurement in thirty-seven states to all GPA parties except Canada highlights the strict reciprocity and conditionality of the MFN obligation under the GPA. The US negotiators had refused to exempt Canadian businesses from the small business set-asides or other exemptions, and in retaliation Canada refused to expand its GPA commitments to include sub-national procurement in 1994. Canada's negotiators argued that those set-asides prevented Canadian businesses from enjoying the same degree of access to US federal procurement markets as the US had to Canadian federal procurement markets.

In other words, just to simply qualify for the full legal protection the US already offered to other GPA parties, Canada had to give additional access to Canadian provincial and territorial government procurement without making any progress on the issue of small business set-asides or other US exemptions at the WTO. Evidently, the detrimental economic effects on Canadian businesses from the Buy American Act gave the US leverage to resolve a longstanding trade spat involving the GPA. But this was bilateral in nature and with strict reciprocity and conditional MFN characterizing the concessions.[3]

4.2.3 SUMMARY CONCLUSIONS

Under the GPA, the strict reciprocity and conditionality of the MFN clause elicits equivalent compensation and indicates that access granted between initial parties

[3] *Canada–US AGP Evidence*, Meeting No. 5, March 23, 2010.

will not automatically be extended. Derogations from MFN are sometimes accompanied with declarations that they will be withdrawn only when the respective signatory has accepted that the other parties have given comparable access to its suppliers. This use of restrictive reciprocity and conditional MFN is a means through which to open up foreign markets and secure equality of opportunities in markets, while protecting against limitless liberalization of their market for foreign exports. It highlights the limits to what the negotiators are prepared to concede.

The concern that emerges from this assessment is whether the strict reciprocity and conditionality of MFN under the GPA has resulted in innumerable derogations. This creates a more fertile environment for selective protectionism rather than for procurement market liberalization. And as such, the GPA is potentially more prone to being a set of bilateral agreements harboring discrimination between parties and non-parties to the GPA and between GPA parties themselves. This approach clearly limits the scope for the liberalization of procurement markets by entrenching the restrictions concerned.

In sum, under the GPA the conditionality of the MFN clause does not serve as an instrument to generalize concessions, but rather brings about a never-ending negotiation of bargains. This does not support the ultimate aim of the GPA and WTO, which is to open up public procurement contracts to international competition under equal commercial conditions, free of any national preferences. This therefore brings to the fore the fundamental dilemma for the GPA: while non-discrimination via open reciprocity and unconditional MFN and national treatment is the guiding principle for the regulation of international trade, reciprocity remains the guiding principle of international trade negotiations.

4.3 The Relationship of Correspondence between the GPA and the Application of the GATS MFN Obligation

This section assesses the effect of the GATS on the GPA. It submits that while government procurement is formally excluded from the coverage of the GATS, the GATS is not, however, without influence on the coverage of the GPA. This analysis examines the MFN principle operating under the GATS with regard to how it conditions access to markets for services and construction services for government procurement purposes, under the GPA. This relationship could, in part, explain why RTA market access commitments in government procurement for services coverage tend to be more extensive than the GPA parties' commitments under the GPA.

4.3.1 THE RELATIONSHIP OF CORRESPONDENCE BETWEEN THE GPA AND THE GATS SCHEDULES

As noted in Section 4.2 in the assessment of MFN under the GPA, pursuant to Article IV of the GPA General Principles:

> With respect to any measure regarding covered procurement, each Party, including its procuring entities, shall accord immediately and unconditionally to the goods and services of any other Party and to the suppliers of any other Party offering the goods or services of any Party, treatment no less favourable than the treatment the Party, including its procuring entities:
>
> (a) domestic goods, services and suppliers; and
> (b) goods, services and suppliers of any other Party.

However, Article IV.7 stipulates that the GPA non-discrimination rules are applicable *only* as regards government procurement and, crucially, *not on measures affecting market access* and competitive conditions for services and service suppliers:

> *GPA Article IV.7 Measures Not Specific to Procurement*
> Paragraphs 1 and 2 *shall not apply* to: customs duties and charges of any kind imposed on, or in connection with, importation; the method of levying such duties and charges; other import regulations or formalities and measures *affecting trade in services* other than measures governing covered procurement (emphasis added).

This provision makes clear that it remains the GATS—and not the GPA—that provides for the general rights of establishment, and regulates the modes of delivery for services. Indeed, the *EC–Bananas III* Panel and Appellate Body Report also confirmed the broad scope of application of the GATS:

> [N]o measures are excluded *a priori* from the scope of the GATS as defined by its provisions. The scope of the GATS *encompasses any measure of a Member to the extent it affects the supply of a service* regardless of whether such measure directly governs the supply of a service or whether it regulates other matters but nevertheless affects trade in services (emphasis added).[4]

In other words, while GATS regulates the market access of services trade, it is the GPA that sets out rules on how governments purchase such services. This provides for the so-called "relationship of correspondence" between the two agreements, and which functions to limit the value of services included under GPA commitments. For given that questions of access to service markets or trade in services in general are addressed by the

[4] Panel Report, *EC–Bananas III*, para. 7.285 and Appellate Body Report, *EC–Bananas III*, para. 220.

GATS, any concessions in services and construction services in the procurement markets of the GPA parties will be subject to whatever conditions on market access apply pursuant to each party's commitments set out under the GATS schedules and subject to the MFN obligation operating under the GATS agreement (Blank and Marceau, 1996: p. 48). Thus, the GPA complements the GATS' general rules on market access in services with access more specifically to procurement markets:

> In general, foreign suppliers not only have to secure the right to participate in tenders on a non-discriminatory basis, but also need to rely on general market access rights to be able to supply services to government. (Anderson et al., 2014: p. 2)

To confirm this tightly controlled scope of application, government procurement remains explicitly excluded from the coverage of the GATS non-discrimination obligations:

> *GATS Article XIII Government Procurement*
> 1. Articles II, XVI and XVII *shall not apply* to laws, regulations or requirements governing the procurement by governmental agencies of services purchased for governmental purposes and not with a view to commercial resale or with a view to use in the supply of services for commercial sale. (Emphasis added)

Accordingly, pursuant to Article XIII, the MFN treatment provided for under Article II GATS and the specific market access and national treatment obligations *do not* apply to the procurement of services for governmental purposes; this is with the notable exception of the Understanding on the Commitments in Financial Services. This Understanding is limited to thirty-one WTO members as signatory parties. The MFN principle that applies under the Understanding is unconditional, and provides MFN treatment even to those WTO members who have not signed up to the Understanding.

Elsewhere under the GATS, the opportunity to schedule MFN exemptions can be utilized only upon joining the agreement and thus occurs only once. Unlike the Understanding, the general MFN obligation under the GATS is narrowed by specific and reciprocal commitments on market access and national treatment. Thus, despite the explicit exemption for public procurement in the GATS, a GPA party's commitments in services and construction services are nevertheless tightly circumscribed by its relationship of correspondence to its GATS commitments. Indeed, some of the GPA parties' notes to Annex 4 Services or to Annex 7 General Notes explicitly reference or indeed reinforce the primacy of the terms and conditions set out in their existing GATS schedules, which are subject to the GATS MFN obligation. For example, Israel's note to Annex 4 Services explicitly states that the GPA is subject to the terms and conditions set out in their Schedule to the General Agreement on Trade in Services:

Note to Annex 4
The offer regarding services (including construction) is subject to the limitation and conditions specified in Israel's schedule of the GATS.

4.3.2 THE CORRESPONDENCE WITH THE GATS MFN

The relationship between the GATS MFN and the GPA suggests that a GPA party can gain market access to another party's services or construction services for the purpose of government procurement only if that party has already opened up that corresponding market under its GATS schedules. This is unless, of course, the GPA party is prepared to expand upon its market access commitments in its GATS schedule as a result of seeking to open up its GPA services or construction services markets, and then apply those additional commitments under an MFN basis.

The GATS Article XVIII regarding additional commitments confirms this dependent relationship in stipulating that:

> Members may negotiate commitments with respect to measures affecting trade in services not subject to scheduling under Articles XVI or XVII, including those regarding qualifications, standards or licensing matters. *Such commitments shall be inscribed in a Member's Schedule.* (Emphasis added)

Accordingly, when in 2006 the EU put forward a draft Annex to the GATS on Government Procurement in Services that included non-discrimination provisions, the legal avenue proposed was through GATS Article XVIII (WTO Working Party on GATS Rules, 2006).

The legal nexus between the two agreements may have potentially significant implications in operating to compel parties to negotiate RTAs if they wish to incorporate commitments in services and construction services that expand upon their GPA schedules. This is due to the limitations that exist by virtue of their correspondence to existing GATS schedules and the need to inscribe their GATS schedules pursuant to Article XVIII. As such, it could be that the GATS schedules effectively act as a ring fence on the further liberalization of the procurement services under the GPA.

Second, it could also be possible that this dependence on existing GATS commitments detracts from the attractiveness of seeking membership of the GPA for developing countries. It stands to reason that if the particular market access concessions desired under the GPA cannot be offered by the respective parties, due to correspondence with their existing GATS schedules, developing country GPA parties cannot hope to redress any imbalance of concessions in the GPA.

As such, modes of interest currently closed to developing countries will also be closed under the GPA until inscribed in the parties' GATS schedules. This is most significant for Mode 4 regulating the supply of a service by a service supplier of one member, through the presence of natural persons of a member in the territory of another member. Mode 4 is the smallest mode of service delivery in terms of both trade flows and the level of scheduled commitments made in the Uruguay Round. Those limited commitments that have been made under Mode 4 refer almost exclusively to higher-level personnel, particularly intra-corporate transferees, whose mobility is essentially an adjunct of FDI liberalization. As a result, most existing Mode 4 commitments have limited significance for developing countries, since their comparative advantage lies primarily in low- and medium-skilled labor-intensive services.

One stocktaking of all RTAs with services commitments noted that there is an average gap of almost 25 percent between services commitments in RTAs and those in the GATS, with variations across sections. Distribution, Transport, and Business Services are each at around 25 percent, whereas Construction and Finance show much lower rates at 17 and 12 percent, respectively. Of further interest here are the significant differences across the modes of supply—on average, Modes 1 and 2 have high gaps of around 24 percent each, whereas both Modes 3 and 4 show lower commitments of around 16 percent. Yet, while Modes 3 and 4 are still very restricted in comparison with Modes 1 and 2, there are interesting variations—RTA Services commitments in Mode 4 are relatively high for Distribution, Transport, and Business Services (van der Marel, 2013).

Yet, additional difficulties emerge in identifying the coverage conditioned by the GPA's relationship of correspondence to the GATS schedules. Any transparent comparison of corresponding substantive market access commitments is hindered by the obvious discrepancies in estimating coverage determined by entities and value thresholds under the GPA, and comparing it with coverage that is determined according to modes of access under the GATS. Clearly, it does not matter under the GATS whether a measure is taken at the central, regional or local government level, nor whether non-governmental bodies are exercising delegated power. Calibration and modulation is achieved through scheduling specific commitments and designating services sectors and subsectors and modes of supply in which members wish to take some level of binding commitments.

Most of the schedules describe the committed service sectors and subsectors based on the Secretariat's Services Sectoral Classification List W/120. As such, access to any particular service sector under the GATS, if subjected to specific commitments, is defined by parameters specifying the levels of market access and national treatment for each of the four modes of supply.

Under the GPA, on the other hand, coverage of services and construction services in government procurement agreements is generally defined by means of a simple list using the UN Provisional Central Produce Classification (CPCprov), and without distinguishing between different modes of supply. Moreover, the GPA regulatory framework does not distinguish between goods and services in the procurement for government purposes, and indeed there is no strict separation between procurement of services and goods pursuant to Article II.2(a), which unequivocally states that:

> 2. For the purposes of this Agreement, covered procurement means procurement for governmental purposes:
>
> (a) *of goods, services or any combination thereof.* (Emphasis added)

4.3.3 SUMMARY CONCLUSIONS

This section has assessed the relationship of correspondence between the GPA and the GATS. It noted that while government procurement is formally excluded from the coverage of the GATS, the MFN principle operating under the GATS continues to function to condition access to markets for services and construction services for government procurement purposes under the GPA. The legal connection between the respective schedules of the parties to both agreements, could, in part, answer those questions concerned with why RTA market access commitments in government procurement, in particular for services coverage, tend to be more extensive than the GPA parties' commitments under the GPA.

Nevertheless, this observation is complicated by the methodological difficulties in comparing the coverage of procurement by designated entities *of goods, services, or any combination thereof*, and scheduling specific commitments and designating services sectors and subsectors and modes of supply according to different levels of binding commitments.

Section 4.4 therefore examines this section's concluding proposition in more detail by examining the GPA parties' commitments in goods, services, and construction services, with reference to their commitments in RTAs with government procurement commitments.

4.4 **The Application of the MFN Principle in the GPA vis-à-vis RTAs with Scheduled GPA+ Commitments in Goods and Services**

Given the conclusions in Section 4.3 on the apparent legal constraints to opening up procurement markets in services and construction services markets under the GPA beyond existing MFN commitments under the GATS schedules, it would seem plausible that those GPA parties wishing to make greater concessions would most naturally turn to the alternative, and indeed more traditional, vehicle of RTAs. This section seeks to test this working hypothesis by comparing the coverage of RTAs with substantive government procurement coverage, as compared with the coverage under the revised 2012 GPA.

4.4.1 MFN EXCEPTIONS UNDER THE GPA

From the outset, a legal quandary can be observed in the relationship between the GPA parties' commitments and those in their RTAs. Unlike GATT Article XXIV[5] and GATS.[6]

Article V of the GPA does not contain a provision explicitly exempting parties from the Agreement's MFN obligations under specified circumstances for reasons of further integration. Under the GATT and GATS, negotiated preferential access is fundamentally based on the definition of a customs union and elimination of substantial trade barriers. However, a comparison of the two indicates that the GATS allows for negotiated preferential access agreements more liberally than its GATT counterpart under Article XXIV. Pursuant to Article VII, the GATS permits a form of MFN based on strict reciprocity and conditional on mutual recognition. As a result, countries can align with one another on a bilateral level in order to confer great advantages over other countries not included in the same negotiated recognition. This GATS approach would seem to suit the strictly reciprocal nature of the GPA negotiations too.

Nevertheless, such a clause was omitted from both the 1994 and 2012 GPA texts. Therefore, it would seem logical that without the inclusion of a similar specific exemption from the GPA's MFN requirements for RTAs, any GPA+ procurement commitments in RTAs is presumably in direct violation of the MFN provision under the GPA Article IV, discussed in Section 4.3.1, which demands that:

> With respect to *all laws, regulations, procedures and practices regarding government procurement covered by this Agreement*, each Party *shall provide immediately and unconditionally* to the products, services and suppliers of other Parties offering products or services of the Parties, treatment no less favourable than: that accorded to domestic products, services and suppliers; and that accorded to products, services and suppliers of any other Party (Emphasis added).

[5] Under GATT Article XXIV, exceptions to the MFN Article I.1 basic rule must fulfil very specific circumstances related to the coverage of substantially all trade. Those exceptions are limited by (a) unspecified preferential arrangements; (b) customs unions or free trade areas; and (c) products originating in developing countries.

[6] With regard to GATS, because the regulation of services prior the Uruguay Round existed at a bilateral level, many countries required a transition period to deal with the temporary elements already agreed upon. During a ten-year period, countries agreed to renegotiate and/or reduce the tariffs into compliance with the MFN rule. Until then, each country had to submit a list of previously existing exemptions they wished to exempt from the MFN rule. For example, countries had to allow for agreements that previously agreed to preferential treatment.

This section therefore seeks to identify whether and where GPA parties have indeed negotiated GPA+ commitments in RTAs, in an apparent (albeit theoretical) conflict with the MFN obligation operating under the GPA in Article IV. For the purposes of methodological comparability, this section bases its analysis on the existing comprehensive findings set out under the OECD and WTO research into government procurement provisions in the GPA and RTAs. Notwithstanding this, the present analysis is a departure from these studies in questioning whether there is any regionalizing dynamic as a consequence of the relationship of correspondence between the GATT commitments and the scope of the GPA Schedules.

A further noteworthy consequence of both the relationship of correspondence with the GATS schedules and the negotiation of access to services markets under the GPA is that any possible regionalizing dynamic emerging from the GPA regulatory framework as submitted can be said to apply also to the procurement for goods. To recall, this is because there is no strict separation between procurement of services and goods pursuant to Article II.2(a). In other words, if access to a particular procurement market cannot be opened because it is *de jure* constrained by the lesser access in its corresponding GATS services commitments, the goods attached to this procurement market will *de facto* also be restricted if they cannot be unbundled from the services part of the particular procurement in question.

4.4.2 IDENTIFYING GPA+ COMMITMENTS IN RTAs AMONG GPA SIGNATORY PARTIES

This section begins to test the working conclusions of this analysis with an examination of GPA+ commitments in RTAs signed between GPA parties. This focus arguably provides the most significant insights into the operation of the MFN obligation within the GPA. The section assesses the commitments in terms of (i) value thresholds; (ii) the coverage of entities; (iii) services commitments; and (iv) other WTO+ commitments.

4.4.2.1 The Value Thresholds

At the most general level, RTA market access commitments signed by the same party are fairly homogeneous. Where some heterogeneity is observed, it is postulated that this is due in large part to the adherence to strict reciprocity in terms of sub-central government entity coverage and the level of thresholds. Reciprocity is observed predominantly in sub-central government entities' commitments. This might suggest the difficulty faced by regional or local governments, possibly due to concerns about the impacts of liberalizing the procurement market for local companies and economies, or reflecting the differing jurisdictional reaches. This is further reflected in the fact that only about half of the parties' commitments cover sub-central government entities in RTAs.

OECD findings (Ueno, 2014) indicate that a number of RTAs between GPA parties achieved better or at least the same level of thresholds compared to those under the GPA. See Table 4.1 and Table 4.2. Thresholds are the minimum estimated values above which a government procurement contract will be subject to non-discrimination and other government procurement obligations under the GPA and RTAs. Thresholds for both the GPA and RTAs are specified for goods, services (except construction services), and construction services, respectively, for the three types of entities mentioned above. The OECD study further observed that of seventy-eight sets of RTA thresholds committed by GPA parties—either in the form of agreements between GPA parties, or the agreements between a GPA party and a non-GPA party—22 percent are GPA+ thresholds.

The Korea–Singapore, Korea–US, and US–Singapore Agreements lower the thresholds for goods and services procured by central government entities to SDR100,000 (Korea–Singapore), $100,000 (Korea–US), and $56,190 USD (US–Singapore). The Japan–Singapore Agreement lowers their thresholds for goods and services procured by both central government entities and other entities to SDR100,000. Of variance here is that the

Table 4.1 RTAs between GPA parties with better or equivalent thresholds than the GPA

	Goods and services			Construction services
	≦ 13 000	≦ 20 000	≦ 400 000	≦ 5 000 000
Central government entities	99.2%	–	–	83.6%
Sub-central government entities	–	71.3%	–	85.2%
Other entities	–	–	96.9%	70.7%

Source: (Ueno, 2014: p. 16)

Table 4.2 Summary of RTA thresholds of OECD GPA parties

	Number of GPA parties' thresholds (n=78)	% of GPA parties' thresholds
GPA-plus thresholds	17	21.8%
GPA-plus/minus thresholds	5	6.4%
GPA-minus thresholds	2	2.6%
GPA-equal thresholds	54	69.2%

Source: (Ueno, 2014: p. 16)

Japanese authority interprets its commitments to relate to the procurement of SDR100,000 or more but less than SDR130,000 covered by the Japan–Singapore RTA, are not subject to the rules of the GPA. This is because, according to the Japanese authority, the GPA provides that non-discrimination treatment shall be given "[w]ith respect to all laws, regulations, procedures and practices regarding government procurement *covered* by this Agreement" (Emphasis added). The GPA applies only to the procurement of not less than SDR130,000, which Japan agrees to procure under the GPA (METI, 2012: p. 925).

Agreements lowering thresholds bilaterally among GPA parties also raise important questions. First, regarding the motivation of GPA parties negotiating such concessions outside of the forum of the GPA, as with the US–Canada GPA (see Section 4.2.2). Second, it raises legal issues as to whether those thresholds might be deemed to apply to all GPA parties by virtue of the MFN clause in the GPA. This Agreement does not provide a general exclusion from the MFN principle for RTAs, discussed further in Section 4.4.2. This is in contrast to the GATT and the GATS.

In assessing the incentives to use an RTA for negotiating such an add-on as opposed to the GPA, it is axiomatic that the nature of negotiating multilateral agreements is drastically different from those of bilateral or regional trade agreement negotiations. Nevertheless, the GPA approach presents negotiating characteristics closer to bilateral negotiations than multilateral because of their emphasis on strict reciprocity. For although WTO Ministerial multilateral negotiations are becoming increasingly open and transparent, albeit increasingly protracted, both the GPA, as a plurilateral agreement standing outside of the single undertaking of the WTO, and RTAs are typically held behind closed doors.

A relative lack of transparency in non-multilateral negotiations does not give a ready explanation for the choice of an RTA for lowering thresholds or covering more procurement entities between two GPA parties. The answer is more likely to lie in the ability of an RTA to provide more scope for cross-sectoral trade-offs than the GPA, with its position outside the WTO's single undertaking and its negotiating scope confined to government procurement. Moreover, RTAs are the traditional vehicle driving inter-governmental trade negotiations. As Hamilton and Whalley's 1996 chronology indicates, RTAs have been a central feature in the development and evolution of the postwar trading system rather than the exception, despite the growth in importance of the GATT/WTO and, more specifically, the GPA (Hamilton and Whalley, 1996). Notwithstanding the presence of both multilateral and plurilateral rules and disciplines in the international trading system, most GATT/WTO contracting parties are parties to at least one regional trade arrangement.

4.4.2.2 The Coverage of Entities

In terms of the entities covered, GPA+ commitments were also observed in the RTAs concluded between GPA parties. Korea offers nine additional central government entities, while the US added one more entity in the Korea–US agreement as compared to the GPA 1994. The EFTA Convention is also GPA+ in being an add-on to their existing respective GPA commitments on sub-central governments, and only lists procurement commitments in relation to other entities. The EFTA Convention includes railway operators in addition to entities covered by the GPA. Under the Japan–Singapore agreement, Japan's offer is based on the GPA 1994 but excluding entities that have been privatized. Under the Korea–Singapore agreement, Korea additionally includes the chemical corporation but excludes the railroad corporation compared to the GPA 1994.

Again, the most obvious explanation for these East Asian "add-ons" in a bilateral or RTA arrangement, as opposed to their inclusion than under the rubric of the GPA, is the ability to use them as trade-offs for concessions in other markets and areas. The extant political economy literature indicates that when East Asian countries began to enter into FTAs from 2001 onwards, most analyses dismissed the economic dimensions of these FTAs and emphasized their foreign policy and security motivations, arguing that the "explosion [of FTAs in East Asia] has been driven by a 'political domino effect'," by "governments unhappy at the prospect of missing out on new diplomatic opportunities" (Ravenhill, 2010: pp. 199–200).

4.4.2.3 The WTO+ Coverage of Build-Operate-Transfer Contracts and Public Works Concessions

The agreements concluded by GPA parties' Korea–US, EU–Korea and US–Singapore also hold GPA+ commitments in the RTAs with explicit coverage of build-operate-transfer (BOT) contracts and public work concessions, although their definition and scope vary from one agreement to another. While the GPA provisions do not refer to the treatment of BOT contracts and public works concessions, Korea added explicit BOT coverage in its commitments under the revised GPA, as did the European Union, albeit in a more restrictive manner (Ueno, 2014).

This assessment also indicates, however, that while there may be a regionalizing dynamic which operates as a function of the strict relationship of correspondence between the GPA schedules and the GATS schedules, there is an incipient and uneven plurilateralizing of regionalism in other areas of government procurement. The lack of simple linearity or deterministic convergence toward either the GPA or RTAs is a reflection of the multiple policy objectives, and therefore negotiating motivations, of governments, as well as an uncertain loyalty to the benefits of an emerging multilateralism over an entrenched mercantilism.

4.4.3 GPA+ SERVICES COMMITMENTS

An important insight for this research is that the OECD study of 130 RTAs with public procurement commitments indicates that the level of commitments under RTAs is considerably better than that under the revised GPA for most services sectors—indeed, 10–40 percentage points higher. As Table 4.3 indicates, the exceptions to this rule are courier services and construction services that are less committed than the GPA. On the other hand, financial services are more committed than the GPA, but only by four percentage points.

Less divergence is observed in the level of commitments under RTAs across services sectors in comparison to those under the revised GPA. In both the GPA and RTAs,

Table 4.3 RTA commitments by sector and comparison with the GPA

W/120		Sectors	All RTAs (a)			GPA2012 with reciprocity (b)			Diffrences (percentage points)
			Full	Partial	Unbound	Full	Partial	Unbound	
1		BUSINESS SERVICES	60.7%	6.2%	33.2%	29.1%	9.9%	60.9%	27.8%
1	A	Professional services	62.2%	5.0%	32.9%	28.3%	9.4%	62.3%	29.4%
1	B	Computer and related services	93.4%	3.2%	3.4%	77.1%	4.6%	18.3%	14.9%
1	C	Research and development services	27.7%	0.0%	72.3%	0.0%	0.0%	100.0%	27.7%
1	D	Real estate services	65.8%	0.4%	33.8%	26.2%	4.8%	69.0%	35.2%
1	E	Rental/leasing services without operators	51.4%	3.2%	45.4%	7.4%	7.6%	85.0%	39.6%
1	F	Other business services	58.4%	9.8%	31.8%	27.7%	14.1%	58.2%	26.4%
2		COMMUNICATION SERVICES	58.4%	1.1%	40.5%	38.4%	2.5%	59.1%	18.6%
2	A	Postal services	43.8%	0.0%	56.2%	1.0%	0.0%	99.0%	42.9%
2	B	Courier services	75.4%	10.0%	14.6%	42.9%	43.8%	13.3%	−1.3%
2	C	Telecommunication services	65.3%	0.1%	34.6%	57.6%	0.2%	42.2%	7.6%
2	D	Audiovisual services	43.8%	2.3%	53.8%	2.1%	2.2%	95.7%	41.9%
2	E	Other	40.0%	0.0%	60.0%	1.0%	0.0%	99.0%	39.0%
3		CONSTRUCTION AND RELATED ENGINEERING SERVICES	91.2%	4.9%	3.8%	94.9%	5.1%	0.0%	−3.8%
4		DISTRIBUTION SERVICES	47.7%	0.0%	52.3%	1.3%	0.0%	98.7%	46.4%

(continued)

Table 4.3 Continued

W/120		Sectors	All RTAs (a)			GPA2012 with reciprocity (b)			Diffrences (percentage points)
			Full	Partial	Unbound	Full	Partial	Unbound	
5		EDUCATIONAL SERVICES	37.1%	4.6%	58.3%	4.8%	0.0%	95.2%	36.9%
6		ENVIRONMENTAL SERVICES	78.7%	6.2%	15.2%	57.9%	13.6%	28.6%	13.4%
7		FINANCIAL SERVICES	38.0%	2.4%	59.5%	29.9%	6.2%	64.0%	4.4%
7	A	All insurance and insurance-related services	42.1%	0.2%	57.7%	40.7%	2.1%	57.1%	−0.5%
7	B	Banking and other financial services	37.4%	3.4%	59.2%	28.7%	8.0%	63.3%	4.1%
7	C	Other	29.2%	0.0%	70.8%	1.0%	0.0%	99.0%	28.3%
8		HEALTH RELATED AND SOCIAL SERVICES	35.2%	4.2%	60.6%	1.0%	0.0%	99.0%	38.5%
9		TOURISM AND TRAVEL RELATED SERVICES	48.7%	2.9%	48.5%	9.5%	8.8%	81.7%	33.2%
10		RECREATIONAL, CULTURAL AND SPORTING SERVICES	44.5%	1.4%	54.2%	1.3%	0.8%	97.9%	43.8%
11		TRANSPORT SERVICES	46.9%	0.7%	52.4%	10.6%	1.6%	87.8%	35.4%
11	A	Maritime transport services	43.2%	0.1%	56.7%	6.2%	0.3%	93.5%	36.8%
11	B	Internal waterways transport	42.2%	0.0%	57.8%	4.9%	0.0%	95.1%	37.3%
11	C	Air transport services	58.3%	1.1%	40.6%	21.9%	2.5%	75.6%	35.0%
11	D	Space transport	63.1%	0.0%	36.9%	20.0%	0.0%	80.0%	43.1%
11	E	Rail transport services	43.8%	0.0%	56.2%	6.9%	0.0%	93.1%	37.0%
11	F	Road transport services	58.5%	3.1%	38.5%	27.6%	7.0%	65.3%	26.9%
11	G	Pipeline transport	36.2%	0.0%	63.8%	0.0%	0.0%	100.0%	36.2%
11	H	Services auxiliary to all modes of transport	38.7%	0.2%	61.2%	0.7%	1.2%	98.1%	36.9%
11	I	Other transport services	37.7%	0.8%	61.5%	0.0%	1.0%	99.0%	37.5%
12		OTHER SERVICES	44.6%	3.1%	52.3%	1.0%	0.0%	99.0%	46.7%
		ALL SECTORS	53.4%	3.1%	43.5%	25.3%	5.1%	69.5%	26.1%

Note: Differences are measured in percentage points by subtracting the aggregate percentage of full and partial commitments of (b) from those of (a).

Source: (Ueno, 2014: p. 58)

research and development services have the lowest level of commitments (less than 30 percent). Health-related and social services, financial services, postal services, distribution services, recreational, cultural and sporting services, audiovisual services, transport services, and educational services also have a low level of commitments, at less than 50 percent. On the other hand, the level of coverage of these services (except for financial services) is much higher than under the GPA (by 30–40 percentage points), and this makes divergence narrower across services sectors under RTAs.

More specifically, the OECD findings displayed in Table 4.3 indicate that in its RTAs with Korea and Singapore, the US bases its offer on its GPA commitments, with slight variations that balance or offset any GPA+ concession with a GPA− element. For example, while the US limits its services exclusion related to maintenance and repair services to ships under NAFTA, it excludes whole repair services of transport equipment under the GPA. Yet the US commits the whole of tourism and travel-related services under the GPA but excludes lodging services under NAFTA.

Further GPA+ commitments are apparent in the area of services RTAs signed between GPA parties, including Japan, the US, Singapore, and Canada. Singapore, for example, uses a negative list approach and offers more than that offered under the GPA. The Japan–Singapore agreement is GPA+, for while it does not include construction, architectural, and engineering services that are covered by their commitments under the GPA, the agreement adds to the existing GPA commitments for further liberalizing goods and services except construction services.

There is a tendency toward using a negative list approach in the RTAs. This can also help to explain how the negotiators have increased the level of RTA services coverage commitments reviewed to be higher than that of the GPA. About 51 percent of RTA commitments reviewed are based on a positive list approach, and 49 percent are on a negative list approach. This result deserves attention because a negative list approach is more frequently used in RTAs, as compared to the GPA. In fact, in the case of GPA commitments, the US is the only GPA party that systematically favors a negative list approach. Indeed, all US RTAs use a negative list. With regard to the other GPA parties applying a positive list approach to their GPA commitments, the EFTA, the European Union, Israel, and Japan also only use a positive list for their RTA commitments, whereas Canada, Korea, and Singapore use both types of approach in their RTAs.

These findings confirm the working hypothesis of this chapter that the correspondence between the GPA and GATS might in some way function to propel GPA parties to negotiate RTAs if they want to move beyond existing GATS commitments to MFN. It is interesting in this regard that in contrast with trade in services, where third-party MFN clauses are incorporated in about 60 percent of the RTAs reviewed, third-party MFN clauses are not found in the government procurement chapters of the OECD member RTAs reviewed. These clauses are found only in the RTAs without coverage commitments. To provide some MFN security, 55 percent of RTAs reviewed instead provide for future negotiation clauses when a party grants more comprehensive access to its procurement markets to a non-party of the RTA. Once again, this could be due to concerns about non-reciprocity and free-riding. Third-party MFN clauses stipulate that the preferential treatment granted in one agreement should in some cases be extended to parties in other agreements. Thus, they tend to limit discrimination among trading partners within RTAs by extending the better treatment of new RTAs to other parties of earlier RTAs. In sum, the absence of third-party MFN clauses in RTA procurement chapters implies that there exists only a limited availability of mechanisms supporting the multilateralization of RTA market access commitments.

This does not imply, however, that there is no multilateralizing dynamic or convergence toward more general principles adhering to good economic governance in public procurement systems. The major principles of transparency, accountability, and increased competition have characteristics that can be said to be public goods, and as a result are non-exclusive and non-exhaustible. Everyone benefits from adherence to such principles whether or not they are parties to the agreement because of their spillover benefits of good governance. Indeed, the growing number of parties negotiating government procurement obligations at either the regional or plurilateral level indicates the broader interest governments have displayed in reforming their procurement systems through opening them up to international competition and greater value for money.

4.5 Identifying GPA+ Commitments in RTAs among GPA and Non-GPA Signatory Parties

4.5.1 OVERVIEW

The following sections identify whether or not there are any salient patterns to be observed in those RTAs including public procurement commitments, first between the GPA parties and non-GPA signatories, and then among exclusively non-GPA signatory parties. Existing studies conducted by the OECD and WTO indicate that on a most basic level, in those RTAs concluded between a GPA party and non-GPA party, GPA parties commit mostly the same level of coverage as is shown under the GPA.

However, beneath this broad statement there is significant heterogeneity in the specific coverage provided by each RTA. Again, this diversity "at the fringes" indicates that the negotiations to these agreements have had more complex policy considerations other than public procurement in play. That is, while the GPA parties calibrate and modulate their commitments through negotiating the coverage of entities, thresholds, and explicit derogations in the Annexes, RTAs have a much wider array of negotiating issues from which to make trade-offs beyond government procurement, or even trade policy as a whole.

4.5.2 RTAs BETWEEN A GPA PARTY AND A NON-GPA PARTY

There is a wide array of different negotiating outcomes set out in those RTAs with public procurement commitments signed between GPA and non-GPA parties. At a most general level, there are as many exceptions as there are emerging patterns or templates from which to generalize. For example, an overview of the existing two major empirical studies discussed here indicates that US RTAs with Australia, Chile, Morocco, and Peru cover approximately eighty entities, which are almost the same entities as covered by the GPA 1994. Yet, the US covers only about fifty entities under NAFTA, the US–Bahrain and US–Oman agreements, and does not offer the Department of Defense, the Department of Homeland Security, and some federal corporations to Oman. The US has GPA-equal coverage commitments with Chile, while having lower coverage commitments with Australia (thirty-one states), Morocco (twenty-three states).

Table 4.4 indicates the fine-tuning and careful calibration at the margins that takes place when negotiating government procurement market access bilaterally with different parties, and in different RTAS. The EU, EFTA, and Japan offer GPA-equivalent commitments to non-GPA parties. Yet this is with the noteworthy exceptions of the EU–CARIFORUM, EU–Mexico, EFTA–Mexico, and Japan–Mexico agreements. While the EU offers GPA 1994-equal commitments to Mexico, it does not offer sub-central government entities. Moreover, the EU limits its coverage to public authorities or undertakings in the field of maritime and inland ports and airports to Chile on a reciprocal basis. The EU–CARIFORUM agreement does not cover any entities other than central government. While the EFTA commits the GPA 1994-equal coverage of other entities with Mexico and Ukraine, it does not cover public authorities or undertakings in the field of electricity with Chile, Colombia, and Peru. Yet this is reciprocal, given that Chile and Colombia likewise do not offer entities in electricity services.

As noted in Section 4.2.2, Canada excludes sub-central government entities for any of its agreements with non-GPA parties. Meanwhile, Japan's offer to Chile, Mexico, and Peru is based on the GPA 1994–2012, but it further excludes tobacco, telecommunications, and privatized railway companies. And while Korea's offer with Chile is considered to be more or less the same as that under the GPA, it also includes additional undertakings that have activities in airports, maritime and inland ports on a reciprocal basis with Chile. Meanwhile, Korea's offer with Peru covers slightly less than under the GPA. Israel added one more entity to the Israel–Mexico agreement than it covers under

Table 4.4 RTAs between the US and non-GPA parties

NAFTA (Goods/ Services)	**Canada**: 78 entities (as in the GPA);	Not covered	**Canada**: 10 entities (as in the GPA);
	Mexico: 86 entities;		**Mexico**: 48 entities;
	US: 53 entities (36 less than the GPA)		**US**: 6 entities (4 less than the GPA)
US–Australia	**US**: 79 entities (10 less the GPA);	**US**: 31 states, (6 less than the GPA);	**US**: 7 entities (3 less than the GPA);
	Australia: similar positive list	**Australia**: extensive list	**Australia**: similar positive list
US–Bahrain	**US**: 52 entities (37 less than the GPA);	Not covered	**US**: 7 entities (3 less than the GPA);
	Bahrain: equivalent list		Bahrain: positive list (17 entities, including Bahrain Petroleum)
US–Chile	**US**: 79 entities (10 less than the GPA);	**US**: 37 states covered, as in its GPA schedule;	**US**: 10 entities
	Chile: 20 entities (19 ministries and the Office of the President of the Republic).	**Chile**: List of 51 entities "Gobernaciones" in 13 different regions + list of 341 municipalities	**Chile**: 11 entities
US–Colombia	**US**: 78 entities (11 less than the GPA);	**US**: 8 states + Puerto Rico (29 less than the GPA);	**US**: 7 entities (3 less than the GPA);
	Colombia: 28 entities	**Colombia**: 38 gobernaciones	**Colombia**: 22 entities
US–DR-CAFTA	**US**: 79 entities (10 less than the GPA);	**US**: 22 states + Puerto Rico (15 less than the GPA) (and for Honduras 16 states + Puerto Rico);	**US**: 7 entities (3 less than the GPA);
	Others: more exceptions than under GPA	**Others**: extensive lists	**Others**: more or less extensive lists.
US–Morocco	**US**: 79 entities (10 less than the GPA);	**US**: 23 states (14 less than the GPA);	**US**: 7 entities (3 less than the GPA);
	Morocco: 30 entities	**Morocco**: extensive list	**Morocco**: extensive list
US–Oman	**US**: 50 entities (39 less than the GPA);	not covered	**US**: 7 entities (3 less than the GPA);
	Oman: equivalent list		**Oman**: positive list (17 entities, including Bahrain Petroleum)
US–Panama	**US**: 78 entities (11 less than the GPA)	**US**: 8 states + Puerto Rico (29 less than the GPA)	**US**: 7 entities (3 less than the GPA);
	Panama: 16 entities	**Panama**: 12 provinces	**Panama**: 30 entities + the Authority of the Panama Canal
US–Peru	**US**: 78 entities (11 less than the GPA);	**US**: 8 states + Puerto Rico covered (29 less than the GPA);	**US**: 7 entities (3 less than the GPA);
	Peru: extensive list (61 entities)	**Peru**: 25 entities	**Peru**: 23 entities

Source: Anderson and Singh (2014).

the GPA 1994, but has also limited coverage to Mexico by excluding entities in the field of urban transport. This further highlights the "trading at the margins" that occurs in bilateral negotiations.

4.5.3 IDENTIFYING GPA+ COMMITMENTS IN RTAs AMONG NON-GPA SIGNATORY PARTIES

The existing studies on procurement commitments among non-GPA parties suggest that there are fairly homogenous commitments in these RTAs in terms of the coverage of central government entities. Yet beyond this, there is also an observable tendency for existing analyses to look for nascent patterns where perhaps none exist except for the adherence to strict reciprocity.

Table 4.5 indicates that among non-GPA parties, the most significant pattern that emerges is the broad liberalization of procurement markets that has been undertaken between Central American countries' RTAs involving Chile, Costa Rica, El Salvador, and Panama. Aside from this deeper regional integration, under the other RTAs the parties continue to tweak their market access commitments according to their negotiating party. For example, Colombia offers about ten entities with the GPA parties Canada, Chile, and EFTA, yet elsewhere it offers thirty entities to the non-GPA party Mexico. Mexico's entity coverage commitments across its RTAs are typically the same—about twenty entities—as those covered under NAFTA, which includes entities in the fields of electricity, railroad, oil, telecommunications, postal, and airport services. Nevertheless, Mexico offers less than what is offered under NAFTA to the GPA parties Israel and the EU, and to the non-GPA party Nicaragua. Under the recent agreements with GPA parties such as the Japan–Mexico and EFTA–Mexico agreements, Mexico also includes newly founded institutions, but continues not to cover any sub-central governments (Table 4.5).

4.6 **Conclusions**

This chapter has observed that while there are potentially negative implications from the strictly reciprocal and conditional approach to the MFN principle operating under the GPA, from the outset it must be acknowledged that it was these same *ex ante* limitations that were instrumental in helping to establish and expand the plurilateral agreement, when full multilateral commitments could not be made.

Nevertheless, as submitted in the introduction to this chapter, governments' continued quest for reciprocity to avoid free-riding has resulted in a myriad of derogations,

Table 4.5 Non-GPA parties' government procurement coverage commitments in RTAs

Agreement	Goods	Services	Construction services
Australia–Chile	All goods covered	All services covered except: AUS: R&D, Plasma fractionation, government advertising services	All construction services, except Chile; Easter Islands
Chile–Colombia	All goods covered	Negative list	All construction services except: Chile: those for Easter Islands Colombia: local content requirement for road and railways
Chile–Costa Rica (Central America)	All government procurement covered	All services that are covered in the trade in services chapter of the agreement	All government procurement covered
Chile–El Salvador (Central America)	All government procurement covered	All services that are covered in the trade in services chapter of the agreement	All government procurement covered
Mexico–Chile	All goods covered, except Mexico, positive list for defense purposes	Mexico: positive list as in NAFTAChile: all services except financial services	Mexico: as in its NAFTA scheduleChile: all construction except those for Easter Island
Mexico–Costa Rica	All goods covered	Provisionally no coverage until parties have elaborated negative lists	Provisionally no coverage until parties have elaborated negative lists
Mexico–Nicaragua	All goods covered	All services covered	All construction services
Panama–Costa Rica (Central America)	All government procurement covered	All services that are covered in the trade in services chapter of the agreement	All government procurement covered
Panama–El Salvador (Central America)	All government procurement covered	All government procurement covered	All government procurement covered

Source: Anderson et al. (2011).

and may have created a framework for selective protectionism. Under the GPA, the conditionality of the MFN clause elicits equivalent compensation and indicates that favors granted between initial parties will not automatically be extended. Derogations from MFN are accompanied with a declaration that they will be withdrawn if and when the respective signatory has accepted that the other parties have given comparable access to its suppliers.

Consequently, the conditionality of the GPA MFN obligation may limit the scope for liberalization of trade by entrenching restrictions, not only among the parties but also with non-parties to the agreement. That is, the ongoing use of restrictive reciprocity and conditional MFN could function to protect national interests rather than to create and maintain an open trading system. Trade liberalization negotiations are conducted, not only in the GPA but also in RTAs, through reciprocal bargaining—contingency and equivalence—rather than unilateral action. The question then revolves around whether these deviations lead to significantly more or less trade liberalization and to more or less scope for trade creation.

The chapter subsequently assessed the relationship of correspondence between the GPA commitments on services and construction services and the GATS MFN obligation. The requirements of the GATS imply that a GPA party cannot gain access to another party's services or construction services markets for the purpose of government procurement unless that party has already opened up under the GATS. This could provide a disincentive for developing countries that are contemplating membership of the GPA but wish to gain access to the procurement markets in services markets in modes of supply that are restricted under GATS, such as Mode 4. Moreover, this could also provide an incentive to negotiate GPA+ RTAs to avoid this legal constraint—that is, a regionalizing dynamic.

Consequently, the remainder of this chapter examined existing comprehensive empirical studies of those RTAs signed by GPA parties with the specific aim of identifying whether any GPA+ commitments had been made, particularly as regards services and construction services. For as hypothesized, these RTAs might be seeking to avoid the relationship of correspondence with the GATS that operates in the GPA by using the most obvious alternative existing negotiating forum of an RTA. Indeed, the review of the OECD analysis of RTAs with procurement commitments in services and construction services markets appears to support this proposition. That study confirmed that those RTAs signed between GPA parties do indeed include GPA+ commitments that are not included under the GPA schedules.

This development would appear to be in conflict with the MFN requirement under the GPA, to which notably there is no formal exception under the GPA, unlike under the GATT and GATS. However, since no challenge has been brought in this regard, and the revised 2012 GPA chose not to include such a provision, it would appear that the questionable legality of GPA+ commitments among its signatory parties is at present academic. This legal uncertainty is tolerated perhaps partly due to the difficulties in going beyond the parties' corresponding GATS schedules, and partly due to the unequivocal adherence to strict reciprocity and conditional MFN. Nevertheless, however theoretical, it must be asked whether such toleration also functions to detract from an automatic *plurilateralization* of regional GPA+ commitments. In other words, is the regionalizing dynamic produced by the GPA and GATS relationship of correspondence in any way confirmed by the lack of MFN provisions included in RTAs with government procurement commitments? These would typically function so as to multilateralize any progressive liberalization that was occurring in government procurement markets at the regional level.

Section 4.5 examined and observed the heterogeneity amongst the coverage commitments of non-GPA parties in the RTAs with both GPA and other non-GPA parties. The findings of this assessment also suggest there are systemic challenges for multilateralizing, or even plurilateralizing, regionalism in the area of government procurement beyond its present bilateral nature. Once again, these challenges are in no small part related to the current practice of negotiating based on strict reciprocity and conditional MFN. Further complications arise from procurement market access negotiations based on entities, rather than on the value of opportunities under offer, and or making linear access across markets. Not only does the current practice of negotiating entities and thresholds not correspond with the general distinction between goods and services observed under the GATT and GATS respectively, but it does not correspond with the modes of supply of services currently governing the negotiation of services market access either.

This chapter's analysis therefore concludes that there are difficulties in the operation of strict reciprocity, conditional MFN, and the GPA's relationship of correspondence with the GATS—with its exclusion of government procurement. These difficulties serve as obstacles to the multilateralization, or even *plurilateralization,* of regional and bilateral government procurement markets. As such, they symptomize the ongoing tension between the optimal trade creation route of unconditional MFN for public procurement regulation and the realistic acknowledgement that at present, this would likely scale down the parties' commitment offers to the level of the lowest common denominator in order to achieve an acceptable balance of concessions.

REFERENCES

Anderson, R. D. and Kovacic, W. E. 2009. "Competition Policy and International Trade Liberalization: Essential Complements to Ensure Good Performance in Public Procurement Markets." *Public Procurement Law Review* 2: 67–101.

Anderson, R. D., Locatelli, C., Müller, A. C., and Pelletier, P. 2014. "The Relationship between Services Trade and Government Procurement Commitments: Insights from Relevant WTO Agreements and Recent RTAs." WTO Staff Working Paper ERSD-2014-21 (available at: <http://www.wto.org/english/res_e/reser_e/ersd201421_e.htm> (accessed July 21, 2016)).

Anderson, R. D. and Müller, A. C. 2008. "Market Access for Government Procurement of Services: Comparing Recent PTAs with Achievements." In M. Roy and J. Marchetti (eds), *Services Trade Liberalization: Preferential Trade Agreements vs. the GATS*. Cambridge: Cambridge University Press, 435–75.

Anderson, R. D., Müller, A. C., Osei-Lah, K., Pardo De Leon, J., and Pelletier, P. 2011. "Government Procurement Provisions in Regional Trade Agreements: A Stepping Stone to GPA

Accession?" In S. Arrowsmith and R. D. Anderson (eds), *The WTO Regime on Government Procurement: Challenge and Reform*. Cambridge: Cambridge University Press, 561–656.

Anderson, R. D. and Singh, H. V. 2014. "Government Procurement and India–US Trade: Why Liberalize? Which Approach Is Best?" Paper Prepared for the Peterson Institute for International Economics, Washington, DC.

Arrowsmith, S. and Trybus, M. 2002. *Public Procurement—The Continuing Revolution*. London: Kluwer Law International 2002.

Blank, A. and Marceau, G. 1996. "The History of the Government Procurement Negotiations Since 1945." *Public Procurement Law Review* 5: 77–147.

Hamilton, C. and Whalley, J. 1996. *The World Trading System after the Uruguay Round*. Washington, DC: Institute for International Economics.

Hoekman, B. and Mavroidis, P. (eds). 1996. *Law and Policy in Public Purchasing: The WTO Agreement on Government Procurement*. Ann Arbor: University of Michigan Press.

Ministry of Economy, Trade and Industry (METI). 2012. "Report on Compliance by Major Trading Partners with Trade Agreements." Government of Japan.

Ravenhill, J. 2010. "The 'New East Asian Regionalism': A Political Domino Effect." *Review of International Political Economy* 17(2):178–208.

Reich, A. 1997. "The New GATT Agreement on Government Procurement: The Pitfalls of Plurilateralism and Strict Reciprocity." *Journal of World Trade* 31(2): 125–51.

Schwartz, W. F. and Sykes, A. O. 1997. "The Economics of the Most Favored Nation Clause." In J. S. Bhandani and A. O. Sykes (eds), *Economic Dimensions in International Law: Comparative and Empirical Perspectives*. Cambridge: Cambridge University Press, 34–79.

Ueno, A. 2014. "Multilateralising Regionalism on Government Procurement." OECD Trade Policy Papers No. 151.

van der Marel, E. 2013. "Why Are Services Commitments in RTAs Stronger Than in the GATS? Trade Policy Implications for TTIP." *ECIPE Bulletin No. 07/2013.*

Yanai, A. 2002. "The Function of the MFN Clause in the Global Trading System." Working Paper Series 01/02—No. 3, APEC Study Centre, Institute of Developing Economies.

Part II
Country studies

5 Public Procurement in the EU

Carlo Maria Cantore and Sübidey Togan

On February 11, 2014 the European Council adopted the legislative package for modernization of public procurement in the EU, which is made up of Directive 2014/24/EU on public procurement repealing Directive 2004/18/EC; Directive 2014/25/EU on procurement by entities operating in the water, energy, transport, and postal service sectors repealing Directive 2004/17/EC; and Directive 2014/23/EU on the award of concession contracts. The member states were to transpose the new rules into their national law by April 2016, except with regard to e-procurement, where the deadline is September 2018. These new regulations build on a set of earlier regulations, namely Directive 2004/17/EC, Directive 2004/18/EC, Directive 2009/81/EC, Directive 89/665/EC, Directive 92/13/EC, and Directive 2007/66/EC.[1]

This chapter first briefly reviews these older regulations (Section 5.1) and then discusses the new directives (Section 5.2) and the EU regime for, and experience with, domestic challenge and review mechanisms (Section 5.3). We do not discuss in any detail the evidence on the extent to which EU member states source internationally, or the drivers of actual EU procurement behavior, as this is a subject taken up in other contributions to this volume. The EU procurement regime is very salient from the perspective of the internationalization of procurement policies, as it applies to a group of now twenty-eight nations that have agreed to adopt common rules of the game in the interest of achieving a single integrated market for goods and services. Thus it offers potential lessons and guidance for what may be desirable and feasible to pursue in the GPA context in the future.

5.1 The Old Regime

The regime in place in pursuance to the older directives is still relevant as it applies, *ratione temporis*, to the procurement procedures launched before the expiry

[1] The following discussion of EU regulations draws on information on EU regulations available at <http://ec.europa.eu/internal_market/publicprocurement/index_en.htm> (accessed July 2016). For more in-depth treatment of EU law and practice in this area see Arrowsmith et al. (2011) and Arrowsmith (2014).

of the period for the transposition of the new directives into the law of the member states.[2]

5.1.1 OBJECTIVES, PRINCIPLES, AND COVERAGE

The main objectives of EU public procurement policy are to increase the efficiency of public spending and to support the attainment of a Single Market. Complementary objectives are the achievement of common societal goals such as the protection of the environment, higher resource and energy efficiency, combatting climate change, promoting innovation and social inclusion, preventing and fighting corruption and favoritism, and ensuring the best conditions for the provision of high-quality public services. The guiding principles of public procurement policy in the EU are competition, non-discrimination, transparency, and objectivity.

Procuring entities covered by the EU regulatory regime (Directive 2004/18/EC) include central government agencies, regional and local authorities, bodies governed by public law, and associations formed by the above. All of these are referred to collectively as "contracting authorities." The bodies governed by public law are set out in Annex III to Directive 2004/18/EC.[3] The Directive also applies to certain works and services contracts which are subsidized by more than 50 percent by contracting authorities, even though the purchaser is a private entity. Rules apply to private bodies holding works concessions to help ensure, in particular, that they do not discriminate in awarding their subcontracts.[4]

Types of Contract: Directive 2004/18/EC covers contracts in writing for pecuniary interest for the procurement of works, supplies, and services, including design contests.[5]

[2] This was also clarified by the Court of Justice of the European Union in the recent Case C-324/14, *Partner Apelski Dariusz v Zarząd Oczyszczania Miasta* (Request for a preliminary ruling).

[3] A body governed by public law is defined as a body with legal personality that meets the following conditions: (a) it meets at least one of the following criteria: (i) it is financed for the most part by a contracting authority, (ii) it is subject to management supervision by a contracting authority, or (iii) it has a board to which more than half of its members are appointed by a contracting authority; and (b) it is established for the specific purpose of meeting needs in the general interest, not having an industrial or commercial character.

[4] Procurement by utilities is discussed in Section 5.1.6.

[5] A "work" is defined as the outcome of building or civil engineering works taken as a whole—such as a hospital, theater, or bridge—that is sufficient of itself to fulfill an economic and technical function and that is fully equipped and completed. Public works contracts are contracts for pecuniary interest concluded in writing between a contractor and a contracting authority, which have as their object either the execution, or both the execution and design, of works related to a work, or the execution of a work corresponding to the requirements specified by the contracting authority. On the other hand, public supply contracts are defined as contracts other than works involving the purchase, lease, rental, or hire purchase—with or without option to buy—of products. Finally, service contracts refer to contracts other than works or supply contracts that have as their object the provision of services referred to in Annex II of the Directive 2004/18/EC.

Service contracts are divided into priority services and non-priority services. While priority services listed in Annex IIA to Directive 2004/18/EC are subject to the full rules under directives, the non-priority services listed in Annex IIB to Directive 2004/18/EC are subject only to the rules on technical specifications, award notices, and certain obligations on provision of statistics.

Financial Thresholds: The Directives regulate only those contracts that are most likely to be relevant from a trade perspective, i.e. contracts that are of sufficiently high value to potentially be of interest to economic operators from other member states, and types of procurement that concern objects that are amenable to cross-border trade, that is are tradable. Thus, the Directives apply only to contracts above a certain threshold financial value. As of 2014, the thresholds were €5.186 million for works (construction), €207,000 for central government priority service contracts, €134,000 for supplies contracts, and €207,000 for supplies contracts not listed in Annex V to Directive 2004/18/EC.

Exemptions: Even if the value of a work, supply, or services contract is above the relevant threshold, the contract may be excluded or there may be limits on the application of the provisions laid on in Directive 2004/18/EC. The Directive excludes contracts in the water, energy, transport, and postal services sectors; contracts in the field of telecommunications; secret contracts and contracts requiring special security measures; contracts awarded pursuant to international rules; service concessions; service contracts awarded on the basis of an exclusive right; reserved contracts; and contracts that concern (i) the acquisition or rental of existing buildings; (ii) the acquisition, development, production, or co-production of program material intended for broadcasting by broadcasters and contracts for broadcasting time; (iii) arbitration and conciliation services; (iv) the purchase, sale, or transfer of financial instruments; (v) employment contracts; or (vi) research and technological development services which do not belong exclusively to the contracting authority or which are not wholly financed by it.

5.1.2 METHODS OF PROCUREMENT AND PROCUREMENT TOOLS

Public procurement authorities covered by EU Directive 2004/18/EC must use one of the following five methods: open procedure, restricted procedure, competitive dialogue, negotiated procedure with a notice, or negotiated procedure without a notice. "Open procedure" is defined as a method of procurement whereby a contracting authority invites providers to bid directly in response to the contract notice. "Restricted procedures" refer to those procedures in which any economic operator may request to participate, but only those economic operators invited by the contracting authority may submit a tender. "Competitive dialogue" is a procedure in which any economic operator may request to participate and whereby the contracting authority conducts a dialogue with the candidate admitted to that procedure, with the aim of developing one or more suitable alternatives capable of meeting its requirements. "Negotiated procedure with a notice" are procedures whereby the contracting authorities consult the economic operators of their choice and negotiate the terms of contract with one or more of these. Finally, under "negotiated procedure without a notice" the contracting authority may simply negotiate a contract without any kind of competition.

EU member states may also use three alternative types of procurement tool: framework agreements, dynamic purchasing systems, and electronic auctions. A "framework agreement" refers to an agreement between one or more contracting authorities and one or more economic operators, the purpose of which is to establish the terms governing contracts to be awarded during a given time limit (in general, not exceeding four years) in particular with regard to price and, where appropriate, the quantity envisaged. The most appropriate use of frameworks is where a contracting authority has a repeated requirement for works, services or supplies, but the exact quantities are unknown. The notice for contracts exceeding the threshold must be published in *Official Journal of the European Union* (*OJEU*) at the start of the process to establish a framework agreement, but not thereafter. A "dynamic purchasing system" is a completely electronic system which can be used for repeat, standardized purchases. We discuss "electronic auctions" in Section 5.1.6.

5.1.3 RULES APPLICABLE TO PUBLIC PROCUREMENT

Advertisement: Under EU Directive 2004/18/EC, contracts—except those awarded by the negotiated procedure without a notice—must be advertised by an EU-wide advertisement. These advertisements, called "contract notices," define the technical specifications in terms of performance and functional requirements. When drawing up the technical specifications, a contracting entity refers to national standards transposing European standards, European technical approvals, and international standards, and the technical specifications are expected not to create unjustified obstacles to competition. The contract notices are sent to the Commission, which publishes the notices free of charge in the Supplement to the *OJEU*. The contract notices can be sent to the Commission by traditional or electronic means via the Information System for Public Procurement (SIMAP). A free online version of the *OJEU* Supplement, called *Tenders Electronic Daily*, is available at <http://ted.europa.eu> (accessed July 21, 2016). The Directive requires that economic operators and others be notified at the end of the contract-specific procurement process that the procurement process has been concluded.

Selecting Economic Operators: Procuring entities may exclude from procurement suppliers for "significant or persistent" deficiencies in past performance, serious crimes or other offenses, professional misconduct, or acts or omissions. In order to check the suitability of economic operators tendering for contracts, the procuring entity may exclude suppliers from procurement if the economic operator is bankrupt, is being wound up, has suspended business activities, or his/her affairs are being administered by the court; has been convicted of any offence concerning his/her professional conduct; has been guilty of grave professional misconduct; has not paid social security contributions or taxes; or has made a false declaration to the contracting authority.

According to Articles 47 of Directive 2004/18/EC, a contracting authority may consider the economic and financial standing of economic operators. The purpose is to assess whether economic operators have adequate financial resources to handle and complete the contract to be awarded. The contracting authority may request from economic operators evidence of their economic and financial standing. The Directive provides a list of the types of evidence, but this list is only indicative and not exhaustive. Therefore, a contracting authority may also require other evidence than that listed in the Directive, subject to compliance of the basic public procurement principles. The Directive explicitly requires the evidence/information sought from economic operators to be related and proportionate to the subject matter of the contract.

The contracting authority may also consider the technical and/or professional ability of economic operators. The Directive lays down an exhaustive list of evidence that a contracting authority may request from economic operators as proof of their technical and/or professional ability. The contracting authority is not obliged to request all of the listed evidence, only the evidence that is necessary to assess the technical and/or professional ability of economic operators in relation to the contract to be awarded.

Setting the Award Criteria: The criterion used by contracting authorities in awarding public contracts is either the lowest price or the most economically advantageous tender. When price is the only award criterion, the contract must be offered to the tenderer that has submitted the lowest price and that has put forward a compliant tender. In cases where a multidimensional criterion is used, the contracting authority takes into account not just overall cost (price), but also factors such as quality, delivery time, technical merit, aesthetic and functional characteristics, environmental characteristics, running cost, or provision of after-sales services. Each such criterion must be given a relative weight by the contracting authority. The premise underlying the use of this approach is to identify the tender that offers the best value for money. In addition, Directive 2004/18/EC requires that the award criteria be established in advance and be disclosed to potential bidders in the tender document.

Tender Evaluation and Contract Award: Evaluation of tenders must be carried out by a suitably competent panel and in accordance with the principles of equal treatment, non-discrimination, and transparency. Confidentiality of the information acquired by those involved in the evaluation process must be preserved. The evaluation panel carries out technical and substantive compliance checks, determines the best tender on the basis of the pre-announced award criteria, and makes a recommendation for the award of the contract. The contracting authority must notify all tenderers and candidates of the contract award decision before it concludes the contract with the winning tender. This notification is followed by a mandatory "standstill" period of ten to fifteen days. This is intended to give other bidders the opportunity to contest the award. If no complaint is received during this period, the contracting authority announces the successful tenderer, and within forty-eight days of the contract award the authority must publish the contract award notice in the *OJEU*.

5.1.4 ELECTRONIC METHODS

Electronic tools can be used for various processes and decisions on a par with more traditional means of communication. Electronic methods reduce the administrative costs of individual procurements, streamline procurement procedures, result in faster procurement procedures and increased transparency, provide better monitoring of procurement, encourage cross-border competition, promote the effectiveness of procurement, encourage the integration of various administrative processes, and support the developments that make the process more efficient.

EU Directive 2004/18/EC places traditional and electronic means of communication on an equal footing. It leaves market operators free to choose which means of communication to use for the procedures. If electronic means are used, the contracting authority is allowed to reduce the time limits. Online submission of tenders is permissible, and a contracting entity may hold an electronic auction to award a contract, except for in the case of certain works and service contracts (such as the design of works that relate to intellectual performances). The electronic auction is to be based either on price (i.e., the contract is awarded to the lowest bidder) or on the most economically advantageous tender. The specifications must contain the quantifiable features whose values are the subject of the electronic auction, the electronic auction process, and the technical specifications for connection. Before proceeding with the electronic auction, the contracting authority is to make a full initial evaluation of the tenders. All tenderers who have submitted admissible tenders are to be invited to take part simultaneously by electronic means, with the invitation specifying the date and time of the auction and, if appropriate, the number of phases. This should include publication of the mathematical formula used to determine automatic re-rankings, incorporating the weighting of the various award criteria. Throughout each phase, the participants are to be informed of their relative ranking compared to other participants, but without knowing their identities. Electronic auctions must close at a date and time that is specified in advance, when a certain amount of time has elapsed after receipt of the last submission, or when the number of phases in the auction has been completed.

5.1.5 CONCESSIONS AND PUBLIC–PRIVATE PARTNERSHIPS

The EU legal framework does not contain a public–private partnership (PPP) law or a specific legal system governing the choice of private partners for PPPs by contracting authorities. A PPP that qualifies as a public contract under Directive 2004/18/EC must be awarded using one of the procedures set out in the Directive applying to public contracts. According to the Directive, the contracting authority must advertise the works concession in the *OJEU*. The contracting authority is free to determine how to run the tender process as long as it runs the process in a transparent manner, ensuring equal treatment and treating economic operators in a non-discriminatory way. Directive 2004/18/EC does not apply to services concessions, but service concessions of cross-border interest will be subject to fundamental EU Treaty principles of transparency, equal treatment, non-discrimination, proportionality, and mutual recognition. Regarding concessions, the current legal framework is fragmented, based on complex case law and divergent national legislations. It lacks basic clarity and thus does not provide sufficient legal certainty. As a result of these considerations, a new Directive 2014/23/EU was issued on February 11, 2014 on the award of concession contracts, within the context of the legislative package for modernization of public procurement. Member states had until March 2016 to transpose the new rules into their national law.

5.1.6 PROCUREMENT BY UTILITIES

Directive 2004/17/EC applies to public as well as private enterprises pursuing activities in the delivery of services such as the provision of water, energy, transport, and postal services to a community as a whole. Since most of these enterprises operate in markets where competition is limited, special rules were introduced regarding how utilities operating in monopolistic, and in some cases monopoly, markets organize their purchases. The Directive covering works, supplies, and services provides for sector-specific exemptions in a number of utility sectors, based essentially on the degree of competition in these markets. The Directive also contains a series of other exemptions specific to the utilities sector, including activities outside the Community, affiliated undertakings exemption, and purchases for resale or hire. The relevant EU financial thresholds for utilities are higher than the thresholds applying to contracts covered by Directive 2004/18/EC. For the two years starting from January 2014, the financial thresholds are €5.186 million for works contracts and €414,000 for supplies and services contracts, as well as for design contests. Directive 2004/17/EC provides for three main procurement procedures: open procedure, restricted procedure, and negotiated procedure with a prior call for competition. When conducting an open procedure, utilities must use a contract notice.

Statutory time limits apply and a standard format contract notice must be used and published in the *OJEU*. On the other hand, when conducting a restricted procedure or a negotiated procedure with a prior call for competition, utilities can choose to use a contract specific notice, an annual "periodic indicative notice," or a notice on the existence of a qualification system.

Utilities are obliged to observe the general principles of equal treatment, transparency, and not distorting competition, and may use purchasing tools such as qualification systems, framework agreements, dynamic purchasing systems, and electronic auctions. Under the qualification system, economic operators interested in contracting with the utility apply to be registered as potential providers for specific works, supplies, or services. The utility—using predefined and published qualification criteria—registers some or all of these economic operators in the system, thus forming a pool for specified works, supplies, or services from which it may draw those who are to be invited to bid or negotiate on contracts. The system is advertised in the *OJEU*. Under framework agreements, the procurement process is much more lightly regulated than under Directive 2004/18/EC and there are no detailed provisions covering how such agreements are to be set up or operated. The dynamic purchasing system—a completely electronic process for making commonly used purchases—uses the open procedure to appoint economic operators who are free to apply to join the system at any time by submitting indicative tenders. Finally, electronic auctions occur at the final stage of a tender process which has been conducted up to that point in accordance with one of the standard procurement procedures provided for in Directive 2004/17/EC.

5.1.7 DEFENSE PROCUREMENT

Defense procurement is the process through which authorities in the field of defense acquire the various goods, services, or works they need in order to perform their duties and missions. Directive 2009/81/EC, the "Defense and Security Directive," aims, among other things, to open up national defense procurement to cross-border competition and thus create a genuine pan-European defense procurement market. The Defense and Security Directive covers two major areas: (i) military equipment, associated services, and works contracts; and (ii) sensitive procurement for security purposes or procurement involving classified information. For the two years starting from January 2014, the financial thresholds in defense procurements are: €5.186 million for works contracts and €414,000 for supplies and services contracts. Contracts whose value is below these thresholds are not covered by the Defense and Security Directive. However, if they are likely to attract cross-border interest, these contracts are covered by the general rules and principles of EU law applying to below-threshold contracts, as explained in more detail in Section 5.1.8.

A significant innovation of the Defense and Security Directive is that contracting authorities in the field of defense are free to choose either the negotiated procedure with prior notice or the restricted procedure. The negotiated procedure with prior notice provides greater flexibility to contracting authorities and more freedom to discuss available solutions with economic operators. In addition, contracting authorities can use the competitive dialogue and the negotiated procedures without prior notice on specific grounds. The latter procedure can be used in urgent situations ensuing from a crisis if compliance with the restricted procedure or the negotiated procedure with prior notice would be incompatible with the urgency of the crisis.

One of the practices used in the defense industry is related to offsets. Under this practice, the foreign defense contractor may be forced to co-produce with domestic producers or subcontract certain activities to domestic producers. The Defense and Security Directive does not deal explicitly with offsets, and EU law does not allow offsets. The Defense Directive includes a set of provisions on subcontracting that aim to address some of the concerns that led member states to adopt offsets in a manner that complies with EU law.

5.1.8 BELOW-THRESHOLD CONTRACTS

Contracts for purchases by contracting authorities that are below the financial value thresholds for works, supplies, and services are regulated mostly by laws and regulations of the member states, and are generally subject to simplified procedures and rules that are less rigorous than those of the Directives.[6] Direct purchasing (buying from an economic operator without a requirement for an advertisement or competitive process) is permitted for contracts between €5,000 and €15,000, depending on what is being purchased. Other procurement methods that may be used include (i) request for quotations, offers, or written tenders from a specified number of tenderers without prior publication of an advertisement; and (ii) seeking two offers through an advertisement on a national portal, but using a simplified procedure.

In the case of below-threshold procurement, contracting authorities must comply with the rules and principles of the Treaty on the Functioning of the European Union (TFEU) insofar as contracts fall under the scope of the Treaty. These principles imply an obligation to ensure adequate advertising on the contracting entity's webpage and/or on portal sites for contracting advertisements and/or national official journals, and/or the *OJEU*. Furthermore, the European Court of Justice has confirmed that the internal market rules of the EC Treaty apply to public procurement contracts outside the scope

[6] The discussion of EU rules for below threshold contracts is based largely on Stockhammer (2008). See also OECD (2010).

of the public procurement directives. In addition, EU Interpretive Communication 2006/C 179/02 rules are applicable to contract awards not, or not fully, subject to the provisions of the public procurement directives. This communication implies obligation to ensure impartiality of the contract award procedures, a non-discriminatory description of the subject matter of the contract, a non-discriminatory description of conditions, observance of mutual recognition principle, appropriate time limits, and a transparent and objective approach. Finally, the EU regulations require that the principle of value for money be observed, implying the observance of the principles of economy, efficiency, and effectiveness. "Economy" refers to satisfaction of the conditions related to appropriate timing, quantity and quality at the best price. "Efficiency" requires the satisfaction of the best relationship between resources employed and results achieved. Finally, "effectiveness" requires the attainment of specific objectives set.

5.1.9 CORRUPTION, SOCIAL, AND ENVIRONMENTAL POLICIES

Procurement markets are often considered a lucrative market for potential bribery. Possible corruption scenarios include the payment of a bribe as a reward for an official who could influence the procurement process, the manipulation of tender documents to favor a specific bidder, or the use of intermediary companies to cover up the illegal activities of a corrupt official. Favoritism may also endanger the integrity of the procurement process. Since EU member states have widely divergent business and national administrative cultures, and since corruption is a highly sensitive issue, it has been difficult to attack the problem at EU level. Instead, the procurement rules of member states contain different mechanisms designed to prevent and combat corruption and favoritism.

In the EU, if the contracting authority wishes to take into account social and environmental considerations, it must refer to them in the contract notice. If it fails to do so, it may not be able to incorporate those considerations at a later stage. It is possible to include social and environmental considerations in tenders to be awarded on the basis of lowest price by incorporating the relevant requirements into technical specifications and contract conditions. Where a contracting authority proposes to award a contract on the basis of the most economically advantageous tender, there are more opportunities to incorporate social and environmental considerations. But in these cases, all award criteria used for assessing the most economically advantageous tender must meet the following four conditions: (i) the criteria must have a link to the subject matter of the contract; (ii) the criteria must be specifically and objectively quantifiable; (iii) the criteria must have been advertised/notified previously; and (iv) the criteria must respect EU law, and thus must comply with the fundamental principles of equal treatment, non-discrimination, and transparency. To sum up, the EU public procurement directives refer to social, environmental, and employment considerations that can be included into different phases of the public procurement procedure. In particular, they can be imposed by the contracting authority as performance conditions of the contract.

5.1.10 COLLECTION OF STATISTICS

According to Articles 75–76 of Directive 2004/18/EC, member states annually have to forward to the Commission a statistical report separately addressing public supply, services, and works contracts awarded by contracting authorities. The statistical report has to detail (i) the number and value of awarded contracts covered by the Directive, and (ii) the number and total value of contracts awarded pursuant to derogations to the Agreement. The data under (i) should be broken down, among others, by the contract award procedures used and the nationality of the economic operator to which the contract was awarded.

5.1.11 SMALL AND MEDIUM-SIZED ENTERPRISES AND PARTICIPATION OF FOREIGN TENDERERS

The purpose of Directives 2004/18/EC and 2004/17/EC is to open up the public procurement market to all economic operators, regardless of their size. Small and medium-sized enterprises (SMEs) are considered to be the backbone of the EU economy. Studies reveal, however, that access of SMEs to the EU public procurement market has been rather restricted (European Commission, 2011: p. 13; PwC, London Economics, and Ecorys, 2011: p. 5). The issue is addressed by the new package of EU directives on public procurement of February 2014, as it will be explained in detail under Section 5.2.2.

The EU approach to public procurement is based on the principles of free movement of goods, freedom to provide services, freedom of establishment, and prohibition of discrimination on grounds of nationality, but these principles apply only to members of the EU. Third-country access to the EU's public procurement market is not automatic. The EU is a member of the WTO Agreement on Government Procurement (GPA). Since it is binding only for signatory parties, the rules of GPA apply only to those members of the WTO that have joined GPA. As such, third countries and the EU can use the GPA to tear down trade barriers. Additionally, third countries can access the EU's public procurement market by signing free trade agreements (FTAs) with the EU that have specific market access clauses for government procurement markets. The Agreement on the European Economic Area (EEA Agreement) is such an agreement that allows the parties access to the other parties' government procurement markets.

5.2 The New Disciplines

As of April 18, 2016, new rules are applicable to public procurement in the EU. This date, in fact, represents the deadline for the transposition of Directives 2014/23, 2014/24, and 2014/25 in the national laws of EU member states. The new directives have radically innovated EU public procurement disciplines, dealing with a number of issues that were not addressed under the previous regime. The following subsections provide a brief account of the main innovations in the legal discipline on government procurement. We will not discuss issues of implementation at the member state level, as it is too early to proceed with such an assessment.

5.2.1 E-PROCUREMENT

The progressive digitalization of procurement procedures is one of the cornerstones of the new directives. In the view of the European Commission, digitalization can achieve different objectives at the same time, as it will reduce the amount of papers produced in the context of bidding procedures, speed up the process, and make it available and more easily accessible to a wider number of enterprises across the EU. Furthermore, the European Commission believes that it could lead to savings of public money in the order of 5–20 percent (European Commission, 2016a: p. 4).

Article 59 of Directive 2014/24 introduces the European Single Procurement Document (ESPD). The Directive requires that when using electronic procurement, contracting authorities use generally available and interoperable IT and systems.[7] The ESPD centers on self-declaration by bidders, replacing the many documents and forms that participants in public procurement procedures had been required to provide at the time of submitting proposals. Under the new disciplines, only the tender winners will have to provide evidence that they meet the requirements spelled out in the tender document. There will be two ways to generate an ESPD. First, the Commission has already developed and put in place a free online service.[8] Second, a structured model for data exchange is available for public buyers and all parties that are interested in being integrated into these solutions.

This innovation is complemented by the establishment of an online repository of certificates (e-Certis), pursuant to Article 61 of Directive 2014/24. The repository helps both European companies and public authorities to identify certificates and attestations

[7] Interestingly, Mavroidis (2016) reports that the clauses of electronic procurement in the GPA were inserted after proposals tabled by the EU and other developed countries.

[8] See <https://ec.europa.eu/growth/tools-databases/espd/filter?lang=en> (accessed May 16, 2016).

that are required across the jurisdictions of the twenty-eight EU member states. The system also covers Turkey and the EEA countries (Iceland, Liechtenstein, and Norway).[9] The new set of rules establishes the so-called "once-only principle." In essence, each document must be provided to public authorities only once. This simplifies the procedures for companies that act as recurrent bidders and helps them save time that they would otherwise devote to the preparation of documentation. By 2018, electronic submissions of offers will be mandatory for all contracting authorities.

5.2.2 SMALL AND MEDIUM-SIZED ENTERPRISES

The new disciplines also mark a change for SMEs, reflecting a desire by the drafters of the new directives to facilitate access to public tenders for such firms. Directive 2014/24 contains explicit provisions about division into lots, reduction of red tape in accessing procedures, access to procedures by groups of economic operators, requirements of economic and financial capacity, and subcontracting. In particular, large contracts can be divided by contracting authorities into smaller portions that allow the participation of smaller undertakings. Contracting authorities may choose not to split contracts into lots, but in that case they would have to explain why. In addition, contracting authorities should accept all bidders with adequate financial status for the contract. In the past, smaller bidders were excluded because the contracting authorities asked for high annual turnover figures even for contracts of a low monetary value. According to the new package, the required annual turnover should normally be no higher than twice the value of the contract. Finally, bidders may prove their suitability, financial status and abilities with self-declarations instead of having to provide full documentary evidence—only the winning bidder will have to provide full documentary evidence.

5.2.3 MODERNIZATION OF PROCUREMENT PROCEDURES: TAMING EXCESSIVE BUREAUCRACY

The new rules introduce shorter minimum time limits for the submission of tenders, which allows the authorities to make the procedures faster. A very important innovation is represented by the new rules for the award of contracts.[10] The system is moving away from price as the main criterion for determining the most advantageous offer for the administration. In fact, EU member states can introduce the "best quality–price ratio,"

[9] See <http://ec.europa.eu/markt/ecertis/login.do> (accessed May 16, 2016).
[10] See Article 67 of Directive 2014/24.

which includes considerations of a different nature, such as qualitative aspects or environmental and social standards.

Authorities will also gain more power, because it will be possible for them to exclude bidders from the procedures if, under the framework of another contract with the same administration, they have not adhered to the terms or have shown deficiencies.[11] More importantly, public authorities will have easier recourse to negotiation with the bidders. There may be situations where the requirements and the conditions for the execution of contracts for particularly complex projects cannot all be clarified at the outset. In such circumstances, Article 29 of Directive 2014/24 makes it easier for contracting authorities to make use of the "competitive procedure with negotiation." Under this procedure, suppliers submit their request to participate and the contracting authority decides—on the basis of grounds of exclusion established in the notice—which of the applicants to invite for negotiations. The final decision of the winning bidder will be the outcome of a process in which the contracting authority and the invited bidder negotiate over how to effectively realize the projects that constitute the object of the notice.

5.2.4 VALUE THRESHOLDS

Pursuant to Article 4, the specific monetary values above which Directive 2014/24 applies remain the same as before (i.e., depending on the subject covered): €5,186,000 for public works, €134,000 for public supply and service contracts awarded by central governments, and €207,000 for public supply and service contracts awarded by sub-central contracting authorities. Notwithstanding the above, a €705,000 threshold applies to social, health, cultural, and educational services, giving local authorities a greater degree of freedom in awarding contracts that deal with these particular areas.

5.2.5 PROCUREMENT COOPERATION AMONG PUBLIC AUTHORITIES

Article 12 of Directive 2014/24 clarifies the requirements for contracts that can be concluded between public authorities without the need to launch a call for tenders. A number of requirements must be met, including the following: the contracting authority must exercise pervasive control over the legal person that is awarded the contract; over 80 percent of the activities of the legal person must be conducted in the pursuit of tasks entrusted to it by the public authority; and there must not be direct

[11] Article 57 of Directive 2014/24.

capital participation of the contracting authority in the capital of the legal person, except for non-blocking forms of participation.

5.2.6 SPECIAL RULES FOR THE UTILITIES SECTOR

The market for utilities is peculiar in that companies that exercise commercial activities relating to utilities (water, energy, transport, etc.) sometimes operate more as commercial entities and less as public administrations. For this reason, Directive2014/25 introduces a dedicated and more flexible set of rules for these entities with regard to public procurement.

Among the main differences, it should be noted that the threshold for simplified arrangements for social, cultural, and health services is set at above €1,000,000, compared to €750,000 for public authorities. Moreover, the Directive does not indicate a preference between awarding either several contracts to various small businesses or one single contract to one large company. Third, the rules on conflicts of interest will not apply to private entities. Finally, the rules for the exclusion of companies as under the general public procurement rules are voluntary, not compulsory.

5.2.7 NEW RULES ON CONFLICTS OF INTEREST, TRANSPARENCY, AND FAIR PLAY

For the first time, the new discipline on EU public procurement introduces a definition of the concept of conflict of interests. Article 24.2 of Directive 2014/24 stipulates that:

> The concept of conflicts of interest shall at least cover any situation where staff members of the contracting authority or of a procurement service provider acting on behalf of the contracting authority who are involved in the conduct of the procurement procedure or may influence the outcome of that procedure have, directly or indirectly, a financial, economic or other personal interest which might be perceived to compromise their impartiality and independence in the context of the procurement procedure.

Member states, pursuant to the Directive, are required to take all necessary measures to ensure that distortions to competition are avoided and that all the participants in procurement procedures are treated in a fair and equitable fashion. Directive 2014/23 reaffirms the rules with regard to the exclusion of companies from procurement procedures when, for instance, the bidder has unduly exercised its influence over the contracting authority, has made fraudulent use of confidential information that should not have been in its possession, or has rendered false statements in order to gain an advantage in the context of the procedures.

Furthermore, the new directives introduce rules with regard to the period following the award. In particular, doubts had emerged with regards to the rules governing the modification of contracts during this period. Article 43 of Directive 2014/23 makes it clear that the contracting authorities will not have to issue a new call if the possibility for modifications and precise review clauses were clearly spelled out in the original call for tender.

Finally, the directives introduce new rules on transparency and on the enhancement of the tools for the exchange of information between national authorities and the European Commission. Article 45 of Directive 2014/23 introduces specific requirements for domestic authorities: they must make the results of their monitoring activities public, and they must submit a report to the Commission every three years containing details on the most frequent causes of incorrect application of the rules.

5.2.8 BEST QUALITY–PRICE RATIO

The new rules make it easier for contracting authorities to take social aspects into account when awarding procurement contracts. In particular, Article 67.2 of Directive 2014/24 clarifies the meaning of the concept of the "most economically advantageous tender":

> The most economically advantageous tender from the point of view of the contracting authority shall be identified on the basis of the price or cost, using a cost-effectiveness approach, such as life-cycle costing in accordance with Article 68, and may include the best price-quality ratio, which shall be assessed on the basis of criteria, including qualitative, environmental and/or social aspects, linked to the subject-matter of the public contract in question.

The express reference to social aspects is particularly relevant, as the decisions of contracting authorities do not have to be based on price alone but can take into account other aspects, permitting the choice of other tenders that provide greater social advantages (e.g., in terms of environmental impact or the effects on employment among disadvantaged sectors of society).

5.3 Challenge and Review Mechanisms

Challenge mechanisms are regulated by the Remedies Directives, which consist of the public sector Remedies Directive 89/665/EC and the utilities sector Remedies Directive 92/13/EC. The Directives were amended by Directive 2007/66/EC. The Directives provide for remedies that are available to any economic operator that has, or has had, an interest in obtaining a particular contract and that perceives itself to have been harmed by an alleged violation of the applicable procurement rules. The

Directives require member states to ensure that three types of remedies are available: interim measures, set asides, and award for damages. Interim measures include (i) the suspension of the implementation of any decision taken by the contracting authority; (ii) the suspension of the whole contract award procedure; and (iii) the provisional correction of a breach. The application of the set-aside remedy cancels or renders ineffective a contracting decision taken unlawfully, or otherwise corrects an unlawful situation. This includes (i) the removal of discriminatory technical, economic or financial specifications in the contract notice, tender documents, or any other document relating to the contract award procedure; (ii) the annulment of an unlawful contracting decision; or (ii) the positive correction of any unlawful document or contracting decision. Damages take the form of compensation to be paid to economic operators found to have been harmed by an infringement of the public procurement rules.

The Directives require that member states provide for a standstill period at the contract award stage—when economic operators participating in the procurement process are notified of a contract award decision. This standstill period allows for the challenge of an award procedure before it is too late. In the implementation of the Directives, review bodies and contracting authorities must observe the general principles of non-discrimination, effectiveness, and transparency. Thus, the Directives allow economic operators to request the enforcement of the public procurement rules, and provide them with rights under those rules in cases where a contracting authority—intentionally or unintentionally—fails to comply with the law. The actions, resulting in increased lawfulness and transparency, build confidence among businesses and facilitate the opening of local public contracts markets to foreign competition. In the case of utilities and defense procurement, the Utilities and the Defense and Security Directives, respectively, include specific provisions on remedies similar to those contained in Directive 89/665/EC as amended by Directive 2007/66/EC.

The discipline on public procurement under EU law also provides for instruments to deal with the coordination of the various systems of review that are in place in the twenty-eight member states of the EU. Two directives set forth minimum standards that have to be respected in the domestic jurisdictions of the member states in order to provide participants in the bid who believe that the procurement procedures did not respect the necessary procedural guarantees the possibility to seek remedies.

The European Commission is actively engaged in efforts toward greater transparency with regard to public procurement. Two elements are of particular importance concerning the present discussion of the review mechanism. First, the European Commission has developed "Public Procurement Indicators," with the aim of achieving a fair overview of the state of public procurement in the EU. In February 2016, the European Commission published a report on Public Procurement Indicators for the year 2014 that contains detailed information concerning the number of notices, contracts awarded, and the value of the tender procedures, broken down by member states (European

Commission, 2016b). Second, the Commission launched a public consultation to solicit views on the effectiveness of the provisions of Directive 2007/66/EC with regard to the review mechanisms.[12]

The European Commission has published annual reports concerning the implementation of the Directives on public procurement at the member state level. The most recent results were made public in the *Annual Public Procurement Implementation Review* for 2013 (European Commission, 2014). This document provides information on, *inter alia*, the use of review mechanisms at the domestic level, including data on the ratio of challenged procedures and the total number of public procurement procedures in place. This ratio is generally low in all member states, although it reaches a peak of 12.3 percent in Latvia. The average success rate of complainants before domestic review mechanisms is around one-third. The limited number of challenges in most member states is difficult to interpret. It could signal that authorities are generally compliant with the rules on public procurement, or that companies are hesitant to engage in a conflict with the domestic authorities.

The sectors that are most commonly affected by problems, and hence more likely to generate challenges, are ICT services and construction (works) contracts. Among the provisions most frequently alleged to be violated are transparency and non-discrimination (equal treatment).

5.4 **Conclusion**

Overall, the EU legal framework governing public procurement is consistent with the GPA, including on the principle of non-discrimination. The exceptions regime is also largely compliant with the GPA. The innovations introduced by the EU in the directives that were approved in 2014 may represent useful blueprints for future negotiations in the context of the GPA. The challenge/review reports compiled by the EU are one dimension in which the EU differentiates itself from other regimes. This is an initiative that should be emulated by other jurisdictions and that, arguably, would greatly enhance transparency in the GPA context. Also noteworthy in the new directives is the greater latitude accorded to competitive negotiations as a procurement tool. Finally, the absence of industrial policy-motivated provisions of the type that are found in procurement legislation in other countries, such as the US, is particularly distinctive in the EU procurement regime.

[12] See <http://ec.europa.eu/growth/tools-databases/newsroom/cf/itemdetail.cfm?item_id=8244> (accessed May 18, 2016).

REFERENCES

Arrowsmith, S. 2014. *The Law of Public and Utilities Procurement*, 3rd edn, vol. 1. London: Sweet & Maxwell.

Arrowsmith, S., Faustino, B., Heuninckx, B., Treumer, S., and Fejo, J. 2011. "EU Public Procurement Law: An Introduction." EU Asia Inter University Network for Teaching and Research in Public Procurement Regulation, University of Nottingham (available at: <http://www.nottingham.ac.uk/pprg/documentsarchive/asialinkmaterials/eupublicprocurementlawintroduction.pdf> (accessed July 21, 2016)).

European Commission. 2011. "EU Public Procurement Legislation: Delivering Results," Summary of Evaluation Reports, Brussels.

European Commission. 2014. "Annual Public Procurement Implementation Review", Brussels, August (available at: <http://ec.europa.eu/internal_market/publicprocurement/docs/implementation/20140820-staff-working-document_en.pdf> (accessed August 4, 2016)).

European Commission. 2016a. "EU Public Procurement Reform: Less Bureaucracy, Higher Efficiency," Brussels, April (available at: http://ec.europa.eu/growth/single-market/public-procurement/rules-implementation/index_en.htm (accessed July 21, 2016)).

European Commission. 2016b. "Public Procurement Indicators 2014," Brussels.

Mavroidis, P. C. 2016. *The Regulation of International Trade*, 2 vols. Cambridge, MA: MIT Press.

OECD. 2010. "Public Procurement in EU Member States—The Regulation of Contract Below the EU Thresholds and in Areas Not Covered by the Detailed Rules of the EU Directives." SIGMA Papers No. 45. Paris: OECD Publishing.

PwC, London Economics, and Ecorys. 2011. "Public Procurement in Europe: Cost and Effectiveness." Report for the European Commission, March.

Stockhammer, K. 2008. "Overview and Principles of Public Procurement." PowerPoint presentation, INTERACT Point Vienna (available at: <http://www.northernperiphery.eu/files/archive/Downloads/Project_Management_Guidance/Public_Procurement/Public_Procurement%20_INTERACT.pdf> (accessed July 21, 2016)).

6 Public Procurement in Global and Regional Trade Agreements

Lessons Learned in Armenia

Eliza Niewiadomska and Astghik Solomonyan

6.1 The EBRD-UNCITRAL Public Procurement Reform Initiative

The EBRD-UNCITRAL Initiative embraces public procurement reform support activities, resorted to due to their potential transition impact, and advocates the benefits of public procurement reform in an era of fiscal restraint.[1] The EBRD-UNCITRAL Initiative is currently active in Armenia, the Kyrgyz Republic, Mongolia, and Tajikistan, and has also encouraged Azerbaijan, Belarus, and Kazakhstan to update their procurement systems. Presently, the EBRD-UNCITRAL Initiative's reform support program comprises of (a) a comparative legal diagnostic; (b) a regional series of policy workshops; and (c) country-specific technical cooperation projects developed with governments in the region to help modernize their public procurement laws and practices (Box 6.1).

6.2 Facilitating Reforms: What Governments Need

With the aim of facilitating interest in reforms, the EBRD-UNCITRAL Initiative ran a series of policy workshops in the CIS region and Mongolia between October 2011 and June 2013. The policy workshops were facilitated by the EBRD-UNCITRAL Public Procurement Reform Initiative in cooperation with the World Bank and the Organisation for Economic Co-operation and Development (OECD) Anti-Corruption Network.

[1] See <http://ppi-ebrd-uncitral.com/> (accessed July 22, 2016).

BOX 6.1 WHAT IS THE NEW POLICY MESSAGE IN THE REFORM CONTEXT?

- Public procurement has a significant impact on economic performance and national development.
- Focus on the efficiency of procurement procedures without compromising on transparency safeguards.
- Fit-for-purpose: providing suitable procurement methods for each project/contract.
- Electronic procurement (eProcurement) tools: improving transparency of procurement (and helping get rid of bureaucracy).
- More professional procurement: better qualified officers for better accountability for procurement decisions.
- Market access: engaging local suppliers, SMEs in particular.

The policy workshops were focused on the 2011 UNCITRAL Model Law on Public Procurement, which is recognized as an effective tool to facilitate reforms in different countries with different backgrounds and levels of economic development. The global appeal of the UNCITRAL Model Law results from UNCITRAL's approach to identifying best practice through intergovernmental meetings, with all regions and countries of the world sharing their experience. As a result, the Model Law reflects international best practice in public procurement as tested by several governments, and its policy standards are suitable for all countries, including transition ones. The objective of the 2011 text of the UNCITRAL Model Law was to present modern procurement policy, based on leading international practice and structured as a drafting template for national procurement legislation. In fact, the UNCITRAL Model Law provisions have sufficient detail to be incorporated into national legislation and are adaptable to allow for different international obligations (e.g., WTO, European Union, international financial institutions) and policy goals of governments undertaking public procurement reforms.[2]

The EBRD-UNCITRAL Initiative team, UNCITRAL Secretariat representatives, and policy advisers participated in the workshops and contributed to the open and constructive discussions, training materials, and publications. Based on the public procurement reform agenda shaped at the policy workshops organized under the EBRD-UNCITRAL Initiative, a public procurement reform agenda, along with proposals for country-specific technical cooperation projects, was developed with the governments of Armenia, the Kyrgyz Republic, Mongolia, and Tajikistan. One lesson learned from the discussions held at these workshops is that no matter how different their political objectives may be, governments are often interested in finding out the answers to questions such as how updating their procurement laws will help in their GPA accession,

[2] For further explanation of the UNCITRAL Model Law provisions, see the "Guide to Enactment of the UNCITRAL Model Law on Public Procurement" at: <http://www.uncitral.org/pdf/english/texts/procurem/ml-procurement-2011/Guide-Enactment-Model-Law-Public-Procurement-e.pdf> (accessed July 22, 2016).

what the modern standards for centralized purchasing and review and remedies procedures are, and how the UNCITRAL Model Law can be utilized to provide a basis for implementing eProcurement tools. These topics were discussed across the EBRD region, from Yerevan to Ulaanbaatar, and Armenia happened to be the first country where the EBRD-UNCITRAL Initiative was engaged in supporting reform activities.

6.3 **Public Procurement Reforms in Armenia**

6.3.1 STARTING POINT

Armenia is a small market with a GDP of US$9.37 billion and a population of 3.1 million (as of 2010). The market is isolated, and international trade is restricted due to the conflict with Azerbaijan and a strained relationship with Turkey. International trade is conducted with the Russian Federation via Georgia, and to a limited extent with the European Union. Armenia's potential growth is constrained by its landlocked position and limited access to neighboring markets, which significantly limits the development of its export industry and lowers its investment attractiveness. The country's dependence on undiversified, low value-added commodity exports and on remittance flows makes it vulnerable to negative terms of trade shocks. In order to increase its competitiveness and prosperity, Armenia still requires substantial investments to diversify its industrial base and improve its physical infrastructure, as well as further efforts to promote openness and liberalization.

The Armenian authorities aim to adopt various measures to enhance the business environment and to promote transparency. The implementation of inspection reforms, the reduction of red tape, and the easing of the tax administration burden have resulted in a tangible improvement in Armenia's business climate. In the World Bank's 2014 *Doing Business* report, Armenia ranked thirty-seventh out of 189 countries.[3] However, the government has not yet taken decisive action against the "black economy" or to tackle corruption issues, especially in procurement and the tax and customs areas.

The public procurement market in Armenia is worth close to 19 percent of GDP (OECD, 2012) thanks to large public sector expenses, the "serving administration" model, and the limited development of the local service sector. Before the reforms, high-value public procurement contracts in Armenia were procured by a central purchasing agency and were conducted traditionally using paper-based procedures, except for notices that were published on the website of the Ministry of Finance. The relevant

[3] Available at: <http://www.doingbusiness.org/data/exploreeconomies/armenia/> (accessed July 22, 2016).

legislation in place was rather basic, but in principle was compliant with the 1994 UNCITRAL Model Law. Small-value contracts were procured by individual contracting entities using requests for quotation, although with lower competition standards compared to the 1994 Model Law—in accordance with Article 43 of the Armenian public procurement law from 2000—it was sufficient to invite two suppliers to provide a price quotation and to receive one quotation in order to sign a public contract.

Influenced by the 2004 EU public procurement directives and the political decision to open negotiations to join the WTO's Agreement on Government Procurement (GPA), the 2009 Armenian government public procurement reform strategy (Government Protocol Decision N17 of April 23, 2009—Strategy on improving procurement system) advocated a new legislation, a new institutional framework, and full decentralization of public procurement, with contracting entities in full charge of their individual budgets. In short, the aim was to join the WTO's Agreement on Government Procurement based on EU directive-oriented legislation, to decentralize the national public procurement system, and to introduce eProcurement tools at the same time.

6.3.2 THE WTO GPA ACCESSION AS A DRIVING FORCE FOR REFORMS

The GPA is a legally binding and enforceable international agreement in the area of public procurement,[4] which is becoming an increasingly important element of the global trade framework.[5] It relates to public contracts—estimated to account for more than 15 percent of GDP in many countries worldwide—and promotes competition and good governance. The fundamental aim of the GPA is to mutually open government procurement markets among its parties. As a result of several rounds of negotiations, the GPA parties have opened procurement activities worth an estimated US$1.7 trillion annually to international competition. The GPA is a plurilateral agreement within the framework of the WTO, meaning that not all WTO members are parties to the Agreement. At present, the Agreement has seventeen parties comprising forty-seven WTO members (including, among others, the European Union and all its twenty-eight member states, the United States, Canada, Japan, Korea, New Zealand, Armenia, and Montenegro). All WTO members are eligible to accede to the GPA. At present, Moldova and Ukraine have completed negotiations and another nine WTO members are in the process of acceding. The driving force of the GPA are the principles of non-discrimination and transparency that apply to public contracts above the GPA thresholds and to the contracting authorities mentioned in the parties' Annexes negotiated with all other member states. The Republic of Armenia was the first developing country to join the GPA's member states

[4] For more about accession to the GPA, see Arrowsmith and Anderson (2011).
[5] For further analysis of the GPA, see Chapters 1 and 4.

on September 15, 2011, and the first developing country that has made its domestic public procurement legislation compliant with international best practice as laid down in the GPA. Armenia also announced market transparency and openness in terms of procurement alongside the reform of electronic procurement to make local procurement opportunities more accessible for foreign suppliers.

Why would a small developing country such as Armenia want to become a GPA member? First, GPA membership for small countries means international recognition and proof that the public procurement legislation of the country is compliant with international best practice. This is very important, especially for cooperation with development partners. Although most big infrastructure projects are contracted in accordance with the procurement rules of the international financial organizations,[6] the fact that it is committed to complying with international best practice definitely scores points for a country receiving a grant or loan. Second, even though the capacities of local suppliers are currently insufficient to bid for contracts in most of the GPA countries, this might change over time, especially if foreign companies participate in local tenders. They can bring know-how and new technologies and subcontract local companies at first, after which the local suppliers will be able to develop the capacity necessary for bidding outside the country. Third, though the GPA is a flexible tool, the basic principles of transparency and non-discrimination are cornerstones that cannot be overruled. Thus, the national legislation will be stable in terms of its basic principles and the main structure of the local procurement system. In addition, GPA member states influence trends in procurement policies and the development of the GPA over time. A developing country can benefit from policy advances in developed countries and become a country that incorporates new regulatory techniques, leading to more effective and efficient procurement practices.

For many countries, the decision to join the GPA can also depend on the bureaucratic requirements related to the process of negotiations, notifications, and participation in the working programs. The example of Armenia provides a good illustration of a speedy process of negotiations, since Armenia joined the GPA less than two years after opening the negotiations process. It is necessary to stress that the process of joining the GPA was accompanied by the current reform of the public procurement sector, including the introduction of electronic procurement. As a result, the new Law on Procurement was adopted on December 22, 2010 and entered into force on January 1, 2011.[7] When negotiating with the GPA members, Armenia significantly opened its market and

[6] For example, the North–South road corridor is divided into several tranches and is financed by the Asian Development Bank (ADB) (Tranche 1, Tranche 2, and co-financing of Tranche 3), the European Investment Bank (EIB) (co-financing of Tranche 3), the Eurasian Development Bank (co-financing of Tranche 4), and the EBRD (a new bridge over the River Debed at the Bagratashen checkpoint).

[7] The Law can be found at: <http://www.arlis.am/DocumentView.aspx?DocID=75494> (accessed July 22, 2016).

included all central government entities and all municipalities (only city communities are included as villages are considered local self government bodies (municipalities) in accordance with Armenian Law but are not included in the Annex 2 offer). There are few restrictions and exclusions, and these mainly relate to procurement for national security and defense (traditionally purchased by the Armenian government from the Russian Federation).[8] Thus, Armenia has decided to open up its market to foreign suppliers, with only very few exceptions, to allow for better competition and enhancement of international trade. It is a policy choice for each country to decide on the level of openness that it wants to offer to the other GPA members, but local suppliers were not harmed as a result of Armenia granting market access to international suppliers.

6.3.3 REFORM IMPLEMENTATION CHALLENGES

The 2009 reform strategy envisaged the adoption of a new regulatory framework, which would be compliant with the GPA standards, and the introduction of the eProcurement reform in two phases: first the implementation of e-tendering, and then e-purchasing tools. It was considered that this radical change—total centralization to decentralization—would be feasible due to the introduction of a single eProcurement platform, available to all contracting entities free of charge and supporting the entire procurement procedure—from the preparation of the procurement, notices, and contract award, through to contract performance review.

However, while the reform strategy envisaged eProcurement tools supporting the entire cycle of the public procurement process, the e-tendering and e-purchasing functionalities mentioned in the strategy did not cover the entire procurement process. This omission in the reform planning caused serious problems at a later stage. Also, to allow for the phased implementation of eProcurement, the 2009 strategy decided on the optional use of eProcurement tools throughout the first two years, with mandatory use of the eProcurement procedures by all contracting entities when the eProcurement platform was to be fully operational. During the first two years, the newly appointed contracting entities could elect to either use the procurement procedures available on the eProcurement platform or to conduct their procurement in a paper-based format.

While this reform plan was reasonable in principle, the reforms revealed the newly appointed contracting entities to be unprepared: government entities and municipalities

[8] The exclusions are listed in Annex 1 of Armenia's offer: "Ministry of Defence of the RA, National Security Service of the RA, Administration of the National Security Council of the RA and Police of the RA adjunct to the Government of the Republic of Armenia: For these entities the Agreement only covers the procurement of the following categories subject to Republic of Armenia determinations under paragraph 1 of Article III." Examples of categories included in the list are vehicular equipment components; construction, mining, excavating, and highway maintenance equipment; medical, dental, and veterinary equipment and supplies, and so on.

had never before conducted high-value procurement, and their staff had no experience in conducting tenders. While some training on how to use the new eProcurement tools had been provided, decentralization of the public procurement system was not supported by a government-sponsored training scheme for public procurement officers, and contracting entities therefore had no trained procurement officers to conduct their procurement procedures, either in paper-based or electronic format. To support decentralization, a public procurement training unit was created in the Procurement Support Centre, but it worked on the assumption that contracting entities would be able to afford to train their procurement officers at their own expense. Training was financed by the state budget and was described as a function of the PSC in the Law of 2010. In 2011, when the new primary law entered into force, no official government-sponsored training program for procurement officers was in place, and no guidelines for contracting entities were readily available.

The reform created new regulatory institutions: a regulatory authority at the Ministry of Finance, a Procurement Support Center, and a procurement review board. However, the primary legislation left the roles of these bodies to be prescribed in secondary legislation and failed to stipulate the competencies and procedures necessary in the decentralized procurement system. For instance, the regulatory authority at the Ministry of Finance was not furnished with the powers to undertake effective *ex ante* control or request accurate information on procurements concluded by newly decentralized contracting entities. In addition, the newly established public procurement review board struggled to perform its duties to the required standard. This was mainly due to the ad hoc system for appointing review panels, which did not provide incentives to take this function seriously, and a lack of expertise in handling procurement complaints.

Also, while the government adopted a reasonable legal framework, it failed to adequately determine the eProcurement system business model, and specifically to decide whether the national eProcurement platform would be government owned and managed, or operated under a mixed system with service level agreement (SLA) contracts with a platform provider. The government-owned model was selected without adequate planning for how the eProcurement platform would be purchased and owned, how its maintenance and future development would be carried out, or how the purchase of additional modules would be financed. Therefore, as a result of cooperation with the World Bank, only an e-tendering system was purchased in 2008, and the government plan did not envisage the way forward. The eProcurement reform, which was launched to improve transparency of the public procurement system and save the resources of contracting authorities and economic operators, did not produce the intended result due to mismanagement, and in fact to mis-procurement of the electronic procurement tools.

As a result of implementation problems, despite significant improvements in the public procurement "law on the books," Armenia ranked at the bottom of

Transparency International's Corruption Perception Index list in 2011 (129th out of 183 countries/territories), with the Control of Corruption Index indicating effectiveness of 31 percent.[9]

6.3.4 OUTCOME OF THE REFORMS

6.3.4.1 Procurement Methods in Armenia

The current Armenian Law on Procurement includes the procurement methods envisaged by the GPA: open tender, restricted tender, and negotiated procedure without publication of notice. However, based on 2014 data provided by the Armenian Ministry of Finance, in practice most of public contracts above the GPA threshold are awarded in the country not via an open tender, but via a price-quotation procedure without notification. This procedure is called "framework agreements" in Armenian law, but is very different from the framework agreement method used in the EU member states or the other GPA countries. In Armenia, the "framework agreements procedure" can be used for purchasing goods, services, or works, as included in the list approved by the Minister of Finance, regardless of their value. Second, the "framework agreements" procedure is accessible only to suppliers registered on the official list at the Procurement Support Centre. This registration comes without any checking for eligibility or qualification. In this "framework agreements procedure," in the absence of any notification, an invitation with a basic technical specification is circulated by the contracting entity to suppliers registered by the Procurement Support Centre and, upon receiving their price proposals, the lowest priced is selected. Foreign companies may potentially register for the "framework agreements procedure," but as of November 5, 2015, only seven foreign suppliers had registered for procurement of foods, and chemical and IT equipment. Five of these companies are from Russia, one is from the Netherlands, and one is from the United States. This system of so-called "framework agreements" in fact precludes open competition and creates an indirect barrier to international trade in the public procurement sector in Armenia.

The annual procurement report reveals that in 2014, 385 open procedures and one restricted procedure were organized in Armenia.[10] In contrast, the negotiated procedure without publication of notice (single sourcing) is used very frequently in the country, with 11,683 such procedures organized in 2014. In addition to the "framework agreements procedure," direct contracting under the "negotiated procedure without publication" is the most frequently used procurement method in the Armenian public

[9] Available at: <http://www.transparency.org/cpi2011> (accessed July 22, 2016).

[10] The report can be found at: <http://gnumner.am/am/category/349/1.html> (accessed July 22, 2016).

Table 6.1 Public contracts awarded above the GPA threshold by procurement procedure (in million euros)

Procurement method	Works	Goods	Services	Total
Open procedure	–	6,393.4	8,161.7	14,555.2
Framework agreements	6,878.9	59,018.9	2,726,1	68,623.9
Negotiated procedure without publication	8,269.4	3,354.2	2,673.1	14,296.9
Negotiated procedure with publication	6,623.1	8,650.7	1,099.4	16,373.3
Competitive dialogue	–	4,453.4	–	4,453.4

Note: The approximate amount in euros is based Central Bank of Armenia rate as of November 15, 2015 (1 euro = 518 Armenian dram).

procurement sector. Table 6.1 provides the complete data on the value of the awarded contracts above the GPA threshold.

The GPA sets out very limited cases where the use of the limited tendering is acceptable, and all GPA countries are required to incorporate these restrictions into their legislation. In the Armenian legislation, "on the books" compliance is achieved in principle, but national procurement practice is a different matter. Cases for limited tendering are not interpreted strictly. In the absence of effective monitoring by the Ministry of Finance, Armenian contracting entities misuse the negotiated procedure without publication and, instead of organizing tenders, apply the negotiated procedure without publication for majority of their procurement.

6.3.4.2 Access to Information on Procurement Opportunities

Armenian legislation provides for certain provisions regarding the availability of information on procurement in a language that is appropriate for foreign suppliers. Contract notices in the open procedure (i.e., contracts estimated at more than 20 million Armenian dram, or AMD) are published in English and Russian. In addition, if the contract's estimated value is more than AMD50 million the tenders can be submitted in English or Russian. Data on procurement contracts reveal that there were twenty such tenders in Armenia in 2014.

6.3.4.3 Review Body in Armenia

One of the major "innovations" of the 2011 law was the creation of the Procurement Review Board (PRB) in charge of the examination of public procurement complaints.[11]

[11] For a detailed analysis of the review body functions in Armenia, see Transparency International (2014).

The PRB was created as an ad hoc body composed of representatives of contracting authorities and civil society. Presently, it consists of seventy-two members, with only three members representing civil society organizations. Reviewing complaints is an (unpaid) additional duty on top of PRB members' regular employment duties at the contracting entity. In addition, since the PRB is not an "organization" in the institutional sense but an ad hoc committee, it was decided that the Procurement Support Center should support the PRB as a Secretariat. Still, on the top of secretarial and administrative duties, the Procurement Support Center was given the power of initial review of complaints and to provide their legal opinion to the PRB member deciding on the complaints. This raised several concerns, the first being that the Procurement Support Center is not independent, but a government agency under direct report to the Prime Minister's Office. Second, the PRB's ad hoc panels almost always follow the opinion of the Procurement Support Center. As a consequence of being only an ad hoc body, the final decisions of the PRB are also drafted by the Procurement Support Center Secretariat, and the panel members merely sign the decisions prepared for them by the Secretariat.

At the same time, the Procurement Support Center provides advice to contracting authorities free of charge, and to local suppliers and contractors as a professional consulting service. The potential for conflict of interest is very real—it could be the case that based on the advice of the Procurement Support Center, a contracting authority or local supplier takes a specific action (or refrains from it), which then results in a complaint. And with the same Procurement Support Center providing the initial reviews of complaints and drafting the review decisions, it is no surprise that local suppliers' and contractors' trust in the review system has not been high since the system was established in 2011.

There are very few complaints submitted in Armenia; Table 6.2 presents the relevant information provided in the records for 2011–14.

The only plausible solution for Armenia to fulfil the GPA standards on domestic review in practice would be the creation of an independent and professional institution

Table 6.2 Quantitative indicators of complaints, 2011–14

N	Received complaints	2011	2012	2013	30.12.2014
1	Satisfied	15	17	19	20
2	Rejected	5	11	20	24
3	Left without examination[a]	6	10	10	2
4	In the process of examination	–	–	–	1
5	Concluded (Restricted procedure*)				1
Total		26	38	49	48

Note: [a] These are the cases when the complaint was revoked. In such a case, the review procedure is terminated.

dedicated to public procurement review. As is demonstrated by the case of Cyprus, such a function can easily be fulfilled by three professionals appointed as an administrative tribunal. It is expected that once such an independent tribunal is created, the trust of suppliers will increase and this will result in more complaints. Again, the case of Cyprus demonstrates that a small administrative tribunal can be capable of handling 400 review cases per year, ten times more than are presently recorded in Armenia.

6.3.4.4 Availability of Procurement Data

According to the annual national public procurement report, contracts above the GPA threshold cover mostly goods (eighty contracts); there have been only three contracts above the GPA threshold for procurement of works, and thirteen contracts for services. Public contracts above the GPA thresholds are usually awarded by central government (eighty-seven contracts). Only one municipality (the City of Yerevan) and eight regional administrative bodies have concluded contracts above the GPA thresholds.

In order to assess the current coverage of the GPA for Armenia, the relative value of these contracts needs to be taken into consideration. The value of above-threshold procurement based on the 2014 national public procurement report constitutes 20 percent of the total annual value of public procurement. The contracting authorities that submitted data have concluded contracts above the GPA thresholds with a total value of AMD61,281.1 million, out of total procurement worth AMD345,076.7 million. It should also be noted that key infrastructure projects in Armenia are not procured under the national public procurement law because they are funded by loans from multilateral development banks. Table 6.3 presents the numbers and value of above-threshold procurement, as well a list of the contracting authorities that have concluded such contracts.

The data collected are not comprehensive because of the lack of appropriate methodology and legal framework. When the procurement system was decentralized, no suitable monitoring and reporting scheme was established. In theory, there is a requirement to report to the Procurement Support Center on awarded contracts (Decree of the Minister of Finance N 1169-N dated December 25, 2012), but it is not effective; there are no sanctions for not reporting. For example, in 2014, twenty-seven out of forty-nine municipalities did not report their procurement at all.

A lack of accurate procurement statistics is one of the outcomes of the decentralization of the Armenian procurement system in 2011.[12] As a result of the total decentralization,

[12] Before decentralization, all tenders were run by the procurement agency in the Ministry of Finance, and requests for price quotations by individual contracting entities were reported on an annual basis. This was abolished by the reform as the electronic system was supposed to collect the data automatically, but this has not yet been introduced.

Table 6.3 Contracts above the threshold concluded in 2014

Annex 1

N	Name of the Contracting Authority	Works		Goods		Services	
		Number of concluded contracts	Value of the concluded contracts (EUR)	Number of concluded contracts	Value of the concluded contracts (EUR)	Number of concluded contracts	Value of the concluded contracts (EUR)
1	2	3	4	5	6	7	8
1	National Assembly			1	255,753		
2	Staff of the Government					1	459,460
3	Ministry of Finance	2	15,148,378	2	1,421,865		
4	Police adjunct to the Government			12	10,905,946	1	7,702,339
5	Ministry of Defence			45	48,614,948	4	1,660,934
6	State National Security Service adjunct to the Government			2	1,055,917		
7	Urban Development PIU of the Ministry of Urban Development	1	6,623,166				
8	State Protection Service			1	287,450		
9	Ministry of Agriculture			1	903,633		
10	Penitentiary Department of the Ministry of Justice			3	1,165,438		
11	Ministry of Regional Administration and Emergency Situations			2	331,197		
12	State Protection General Department			2	399,166		
13	Ministry of Labour and Social Affairs					1	1,065,152

(continued)

Table 6.3 Continued

N	Name of the Contracting Authority	Works		Goods		Services	
		Number of concluded contracts	Value of the concluded contracts (EUR)	Number of concluded contracts	Value of the concluded contracts (EUR)	Number of concluded contracts	Value of the concluded contracts (EUR)
1	2	3	4	5	6	7	8
14	Ministry of Education and Science					3	1,443,494
15	Ministry of Health			3	1,424,160		
16	Yerevan Municipality			1	2,716,726		
17	Organisations under the supervision of Yerevan Municipality			1	829,689		
18	Organisations under the supervision of the Ministry of Energy and Natural Resources			3	2,908,422	2	1,229,795
19	Organisations under the supervision of the Ministry of Transport and Communication			1	8,650,876	1	1,099,421
	Total, including						
	Works	3	**21,771,544**				
	Goods			**80**	**81,871,186**		
	Services					13	**14,660,596**

Source: Annual procurement report prepared by the Procurement Support Centre (available at: <http://gnumner.am/am/category/349/1.html> (accessed July 22, 2016), in Armenian only).

around 4,000 contracting authorities were newly created, and their main problems are clear: procurement officers did not receive proper procurement training; the national electronic procurement system was lacking in functionalities due to technical problems; and procurement monitoring and budgetary supervision were almost impossible in a system where each and every school and kindergarten is an independent contracting authority and may not be accountable for the way it spends its budget. The appropriate authorities are now trying to solve the problems by introducing a new module on reporting that will be connected to the e-tendering system and will use the data available on the platform to produce statistical reports.

6.3.4.5 Market Access after GPA Accession

In total in 2015, the Ministry of Finance of Armenia approved thirty-one contracts with twenty foreign suppliers with no subsidiaries in Armenia (as of November 6, 2015). It is important to note that these suppliers are different from those registered under the framework agreements scheme.

Twenty-five of the above-mentioned public contracts were concluded using the negotiated procedure without publication (direct contracting); there were three open procedures, one competitive dialogue, and one negotiated procedure with announcement. The main contracting authorities procuring from foreign suppliers were the General Department of Civil Aviation, adjunct to the Government of Armenia (nine contracts); the Staff of the President (six contracts), the Ministry of Health (four contracts); the Ministry of Agriculture (three contracts), the police, adjunct to the Government of Armenia (three contracts); Staff of the Government (two contracts); the Ministry of Finance (two contracts); the Ministry of Defence (one contract); and the Central Electoral Commission (one contract). Unfortunately, there are no comprehensive data available on foreign participation due to the decentralization of the procurement system and contracting entities not being required to report whether their supplier is local or foreign.

6.3.4.6 Implementation of Equal Treatment and Non-Discrimination Principles

The latest amendments to the Armenian legislation adopted by the government in the secondary legislation in April 2015 unfortunately contradict the principle of non-discrimination and set a 15 percent price preference for goods originated from the EEU countries (Armenia, Russia, Belarus, Kazakhstan, and the Kyrgyz Republic) if the procurement value is below AMD70 million (approximately the GPA threshold in national currency). This is a new form of preference, as price preference is given not only to local goods but also to goods from other countries that are in the same regional trade agreement (in this case, the Eurasian Economic Union Treaty). Even taking into account that the newly introduced price preference relates to procurement below the GPA thresholds, this norm of the secondary legislation clearly contradicts the primary legislation (Article 6), which explicitly provides that any entity, regardless of being a foreign natural person or a legal entity, has equal right to participation in the public procurement process. It needs to be underlined that the Eurasian Economic Union Treaty did not require the introduction of any such provisions; in fact, the Eurasian Economic Union

Treaty acknowledges that whenever national legislation provides for any price preference, it should be extended to suppliers from the Eurasian Economic Union Treaty countries.

6.4 External Implications of the Public Procurement Reform Project in Armenia

At the trade level, setting compliance and implementation issues aside, Armenia completed the GPA negotiations and was accepted as a GPA member on condition of the adoption of a new public procurement primary legislation compliant with the 1994 GPA. Such legislation was adopted and entered into force in 2011 and, except for the "framework agreements procedure," can be considered to fulfil the 1994 GPA mandatory obligations. Simultaneously, Armenia was negotiating a chapter on public procurement within a regional trade agreement (RTA) with the European Commission. The Deep and Comprehensive Free Trade Agreement (DCFTA)—requiring, in principle, harmonization with the EU policies to the level of compliance with the 1994 GPA mandatory standards—was abandoned in 2013. As a replacement for the DCFTA, in October 2015 the EU Commission announced the opening of negotiations of a new "framework" with Armenia, within the EU Neighbourhood instruments. It is yet to be confirmed whether this framework will be reflected in national public procurement policies.

At the same time as the DCFTA with the EU Commission was abandoned, a customs union (CU) with the Russian Federation, Kazakhstan, and Belarus came into negotiations in 2013. The customs union included an agreement on public procurement which, in the agreement's language, "*aimed at harmonizing the public procurement regime of the CU members and conducting a common policy in the area of public procurement*," while in fact requiring full harmonization of procurement policies with the newly adopted federal government contracts law of the Russian Federation.

Next, the Eurasian Economic Union Treaty (EEUT) was signed in Astana in May 2014, as a general agreement with a chapter on public procurement. This chapter specifies harmonization requirements for public procurement laws of signatory countries and creates a requirement for each country to adopt a roadmap for accession, which would formulate actual terms of joining the EEUT. Armenia adopted it in October 2014, accepted a road map for EEUT implementation imposed by the EEUT Commission, and faced an obligation to harmonize its public procurement system with the EEUT requirements in November 2014, while both Kazakhstan and the Kyrgyz Republic requested (and were granted) a transition period of twenty-four months.

On the GPA side, the WTO adopted a revised GPA text in 2012, and the ratification process reached Armenia in autumn 2014 (at the same time as the obligation to implement the EEUT was made mandatory). Ratification of the revised 2012 text of the GPA was completed in Armenia in June 2015.

6.5 Are Global and Regional Trade Regimes Compatible in Terms of Procurement Policy?

With all the above-described trade developments taking place and the international agreements being signed and ratified, the EBRD-UNCITRAL Initiative team was working hand-in-hand with the Ministry of Finance of Armenia on a comparative analysis of trade regimes and their impact on the public procurement system in Armenia.

Completed in early spring 2014, the legal analysis of the 2012 text of the GPA and the 2013 text of the customs union's agreement on public procurement suggested that public procurement requirements of the customs union—very detailed in terms of procurement methods and procedures and focused on implementing specific electronic tools such as the Russian model of electronic reverse auction—were rather incompatible with the GPA system.

With the signing of the EEUT in August 2014, a comparative analysis of the 2012 GPA and the EEUT regimes in terms of their specific requirements for public procurement policies was undertaken. Soon after, in September 2014, SIGMA (a joint program of the OECD and the European Commission) undertook a review of compliance of the Armenian public procurement legislation with the 2014 EU Public Procurement Directives. These two analytical works served as a basis for the analytical exercise determining whether the 2012 GPA standards, the 2014 EU Directives on public procurement, and the 2014 EEUT regimes can be satisfied within a single and implementable public procurement legal framework. Key points from the comparative review are presented in Section 6.6.

6.6 Comparative Analysis of the 2012 GPA and the EEUT Mandatory Requirements

Although the WTO system and the EEUT are very different, in terms of their requirements for public procurement the 2012 GPA and the EEUT are, in principle, not contradictory and can "coexist" at the level of national public procurement policy. This is not only important for a country wishing to remain in both trade regimes, but it also means that a careful choice of legal instruments needs to be made that does not contradict any of the above-mentioned international treaties.

The 2012 GPA and the EEUT regulate different phases of the public procurement process with different depth, thus making it possible to maneuver between the mandatory and facultative rules of both agreements. As an example, from the 2012 GPA perspective, institutional provisions on domestic review procedures are highly accentuated, with mandatory requirements for procedural fairness and public procurement review bodies that are not courts. In the EEUT, domestic public procurement review is very lightly regulated. As such, the institutional framework and procedures for review bodies are left to be developed by national legislators. This way, it is possible to design a public procurement review framework which is in compliance with both the 2012 GPA and the EEUT.

6.6.1 GENERAL PRINCIPLES

The GPA and the EEUT build their general approach to public procurement upon the same principles of non-discrimination, transparency, equal treatment, and competition. However, the GPA and the EEUT have different memberships, except for Armenia, and some differences exist with respect to implementing these principles in procedural requirements arising from different objectives of these legal acts and the legislative choices available to their member countries. However, as explained below, requirements arising from international agreements can be combined in a single and coherent legal framework for public procurement.

As we can see from the analysis in this section, the approaches to fulfilling the general principles are different, but usually do not create practical problems. The exception can be publication and language requirements, examples of which are provided later in the text.

6.6.2 THRESHOLDS OF APPLICATION

The EEUT does not prescribe thresholds for its application, which means that its mandatory regulations apply to all public procurement of the EEUT countries, except for state secrets. However, the EEUT contains a provision (point 12, Sub-Annex 3 of Annex 25): "Determination of the maximum amount of transactions (or quarterly or annual limit volume) that may be set by the legislation of a Member State" that allows procurement without competition (single source/direct contracting); in this case, "said amount shall not be determined by contracting entities and the Member States shall seek to minimize this threshold in order to maximize access to procurement for potential suppliers." This provision is generally interpreted as giving permission for the member states to decide individually on the national thresholds for single-source contracting. In practice, the member states may decide on very high thresholds, thus avoiding competitive public procurement procedures for lower-value procurement.

The absence of thresholds creates practical problems for countries with fully decentralized systems and, as in the case of Armenia, a high volume of low-value procurement and a low volume of high-value procurement. For example, the EEUT requires that all procurement information also be published in Russian (the definition of "procurement information" in accordance with the Treaty includes not only contract notices, contract award decisions, and other information necessary for the potential and actual bidders, but also internal documents such as protocols). We do understand that this information is necessary in Russian for the EEUT suppliers, but from the point of view of the Armenian contracting authorities, it is a heavy burden for small contracting entities that handle only low-value procurements. While Russian is widely spoken in the region, it creates an entry barrier to EU or other GPA party suppliers, which are not provided with the same information in English or any of the WTO languages. In case of proportional thresholds, the language requirements would apply only to the high-value procurements and would not be burdensome.

Nonetheless, in the absence of thresholds in the EEUT and the 2012 GPA requirements applicable above to thresholds established during the negotiations with the GPA parties, it is relatively easy to combine both regimes into a single and coherent legal framework.

Procedural deadlines stipulated in the EEUT are also very strict and inflexible. For example, public contracts shall be signed no earlier than ten days from the date of the award decision by the evaluation panel. First of all, it is not clear from the text whether this provision relates to a standstill period, i.e. a period that allows bidders that did not win the procurement contract to find out about the award decision and mount a challenge if need be. Assuming this is the case, the standstill period is calculated not from the date of public announcement of the contract award decision, but from the day the decision was adopted by the evaluation panel. This means that in order to comply with the 2012 GPA (in which the standstill period is at least ten days from the date of publication of the notice), the award decision should be adopted and published on the same day.

6.6.3 RULES REGARDING ESTIMATED VALUE OF THE PROCUREMENT

The GPA (Article II, paras 6–8) stipulates detailed rules on determining the estimated value of the procurement, in order to favor aggregation of procurement and prohibit the splitting of contracts below the thresholds of the GPA application. The EEUT does not contain provisions regarding the determination of the estimated value of a public contract and gives freedom to legislative choices of its member states.

6.6.4 ELIGIBILITY, GROUNDS FOR EXCLUSION, AND QUALIFICATION CRITERIA

The EEUT allows its member states to decide individually on the specifics of eligibility rules, grounds for exclusion, and supplier and contractor qualification criteria. At the same time, it requests any existing domestic preferences to be extended to suppliers and contractors from the EEUT member states. In addition, blacklisting schemes are required to be mandatory and, according to Article 14 of Annex 25 of the EEUT, should be formed and maintained as common across the EEUT member countries. From the reading of Article 14 of the Annex 25, it seems that members are given a choice to use only their own or other members states' blacklists. However, the language of this Article can be misleading. The EEUT provides for conditions, time limits, and appeals against the decisions of inclusion in blacklisting registers.

The EEUT requires that the decision on the blacklisting needs to be adopted by the court and (or) by the authorized regulatory and (or) controlling organ, meaning that individual contracting authorities shall not have powers to decide on the blacklisting of a specific supplier. The main reason for blacklisting is non-performance or inadequate performance of contractual obligations. The text of the treaty does not provide for more detail, which may allow blacklisting even for an insignificant breach of a contract. The period of blacklisting is fixed at two years from the date the grounds for blacklisting are confirmed.

By contrast, the 2012 GPA incorporates general eligibility rules and a limited list of grounds for exclusion, with a rather general description of "significant or persistent deficiencies in performance of any substantive requirement or obligation under a prior contract or contracts." It also incorporates general rules for qualification criteria and allows for exclusions of the tenderer from the procurement procedure based on a transparent blacklisting scheme (Article VIII, para. 4). Without contradicting any of the international instruments, it is therefore possible to develop procurement legislation following the 2012 GPA mandatory requirements on eligibility, qualification, and allowed exclusions and at the same time satisfy the EEUT by introducing an appropriate national blacklisting scheme.

6.6.5 PROCUREMENT METHODS

The GPA and the EEUT incorporate different approaches to the available procurement methods.

Article 4 of Annex 25 of the EEUT lists the following applicable procurement methods:

1. open procedure (which may include also pre-qualification and a two-stag procedure);
2. price quotation;

3. closed procedure—quotation of bids (optional);
4. open electronic auction;
5. commodity market negotiations (optional); and
6. single-source procurement.

The wording used in Article 4 suggests that the list of procurement methods is exhaustive, that is, no other procurement methods are permitted. The EEUT also sets out mandatory procurement procedures that need to be transposed into the legislations of the EEUT member states. The EEUT prescribes six procurement procedures, with the implementation of four procedures mandatory for its member states. The mandatory procedures are open tender (which may include pre-qualification and two-stage procedures), request for quotation, reverse electronic auction, and single sourcing. Requests for proposals and exchange trading can be used if envisaged in the legislation of the member states. The EEUT exhaustively regulates all procedures, and in some cases regulation differs from the standards recommended by the 2011 UNCITRAL Model Law on Public Procurement (for electronic reverse auction, in particular).

The 2012 GPA does not mention specific procurement methods, instead laying down common basic rules for every procurement method. Thus, a country wishing to comply with both the EEUT and the 2012 GPA needs to opt for the EEUT mandatory list of procedures. However, based on the specific procedural requirements pertaining to each procurement method allowed by the EEUT, we believe it is possible to make a selection of procedures from the 2011 UNCITRAL Model Law on Public Procurement that is sufficient for the local market in Armenia and compliant with both the 2012 GPA and the EEUT.

From the Armenian perspective, the major legislative amendment will be the elimination of the "framework agreements procedures," instead of which electronic reverse auction will be introduced. More detailed analysis of the electronic reverse auction under the EEUT is presented below. Among other amendments, the existing simplified procedure for small value contracts will be transformed into price quotation; instead of competitive dialogue, there will be an open tender with a two-stage procedure; and the restricted procedure will be renamed "closed procedure" in the new legislation.

6.6.6 DIRECT CONTRACTING/SINGLE-SOURCE PROCUREMENT

The GPA specifies strictly limited cases for single-source procurement (Article XIII). The EEUT contains a wide list of cases where single-source procurement is permitted (Sub-Annex 3 of Annex 25). However, there is also the possibility for a member country to incorporate a reduced list into its legislation (provided in Article 10 of Annex 25 of the EEUT), and this list can be made compatible with the cases for direct contracting in the 2012 GPA.

The 2012 GPA allows for limited cases when a country may procure using the non-competitive procedures, as does the EEUT but with one big difference. Though the EEUT list of single sourcing is also exhaustive (i.e., countries cannot increase the number of single-sourcing possibilities specified in the list), the length of the list of allowed single sourcing raises doubts—sixty-three provisions on allowed single sourcing are included. Moreover, the list in the EEUT does not need to be rigorously interpreted and several provisions describe a number of situations when single sourcing is permitted, such as purchasing goods, works, and services required to ensure the safety and security of a head of a member state and other protected persons, including household services, hotel services, transportations, maintenance of computer equipment, sanitary and epidemiological well-being, safe meals, as well as services for the creation of a video archive and information support of activities of the head of the member state.

At first glance, the requirements of the treaties seem contradictory, but since it is allowed for the EEUT member state to shorten the list of single sourcing in their national legislation, the solution proposed for Armenia is to cut it down to the 2012 GPA list of limited tendering. This could raise the issue of unequal terms compared to other EEUT member states—one EEUT member state may include all sixty-three provisions, while Armenia, being a party to the GPA, will be limited to the rather short GPA list of limited tendering. In practical terms, the list included in the current legislation is compliant with the 2012 GPA, and it has been decided not to enlarge it. However, as has been explained above, with 11,683 cases of negotiated procedures without publication in Armenia in 2014, it is not the wording but the implementation of the law that remains a challenge.

6.6.7 ELECTRONIC PROCUREMENT

Though the EEUT and the 2012 GPA are very different with regards to the overall rationale of the treaties, mandatory provisions, and possible outcomes for the member states, there is also a very important similarity across both international instruments. Both agreements place a lot of emphasis on electronic procurement procedures, electronic reverse auctions, and a single, online point of access for information on procurement opportunities and procurement decisions. The 2012 GPA was updated to allow for electronic communication in public sector purchasing and the EEUT has been based on the Russian procedural model, which in turn is heavily based on the use of electronic reverse auctions.

Some differences notwithstanding, both treaties promote the use of ITC technologies as a means of increasing access to procurement markets across borders. The EEUT is detailed and contains definitions of the web portal, e-platform, and electronic procedures, and the 2012 revised text of GPA defines electronic auctions. Another similarity from the point of view of electronic procurement is the requirement to have a single point of access for all procurement information—this is mandatory from both the EEUT and the GPA perspective. The definition of "web portal" in the EEUT refers directly to the single official website of the member state providing a *single point of access* to information on procurement. The 2012 GPA in its Article VII, when referring to notifications, makes it clear that the information on procurement of the central government entities (covered under Annex 1) needs to be accessible through a single point of access, and sub-central governmental entities and other entities (the bodies in Annexes 2 and 3) are also encouraged to publish their notifications through a single point of access.

The EEUT requires that open procedures and reverse electronic auctions must be organized only using electronic procedure. The EEUT member countries are also required to implement all their procurement methods using electronic procedures (EEUT, Article 4 of Annex 25), as well as to introduce concluding procurement contracts in electronic form (Article 28 of Annex 25). From the point of view of the EEUT, an electronic auction is a stand-alone procedure required for specific procurements, with a list of goods, services, and works prescribed for auction in the annex to the treaty. This stipulates that the use of electronic auctions is mandatory depending on the type of procurement. The list of goods, services, and works to be procured via electronic auctions is mandatory but not exhaustive; EEUT member states are allowed to extend the list and make more widespread use of electronic auctions.

From a procedural point of view, the EEUT describes electronic auctions as having the same procedural steps as the open procedure, but with shortened submission deadlines of fifteen or seven days from the publication of the procurement. In order to participate in the auction, interested suppliers should register on the accredited electronic procurement platform, and it is the prerogative of the member state to decide whether pre- or post-qualification will be applied.

From the GPA perspective, the use of electronic auctions is not mandatory but when incorporated in the national legislation, the electronic auction procedure should ensure that participants in the auction are well informed on their ranking and can take appropriate decisions during the auction. As previously mentioned, this is another example of both agreements regulating the same process from different angles and with different perspectives, and thus allowing for the design of electronic procedures that are compliant with both regimes. Armenia has used its ARMEPS electronic procurement platform since January 2012, and competitive procedures (except for competitive dialogue) are presently conducted on the ARMEPS platform. The ARMEPS also provides an electronic auction module, which has never been used in Armenia. Initial review of the electronic auction procedure on ARMEPS confirmed that it is compliant with the 2011 UNCITRAL Model Law and it should be possible to employ it under the EEUT procedural model.[13]

[13] See <http://www.ppi-ebrd-uncitral.com/images/stories/pdf/Armenia_EBRD_UNCITRAL_Initiative_progress_report.pdf> (accessed July 22, 2016).

The EEUT mandatory requirements also include certified electronic signatures for participating in public procurement procedures. The EEUT requires member states to work together on establishing mutual recognition of certified electronic signatures among the EEUT member states. As reported by the EEUT Commission, only Belarus and Russia have been successful in reaching the point of mutual recognition of e-signatures; the other member states are still working on this matter. As an EEUT member state, Armenia also has the obligation to mutually recognize certified electronic signatures; however, the existing electronic procurement platform in Armenia does not require the use of a certified signature for bidding, and procurement contracts are still signed on paper. Scanned versions of hardcopy official documents are uploaded, and alternative verification procedures are used to register. Thus, in principle, participation in procedures conducted on ARMEPS is open to foreign suppliers. The problem arises for Armenian suppliers wishing to participate in procurement in other EEUT member states. Without a recognized certified signature, they will not be able to participate in any electronic procurement procedures. Though the 2012 GPA does not refer to the use of certified electronic signatures, a requirement for specific e-signatures discriminates against foreign suppliers and contractors. This problem should also be taken into account when amending legislation and the system.

In conclusion, the obligatory requirements of the EEUT for electronic procedures can be easily accommodated under the 2012 GPA rules, which encourage electronic procurement, establish standards for electronic auctions, and prescribe minimum tender deadlines for electronic procedures. Hence, both regimes can be accommodated into a single legal framework, if deadlines for electronic procedures are adopted in compliance with the 2012 GPA requirements.

6.6.8 TECHNICAL SPECIFICATIONS

The GPA specifies minimum standards for technical specifications (Article X, paras 1–6). According to these, specifications shall be non-discriminatory and preference—where appropriate—should be given to functional (output) specifications. Also, the notion "or equivalent" should always accompany the design and descriptive characteristics in technical specifications, as well as references to trademarks, patents, and similar notions.

The EEUT (Article 19 of Annex 25) incorporates a provision against the inclusion in tender documents of requirements in relation to trademarks, company names, patents, and similar notions, unless there is no other option for describing the subject matter of a contract. This wording is covered by the UNCITRAL Model Law, which also considers it mandatory for the contracting authority to include the notion "or equivalent (analogue)" in the technical specification. Contracting authorities are entitled to use technical standards according to international acts being part of the EEUT, as well as legislation of a particular EEUT member country.

6.6.9 CONTRACT AWARD CRITERIA

The EEUT contains indirect remarks regarding the possibility of using not only price as a tender award criterion, but also quality-related criteria. For instance, point 1 of Sub-Annex 1 of Annex 25 of the EEUT rules that the successful bidder shall be the potential supplier offering the best terms for the implementation of the procurement agreement (contract). For other procurement procedures, the EEUT explicitly requires the lowest price to be the sole award criterion; for example, point 5 of Sub-Annex 1 of Annex 25 provides that the successful bidder under request for pricing (request for quotations) shall be the potential supplier offering the lowest price of the procurement agreement (contract). The GPA establishes two tender award criteria: the most economically advantageous tender, and the lowest price (Article XV, para. 5).

6.6.10 REVIEW PROCEDURES

According to the provisions of the EEUT, the public procurement review function is considered to be an administrative enforcement mechanism, and rules regarding the review procedure are left to the discretion of member countries (Article 37, point 2 of Annex 25). In contrast, the GPA contains general requirements regarding domestic review procedures, which should be available to private sector stakeholders and mandatory for parties to the agreement (Article XVIII). The GPA mandatory standard corresponds to the 2011 UNCITRAL Model Law provisions, and in essence requires independence and impartiality of a review body, swiftness of the review proceedings, and availability of appeal to the review decision.

6.6.11 PROCUREMENT CONTRACTS AND FRAMEWORK AGREEMENTS

The GPA does not regulate procurement contracts and framework agreements, as this procedure for repetitive contracting of goods and services is understood in the 2011 UNCITRAL Model Law or in the 2014 EU directives on public procurement. There is, however, a provision prohibiting modifications to already awarded contracts in a manner that circumvents the obligations under the GPA (Article XV, para. 7). The EEUT contains provisions regarding mandatory minimum content of procurement contracts (Article 21 of Annex 25) and mandatory rules prohibiting contractual conditions limiting competition, unilateral stepping back from the contractual obligations by the supplier, and particular amendments to procurement contracts (Article 22 of Annex 25). The EEUT does not envisage the use of framework agreements in public procurement, and online framework agreements in particular. The only procedural option for designing a procedure similar to framework agreements is to establish a pre-qualified suppliers' list, which is allowed under the EEUT.

6.7 **Lessons Learned**

Joining the GPA in 2011 did not enhance cross-border trade for Armenia, and neither did it increase the amount of foreign participation or lead to significant positive effects on the Armenian economy. We believe that the reasons lie mainly in the overly permissive legislation allowing for procedures without publication of contract notices, and in implementation difficulties (problems with operating the electronic procurement platform; inadequate regulation for switching from a centralized to decentralized procurement system; and thresholds that generated a high volume of low-value procurement, which ended up contracted without any competition). Nonetheless, GPA membership proved to be a vehicle to keep Armenia's public procurement policies under the influence of international best practice. If not for the GPA membership, it is likely that Armenia would have abandoned its public procurement reform project and joined the customs union in 2013.

Policy choices in the primary legislation should be consistent, and be based on international best practice. In Armenia, the new primary law envisaged a fully decentralized system, incorporating framework agreements. However, a balanced decentralization—with central purchasing based on framework agreements—represents current best practice in procurement, as has been successfully implemented in the eProcurement environment across the EU member states.

Decentralization of a public procurement function requires a new institutional framework and new, efficient operational procedures (monitoring, in particular). Prior to the reforms—when the procurement function in Armenia was centralized and was delivered by an internal department of the Ministry of Finance—there was no need for laws regulating the allocation of roles and responsibilities in the procurement process, procurement planning, or reporting on the procurement results. All of these matters were internal matters of the Ministry of Finance and were regulated by internal procedures. In this centralized system, public procurement officers were personnel of the Ministry, accountable to the department director, and their management reported on their performance directly to the Minister of Finance.

In a decentralized procurement system, secondary legislation must prescribe how contracting entities should perform the procurement function, what their planning and reporting obligations are, and how they should report to the national regulatory authority. Without these regulations, the national regulatory authority has no access to information on how the procurement function is conducted. In a decentralized system, the national regulatory authority does not conduct public procurement, but rather ensures that the procurement procedures of individual contracting entities are compliant with the law. This is achieved through monitoring and audit procedures, which need to be prescribed by law and must be efficiently implemented. The experiences of several countries have demonstrated that, in a decentralized system, efficiency of monitoring is a key policy issue. In order not to create unnecessary bureaucracy, delays, and massive costs from human resources allocated to reviewing reports submitted by contracting entities upon the completion of procurement procedures, governments should employ more transparent and less expensive computerized systems, with real-time, online reporting conducted at the central level by a few, well-trained and well-paid analysts of the national regulatory authority.

Decentralization of a public procurement system can be combined with the implementation of eProcurement tools if the newly appointed contracting entities are trained in both how to conduct procurement and how to use the eProcurement tools. There is a high risk of irregularities and non-compliance if insufficient training is provided in conducting procurement processes, and where there are no professional procurement officers at the contracting entities. If the eProcurement system is not implemented in tandem with sufficient support for conducting procurement procedures on the platform, the contracting entities will experience operational difficulties, since they have no previous procurement experience and skills, and are learning both how to conduct procurement procedures and how to use new IT systems with which they are unfamiliar.

The story of public procurement reform in Armenia clearly demonstrates that high-level political support is essential in order to initiate reforms in the public sector, and sufficient and well-prepared human resources are necessary to implement them. If the reforms are ambitious, and will affect the entire public procurement sector, they should be very well thought through and necessary change-management instruments must be put in place—and be made effective—well in advance of the entry into force of the new primary legislation. In the case of Armenia, the political objective of the reforms—accession to the GPA—has been accomplished, but the goal of a more efficient and modern public procurement system will take longer to achieve.

Presently, with the different trade regimes applicable to public procurement in Armenia, the direction of public sector procurement development in Armenia is dependent on the political decisions regarding new legislation.

The comparative review summarized here confirms that there is no legal contradiction between the 2012 GPA and the EEUT standards. Incorporating the 2012 GPA and EEUT requirements for public procurement policies into a single public procurement framework may create some minor implementation issues, but these can be easily resolved by making smart policy choices and developing national public procurement legislation based on the 2011 UNCITRAL Model Law.

We have found that the EEUT chapter on public procurement regulates a different level of policy as it contains detailed provisions regarding procedural aspects of procurement methods, whereas the GPA regulates the same aspects in a very general manner. Moreover, most of detailed provisions of the EEUT are generally compatible with the 2011 UNCITRAL Model Law and are not in conflict with the general rules and spirit of the 2012 GPA's mandatory requirements.

At the same time, it is necessary to acknowledge that it is difficult to consolidate the EEUT requirements with all the standards of the 2014 EU directives on public procurement. While compatible on the level of general policy principles (competition, transparency, and non-discrimination), these principles are understood differently, and several key procedural requirements in these regional standards are distinct and incompatible.

The government of Armenia is now in the process of drafting new primary legislation that is compliant with the global standard of the GPA and the EEUT regional standard. It is expected that the new law will be adopted in 2016.

REFERENCES

Arrowsmith, S. and Anderson, R. (eds). 2011. *The WTO Regime on Government Procurement: Challenge and Reform*. Cambridge: Cambridge University Press.

OECD. 2012. "Armenia Progress Report." Report Presented by Armenia at the Eleventh Monitoring Meeting for the Istanbul Anti-Corruption Action Plan, February 22–24.

Transparency International. 2014. "Monitoring of Public Procurement System in 2011–2013," Berlin.

7 Public Procurement in Turkey

Sübidey Togan, Bedri Kamil Onur Taş, and Servet Alyanak

7.1 Introduction

This chapter discusses Turkey's public procurement regime. Turkey is not a member of the World Trade Organization (WTO) Agreement on Government Procurement (GPA) but is an EU accession candidate country, and as such will be required to have a procurement regime that conforms to EU norms and regulations. It is unclear if and when Turkey will accede to the EU, however, and as discussed in this chapter the extent of convergence to the EU *acquis* has been limited in a number of important areas.[1]

The chapter is organized as follows. Section 7.2 studies the main characteristics of the Turkish public procurement system, and Section 7.3 studies the government procurement markets. Section 7.4 concentrates on the primary goals of a sound public procurement and analyzes how successful the Turkish public procurement regime has been in achieving these goals. Section 7.5 concentrates on empirical analysis of public procurement, and Section 7.6 concludes.

7.2 The Characteristics of Turkish Public Procurement

The legal framework for the current Turkish public procurement system comprises the Public Procurement Law (PPL) No. 4734 of 2002 and the Public Procurement Contracts Law (PPCL) No. 4735 of 2002. The PPL establishes the principles and procedures to be applied in public procurements. Implementation of public procurement contracts is regulated by the PPCL, which applies to contracts awarded through the application of

[1] At the European Council meeting held in Helsinki on December 10–11, 1999, Turkey was officially recognized as an EU candidate country. After the approval of the Accession Partnership by the European Council and adoption of the Framework Regulation on February 26, 2001, the Turkish government announced a National Program for the adoption of the *acquis communautaire* on March 19, 2001. Progress toward accession continues along the path set by the National Programs of 2001, 2003, and 2008. According to these programs Turkey intends to adopt and implement Community's *acquis* in the public procurement area.

procurement procedures carried out in accordance with the provisions of the PPL. Both the PPL and the PPCL were prepared taking into account the 1994 United Nations Commission on International Trade Law's (UNCITRAL) Model Law on Procurement of Goods, Construction, and Services, the 1994 WTO GPA, and the then prevailing European Community's (EC) Directives on public procurement.

The PPL consists of seventy articles structured in six chapters, a set of interim articles, and an additional article, and covers all stages of procurement procedures, except for the execution and termination of contracts, which are covered exclusively by the PPCL. The major features of Turkish procurement legislation are presented in what follows.[2]

7.2.1 PRINCIPLES AND COVERAGE

The PPL lays out a number of core principles for government purchases. Contracting authorities are responsible for ensuring transparency, competition, equal treatment, reliability, confidentiality, public supervision, fulfillment of needs appropriately and promptly, and the efficient use of resources.

Article 2 of PPL states that most public entities and institutions governed by public law or under public control or using public funds are subject to the PPL. Thus, the "contracting authorities" include public entities of the central government, special provincial administrations, municipalities and their related revolving fund organizations, unions, and legal entities; state economic enterprises (SEEs); social security establishments; funds, entities of legal personalities that are established in accordance with special laws and that are assigned with public duties and establishments with independent budgets; and any institution, organization, association, enterprise, and corporation which—directly or indirectly, and together or separately—has more than half of the capital owned by the authorities mentioned above. The scope of application of PPL includes public supply contracts, public service contracts, and public works contracts.

The PPL applies only to contracts above a certain financial value. The threshold values for the period February 2014 to January 2016 were approximately €274,000 for procurement of goods and services by contracting entities operating under the general or the annexed budget; €456,000 for the purchase of goods and services by other contracting

[2] The Turkish legislation on public procurement is available at: <http://www.ihale.gov.tr/Mevzuat.aspx> (accessed July 22, 2016). The Turkish regulations are discussed in the annual *Turkey Public Procurement Assessment Reports* of the OECD Support for Improvement in Governance and Management (SIGMA) initiative over the period 2005–9, in annual *Assessment Turkey* reports of SIGMA over the period 2010–13, in Gözel (2004), Alyanak (2007), and Public Procurement Authority (2014).

entities within the scope of the PPL; and €10 million for constructions for administrations covered by the PPL.[3]

Certain categories of procurement are not covered by the PPL. Article 3 of the PPL spans nineteen paragraphs specifying exceptions, including procurements related to defense, security, and intelligence needs; purchases of SEEs and of economic enterprises of the municipalities not exceeding €2.5 million; and procurements of agriculture or livestock products by contracting authorities. Article 68/c exempts the Housing Development Administration (TOKI) from the provisions of PPL as regards all projects.[4] In addition to the exemptions stipulated in PPL, several other laws introduce more exemptions, either for individual institutions or for specific types of contracts, or even for individual projects.

7.2.2 THE PUBLIC PROCUREMENT AUTHORITY

There are various functions of a public procurement system that need to be tackled at the central level. These functions concern the preparation of national public procurement legislation, the publication of contract notices, cooperation with other international institutions, advice to contracting authorities and economic operators on the application of legislation, the provision of public procurement training, and monitoring and compliance assessment. Article 53 PPL establishes the Turkish Public Procurement Authority (PPA) as an administratively and financially autonomous body with a link to the Ministry of Finance. The mandate of PPA is to ensure the proper implementation of the PPL, to support participants in the procurement process, and to provide legal resolution of disputes over public procurement. PPA—realizing that the announcement of contract opportunities is vital to secure the transparency, competition, and equal treatment of economic operators in awarding public contracts—is mandated to publish procurement notices of the contracts covered by the PPL.[5] PPA performs this duty by publishing the Public Procurement Bulletin, which is available in electronic format.[6] PPA is financed mainly by contracting authorities through a fee of 0.05 percent of the value of the public contracts above €106,500.

[3] The thresholds, updated every two years, are in Turkish lira (TL). The euro figures stated here are approximate figures using the exchange rate of 2.9659 lira to the euro.

[4] TOKI, founded by Mass Housing Law No. 2985 of 1984, is the leader official institution of Turkey in terms of dealing with housing and settlement issues.

[5] If the contract in question is not covered by the PPL or its value is below the thresholds for publication of notices stated in the PPL, then the announcements of these contract opportunities are made through either the *Official Gazette* or national and/or local newspapers.

[6] The Public Procurement Bulletin publishes the following tender notices: contract notices, pre-qualification notices, correction notices, cancellation notices, and contract award notices. The Public Procurement Bulletin is published in electronic media and is accessible online and free of charge.

The PPA consists of the Public Procurement Board (PPB), the presidency, and the service units. The PPB is the main decision-making body of the PPA. In addition, the PPB examines complaints and may take corrective action and determine the remedies, cancel the tender decision, and terminate the tender proceedings, or decide that the complaint is irrelevant. The PPB has nine members including the chairperson, who is appointed by the Council of Ministers on the recommendation of the Minister of Finance. The Council of Ministers selects the chairperson of the PPB from among its members.

7.2.3 METHODS OF PROCUREMENT AND PROCUREMENT TOOLS

Four procurement procedures are specified in Articles 18–22 of the PPL: (i) open procedure, (ii) restricted procedure, (iii) negotiated procedure, and (iv) direct procurement. While under the "open procedure" all tenderers can submit their qualification documents and bids, under the "restricted procedure" only tenderers who, following an open invitation to pre-qualify, are evaluated as qualified are invited by the contracting entity to submit tenders. Under the "negotiated procedure," following Article 21 of PPL, at least three tenderers will be invited to submit their qualification documents and price offers, and in those cases there is no need for the advertisement of contract notice.[7] Under "direct procurement" applied in cases specified in Article 22 of PPL, there is no need for the fulfillment of most of the requirements specified in PPL such as advertisement of contract notice. A legislative amendment in 2008 introduced provisions regarding the use of framework agreements, dynamic purchasing systems, and electronic auctions into Turkish legislation. The related regulations are on the whole consistent with the equivalent provisions that apply in EU law, although some differences exist.

7.2.4 RULES APPLICABLE TO PUBLIC PROCUREMENT

To procure goods, services, or works in Turkey, a contract notice must be published except in those cases when the award was made by "direct procurement" or by "negotiated procedure" in certain cases specified in PPL. The technical criteria specified in the technical specifications of the contract notice must aim for efficiency and functionality,

[7] Under the "negotiated procedure," at least three tenderers will be invited to submit their qualification documents and price offers in the following cases: (i) the tender procedure has to be conducted immediately due to unexpected and unforeseen events such as natural disasters, epidemics, risk of loss of lives or properties, or events that could not be predicted by the contracting authority; (ii) specific events relating to defense and security; and (iii) procurements of goods, material and services by contracting authorities not exceeding €53,000.

must ensure equal opportunities for all tenderers, and must not contain conditions impeding competition. Technical specifications, where possible, must refer to national and/or international technical standards. No specific brand, model, patent, origin, source, or product can be specified, and no feature or definition indicating any brand or model can be included in them. The contract notice period and the relevant media for publication differ depending on the estimated cost of the contract. The contract notice period is forty days for contracts in open procedure, which can be reduced to twenty-four days if a pre-qualification notice is published. All contract notices are published online on the Electronic Public Procurement Platform (EPPP).

Article 11 PPL excludes certain persons or authorities from participation in any procurement, directly or indirectly or as a sub-contractor, either on their own account or on behalf of others. Furthermore, the tenderers participating in the procurement proceedings are required to submit information and documents for evaluation of their economic and financial standing, as well as for the evaluation of their professional and technical qualifications (Article 10). Award procedures are similar to those that apply in the EU. Only two criteria are permissible: either the most economically advantageous tender (MEAT), or the lowest price bid that satisfied the performance requirements specified in the call for proposals. When the MEAT criterion is used, the relative weighting of the different factors, as well as the method of calculation of the best tender, must be expressed in the tender document.

The procurement process starts when the contracting authority determines its needs. The properties of the needs are described by the contracting entity, specifying in detail the technical requirements of the goods, services, or construction works. The contracting entity performs detailed market research and estimates the procurement cost. The public institution that is associated with the contracting entity determines the procurement method. Article 5 of PPL specifies that government agencies will not be able to issue tender notices unless adequate funds have been allocated in the budget and an Environmental Impact Assessment report is prepared. Thereafter, auction documents are prepared. The contracting authority applies to PPA for the permit to conduct the procurement process. Once the permit is granted, the tender commission is constructed by the contracting entity, and auction details are announced to the public. Tender documents can be viewed at the premises of the contracting authority and online on the Electronic Public Procurement Platform (EPPP). It is possible to acquire a tender document through EPPP by using an e-signature or m-signature free of charge. Otherwise, the document has to be purchased by tenderers willing to participate in procurement. Next, the tenders are prepared and submitted to the contracting entity according to the conditions that had been announced.

Regarding the assessment of tenders, we note that tenders are opened at the place and time stated in the tender documentation. The session for the opening of tenders is open to the public. Prices submitted by each tenderer are announced to all tenderers in this session. The tender commission checks if there are any missing documents in the tenders and if the offer letters and the bid guarantees are proper. Before closing the first session, the documents submitted by tenderers and their bids are recorded in official minutes and a copy of these is provided to those who request it. A detailed assessment of the documents submitted by the tenderers is carried out by the tender commission in a closed session. Tenders that do not meet the qualification criteria specified in the tender document are rejected, and valid tenders are evaluated based on the contract award criteria. All decisions and transactions regarding the assessment and evaluation of tenders must be recorded in official minutes by the commission. The contract is awarded after all the assessments are completed. As indicated here, only two criteria are permissible: MEAT and the lowest price. The contract award decision must be notified to the parties within three days of the decision being approved by the authorized official. Contract award decisions are published online in the Public Procurement Bulletin.

7.2.5 ELECTRONIC METHODS

Electronic tools can be used for various processes and decisions on a par with more traditional means of communication. Electronic methods reduce the administrative costs of individual procurements, streamline procurement procedures, result in faster procurement procedures and increased transparency, provide better monitoring of procurement, encourage cross-border competition, promote the effectiveness of procurement, encourage the integration of various administrative processes, and support developments that make the process more efficient.

The concept of e-procurement was introduced in 2008 in order to improve the efficiency of state purchases. Following the legislative changes, the EPPP has been established as a part of the e-government project, and an E-procurement Research and Development Centre has been established. The PPA has started to provide training for the public agencies through the cooperation agreements with universities for professional assistance for training, and a call center has also been established to provide the procuring entities with advisory services. EPPP became operational in 2010 and since then, transactions related to public procurement have been carried out through or registered on the platform. Contract notices are published on EPPP, and contract documents of contracting authorities are made available on EPPP. Economic operators can download the contract documents from EPPP, and they can access information on their tax liabilities and social security premium debt, as well as information on their balance sheets and income statements. Alsaç (2012) emphasizes that since March 2012, e-notice preparations and electronic access to tender documents have been possible. However, electronic auctions have not started yet. Finally, note that in the case electronic methods, similar rules apply in Turkey as in the EU.

7.2.6 CONCESSIONS AND PUBLIC–PRIVATE PARTNERSHIPS

The legal framework governing concessions and PPPs has not yet been established, and separate regulations govern different sectors. The main regulation is the law on projects carried out under build-operate-transfer (BOT) contracts and a decree, revised in the middle of 2011, regulating the application of this law. Other related laws are Law No. 3465 on Assignment of Institutions for Highway Construction with Tolls, Maintenance and Operation; Law No. 6428 on Building, Renovating Facilities and Receiving Service on PPP Model; and Law No. 3096 on the Assignment of Institutions for Electricity Production Generation, Transmission, Distribution and Trade.

7.2.7 PROCUREMENT BY UTILITIES

The PPL does not explicitly deal with entities operating in the utilities sector. It is stated in Article 2 of the PPL that enterprises, establishments, and corporations that carry out activities in the energy, water, transport, and telecommunications sectors are outside the scope of PPL. Nevertheless, Interim Article 4 of PPL states that enterprises, establishments, and corporations that carry out activities in the energy, water, transport, and telecommunications sectors, until their special laws enter into force, shall be subject to the provisions of PPL for procurement of goods, services, and works. Sub-paragraph (g) of Article 3 of PPL stipulates that goods or services procurements of the institutions listed in sub-paragraphs (b) and (d) in Article 2 of PPL for their commercial and industrial activities in contracts not exceeding €2.45 million, except those financed by treasury guarantee or by means of transferring directly from the transfer order of budget, shall not be governed by PPL except for those requirements of the PPL concerning prohibitions and criminal provisions.[8]

[8] While sub-paragraph (b) of Article 2 of PPL concerns state economic enterprises, consisting of public corporations and state economic establishments, sub-paragraph (d) concerns any institutions, organizations, associations, enterprises, and corporations of which more than half the capital—directly or indirectly, together or separately—owned by those stated in items (a), (b) and (c). Note that sub-paragraph (a) of Article 2 of PPL concerns public administrations included in the general budget, administrations with special budgets, special provincial administrations and municipalities and their related revolving funds organizations, associations (except those operating as professional organizations and their supreme institutions), and legal persons. Sub-paragraph (c) of Article 2 of PPL concerns social security establishments, funds, legal persons that are established in accordance with special laws and that are assigned with public duties (except for professional organizations and foundation institutions of higher education), and institutions with independent budgets.

7.2.8 DEFENSE PROCUREMENT

Special exclusions are provided in PPL for the state's defense and security needs, but non-defense procurement must be done according to PPL. This also applies to the armed forces under the Ministry of Defense. However, no formal efforts appear to have been made to transpose the Defense Procurement Directive of the EU to date. In February 2014, the "omnibus" law amended various aspects of Turkish public procurement legislation. The law amendment introduced an offset option in public tenders and exempted acquisitions involving offsets from PPL.

7.2.9 BELOW-THRESHOLD CONTRACTS

The PPL applies to tenders regardless of the thresholds set out in Article 8. Therefore, contracts below the thresholds are still subject to the provisions laid down in the PPL, but they are not subject to the PPL requirements on transparency and equal treatment. The particular rules regarding transparency are specified in Article 13/B of PPL and Communique 2014/1.

According to Article 21 of PPL and communiqué 2014/1 of PPA, negotiated procedures will be used in Turkey as long as estimated costs of procurement do not exceed €53,300. In such cases, there is no need for advertisement of the contract notice. According to Article 22 of PPL and communiqué 2014/1 of PPA, direct procurement can be used for purchases relating to accommodation, trips, and subsistence within the scope of representation expenses, and procurements not exceeding €16,000 for the needs of authorities within the boundaries of metropolitan municipalities, or €5,300 for the needs of other contracting authorities. In these cases, there is no need for either the advertisement of contract notice or the fulfillment of requirements specified in PPL.

7.2.10 CORRUPTION, TRANSPARENCY, AND ENFORCEMENT

Procurement markets are often considered lucrative markets for potential bribery. Corruption may take the form of payment of a bribe as a reward for an official who can influence the procurement process, manipulation of tender documents to favor a specific bidder, or the use of intermediary companies to cover the illegal activities of the corrupt official. In addition, favoritism may also endanger the integrity of the procurement process. The PPL contains significant provisions that aim to combat corruption. It defines and prohibits forms of bribery and corruption in a separate article. In addition, the PPL provides for sanctions and penalties in the event of discovery of corruption, which apply to both individuals and companies. The PPL and PPCL also require the collection of detailed information on all public procurement auctions that are held in Turkey by the PPA. The PPA dataset contains detailed information on public procurements conducted within the country.

Articles 55–57 of the PPL establish a three-tier system for reviewing complaints lodged by disappointed suppliers. In the first stage, a complaint is submitted and reviewed by the contracting authority itself. A complainant who is dissatisfied with the decision of the contracting authority may, as a second step, appeal this decision to the PPA, and the decision on this appeal is made by the PPB. The final decision on the appeal made by the PPB is then subject to the jurisdiction of the regular courts.

7.2.11 PARTICIPATION OF FOREIGN TENDERERS

Foreign economic operators can access the contract notices and tender documents through EPPP, and they can submit their tenders in person or by post. When applying, they can use qualifications obtained in a foreign country. They also have the right to submit a complaint against decisions of the contracting authorities to the PPA and to the courts. In case of below-thresholds procurements, participation of foreign tenderers may be prevented by the contracting authority if this condition is stated explicitly in the tender document.

In September 2011, the Prime Ministry published a circular stipulating that the implementation of the PPL should favor the participation of domestic bidders. In the case of above-threshold procurements, the contracting authorities cannot block the participation of foreign tenderers, but a price advantage up to 15 percent could be applied in favor of domestic tenderers or to tenderers offering domestic goods in the procurement of goods above threshold if this condition was stated explicitly in the tender document. Domestic preference was not applied automatically, and contracting authorities could choose not to apply the domestic preference. Since the maximum domestic preference was 15 percent, contracting authorities could choose to apply a smaller rate. However, this provision was not applicable to domestic bidders that participated in the tender proceedings by forming joint ventures with foreign tenderers.[9] In February 2014, the "omnibus" law amended various aspects of Turkish public procurement legislation and introduced language that makes the previously optional domestic price advantage of up to 15 percent compulsory for "medium and high-technology industrial products."

[9] In order to benefit from the price advantage, in the case of goods procurements the tenderer had to be of Turkish nationality and the goods concerned had to be of domestic origin; in the case of services and works procurements, the tenderer had to be of Turkish nationality.

In contrast to many other countries, the PPL does not include specific provisions favoring small and medium-sized enterprises.

7.2.12 PREFERENTIAL TRADE AGREEMENTS

Although Turkey has a customs union agreement with the EU, this does not span public procurement policies. The Turkey–EU Customs Union Decision (CUD) of 1995 covers only trade in industrial products, and does not cover—among other things—agriculture, services, or government procurement. The Accession Partnership with the EU provides a venue for cooperation and assisting Turkey to adopt the *acquis communautaire*, but the extent to which this is pursued hinges upon the political will of both sides—the EU and Turkey.

7.3 **Public Procurement Markets in Turkey**

Public procurement is very important in Turkey. As shown in Table 7.1, total procurement as a share of GDP over the period 2007–13 fluctuated between 6.3 percent and 8.8 percent; the average value was 7.2 percent. However, TEPAV (2009) emphasizes that this value represents a minimum value for the period 2011 onwards, since the table does not include the statistics on housing and other construction procurements by the Mass Housing Administration (TOKI) for the years after 2011. TOKI was initially included in Chart No. II of the Public Financial Management and Control Law No. 5018 of 2003 as a special budget public administration, and was subject to PPL. In 2011, TOKI was removed from this chart. Furthermore, according to Article 68/c of PPL, TOKI, as emphasized in Section 7.2.2, was exempted in 2003 from the provisions of PPL as regards mass housing projects. In 2011, the exemption was extended to all projects conducted by

Table 7.1 Public procurement as a fraction of GDP

Year	Total procurement value (million TL)	GDP (million TL)	Share of total procurement in GDP (%)
2007	65,978.3	843,178	7.82
2008	83,915.3	950,534	8.83
2009	66,224.8	952,559	6.95
2010	69,510.3	1,098,799	6.33
2011	91,771.4	1,297,713	7.07
2012	94,398.7	1,416,798	6.66
2013	105,504.1	1,565,181	6.74
Average			7.20

TOKI. Since after 2011 TOKI was no longer a special budget public administration, it no longer fell within the scope of PPL, and the large tenders it was conducting were not reported in the statistics provided by PPA after 2011.

Another reason for the relatively low value of public procurement as a fraction of GDP is the exclusion of concessions, such as the construction of highways and bridges, from the public procurement statistics. The problems related with concessions should be carried out by considering the provisions of Law No. 3996/1994 (including Amending Law No. 4993/1999) on the build-operate-transfer (BOT) model and the related Decree No. 5907/1994. Other laws also contain provisions related to concession, such as Law No. 5272/2004 on Municipalities, Law No. 3096/1984 on the Electricity Market, Law Nos. 406/1924 and 2813/1983 on Telecommunications, and Law No. 3465/1988 on Transportation and Motorways.

Once TOKI is subject to the provisions of PPL, and the Turkish legislation on concessions is brought in line with EU Directive 2014/23/EU on the award of concession contracts, one can expect the value of public procurement as a fraction of GDP to increase considerably from its present value of 7.2 percent. In addition, the country will derive efficiency gains, as those procurements will no longer be outside the scope of the rules of PPL.

Table 7.2 shows the developments in the shares of different procurement types—such as open procedure, restricted procedure, negotiated procedure, and direct procurement—in terms of total number as well as total value of public sector procurements over the period 2007–13. The table reveals that the number of exemptions as a percentage of the total number of procurements fluctuated between 17.2 percent and 27 percent, with an average value of 24 percent. There are no figures on the total number of direct procurements. The share of negotiated procedures fluctuated between 11.6 percent and 19.5 percent of the total number of procurements, the share of restricted procedures fluctuated between 0.3 percent and 0.5 percent, and the share of open procedures fluctuated between 55.9 percent and 70.8 percent. The average figures are 59.6 percent for open procedures, 0.4 percent for restrictive procedures, and 15.9 percent for negotiated procedures.

When we consider the shares of the different procurement types of the total value of public sector procurements, we note that the share of exemptions in the total value of procurements fluctuated between 7.5 percent and 13.5 percent. Direct procurement fluctuated between 5.9 percent and 18.4 percent of the total value of public procurement, the share of negotiated procedures fluctuated between 4.9 percent and 10 percent, and the share of restricted procedures fluctuated between 1.5 percent and 8.8 percent. Finally, the share of open procedures fluctuated between 57.4 percent and 70.8 percent. The average figures are 66.6 percent for open procedures, 4.6 percent for restrictive procedures, 8 percent for negotiated procedures, 9.3 percent for direct procurement, 11.4 percent for exemptions, and 0.2 percent for other procurement types. Turkey, in comparison to the EU as reported by the European Commission (2011), is

Table 7.2 Public procurement statistics

	Quantity						
	Open procedure (quantity)	Restricted procedure (quantity)	Negotiated procedure (quantity)	Direct procurement (quantity)	Exemptions (quantity)	Others (quantity)	Total procurement value (quantity)
2007	127,307	856	20,806	–	30,859	–	179,828
2008	93,383	600	22,629	–	33,175	–	149,787
2009	77,309	679	20,154	–	32,686	–	130,828
2010	68,551	560	18,865	–	32,475	–	120,451
2011	77,151	616	22,479	–	36,585	95	136,926
2012	71,414	624	22,135	–	33,440	88	127,701
2013	72,414	435	25,158	–	30,958	128	129,093

	Share of different procurement types in total number of procurement (%)						
	Open procedure	Restricted procedure	Negotiated procedure	Direct procurement	Exemptions	Others	Total
2007	70.8	0.5	11.6	–	17.2	–	100
2008	62.3	0.4	15.1	–	22.1	–	100
2009	59.1	0.5	15.4	–	25.0	–	100
2010	56.9	0.5	15.7	–	27.0	–	100
2011	56.3	0.4	16.4	–	26.7	0.1	100
2012	55.9	0.5	17.3	–	26.2	0.1	100
2013	56.1	0.3	19.5	–	24.0	0.1	100
Average	59.6	0.4	15.9	–	24.0	0.1	

Value

	Open procedure (million TL)	Restricted procedure (million TL)	Negotiated procedure (million TL)	Direct procurement (million TL)	Exemptions (million TL)	Others (million TL)	Total procurement value (million TL)
2007	46,022.1	1,639.4	5,154.2	5,009.3	8,153.3	–	65,978.3
2008	59,413.1	1,348.7	7,418.0	4,989.3	10,746.3	–	83,915.3
2009	45,850.5	983.0	6,629.2	4,806.1	7,956.0	–	66,224.8
2010	46,749.2	2,242.1	5,299.9	5,866.9	9,352.2	–	69,510.3
2011	52,680.9	5,757.2	4,520.8	16,913.0	11,870.2	29.4	91,771.4
2012	61,977.9	7,749.4	6,907.4	10,554.3	7,121.7	88.0	94,398.7
2013	69,690.8	9,272.6	10,274.2	6,433.8	9,213.5	619.3	105,504.1

Share of Different Procurement Types in Total Procurement (%)

	Open procedure	Restricted procedure	Negotiated procedure	Direct procurement	Exemptions	Others	Total
2007	69.8	2.5	7.8	7.6	12.4	–	100
2008	70.8	1.6	8.8	5.9	12.8	–	100
2009	69.2	1.5	10.0	7.3	12.0	–	100
2010	67.3	3.2	7.6	8.4	13.5	–	100
2011	57.4	6.3	4.9	18.4	12.9	0.0	100
2012	65.7	8.2	7.3	11.2	7.5	0.1	100
2013	66.1	8.8	9.7	6.1	8.7	0.6	100
Average	66.6	4.6	8.0	9.3	11.4	0.2	

Note: Others refer to procurements conducted according to State Tender Law No. 2886 of 1983, and Build-Operate-Transfer Law No. 3996 of 1994, and all reported to EPPP.

thus an extensive user of exceptional procedures (negotiated procedures and direct procurement). What are the advantages of these procedures?

As emphasized in Section 7.2.4, procedures other than open and restricted may be used in Turkey under special circumstances set in Articles 21 and 22 of PPL. Procurement of the consulting services with the restricted procedures are subject to special regulations (Article 48–52 of PPL) and competitive dialogue procedure does not take place in PPL. Furthermore, "direct procurement," as emphasized in Section 7.2.4, does not require the advertisement of contract notice and can be applied under certain specified conditions stated in Article 22 of PPL. Tenderers participating in the procurement proceedings are no longer required to submit information and documents for evaluation of their economic and financial standing or for the evaluation of their professional and technical qualifications. Similarly, the "negotiated procedure" is used under certain specified conditions stated in Article 21 of PPL. In some of these cases, there is even no need for advertisement of the contract notice. Since the requirements of "direct procurement" and "negotiated procedure" are less restrictive than those of "open procedure" and "restricted procedure," the efficient functioning of public procurement may be distorted by collusion or corruption, or both, reducing competitiveness and efficiency in the public sector and violating the primary goals of sound procurement.

Table 7.3, showing the shares of procurements below and above the thresholds, reveals that on average 94.6 percent of the total number of public procurements (35.5 percent in terms of value) are below thresholds. These are high figures, and they are partly the result of high threshold values adopted in comparison to those of the EU. From Section 7.2.10, we know that for below-threshold contracts the rules for publication of advertisements and time limits are less demanding than those for above-threshold contracts. As a result, there is less competition for those procurements. Furthermore, the high limits reduce the opportunities for foreign bidders to apply. Thus, the high threshold values adopted lead to violations of all of the primary goals of sound procurement systems. In addition, complicated qualification procedures form bureaucratic obstacles and increase the cost of participation in public tenders. As indicated in Section 7.2.5 on selecting economic operators, the Turkish regulations require more information and documents than are required by the EU regulations. They thus form an obstacle to wider competition in public tenders.

We note that the Turkish legislation is not in line with the principle of equal treatment, given that below-threshold procurement is reserved mostly for domestic bidders, while a 15 percent national preference applies above the thresholds. The existence of such a preferential provision presents an obstacle to fair competition. Furthermore, the offset option in public tenders introduced in 2014 contradicts the EU *acquis*, violating the principle of non-discrimination.

Table 7.4 shows data on challenge procedures. The table reveals that over the period 2008–13, there were on average 4,646 challenges, with the number of challengeable

Table 7.3 Procurements below and above thresholds

	Below thresholds (quantity)	Percentage distribution	Above thresholds (quantity)	Percentage distribution	Below thresholds (million TL)	Percentage distribution	Above thresholds (million TL)	Percentage distribution
2007	174,617	97.1	5,211	2.9	20,013.2	32.8	40,955.8	67.2
2008	141,749	94.6	8,038	5.4	21,196.4	26.9	57,729.6	73.1
2009	124,229	95.0	6,599	5.0	18,156.9	29.6	43,261.9	70.4
2010	83,303	94.7	4,673	5.3	19,978.9	36.8	34,312.3	63.2
2011	94,285	94.1	5,961	5.9	26,786.7	42.5	36,172.1	57.5
2012	88,082	93.5	6,091	6.5	30,273.5	39.5	46,361.2	60.5
2013	91,075	92.9	6,932	7.1	36,163.4	40.5	53,074.2	59.5
Average		94.6		5.4		35.5		64.5

Table 7.4 Challenge procedures

	Number of challenges in goods contracts	Number of challengeable tenders	Share in number of challengeable tenders	Number of challenges in work contracts	Number of challengeable tenders	Number of challengeable tenders	Share in number of challenges in services contracts	Number of challengeable tenders	Number of challengeable tenders	Share in number of total challenges	Number of challengeable tenders	Share in number of challengeable tenders
2008	1,096	68,715	1.60	1,009	28,095	3.60	3,487	53,784	6.48	5,592	150,594	3.71
2009	535	58,043	0.92	721	20,633	3.49	1,698	48,829	3.48	2,954	127,505	2.32
2010	747	57,643	1.30	1,650	24,047	6.86	1,884	51,651	3.65	4,281	133,341	3.21
2011	839	54,470	1.54	1,423	24,145	5.89	2,408	46,011	5.23	4,670	124,625	3.75
2012	913	50,331	1.81	1,463	23,500	6.23	2,906	45,917	6.33	5,282	119,748	4.41
2013	854	45,781	1.87	1,205	25,227	4.78	3,034	45,560	6.66	5,093	116,929	4.36
Average	831	55,831	1.51	1,245	24,275	5.14	2,570	48,625	5.31	4,645	128,791	3.63

tenders amounting to 128,791. The average challenge rate was therefore 3.63 percent. The challenge data show a considerable degree of variation among goods, works, and services contracts. The average challenge rate for goods contracts was 1.51 percent, the challenge rate for works contracts was 5.14 percent, and the challenge rate for services contracts was 5.31 percent. According to the OECD (2009), the number of complaints lodged by dissatisfied tenderers amounted to some 900 in 2003. Table 7.4 reveals that the number grew to about 5,000 in 2013—a considerable increase. The OECD (2009) further asserts that from 2003 to May 2009, 1,585 decisions of the PPB were brought to the courts, and that of the court cases opened against decisions of PPA, 198 have been finalized, of which 138 were concluded in favor of the of the PPA and 60 in favor of the complainant.

Alyanak (2006) points out that the Turkish review system summarized in Section 7.2.10 is very intricate and formalistic. Turkey can be criticized mainly due to the complexity of the review system and the absence of fully effective rules on review. In fact, the related Turkish legislation has to ensure that the review provisions are clear, precise, and binding, and that the implementing legislation is properly fulfilled.

7.4 International Good Practices and Turkish Public Procurement

Countries crafting a sound public procurement system must balance a number of goals. Of these, competition, transparency, non-discrimination, and integrity are probably the most important.

The economic literature emphasizes the importance of *competition* for achieving an optimal allocation of resources. Competition leads to lower prices and higher-quality products for a given price. In public procurement, the main issues are preserving free entry and the absence of collusion. Competition will be promoted in procurement markets by prohibiting discrimination, adopting transparent procedures and standardization of the procedures for awarding procurement contracts, and opening procurement markets to international trade. In preventing collusion among alternative suppliers, national competition laws and policies play an essential role. This role encompasses the adoption and enforcement of effective competition rules to prevent collusive tendering, and the progressive elimination of regulatory and other barriers to competition in public procurement.

The concept of *transparency* in the context of procurement involves five main elements: the public disclosure of the rules that apply in the procurement process; the publication of procurement opportunities; the prior determination and publication of what is to be procured and how submissions are to be considered; the visible conduct of procurement according to the prescribed rules and procedures; and the existence of a system to monitor that these rules are being followed. The major aim of transparency is to ensure that the rules are followed and that non-compliance can be ıdentified and addressed. The effect of transparency is a higher level of competition. Since the contracting authorities must make procurements publicly known, more suppliers will be aware of the opportunities. Furthermore, suppliers that are aware of the fact that their possible rivals have access to the same information will come up with proposals that are competitively superior to those of their opponents. This ensures that the contracting authority can pick the best possible proposal.

Non-discrimination in public procurement refers to avoiding provisions that limit, bar, or discourage firms from bidding on the basis of location, sourcing decisions, and employment practices. The principles of equal treatment and transparency are closely related to the principle of non-discrimination. Equal treatment requires that comparable situations are not treated differently and that different situations are not treated similarly unless such a difference or similarity in treatment can be justified objectively. Thus, a contracting authority must act fairly in the course of public procurement; all competitors must have an equal opportunity to compete for the contract. On the other hand, the principle of transparency requires transparent decision-making in order to show that the contracting authority is following the principle of equal treatment. Finally, we note that discrimination against foreign firms in an international trade context includes price preferences, outright bans on foreign bidders, local-content related restrictions such as offsets, and standards adopted in the procurement process that raise the costs of foreign firms.

Integrity in procurement involves both the avoidance of corruption and abuse and the notion of personnel involved in procurement acting ethically and fairly, avoiding conflicts of interest. Corruption practices involve different forms of collusion between government and bidders, such as awarding contracts on the basis of bribes; awarding contacts to firms in which one has a personnel interest; awarding contracts to firms in which one's friends, family, or business acquaintances have an interest; and awarding contracts to political supporters. Such corruption, which can occur in the execution as well as award of contracts, may prevent authorities from achieving value for money in their acquisitions, since under corruption contracts will not be awarded to the best firms.

7.4.1 ASSESSMENT

Turkey's public procurement system has significantly improved since the adoption of PPL and PPCL in 2002 in achieving the primary goals of a sound public procurement system.[10] The new system of public procurement introduced through PPL and PPCL of 2002 was of a high standard, and during the period since 2002 Turkey has shown remarkable progress in adjusting to the new system of public procurement. Furthermore, considerable progress has been made in improving the efficiency and effectiveness of the PPA operations through the use of IT technologies and through e-procurement tools.

But over time, problems started to accumulate. Economic units adversely affected by the changes in government procurement legislation started to complain. Policy-makers responded to these complaints by making amendments to PPL directly and indirectly. While in the case of direct method the government has introduced changes in PPL by amending Law No. 4734 of 2002 through a separate legislation, indirect methods were used when the government inserted the amendments to PPL to other laws adopted and also inserted these amendments to different government decrees. According to Odabaşı (2014), as of 2014 there were thirty-seven direct and 138 indirect amendments to PPL. Some of the changes to PPL were made in order to align the public procurement legislation to EU public procurement *acquis*. But other changes were introduced that led to further deviations from satisfying the primary goals of a sound procurement system, and most of these amendments concerned exemptions discussed in Section 7.2.2. In addition, the Mass Housing Administration, TOKI, as emphasized in the previous section, is no longer within the scope of PPL.

The growing number of exemptions means that many contracts that would normally be covered by PPL rules remain outside the scope of PPL. Such derogations not only deteriorate the integrity of PPL, but also undermine the uniform implementation of the PPL. Furthermore, they hinder the realization of the objective of providing a comprehensive framework for public procurement in Turkey. Once a sector becomes exempt from the rules of PPL, the principles and procedures concerning public procurement are determined with the regulations prepared by the related ministries or institutions taking account of the opinions of PPA. Accordingly, these rules should reflect the main principles of public procurement, such as equal treatment, transparency, and competition of PPL, when awarding the contracts. However, it is hard to say that these regulations are in full compliance with the main principles of the PPL. In particular, the transparency requirements for advertising the contracts are in most cases violated. Besides, tender procedures are not similar to the PPL tender procedures. Under exemptions, the efficient functioning of public procurement is distorted by collusion or corruption, or both, reducing competitiveness and efficiency in the public sector. Thus, the increased use of exemptions is violating all of the goals of a sound public procurement system.

[10] For a discussion of public procurement system prior to 2002 and its shortcomings see World Bank (2001) and Gözel (2004).

On the other hand, PPL does not contain provisions on works and services concessions such as construction of highways and bridges by the private sector. As a result, tender procedures, award criteria, and the inclusion of social and environmental considerations in public contracts are different from those stipulated in EU public procurement directives. Thus, a significant difference exists between the EU public procurement directives and the Turkish legislation. For example, the Build, Operate and Transfer Law (Law No. 3996) does not provide the principles and procedures established in European legislation. In addition, the temporary coverage of entities operating in the utilities sectors does not comply with the EU legislation. Thus, uniform and coherent laws on utilities are still missing. As a result of opaque tendering procedures and poor governance, contract prices tend to be higher and delays and cost over-runs affect taxpayers negatively, as they end up paying more for less. Although more than seven years have passed since the preparation of the Draft Law on Utilities, which had been submitted to Ministry of Finance for enactment through the legislative process, the Law on Utilities has until now not been enacted, showing the lack of political will on this issue.

Concentrating on some specific issues related to PPL, we note that in the definition of "state authorities," the approach is formal referring to the method of financing. However, the approach of EU directives is functional and refers to the composition, the function of the institution, and the way of establishment. Furthermore, Turkish PPL does not contain the concept of a body governed by public law (Art. 1 (9) of the Directive 2004/18/EC). The corresponding item in Turkish Law (Art. 2 (d) of PPL) is less comprehensive than the concept of body governed by public law developed by the European Court of Justice. In addition, Turkish PPL does not contain an indicative list of contracting entities, and neither does it contain a provision stating that in the case of contracts subsidized more than 50 percent by a public contracting entity the rules of the PPL are mandatory. Moreover, the definition of "public contract" deviates from the definition of the EU Directives in the sense that the element of "pecuniary interest" is omitted, which is fundamental in the definition of a procurement contract in the EU.

These considerations reveal that Turkey, instead of aligning its public procurement legislation over time with the EU public procurement *acquis,* has chosen to deviate more and more from the EU *acquis.* It seems that the complexity and variety of different interest groups within society and within public administration complicates the pursuance of the satisfaction of primary goals of sound procurement, namely competition, transparency, non-discrimination, and integrity.

7.5 **Empirical Analysis of Government Procurement**

This section examines empirically the efficiency of three procurement methods implemented by PPA: open, restricted, and negotiated procedures. We are fortunate to have access to detailed information about government procurement auctions in Turkey collected by PPA. We make use of this unique data set covering the period 2004–10. The following variables are employed in the empirical analysis:

- Winning bid: The PPA dataset contains the winning bids (i.e., the lowest bids) for each of the public procurement auctions run during the 2004–10 period. The PPA law requires collection of only the value of the winning bid and the number of bidders. Thus, we do not have information on losing bids in the dataset.
- Estimated cost: Experts estimate the cost of the procurement before the auction is announced. The PPA controls the accuracy of these estimates.
- Number of firms (N): The number of valid bids submitted by the bidders.

We add additional variables that are necessary for our analysis. First, we construct a dummy variable, "Above Threshold." After collecting the threshold values announced by PPA, "Above Threshold" equals unity if the estimated cost is above the threshold value, and zero otherwise. Second, we construct a dummy variable, "Foreign Winner," which has a value of unity if the winner in an auction is a foreign firm and zero otherwise. Next, we define another variable by identifying all the Turkish cities in which auctions take place. We group the auctions into regional dummies depending on which region the city is located in. The Turkish government provides financial support to investors that invest in less-developed regions. The Ministry of Development has identified six regions according to the economic development of those regions, with the first being the most-developed and the sixth the least-developed region. Firms that invest in region one are not eligible for any financial support, whereas firms that invest in region six get tax refunds and financial support for employment, and they can even be eligible for rent-free land. Following Onur et al. (2012), we classify the city in which the auction took place as a "Big City" if the population is greater than or equal to one million. Finally, we construct the "Education" variable, which represents the percentage of the population in each city with at least a high school diploma.

Using the dataset, we examine the following questions:

- Which procurement procedure yields the lowest procurement cost, and which procedure results in the greatest competition (in terms of number of firms)?
- What is the effect of competition on procurement costs?
- Which factors determine the participation of tenderers?
- What is the effect of opening a procurement to foreign firms on procurement costs and also on the level of competition?
- What is the effect of adopting an electronic procurement system on procurement costs and also on the level of competition?

Several studies investigate the efficiency of government procurement auctions. Paarsch (1992) shows that the winning bid declines until the number of bidders reaches between five and ten for the tree-planting contract auctions held in British Columbia, whereas Gupta (2002) analyzes the Florida highway construction auctions and finds that the market becomes competitive with eight bidders. Iimi (2006) reports that the winning bid decreases as the number of bidders increases in the Japanese Official Development Assistance (JODA) auctions up to about eight firms. Estache and Iimi (2008) conclude that seven bidders are required to take full advantage of competition in the roads and water sectors, whereas the optimal number of bidders for the power sector is three.

We contribute to this literature by comparing the efficiency of alternative procurement methods. We also examine the impact of the adoption of an electronic procurement system on procurement costs and on the number of firms participating in the procurement procedures. We provide empirical support for the adoption of electronic systems by showing that electronic procurement systems promote competition and that lower procurement costs are achieved after the adoption of such a system.

Table 7.5 displays the summary statistics of the variables for different types of procurement procedures. In the dataset, three procurement methods are recorded: open procedure, restricted procedure, and negotiated procedure.[11] The table allows us to examine the differences between different procurement methods. One important piece of information is the mean of the dependent variable, defined as $ln\left(\frac{wb_i}{ecost_i}\right)$ where ln denotes the natural logarithm, wb_{it} the procurement cost of procurement i, and $ecost_{it}$ the estimated cost of procurement i. Table 7.5 reveals that the mean value of the dependent variable is -0.167 for the open procedure, and is higher for the other methods. This indicates that lower procurement prices are achieved when the open procedure is used. Also, the number of bidders is significantly higher for the open procedure, suggesting that the open procedure is much more competitive than the restricted and negotiated procedures. Finally, 4.5 percent of the winners are foreign firms in the open procedure, and this percentage is significantly lower in the other procedures.

Table 7.5 also displays statistics about foreign participation in Turkish public procurement. Out of 572,760 procurements, 24,626 procurement contracts have been awarded to foreign firms (4.2 percent). The open procedure had the highest percentage of foreign suppliers—458,660 procurements were conducted using the open procedure, and foreign firms won 20,744 (4.5 percent) of these contracts. The percentage was significantly lower for the restricted and negotiated procedures. Foreign firms were awarded 3.15 percent of the contracts when the restricted procedure was implemented, and 3.41 percent when the negotiated procedure was implemented.

[11] The data set does not contain information about direct procedure.

Table 7.5 Summary statistics

	Open procedure			Negotiated procedure					
	Number of obs.	Mean	Std. dev.	Number of obs.	Mean	Std. dev.	Number of obs.	Mean	Std. dev.
Winning bid (WINBID)	458,660	1,792,098	6.65E+08	3,051	2,230,026	1.17E+07	111,049	195,995	2,955,148
Estimated cost (ESTIMATE)	458,660	2,165,177	7.76E+08	3,051	3,117,951	1.62E+07	111,049	217,443	3,265,992
Dependent variable*	458,660	−0.167	0.2	3,051	−0.074	0.157	111,049	−0.101	0.148
Number of bidders (N)	458,660	3.21	3.57	3,051	2.67	3.82	111,049	2.21	1.63
Foreign	In 20744 auctions foreign firms are selected. (4.5%)			Foreign firms are selected in 96 procurements. (3.15%)			Foreign firms are selected in 3786 procurements. (3.41%)		

* Dependent variable = log(winning bid)-log(estimated cost)

Table 7.6 Domestic and foreign suppliers by procurement method

	Procurement method								
	Open procedure			Restricted procedure			Negotiated procedure		
Year	Domestic	Foreign	Percent	Domestic	Foreign	Percent	Domestic	Foreign	Percent
2005	49,348	2,296	4.45	50	1	1.96	8,754	334	3.68
2006	84,495	4,036	4.56	644	37	5.43	16,476	592	3.47
2007	82,009	4,027	4.68	749	25	3.23	19,488	700	3.47
2008	86,971	4,177	4.58	591	17	2.8	23,656	806	3.29
2009	77,692	3,673	4.51	602	7	1.15	23,265	831	3.45
2010	55,815	2,557	4.38	35	6	14.63	15,283	513	3.25

Table 7.7 Auction characteristics and auction results

	Auction result	
Procurement characteristic	Dependent variable	Number of bidders
Open procedure	−0.072 (120.38)**	1.009 (97.26)**
Above threshold	−0.01 (9.06)**	1.350 (71.35)**

* p<0.05; ** p<0.01. Constant is not displayed.

Table 7.6 shows the change in the origin of suppliers over time. The percentage of foreign suppliers does not change very much in the cases of open and negotiated procedures. However, the percentages vary significantly for the restricted procedure.

Next, we estimate the following regression equation to gauge the effects of different procurement specifications on the procurement price and the competitive environment (i.e., the number of bidders):

$$Auction\ Result_i = \beta_0 + \beta_1 Auction\ Characteristic_i + \epsilon_{i.}$$

Table 7.7 displays the estimation results. The coefficient of the open procedure dummy variable is significant, with a negative coefficient for the dependent variable, indicating that when the open procedure is implemented, the procurement price is significantly lower compared to the price under other procurement procedures, and the number of bidders is significantly higher. On average, 1.35 more firms participate in procurements when the estimated cost is above the threshold level, resulting in a lower procurement price.

7.5.1 DETERMINANTS OF PROCUREMENT PRICES

We now turn to investigation of the effects of the number of bidders (i.e., competition) and the participation of foreign tenderers on procurement prices, and estimate the following regression equation:

$$ln\left(\frac{wb_i}{ecost_i}\right) = X_i\beta + \Phi\ Control_i + \epsilon_{i.}$$

The vector of factors X_i contains the variables of interest. The regression specification also contains vector of control variables, $Control_i$.

We take into account the possible endogeneity of the variables while conducting the regression analysis. We treat the number of bidders (N) as endogenous. Therefore, we use the "Education" and the "Big City" dummy variables as instruments in our regression, using the GMM methodology suggested by Onur et al. (2012). We select these variables since they are closely related to the number of bidders and they are strictly exogenous. Statistical analysis concludes that these variables are valid instruments.

In Table 7.8, we regress the normalized winning bid on auction specific variables. Each column presents a different procurement procedure. The table shows that the number of bidders is a significant determinant of procurement prices for the open procedure and restricted procedure. As expected, an increase in the number of bidders significantly lowers procurement prices, since the coefficient of the number of bidders is negative and significant. In addition, Table 7.8 shows that when the winner of the procurement process is a foreign firm, the procurement price is lower for the open procedure. The coefficient of the foreign winner dummy variable is not significant for the other procedures.

The above considerations reveal that the number of bidders (i.e., competition) is important in determining the procurement prices. Government agencies can lower the procurement cost by promoting participation in government procurements.

7.5.2 ENTRY DECISION OF FIRMS

We now study the determinants of the number of bidders for different procedures. The determinants of entry for firms in Turkish procurement are examined using a count data model, as in Bajari and Hortacsu (2003). We regress the number of bidders in an auction on various covariates, and the results are presented in Table 7.9. The table shows that the estimated cost of a procurement is a significant factor for the number of bidders, especially for the open procedure. When the estimated cost is higher, more firms submit

Table 7.8 Determinants of procurement prices GMM analysis

	Procedure		
Variable	Open procedure	Restricted procedure	Negotiated procedure
Number of bidders (N)	−0.025	−0.070	0.004
	(16.58)**	(2.90)**	(0.97)
Stimulus Region 2	0.008	−0.052	−0.000
	(6.35)**	(1.77)	(0.19)
Stimulus Region 3	0.005	−0.041	−0.007
	(3.68)**	(1.12)	(3.51)**
Stimulus Region 4	0.011	−0.048	−0.018
	(9.11)**	(1.18)	(10.48)**
Stimulus Region 5	0.021	−0.074	0.005
	(17.00)**	(2.06)*	(2.48)*
Stimulus Region 6	0.029	−0.026	−0.007
	(28.01)**	(1.30)	(2.97)**
Goods dummy	−0.063	0.014	−0.026
	(87.34)**	(1.55)	(21.08)**
Construction dummy	−0.057	0.261	−0.049
	(11.26)**	(1.75)	(8.72)**
Above threshold dummy	0.019	0.037	−0.014
	(6.08)**	(0.95)	(3.83)**
Foreign winner dummy	−0.007	−0.011	−0.001
	(3.34)**	(0.37)	(0.33)
Constant	−0.045	0.088	−0.093
	(9.49)**	(1.08)	(8.61)**
N	458.659	3.051	111.049

*p<0.05; ** p<0.01. Year dummy variables not displayed

bids. Additionally, more firms participate in construction procurements. The construction dummy variable is significant with a positive coefficient for all procedures.

7.5.3 PROCUREMENTS OPEN TO FOREIGN TENDERERS

Another important concept in government procurement auctions is equal treatment of firms, calling for equal treatment of foreign and national firms. The PPA dataset contains information about whether the procurement is open to foreign firms for the 2004–6 period. Table 7.10 displays the procurement costs of procurements open to foreigners. The mean of the natural logarithm of the winning bid to estimated cost is shown for

Table 7.9 Determinants of auction entry: Bidder entry-negative binomial regression

	Procedure		
Variable	Open Procedure	Restricted Procedure	Negotiated Procedure
Estimated Cost	0.215	0.074	0.077
	(182.94)**	(7.67)**	(36.18)**
Stimulus Region 2	−0.044	−0.331	−0.158
	(9.71)**	(5.81)**	(24.11)**
Stimulus Region 3	−0.079	−0.232	−0.122
	(16.91)**	(4.53)**	(17.62)**
Stimulus Region 4	−0.033	−0.503	−0.025
	(8.31)**	(11.79)**	(3.49)**
Stimulus Region 5	−0.023	−0.302	−0.079
	(5.57)**	(5.91)**	(11.31)**
Stimulus Region 6	0.212	−0.059	0.199
	(47.33)**	(1.27)	(29.15)**
Goods Dummy	0.062	−0.013	0.080
	(17.46)**	(0.32)	(16.64)**
Construction Dummy	0.592	0.906	0.364
	(155.21)**	(16.22)**	(45.85)**
Above Threshold Dummy	−0.138	−0.086	−0.009
	(20.73)**	(1.19)	(0.70)
Foreign Winner Dummy	−0.061	−0.046	−0.036
	(5.38)**	(0.48)	(1.14)
Constant	−1,318	0.143	0.070
	(72.23)**	(0.74)	(1.84)
N	458.659	3.051	111.049

*p<0.05; ** p<0.01. Year dummy variables not displayed

Table 7.10 Effect of being open to foreign firms on procurement costs

	Procedure					
	Open procedure		Restricted procedure		Negotiated procedure	
	Number of obs.	Mean	Number of obs.	Mean	Number of obs.	Mean
Open to foreign firms*	10,033	−0.204	12	−0.067	2061	−0.143
Not open to foreign firms	79,781	−0.172	113	−0.161	13,931	−0.114
T-test	T-test = 13.02		T-test = −1.51		T-test = 6.87	
	P-Value = 0		P-Value = 0.13		P-Value = 0	

* Data is available for the 2004–6 period.

Table 7.11 Effect of being open to foreign firms on number of bidders

	Procedure					
	Open procedure		Restricted procedure		Negotiated procedure	
	Number of obs.	Mean	Number of obs.	Mean	Number of obs.	Mean
Open to foreign firms	10,033	3.44	12	4.25	2061	2.66
Not open to foreign firms	79,781	3.05	113	4.23	13,931	2.31
T-test	T-test = −9.54		T-test = −0.02		T-test = −4.85	
	P-Value = 0		P-Value = 0.99		P-Value = 0	

different procedures. The hypothesis test reveals that procurements open to foreign firms have significantly lower procurement costs under the open procedure and the negotiated procedure.

Table 7.11 displays the number of firms in procurements open to foreigners. The mean of the number of firms is shown for different procedures. The table shows that the procurement process is more competitive when it is open to foreign firms under open procedure and under negotiated procedure. The open and negotiated procedures lead to significant savings in the economy.

7.5.4 EFFECT OF THE ELECTRONIC PUBLIC PROCUREMENT SYSTEM

After the introduction of EPPP, a significant portion of the government procurements is conducted by electronic methods. The extensive structure of the PPA dataset allows us to perform an empirical analysis of EPPP adoption. Tables 7.12 and 7.13 present information about the electronic procurement, and investigate the effect of EPPP implementation on procurement prices and on the number of firms. Table 7.12 reveals that procurement costs are significantly lower after EPPP adoption for the open and restricted procedures. Table 7.13 shows that the procurement process is more competitive for all procedures after EPPP implementation.

Summarizing the above results, the empirical analysis of the PPA dataset allows the following observations:

- Procurement costs are significantly lower and the level of competition is significantly higher for the open procedure compared to the restricted procedure and negotiation.
- An increase in the number of firms significantly decreases procurement costs for the open and restricted procedures, but has no effect in the case of the negotiated procedure.

Table 7.12 Effect of electronic procurement system on procurement prices

	Procedure					
	Open procedure		Restricted procedure		Negotiated procedure	
	Number of obs.	Mean	Number of obs.	Mean	Number of obs.	Mean
Paper-based procurement	472,561	3.44	3119	4.25	112,959	2.66
Electronic procurement	115,896	3.05	173	4.23	37,184	2.31
T-test	T-test = 17.51		T-test = 5.37		T-test = −0.07	
	P-Value = 0		P-Value = 0		P-Value = 0.94	

Table 7.13 Effect of electronic procurement system on number of firms

	Procedure					
	Open procedure		Restricted procedure		Negotiated procedure	
	Number of obs.	Mean	Number of obs.	Mean	Number of obs.	Mean
Paper-based procurement	472,561	3.28	3119	2.68	112,959	2.22
Electronic procurement	115,896	3.80	173	9.19	37,184	2.31
T-test	T-test = −42.99		T-test = −20.67		T-test = −7.71	
	P-Value = 0		P-Value = 0		P-Value = 0	

- More firms participate in larger procurements when the estimated cost is above the threshold, and also in construction procurements.
- Under the open procedure, procurement costs are lower when the winner is a foreign firm. Also, when procurements are open to foreign firms the costs are significantly lower for all procedures, and competition is significantly higher.
- Procurement costs are significantly lower after the electronic procurement system is adopted for all procurement methods. More firms participate in the processes after the adoption.

7.6 **Conclusion**

Public procurement concerns how public authorities spend taxpayers' money when buying goods, services, and works. While countries in general may have rules aimed at ensuring that public money is spent in a transparent, efficient, and non-discriminatory way, thus securing competition and integrity, some countries may not observe these goals of a sound public procurement system. One such country that did not observe the goals of sound public procurement was Turkey prior to the adoption of the Public Procurement Law (PPL) in 2002. PPL was prepared by taking into account the then prevailing EC Directives on public procurement, the 1994 UNCITRAL Model Law, and the WTO's 1994 GPA. However, the high standard of the initial PPL could not be maintained over time. Instead of aligning the public procurement legislation closer to EU public procurement *acquis,* Turkey chose to deviate more and more from the EU *acquis* over time. As a result, the Turkish system of public procurement as of 2015 is in need of major reform.

There are three "paths" that could be followed to provide a framework for the needed reforms. The first is refocused efforts to adopt the evolving EU *acquis.* The second is to participate in one of the new mega-regional trade agreements that the EU and the US form part of. The most obvious and likely focal point for such an initiative would be seeking to join the TTIP if and when these talks between the EU and the US are concluded. This will be a GPA+ agreement and thus will be challenging to implement, although it would drive efficiency gains through the strengthening of competition, improved deterrence of corruption, and locking-in of internal reforms through legally binding commitments. Turkey would benefit from improved governance and would derive gains from achieving better value for money for government and citizens in its domestic procurements through greater transparency and non-discriminatory conditions of competition between suppliers.[12] As under accession, Turkish producers would have the legal right to access EU government procurement markets, generating potential export market gains and safeguarding against protectionist measures by EU member states.

Given the uncertainty and time that pursuing the trade agreement strategy entails, the third option—to start negotiations to join the WTO Agreement on Government Procurement (GPA)—could be pursued. By joining the GPA, Turkey would enhance its chances of concluding an FTA with the EU covering, among others, government procurement, since the requirements imposed by the government procurement *acquis* of the EU are much more demanding than those imposed by the GPA. Thus, it would be a step-by-step approach to concluding the FTA with the EU covering, among others, government procurement. The advantages of joining the GPA would include—as emphasized by Anderson et al. (2011)—the chance to enhance competition internationally, to promote competition in internal procurement markets, and to obtain right of access to GPA members' government procurement markets, as well as the possibility of deterring corruption in national procurement systems.

[12] According to Wade (1990), corruption and clientism in state procurement policies is a barrier to efficient and sustainable development.

ACKNOWLEDGMENTS

The views expressed in this chapter are those of the authors and do not necessarily represent the views of the Turkish Ombudsman Institution. Bedri Kamil Onur Taş gratefully acknowledges the research support (113K743) provided by the Scientific and Technological Research Council of Turkey.

REFERENCES

Alsaç, Ü. 2012. "Electronic Public Procurement Platform." PowerPoint presentation. Public Procurement Authority, Public Procurement Monitoring and Information Services Department, Ankara.

Alyanak, S. 2006. "An Overview of Turkish Remedies in Public Procurement in Turkey." *Public Procurement Law Review* 15(5): 286–305.

Alyanak, S. 2007. "The Public Procurement System of Turkey in Comparison to European Community Procurement Legislation." *Public Contract Law Journal* 36(2): 203–27.

Anderson, R. D., Pelletier, P., Osei-Lah, K., and Müller, A. C. 2011. "Assessing the Value of Future Accessions to the WTO Agreement on Government Procurement (GPA): Some New Data Sources, Provisional Estimates, and an Evaluative Framework for Individual WTO Members Considering Accession." WTO Staff Working Paper ERSD-2011-15, Geneva.

Bajari, P. and Hortaçsu, A. 2003. "The Winner's Curse, Reserve Prices, and Endogenous Entry: Empirical Insights from eBay Auctions." *RAND Journal of Economics* 34(2): 329–55.

Estache, A. and Iimi, A. 2008. "Procurement Efficiency for Infrastructure Development and Financial Needs Reassessed." World Bank Policy Research Working Paper No. 4662, Washington, DC.

European Commission. 2011. "EU Public Procurement Legislation: Delivering Results." Summary of Evaluation Reports, Brussels.

Gözel, K. A. 2004. "Reforming Public Procurement Sector in Turkey." In *Challenges in Public Procurement: International Perspectives*, vol. 3. Boca Raton, FL: PrAcademics Press, 49–62.

Gupta, S. 2002. "Competition and Collusion in a Government Procurement Auction Market." *Atlantic Economic Journal* 30(1): 13–25.

Iimi, A. 2006. "Auction Reforms for Effective Official Development Assistance." *Review of Industrial Organization* 28(2): 109–28.

Odabaşı, H. 2014. "Kamu İhale Kasası." *Aksiyon* No. 1037, October.

Onur, I., Ozcan, R., and Taş, B. K. O. 2012. "Public Procurement Auctions and Competition in Turkey." *Review of Industrial Organization* 40(3): 207–23.

Organization for Economic Cooperation and Development (OECD). 2009. "Turkey Public Procurement Assessment May 2009." Support for Improvement in Governance and Management (SIGMA) (available on request from: <www.sigmaweb.org>).

Paarsch, H. 1992. "Deciding between the Common and Private Value Paradigms in Empirical Models of Auctions." *Journal of Econometrics* 51(1/2): 191–215.

Public Procurement Authority. 2014. "Turkish Public Procurement Law." PowerPoint presentation, Department of International Relations, Ankara.

TEPAV. 2009. "Kamu İhale Kanunu'nda Yapılan Değişiklikler Ne Anlama Geliyor?", Ankara.

Wade, R. 1990. *Governing the Market: Economic Theory and the Role of Government in East Asian Industrialization.* Princeton, NJ: Princeton University Press.

World Bank. 2001. "Turkey Country Procurement Assessment Report," Europe and Central Asia Region, Washington, DC.

8 Israel's Public Procurement Regime

International and Comparative Aspects

Arie Reich

8.1 Introduction

Public procurement in Israel amounts to around $25–35 billion, which represents about 10–15 percent of the country's gross domestic product.[1] Given this large share of the country's economic activity, as well as the potential for improper influence and corrupt abuse, one can understand the importance of effective regulation and independent judicial review over the field. Indeed, some of the regulation of procurement activities is as old as the state itself, and even precedes it,[2] and judgments conducting judicial review of procurement decisions were among the first issued by the young state's Supreme Court.[3]

This chapter aims to describe and analyze Israel's public procurement regime, including the system for judicial review of this regime, with a special emphasis on its international and comparative aspects. By "international aspects," I mean primarily the international agreements concluded in this field, how they have been implemented, and the impact that they have had on the country's procurement rules. By "comparative aspects," I mean the relationship between Israeli procurement regulations and those of other legal systems. Here I intend to discuss the possible influence that foreign legal systems have had on Israeli regulation, and in particular on the procedural amendments

[1] The figure is taken from the Report of the Team for Improvement of the Administrative Work and Operational Capacity of the Government Ministries ("The Governability Committee") (Jerusalem, March 2013) (available at: <http://www.pmo.gov.il/SiteCollectionDocuments/meshilut2013.pdf> (accessed July 22, 2016).

[2] The duty on Israeli municipalities to conduct public tenders was imposed by the British Mandate in Article 94 of the Municipalities Ordinance of 1934, whereas the State of Israel was established in 1948.

[3] See, for instance, H.C.J. 123/58 *Shlomo Valeiro v. Chairman and Members of the Tenders Committee of Tel-Aviv Municipality* P.D. 13, 715 (judgment rendered on May 8, 1959). There, the Supreme Court, in its capacity as High Court of Justice, annulled an award decision of the Tel-Aviv Municipality because of procedural irregularities.

introduced in the 2009 reform. Also, special attention will be paid to whether technological changes have had an impact and to what extent the Israeli procurement system is taking advantage of modern technology.

8.2 The History of Israel's Public Procurement Regime

Long before Israel's central government procurement was regulated by legislation, it was regulated by court-made jurisprudence, also known as "Israeli Common Law." The courts considered the procurement activities of the government as part of its governmental functions and, as such, subject to the general principles of public administrative law. One of the first and leading judgments in this regard was issued by the Supreme Court in 1961 in the *Rehovot Packing House* case.[4,5] It dealt with a tender for packing and marketing services published by a unit for agricultural experimental research, owned by the Ministry of Agriculture. The petitioner lost the tender to another firm that had performed the same services for this unit during the five years that preceded the tender. The petitioner claimed that it should have won the contract, since its bid was less expensive than that of the winning firm. The state claimed that this case was not under the jurisdiction of the High Court of Justice but of the general courts, just like any other commercial or contractual dispute. Although the tender was conducted by a governmental agency, the state argued, it was in essence conducting a commercial transaction that is governed by private law. The court rejected this argument and held that in the pre-contractual phase the government's actions are governed by public law, thus requiring it to act fairly and without favoritism toward all potential suppliers, ensuring them all equal opportunity to compete for the public contract (see p. 27 of the judgment). The court ruled that this duty exists even if there is no law requiring the government to conduct tenders, nor prescribing how to conduct them. It stems from the agency's obligation under public administrative law to act according to principles of fairness and equality.[6]

Based on these principles, the Israeli Supreme Court developed over a period of thirty years a detailed body of public procurement law. This body of court-made law included

[4] Israel's Supreme Court, in addition to being the highest appeal court in the country for all matters (civil law, criminal law, administrative law, etc.), also serves in the capacity of the High Court of Justice, meaning that it is the first (and final) instance for petitions filed by citizens against governmental agencies based on public law.

[5] H.C.J. 292/61 *Rehovot Packing House Ltd. v. Minister of Agriculture* P.D. 16, 20 (judgment rendered January 8, 1962).

[6] H.C.J. 292/61 *Rehovot Packing House Ltd. v. Minister of Agriculture* P.D. 16, 20 at p. 30. The court also noted that there was an official policy of the Ministry of Agriculture to conduct tenders for its contracts. Once such policy exists, the agency is obliged to implement it fairly and non-discriminatorily.

rules on the duty to conduct public tenders,[7] the prohibition against negotiations with only one of the bidders,[8] the rule against conflict of interest of any of the members of the tendering committee,[9] the duty to award the contract to the least expensive or otherwise economically most advantageous bid,[10] and the right of the losing bidders to inspect the records of the tendering committee and all other relevant tender documents,[11] to mention just a few. These rules are based on three central principles, all of which have their roots in general administrative law: (i) the obligation of the agency to act with integrity and probity and to avoid favoritism; (ii) the prohibition against discrimination and the obligation to ensure equal opportunity to all potential bidders; and (iii) the agency's duty to ensure economic efficiency and to prevent waste of taxpayers' money.[12] These court-made procurement rules applied to all types of government agencies, including government corporations.

In addition, there were (and still are) internal directives (the so-called "TAKAM") issued by the Accountant-General of the Ministry of Finance, which prescribe detailed rules on how to conduct tenders and conclude purchase and sales contracts for the government.[13] These directives are updated from time to time based on experience and rulings by the courts. However, they do not have the status of legislation, they are not published in the official gazette,[14] and bidders cannot rely on them in court if they are breached in the same way as they could if a legislated rule were breached.[15]

Until 1992, the only public agencies in Israel whose procurement activities were regulated by legislation were the local government authorities. This goes back as far as the time of the British Mandate[16] and is probably attributed to the fact that the "natives"

[7] H.C.J. 5023/91 *Poraz v. Minister of Housing* P.D. 46(2) 793.

[8] H.C.J. 688/81 *Migda v. Minister of Health* P.D. 36(4) 85.

[9] H.C.J. 55/82 *Isfar Ltd. v. Minister of Defense* P.D. 37(2) 505.

[10] In *Rehovot Packing House* (p. 27), Berenson J. held that this duty applies even if the tender notice states that the procuring agency is not obliged to choose the least expensive bid or any other bid. See also D.N. 22/88 *Beit Youles v. Raviv* P.D. 43(1) 441 (p. 487).

[11] C.A. 6926/93 *Israel Shipyards Ltd. v. Israel Electric Company* P.D. 48(3) 749.

[12] Omer Dekel, *Procurement Law: Theory and Practice*, vol. 1, 173 (2004) (Hebrew).

[13] "TAKAM" is short for Takanon Ksafim uMeshek (loosely translated as "Regulations on Economy and Finances"). They can now be found at <http://takam.mof.gov.il/doc/hashkal/horaot.nsf> (accessed July 22, 2016).

[14] In the past, they were known mainly to procurement officers and were difficult for the general public to obtain.

[15] According to case law, the government agency is usually required to follow these directives. However, if there are circumstances that justify deviating from them, the agency may do so and cannot be challenged by a bidder on such account. On the contrary, the agency is under the obligation to consider each time whether such special circumstances exist and, if so, deviate from the directives. See Y. Dotan (1996) and H.C.J. 2709/91 *Hefzibah v. Israel Land Authority* P.D. 45(4) 428.

[16] Between 1922 and 1948, the area of so-called Palestine was administered by Britain pursuant to a mandate granted to it by the League of Nations. The Municipalities Ordinance, which requires municipalities to conduct public tenders, was enacted in 1925.

ran the local authorities (municipalities, regional councils and local councils) and thus needed to be controlled, while the central government was run by the British. Under Article 197 of the Municipalities Ordinance (New Version),[17] a municipality "may not enter into a contract to transfer land or goods, to order goods or to perform work except for through a public tender." The Ordinance authorized the Minister of the Interior to issue regulations that will set out detailed rules on the form of the public tender, and on how bids are to be summoned and accepted.[18] It also authorized the Minister to determine certain contracts that the municipality could enter without a public tender. Similar provisions are found in the legislation that applies to the regional councils and to the local councils.[19,20]

In 1973, the Knesset (the Israeli parliament) passed a new law on contracts—the Contract (General Part) Law, 1973—to replace the English Common Law that had been the main source of Israeli contract law until then.[21,22] One of the most radical innovations of this law was the duty that it imposed upon the contracting parties to act "in customary manner and in good faith" during the negotiation of the contract (Article 12(a)), that is, in the pre-contractual stage. This duty of course has a bearing on the law of tendering, which also deals with the pre-contractual stage and is in essence a method of negotiating and reaching agreement on a contract. This new law thus added private law norms to the public law norms that already applied to this field. The new contract law also contributed important tools to deal with various contractual issues that often come up in procurement, such as how to interpret the tendering documents, how to relate to a procurement contract concluded as result of a mistake, and what remedies should be granted to an aggrieved bidder, especially when the contract has already been wrongfully awarded to another bidder.[23] The fact that both of these sources of law apply

[17] The Municipalities Ordinance (New Version), published in *Diney Medinat Yisrael* No. 8 of August 9, 1964, p. 197. This is an official amended translation into Hebrew of the original British Mandate Ordinance.

[18] The Municipalities Ordinance (New Version), published in *Diney Medinat Yisrael* No. 8 of August 9, 1964, Article 198. Based on this authority, the Minister issued the Municipalities Regulations (Tenders), 5748-1988, which sets out detailed tendering rules.

[19] The Local Councils (Regional Councils) Order, 5718–1958, Second Annex, enacted pursuant to the Local Councils Ordinance.

[20] The Local Councils Order (A), 5710–1950, Fourth Annex.

[21] The Contracts (General Part) Law, 5733-1973, published in *Sefer HaChukkim* 5733 No. 694 of April 19, 1973, p. 118.

[22] For a general discussion of the law in English, see Shalev (1974).

[23] For instance, one way of looking at the tender is through the "Contract A-Contract B" doctrine (or "Annexed Contract" doctrine, as it is called in Israel). Under this doctrine, the submission of an offer in response to a call for tenders constitutes a contract (Contract A) separate from the eventual contract awarded at the end of the process (Contract B). The principal term of Contract A is that the agency that published the call for tenders will respect the rules of the tender and award the final contract according to the criteria set out in the call. By submitting its bid, a bidder relies on these terms and enters into a contract with the agency, and if the rules are broken, this amounts to a breach of contract. This doctrine was first adopted by the Supreme Court in the late 70s in C.A. 207/79 *Raviv v. Beit Youles* P.D. 37(1) 533. A similar approach

to public procurement has led courts and commentators to characterize public procurement law as a prime example of "normative duality," that is, a field that is governed by both private and public law norms.[24]

After more than forty years, the Knesset finally decided in 1992 that it was time that Israel's central government procurement should also be regulated by more detailed statutory rules, and not only court-made principles and internal directives. It therefore passed the Mandatory Tenders Law, 1992,[25] which requires all government agencies to conduct their procurement by means of a public tender. The Law itself is a "skinny" law that had only nine original provisions, with four more that have been added over the years. It sets out the basic duty to conduct non-discriminatory public tenders and imposes it on the state, government corporations, and several other types of public entities,[26] as well as private entities funded by the state (such as universities). The Law applies both to purchases and to sales conducted by these entities. It then goes on to authorize the executive branch to exempt—by way of regulations—certain types of procurements from this duty and also to determine the form of the tenders and ways of inviting and receiving price bids, and the manner of publication of the tenders. The Law also authorizes the regulator to provide for various types of preferences in order to promote certain industrial and socio-economic policies through the use of procurement. These include domestic preferences,[27] offsets,[28] preferences and set-asides for national preference regions,[29] and preferences for women-owned businesses.[30]

Hence, the detailed rules of procedures pertaining to public procurement are to be found in the regulations. The most important are the Mandatory Tenders Regulations,

was adopted by the Supreme Court of Canada in the landmark case of *R.(Ont.) v. Ron Engineering* [1981] 1 S.C.R. 111.

24 H.C.J. 492/79 *Plonit Company v. Ministry of Defense* P.D. 34(3) 706, p. 715; and H.C.J. 688/81 *Migda v. Minister of Health* P.D. 36(4) 85, p. 90.

25 The Mandatory Tenders Law, 5752-1992, Published in *Sefer HaChukkim* 5752 No. 1387 of March 12, 1992, p. 114. The bill was published in *Hatza'ot Chok* 5751 No. 2073, p. 354. The Law has been amended twenty-one times since its adoption.

26 For instance, religious councils (municipal bodies in charge of providing religious services to the local public) and *Kupot Cholim* (public health providers/insurers). Pursuant to an amendment from 2002, the Law shall also apply to municipal corporations, as soon as special regulations pertaining to their procurement activities have been issued. However, such regulations are yet to be made.

27 These preferences are subject to Israel's international obligations and are discussed further in Section 8.4.3.

28 Offsets are discussed in Section 8.4.4.

29 Article 3A(A1) of the Mandatory Tenders Law. These preferences are given only in tenders conducted by the Ministry of Defense. The Government has the authority to extend them to other ministries, but this has never been done.

30 Article 2B of the Mandatory Tenders Law. It provides that in a tender in which two or more bids receive identical scores that are the highest ones, if one of them is a firm owned and managed by a woman, it will prevail over the other bids and receive the contract.

1993,[31] (hereafter the "Regulations"). The Regulations apply to the procurement activities of all central government entities, except for the defense establishment, as well as to other entities not falling under other special regulations. Two other sets of tendering regulations are those that apply to the defense establishment,[32] and those that apply to institutions of higher education.[33]

Originally, before the 2009 amendments, the Regulations allowed only four types of competitive tendering procedures:

i. Public tenders, where a call for proposals is openly published in a designated publication and any supplier can submit a bid. These procedures were the rule—at least from a normative perspective—and had to be used unless one of the exceptions set out in the Regulations applied.
ii. A closed tender, where the call for proposals is directed only to certain suppliers, usually drawn from a previously established list. Such a tender may be used only in the special circumstances listed in Article 4 of the Regulations.
iii. A negotiated tender, where the public tender also includes the right to conduct negotiations with the suppliers whose bids are found to be suitable, as set out in Article 7 of the Regulations.
iv. A request for proposals, for the procurement of professional services from experts or for granting of trust positions, if the procurement falls into one of the categories listed in Article 5.

The Regulations also set out a long list of circumstances where the procuring agency can be exempt from the duty to conduct a competitive tender (Article 3). These include, among others, low-value procurements (Article 3(1)); urgent procurements (Article 3 (2)); circumstances where conducting a public tender might significantly harm national security, foreign relations, the economy, public safety, or a commercial or professional secret of the government agency (Article 3(3)); a procurement that is a continuation of a

[31] The Mandatory Tenders Regulations, 5753-1993, Published in *Kovetz Hatakanot* No. 5523 of May 19, 1993, p. 826. These regulations were issued by the Minister of Finance, with the approval of the Knesset Constitution, Law and Justice Committee. They have been amended twenty-three times since their adoption.

[32] The Mandatory Tenders Regulations (Contracts of the Defense Establishment), 5753-1993, published in *Kovetz Hatakanot* No. 5523 of May 19, 1993, p. 841. These regulations were issued by the Minister of Defense, after consulting the Minister of Finance, and with the approval of the Knesset Constitution, Law and Justice Committee. They are parallel to the previous ones in terms of their material scope, but they apply to procurements of the Ministry of Defense, including the Israel Defense Forces. They have been amended five times since their adoption.

[33] The Mandatory Tenders Regulations (Contracts of Institutions of Higher Education), 5770-2010, Published in *Kovetz Hatakanot* No. 6867 of February 11, 2010, p. 774. These regulations were issued jointly by the Minister of Finance and the Minister of Education, after consulting the Council for Higher Education, and with the approval of the Knesset Education Committee. These regulations are also parallel to the previous ones in terms of their material scope, but they apply to procurements by universities and other public institutions of higher education. They have been amended only once since their adoption.

previous procurement (such as an additional delivery by the original supplier), under certain conditions (Article 3(4)); a contract between a government agency and a government corporation under certain circumstances (Arts. 3(5), 3(7), 3(8)); procurement of special cultural or entertainment services (Article 3(11)); situations when, for legal or other reasons, the goods or services can be supplied only by a particular supplier (Article 3(29)); and other extra-ordinary circumstances (Article 3(28)). For many of these circumstances, an approval by the Accountant-General or by a central exemption committee in the Ministry of Finance was required. This was intended to ensure that the conditions of the exemptions were met and that procurement by non-competitive or less competitive procedures was justified. Thus, while the conduct of the procurement itself was decentralized—each government agency has its tenders committee—the authority to grant most of the exemptions was centralized.[34]

8.3 **The 2009 Reform of the Regulations**

8.3.1 THE BACKGROUND TO THE REFORM

As the Mandatory Tenders Law and Regulations entered their second decade, the Israeli government felt that it was time to review the functioning of the procurement regime. Over the years, there was a growing dissatisfaction among government officials (from ministries other than Finance) with the exemptions regime. Their claim was that the central exemption committee had become a "bottleneck" in the system that slowed down the process and created unnecessary delays and obstacles in the path of government agencies to fulfill their tasks of serving the public. Indeed, this committee had to deal with about 1,600 requests for exemptions every year,[35] and decisions took their time. It would also seem that some ministers were unhappy with the refusal of the central exemption committee to approve some of the exemptions that their ministry had requested, and were behind the move to move the authority back to their own ministry.[36]

[34] According to official figures of the Ministry of Finance, the number of exemptions in 2008 (prior to the reform) was 3,102. As explained in footnote 36, the number of exemption requests dealt by the central exemption committee for 2007 was around 1,600 and for 2008 was probably around 2,000. To this figure one needs to add exemptions or approval of exemptions given by the Accountant General himself. Hence our statement that "the authority to grant most of the exemptions was centralized." Certainly, in terms of contract value, most of the authority to exempt was vested at the central level.

[35] The figure is taken from the explanations to the 2008 proposal for amendment of the Mandatory Tenders Regulations (p. 1). It probably relates to the year 2007. From the figures I have received from the Ministry of Finance, it would seem that for 2008 the number is more like 2,000 requests for exemptions per year.

[36] According to press reports, it was the stringent policy of the then Accountant-General Yaron Zelekha, and in particular the refusal to approve huge contracts between the Ministry of Construction and Housing

On the other hand, there were also those who thought that too many requests for exemptions were made and that some were motivated by the considerable administrative burden involved in conducting a public tender. They argued that the existing procurement rules were too stringent and did not grant enough flexibility to the agency's procurement committee to choose a procurement procedure that would best serve each case. Hence, if the rules were made more flexible and less bureaucratic, it would lead to fewer requests for exemptions.

The government therefore decided in 2004 to appoint a committee of directors-general of several government ministries, headed by the Director-General of the Prime Minister's Office and the Accountant-General, to examine ways to improve and streamline the public purchasing mechanism and submit their recommendations to the government.[37] The mandate of the team spoke of the need to "examine economic and technological developments and relevant international treaties." The team appointed a sub-committee (the Weinshall-Lifshitz Committee), which, after deliberations, produced a report with recommendations on several amendments to the Regulations.[38] The thrust of the recommendations was that the tendering procedures should be more flexible and offer more alternative means of conducting a competitive procedure. The tendering committees should have the discretion to choose from these alternatives, but without harming the appropriateness of the procedures, the equality of opportunity, and the integrity of the procurement system.

The recommendations were deliberated by the government for some time and eventually adopted.[39] However, at the same time the government decided in 2007 to appoint another committee, the "Ariav Committee," headed by the Director-General of the Ministry of Finance. The original mandate of this committee was to examine the need for additional amendments in connection with contracts between the government and government corporations that act as executive arms of the government,[40] as well as with

and the government corporation Arim, that prompted the Minister of Housing at the time, Meir Sheetrit, to initiate a reform of the system. See, for instance, Stella Korin Lieber, "Zelecha versus Sheetrit: Rejected Exemption from Tender for Arim Corporation of a 380 Million Shekel Contract," *Globes* June 26, 2007, available at: <http://www.globes.co.il/news/article.aspx?did=1000224067> (Hebrew) (accessed July 22, 2016). According to this newspaper story, Zelekha refused to approve the exemption so that the construction contract could be granted to Arim because there were many private construction companies that could perform the contract and therefore a tender was required. As a result, Sheetrit asked the government to transfer the authority to grant the exemption to the ministries.

[37] Government of Israel, Decision No. 2045 of June 13, 2004.

[38] Report of the Sub-Team of the Committee of Director-Generals for the Streamlining of the Governmental Procurement (the "Weinshall-Lifshitz Report" or the "Zelekha-Cohen Report"), October 28, 2004.

[39] Government of Israel, Decision No. 972 of December 31, 2006. See also Decision No. 43 of February 18, 2007.

[40] See Lieber (2007).

local authorities in their respective fields of jurisdiction.[41] In practice, however, the Ariav Committee made rather sweeping recommendations, the essence of which was to decentralize the procurement system even further and vest most of the authority and the responsibility—both in relation to the choice of method of competitive procurement and to whether to exempt the procurement from any type of competition whatsoever—with the individual agencies.[42] The committee recommended strengthening the role of the Accountant-General as an advisor and educator of the procuring entities, as well as a controller and supervisor over the tendering and procurement procedures conducted by these entities.

The Ariav Committee's recommendations were also adopted and in 2007, the government decided to instruct its legal advisors to prepare the amending legislation.[43] The work on this amendment, including lengthy deliberations in the Knesset Constitution, Law and Justice Committee, took some time, but the amendments were eventually adopted in 2009.

The Mandatory Tenders Regulations (Amendment), 5769-2009 (hereafter the "Amending Regulations") were adopted in February 2009 and came into force in June 2009.[44] However, many of their important amendments were adopted only on a temporary basis for a trial period of two and half years (until January 1, 2012),[45] that later became permanent.[46] I will discuss below the main changes introduced by these amendments, with a special emphasis on those that were meant to take advantage of new technologies and e-procurement, changes in approaches toward public sector governance and accountability, and attempts at improving the efficacy and efficiency of the procurement processes. I will also try to point to instances where the amendments were inspired or influenced by international or foreign practices, to the extent that such influence can be shown to exist. In this context, it should be mentioned that the Weinshall-Lifshitz Committee commissioned a comparative law study by an Israeli scholar with expertise in public procurement in order to learn from the experience of other jurisdictions (hereafter the "Dekel Report").[47]

[41] The mandate was broadened in a later Government Decision.

[42] Report of the Inter-Ministerial Team for Improving the Efficiency of Governmental Procurement, March 28, 2007 (hereafter the "Ariav Committee Report"). Yarom Ariav, the then Director-General of the Ministry of Finance, was the Chairman of the Committee.

[43] Government of Israel, Decision No. 1576 of April 15, 2007. See also Decision No. 1413 of March 18, 2007; and Decision 1538 of April 1, 2007.

[44] Published in *Kovetz Hatakanot* No. 6750 of February 9, 2009, p. 442.

[45] See Article 45 of the Amending Regulations.

[46] The Mandatory Tender Regulations (Amendment) (Amendment), 5774-2014, *Kovetz HaTakanot* No. 7332 of January 21, 2014, p. 545.

[47] The study was performed by Dr. Omer Dekel from the College of Law and Business in Ramat Gan, Israel.

8.3.2 A NORMATIVE HIERARCHY: COMPETITIVE, LESS-COMPETITIVE, AND NON COMPETITIVE TENDERS

The Weinshall-Lifshitz Committee recommended that the Regulations should create a clear normative hierarchy between the competitive and less competitive procedures so that it would be clear that the public tender open to all interested suppliers was the preferred method. In doing so, the Committee noted the commitment of the State of Israel to its international obligations under relevant treaties.[48] This comment is rather surprising considering the fact that none of the international agreements to which Israel is a party requires it to prefer so-called open tendering over selective (also known as "restricted") tendering procedures. Neither the version of the WTO Agreement on Government Procurement that was in force when the Committee made its recommendation,[49] nor the revised version currently in force,[50] requires such a preference.[51] Rather, signatories or their procuring entities are free to choose between open tendering ("a procurement method where all interested suppliers may submit a tender")[52] and selective tendering ("a procurement method where only suppliers satisfying the conditions for participation are invited by the procuring entity to submit a tender").[53]

Nevertheless, the recommendation, which was also supported by the Ariav Committee, was adopted and implemented in Article 1B of the Regulations. This provision clarifies the normative hierarchy between the various methods.[54] The public tender is at

[48] Report of the Sub-Team of the Committee of Director-Generals for the Streamlining of the Governmental Procurement ("Weinshalll-Lifshitz Report"), October 28, 2004, chapter 3, para. 3.

[49] Agreement on Government Procurement, April 15, 1994, Marrakesh Agreement Establishing the World Trade Organization, Annex 4 (hereinafter "GPA"), reprinted in WTO (1994: p. 438).

[50] The Revised Agreement on Government Procurement came into force on April 6, 2014. It is available at <http://www.wto.org/english/docs_e/legal_e/rev-gpr-94_01_e.htm> (accessed July 22, 2016).

[51] Article IX:4 of the Revised GPA, which deals with selective tendering under the agreement, does not impose any condition for the use of this method instead of open tendering. For some time in the European Community, the EC-amended Supplies Directive (Council Directive 88/295/EEC of March 22, 1988) gave clear preference to open tendering procedures, and required special justifications for using restricted procedures (see Article 6(2) and 6(5) of this Directive). However, a few years later the EC authorities withdrew this amendment and changed the provisions back to their previous position whereby the choice was completely that of the procuring agency. For a discussion of this, see Reich (1999: p. 203).

[52] Definition found in Article I(l) of the 2014 GPA.

[53] Revised GPA, Article I(p).

[54] To a certain extent this hierarchy existed before the 2009 reform as well, and was implicit in the requirement to conduct "a regular tender" (i.e., a public tender) unless various exceptional circumstances exist or certain conditions have been met that allow the use of other methods. One should also mention Article 42 in the previous version of the Regulations, which provided that even when these conditions have been met, a public agency should prefer the use of a regular tender, if this is possible. The revised regulations, however, are more explicit in setting out this normative hierarchy at the front of the regulations and in clear language in Article 1B, even if its significance is merely declaratory.

the top and should always be preferred, even where the agency has the permission to conduct the procurement in a less competitive way.[55] Second comes the limited public tender, which includes two types of tenders:[56] (i) an expedited online tender, explained below; and (ii) a public tender where negotiation can be conducted with the bidders.[57] Such a tender shall be used only when it is justifiable not to use the regular public tender.[58] As part of the reform, more detailed rules were set out on how to conduct these negotiations in a fair and equitable manner.[59] Third comes the closed tender (similar to the "selective tendering" of the GPA), which may only be used when neither of the two previous methods is viable.[60] At the bottom of this normative hierarchy is the non-competitive method, that is, not by a tender, and a decision to use such a method requires special justification only after the three previous methods have been considered and ruled out.[61] As we will show in Section 8.3.8, this normative hierarchy seems to have remained a mere declaration devoid of any real substance, with the reality being that the public tender has become the exception and non-competitive procurement procedures the rule.

8.3.3 INTRODUCTION OF NEW PROCUREMENT METHODS

The Weinshall-Lifshitz Committee was of the opinion that the existing Israeli Regulations were too stringent in imposing on the procuring agency the type of procurement procedure it must use. Generally, this had to be the public tender method, unless conditions for using one of the other three (less) competitive methods were fulfilled, or that the procurement was eligible for an exemption, in which case no tender needed to be conducted. The Committee therefore recommended that the arsenal of possible procurement methods should be enlarged, and that greater discretion should be given to the procuring agency to decide which method to use for each case. In making this recommendation, the Committee noted:

> Our comparative study of government procurement law in Western countries show that there is a trend of granting more flexibility to the procuring entity to adapt the competitive procedure to the type of transaction and its complexity.[62]

[55] Regulations, Article 1B(1), as amended in 2009.
[56] See definition of the term "limited public tender" in Article 1 of the Regulations.
[57] The conditions for this to be permitted are set out in Article 7 of the Regulations, as well as how negotiations are to be carried out in a fair and non-discriminatory manner.
[58] Regulations, Article 1B(2).
[59] These rules are set out in the amended Article 7 of the Regulations.
[60] Regulations, Article 1B(3).
[61] Regulations, Article 1(B)(4).
[62] The Weinshall-Lifshitz Report, para. 27.

The new procurement methods that were introduced into the Regulations by the 2009 reform are the following:[63]

i. **A tender with a two-phase examination.**[64] This is in essence a public tender, but differs from the "regular" public tender in that the assessment is divided into two phases. In the first phase, only the quality of the various bids is assessed and each bid is graded for its quality before its proposed price is known. In the second phase, the price proposals of those bids that passed the quality threshold are opened and a final score is given based on the score given for quality and the score for price. This separation of the quality examination from the price examination prevents bias—whether conscious or subconscious—when the tendering committee assesses the quality of each bid, as well as the appearance of such a bias.[65] The detailed procedures for conducting a tender with a two-phase examination are set out in a new Article 17D. This proposal was among those suggested by the Dekel Report (2004) noting that this method is used in US federal tendering procedures.[66] One should add that it is also found in the UNCITRAL Model Law.[67]

ii. **A tender with a preliminary selection phase.**[68] This procedure also has two phases, but here the first phase is aimed at selecting from the bids that are submitted to the preliminary selection phase those that will continue to the next, final phase.[69] In this phase, the tendering committee examines all the bids in order to ensure that they meet the threshold conditions of the tender, including any minimum quality score that was fixed for this tender. Those that do meet these conditions are then invited to submit a bid in the next phase. This procedure enables the tendering committee to find out whether there are enough qualified bidders to proceed with a full-fledged public tender. It also allows potential bidders to verify that they comply with the tender prerequisites before investing substantial funds and efforts in the preparation of their bids. According to the Regulations, the tendering committee may provide in the tendering documents that it may fix new threshold conditions and new minimum scores for this second phase.[70] This permission may be problematic, as it can allow the tendering committee to favor a

[63] Some of these methods were sometimes utilized in practice even before the reform, but without the express authorization to do so. By introducing them into the Regulations and setting out detailed rules on how to use them, the Weinshall-Lifshitz Committee hoped to spread their use and prevent abuse.

[64] Proposed by the Weinshall-Lifshitz Committee, chapter 3, para. 1

[65] For a study demonstrating and analyzing this bias, see Dekel and Schurr (2014).

[66] Omer Dekel, Proposals for Amendments to the Mandatory Tenders Law and the Mandatory Tenders Regulations (on file with author), para. 3.

[67] Article 48 of the UNICTRAL Model Law on Public Procurement, available at: <http://www.uncitral.org/pdf/english/texts/procurem/ml-procurement-2011/2011-Model-Law-on-Public-Procurement-e.pdf> (accessed July 22, 2016).

[68] This procedure was not mentioned in the Weinshall-Lifshitz Committee's recommendations, and was added by the drafters at a later stage.

[69] Article 17C of the Regulations.

[70] Regulations, Article 17C(c).

certain bidder by designing new threshold conditions based on what has been revealed about all of the eligible bids in the preliminary selection phase. It is therefore submitted that one should consider omitting the option of fixing new threshold conditions. Instead, the various pros and cons of each qualifying bid can be evaluated in the award procedure.

iii. **A tender with an additional competitive phase ("best and final offer").**[71] This is a procedure wherein after having conducted a regular public tender, the procuring agency requests the best bidders to improve their prices and to submit their best and final offer. Before the reform, such a procedure could not be used for regular public tenders, but only for tenders where negotiations were permitted, that is those that qualify under Article 7. The concern was that negotiations after submission of bids could violate the principle of equality between the bidders and could be abused for the purpose of favoring a certain supplier over another. If discretion was left to the procuring agency, it was thought that it might abuse such discretion and revert to negotiations whenever the favored supplier was found not to have submitted the lowest bid.[72] Therefore, Article 17E provides that in order to use this method, the procurement notice must set out the objective conditions wherein the additional competitive phase will be used. It may also be used whenever all the submitted bids are higher than the estimate of the contract price made prior to the tender.[73] If those conditions occur, the tendering committee must notify all the bidders who, according to the above conditions, are entitled to submit an improved bid that they may do so. The committee will then consider the new bids (or the original one, if a bidder decided not to improve his bid) and choose the best one among them. However, under the new Israeli provision it appears that in the additional competitive phase, a bidder may only improve the price component of his bid, not the quality or performance component. This limitation, which stems from the wording of the provision, is not necessarily justified. Often a procuring entity can discover from the bids submitted that there are additional functions or better solutions to the problems that they face of which they were not aware when they formulated their call for bids. An additional competitive phase could thus have been used to allow other bidders to improve their bids by including such additional functions, but such a possibility appears to be prohibited under the current Regulations.[74]

[71] Proposed by the Weinshall-Lifshitz Committee, chapter 3, para. 2.

[72] Omer Dekel, *Procurement Law: Theory and Practice*, vol. 2 (2006: pp. 154–5) (Hebrew).

[73] Article 21(A1) of the Regulations. See also the amended Article 23, which deals with a situation where only one bid is left before the tendering committee, but this bid is higher than the estimate. The provision allows the committee to inform the bidder that his bid cannot be accepted unless he improves it, and invites him to do so.

[74] It would seem that under the previous GPA such changes were permitted, provided that all remaining participants are afforded an opportunity to submit new or amended submissions on the basis of the revised requirements (see Article XIV:4(c) of the 1994 GPA). In the revised GPA, there is no similar provision, and Article XII:2(a) dealing with negotiations provides that procuring entities must ensure that any elimination of suppliers participating in negotiations is carried out in accordance with the evaluation criteria set out in

iv. **Online tendering.** An important innovation was the introduction of online procedures as an officially recognized way of conducting procurements, as already done in many countries and now provided for in Article V:3 of the Revised GPA. The Weinshall-Lifshitz Committee notes in its report that the experience in other countries has shown that the use of online tenders has helped to reduce bureaucracy and increase transparency, and has caused an increase in the number of suppliers who participate in the tenders. It also allows for more dynamic and efficient methods of procurement.[75]

The amended Regulations offer three types of such procedures. The first is a regular online tender, which is essentially an electronic version of a regular one-stage public tender.[76] The second is called a "developing online tender," and appears to be a kind of electronic auction.[77] Article 19D:1 provides for the possibility for the tendering committee to use one of the two-phase methods already provided for by the amended regulations and discussed in Sections 8.3.3(ii) and (i) respectively: a tender with a preliminary selection phase (Articles 17C(1) and (2)), or a tender with a two-phase examination (Articles 17D(1) and (2)). The bidders that are thus selected in the first phase are then invited to submit their bids in the ensuing electronic auction. Alternatively, it would seem,[78] the tendering committee can decide that there is no need for a preliminary stage and publish calls for the electronic auction immediately.

The possibility of conducting an electronic auction has also been adopted by the Revised GPA.[79] This agreement defines an "electronic auction" as "an iterative process that involves the use of electronic means for the presentation by suppliers of either new prices, or new values for quantifiable non-price elements of the tender related to the evaluation criteria, or both, resulting in a ranking or re-ranking of tenders."[80] The advent of modern computer technology has made auctions quite popular, both in the private and public sectors, since it enables the conduct of auctions in an effective manner with remote parties, without gathering them into one room like in traditional auctions, and

the notice or tender documentation, that is the original criteria and not revised ones. A similar approach can be found in the UNCITRAL Model Law, under the tendering method called "Request for Proposals with Consecutive Negotiations" (Article 50) where the bidder with the highest ranking is invited to negotiations "on the financial aspects of its proposal." However, under the "Competitive Negotiation" method (Article 51), after the completion of the first stage of the negotiations, all bidders are invited to present "best and final offer with respect to *all aspects* of their proposals."

[75] Weinshall-Lifshitz Report (2004), chapter C, para. 4:VIII.

[76] These procedures are provided for in Article 19C.

[77] These procedures are provided for in Article 19D. The provision is a bit cryptic, and does not give very much guidance about how to conduct this tender, but since it talks about the possibility of several phases of bidding, it appears to be dealing with an online auction.

[78] As noted previously, the provision is not very clear on this, but since Article 19D(1) is worded as an option, it appears that this stage is not required and that the procurement could proceed immediately to the "developing" multi-stage online tendering procedures.

[79] Revised GPA, Article XIV.

[80] Revised GPA Article I(e).

while enabling procuring entities to "push the bidders to the limit" of what they are able to propose. Compared to the Revised GPA, the text of the amended Regulations on this method is very cryptic and does not even use the word "auction." Article 19D is also not very clear on how such auctions should be conducted. In particular, it fails to clarify that the bids submitted are open to all the other bidders, so as to push them to improve their own bids continuously until the deadline.

The third type of procedure, called the "expedited online tender," is highly innovative.[81] It offers something that can only be done by online tendering,[82] namely, allowing a procuring agency to conduct an expedited tender where the submission date may be as short as five days after publication of the tender, depending on the urgency of the case.[83] However, unlike the other two online procedures, which the tendering committee can choose at its discretion, the expedited tender may only be used for procurements valued at no more than 400,000 shekels (approximately US$100,000) when the contract is urgently needed in order to avoid material damage.[84] In extraordinary urgent cases,[85] the tendering committee may even set the submission date for as little as four hours following publication. The expedited online tender has the important potential of reducing the number of exemptions from public tenders given for reasons of urgency (Article 3(2)). Now, urgent procurements can be conducted through competitive online procedures and there is no longer a justification to exempt them from all types of tenders. Indeed, Article 3(2) was amended so that it can now be used only in the very rare case where a contract is needed within two working days or fewer, and after receiving an exemption by the agency's exemption committee.[86]

[81] Regulations, Article 19E.

[82] This procedure was proposed by the Weinshall-Lifshitz Committee. See its report (2004), footnote 40 (supra), chapter 3, para. 4:III.

[83] Article 19E(b)(2). The Revised GPA also allows for significant shortening of time periods when electronic communication is used. Article XI:5 of the Revised Text provides that a procuring entity may reduce the time period for tendering by 5 days for each one of the following circumstances: (i) the notice of intended procurement is published by electronic means; (ii) all the tender documentation is made available by electronic means from the date of the publication of the notice of intended procurement and (iii) the tenders can be received by electronic means by the procuring entity. Thus, the total reduction can be fifteen days, as long as the time period for tendering is no less than ten days from the date on which the notice of intended procurement is published (Revised GPA, Article XI:6). This provision, however, is not conditioned upon urgency, as in the case of the Israeli Expedited On-Line Tender.

[84] Article 19E(a)(1) and (2) of the Regulations.

[85] Article 19E(b)(2). The wording "extra ordinary cases" is not used in the provision, which surprisingly repeats the same term as used for "regular" urgency cases (where there is a minimum time frame of five days), namely, that the contract is "urgently needed in order to avoid material damage." However, the provision uses the words "considering the date required for the conclusion of the contract and its urgency," so that the circumstances must justify employing such a short time frame for submissions. It would have been better, however, if the drafters had made a clearer distinction between "regular" urgency and extraordinary urgency.

[86] Before the amendment, any type of urgency could justify an exemption from tender, subject to an approval of the Accountant-General. If the urgency was such that a contract was required within forty-eight

The new provisions set out detailed rules on how online procedures are to be conducted in order to ensure fairness, confidentiality, and efficiency, similar to what is provided for in the Revised GPA[87] but in a more detailed manner. They require a special secured website; software that records the exact time of any action, including the sending and reception of messages and the identity of each sender;[88] a virtual "bid box" to which bids are submitted and that can only be opened by an authorized official in the presence of the tendering committee and after a set time; and so on.[89] The system must be protected from outside invasion ("hacking") and have a secure backup. Electronic bids can be submitted only by identified bidders and must be signed by them with a secured electronic signature.

The amended Regulations also require each public agency to establish a special secured website where *all* of its tender notices must be published,[90] in addition to the regular publication in both Hebrew and Arabic newspapers.[91] The notices must be published in both Hebrew and Arabic and there are detailed rules on how such a website should be managed and supported in a secure and transparent manner.[92] The agency is also under various obligations to ensure that the existence of the website is publicized properly and that the public can receive technical assistance to access and communicate with it.[93]

While the introduction of online procedures in the Regulations marks an important improvement, unfortunately, as we will show at the end of Section 8.3.8, they have barely been introduced in practice because of budgetary constraints.

v. **Framework tender.**[94] Another new type of tender that was officially introduced by the 2009 amendments is the framework tender.[95] Here, there is first a public tender in which several suppliers are chosen, after which framework agreements for the supply of certain products, work or services will be concluded with all those suppliers ("framework suppliers"). This, then, is a so-called "multi-provider framework."[96] The framework agreements are usually concluded for long periods of time, but they may not be longer

hours, the exemption could be given by the Director-General of the procuring agency. There was also no cap on the value of such a procurement.

87 Article V:3 of the Revised GPA.

88 Article 19B(b) and (c) of the Regulations.

89 Article 19C of the Regulations.

90 Article 24A of the Regulations.

91 Article 15(a) of the Regulations.

92 Article 24B of the Regulations.

93 Article 24B(e) of the Regulations.

94 Article 17f of the Regulations.

95 Such tenders were already used by some Israeli government agencies and recognized by the internal directives of the Accountant-General (the "TAKAM"), but not by the Regulations. It was felt that these procedures needed to be regulated explicitly by the Regulations.

96 See extensive discussion of the various types of frameworks agreements in Arrowsmith (2014: pp. 1006–10).

than five years.[97] The government agencies may then make individual calls under those framework agreements for the products, works, or services in question, but must request offers from all of the framework suppliers. In their bids, they are limited by the maximum price that was agreed in their framework agreement, but they may also bid for less, so the competition is maintained also at this stage. This type of tender was proposed by the Weinshall-Lifshitz Committee, but only as a central tender performed by the government procurement administration in the Accountant-General's office.[98] The idea was to take advantage of the government's purchasing power when it consolidates the needs of all of its agencies and thus obtain lower prices. In practice, however, the Regulations allow framework tenders to be conducted by every individual procurement agency, presumably as part of the decentralization strategy of the Ariav Commission. This may be problematic if, on the one hand, some competitors are shut out of the business for several years until the framework agreement expires, and, on the other hand, the government is not taking full advantage of economies of scale by purchasing large quantities for all of its units. Procedures for framework tenders are found in many foreign and international procurement regimes, such as the EU procurement directives,[99] the US Federal Acquisition Regulations,[100] and the UNCITRAL Model Law.[101] The proposal to introduce them into Israel's procurement regulations was most probably influenced by these foreign regimes.[102]

vi. **A limited version of the competitive dialogue.** The Weinshall-Lifshitz Committee recommended the introduction of the competitive dialogue method of tendering, relying expressly on Article 29 of the EU Public Sector Directive, which was in force at the time.[103] The rationale of the proposal was to allow procuring agencies to collaborate with

[97] Article 17f(c).

[98] Weinshall-Lifshitz Committee Report (2004), para. 14:IV.

[99] See Article 33 of Directive 2014/24/EU of the European Parliament and of the Council of February 26, 2014 on Public Procurement and repealing Directive 2004/18/EC, *O.J.* L 94/65 (March 28, 2014). In the EU, the term of framework agreements shall normally not exceed four years. For a discussion of this provision and of framework tenders in the EU in general, see of Arrowsmith (2014: chapter 11).

[100] One such form is the "Blanket Purchase Agreement," defined as "a simplified method of filling anticipated repetitive needs for supplies or services by establishing 'charge accounts' with qualified sources of supply" (Federal Acquisition Regulation, para. 13-303-1). This type can be used by the individual agency. There are also so-called GSA Schedules, which are centralized framework agreements concluded by the US General Services Administration.

[101] See chapter VII of the UNCITRAL Model Law on Public Procurement, available at: <http://www.uncitral.org/pdf/english/texts/procurem/ml-procurement-2011/2011-Model-Law-on-Public-Procurement-e.pdf> (accessed July 22, 2016).

[102] The proposal is included in the Dekel Report (2004, (para. 5), which was based on Dr. Dekel's comparative law research—see Section 8.3.1.

[103] Weinshall-Lifshitz Report (2004), para. 14:V. The directive in question is Directive 2004/18/EC of the European Parliament and of the Council of March 31, 2004 on the coordination of procedures for the award of public works contracts, public supply contracts and public service contracts, *O.J.* L 134/114 (April 30, 2004) ("the Public Sector Directive").

potential suppliers in defining the project, its scope and components, in particular for complex projects where the agency needs help from the industry to define the technical, financial, or legal aspects of the project. However, in practice, the amended Regulations did not adopt the competitive dialogue as a distinct type of tendering method,[104] nor do they use this term. Rather, Article 14A, titled "Preliminary Request for Information" (RFI), was added, providing that a procuring agency may decide to make a preliminary request for information that it needs in connection with a procurement. Such a request must be made public, and the dialogue and exchange of information between the agency and the potential suppliers must ensure equality of treatment of the participants. The tendering committee must document all information received and every discussion held with the participants. This documentation may be open for perusal by other participants, but only after the contract award and subject to business confidentiality.[105] Once this preliminary request and the ensuing dialogue has been concluded, the tendering committee can choose whichever method of tender it wants, subject to the regular rules, and participation in the preliminary request procedure shall not serve as a condition for participation in the actual tendering procedure.[106] In that sense, these procedures are different from the EU procedures, where the contracting authority may select from among the economic operators that submitted information in response to the call those who may participate in the dialogue (Directive 2014/24/EU, Article 30(1)). Moreover, only these selected participants may then submit their final tenders on the basis of the solution or solutions presented and specified during the dialogue (Article 30(6)). Another important difference is that in Israel, the use of a preliminary request for information is not limited to specific circumstances, as it is in the EU,[107] but may be used whenever the tendering committee feels it could be of assistance. A somewhat similar, but more complicated, procedure can be found in the UNCITRAL Model Law.[108]

[104] Thus, for instance, the method is not mentioned in Article 1 of the Regulations that define the various types of tenders.

[105] Article 14A(f) provides that Article 21(e) shall apply to this information, *mutatis mutandis*. Article 21 (e) provides that within thirty days of contract award notice, a bidder has the right to see the protocol of the tendering committee, its correspondence with the bidders, professional opinions prepared at the request of the tendering committee, the position of the legal advisor to the committee, and the winning bid, and to receive copies of these documents. However, parts of the decision or the bid which in the tendering committee's opinion may reveal commercial or professional secrets, or harm national security, or the state's foreign relations, economy or public security, may be withheld.

[106] Article 14A(e) of the Regulations.

[107] Under the 2004 EU Public Sector Directive, this procedure may only be used "in the case of particularly complex contracts" (Article 29). In the 2014 Directive, the circumstances justifying its use have been redefined and include more types of circumstances; see Article 26(4).

[108] See Article 49 of the UNCITRAL Model Law on Public Procurement.

8.3.4 DECENTRALIZATION OF THE EXEMPTION AUTHORITY

Another central component of the 2009 reform, which has proved to be much more controversial than the previous one, was the decentralization of the authority to grant exemptions from the duty to conduct public tenders. As mentioned above, the Regulations have a very long list of exemptions from public tenders that before the reform included no less than thirty-three different grounds for exemption. The decision of whether for a particular procurement the circumstances justify an exemption under one of those grounds was, for most cases, vested with the agency's tendering committee,[109] but provided that the value of the procurement did not exceed 400,000 shekels (approximately $100,000),[110] or 1,500,00 shekels for the purchase of real estate.[111] For procurements valued over those caps, the procuring agency was required to submit a request for exemption to a central exemption committee headed by the Accountant-General or his representative. The central exemption committee's approval was also required in order to perform a restricted tender for a procurement valued over those caps.

Following the Ariav Committee's recommendation, the 2009 reform established exemption committees in each government ministry (hereafter "agency exemption committees").[112] The agency exemption committees are headed by the Director-General of the ministry in question, and have as their other members the ministry's legal advisor and its accountant. In order to ensure their personal responsibility for the decisions taken, these three members may not delegate their authority to any of their subordinates.[113] The agency exemption committee is authorized to grant exemptions from public tendering, or to approve restricted tendering, for procurements valued up to 4,000,000 shekels (approximately $1 million),[114] that is ten times more than what the ministry's tendering committee had been authorized to exempt before the reform. Exemptions that previously required the approval of the Accountant-General himself (not the central exemption committee) could now be exempted by the ministry's exemption committee up to a cap of 2,500,000 shekels. The 2009 amendments also limited the tendering committees' authority to grant exemptions, by lowering the value cap of their authority from 400,000 shekels to 150,000 shekels per transaction, thereby basically transferring the authority to exempt procurements valued between these two sums from the

[109] Article 9(a) of the Regulations.

[110] For certain types of procurements included in a list published by the Accountant-General, the authority was extended to 700,000 shekels.

[111] Article 12(a) of the Regulations, before their amendment in 2009.

[112] Article 10A(a) of the Amended Regulations.

[113] Except for cases where a member is in conflict of interests in relation to a certain procurement; see the Ariav Committee Report (p. 13).

[114] Article 12 of the Amended Regulations.

ministry's tendering committee to its exemptions committee. The *de minimis* cap of 25,000 shekels found in Article 3(1), whereby there is an automatic exemption from a public tender for low-value procurements, was raised to 50,000 shekels.[115]

The Ariav Committee explained that these changes were required in order to solve the "bottleneck" problem that had been created at the level of the central exemption committee. But the Committee also advocated a fundamental change of paradigms, whereby not only the procurement decision and management is decentralized, but also the exemption authority. This new authority, said the Committee, would be coupled with increased accountability and higher standards of transparency and reporting obligations. The central exemption committee would only have to deal with a small number of high-value procurements, and instead it would be vested with strengthened powers of supervision of the work of tendering committees and the ministries' exemption committees. One way in which this power would be exercised is by giving a right of appeal to any member of the exemption committee who was in disagreement with the decision of the committee. Such a member, who presumably had been outvoted by the other two members, could then appeal the decision to the central exemption committee or to the Accountant-General, depending on the circumstances.[116] In practice, such appeals are very rare (amounting to about one or two per year).[117]

To complete the discussion of the exemptions, one should also mention that many amendments were made to the Article 3 list of exemptions from the obligation to perform a public tender. First, several (eight) exemption grounds were repealed.[118] However, most of them were exemptions that were rarely or never used.[119] On the other hand, four new exemptions were added.[120] Finally, several exemption grounds

[115] The Ariav Committee recommended raising it to 43,000 shekel, but in the final version of the 2009 Regulations the cap was set at 50,000.

[116] This recommendation was implemented in Article 10A(f)(1) of the Regulations, which provides: "A decision by the ministry's exemption committee that was not taken by consensus, except for a decision under Article 3(2) [extreme urgency, A.R.], may be appealed by any member of the ministry's exemption committee within three working days of the decision."

[117] Information obtained from the Ministry of Finance.

[118] The following is the list of the exemptions repealed: Article 3(9)—A contract with a winner of a lottery conducted by the Ministry of Housing as part of a residential building project; Article 3(15)—Short-term, low-value lease of real estate; Article 3(17)—A contract with an army invalid to run a snack bar in a ministry; Article 3(21)—A contract by the Educational Television Authority; Article 3(23)—A contract concerning marketing of frozen meat imported from abroad; Article 3(24)—Certain types of procurement of printing services; Article 3(26)—A contract for construction development work with a company that was retained before the coming into effect of the Law; Article 3(27)—A contract to execute an option included in a contract awarded through a public tender.

[119] On the limited use of these exemptions, see Explanations to the Proposal to Amend the Regulations (2008: p. 3).

[120] Article 3(31) and Article 3(32) were added in 2009, and Article 3(33) and (34) in 2012. They all relate to very specific and rare circumstances.

were severely restricted or conditioned upon approval by a central authority.[121] One seemingly important amendment was made to Article 3(29) that is an often used exemption: "A contract with someone who pursuant to legal rights or to the actual circumstances is the only one who is able to perform the contract," and to Article 3(31)—purchase abroad or from a foreign supplier under certain conditions. The use of these exemptions was made conditional upon a prior examination against the market by a public notification that indeed there is no other potential supplier,[122] an improvement that the present author has advocated in relation to the GPA.[123] Likewise, the use of Article 3(3) for non-profit projects for educational, cultural, religious, or other similar purposes was also made conditional upon a similar prior examination of alternative suppliers.[124]

8.3.5 INCREASED TRANSPARENCY

Finally, one should mention two important amendments that were introduced in order to improve the transparency of the procurement system. One is the obligation of the tendering committee to publish in advance, as part of the tendering documents, the relative weight that will be given to each of the award criteria, in the course of choosing the winning bid (Article 22(b)). Under Article 21, the tendering committee is usually obliged to award the contract to the lowest bid (for a procurement, or the highest, when we are dealing with a sale), unless it has employed its right under Article 22 to set out other award criteria that will grant the procuring agency maximum advantages from the procurement.[125] In such a case, it must usually award the contract according to these criteria, after having given each of them the relative weight that was allocated to them in the tendering documents.[126] This amendment, that was proposed by the Weinshall-Lifshitz Committee, is not entirely revolutionary, since the Supreme Court had already stated in several judgments that the procuring agency is under the duty to act accordingly.[127] Rather, the amendment codifies these judicial holdings and makes them an

[121] One of them was Article 3(2) in relation to urgent requirements.

[122] The procedure for this examination and the conditions for using these two exemptions are set out in detail in the new Article 3A of the Regulations.

[123] See Reich (2009: pp. 1009–10).

[124] The procedure for this examination and the conditions for using it are set out in detail in the new Article 3B of the Regulations.

[125] Article 21(b) of the Regulations.

[126] The committee may in exceptional circumstances refrain from deciding in accordance with the award criteria, for reasons that must be recorded and after giving the affected bidder the opportunity of appearing before the committee and presenting its arguments in this regard.

[127] See in particular A.P.A. 7357/03 *Ports Authority v. Tzomet Engineers*, p. 20.

express part of the Regulations, thus improving the predictability and fairness of the procurement process.

The second amendment grants all bidders the right of access to the protocols of the tendering committee, its correspondence with the bidders, professional opinions prepared pursuant to the committee's request, and to the position of the legal advisor of the committee.[128] This right may be exercised by the bidder, and sometimes even by other interested parties[129] (subject to certain restrictions),[130] within thirty days of receiving the notice on the results of the tender. While this right, too, may have existed in principle even without the amendment—pursuant to the Freedom of Information Law, 1998—its detailed incorporation into the Regulations is an important improvement.[131]

8.3.6 TWO COMMITTEES, TWO APPROACHES?

Interestingly, both the Weinshall-Lifshitz Committee and the Ariav Committee were grappling with the same problem, namely, a public procurement regime that was claimed to be too rigid and that made it too difficult for government agencies to implement their programs. However, the two committees recommended very different solutions to this problem. The Weinshall-Lifshitz Committee recommended introducing more types of tendering procedures and allowing the tendering committees of the government agencies to decide which one to employ. It also recommended modernizing the procurement system by introducing new technologies, including electronic procurement. It was willing to expand the authority of the tendering committee to decide on exemptions from public tendering, but only to a limited degree (to raise the cap from between 400,000–700,000 to 1,200,00 shekels). The Ariav Committee, in contrast, did not believe that a wider and more flexible range of methods would solve the problem, and recommended complete decentralization of the exemption authority. As we have seen, it actually recommended narrowing the exemption authority of the tendering

[128] Article 21(e) of the Regulations.

[129] Recently, it was held by the Supreme Court that even a firm that did not submit a bid, but expressed interest in the tender may be entitled to access to the committee protocols. The case dealt with a firm that had decided to refrain from submitting a bid once it was told by the procuring agency that it insists on a certain precondition. When the contract was awarded, it discovered that the winning bidder was a competitor that also did not meet this precondition. The court held that the firm was "a classic potential bidder," because if it were not for the precondition, the firm would have submitted a bid. C.A.A. 3888/15 *Afcon Control & Automation Ltd. v. Arad Ltd.* (judgment of Solberg J. of July 22, 2015).

[130] The right to read these documents and to receive copies of them may be restricted in relation to documents that the tendering committee thinks may infringe on business or professional confidentiality, or to harm national security, the national economy or foreign relations. Legal opinions rendered as part of the legal advice given to the committee may also be restricted.

[131] Freedom of Information Law, 1998-5758 published in *Sefer HaChukkim* 1667.

committees and creating a clear separation between the body authorized to conduct the procurement and the body authorized to exempt it from public tendering, although both of them were to be in the same ministry. Eventually, both the decentralization approach and the enlargement of the arsenal approach were adopted by the regulator and implemented in the 2009 amendments.

8.3.7 CONCERNS FOR SURGE IN EXEMPTIONS AND ATTEMPTS TO ALLEVIATE THEM

The Ariav Committee's proposal to transfer the authority to grant most of the exemptions from the central exemption committee in the Ministry of Finance to agency exemption committees was not welcomed by everyone. Even within the Committee, there was dissent based on the concern that such a change would lead to a significant increase in the volume of exemptions, at the expense of competitive tendering procedures, and that this might seriously harm the integrity of the procurement system and the right to equal opportunity for potential bidders.[132] The opponents were of the opinion that there has to be a central independent body that supervises the procurement activities of government agencies and ensures that exemptions from public tenders are granted only when this is justified and absolutely necessary. To allow the agency to decide when to exempt itself from the tendering duty, it was argued, is like asking the cat to guard the cream. A central authority was also essential in order to ensure uniformity in the administration of the exemptions. Similar concerns were also raised in the Knesset.[133] This, however, did not stop the adoption of the amendments.

[132] The Accountant-General at the time, Dr. Yaron Zelekha, wrote a lengthy letter to the Ariav Committee expressing his disagreement with the draft proposals and warning about the consequences (see his letter of March 27, 2007, to Yarom Ariav, Director-General of the Ministry of Finance, the Chairman of the Committee). His deputy, Gabriel Shochat, who was a member of the committee, therefore voted against it, and the letter was attached to the Committee's report at their request, as a dissent opinion. There was also another dissent, by the Director-General of the Ministry of Construction and Housing, Arie Bar, but his dissent was motivated by the opposite position: that the recommendations for decentralization did not go far enough. He demanded that the authority of the agencies' exemption committees should be extended to 7 million shekel, that there should be no right of appeal by a Committee member, and that the right to contract with a government management corporation should be completely exempted from tender (see his letter of March 27, 2007, to Yarom Ariav, Director-General of the Ministry of Finance, also attached to the Ariav Committee Report).

[133] MK Shelly Yechimovitz (Labor) and MK Zevulun Orlev (NRP) were opposed to the proposal, and expressed their opinion that it would lead to more corruption in the public service. They said also that this was an attempt to circumvent the Accountant-General, Zelekha, who they said was standing in the way of exempting many of the ruling government's "corrupt procurements." See <http://www.ynet.co.il/articles/0,7340,L-3429249,00.html> (accessed July 22, 2016).

The Ariav Committee rejected the claim that the reform would necessarily lead to an increase in the number of exemptions.[134] On the contrary, it wrote, the agencies' exemption committees would be able to examine the requests more thoroughly, and with greater professional familiarity with the subject matter, than the central committee could. To counter the criticism that the reform may foster corruption, the Ariav Committee proposed strengthening the conflict of interest provisions of the Regulations and toughening the sanctions for breach of these provisions. In relation to the former, the proposal was to require each of the members of the exemption committees (both the central and the agency committees) to declare before every decision that neither the member nor any of his or her family members have any personal interest in the procurement in question, and that he has not been approached by the minister or deputy minister, or by anyone on their behalf, in connection with the procurement. In relation to the latter, the Committee proposed to create a disciplinary offence for any of the following actions: (i) participation in the deliberations on a procurement in which the civil servant has a personal interest; (ii) misleading the exemption committee by presenting incomplete or imprecise information; and (iii) a willful decision to grant an exemption contrary to the law. The Committee also recommended requiring the exemption committee to keep full records of their deliberations and to publish them within five days of the decision to grant an exemption.

Unfortunately, of these recommendations only the last was implemented.[135] No duty to declare the lack of personal interest or the fact of being approached or contacted by the minister or deputy minister has been added to the Regulations. As for the proposal to toughen the sanctions against misbehavior and breach of the prohibition against conflict of interest by exemption and tendering committee members, it was met with opposition by Knesset members and therefore omitted. Thus, although the Ariav Committee had emphasized several times in its report that the recommendations reflect a delicate balance between conflicting values and therefore must be adopted as a whole,[136] this warning was not heeded. Consequently, while the agency's own head management (Director-General, accountant and legal advisor) received the authority to exempt the agency's procurements from the duty (and hassle) of conducting a public tender, the safeguards that the Ariav Committee had recommended in order to prevent abuse of this new-found authority were never adopted.

[134] Ariav Committee Report (p. 15).

[135] Article 10A(d) of the Regulations (as amended in 2009) requires the agency's exemption committee to record its decision in writing, along with the reasons for granting the exemption, and have it signed by all its members. Article 1C requires that all exemption decisions be published on the relevant agency's website within five working days of the decision.

[136] Ariav Committee Report (p. 11).

8.3.8 ASSESSMENT OF THE 2009 REFORM

An article published recently by the present author presents a detailed statistical analysis of the results of the 2009 reform (Reich, 2015). The analysis is based on detailed statistical data obtained from the relevant ministries with the objective of understanding whether the concerns over a surge in exemptions as a result of the reform were justified.

According to the findings of this research, the five years that have passed since the implementation of the reform have indeed seen a significant surge in the number of exemptions. While in 2008—that is, prior to the reform—the percentage of exempted contracts, in terms of volume, was around 65 percent, in 2009 it soared by ten points and passed 75 percent (note that the reform came into effect in the middle of the year). In 2010–12 the ratio continued to rise and was around 79 percent, and in 2013 it reached as much as 85 percent. Hence, only around 15 percent of government contracts in Israel were awarded through public tenders. This would appear to fly in the face of the central principle of the Mandatory Tenders Law, expressed in its Article 2, whereby contracts must be awarded through public tenders. The same applies to the "normative hierarchy" provision added by the 2009 reform to the Regulations (Article 1B), to clarify that the public tenders must be preferred over less-competitive forms of procurements.[137]

In contrast, figures obtained from the Ministry of Defense, which was not subject to the reform, do not indicate any surge in exemptions since 2009. The figures, that cover the years 2009–13, show instead a slight a reduction in the volume of exempted contracts, from 57.7 percent to 50 percent,[138] far from the current 85 percent of the other ministries who had been put in charge of exempting themselves from the duty to perform public tenders.

The research also examined which exemptions were most commonly used. It found that the most popular exemptions, both before and after the reform, are Article 3(4) (continuation of a previous procurement), and Article 3(29) (where there is only one supplier available). These exemptions represent 41 percent and 28 percent, respectively, of the total number of Article 3 exemptions, and 50 percent and 9 percent, respectively, of the monetary value of the exempted contracts.[139] To be fair, one should acknowledge that a large part of the contracts that were exempted under Article 3(4) were continuations of a contract originally awarded following a public tender or a competitive RFP.[140] Thus, they are not entirely non-competitive. However, the procurement market suffers

[137] For a complete discussion of the results, possible doubts about their accuracy, and their significance, see Reich (2015: p. 211).

[138] Reich (2015: pp. 211–12 and table 2).

[139] These figures are based on a multi-year average for 2008–13.

[140] This is one of the conditions of Article 3(4)(b)(2), but there are circumstances where exemptions under Article 3(4) can be granted even if this condition has not been fulfilled.

from many market failures and just because a contract was awarded some years ago to a certain supplier,[141] it does not mean that today this is the optimal contract the procuring agency could obtain—prices may have gone down, products or services may have improved, and a public tender conducted today might have obtained better terms. Furthermore, given that the number of contracts awarded under Article 3(4) has not increased, but has actually slightly decreased since the reform, the clear increase in the number and percentage of total exemptions granted following the reform, which is the most important finding of this study, cannot be attributed to Article 3(4) exemptions.

These figures on the extensive use of these two exemptions would seem to imply that the attempts of the Ariav Committee to limit their use have not been very successful. Hence, with regards to Article 3(29), the conditioning of its use upon a prior examination against the market by a public notification has not had a significant impact on the volume of exemptions under this provision.[142] As for Article 3(4), the results are more ambivalent.[143]

There were several provisions that were never used[144] and some that were used very rarely.[145] One should therefore consider omitting them entirely and shortening the list, which is much too long and much too specific. One of the more general exemptions could always deal with special circumstances that are rare but justify the exemption from a public tender.

Another issue that was examined by the research was the extent to which the new procurement methods introduced by the 2009 reform were used in practice. It found a very limited use of these methods over the years 2009–13. As much as 88 percent of the public tenders were still conducted in the regular way, and fewer than 12 percent of them utilized any of the other eight methods. One could also not discern any tendency for increase in these numbers over the years since the reform came into force. Of the new methods, the most popular is the public tender with two phases of examination (Article 17D)—with 4 percent use—followed by the preliminary request for information (Article 14A) and limited public tender (Article 7)[146] with roughly 2 percent each. That would

[141] Under Article 3(4)(b)(2)(b) the follow-up contract can be awarded up to five years after the original contract.

[142] On the contrary, there is even a certain increase in the percentages. Before the reform (2008–09), Article 3(29) was used for 20 percent of the exempted contracts, which represented 7 percent in terms of contract value. After the reform (2010–13), this exemption was used for 28 percent of the exempted contracts, which represented 9 percent in terms of contract value.

[143] Before the reform (2008–09), Article 3(4) was used for 50 percent of the exempted contracts, which represented 29 percent in terms of contract value. After the reform (2010–13), this exemption was used for only 41 percent of the number of exempted contracts, which is a certain reduction in volume, but in terms of contract value these exempted contracts represent as much as 50 percent of the exempted contracts, which is almost twice as much as before the reform.

[144] Articles 3(6), 3(25) and 5(b).

[145] Articles 3(20a), 3(12), 3(10), 3(32), 3(20), 3(33), 3(14b).

[146] This refers mainly to cases where as part of a regular public tender, fair and non-discriminatory negotiations are permitted with bidders. It does not refer to the expedited online tender, which is extremely rare.

seem to reflect a very limited impact of all of the Weinshall-Lifshitz recommendations and a lack of integration of the new, more flexible procurement methods. It may mean that the government has not done enough to educate the agencies' procurement officials about the new methods and to train them in using them.

The study also found that use of electronic tendering was very limited, partly because of budgetary constraints that prompted the government in 2013 to stop any further integration, development, or support for the new electronic tendering system. As for the electronic auction system, it has only been made available to the Government Procurement Administration in the Ministry of Finance, again because of budgetary constraints. During the years 2009–13, this system has conducted 183 auctions, most of them central tenders (71 percent) and the rest for other agencies. Overall, however, the use of electronic tendering is disappointingly low and is expected to decline even further until proper technological infrastructure is provided.

8.4 **Israel's International Public Procurement Commitments**

8.4.1 THE WTO AGREEMENT ON GOVERNMENT PROCUREMENT

Israel has been a signatory of the WTO Agreement on Government Procurement ever since 1983, before there was a WTO and when the agreement was still called a "Code."[147] This first version of the agreement originated in the Tokyo Round that was concluded in 1979.[148] Israel joined four years after its conclusion, because of problems encountered by Israeli suppliers to the US government following the prohibition imposed by the US on suppliers from non-GPA countries participating in federal tenders.[149] At the time of accession, Israel was one of very few developing countries that were a party to this agreement, and it was permitted to accede with a quite limited list of covered entities, as well as with a special authorization to use offset policies.

When the Uruguay Round GPA was concluded in 1994, Israel was an original signatory, this time with a much more extensive list of covered entities. The list included all central government entities, except for the Ministry of Defense and the Ministry of Internal Security (in charge of the police). It also included the three biggest

[147] See Report of the Committee on Government Procurement, GATT *BISD* Thirtieth Suppl. (p. 34, para. 4). The accession of Israel to the Code came into effect on June 29, 1983 (See GATT, Status of Legal Instruments, 165.2).

[148] Agreement on Government Procurement, General Agreement on Tariffs and Trade, April 12, 1979, published in GATT *BISD* Twenty-sixth Suppl. (1979: p. 33); 1235 UNTS 258.

[149] See the full account in Reich (1999: p. 153).

municipalities (Jerusalem, Tel-Aviv, and Haifa) and the central purchaser for all the smaller municipalities,[150] as well as many "Other Entities" set out in Annex 3. Some of these entities have extensive procurement budgets, such as the Israel Airport Authority, the Israel Port Authority, and the Israel Electric Company. However, Israel was allowed to retain its offset policies, subject to certain caps and conditions.

In the context of the Revised GPA that came into force in 2014, Israel's coverage continued to grow, in particular in the context of the Annex 3 entities, which grew from fourteen to twenty-three entities.[151] Israel also committed to open up all entities operating in the field of urban transport, except those operating in the field of bus services, on the condition of mutual reciprocity. As for offset policies, Israel was pressured into agreeing to phase out gradually all of its offset requirements by 2029. During the transitional stage, instead of the original 35 percent[152] cap that was in place between 1995–2000, the current cap of 20 percent of the contract value would go down to 18 percent in 2023. Offsets could only be required for procurement of certain entities and only if they are valued above a threshold of Special Drawing Rights (SDR) 3 million.[153]

8.4.2 BILATERAL AGREEMENTS

In addition to the plurilateral GPA, some of Israel's free trade agreements (FTAs) have chapters on government procurement. The most significant of these FTAs are those with Mexico and Columbia, concluded in 2000 and 2013, respectively, which create full-fledged bilateral procurement regimes parallel to—and, to a certain extent, modeled on—the GPA.[154] Since these countries are not GPA parties, unlike most of Israel's other FTA partners, it was necessary to formulate a detailed body of substantive and

[150] This is a company owned by the Center for Local Government called Local Government Economic Services Ltd.

[151] Israel, Annex 3 "Other Entities," of the original GPA as compared to that of the Revised GPA. Both annexes are available at <https://www.wto.org/english/tratop_e/gproc_e/gp_app_agree_e.htm> (accessed July 22, 2016). Four more entities were also added to Israel's Annex 1: the Central Bureau of Statistics, the Geological Survey of Israel, the Administration for Rural Residential, Education and Youth Aliyah, and the Survey of Israel.

[152] This was the original cap in the Code and during the first five years of the Uruguay Round GPA. It was lowered gradually, and in the Revised GPA Israel undertook to continue to lower it until all offsets were completely eliminated.

[153] The full details are set out in Israel's Note on Offsets, of the Revised GPA. The SDR 3 million cap is insignificant, since in any case Israel's regulations only require offsets for contracts valued over $5 million. See the discussion in Section 8.4.4.

[154] The Israel–Mexico Free Trade Agreement was signed on April 10, 2000, and entered into force on July 1, 2000. The text of the agreement can be found at <http://www.sice.oas.org/Trade/meis_e/isr_mexind_e.asp#Government> (accessed July 22, 2016); the procurement provisions are found in chapter VI of the FTA. The Colombia–Israel Free Trade Agreement was signed on September 30, 2013, but has still not entered into force; its procurement provisions are found in chapter 9 of the FTA.

procedural provisions, along with detailed coverage annexes, in order to facilitate the reciprocal opening up of their respective procurement markets. Israel's coverage under both agreements is similar, although not identical, to its coverage under the Uruguay Round GPA. However, under the Columbia–Israel FTA, provisions were made to extend it as in the Revised GPA once it enters into force.[155] There is also a chapter on government procurement in Israel's 1985 FTA with the US,[156] but it has limited significance today.[157]

Finally, one should mention that there is a bilateral Memorandum of Understanding (MOU) on defense procurement between Israel and the US, signed in 1987,[158] similar to the ones that the US has with its NATO allies. These MOUs waive domestic preference policies (such as the Buy American Act) in relation to suppliers from the other party.[159] This agreement applies to the ministries of defense of the two countries, including their procurement of military equipment, which of course is not included in the GPA. Annex IV of the MOU, which was amended in 2008, provides for reciprocal government quality assurance services in support of the procurement of defense products.[160] Given the huge size of the defense procurement budgets of both countries, as well as the sophistication of their respective defense industries, one can easily understand the paramount importance of this bilateral agreement.

The obligations under the GPA, as well as those under the various bilateral agreements, can be divided into two categories: substantive and procedural. The category of substantive obligations includes primarily the prohibition against discrimination, or in trade law jargon, the obligation to provide national treatment and most-favored-nation

155 In 2013, when this FTA was concluded, Israel's coverage schedules under a future revised GPA had already been determined and they were awaiting the conclusion and entry into force of this revised GPA. That is the reason that an automatic mechanism for such an extension was included in the FTA.

156 Agreement on the Establishment of a Free Trade Area between the Government of Israel and the Government of the United States of America, signed May 22, 1985. The government procurement provisions are found in Article 15 of the FTA (the agreement is available at: <http://www.mfa.gov.il/mfa/mfa-archive/1980-1989/pages/israel-us%20free%20trade%20area%20agreement.aspx> (accessed July 22, 2016).

157 For more details on this chapter, see Reich (1999: pp. 156–61). The chapter lowered the threshold for goods procurement between the two parties from the SDR 130,000 of the GPA to US$50,000. However, since it was concluded in 1985, it referred to the entities covered by the Tokyo Round GPA, and the coverage under the FTA has not been extended since then. Given Israel's very limited entity list under this agreement, this has seriously undermined the significance of the FTA for Israeli public procurement.

158 Memorandum of Understanding between the Government of the United States of America and the Government of Israel Concerning the Principles Governing the Mutual Cooperation in Research and Development, Scientist and Engineer Exchange, Procurement and Logistics Support of Defense Equipment (MOU) signed in Washington, DC, on December 14, 1987. This MOU was later amended at the end of 1997. Both the original MOU and its amendment can be found at: <http://www.acq.osd.mil/dpap/Docs/mou-israel.pdf> (accessed July 22, 2016).

159 These MOUs are implemented in the US by the special Department of Defense Supplement to the Federal Acquisition Regulations, known as DFARS (para. 225.872-1).

160 This amended Annex is found at: <http://www.acq.osd.mil/dpap/Docs/mou-isreal2008AnnexIV.pdf> (accessed July 22, 2016).

treatment.[161] The prohibition against offsets also falls under this category.[162] The category of procedural obligations includes a detailed body of rules and provisions prescribing how covered government entities should go about performing their procurements, that is through competitive, transparent, and impartial tendering procedures.[163] These procedures are aimed at ensuring open and fair competition for government contracts by potential suppliers of the goods or services in question from all the countries that are signatories to the GPA, domestic and foreign alike. The obligation to provide effective domestic review procedures for supplier challenges also falls under this category.

Before turning to the issue of how the substantive obligations of these agreements have been implemented in Israel, we first need to understand Israel's existing domestic preference and offset policies. As for the procedural obligations, they will be understood against the backdrop of Israel's existing tendering rules and bid challenging procedures.

8.4.3 DOMESTIC PREFERENCE POLICIES IN ISRAEL

Israel's domestic preference policies are set out in the Mandatory Tenders Regulations (Preference for Domestic Production), 1995,[164] issued by the government.[165] These regulations impose an obligation to give preference to domestic products over foreign-

[161] In the Revised GPA, this obligation is found in Article V:1, titled "National Treatment and Non-Discrimination," which provides: "With respect to any measure regarding covered procurement, each Party, including its procuring entities, shall accord immediately and unconditionally to the goods and services of any other Party and to the suppliers of any other Party offering the goods or services of any Party, treatment no less favorable than the treatment the Party, including its procuring entities, accords to: (a) domestic goods, services, and suppliers [i.e. national treatment] and (b) goods, services, and suppliers of any other Party [i.e. most-favored-nation treatment]."

[162] In the Revised GPA this prohibition is found in Article V:6, which provides: "With regard to covered procurement, a Party, including its procuring entities, shall not seek, take account of, impose, or enforce offsets." "Offsets" are defined in Article I(k) of the Revised GPA to mean "any condition or undertaking that encourages local development or improves a Party's balance-of-payments accounts, such as the use of domestic content, the licensing of technology, investment, counter-trade, and similar actions or requirements." However, Article IV:3 permits a developing country, with the agreement of the other signatories, to adopt or retain offsets for a transitional period and in a manner that does not discriminate among the parties.

[163] Most of the GPAs provisions are devoted to this goal. The guiding principles of these detailed provisions are set out partly in GPA Article V:4.

[164] The Mandatory Tenders Regulations (Preference for Domestic Production), 5755-1995, published in *Kovetz Hatakanot* No. 5653 of January 15, 1995, p. 562 (hereafter the "Preference Regulations"). The Preference Regulations have been amended three times since their adoption.

[165] It is quite rare to find regulations issued by the entire government, as opposed to a certain minister. In this case, it is a result of an unresolvable dispute that erupted between the Minister of Industry and Trade (who traditionally is more protectionist) and the Minister of Finance (who usually is more free-market oriented) on who should be authorized to issue the regulations. In order to solve the deadlock, the law authorized the government as a whole to issue them.

made products up to a maximum difference of 15 percent for regular Israeli-made products, and 20 percent for goods produced in the region close to the Gaza Strip.[166] The latter preference is a result of a provisional amendment passed in August 2015 for a period of five years,[167] whose objective is to assist industries in Southwest Israel that have been seriously harmed by the missile bombardment from Gaza. For procurement by government corporations or other governmental entities that export more than 30 percent of their production, the preference margin is only 10 percent.[168]

The way these preference margins work is that when evaluating the bids according to the various award criteria (price, quality, experience, etc.), the price component of bids offering domestic products is divided by 1.15, 1.20 or 1.10—as the case may be—so that the price taken into account in the evaluation is lower than it actually is.[169] However, if the bid that received the highest score according to this method of evaluation is one offering a domestic product that prevailed over a foreign bid only because of the price preference, it does not mean that it will automatically win the contract. Rather, the procurement officer will contact the bidder in question and propose that he sell the product at the same (lower) price as the foreign bidder with the highest score.[170] If he refuses, the officer is authorized to make the same offer to two other domestic bidders, first to the one that received the second highest score out of the domestic bidders, and then to the third highest.[171] The first of these domestic bidders to accept the proposal will win the contract on the spot. Only if none of them agrees will the procurement officer return to the first domestic bidder and award the contract to him at the price he had originally proposed.[172] The purpose of this procedure is to try to bring down the price of the winning domestic bidder, so as to cancel out the effect of the domestic price preference on the public treasure. When this bidder receives such a proposal, he is faced with a dilemma: either he agrees to lower his price in order to be certain that he wins the contract; or he refuses and risks that one of the other two domestic bidders will accept the proposal and win the contract instead. If he has good reason to believe that none of them will do so, or if he knows that there are no other eligible bidders,[173] he is

[166] Article 3(a) of the Preference Regulations.

[167] *Kovetz Hatakanot* No. 7543 of August 16, 2015, p. 1818.

[168] Article 3(b) of the Preference Regulations.

[169] Article 3(d) of the Preference Regulations.

[170] Or to be more precise, at the price that will result in his bid receiving the same score as the best foreign bid, without using the price preference formula. This formulation takes into account that there may be several criteria determining the score, not only the price; see Article 3(f) of the Preference Regulations.

[171] Article 3(g) of the Preference Regulations. These domestic bidders will receive this proposal only if their bids, when calculated using the domestic preference, received a score equal to or higher than the highest scored foreign bid.

[172] Article 3(h) of the Preference Regulations.

[173] If the winning bidder knows that there are no other domestic producers of the goods in question, he will certainly refuse to reduce his price. If there are other domestic producers but the winning bidder

better off holding out and refusing to go down, in which case the contract will eventually be awarded to him at the original high price.

In addition to these Preference Regulations, there are also the Mandatory Tenders Regulations (Preference for Products from National Preference Regions), 1998,[174] issued by the Minister of Defense. These regulations apply only to procurements by the Ministry of Defense and grant certain preferences to suppliers established in disadvantaged regions or conflict zones, so-called "National Preference Regions." Such suppliers, provided that at least 40 percent of their workers are residents of one of these regions, can enjoy a price preference of between 5 and 15 percent over other suppliers (domestic and foreign alike).[175]

What is considered as a "domestic product" for the purpose of the Preference Regulations? The definition, found in Article 1 of the regulations, is based partly on the rules of origin of the Israel–US FTA.[176] These rules demand, in principle, the fulfillment of two requirements for an Israeli product that includes foreign components to be considered as "originating in Israel":

i. the product has been manufactured in Israel in a way that has *substantially transformed* it into a new product with a different name, character, or use than the components and raw materials from which it was produced (para. 1a); and
ii. the sum of the cost or value of the materials produced in Israel plus the direct costs of processing operations performed in Israel constitutes at least 35 percent of the appraised value of the product at the time of import (para. 1c).

At first blush, the Preference Regulations seem to have adopted the same formula, and the English words "substantial transformation" even appear in parenthesis, after the Hebrew translation, in the text of the regulations (a rather rare phenomenon).[177] However, a closer examination of the definition will show that there is a significant difference between it and the FTA definition in the method used to calculate the 35 percent. Whereas the FTA requires this minimum domestic content to be made up of Israeli-made materials and Israeli labor, the Preference Regulations calculates it "going backwards"—domestic content is calculated based on the ex-works price of the product,

estimates that they are unable, because of their cost constraints, to offer a price as low as the winning foreign bidder, he will also refuse to accept the proposal to reduce his price.

[174] The Mandatory Tenders Regulations (Preference for National Preferential Regions), 5758-1998, Published in *Kovetz Hatakanot* No. 5911 of July 16, 1998, p. 1020. The Regulations have been amended six times since their adoption.

[175] Mandatory Tenders Regulations, Article 4. A judgment discussing and interpreting these conditions is A.P. (Tel-Aviv) 1436/08 *Orlite Industries (Millenium 2000) Ltd. v. State of Israel—Ministry of Defense* (judgment issued September 7, 2009).

[176] Israel-US FTA, Annex 3 ("Rules of Origin").

[177] The Preference Regulations, Article 1 (definition of "production"). See also Article 1, definition of "domestically produced goods" ("Tuvin Mitotzeret Ha'aretz").

minus any foreign components or foreign labor that has been used to produce it. The main difference between these two methods lies in how to relate to the bidder's profit on each product. Under the FTA, it is not taken into account when calculating the 35 percent domestic content, whereas under the Preference Regulations it is.

To illustrate this, consider the following example. A product is produced in Israel in a manner that constitutes "substantial transformation." It is made entirely of foreign materials and the cost of labor to produce it is 5 percent of the ex-work price of the product. The total cost of production (materials + labor) is 70 percent of the ex-work price (i.e., the foreign material makes up 65 percent of the price, and the profit to the bidder is 30 percent). This product will meet the requirement of 35 percent domestic content under the Preference Regulation (100-65 = 35 percent). Under the FTA, in contrast, it has no more than 5 percent domestic content and will not be considered as originating in Israel.

One can therefore rightfully criticize the Preference Regulations as being much too lenient in their definition of domestic content. If the purpose is to encourage the creation of domestic jobs and domestic manufacturing by using funds from the procurement budgets of government agencies, one would expect the regulations to require more significant amounts of domestic labor and domestic materials in order to justify the extra spending. Looking at the hypothetical example described above, one may rightfully wonder why Israeli taxpayers' money should be wasted, up to a difference of 15 percent of the contract price, on a product that has only 5 percent worth of domestic labor in it? Moreover, the existing formula actually encourages the bidder to raise his price in order to qualify for domestic preference, because his profit margin is counted in the 35 percent domestic content.

8.4.4 ISRAEL'S OFFSET POLICIES

The objectives of Israel's offset policies is to promote long-term cooperation between Israeli industry and the large foreign corporations who compete for high-value Israeli government contracts, and thereby lead to job creation, technology and knowhow transfer, and the development of new markets. The policies are implemented through the Mandatory Tenders Regulations (Mandatory Industrial Cooperation), 2007,[178] issued by the government. These regulations require government agencies, government corporations, municipal corporations, and the public health providers that conduct large-scale procurements (valued over $5 million)[179] to include certain offset

[178] The Mandatory Tenders Regulations (Mandatory Industrial Cooperation), 5767-2007, published in *Kovetz Hatakanot* No. 6586 of May 10, 2007, p. 826 (hereafter the "Industrial Cooperation Regulations"). The Regulations have been amended once since their adoption. These regulations replace a chapter on mandatory industrial cooperation that was part of the domestic preference regulations from 1995.

[179] The Industrial Cooperation Regulations, Article 3(b)(1). The offset requirement also applies to contracts valued over $500,000 if they are a continuation of a previous contract valued over $5 million that was awarded within the previous five years (The Industrial Cooperation Regulations, Article 3(b)(2)).

requirements from foreign contractors as part of the contract. A special agency, the Industrial Cooperation Authority (ICA), is in charge of facilitating such offset purchases and making sure that they are enforced.[180]

The offset requirements are of several kinds, depending on the type of contract. Generally, a foreign contractor can choose to perform its offset commitments by any or all of the following means: local sub-contracting, direct investment, research and development, technology transfer, the purchase of domestic goods or services or otherwise as agreed upon with the ICA.[181] In such case, the rate of the required offset commitment is 35 percent for civil purchases and 50 percent for defense-related purchases. For purchases subject to the GPA, the rate is only 20 percent.[182] However, if the contract is one that the ICA determines as of special importance for the promotion of the industry and the technological development of the country, the procurement must be published as one requiring local sub-contracting at the amount of 20 percent of the contract value.[183] In other words, if a foreign bidder wins the contract, it will be required to sub-contract at least 20 percent of the contract project to an Israeli manufacturer.

8.4.5 IMPLEMENTATION OF ISRAEL'S INTERNATIONAL OBLIGATIONS

There are no detailed regulations implementing Israel's international obligations under the GPA or under any of the other relevant agreements. There is, however, an important provision in the primary legislation that does the job,[184] namely, Article 5A(b) of the Mandatory Tendering Law, which provides:

> Regulations pursuant to this law will apply to the extent that they do not conflict with a commitment of the state in an international treaty.

Since all of Israel's domestic preference policies, as well as its offset policies, are prescribed by regulations issued under the Mandatory Tendering Law, the implication of Article 5A(b) is that these policies will yield whenever they conflict with a provision of any of the relevant government procurement agreements. Hence, whenever a procurement is covered by the GPA or by any other agreement, the obligation under the Preference Regulations to give preference to domestic products does not apply. Rather,

[180] The ICA is an independent unit of the Ministry of Economy. For more information on the ICA, see <http://www.moital.gov.il/NR/exeres/7E2BB77E-A0C8-4EF9-9664-5B065657A5F3.htm> (accessed July 22, 2016).

[181] The Industrial Cooperation Regulations, Article 4(a).

[182] As per Israel's commitment under the Revised GPA; see the discussion in Section 8.4.1.

[183] The Industrial Cooperation Regulations, Article 7(a).

[184] There are also internal directives of the Ministry of Finance, in particular TAKAM, Directive 7.12.3, "Undertaking to Purchase from Abroad under International Agreements," available at: <http://hozrim.mof.gov.il/doc/hashkal/horaot.nsf/ByNum/7.12.3> (accessed July 22, 2016).

as prescribed by the TAKAM internal directives, all of the GPA provisions will apply.[185] In such case, the procuring entity will publish the tender as a "GPA tender" and will indicate in the tender notice that it is subject to the GPA and that the domestic preference policy does not apply in relation to suppliers from other GPA countries. Pursuant to Revised GPA Article VII:3, a summary notice of such a procurement will also be published in English in one of the English-language daily newspapers published in Israel (the *Jerusalem Post* or the *International Herald Tribune—Ha'aretz*).[186] To the extent that the Industrial Cooperation Regulations apply (i.e., when the contract is valued above $5 million), the procuring entity will only require an offset obligation of 20 percent, as opposed to 35 percent for non-covered procurements, in line with Israel's GPA commitment, going down to 18 percent in in 2023 and eventually disappearing entirely.[187]

A similar, but not identical, arrangement is found in the tendering regulations of the municipalities.[188] Article 22 of these regulations provides for the 15 percent domestic preference requirement, while Article 24 stipulates that these regulations "will apply to the extent that they do not conflict with a commitment of the State in an international treaty." Article 24(2), however, also provides that when such conflict occurs, the TAKAM internal directive on international agreements will apply *mutatis mutandis.*[189] Here, then, the more detailed implementation rules of the TAKAM are given the status of (secondary) legislation that can be more easily relied upon by bidders.[190]

As for the procedural obligations of the GPA and other international agreements, these are also taken care of through Article 5A(b), since all of the tendering rules are also prescribed by the Mandatory Tendering Regulations. There are, however, very few conflicts between these regulations and the international agreements, since they are all based on similar principles of fair competition, predictability, and transparency. In some aspects, the Israeli regulations are even more competition-oriented than the GPA. For instance, Israeli government agencies are not permitted to use selective tendering procedures except for in specific circumstances and after obtaining an authorization from one of the exemption committees,[191] whereas under the GPA there are no

[185] Ministry of Finance Directive 7.12.3, Article 2.8.

[186] See also Article VI:2(b) which requires parties to list in Appendix III to the GPA, the electronic or paper media in which each party publishes the notices required by Articles VII, IX:7 and XVI:2. In its Appendix III Israel has listed these two newspapers. See also the internal Ministry of Finance directive, Article 2.12.3.

[187] See the discussion in Section 8.4.1.

[188] The Municipalities Regulations (Tenders), 5748-1987, *Kovetz Hatakanot* 5748, 5069, December 10, 1987, p. 229.

[189] While the TAKAM is generally formulated to apply to central government agencies, here its provisions will be adapted to apply to municipalities.

[190] See also the discussion of the *Dolev v. Tel-Aviv Municipality* case, in Section 8.6.

[191] Article 4 of the Mandatory Tendering Regulations, note 33 (supra). The requirement to obtain authorization from the central exemption committee applies only to procurements valued over 4 million shekel (Article 12(a)). For procurements valued over 300,000 shekel, the Ministry exemption committee's

restrictions on their use. As for the date for submission of bids under open tendering, while the Mandatory Tendering Regulations only require "a reasonable time period,"[192] the minimum time under the GPA is forty days, except for in certain circumstances.[193] Therefore, the TAKAM internal directive provides that for GPA procurements the procuring agency must allow for at least forty days from the date of publication of the tendering notice for an open tender, except for in the circumstances set out in the GPA,[194] and twenty-five days for selective tendering.[195]

On the other hand, the long list of circumstances that may permit an exemption from conducting any type of competitive tendering, found in Article 3 of the Regulations and discussed extensively above, is clearly in conflict with the GPA. This is so because the parallel provision in the GPA ("limited tendering") has a much shorter list of circumstances that justify awarding a contract without competition (eight, instead of thirty-three).[196] Granted, some of the circumstances listed in Article 3 are not relevant to the GPA—for instance, contracts valued under 50,000 shekels that are exempted under Article 3(1) of the regulations, or contracts for sale or purchase of certain real estate rights exempted under Article 3(14A). There are still, however, many exemptions that could be relevant but that have no parallel in the GPA's exemption lists—for instance, procurement of medicines, serums or vaccines that are "unique," exempted under Article 3(13); or procurement of various financial services, exempted under Article 3(14).[197] It is therefore clear that these exemptions cannot apply for procurements covered by the GPA by virtue of Article 5A(b) of the primary law, which provides that the regulations will not apply whenever they conflict with an international agreement. Thus, limited tendering can be permitted for such procurements only if they fall under one of the GPA exemptions. A procuring entity could, however, request an exemption from conducting a public tender, based on one of the provisions of Article 3 that does not have a GPA parallel, and conduct a selective tendering process instead, since selective tendering does not require a special justification under the GPA.

authorization is required. Under that, the tendering committee can decide on its own to undertake a selective tendering process.

[192] Article 15(a) of the Mandatory Tendering Regulations.

[193] Revised GPA, Article XI:3. The time period may be reduced to as little as ten days when a notice of planned procurement has been published, provided that certain conditions have been met (Article XI:4), or when electronics means have been used (see Article XI:5).

[194] Ministry of Finance internal directive, para. 2.12.6.

[195] Ministry of Finance internal directive, Annex B, implementing GPA, Article XI:2.

[196] Revised GPA, Article XIII.

[197] This provision exempts "contracts dealing with granting of credit or receiving it, investment of funds, receiving banking services, sale or purchase of stocks, or other activities in the financial markets, provided that the Accountant-General, or anyone authorized by him, has approved it." Financial services (insurance services, banking and investments services) are covered by the GPA under Israel's Annex 5, subject to its GATS commitments. Hence, this exemption could certainly not apply whenever the procurement of such services is valued over the applicable threshold and made by a covered entity.

In view of the high percentage of exemptions from public tenders found in our research and described above,[198] one may ask oneself whether this is an indication of widespread violations of the GPA. The answer is that there is no way of knowing. It is very possible that none of those exemptions was granted in relation to procurements covered by the GPA, or that those that were GPA-related were justified under one of the exemptions listed in GPA Article XIII. Unfortunately, the statistics obtained from the government do not distinguish between GPA-covered procurement and other procurement. In fact, my inquiries with the Ministry of Finance have found that there are no statistics available at all on how many GPA procurements are concluded in Israel each year, under which types of procedures they are conducted, or to whom they are awarded. It is said that they do not yet have the facilities in place to collect such information, but hope to develop them soon, in view of the collection and reporting obligation under Revised GPA Article XVI:4.[199]

8.4.6 BID CHALLENGING IN ISRAEL, IN GENERAL AND UNDER THE GPA

Bid challenging in Israel today is handled mainly by the administrative courts, which are part of the District Courts. These courts were established in 2000 by the Courts for Administrative Matters Law.[200] Until 1991, all bid challenges were handled by the Supreme Court in its capacity as High Court of Justice. In 1991, in the landmark Pasternak case,[201] in order to lighten its heavy caseload, the Court ruled that from now on these challenges could be handled by the regular civil courts (i.e., the Magistrate or District Courts) according to the money value of the dispute. One of the criticisms leveled at this change was that these courts did not have much experience in administrative law and that it would be hard for them to develop expertise, since the authority was spread over almost all the judges in the country. In view of this, the Knesset decided to create specialized courts for administrative matters.

The Law provides for two types of actions that are relevant to public procurement: an "administrative petition," which is a petition challenging a decision of an administrative

[198] See Section 8.3.8.

[199] A similar obligation existed also under the previous GPA, under Article XIX. The level of compliance with the collection and reporting obligation of statistics under the GPA has not been very good for many other GPA parties. The US, for instance, has not submitted a report since 2008, and Iceland and Israel have not done so at all for the last twenty years (see <https://www.wto.org/english/tratop_e/gproc_e/notnat_e.htm#statPro> (accessed July 22, 2016)). It seems, however, that the level of compliance is picking up over the last few years, so Israel will have to get organized to fulfill its obligations.

[200] Courts for Administrative Matters Law, 5760-2000, published in *Sefer HaChukkim* 5760 No. 1739 of June 11, 2000, p. 190.

[201] H.C.J. 991/91 *David Pasternak Ltd. v. Minister of Housing*, P.D. 45(5) 50.

agency;[202] and an "administrative action," which is an action for damages resulting from an infringement of public procurement rules.[203] The procedural rules regarding the submission and review of administrative petitions are set out in the Courts for Administrative Matters (Procedures) Regulations,[204] whereas administrative actions are reviewed in accordance with the Civil Procedure Regulations, 1984,[205] which provide the procedural framework for most civil actions in Israel.[206] An important and distinctive feature of an administrative action is that it cannot be lodged in parallel to lodging an administrative petition to the court. In practical terms, this means that an aggrieved tenderer is expected to first lodge an administrative petition requesting the court to repeal the allegedly unlawful decision of the government agency, or to correct it in any other way. Only if this petition has been exhausted can he turn again to the court and sue for damages for his losses in an administrative action.[207,208]

Judicial review of procurement decisions is quite common in Israel. Judgments in this field, both by the administrative courts and by the Supreme Court (mainly in its capacity as the administrative appeal court), are published regularly. According to figures obtained from the Israeli Courts Administration, between the years 2010 and 2014 an average of 434 administrative petitions in relation to procurement decisions were filed each year.[209] These figures do not include administrative actions and petitions to the High Court of Justice in procurement matters, both of which are less common than the administrative actions. Between 14 and 22 percent of these administrative petitions are

[202] For example, a petition in which the petitioner asks the court to set aside an agency's contract award decision.

[203] Article 5 of the Court for Administrative Matters. The Court for Administrative Matters is the competent court for adjudicating Administrative Actions. However, some actions for damages in connection with public tenders may be submitted to the Civil Courts.

[204] Courts for Administrative Matters Regulations (Procedure), 5761-2000, *Kovetz Hatakanot* 5761 No. 6070 of December 7, 2000, p. 171.

[205] Hereinafter referred to as the "Civil Procedure Regulations."

[206] However, in the case of a discrepancy between the provisions of the Courts for Administrative Matters Act and the Courts for Administrative Matters Regulations (Procedure), 2000, on the one hand, and the Civil Procedure Regulations 1984 on the other hand, the former will prevail (see Article 30 of the Courts for Administrative Matters Regulations (Procedure), 2000).

[207] Very recently, the Supreme Court changed its previous position and ruled that once a petitioner's request for interim relief, as part of his administrative petition, has been denied, this can be considered as exhaustion and he will be allowed to file an administrative action without pursuing the administrative petition to its formal end; see A.A.P. 7401/14 *Kessem HaMilennium Ltd. v. Airport Authority* issued on September 9, 2015, para. 24.

[208] This was held by the Supreme Court in the A.A.P. 9423/05 *The Broadcasting Authority v. Katimora Ltd,* Tak-Al 2007(3) 2403 (2007). For a critique of this decision and a proposal on how to reform the rules on damages in public procurement, see Reich and Shabat (2014).

[209] Information obtained by Advocate Oren Shabat, the author's doctoral student here at Bar Ilan University, Faculty of Law, on file with author.

successful, in the sense that they are fully or partly accepted by the courts, or are resolved through an agreed compromise.[210]

This judicial review of procurement decisions is also available for foreign and domestic suppliers who would like to challenge a procurement decision for not abiding by the provisions of the GPA or any other international agreement. This is so despite the fact that Israel has a so-called dualistic legal system, which does not recognize norms originating from international treaties as part of its internal legal system unless they have been incorporated by way of legislation into the domestic system.[211] Here the international agreements are considered to have been incorporated, since Article 5A(b) of the Mandatory Tendering Law granted them priority over regulations issued under this law. Israel therefore considers itself as having fulfilled its obligation under GPA Article XX (and Revised GPA Article XVIII) to provide for "timely, effective, transparent, and non-discriminatory administrative or judicial review procedure" through its existing system of judicial review.

An interesting case that illustrates how Israel's bid challenge procedures work is *Dolev v. Tel-Aviv Municipality*.[212] The case dealt with a public tender for a framework agreement for various recycling and garbage containers. At first, the municipality had published it as a regular tender, including a clause providing that the domestic preference policy will apply. One of the interested bidders (an Israeli company who presumably intended to offer foreign products originating in another GPA country) then sent a letter to the municipality demanding that this clause be deleted. The firm claimed that in view of the option clauses in the contract, its potential value exceeded the GPA threshold of SDR 250,000, and therefore the tender was subject to the GPA. It threatened to petition the administrative court if the municipality refused to delete the domestic preference clause. The municipality accepted this claim, and notified all of the potential suppliers that the tender would be subject to the GPA and therefore there would be no domestic preference. This was met by opposition by another potential supplier, who denied that the procurement was covered by the GPA and demanded that the domestic preference clause be reinstated. This supplier argued, among other things, that this procurement should in fact be seen as three separate procurements for three different types of containers and, as such, none of them was valued above the GPA threshold.

[210] Most of this "success rate" is made up of cases where the petition has been fully accepted by the court.

[211] Israel "inherited" this approach from English Law. It is connected to the fact that the Executive Branch, the Israeli Government, has exclusive competence to conclude international treaties without the need for authorization or ratification by the Knesset, the Legislative Branch. If norms from these treaties were to become binding within the Israeli legal system, it would mean that the Executive Branch could circumvent the Legislative Branch in creative binding domestic legal norms (see, for example, C.A. 145/55 *The Custodian for the Property of Missing People v. Samara*, P.D. 10 1825).

[212] A.P. 54507-08-10 *Dolev Plastic Products (Holdings) Ltd. v. Tel-Aviv Municipality et al.* issued by the Tel-Aviv District Court (Stoffman, J.), in its capacity as Court for Administrative Matters (judgment of August 1, 2011).

When the municipality refused to accept this claim, noting that it was prohibited under the GPA to divide procurements with the intention of avoiding the application of the agreement,[213] the supplier filed his petition to the administrative court.

In dealing with the dispute, the court held:[214]

> There is no doubt that preference for "blue and white" products over foreign products has a significant contribution to the growth of the Israeli economy. However, international trade agreements, such as the GPA, promotes Israeli interests, and among them the creation of political and commercial ties between Israel and the various states that are signatories of the agreement, opening up opportunities for Israeli manufacturers to move into new markets abroad, the diversification of products, intensifying the competition and hence reducing prices for the Israeli consumer.
>
> Therefore, the balancing formula found in Article 24 of the Municipalities Tendering Regulations provides that these regulations will apply to the extent that they do not conflict with commitments of the State of Israel under an international treaty. In our case, preference will be given to domestically manufactured goods, only as long as there is no conflict with the application of international treaties such as the GPA.

Based on this, the critical question was therefore whether or not the procurement in question was subject to the GPA. This question depended on how to determine the value of the contract, in order to know if it was valued over the threshold. The court reached the conclusion that the contract was subject to the GPA based on GPA Article 2:6, which provides that where the intended procurement includes option clauses, the basis for valuation shall be the total value of the maximum permissible procurement, inclusive of optional purchases. The court rejected the claim that this provision should be read together with Article 2:4 that limits additional contracts to a period of twelve months or a fiscal year, holding that although the options in this case could be executed over a period of three years, they should still be included in the valuation of the procurement. The court therefore rejected the petition and allowed the municipality to proceed with the procurement in accordance with the GPA rules.

8.4.7 SUMMARY AND CONCLUSIONS

This chapter has discussed the history and origins of Israel's public procurement law. It has shown the central role played by the Israeli Supreme Court in creating and developing this law, even in the absence of any procurement legislation, based instead on general principles of administrative law. The Court's role in this context is reminiscent of its role in the development of the country's constitutional law—there too, the Court

[213] GPA, Article II:3. This procurement was governed by the previous GPA.

[214] *Dolev v. Tel Aviv*, p. 8.

created constitutional norms almost *ex nihilo*, preceding the legislator by several decades and prompting him to eventually fulfill his role as the regulator. Once the project of creating a detailed body of public tendering law had been completed, and the legislator was about to step in, the Supreme Court was prepared to step out and transfer the jurisdiction to lower courts. This all happened in the beginning of the 1990s, when the Court issued the Pasternak decision,[215] the Knesset passed the Mandatory Tenders Law, and based on this the government issued the various tendering regulations. This was later followed by the establishment of the administrative courts in 2000, which received almost exclusive jurisdiction over bid challenges.

As is often the case, when regulation moves from general (judge-made) principles to detailed (legislated) rules, the system sometimes becomes too rigid and too legalistically bureaucratic, and agencies feel they are unable to accomplish their objectives. This led to the establishment of two different committees, both assigned with the mandate to propose reforms to the tendering rules. One recommended expanding the arsenal of tendering procedures available to procuring agencies so that they would be more flexible, and modernizing the procurement system by introducing new technologies, including electronic procurement. The other recommended decentralizing the exemption authority. As I have shown (Section 8.3), both of these approaches were adopted in the 2009 reform of the Regulations. I have also shown how the new tendering procedures were influenced both by foreign legal systems (mainly the EU and the US) and by international instruments, such as the UNCITRAL Model Law and the GPA. While there are some problems with these new procedures that I pointed out during their discussion, their addition to the tools available to tendering committees definitely represents an improvement. Nevertheless, my assessment of the effects of the reform shows that they have not yet been very positive. The new tendering procedures are seldom used, the pace of introducing electronic procurement is painfully slow, and there has been a dangerous surge in the number of exemptions from public tendering, which probably is a result of the decentralization.

The chapter also discusses Israel's international commitments in this field, mainly under the plurilateral GPA, but also under other bilateral international agreements, such as the FTAs with Mexico and Colombia, as well as the FTA and MOU with the US. The practical significance of these commitments can only be understood against the backdrop of Israel's domestic preference and offset policies. These policies were therefore discussed and analyzed as they apply when none of the international agreements applies. I then went on to examine how these discriminatory measures are set aside whenever an international agreement covers the procurement and how the regular tendering rules are adapted to comply with the agreement.

[215] H.C.J. 991/91 *David Pasternak Ltd. v. Minister of Housing*, P.D. 45(5) 50.

Finally, the chapter discusses Israel's bid challenge system, which is found exclusively within the judiciary. I explained how the system works and how it serves to satisfy the obligation under the GPA to provide for an effective and independent bid challenge system. I also presented figures on the actual use of administrative petitions in the field of public procurement and on the average success rate of petitioners. I concluded with the discussion of a recent case, which implemented GPA rules and dismissed the demand of the local producer to receive preferential treatment.

One can therefore wrap up with the conclusion that Bileam's characterization (or perhaps curse) of the Children of Israel, in the Book of Numbers 23:9, as "lo, it is a people that dwells alone, not reckoned among the nations," and translated by Jonathan as "they shall not be led in the laws of the nations," does not apply to the public procurement field. Israel's laws in this field are closely integrated with, and influenced by, those of other nations, and we can hope that its experience with procurement regulation, as expounded in this chapter, can be helpful to other nations as well.

ACKNOWLEDGMENTS

Section 8.3 of this chapter draws heavily on Reich (2015). I am indebted to my research assistants, Elichai Shilo and Omri Segev, and to my doctoral student Oren Shabat, for their assistance. Thanks are also due to Omer Dekel and Benjamin Shmueli for their comments on a previous draft of this chapter. The regular caveats apply.

REFERENCES

Ariav Report 2007. *Report of the Inter-Ministerial Team for Improving the Efficiency of Governmental Procurement*, March 28 (Hebrew).

Arrowsmith, S. 2014. *The Law of Public and Utilities Procurement: Regulation in the EU and UK*, vol. 1, 3rd edn. London: Sweet & Maxwell.

Dekel, O. 2004. *Procurement Law: Theory and Practice*, (Hebrew). vol. 1, Lapid, Shurat Hadin (Hebrew).

Dekel, O. 2006. *Procurement Law: Theory and Practice*, (Hebrew). vol. 2, Lapid, Shurat Hadin (Hebrew).

Dekel, O. and Schurr A. 2014. "Cognitive Biases in Government Procurement: An Experimental Study." *Review of Law and Economics* 10(2): 169–200.

Dekel Report 2004. *Proposals for Amendments to the Mandatory Tenders Law and the Mandatory Tenders Regulations* (on file with author) (Hebrew).

Dotan, Y. 1996. *Administrative Guidance*. The Harry and Michael Sacher Institute for Legislative Research and Comparative Law, Faculty of Law, Hebrew University, Jerusalem (Hebrew).

Governability Report, 2013. *Report of the Team for Improvement of the Administrative Work and Operational Capacity of the Government Ministries ("The Governability Committee")* (Jerusalem, March 2013) (available at: <http://www.pmo.gov.il/SiteCollectionDocuments/meshilut2013.pdf> (accessed July 22, 2016)).

Lieber, S. K. 2007. "Zelecha versus Sheetrit: Rejected Exemption from Tender for Arim Corporation of a 380 Million Shekel Contract," *Globes*, June 26 (available in Hebrew at: <http://www.globes.co.il/news/article.aspx?did=1000224067> (accessed July 22, 2016)).

Reich, A. 1999. *International Public Procurement Law*. Leiden: Kluwer International.

Reich, A. 2009. "The New Text of the Agreement on Government Procurement: An Analysis and Assessment." *Journal of International Economic Law* 12(4): 989–1022.

Reich, A. 2015. "The 2009 Reforms of Israel's Mandatory Tendering Regulations: One Step Forward, Two Steps Backward?" *Public Procurement Law Review* 24(6): 193–220.

Reich, A. and Shabat, O. 2014. "The Remedy of Damages in Public Procurement in Israel and the EU: A Proposal for Reform." *Public Procurement Law Review* 2: 50–77.

Shalev, G. 1974. "General Comments on Contracts (General Part) Law, 1973." *Israel Law Review* 9: 274.

Weinshall-Lifshitz Report 2004, *Report of the Sub-Team of the Committee of Director-Generals for the Streamlining of the Governmental Procurement* October 28, 2004 (Hebrew).

WTO. 1994. "The Results of the Uruguay Round of Multilateral Trade Negotiations," Geneva.

9 US Government Contracting in the Context of Global Public Procurement

Christopher R. Yukins

9.1 Introduction

One could, in principle, assess the internationalization of US procurement law from the top down, from a global perspective down to the individual state level.[1] On reflection, however, there seems little to be gained in attempting to divine how international influences—through vehicles such as the World Trade Organization's (WTO's) Government Procurement Agreement (GPA),[2] the United Nations Commission on International Trade Law (UNCITRAL) model law on public procurement,[3] regional free trade agreements (such as the North American Free Trade Agreement, or NAFTA),[4] or even bilateral agreements—have impacted US government procurement policy, law, regulation, or practice, because the answer is, ultimately, hardly at all. While the United States has been a leader in pressing other countries to open their markets and to adopt what are considered best practices in procurement (e.g., Marceau and Blank, 1996), procurement law in the United States has evolved with little input from abroad.

The US experience, while it may be unique, suggests that the question is better understood from the bottom up. In other words, the US federal government has a rich and lengthy history of heavily regulated public procurement,[5] and the primary global instruments that

[1] An earlier piece suggested a conceptual framework for better integrating US procurement law with international norms; see Yukins and Schooner (2007).

[2] World Trade Organization, Agreement on Government Procurement (2012) (available at: <http://www.wto.org/english/tratop_e/gproc_e/gp_gpa_e.htm> (accessed July 23, 2016)); see generally Arrowsmith and Anderson (2011).

[3] UN Commission on International Trade Law (UNCITRAL) Model Law on Public Procurement (2011) (available at: <http://www.uncitral.org/uncitral/en/uncitral_texts/procurement_infrastructure/2011Model.html>(accessed July 23, 2016)).

[4] See, for example, Yukins (2015).

[5] The focus here will be on the US federal procurement regime, as state and local governments in the United States (with some notable exceptions) generally develop their own procurement laws. The federal government procures approximately $500 billion worth of goods and services every year (see <www.USASpending.gov>),

appear to be driving international harmonization evolved, in large part, based upon and/or consistent with the US federal experience. Indeed, with few exceptions—for example, in nomenclature ("bids" versus "tenders") and emphasis (the US system, unlike most, has also developed unique rules for contract performance, not just formation)—a US-centric analysis could conclude that procurement regimes around the world are slowly, but inexorably, evolving toward primary aspects of the US federal model.

The lesson here is not that other systems are adopting the US model, but that procurement systems, to a remarkable extent, seem to evolve in parallel. As the discussion below reflects, while the *process* of developing US procurement law is largely isolated from foreign influence, the US federal procurement regime is strikingly similar to the procurement directives used to guide laws in the European Union (e.g., Arrowsmith, 2014; Bovis, 2012), and to procurement regimes in other developed and developing nations.[6] This convergence has important ramifications, both for international procurement markets and for the development of best practices in procurement, around the globe. Having acknowledged this "convergent" evolution of procurement regimes, the logical next questions are:

- *Why are procurement systems so similar*—do the rules evolve to address common pathologies? This is a deeply complex question, which implicates many disciplines within law, economics, political science, and sociology. The question is, therefore, largely beyond the scope of this chapter, although a rich body of literature is emerging to address this critical puzzle.[7]
- *Should the minor, almost vestigial differences between rules systems be smoothed away,* as unnecessary impediments to competition and trade? Put differently, is it possible to nudge forward the process of convergent evolution?[8]

and those procurements are (for the most part) covered by a unitary scheme of statutes and regulations, under the statutory US Code and the Federal Acquisition Regulation (FAR) (codified at Title 48 of the Code of Federal Regulations).

[6] While one could, in theory, argue whether this is what natural scientists might call *homology* (corresponding features in different systems due to inheritance from a common ancestor) or *analogy* (corresponding features due to similar functions but not derived from a common ancestor) (see "Evolution," *Encyclopedia Britannica,* (2014), available at: <http://www.britannica.com/EBchecked/topic/197367/evolution/49899/Convergent-and-parallel-evolution> (accessed July 23, 2016)), the point is that procurement rules—on either side of the Atlantic, and around the world—are increasingly, and extraordinarily, similar.

[7] See, for example, Trepte (2004), discussing special problems presented by the government as a purchaser; Arrowsmith, Linarelli, and Wallace (2004); Sanchez Graells (2011); Schooner (2002); and Yukins (2010).

[8] The antitrust (competition) community faced many of the same challenges when competition agencies from around the world launched the International Competition Network (<www.icn.com>) approximately fifteen years ago. Hugh Hollman and William Kovacic, both then at the US Federal Trade Commission, described the ICN's goal, to spur "convergence" in competition law internationally:

To provide context for studying the ICN's experience, we first define "convergence"—the main objective that motivated the ICN's creation and sustains its operations today. By convergence we mean the broad

To assess the latter question in the context of the United States' national experience, this chapter discusses how procurement regulation has thrown up unique differences which work as trade barriers in the US procurement system, and it reviews why traditional solutions to such barriers—enhancing transparency, for example, or allowing bidders to challenge barriers—have not fully succeeded. The chapter concludes by suggesting a new way forward: that the United States and its trading partners ease convergence, and reduce unnecessary trade barriers, by opening channels for cooperation and harmonization in their respective procurement regimes.

In Section 9.2, this chapter will first describe the "state of play" in US procurement, focusing (as noted) on the federal procurement system.[9] Section 9.2 will also discuss how various major reforms in US federal procurement law and policy have generated barriers to trade, and Section 9.3 will describe how US approaches to transparency, public reporting, and e-procurement (normally stock solutions for trade barriers) have fallen short. Section 9.4 will review the influence that international norms and texts have had on US procurement law (surprisingly little, despite the prominent role that the United States has played in international efforts at procurement harmonization). A special focus in Section 9.4 will be on dispute settlement mechanisms and e-procurement systems in US federal procurement. Finally, the chapter will suggest a concerted effort, through trade negotiations or otherwise, to ease residual differences between procurement regimes.

9.2 State of Play—The US Federal Procurement System

The United States has a strong federal government and fifty state governments which enjoy substantial autonomy.[10] Local governments, which draw their authority from the

acceptance of standards concerning the substantive doctrine and analytical methods of competition law, the procedures for applying substantive commands, and the methods for administering a competition agency. Administration encompasses the techniques a competition agency uses to organize its operations, set priorities, and evaluate its effectiveness.

Convergence as we see it does not anticipate the establishment of identical policies and enforcement mechanisms across the world's competition policy systems. Complete uniformity—which we associate with the term "harmonization"—is probably unattainable. Variations in the economic conditions, history, legal process (e.g., civil law versus common law), and political science of individual jurisdictions are enduring sources of difference among competition systems (Hollman and Kovacic, 2011, footnotes omitted).

Bill Kovacic now serves as the Global Competition Professor of Law and Policy at the George Washington University Law School, and as director of the school's Competition Law Center.

[9] For a comprehensive review of most of the fifty US states' procurement laws, see ABA Public Contract Law Section (2011).

[10] The US federal government also oversees the District of Columbia (which contains Washington, the capital city) and a number of territories and associated states; see <http://www.usa.gov/Agencies/State-and-

states, also have independent authority. State and local governments across the United States have procurement laws which are generally not subject to interference by the federal government,[11] and which are notably diverse.[12] While federal grant rules do require state, local, and other governments to follow certain minimum procedures when they procure using federal grant funds,[13] and the American Bar Association has published a model procurement law which has been adopted, in whole or in part, by seventeen states and hundreds of local governments,[14] as a practical matter—and completely unlike the European Union—there is little if any harmonization in US procurement law across federal, state, and local governments.

Viewed on its own, however, the federal government is strikingly monolithic in its approach to procurement regulation. Almost all federal executive agencies procure under the Federal Acquisition Regulation (FAR),[15,16] which (with its agency-specific supplements) is several thousand pages long.[17] As Figure 9.1 reflects, federal agencies spend approximately $500 billion per year on procurement; that amount has roughly doubled since the terrorist attacks of September 11, 2001, and the launch of the wars in Iraq and Afghanistan. Federal procurement spans construction, supplies, and services, though recent decades have seen a pronounced increase in service spending, as the federal government has moved to outsource more service-based functions to the private sector.[18]

Spending by the Department of Defense (DoD) plays a very prominent role in US procurement, generally accounting for more than half of federal procurement (Figure 9.1). With the launch of the unified FAR in 1984, the United States established itself as a leader in what is now more commonly accepted internationally[19]—the merger of defense

Territories.shtml> (accessed July 23, 2016). The focus here, however, will be on procurement by the federal government's executive agencies.

[11] See, for example, *Trojan Technologies, Inc. v. Commonwealth of Pennsylvania*, 916 F.2d 903, 908 (3d Cir. 1990) (states' prerogative to impose procurement preferences not preempted by US commitments under the WTO Government Procurement Agreement).

[12] See generally Conway (2012).

[13] See Yukins and Priess (2014), discussing federal grant rules' requirements regarding procurement.

[14] see <http://apps.americanbar.org/dch/committee.cfm?com=PC500500> (accessed July 23, 2016).

[15] A very few elements of the federal government are exempt from the Federal Acquisition Regulation. The Federal Aviation Administration (FAA), for example, won its independence from the FAR in 1995. See the FAA Acquisition Management Policy, available at <http://fast.faa.gov/AcquisitionMgtPolicy.cfm>; and Allen and Yukins (1997).

[16] For a brief history of the birth of the Federal Acquisition Regulation, see Nagle (1999: pp. 481–91).

[17] The FAR is available online at <www.acquisition.gov/far>; that online version is regularly updated. The FAR also appears, with its various agency supplements, at Title 48 of the Code of Federal Regulations.

[18] *Report of the Acquisition Advisory Panel to the Office of Federal Procurement Policy and the United States Congress* (p. 414) (January 2007) (hereinafter "Acquisition Advisory Panel Report"), available at: <http://www.acquisition.gov/comp/aap/24102_GSA.pdf> (accessed July 23, 2016).

[19] See, for example, UN Commission on International Trade Law (2014: pp. 41–9).

and civilian procurement rules.[20] As a result, while there are military agency-specific supplements to the FAR (much as civilian agencies also have their own supplements to the FAR), absent special authorization[21] those agency-specific supplements must be in accord with the government-wide FAR regulation (e.g., Cibinic, Nash, and Yukins, 2011: pp. 34–7).

Procurement spending is also highly concentrated in a relatively small number of large contractors.[22] The top five companies—Lockheed Martin, Boeing, General Dynamics, Raytheon, and McKesson Corporation—accounted for $73 billion in DoD contracts in 2014. This high degree of concentration affects how the regulatory regime evolves, for the largest contractors—which often are significant stakeholders in any reform process—are best able to take on additional regulatory burdens.[23] In practice, this means that additional regulation can help to reinforce market concentration. This may be one of the reasons why, despite extensive procurement measures to favor small businesses, small businesses often argue that regulatory requirements remain a durable barrier to their growth in federal markets.[24] As can be seen in Figure 9.1, small businesses' share of the federal procurement market is less than 20 percent of the total.

The uniform procurement law regime has helped to strengthen the federal procurement workforce because, once trained in the FAR, professionals can move relatively easily from one agency to another, and from the government to the private sector and back (Schooner, 2002). The federal procurement community, broadly understood, now probably numbers several hundred thousand persons. For the fiscal year 2012, the Federal Acquisition Institute reported that, in the civilian agencies, there were over 73,000 acquisition professionals in the core categories of federal acquisition personnel (Federal Acquisition Institute, 2013: p. 1). As of 2006, the RAND Corporation reported that there were over 126,000 civilian and military personnel in the Defense Department's acquisition workforce (Gates et al., 2008).

[20] While the European Union has separate procurement directives for "classic" civilian procurement, Directive No. 2014/24/EU, and for defense procurement, Directive No. 2009/18/EC (e.g., Arrowsmith, 2014: paras. 6–141 to 6–151), there has been serious discussion of eventually merging civilian and defense procurement directives in Europe. For a review of some of the barriers created by the European defense directive, see Yukins (2009: p. 383).

[21] *See* FAR Subpart 1.4.

[22] Concentration in the defense industry has long been a policy concern in the United States (see, for example, McKie, 1970).

[23] The Acquisition Reform Working Group, which includes a cross-section of US associations for large and small businesses, is a prominent voice in commenting on the annual defense authorization bill, which is the most important vehicle for procurement reform. For examples of the group's submissions on annual defense authorization legislation, see the National Defense Industrial Association website (<http://www.ndia.org/advocacy/resources/pages/arWG.aspx>.

[24] See generally Beale (2014), discussing barriers to small business participation in federal procurement market).

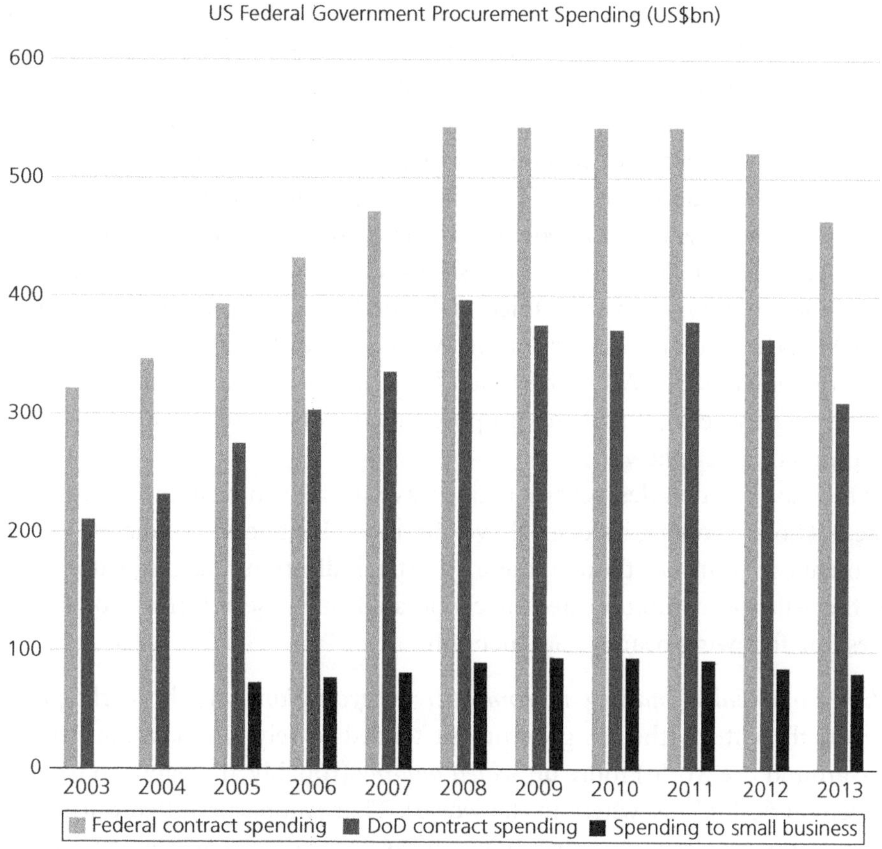

Figure 9.1. Size, trend, and composition of US federal procurement

Source: Draws on data from www.usaspending.gov.

There are two primary sources of regulatory change in the federal procurement regime: Congress, and the regulators themselves. While technically a new revision to the FAR could be launched by any person,[25] in practice regulatory reforms come primarily from Congress (usually as part of annual legislation authorizing defense spending), or through proposed changes to the FAR launched by the regulators themselves.

The defense authorization bill plays a critical role in the operations of the US Department of Defense, and as a result the House and Senate armed services committees have succeeded in passing annual defense authorization legislation through Congress for over fifty years (e.g., *Defense News*, 2013). Because agencies, associations, and firms interested in the procurement system know that Title VIII of the annual national defense authorization bill is likely to carry significant procurement law reforms, they (and other

[25] See FAR 1.502.

interested stakeholders) generally focus their lobbying efforts on the key members of Congress and staff on the armed services committees.[26] The procurement reforms mandated by Title VIII in each year's defense authorization legislation are then generally implemented into regulation—typically, into the FAR—over the following year.

The other major source of federal procurement reform is the Federal Acquisition Regulatory Council (known as the "FAR Council") itself, a coordinating body between the three leading agencies in federal procurement—the Defense Department, the National Aeronautics & Space Administration (NASA), and the General Services Administration (GSA)—and the Office of Federal Procurement Policy (a unit of the Office of Management and Budget, in the White House).[27] The FAR Council publishes proposed revisions to the FAR in the *Federal Register* (the daily administrative journal of the federal government),[28] and the proposed regulatory changes should be subject to public comment and review.[29]

Over the past few decades, several major waves of reform have moved through these processes. Those evolving reforms have, in most instances, paralleled very similar developments in Europe, though there is little indication that regulators on either side of the Atlantic communicated or cooperated on these reforms. For comparative purposes, the following bear special mention:

- *Shift from sealed bidding to competitive negotiations.* In the early part of the twentieth century, the US government tended to rely (as most governments still do, around the world) more on *sealed bidding* (roughly analogous to what is called "open tendering" elsewhere in the world). That emphasis shifted during the latter part of the twentieth century, however, as the federal government came to rely much more heavily upon "competitive negotiations" under FAR Part 15—analogous to "competitive procedures with negotiations" or "competitive dialogues" under the most recent EU procurement directives.[30] Today, only a relatively small portion of federal procurement (primarily construction) is done using sealed bidding against set specifications under FAR Part 14 (Cibinic, Nash, and Yukins, 2011: p. 501). Instead, whenever a federal agency is procuring complex goods (information technology, for example, or weapons systems), the agency is much

[26] This process is a focus of the George Washington University Law School's procurement reform seminar, which each year meets with officials, stakeholders and experts to discuss the current crop of proposed reforms in the defense authorization bill.

[27] See 41 USC. para. 1302; FAR 1.103, 1.201; <http://www.whitehouse.gov/omb/procurement far coun cil> (accessed July 23, 2016).

[28] The *Federal Register* is available at <www.federalregister.gov>.

[29] See FAR Subpart 1.5. The regulatory history of new rules, including submitted public comments, is generally available at <www.regulations.gov>.

[30] See, for example, Articles 29 and 30 of the "classic" directive, used generally for agencies' purchases of supplies and services, Directive No. 2014/24/EU; Arrowsmith (2006: pp. 337 and 340); Yukins (2013).

more likely to use the more liberal competitive negotiations, which will allow members of industry to present (and negotiate) widely divergent technical solutions. It appears that the European Union is following this same trend towards open, multilateral negotiations, and the World Bank has adopted reforms that would open the door to this more liberal—and, from an anti-corruption standpoint, riskier—method of procurement in World Bank-financed projects.[31,32]

- *The "commercial item" revolution.* In 1994, Congress passed the Federal Acquisition Streamlining Act (FASA),[33] a major milestone in federal procurement. In order to match the norms of the commercial marketplace, FASA required agencies to impose far fewer regulatory and contractual burdens on "commercial items"—commercial off-the-shelf items, and goods and services that were at or near commercial availability (Vacketta and Pope, 1998; Schooner, 2003). The reforms of the 1990s also propelled much broader use of purchase cards (which allow government end-users to make purchases directly in the commercial marketplace)[34] and micro-purchases (generally open market purchases below $3,500,[35] which are almost completely free of regulatory requirements) (Schooner, 2001: pp. 627 and 660). While Europe has not experienced a similar regulatory "revolution" around commercial items, the US "commercial item" reforms *were* grounded in the same core concern that drove the European procurement directives—the desire to better integrate government procurement into a broader commercial economy (Telles, 2013: p. 3; Yukins and Cora, 2013: p. 64).
- *Anti-corruption and contractor compliance.* For several decades after the widespread scandals of the 1980s (McGarry, 1993: p. 249), contractors resisted instituting the compliance controls that became, after the US Sentencing Commission issued its organizational sentencing guidelines in 1991, a standard part of the US corporate landscape (Murphy, 2002: p. 697). In 2008, however, after long debate (Yukins, 2003), the FAR Council published a final rule which required most contractors to institute internal compliance controls,[36] and to report to the government when the contractor finds compelling evidence of fraud, significant overpayments, or certain kinds of criminal activity.[37] Notably, only a short time later, the United Kingdom

[31] See, for example, Gordon and Racca (2014), discussing greater corruption risks of more "subjective" selection approach prevalent in the US system.

[32] World Bank (2014: pp. 12–13); new World Bank approved procedures would include competitive dialogue. The new World Bank procurement framework, formally adopted on July 1, 2016, is discussed at <www.worldbank.org/en/projects-operations/products-and-services/brief/procurement-new-framework>.

[33] Public Law No. 103-355, 108 Stat. 3243 (1994).

[34] 10 USC. para. 2784 (on use of purchase cards in the Department of Defense); 41 USC. para. 1909 (purchase cards in civilian agencies); Gupta and Palmer (2007).

[35] 41 USC. para. 1902; FAR Subpart 13.2.

[36] See 73 Fed. Reg. 67064 (2008); Levy and Huffman (2010).

[37] See, for example, FAR 52.203-13; Kathuria (2009: p. 803).

enacted the UK Bribery Act of 2010, and the UK Ministry of Justice the following year issued guidance on corporate compliance which in many ways paralleled the US guidelines on appropriate corporate compliance systems.[38] Perhaps because of the obvious need to coordinate multinational corporations' compliance efforts, in this area—uniquely—there has been extensive cooperation between regulators in setting what are, in fact, remarkably similar standards in corporate compliance.[39]

- *Spread of indefinite-delivery/indefinite-quantity (IDIQ) ("framework") contracts.* "Catalog" contracting using "IDIQ" agreements—what are known as "framework" agreements in Europe and elsewhere[40]—exploded in US federal procurement in the late 1990s, after FASA specifically endorsed the use of this novel contracting method.[41] At the same time, "framework" contracting was taking hold in Europe.[42] IDIQ (or framework) contracting allows agencies— especially centralized agencies—on both sides of the Atlantic to offer standardized goods and services, generally at commercial market prices, to other agencies. This reduces transaction costs, and allows centralizing purchasing agencies to flex their comparative advantages in procurement, while harnessing the broader government's enormous purchasing power.[43] Despite the parallels between the two systems, however, and the practical barriers to trade that this type of contracting could pose, there was no apparent coordination between the US and European procurement regulators regarding IDIQ contracting and framework agreements.
- *Emergence of cybersecurity.* In the face of unprecedented threats of espionage and data theft across the internet, the US government has mandated a wide variety of cybersecurity measures which affect firms doing business with the federal government.[44] Those US requirements are rapidly evolving, and they generally involve both (i) measures to exclude suppliers that could potentially open security risks in the supply chain,[45] and (ii) broader requirements for security precautions in contractor and

[38] UK Ministry of Justice (March 2011), The Bribery Act 2010 (available at: <https://www.gov.uk/government/uploads/system/uploads/attachment_data/file/181762/bribery-act-2010-guidance.pdf> (accessed July 23, 2016).

[39] US Department of Justice and US Securities & Exchange Commission (2012), noting parallel compliance system requirements around the world.

[40] See, for example, Yukins (2008: p. 545) and Horska (2010: pp. 697 and 691–5), comparing US and foreign practices under frameworks agreements.

[41] See, for example, Beale (2014: p. 81), discussing impact of IDIQ growth on small businesses.

[42] Framework agreements are now an established part of the European procurement regime; see Arrowsmith (2014: paras 11-01 to 11-03).

[43] See, for example, Racca, Cavallo Perin, and Albano (2011: p. 89), discussing benefits of post-award competition in framework contracting.

[44] See, for example, Nichols et al. (2014).

[45] See, for example, Section 806 of the National Defense Authorization Act for Fiscal Year 2011, Pub. L. No. 111-383, 124 Stat. 4137 (2011), which gave the military services broad authority (subject to limited procedural safeguards) to exclude sources which are perceived to pose "supply chain risk," that is risk

agency information technology systems.[46] Importantly, these cybersecurity requirements in US procurement are not necessarily in sync with similar requirements emerging in Europe and elsewhere,[47] and this poses a serious possibility—again—that differing requirements will raise a serious barrier to trade. Nor is it clear that the differences in security requirements are grounded in differing risks; instead, at least for now, the divergence in cybersecurity requirements internationally seems more likely a product of uncoordinated efforts. In practice, this may raise an unnecessary barrier to trade; more seriously, a failure to cooperate could mean that public purchasers will not have access to the best technical solutions in cybersecurity, which in turn could retard development, and expose public agencies to increased security risks.

While they were not always "reforms" per se, it is important here to discuss the proliferation of socioeconomic programs and domestic preferences in the federal procurement system. Since 1933, with the passage of the Buy American Act, and 1953, with the passage of the Small Business Act,[48] the United States has put into place a remarkable array of domestic and small business preferences, and other socioeconomic requirements, in federal procurement.

- *Domestic content.* The domestic preferences have evolved over time, and tend now to be targeted on specific industries or types of procurement (Manuel et al., 2014). While other nations have patterned their own domestic preferences on the Buy

that "an adversary may sabotage, maliciously introduce unwanted function, or otherwise subvert the design, integrity, manufacturing, production, distribution, installation, operation, or maintenance of a covered system so as to surveil, deny, disrupt, or otherwise degrade the function, use, or operation of such system." Section 806 was not implemented for several years, when the DoD issued an interim rule, published at 78 Fed. Reg. 69268 (November 18, 2013), and now incorporated into the Defense Federal Acquisition Regulation Supplement (DFARS). Procurement in the US intelligence community is governed by a similar requirement, per Intelligence Community Directive 731, issued by the Director of National Intelligence on December 7, 2013 (available at: <http://www.dni.gov/index.php/intelligence-community/ic-policies-reports/intelligence-community-directives> (accessed July 23, 2016)). In early 2014, the Defense Department and the General Services Administration issued a joint report on reducing cybersecurity risk through the acquisition process, in response to President Obama's Executive Order 13636, which called for improved security for critical infrastructure. See US Department of Defense and US General Services Administration (2014); Bosco (2014: p. 41).

[46] See, for example, Nichols et al. (2014: p. 3–14), reviewing standards.

[47] For example, the "No-Spy-Decree" issued by the German government, which requires contractors to certify that the technology sold to covered units of the German government will not make secure data available to foreign intelligence agencies (Haak and Westerwelle, 2014; Gleeson and Demmel, 2014, with links to decree and implementing guidelines). Taken alone, this German requirement is a much narrower approach to cybersecurity than the US initiatives outlined above, one born partly of Germany's unique frustrations with alleged US spying, and of Germany's acute recognition of the dangers of uncontrolled surveillance.

[48] For a short history of the Small Business Act and its implementation, see the US Small Business Administration website (<https://www.sba.gov/about-sba/what_we_do/history> (accessed July 22, 1010)).

American Act and other similar barriers,[49] the US preferences are typically born legislatively, often in a highly charged political environment, with little discussion of international best practices or the preferences' impact on international trade.[50]

- *Small business preferences.* While explicit preferences for domestic content have tended to grow narrower and more focused in US federal procurement over the decades, US small business preferences (which would be known as "small and medium-sized enterprise", or SME, preferences in other nations)[51] have tended to proliferate, to address a broad variety of social and political goals. Beyond a general preference for small business, there are, for example, preferences in federal procurement now for small businesses owned by women, service-disabled veterans, socially disadvantaged businesspeople, and entrepreneurs in historically underutilized business zones (Manuel and Lunder, 2012). Since generally only US-based businesses qualify for these preferences,[52] and fully 23 percent of all federal procurement dollars are to go to small business,[53] these preferences (and *de facto* trade barriers) are a continuing irritant with the United States' most important trading partners, including the European Union. As with the domestic content preferences discussed above, these small business preferences are generally born in Congress, with little public reference to international trade issues or best practices abroad (including, notably, initiatives to support small business which have evolved in other procurement systems, in parallel with the US preferences) (Kidalov, 2011: p. 443).

[49] See, for example, Novais (2012), tracing how a Brazilian domestic preference was based upon the Buy American Act.

[50] See, for example, Schooner and Yukins (2009: p. 78), discussing the need to be sensitive to international trade obligations in rules implementing the American Recovery and Reinvestment Act. In order to comply with existing US trade obligations, typically new trade preferences will be made subject to existing thresholds and trade agreements. See, for example, Section 1605 of the American Recovery & Reinvestment Act (ARRA), Public Law 111-5 (2009), which stated that none "of the funds appropriated or otherwise made available by this Act [nearly $800 billion in emergency fiscal stimulus] may be used for a project for the construction, alteration, maintenance, or repair of a public building or public work unless all of the iron, steel, and manufactured goods used in the project are produced in the United States," but also provided that this requirement "shall be applied in a manner consistent with United States obligations under international agreements."

[51] The US Small Business Administration defines "small" businesses relatively expansively, to include (depending upon the industry) potentially firms with hundreds of employees and many millions of dollars in annual revenues. See, for example, the US Small Business Administration, Table of Small Business Size Standards (<https://www.sba.gov/content/small-business-size-standards> (accessed July 23, 2010). Those expansive standards have been the subject of some criticism (e.g., Cooper, 2012).

[52] See, for example, 15 USC, para. 632 (requiring that majority interests of enterprises under certain preference categories be held by US citizens); 13 C.F.R., para. 121.105 (US Small Business Administration defines eligible "business concern or concern" as a small business which "is a business entity organized for profit, with a place of business located in the United States, and which operates primarily within the United States or which makes a significant contribution to the US economy through payment of taxes or use of American products, materials or labor").

[53] See 15 USC, para. 644(g) (goals for participation of small business concerns in procurement contracts).

- *Environmental concerns.* In the US federal government, as in Europe, the government has struggled with how to address "sustainability" issues in procurement. While some governments have taken a broader approach to sustainability, to include issues of economic sustainability and social justice,[54] the US government, in political prudence, has focused more narrowly on *environmental* issues—a subpart of sustainability.[55] The federal government's efforts to reduce greenhouse gases in procurement have slowed substantially,[56] but as an interim measure the federal government (much like the European Union) has embraced "eco-labels" in procurement.[57] "Eco-labels" signify that a good has met certain environmental standards, and assure the buyer that the good will have a lower environmental impact. The problem, however, is that "eco-labels" are likely to differ from one jurisdiction to another; as a result, these differing

[54] The United Nations Environment Programme defines "sustainability" in the context of public procurement as follows, to include economic, social justice, and environmental goals: "Sustainable Procurement is a process whereby organisations meet their needs for goods, services, works and utilities in a way that achieves value for money on a whole life basis in terms of generating benefits not only to the organisation, but also to society and the economy, whilst minimising damage to the environment" (available at: <http://www.unep.org/resourceefficiency/Consumption/SustainableProcurement/WhatisSustainablePublicProcurement/tabid/101245/Default.aspx> (accessed July 23, 2016)).

[55] See, for example, Anderson (2012), discussing various branches of sustainability in procurement.

[56] For an update on current initiatives, see the US General Services Administration's "Greening the Supply Chain" (available at: <http://www.gsa.gov/portal/content/285653> (accessed July 23, 2016)).

[57] FAR 23.103, Sustainable Acquisitions, provides as follows:

(a) Federal agencies shall advance sustainable acquisition by ensuring that 95 percent of new contract actions for the supply of products and for the acquisition of services (including construction) require that the products are—
  (1) Energy-efficient (ENERGY STAR® or Federal Energy Management Program (FEMP)-designated);
  (2) Water-efficient;
  (3) Biobased;
  (4) Environmentally preferable (e.g., EPEAT®-registered, or non-toxic or less toxic alternatives);
  (5) Non-ozone depleting; or
  (6) Made with recovered materials.

(b) The required products in the contract actions for services include products that are—
  (1) Delivered to the Government during performance;
  (2) Acquired by the contractor for use in performing services at a Federally-controlled facility; or
  (3) Furnished by the contractor for use by the Government.

(c) The required products in the contract actions must meet agency performance requirements.

(d) For purposes of meeting the 95 percent sustainable acquisition requirement, the term "contract actions" includes new contracts (and task and delivery orders placed against them) and new task and delivery orders on existing contracts.

For a discussion of the use of "eco-labels" under the prior European procurement directives (2004), see <http://ec.europa.eu/environment/ecolabel/ecolabel-and-green-public-procurement.html> (accessed July 23, 2016). Recital (88) to the revised 2014 directive, 2014/24/EU, provides, in relevant part: "Contracting authorities should be able to require that environmental management measures or schemes be applied during the performance of a public contract. Environmental management schemes . . . can demonstrate that the economic operator has the technical capability to perform the contract. This includes Ecolabel certificates involving environmental management criteria."

"eco-labels" are likely to pose a significant barrier to trade between procurement markets.[58]

- *Other socioeconomic requirements.* Over the past decades, additional trade-distorting preferences have crept into US procurement rules, again with no probing consideration of their effects on international trade, or reference to practices in other countries. Thus, for example, while Section 508 of the Rehabilitation Act requires that all information technology bought by the government be accessible to persons with disabilities, and similar requirements have begun to crop up in Europe,[59] there was no public effort to coordinate the US and European standards for accessibility—indeed, regulators specifically *rejected* using certain international technical standards when the "Section 508" standards were originally published.[60] Here, as elsewhere, socioeconomic requirements have been imposed on federal

[58] To address this serious problem, at least within the European market, the Court of Justice for the European Union, in the "*Max Havelaar*" decision, wrote that while procuring entities may require that vendors be able to present such "labels," vendors also must be afforded the chance to meet this requirement by demonstrating that they can meet *equivalent* standards. The *Max Havelaar* decision's popular name derives from the "fair trade" label at the center of the case, the "Max Havelaar" label, signifying fair trade (trade in which fair prices are paid to producers) in coffee; the Max Havelaar label was originally launched by a development agency in the Netherlands (Helms, 2011: p. 79). In that decision, *European Commission v. Kingdom of the Netherlands,* Case C-368/10, Court of Justice of the European Union, the court concluded the government of North Holland violated the relevant European procurement directive when it:

- established a technical specification incompatible with Article23(6) of Directive 2004/18 by requiring that certain products to be supplied were to bear a specific eco-label, rather than using detailed specifications;
- established award criteria incompatible with Article53(1)(a) of that directive by providing that the fact that certain products to be supplied bore specific labels would give rise to the grant of a certain number of points in the choice of the most economically advantageous tender, without having listed the criteria underlying those labels and without having allowed proof that a product satisfies those underlying criteria by all appropriate means.

The *Max Havelaar* approach—read broadly, to allow vendors to enter new markets by showing that they can meet functionally equivalent standards—squares with the World Trade Organization's GPA, *see* Article X(3) (2012) ("Where design or descriptive characteristics are used in the technical specifications, a procuring entity should indicate, where appropriate, that it will consider tenders of equivalent goods or services that demonstrably fulfil the requirements of the procurement by including words such as 'or equivalent' in the tender documentation"), and points a way forward for breaking technical barriers to procurement markets worldwide.

[59] See, for example, European Procurement Directive 2014/24/EU, Art. 42(1) ("For all procurement which is intended for use by natural persons, whether general public or staff of the contracting authority, the technical specifications shall, except in duly justified cases, be drawn up so as to take into account accessibility criteria for persons with disabilities or design for all users").

[60] See Yukins (2004: pp. 667, 692, and n.95), discussing regulatory history. The accessibility standards under section 508 are currently being revised, and the revised standards are being drafted with an eye to harmonization with international technical standards; see US Access Board, *Operating Protocols: Telecommunications and Electronic and Information Technology Access Advisory Committee* (available at: <http://www.access-board.gov/guidelines-and-standards/communications-and-it/about-the-ict-refresh/background/advisory-committee-operating-protocols> (accessed July 23, 2016)).

procurement without thorough public consideration of their practical effect on international trade flows.[61]

Taken in sum, these important changes in US procurement—regulatory innovations which may, in practice, raise serious potential non-tariff barriers to trade—show that change in federal procurement consistently comes from within, almost always with no serious discussion of international norms or best practices. Those working to reform federal procurement (through Congress, or through the regulatory process) have no ready means of exchanging information with foreign stakeholders or regulators. Members of Congress and their staff members, in a democratic institution driven largely by domestic political concerns, have few incentives to accommodate foreign interests, and are not focused on opening international procurement markets. The regulators (including the FAR Council), for their part, have no clear mandate to consider open markets or international best practices in shaping procurement rules.[62] As a result, the US federal procurement system regularly evolves unique requirements which can, and do, serve as durable barriers to trans-border trade. The discussion above shows, however, that those barriers often could be reduced, and the quality of procurement regulation could be improved, if regulators in different systems compared notes during the rule-writing process.[63]

[61] The socioeconomic requirements have included several which address labor and employment practices, including the "Fair Pay and Safe Workplaces" Executive Order, E.O. 13673, issued by President Barack Obama on July 31, 2014. That executive order will require contracting officers to consider whether potential contractors have engaged in serious, repeated, willful, or pervasive violations of certain labor laws and, if so, possibly to exclude those contractors as unqualified to contract ("non-responsible," in US procurement terms). The order has only recently passed through the rulemaking process (see <http://www.dol.gov/asp/fairpay/> (accessed October 2, 2016), but it has already proven extremely controversial, as it could create a cumbersome layer of review before award of the affected contracts. Because the executive order calls for contracting officers to assess contractors' violations of *domestic US* labor laws, the order may have the unintended effect of favoring new market entrants from abroad, which may have no experience with US labor laws.

[62] Regulators are, technically speaking, supposed to consider the market impact that significant rules may have; in practice, however, that required review is often ignored in rulemaking regarding procurement. See, for example, Yukins and Cora (2013), discussing executive order requiring assessment of impacts.

[63] Although Congress (and sometimes the President) may impose domestic preferences in response to political pressures, it is worth noting that the procuring agencies, over time, will tend to gently resist domestic preferences, because federal buyers want access to the best technologies and vendors available on world markets. See, for example, Yukins and Schooner (2007: p. 538): "The agencies typically have been willing to bear the additional costs of domestic preferences in order to further other social or political goals. Now... purchasing agencies' new decision to demand flexibility (rather than slavishly adhere to a domestic preference mandate) highlights the internal fissures that undermine traditional domestic preferences. Agencies and contractors, under pressure to utilize the collective strength of a global supply chain, cannot indefinitely abide arbitrary political demands to accommodate self-interested domestic industries."

9.3 US Federal Approaches in Transparency, Reporting, and e-Procurement

As the discussion above reflects, the US federal procurement regime has evolved a broad array of highly developed procurement rules—rules which were generally designed to serve other ends, and may in practice serve as significant non-tariff barriers to trade. The next question, then, is whether the tools most commonly championed in international trade to reduce barriers to trade in procurement—transparency, regular reporting, and electronic procurement ("e-procurement")—have been brought to bear in the US system. As the discussion here will show, although these tools *have* been deployed, and the United States has often led the way in developing new techniques and technologies, these improvements have come with almost no apparent reference to their impact in opening international competition.

Transparency. There is broad recognition in the US procurement community that procurement opportunities and awards should be adequately publicized.[64] That policy goal, however, has not been fully met. For example, though most federal procurement opportunities and awards over $25,000 are publicized through the *Federal Business Opportunities* website,[65] there is no general requirement that individual opportunities and awards under most framework agreements (i.e., in US terms, "orders" under "indefinite-delivery/indefinite-quantity" (IDIQ) contracts) be published, as well.[66] As a result, it is very difficult to track billions of dollars in orders awarded under standing IDIQ (framework) agreements—both the opportunities and awards are often invisible to outsiders.[67] This means, in practical terms, that the growth of framework agreements (IDIQ contracts) has created a major non-tariff barrier to trade (a large, non-transparent sphere of activity) in the federal procurement market. While it is generally recognized that this lack of transparency in frameworks contracting is a serious policy issue, the debate over the problem, and the limited solutions that have been adopted, have almost never cited the impact that this lack of transparency may have on international trade. Thus, though the US procurement system is slowly remedying these and other

[64] See, for example, Gordon and Racca (2014: p. 139), discussing history of transparency in US procurement.

[65] See FAR 2.101 (Government-wide point of entry (GPE) "means the single point where Government business opportunities greater than $25,000, including synopses of proposed contract actions, solicitations, and associated information, can be accessed electronically by the public." The GPE is located at: <http://www.fedbizopps.gov> (accessed July 23, 2016); FAR 5.101 (threshold for publication); FAR 5.201 (publication requirement).

[66] See, for example, FAR 16.505(a)(1) ("In general, the contracting officer does not synopsize orders under indefinite-delivery contracts").

[67] See, for example, the Acquisition Advisory Panel Report, pp. 430–2 and 441–2.

"blank" zones of non-transparency, it is doing so from within, largely without reference to international markets.

Reporting. As noted, the US government data on awarded contracts are not always complete, and the main US data repository, the Federal Procurement Data System (FPDS),[68] has been roundly criticized over the years.[69] Because it is so difficult for laypersons to access data through FPDS, the federal government adopted a more user-friendly website to access the FPDS procurement data.[70] That website, USASpending.gov, is now the primary public source of data on federal procurement and grants. Although the USASpending website is quite sophisticated and useful, as noted some gaps remain, and the efforts to correct the blind spots in the data are, again, being made without reference to international obligations of the United States.

Reporting issues are more acute in the public databases used to track contractor qualification (called "contractor responsibility" under US law). There have been embarrassing technical failures (e.g., Bernhart Walker, 2014) as databases containing contractor qualification information have been rebuilt and consolidated in a new "System for Award Management," at <www.sam.com>.[71] While the list of debarred and suspended contractors (formerly known as the "Excluded Parties List System," or EPLS) has long been maintained, recent legislative and regulatory changes have made more data regarding contractor qualification (such as reports of poor performance and defaults) available on the www.sam.gov public website (Richard, Whiteman, and Gleic, 2013). This nominally makes the qualification process more transparent, and thus more accessible, but the regulatory complexity which surrounds this public reporting—the nature of the reports, for example, and the procedures for challenging adverse reports—means, in practice, that experienced domestic firms have a natural advantage in navigating the system. Notably, though debate continues on how (and to what extent) contractor qualification information will be made public, no serious consideration has been given to the effect that uneven reporting may have on international trade.

e-procurement. In the mid-1990s, the US government undertook an early effort—and failed—to erect a comprehensive e-procurement system, the ill-starred Federal Acquisition Computer Network (FACNET) (Godes, 1997: p. 663). After FACNET failed (it was overtaken by the internet) (Yukins, 1998), the federal government's approach to e-procurement was more cautious and incremental, from the databases described earlier to much more ambitious efforts to secure transactions between contractors and the government (Hordell and Hoffman, 2000). The US government has generally favored

[68] Available at: <https://www.fpds.gov> (accessed July 23, 2016).

[69] See, for example, the Acquisition Advisory Panel Report, pp. 435–8, recounting criticism.

[70] See, for example, White House, "Frequently Asked Questions Regarding Procurement Data," <http://www.whitehouse.gov/omb/procurement_pro_data_faq> (accessed July 23, 2016) (discussing FPDS and USASpending.gov).

[71] A play on the term "Uncle Sam," a nickname used since the nineteenth century for the US government.

technology-neutral solutions in e-procurement, and has, as a practical matter, tried to minimize the market disruptions caused by the shift to online procurement. Although these more cautious policies are less likely to create artificial barriers to trade, the discussion of e-procurement has been an almost exclusively domestic one, with little real assessment of how e-procurement can, as a practical matter, open international procurement markets.

9.4 **Impact of International Dispute Settlement Mechanisms on Federal Procurement**

Given the issues outlined above, in theory the US procurement system could be a robust target of challenges asserting violations of international trade agreements. Under small business preferences, for example, the government's requirement that prime contractors subcontract with small businesses to the greatest extent practical might be read as an informal offset requirement; a foreign vendor might argue, for example, that forcing prime contractors to use small businesses (by definition, US domestic small businesses) is, in effect, a prohibited offset, which discriminates against foreign firms.[72] While these and other practices in US procurement could, at least theoretically, have spawned challenges from affected foreign vendors over the years, there have been few formal challenges. Only one procurement-related case has reached full decision under the WTO's dispute procedures,[73] and there have been *no* cases in the US Court of Federal Claims or the Government Accountability Office (GAO)—the two most popular forums for bid challenges in federal procurement—stemming from the Government Procurement Agreement.

[72] Under FAR 19.702, which implements the government's small business subcontracting plan, any contractor receiving a substantial federal contract "must agree in the contract that small business, veteran-owned small business, service-disabled veteran-owned small business, HUBZone small business, small disadvantaged business, and women-owned small business concerns will have the maximum practicable opportunity to participate in contract performance consistent with its efficient performance." As noted above, only US-based firms will qualify as eligible small businesses, and so qualify for this subcontracting preference. The US government is likely to defend this small business subcontracting preference by pointing out, however, that the United States' general notes to the revised (2012) Government Procurement Agreement (Annex 7) (<www.wto.org/gpa> (accessed July 23, 2016)) provide in paragraph 1: "This Agreement does not apply to any set aside on behalf of a small- or minority-owned business. A set-aside may include any form of preference, such as the exclusive right to provide a good or service, or any price preference." Assessing the impact of that reservation, and any similar reservation for small business preferences under other US trade agreements, is beyond the scope of this chapter.

[73] The United States' challenge to South Korean procurement practices at the Inchon International Airport reached a panel decision in *Korea–Procurement*, WTO DS163; the docket and decision are available through the WTO website (<http://www.wto.org/english/tratop_e/gproc_e/disput_e.htm#gpadisputes> (accessed July 23, 2016)).

There are at least two possible explanations for this relative lack of litigation (which is surprising in what is normally a very litigious marketplace).

- First, the texts of the free trade agreements are modeled, to an important extent, on the procurement law regime of the United States. A key goal of US negotiators is to minimize the regulatory change that any procurement-related agreement may cause. Because the trade agreements' texts align with the existing US procurement regime, a challenge to the explicit terms of US law is less likely.
- Second, a judicial or administrative challenge to the *discriminatory impact* of US procurement rules would not be simple, for the jurisdiction of the Court of Federal Claims and the GAO to hear challenges under the trade agreements is generally untested and unsure. Although the United States' trade agreements which address procurement typically require the parties to ensure that a judicial or administrative body is available to hear challenges to discriminatory violations of the agreements,[74] neither the Court of Federal Claims nor the GAO has squarely addressed its jurisdiction to hear those challenges,[75] and broader challenges (for example, to enforce states' obligations under the GPA) could face significant statutory obstacles.[76]

This reality—that existing US barriers to trade are unlikely to be addressed or resolved through judicial or administrative bid challenges—has important collateral consequences. The European Union and the United States parties are currently negotiating

[74] Section 9.13(1) of the United States-Chile Free Trade Agreement (<http://www.ustr.gov/sites/default/files/uploads/agreements/fta/chile/asset_upload_file926_4003.pdf> (accessed July 23, 2016)) provides, for example, regarding required fora for bid challenges:

Each Party shall establish or designate *at least one impartial administrative or judicial authority* that is independent from its entities *to receive and review challenges that suppliers submit relating to the Party's measures implementing this Chapter in connection with a procurement covered by this Chapter and make appropriate findings and recommendations.* Where a challenge by a supplier is initially reviewed by a body other than such an impartial authority, the Party shall ensure that the supplier may appeal the initial decision to an impartial administrative or judicial authority that is independent of the entity that is the subject of the challenge (emphasis added).

[75] In two GAO decisions which have addressed the Government Procurement Agreement's non-discrimination obligations, the GAO applied the requirements of the implementing US statutes and regulations—not the trade agreement itself—is assessing the federal government's obligations. *Hid Global, Inc.*, Comp. Gen. B-403103, 2010 CPD p. 215 (September 15, 2010); *Olympic Container Corp.*, Comp. Gen. B-250403, 93–1 CPD p. 89 (January 29, 1993). In a 2015 bid challenge which asked the US Court of Federal Claims to enforce a US–Denmark agreed preference for Danish and Greenlandic firms at Thule Air Base, Greenland, the court largely sidestepped the US Justice Department's argument that under 28 U.S.C. 1502 the Court of Federal Claims lacks jurisdiction to hear "claims" arising under international executive agreements. *Per Aarsleff A/S V. United States*, 121 Fed. Cl. 603, 621–2 (2015) *rev'd on other grounds*, Fed Cir. Nos. 2015–5111 et al. (June 23, 2016). The court looked to the international agreement, not as binding, but rather as guidance in interpreting the governing solicitation.

[76] Section 3512 of Title 19, US Code, for example, appears to bar any direct suits against the states to enforce the states' obligations under the GPA.

a potential Transatlantic Trade and Investment artnership (TTIP) agreement which would address, among other things, procurement rules. While the United States has suggested that it has more modest goals for procurement under TTIP, both the European Union and the US business community have suggested that the TTIP agreement should go further.[77] Among other things, this may mean broadening the TTIP, to include procurement among other spheres of regulation that would be discussed regularly between the United States and the European Union, in an ongoing effort to improve harmonization and coordination between the two economies (Yukins and Priess, 2014). The TTIP agreement could, in other words, establish a permanent negotiating structure for resolving barriers to trade in procurement.[78] Given the serious potential barriers identified above, and the relative weakness of the classic solutions to such barriers—transparency and contractor challenges—this new approach, to open a permanent channel for cooperation on procurement, could bear special promise.

9.5 **Conclusion**

Since the end of World War II, the United States has consistently pressed to open procurement markets abroad. That commitment to open international procurement markets has, however, been shadowed by a stubborn reluctance to fully open procurement markets at home. Those market barriers have been exacerbated because, although the US federal procurement regime has evolved in parallel to other regimes abroad, US regulators have generally not referenced or communicated with regulatory regimes abroad (including, importantly, the European Union) to harmonize rules and maximize competition. By the same token, the US procurement regime has evolved without much reference to the United States' obligations under its international trade agreements. Nor have the tools that would normally work to break down barriers—such as transparency

[77] See, for example, "Procurement" on the Business Coalition for Transatlantic Trade website (<http://www.transatlantictrade.org/issues/procurement/> (accessed July 23, 2016)), discussing goals of US business community for procurement in TTIP negotiations.

[78] This may mean stretching the TTIP agenda, even measured against the European Union's more ambitious goals for procurement under the agreement. While the European Union has emphasized that the parties "continue[] to discuss how to ensure close regulatory cooperation between our respective regulators on different areas of regulations including standards and conformity assessment" (statement of the European Union's Chief TTIP Negotiator, Ignacio Garcia Bercero, on July 18, 2014), and the European Union was careful to leave open the possibility that such institutionalized cooperation could occur outside specific trade sectors (European Commission, 2013a), the European Union's initial statements of TTIP negotiating goals did not specifically cite procurement as one of the areas of regulation that should be an ongoing focus of discussions and cooperation between the United States and the European Union. Instead, the European Union's statement of goals for public procurement focused on expansion of the terms of the GPA, and did not include establishment of a consultative body for cooperation in procurement regulation between Europe and the United States (European Commission, 2013b).

and e-procurement, or bidders' challenges to enforce non-discriminatory trade commitments—proven fully effective in reducing the explicit and practical barriers to international competition in the US procurement market. A possible first step to ease these problems would be to expand regulatory cooperation across the Atlantic, so that European and US procurement regulators could, on an ongoing basis, communicate and cooperate to reduce avoidable regulatory differences that could otherwise raise barriers to international trade. This first small step, which could in time be expanded to include other nations (under the WTO or otherwise),[79] would reduce compliance costs and enhance competition in international procurement markets, and improve best value for governments procuring goods and services around the world.

ACKNOWLEDGMENTS

Special thanks to Steven Schooner for his insightful comments on an earlier draft of this chapter; any mistakes are, of course, my own.

REFERENCES

Allen, R. and Yukins, C. 1997. "Bid Protests and Contract Disputes under the FAA's New Procurement System." *Public Contract Law Journal* 26(2): 135–55.

Anderson, R. D. 2012. "Government Procurement in the World Trade Organization (WTO): 2011 as a Watershed Year." West Government Contracts Year in Review Briefs 4, Thompson Reuters.

Arrowsmith, S. 2006. "The Past and Future Evolution of EC Procurement Law: From Framework to Common Code?" *Public Contract Law Journal* 35(3): 337–84.

Arrowsmith, S. 2014. *The Law of Public and Utilities Procurement: Regulation in the EU and UK*, vol.1, 3rd edn. Andover: Sweet and Maxwell.

Arrowsmith S. and Anderson, R. D. (eds). 2011. *The WTO Regime on Government Procurement: Challenge and Reform*. Washington, DC: WTO.

Arrowsmith, S., Linarelli, J., and Wallace, D. 2004. *Regulating Public Procurement: National and International Perspectives*. Alphen aan den Rijn: Kluwer Law International.

Beale, H. B. R. 2014. "Evaluation of the Small Business Procurement Goals Established in Section 15(g) of the Small Business Act: A Report Pursuant to Section 1631(d) of the National Defense Authorization Act of 2013." Report produced under Contract to the Small Business

[79] Although chapter 15 of the Trans-Pacific Partnership ("TPP") regional trade agreement, released for public review in November 2015, would include extensive procurement-related provisions built largely on the text of the GPA, chapter 15 would not appear to erect new negotiating means for ensuring regulatory harmonization regarding procurement amongst the Pacific member nations. See https://ustr.gov/tpp/.

Administration (available at: <https://www.sba.gov/sites/default/files/files/rs423tot.pdf> (accessed July 22, 2016)).

Bernhart Walker, M. 2014. "SAM 'Inelegant and Cumbersome' Says GSA CI." FierceGovernmentIT, April 16 (available at: <http://www.fiercegovernmentit.com/story/sam-inelegant-and-cumbersome-says-gsa-cio/2014-04-16>).

Beth Bosco, M. B. 2014. "Acquisition Working Group Releases Recommendations on the Role of Cybersecurity in Government Procurement." *The Government Contractor* 56.

Bovis, C. 2012. *EU Public Procurement Law*, 2nd edn. Cheltenham: Edward Elgar.

Cibinic, Jr. J., Nash, Jr., R. C., and Yukins, C. R. 2011. *Formation of Government Contracts*, 4th edn. New York: Wolters Kluwer Law & Business.

Conway, D. M. 2012. *State and Local Government Procurement.* Chicago, IL: American Bar Association.

Cooper, S. 2012. "The Government Definition of Small Business is B.S." Forbes.com, September 20 (available at: <http://www.forbes.com/sites/stevecooper/2012/09/20/the-government-definition-of-small-business-is-b-s/> (accessed July 22, 2016)).

Defense News. 2013. "With Just Days to Spare, Senate Extends NDAA Streak." December 20 (available at: <http://www.defensenews.com/article/20131220/DEFREG02/312200014/With-Just-Days-Spare-Senate-Extends-NDAA-Streak> (accessed July 22, 2016)).

European Commission. 2013a. "Trade Cross-cutting Disciplines and Institutional Provisions," Initial EU Position Paper, Brussels (available at: <http://trade.ec.europa.eu/doclib/docs/2013/july/tradoc_151622.pdf> (accessed July 22, 2016)).

European Commission. 2013b. "Public Procurement," Initial EU Position Paper, Brussels (available at: <http://trade.ec.europa.eu/doclib/docs/2013/july/tradoc_151623.pdf> (accessed July 22, 2016)).

Federal Acquisition Institute. 2013. "Annual Report on the Federal Acquisition Workforce 2012," Fort Belvoir, VA.

Gates, S. M., Keating, E. G., Jewell, A. D., Daugherty, L., Tysinger, B., Robbert, A. A., and Masi, R. 2008. "The Defense Acquisition Workforce: An Analysis of Personnel Trends Relevant to Policy, 1993–2006," RAND National Defense Research Institute (available at: <http://www.rand.org/content/dam/rand/pubs/technical_reports/2008/RAND_TR572.pdf>(accessed July 22, 2016)).

Gleeson, M. and Demmel, A. 2014. "New Guidelines on 'No Spy Decree'," Lexology.com, October 6 (available at: <http://www.lexology.com/library/detail.aspx?g=0e70d871-3547-499a-8f66-02b291f22170>(accessed July 22, 2016)).

Godes, S. N. 1997. "Government Contracting on the Internet: Abandoning FACNET as the Government's Network for Electronic Commerce." *Public Contract Law Journal* 26(4): 663–82.

Gordon, D. I. and Racca, G. M. 2014. "Integrity Challenges in the EU and US Procurement Systems." In G. M. Racca, and C. R. Yukins (eds), *Integrity and Efficiency in Sustainable Public Contracts: Balancing Corruption Concerns in Public Procurement Internationally.* Brussels: Bruylant, 117–46.

Gupta, M. and Palmer, R. J. 2007. "Government Efficiency versus Accountability: How an Emerging Control Model for Purchase Card Use May Enable US Government Agencies to Achieve Both Goals." *Public Contract Law Journal* 36(2): 175–201.

Haak, A. and Westerwelle, K. 2014. "The Brand New 'No-Spy-Decree'—Consequences for Public Contracts with Foreign Undertakings." Lexology.com, September 12 (available at: <http://www.lexology.com/library/detail.aspx?g=867949c4-3ede-4afb-b70a-be278e99951b> (accessed July 22, 2016)).

Helms, G. E. 2011. "Fair Trade Coffee Practices: Approaches for Future Sustainability of the Movement." *Indiana International and Comparative Law Review* 21(1): 79–109.

Hollman, H. M. and Kovacic, W. E. 2011. "The International Competition Network: Its Past, Current and Future Role." *Minnesota Journal of International Law* 20: 274.

Hordell, M. A. and Hoffman, L. L. 2000. "Federal E-Commerce: Where We've Been, Where We're Going." *Public Contract Law Journal* 35(3).

Horska, K. 2010. "Curbing the World Bank's Problems with Patronage and Corruption Through the Use of Open Framework Agreements." *Public Contract Law Journal* 39(3): 679–99.

Kathuria, S. 2009. "Best Practices for Compliance with the New Government Contractor Compliance and Ethics Rules Under the Federal Acquisition Regulation." *Public Contract Law Journal* 38(4): 803–56.

Kidalov, M. V. 2011. "Small Business Contracting in the United States and Europe: A Comparative Assessment." *Public Contract Law Journal* 40(2): 443–510.

Levy, F. and Huffman, R. (eds). 2010. *Guide to the Mandatory Disclosure Rule: Issues, Guidelines, and Best Practices.* Chicago, IL: American Bar Association.

McGarry, M. S. 1993. "Winning the War on Procurement Fraud: Victory at What Price?" *Columbia Journal of Law and Social Problems* 26: 249–89.

McKie, J. W. 1970. "Concentration in Military Procurement Markets: A Classification and Analysis of Contract Data." RAND Memorandum RM-6307-PR (available at: <http://www.rand.org/content/dam/rand/pubs/research_memoranda/2006/RM6307.pdf> (accessed July 22, 2016)).

Manuel, K. M., Dolan, A. M., Murrill, B. J., and Perry, R. M. 2014. "Domestic Content Restrictions: The Buy American Act and Complementary Provisions of Federal Law," Congressional Research Service, January 6.

Manuel, K. M. and Lunder, E. K. 2012. "Small Business Set-Aside Programs: An Overview and Recent Developments in the Law," Congressional Research Service, June 15.

Marceau, G. and Blank, A. 1996. "History of the Government Procurement Negotiations Since 1945." *Government Procurement Law Review* 4.

Murphy, D. E. 2002. "The Federal Sentencing Guidelines for Organizations: A Decade of Promoting Compliance and Ethics." *Iowa Law Review* 87(2): 697–719.

Nagle, J. F. 1999. *History of Government Contracting*, 2nd edn. Washington, DC: George Washington University.

Nichols, R., Booth Cassidy, S., Vohra, A., Scalzo, K., and Meade, C. 2014. "Cybersecurity for Government Contractors." Briefing Papers No. 14-5, Thomson Reuters.

Novais, A. 2012. "Introduction to the Buy Brazilian Act." *The Brazil Business*, September 10 (available at: <http://thebrazilbusiness.com/article/buy-brazilian-act> (accessed July 22, 2016)).

Racca, G. M., Cavallo Perin, R., and Albano, G. L. 2011. "Competition in the Execution Phase of Public Procurement." *Public Contract Law Journal* 41(1): 89–108.

Richard, D. G., Whiteman N. S., and Gleic, S. B. 2013. "Contractor Reporting Requirements in the Wake of Implementation of the System for Award Management." Briefing Papers No. 13-6, Thomson Reuters.

Sanchez Graells, A. 2011. *Public Procurement and the EU Competition Rules*. Oxford: Hart.

Schooner, S. L. 2001. "Fear of Oversight: The Fundamental Failure of Businesslike Government." *American University Law Review* 50: 627–722.

Schooner, S. L. 2002. "Desiderata: Objectives for a System of Government Contract Law." *Public Procurement Law Review* 11: 103–12.

Schooner, S. L. 2003. "Commercial Purchasing: The Chasm Between the United States Government's Evolving Policy and Practice." GW Law Faculty Publications & Other Works Paper No. 103 (available at: <http://scholarship.law.gwu.edu/faculty_publications/103> (accessed July 22, 2016)).

Schooner, S. L. and Yukins, C. R. 2009. "Tempering 'Buy American' in the Recovery Act—Steering Clear of a Trade War". *The Government Contractor* 51(10): 4–10.

Telles, P. 2013. "The Good, The Bad, and the Ugly: The EU's Internal Market, Public Procurement Thresholds, and Cross-Border Interest." *Public Contract Law Journal* 43: 3–25.

Trepte, P. 2004. *Regulating Procurement: Understanding the Ends and Means of Public Procurement Regulation*. Oxford: Oxford University Press, chapter 2.

UN Commission on International Trade Law. 2014. *Guide to Enactment of the UNCITRAL Model Law on Public Procurement*, Washington, DC (available at: <http://www.uncitral.org/pdf/english/texts/procurem/ml-procurement-2011/Guide-Enactment-Model-Law-Public-Procurement-e.pdf> (accessed July 22, 2016)).

US Department of Defense and US General Services Administration. 2014. "Improving Cybersecurity and Resilience through Acquisition." Washington, DC (available at: <https://acc.dau.mil/adl/en-US/694372/file/75816/IMPROVING_CYBERSECURITY_AND_RESILIENCE_THROUGH_ACQUISITION.pdf> (accessed July 22, 2016)).

US Department of Justice and US Securities and Exchange Commission. 2012. *A Resource Guide to the US Foreign Corrupt Practices Act 63*, Washington, DC.

Vacketta, C. L and Pope, S. H. 1998. "Commercial Item Contracts: When Is a Government Contract Term or Condition Consistent with 'Standard' or 'Customary' Commercial Practice." *Public Contract Law Journal* 27(2): 291–314.

World Bank. 2014. "Procurement in World Bank Investment Project Finance. Phase II: Developing the Proposed New Procurement Framework." Framework Paper for Consultation, Washington, DC (available at: <http://consultations.worldbank.org/Data/hub/files/consultation-template/procurement-policy-review-consultationsopenconsultationtemplate/phases/procurement_in_world_bank_investment_project_finance_-_phase_ii.pdf> (accessed July 22, 2016)).

Yukins, C. R. 1998. "FACNET: Has Congress Struck a Mortal Blow?" *Washington Technology*, January 12.

Yukins, C. R. 2003. "Ethics in Procurement: New Challenges after a Decade of Reform." *The Procurement Lawyer* 38(3).

Yukins, C. R. 2004. "Making Federal Information Technology Accessible: A Case Study in Social Policy and Procurement." *Public Contract Law Journal* 33(4): 667–724.

Yukins, C. R. 2008. "Are IDIQs Inefficient? Sharing Lessons with European Framework Contracting." *Public Contract Law Journal* 37(3): 545–68.

Yukins, C. R. 2009. "The European Defense Procurement Directive: An American Perspective." *The Government Contractor* 51(41).

Yukins, C. R. 2010. "A Versatile Prism: Assessing Procurement Law Through the Principal-Agent Model." *Public Contract Law Journal* 40(1): 63–86.

Yukins, C. R. 2013. "Coordinating Compliance and Procurement Markets in a Shrinking World: The Case for a Transatlantic Dialogue." West Government Contracts Year in Review Briefs, Thomson Reuters.

Yukins, C. R. 2015. "International Protection of Free Trade in Procurement under NAFTA's Chapter 10 on Public Procurement: The Pathway from NAFTA to the WTO Government Procurement Agreement to a Potential European–U.S. Transatlantic Trade & Investment Partnership." In M. Audit and S. Chil (eds), *Transnational Law of Public Contracts*. Brussels: Bruylant.

Yukins, C. R. and Cora, J. A. 2013. "Considering The Effects of Public Procurement Regulations on Competitive Markets." *The Government Contractor* 55.

Yukins, C. R. and Priess, H.-J. 2014. "Breaking the Impasse in the Transatlantic Trade and Investment Partnership (TTIP) Negotiations: Rethinking Priorities in Procurement." *The Government Contractor* 56.

Yukins, C. R. and Schooner, S. L. 2007. "Incrementalism: Eroding the Impediments to a Global Public Procurement Market." *Georgetown Journal of International Law* 23.

10 Government Procurement in US Trade Agreements

Gary Hufbauer and Tyler Moran

10.1 Introduction

The US public sector commands one of the world's largest procurement markets. In 2013, the total was roughly $600 billion at the federal level and $1 trillion at the state and local level, by our estimation, amounting to $1.6 trillion for all levels of government.[1] This represented about 10 percent of US GDP, which is considerably lower than other developed countries. The OECD estimated that general government procurement (federal plus sub-federal) accounted for 17 percent of GDP in Germany, 18 percent in France, and 19 percent in the United Kingdom when state-owned utility procurement was included. For comparison, the same dataset reports US general government procurement as 11 percent of GDP, somewhat higher than we have estimated above. But even so, government procurement is clearly a meaningful share of US economic activity and an important market for both foreign and domestic producers.

In terms of import penetration, Messerlin and Miroudot (2012) calculated that around 4.6 percent of US government procurement was sourced from foreign producers. This was roughly equal to the figure for Japan (4.7 percent), notably higher than that for the EU (2.7 percent, with member countries weighted by their gross domestic product (GDP)), and notably lower than the figures for Canada and China (6.9 percent and 6.1 percent, respectively). These figures do not include foreign procurement for investment purposes, such as infrastructure construction. However, the study noted that import penetration ratios were steadily increasing for most individual countries and for the world as a whole.

The increasing globalization of procurement markets has, in part, been driven by the same forces that drive globalization in general. Falling transportation costs and

[1] Figures calculated based on the Bureau of Economic Analysis's National Income and Product Account (NIPA) tables. For our purposes, procurement is equal to expenditures on intermediate goods and services (less own-account investment) plus gross investment, for both federal and state and local procurement. The data are located in NIPA tables 3.9.5 and 3.10.5 (available at <www.bea.gov/national/pdf/dpga.pdf> (accessed July 23, 2016)).

improved communications technology encourage international supply chains for all purchasers, governments included. But the increasing internationalization of government procurement has also coincided with substantial liberalization programs undertaken by some of the world's largest markets, the United States included.

10.2 **US Law, Federal and State**

The Buy American Act of 1933 and the executive orders that followed it are the basis for much of the discrimination faced by foreign entities seeking to compete in US federal procurement markets. The specifics of the Act's implementation have varied substantially across government entities and different time periods, but generally US producers are given some quantitative price advantage over foreign producers in awarding contracts. These preferences can be expanded for projects that will generate employment in so-called "Labor Surplus Areas" designated by the Department of Labor, as stated in Executive Order 10582.[2] The "Buy American Act of 1988" (Title VII of the Omnibus Trade and Competitiveness Act of 1988) amended the 1933 Buy American Act, limiting US procurement of goods and services from countries which discriminate against US suppliers in their procurement procedures.

US authority for implementing commitments in WTO agreements and free trade agreements (FTAs, also known as preferential trade agreements or PTAs) generally falls under the umbrella of the Trade Agreements Act of 1979. The stated purpose of the Act was to "approve and implement the trade agreements negotiated under the Trade Act of 1974." One such agreement was a predecessor of today's Government Procurement Agreement (GPA). In order to allow the United States to comply with its commitments in the 1979 Agreement on Government Procurement, as well as future agreements on procurement, the Act gave the president the authority to waive discriminatory requirements associated with federal government procurement. Waivers can be issued for countries that provide similar treatment to US products and suppliers, including WTO GPA members and most US FTA partners, or for least developed countries. Although the Code did not initially apply to some government enterprises, such as the Tennessee Valley Authority, coverage was later extended to most of these entities in subsequent trade agreements that covered government procurement.

These waivers do not, however, cover all procurement. First, programs designed specifically to benefit small and minority-owned businesses are exempt from waivers authorized by the Trade Agreement Act of 1979. Even for covered entities, the GPA and

[2] Section 10.4; text available at: <http://www.archives.gov/federal-register/codification/executive-order/10582.html> (accessed July 23, 2016).

procurement chapters in US FTAs always establish some threshold for coverage, with smaller contracts being exempt. Thresholds are typically expressed in terms of Special Drawing Rights (SDRs), an accounting unit established by the IMF. The US Trade Representative (USTR) is tasked with reporting an equivalent US dollar amount on an annual basis.

The USTR is also tasked with interpreting US commitments on procurement, with the exception of commitments covering the Department of Defense, for which the Secretary of Defense controls the interpretation. In the fiscal year 2013, the Department of Defense purchased roughly $965 million worth of goods under waivers to the Buy American Act, out of $19 billion in total purchases from foreign entities.[3] About half of the $965 million worth of products purchased under waivers were from GPA members and FTA partners, while the remaining goods were purchased from other designated countries.

With respect to state government procurement, there is little doubt that the US federal government has the authority to impose restrictions on state "Buy American" rules or similar measures. The Commerce Clause of the US Constitution grants Congress the power to regulate interstate and foreign commerce, a provision that covers the procurement of foreign goods and services by state and local governments. Therefore, an agreement or federal law limiting state and local "Buy American" provisions could preempt sub-federal practices. However, the federal government is generally unwilling to "meddle" in the affairs of the states without a strong imperative, so no existing agreements have forced procurement rules on state and local governments. Moreover, US Supreme Court decisions have allowed states to enact numerous preferences for their own residents and business firms, such as lower college tuition fees and preferential procurement from small and medium-sized in-state firms, even without explicit authorization from the US Congress.[4] Since states have enjoyed a somewhat free hand in discriminating against each other, they expect to enjoy the same latitude in discriminating against foreign firms.

The US federal government might be willing to impose more serious commitments on the states if partner countries offered comparable access to large sub-federal procurement markets. However, there is a political trade-off between how desirable a country's sub-federal procurement markets are to US negotiators and how difficult it is for foreign negotiators to liberalize those markets. Sub-federal governments with large budgets are

[3] Source: Department of Defense report on purchases from foreign entities, available at: <http://www.acq.osd.mil/dpap/cpic/cp/docs/RTC_FY13_Foreign_Entities_(Auth)_signed_7_May_14.pdf> (accessed July 23, 2016).

[4] Some states have a policy of reciprocal treatment, requiring them to keep track of procurement policy; for reference, see the State of Oregon's "Procurement Services and Policy, State by State Preference Data" (available at:<http://www.oregon.gov/DAS/EGS/ps/Pages/detail_a_main_page.aspx> (accessed July 23, 2016)).

more likely to enjoy substantial political independence, making it more difficult for negotiators to make commitments on their behalf (as is true in the United States). On the other hand, sub-federal governments abroad that are more easily cajoled are less likely to enjoy the degree of spending power that would tempt US federal policymakers. We discuss potential solutions to this conundrum at the end of this chapter.

10.3 The Government Procurement Agreement

The Tokyo Round of Multilateral Trade Agreements, which ran from 1973 to 1979, established a number of agreements (commonly known as "codes") among participants. One such code was the Tokyo Round Code on Government Procurement, which was signed at the conclusion of the Round in 1979. In addition to restricting outright discrimination by covered entities, the Code also tackled more clandestine methods of putting foreign suppliers at a competitive disadvantage. The Code mandated that technical specifications in procurement contracts "be in terms of performance rather than design" and that they "be based on international standards, national technical regulations, or recognized national standards." Moreover, the Code required that national government adopt transparent tendering procedures for selecting qualified suppliers.[5] These rules, along with several others, reduced the risk of cronyism in the procurement process. The threshold for coverage was initially set at 150,000 SDR, roughly $220,000 in 2014.

Not all entities were covered by the Code; notably, sub-federal government entities were not covered. The text, however, did instruct members to attempt to bring their non-covered entities on board by "draw[ing] their attention to the overall benefits of liberalization of government procurement," but no formal targets or requirements were established. The United States had initially sought to extend coverage to "all entities under the direct or substantial control of [central] governments,"[6] but instead negotiations took place on an agency-by-agency basis. Ultimately, the United States excluded the following federal entities in the Tokyo Round Code: the Department of Transportation; the Department of Energy; the Bureau of Reclamation of the Department of the Interior; the Army Corp of Engineers; the Tennessee Valley Authority (TVA); three parts of the General Services Administration (Automated Data and Telecommunications Service, Region 9, and the National Tool Center); COMSAT, AMTRAK; CONRAIL; and the US Postal Service.[7] Even among the covered entities, construction contracts were

[5] Agreement on Government Procurement, available at: <http://www.wto.org/english/docs_e/legal_e/tokyo_gpr_e.pdf> (accessed July 23, 2016).

[6] Code of Federal Regulations, 1979, Compilation and Parts 100 and 101.

[7] Oversight on Government Procurement Code and Related Agreements: Hearing Before the Subcommittee on Finance of the United States Senate. 97th Cong. 2 (1982).

wholly excluded and services contracts in general were excluded unless "incidental to the purchase of goods, provided that the value of such services does not exceed the value of the goods." State and local governments were explicitly excluded. The Tokyo Round Code was amended in 1987 to, among other things, extend coverage to leasing contracts. The update also lowered the minimum contract value to 130,000 SDR, which would be equal to roughly $190,000 at present.

When the WTO was created in 1995, several parties drafted the Agreement on Government Procurement, commonly referred to as the "Government Procurement Agreement," or GPA. Six parties acceded to the new GPA on January 1, 1996 (counting the European Union as a single party; the EU included fifteen countries at the time). Since then, nine more parties have implemented the agreement, bringing the total number to fifteen.[8] These countries made commitments beyond those of the Tokyo Round Code in several regards. Service contracts were included for covered entities, as well as construction contracts (albeit at higher thresholds). Moreover, the number of covered entities was sharply increased. Some previously excluded entities, such as the TVA, were added to the US schedule of commitments. The United States still maintains a few exceptions carried forward from the Tokyo Round Code, such as procurement by the Federal Aviation Administration.

More significantly, several US states made commitments under the GPA. In fact, thirty-seven states made varying commitments. Some listed specific covered agencies, while others simply stated that "all executive agencies" were subject to the agreement. Some states went further and added state universities to their commitments. There were some exceptions: for example, Mississippi excluded services and Montana covered only services and construction. Moreover, twelve states specifically excluded construction grade steel, motor vehicles, and coal. Several states specifically excluded all construction contracts. State commitments are listed in Annex 2 of US schedules to the GPA. The following states made some level of commitment: Arizona, Arkansas, California, Colorado, Connecticut, Delaware, Florida, Hawaii, Idaho, Illinois, Iowa, Kansas, Kentucky, Louisiana, Maine, Maryland, Massachusetts, Michigan, Minnesota, Mississippi, Missouri, Montana, New York, Nebraska, New Hampshire, Oklahoma, Oregon, Pennsylvania, Rhode Island, South Dakota, Tennessee, Texas, Utah, Vermont, and Washington.

In addition to the expansion of coverage, the GPA also required countries to improve their procurement procedures. For example, the so-called "offsets" (defined as "measures to encourage local development or improve the balance-of-payments accounts by means

[8] See <http://www.wto.org/english/tratop_e/gproc_e/memobs_e.htm#parties> (accessed July 23, 2016). The parties are Armenia, Canada, the EU for its twenty-eight member states, Hong Kong, Iceland, Israel, Japan, South Korea, Lichtenstein, Aruba (via the Netherlands), Norway, Singapore, Switzerland, Taiwan, and the United States.

of domestic content, licensing of technology, investment requirements, counter-trade or similar requirements"[9]) are specifically forbidden, except for developing countries that negotiated such an exception. The agreement also reaffirmed the Code's commitment to transparency, requiring that laws, decisions, and rulings be made public when they are relevant to procurement by a covered entity. GPA Article XIX took an additional step, requiring that members collect and report statistics on the total amount of procurement that was subject to the agreement on an annual basis. Statistics are supposed to be broken down by the purchasing entity and the category of good or service that was procured. The reports must also, to the greatest extent possible, identify the countries of origin for procured goods and services. Some of these reports are available, although there is significant lag for many countries.[10] For the United States, reports are only available for 1996 through 2008.

In 2013, the GPA parties completed an update to the GPA, which was centered on general improvements to increase user friendliness. The update amended provisions to better reflect changing procurement practices that governments have adopted in recent years, primarily driven by increasing adoption of digital technology. Many countries also expanded the scope of their commitments in the 2013 update, although the United States does not appear to have made major changes in this area. Of the fifteen parties to the agreement, all but Armenia, South Korea, and Switzerland had opted to join the revised GPA by July 2014.

10.4 **Procurement under US Free Trade Agreements**

10.4.1 US–ISRAEL

The first US FTA to touch on government procurement, and indeed the first modern US bilateral free trade agreement, was the agreement with Israel. The "Israel Free Trade Agreement," as it is known in the United States, was concluded, signed, and entered into force in 1985, after just over one year of negotiations. The agreement contains a section on government procurement, although it is very brief. In that section, the United States resolved to waive all "Buy National" restrictions for all government agency purchases exceeding $50,000 "which would be subject to the Agreement on Government Procurement at the time of entry into force of this Agreement but for the threshold provided for in Article I (l) (b) of the Agreement on Government Procurement."[11] In other words, the

[9] See <http://www.wto.org/english/tratop_e/gproc_e/gpa_overview_e.htm> (accessed July 23, 2016).

[10] See <http://www.wto.org/english/tratop_e/gproc_e/gpstat_e.htm>(accessed July 23, 2016).

[11] See <http://tcc.export.gov/Trade_Agreements/All_Trade_Agreements/exp_005439.asp> (accessed July 23, 2016); note that the linked text refers to "Article I'll) (b)," which is assumed to be a typo.

Israel FTA effectively lowered the threshold for the then-current Tokyo Round Code. Israel made comparable commitments, agreeing to waive "Buy National" requirements for covered entities.

Israel was permitted to make exceptions for certain purchases made by its Ministry of Defense, so long as those exceptions were comparable to exceptions made by the US Department of Defense. Moreover, Israel agreed to relax its offset arrangements, except for those employed by the Ministry of Defense. Currently, Israel still imposes offsets on its military purchases to a notable degree.

Both countries implemented the WTO Government Procurement Agreement at its inception in 1996, which superseded the earlier Tokyo Round Code. Under current US law, Israel maintains its preferential threshold for supply contracts ($50,000).[12] Israeli suppliers do not benefit from a lower threshold with respect to construction contracts, relative to other GPA parties.

10.4.2 CANADA–US FTA AND NAFTA

The Canada–US FTA (CUSFTA) was more comprehensive than the Israel FTA, both in general and with respect to government procurement. CUSFTA was the culmination of sectoral trade pacts that Canada and the United States had forged over the several prior decades, most notably the Canada–United States Automotive Products Agreement. The agreement came more or less on the heels of the agreement with Israel, with negotiations finishing late in 1987 and implementation occurring in 1989. CUSFTA has since been supplemented, in a major way, by the North American Free Trade Agreement (NAFTA).

Procurement obligations under CUSFTA were detailed in Part Three of the Agreement, Chapter Thirteen (both of which were titled "Government Procurement"). As a statement of principle, the introduction of Part Three states that "[t]he chapter broadens and deepens the obligations both countries have undertaken in the Tokyo Round Code, commits each country to work toward the multilateral liberalization of government procurement and to negotiate further improvements in the bilateral agreement once multilateral negotiations are concluded."

As noted, treatment of foreign suppliers in government procurement markets was already subject to the Tokyo Round Code, discussed in Section 10.3. The most significant change resulting from CUSFTA was the decrease in the threshold for coverage. Both

[12] See <http://www.law.cornell.edu/cfr/text/48/25.406> (accessed July 23, 2016). Specifically, the text reads: "Acquisitions of supplies by most agencies are covered by the Israeli Trade Act, if the estimated value of the acquisition is $50,000 or more but does not exceed the WTO GPA threshold for supplies."

Canada and the United States adopted a $25,000 threshold for national treatment obligations to apply, some 80 percent lower than the threshold set in the Code. The thresholds only applied to the entities listed under Annex I of the Government Procurement Code (central government entities), and were subject to the same exclusions and exceptions. Thus, services contracts and construction were not covered initially and procurement by US states was wholly excluded, since these were not covered under the Tokyo Round Code. Moreover, the same US government entities were excluded, and the exceptions for certain defense spending and small business programs persisted.

In 1994, NAFTA supplemented CUSFTA for the United States and Canada, in addition to, and most importantly, adding Mexico. Chapter 10 of NAFTA ("Government Procurement") substantially expanded on the procurement obligations present in CUSFTA, much like the 1996 Government Procurement Agreement would improve on the Tokyo Round Code. For goods and services contracts, and for covered entities, the threshold was set at $50,000 and indexed to the US inflation rate. Government enterprises were also bound by NAFTA with a threshold of $250,000, with the same indexing scheme. The United States scheduled seven such enterprises for coverage, including the TVA and the four federal Power Marketing Administrations (Bonneville Power Administration, Southeastern Power Administration, Southwestern Power Administration, and the Western Area Power Administration). Construction contracts were covered with substantially higher thresholds for both government entities and enterprises ($6.5 million and $8 million, respectively).

Some provisions of CUSFTA have persisted exclusively for the United States and Canada, bilaterally. One such provision is the aforementioned $25,000 threshold, which still applies to the purchase of goods by US and Canadian federal government agencies. Mexican suppliers face the higher standard threshold applied by both of the other two NAFTA partners, and vice-versa.[13]

NAFTA Chapter 10 also contained provisions to encourage sub-central governments to join the agreement on a voluntary basis. Specifically, Article 1024 states that, upon completion of NAFTA Chapter 10, parties shall: "immediately begin consultations with their state and provincial governments with a view to obtaining commitments, on a voluntary and reciprocal basis, to include within this Chapter procurement by state and provincial government entities and enterprises." Thus far, the effort to induce voluntary participation by sub-federal governments has not been successful within NAFTA. Canada and the United States have substantial access to each other's sub-federal procurement

[13] See <http://tcc.export.gov/trade_agreements/exporters_guides/list_all_guides/nafta_chapter10_guide.asp> (accessed July 23, 2016).

markets through the 1996 GPA, following an agreement dated February 2010 covering Canadian provinces,[14] but Mexico has concluded no such arrangement.

The February 2010 US–Canada Agreement resulted from bilateral disputes over US implementation of the American Recovery and Reinvestment Act (ARRA), the $800 billion stimulus law that was passed following the economic turmoil of 2008. Among other objectionable provisions, the ARRA only waived the Buy American requirements for projects involving "iron, steel, or manufactured goods" when the use of US-produced equivalents would raise the overall cost of a project by more than 25 percent. This ran afoul of multiple US commitments and caused concern among several US trade partners, most notably Canada.

To assuage Canadian concerns, the two governments reached the aforementioned agreement in 2010. In theory, the agreement precluded restrictions on purchases of Canadian goods through the ARRA. However, the federal government also took measures to ensure that the bulk of funds were committed before the agreement actually entered into force, so Canadian manufacturers were largely shut out from stimulus spending (Hufbauer et al., 2013).

10.4.3 OTHER US TRADE AGREEMENTS

Almost all US FTAs negotiated after NAFTA contain substantive procurement obligations. Most contain procurement obligations similar to those in the Government Procurement Agreement. Of these, South Korea and Singapore are already parties to the GPA, so those two free trade agreements offer lower thresholds similar to the Canada–US FTA. The agreement with Jordan contains its own set of procurement obligations, recognizing that Jordan is seeking to join the GPA. Jordan originally applied for accession in July 2000, but has yet to become a member nearly fifteen years later; meanwhile Jordan maintains its observer status in the GPA.

While procurement obligations under these US agreements are not identical, they tend to be very similar in structure. Therefore, giving each individual agreement the same description offered for NAFTA and US–Israel would be highly repetitive. Instead, procurement commitments in US FTAs are summarized in Table 10.1. US FTA partners that are also GPA signatories are denoted by asterisks.

Evidently, despite agreements in the GATT and WTO, and in FTAs, much US federal and sub-federal procurement remains "off limits" to foreign suppliers. We wrap up this

[14] See <https://ustr.gov/about-us/policy-offices/press-office/press-releases/2010/february/us-canada-sign-agreement-government-procurement> (accessed July 23, 2016).

Table 10.1 Government procurement obligations in concluded US FTAs

	Threshold for coverage		
	Goods and services	Construction	States covered
Israel*	50,000	7 864,000	0
Canada*	25,000	n/a	0
NAFTA	79 507	10 335 931	0
WTO GPA	204,000	7 864,000	37
Jordan	n/a	n/a	n/a
Australia*	79 507	7 864,000	31
Chile	79 507	7 864,000	37
Singapore*	79 507	7 864,000	37
Bahrain	204,000	10 335 931	0
Morocco	204,000	7 864,000	23
Oman	204,000	10 335 931	0
Peru	204,000	7 864,000	10
CAFTA-DR	79 507	7 864,000	22
Panama	204,000	7 864,000	8
Colombia	79 507	7 864,000	8
Korea*	100,000	7 864,000	0

Note: * designates GPA signatories.

chapter with thoughts as to what can be done to expand coverage, thereby benefiting US taxpayers as well as foreign firms.

10.5 **What Can Be Done?**

The United States should expect to face increased demands from trade partners in future trade negotiations. Already, the European Union is seeking broad access to state and local procurement, as well as entities operating under those governments.[15] However, requests from foreign governments do not do much to change the US political context, particularly with respect to the states. If US negotiators are going to make offers that match the new requests, while also making agreements that can pass muster in Congress, innovative approaches will be required.

[15] "EU Seeks Broad Access to Local U.S. Procurement Under TTIP, Paper Shows," *Inside U.S. Trade*, December 12, 2014 (available at: <http://insidetrade.com/inside-us-trade/eu-seeks-broad-access-local-us-procurement-under-ttip-paper-shows> (accessed July 23, 2016)).

10.5.1 STATE-LEVEL RECIPROCITY

One solution, attempted in the past, is state-level reciprocity. Under this approach, suppliers from a state only gain non-discriminatory access to sub-federal procurement in the partner's market if the state itself offers comparable access. This was implemented in US FTAs with Peru, Colombia, and Panama. However, US partners might be skeptical of this system, since states have been relatively unwilling to sign up—very few states signed the aforementioned agreements, so some additional legwork might be needed in future agreements. As for the TTIP, it seems likely that states will be more eager to gain access to sub-federal markets in Europe than in Latin America.

10.5.2 FIRM-LEVEL RECIPROCITY

A related, untested concept would be relying on firm-specific characteristics to determine a firm's eligibility to bid on foreign contracts. FTA commitments could require that a firm would gain access to sub-federal procurement markets in the partner country if and only if the majority of its employment was located in states that voluntarily subscribed to the FTA procurement chapter.

10.5.3 TRACING FEDERAL FUNDS

Another approach could entail "tracing" federal funds. Projects which rely on funding from the federal government to a significant degree could be required to abide by the federal government's agreements with respect to procurement, even if the project is administered by a state or city government. If it had been in force, this provision would have ruled out the abuses involved in ARRA projects.

10.5.4 EXPEDITED DISPUTE RESOLUTION

Another aspect deserves mention—as happened with the ARRA, governments take advantage of the fact that enforcement mechanisms generally act very slowly. If an individual government program, such as the ARRA, can be carried out to completion before the cheated party can win a judgment, then ultimately the rules have little practical impact when a government is determined to skirt its obligations.

A possible solution to this problem would be a "fast-track" system for dispute resolution, designed to resolve procurement commitments in a timely manner. Ideally, this service would be provided by the WTO, possibly in the next iteration of the GPA. If built into the GPA, the same fast-track process could be made available to government procurement disputes in FTAs, with costs paid by the litigating parties.

ACKNOWLEDGMENT

The views expressed are authors' own.

REFERENCES

Hufbauer, G. C., Schott, J. J., Cimino-Isaacs, C., Vierio, M., and Wada, E. 2013. *Local Content Requirements: A Global Problem*. Washington, DC: PIIE.

Messerlin, P. and Miroudot, S. 2012. "EU Public Procurement Markets: How Open Are They?" Mimeo, Groupe d'Economie Mondiale (GEM), July (available at: <https://www.jetro.go.jp/ext_images/france/pdf/messerlin_miroudot_en.pdf> (accessed July 23, 2016)).

11 The Internationalization of Canada's Public Procurement

Paul M. Lalonde

11.1 Introduction

Canada's procurement laws are difficult to analyze because they vary by jurisdiction, and by the entity carrying out the procurement. For example, procurement rules that apply to federal government departments differ significantly from those that apply to provincial government departments, which in turn differ from those that apply to sub-provincial entities such as municipalities. While there are common threads (obligations to compete requirements above certain value thresholds, obligations to publicize opportunities, etc.), the manner in which procurement is carried out, the degree to which procurement activity is regulated, and the extent to which prejudiced suppliers are provided with recourses vary widely across the country.

In addition, there is no central repository of public procurement data in Canada. Meaningful statistics are difficult to obtain and are not published on a proactive basis by public authorities. For example, while the information could be obtained through a formal access to information request, deciphering who are the biggest defense industry suppliers to the Government of Canada is not an easy task. Analyzing procurement statistics by nationality of the suppliers is even more challenging.

At the federal level, the authority for disbursement of Government of Canada funds is derived from the Financial Administration Act (FAA).[1] The Government Contracts Regulations (GCR),[2] which were adopted under the FAA, provide a general obligation to purchase on a competitive basis and establish how contracts must be entered into, but they do not provide specific guidelines on the procurement process that should be followed or on the post-award administration of government contracts.

Ultimately, the Treasury Board of Canada and the courts—namely, the Federal Court of Canada or the provincial superior courts—are responsible for the enforcement of the FAA and the Government Contracts Regulations. The majority of federal government

[1] RS 1985, F-11.
[2] SOR/87-402.

purchasing is centralized through Public Works and Government Services Canada (PWGSC). The Minister of Public Works and Government Services has implemented the Supply Manual and the Standard Acquisition Clauses and Conditions (SACC) under the auspices of the Department of Public Works and Government Services Act.[3] Together, these provide additional policy (non-statutory) guidance on how PWGSC officials are to carry out purchasing.

Under Canada's constitution, legislative powers are exclusively divided between the federal and provincial governments.[4] The federal government has no authority to dictate how the provinces spend their budgets or how they carry out public procurement. Every province is subject to individual provincial legislative frameworks, which have varying degrees of complexity and formality. In Quebec, for example, the province has passed the Act Respecting Contracting by Public Bodies,[5] which details the procurement practices to be used by public bodies in that jurisdiction. In comparison, Ontario's provincial legislative framework dealing with procurement is not well developed. Pursuant to the general directives of the Financial Administration Act,[6] the Treasury Board of Ontario (TBO) controls the expenditure of public funds. As part of this mandate, the TBO has issued, among other things, the Supply Chain Guideline (SCG),[7] which provides detailed instructions on how Ontario departments and agencies *should* carry out procurements. But the SCG is not a statutory instrument and there is no clear sanction or remedy in the event that it is contravened. The SCG also does not apply to the entities that are not departments or agencies of the Government of Ontario but that receive significant public funding, such as school boards, the health care sector, and other government-funded entities (referred to in Ontario as the "broader public sector").

In response to chronic problems and high-profile scandals in broader public sector procurement, Ontario adopted the Broader Public Service Procurement Directive (BPSPD) in April 2011.[8] Initially, the BPSPD applied to hospitals, school boards, colleges, universities, community care access corporations, and children's aid societies. From January 1, 2012 onward, the Directive has also applied to any other publicly funded organizations that are in receipt of $10 million or more in public funds.[9]

[3] SC 1996, c 16.

[4] Constitution Act, 1867, 30 and 31 Victoria, c. 3 (UK), sections 91 and 92.

[5] RSQ, c C-65.1

[6] RSO, c F12.

[7] See <https://www.doingbusiness.mgs.gov.on.ca/mbs/psb/psb.nsf/0/e96ea292fdfdb2b58525803d00655ee8/$FILE/Supply_Chain_Guideline.pdf>.

[8] See <www.fin.gov.on.ca/en/bpssupplychain/documents/bps_procurement_directive.html> (accessed July 23, 2016).

[9] All values in this chapter are expressed in Canadian dollars. As at January 20, 2016, one Canadian dollar was equal to approximately US$0.69. Source: Bank of Canada Daily Currency Converter, available at: <http://www.bankofcanada.ca/rates/exchange/daily-converter/> (accessed July 23, 2016).

Access to information laws apply to public procurement-related records at both the provincial and federal level. The federal Access to Information Act is the relevant statute in relation to the records of the Government of Canada.[10] Pursuant to this Act, government records and information will be disclosed upon request, subject to certain exceptions, including where the records in question enclose sensitive third-party commercial or financial information, disclosure of which would prejudice the third party. Most of the equivalent provincial statutes contain similar provisions. The nature and content of the document will determine the extent to which tenders or third-party proposals are disclosed, and this varies from province to province.

There are also federal and provincial laws governing the conduct of lobbyists, which may impact procurement activities. For example, the federal Lobbying Act and its equivalent in Quebec both prohibit success fees (contingency payments) for lobbyists in situations where the client secures a government contract.[11]

Canada is a signatory to several international agreements that relate to procurement, including the World Trade Organization Agreement on Government Procurement (GPA), the February 2010 Canada–United States Agreement on Government Procurement (Canada–US GPA),[12] and the North American Free Trade Agreement (NAFTA), which also contains significant procurement-related commitments.[13] As is explained in greater detail in Section 11.2, a procurement review process under the terms of the Canadian International Trade Tribunal Act ensures compliance with the GPA and NAFTA (and other agreements).[14] This Act endows the Canadian International Trade Tribunal (CITT) with the power to investigate complaints from suppliers about non-compliance with the trade agreement commitments. The Tribunal's jurisdiction is limited to the procurement process related "designated contracts," which means procurements that are:

a. by federal departments, agencies, and state enterprises that are specifically listed in prescribed international agreements; and
b. for purchases above the value thresholds stipulated in the relevant agreements.

Several exemptions further restrict the scope of review where contracts deal with, among other things, national security, shipbuilding, certain transportation equipment, financial services, health services, engineering and architectural services, and certain agricultural arrangements.

[10] RSC, 1985, c A 1 (as amended).
[11] RSC, 1985, c 44 (4th Supp.).
[12] See <http://www.international.gc.ca/trade-agreements-accords-commerciaux/agr-acc/other-autre/us-eu.aspx?lang=eng>(accessed July 23, 2016).
[13] Chapter 10, available at <http://www.international.gc.ca/trade-agreements-accords-commerciaux/agr-acc/nafta-alena/text-texte/toc-tdm.aspx?lang=eng> (accessed July 23, 2016).
[14] RSC, 1985, c 47 (4th Supp.).

Canada has not made commitments under the auspices of the GPA or NAFTA with respect to procurement by sub-national entities (namely the provinces and territories and their entities). However, pursuant to the recent Canada–US GPA, the provinces have committed to comply with the terms of the 2007 draft of the GPA, but only to the benefit of US suppliers. Although these new commitments were intended to be implemented by February 2011, compliance by the provinces is unclear and inconsistent. For example, many provinces have still not adopted formal, effective bid challenge processes.

Most recently, Canada and the European Union have negotiated a Comprehensive Economic and Trade Agreement (CETA) that will cover federal, provincial, and local procurement, including goods and services that were previously excluded, such as rolling stock for public transit. Although it has not yet been implemented, it is expected that the CETA procurement chapter will go further than NAFTA and the GPA in terms of the scope of its application and the substance of the obligations, which will be discussed in greater detail in Section 11.4.

The federal, provincial, and territorial governments are all signatories to the Agreement on Internal Trade (AIT). Chapter 5 of the AIT sets out general commitments pertaining to non-discrimination and transparency in procurement. At the federal level, compliance is ensured through the CITT. At the provincial and territorial level, although the AIT does provide a dispute resolution process, it is not generally considered to offer an effective remedy for non-compliance from the perspective of suppliers. In general, the provinces do not have effective complaint-based bid challenge processes. Several of the provinces have entered into supplemental agreements that further ensure that procurements are executed in an open, non-discriminatory, and transparent manner. These agreements typically provide general non-discrimination commitments and do not offer suppliers effective remedies in the event of non-compliance.

11.2 **Procurement Data in Canada**

11.2.1 THE GPA AND TRANSPARENCY OF PROCUREMENT DATA

As noted above, Canada is a party to the GPA. Originally adopted in 1994, the GPA underwent significant changes in March 2012.[15] Canada announced its ratification of the 2012 revised GPA on December 3, 2013, and the revised GPA came into force on April 6, 2014.[16] One of several key areas of change in the modernization of the GPA was

[15] World Trade Organization, "The re-negotiation of the Agreement on Government Procurement (GPA)," available at: <http://www.wto.org/english/tratop_e/gproc_e/negotiations_e.htm> (accessed July 23, 2016).

[16] World Trade Organization, "Agreement on Government Procurement," available at: <https://e-gpa.wto.org/en/Agreement/Latest> (accessed July 23, 2016).

enhanced transparency with respect to procurement and reporting practices. Specifically, the revised GPA allows for procurement notices to be published electronically, as opposed to in print media, as long as the electronic version is readily accessible to potential bidders. Further, electronic posting allows for greater flexibility through the reduction of notice times for the purchase of commercial items. In terms of awards, the GPA requirement that pertinent information be posted in an appropriate paper or electronic medium is also intended to encourage greater transparency.

The heightened use of electronic media at every stage of the procurement process is expected to increase procurement transparency by providing member countries with an easier means of verifying compliance with terms of the GPA. Ideally, these changes were meant to promote flexibility, accountability, efficiency of processes associated with procurement practices, and to combat corruption among the countries party to the GPA.

11.2.2 WHERE ARE DATA LOCATED FOR CANADA?

Canada is a relatively decentralized federal state, meaning that much of the public procurement carried out is at the provincial and sub-provincial level. This makes collecting and analyzing procurement data very challenging in Canada. Although the federal government has emphasized on its sites and resources that its objective is to increase transparency and make information more accessible, Canada has no centralized clearing house for procurement statistics. To the extent data are available, the following provides information on how to locate them.

The Integrated Government Procurement Market Access Information (e-GPA) portal on the WTO website is intended to act as a single point of access to information under the GPA,[17] along with related information that signatory states have committed to provide. Currently, the site contains information on the coverage of the revised GPA. Further content is expected to be added periodically in consultation with modifications to coverage, information on national legislation, media for publication of procurement information by parties, and information on covered procurement statistics. Additional information that is anticipated to be accessible from the e-GPA portal includes information on current commercial opportunities and contract award notices regarding covered procurement that is published within the parties' respective jurisdictions. At this time, however, Canada has not yet provided such detailed data.

[17] Available at <http://e-gpa.wto.org/> (accessed July 23, 2016).

The WTO website also features a Statistics Database,[18] which allows users to extract statistical information that falls under the following categories:

- *Trade Profiles* containing predetermined information leaflets that detail the trade situation of members, observers, and selected economies;
- *Tariff Profiles* detailing the market access situation of members, observers, and selected economies;
- *Services Profiles* providing statistics pertaining to key infrastructure services for selected economies, including transportation, telecommunications, finance and insurance;
- *Aid for Trade Profiles* explaining trends of aid for trade, costs of trade, and trade performance and development for specific Aid for Trade recipients; and
- A *Time Series* section providing interactive data retrieval of international trade statistics. Short-term trade statistics are also available on the WTO website, and include monthly data with daily updates, and quarterly data updated every three weeks.

Canada has provided the required statistical trade data, but it does not provide data specific to public procurement as part of this disclosure.

The TBC's stated goal for its *Contracting Policy* is to ensure that the federal government's acquisition of goods and services is executed in a way that provides increased access, competition, and fairness, and leads to the greatest value or the best balance of benefits to Canada and its citizens. Moreover, contracting must support long-term national objectives, such as the development of different industries and regions, as well as abide by international and domestic trade obligations. As such, the Government of Canada has required public notice of contracts of more than $10,000 since 2004.[19] Lists of federal contracts and contract amendments can be accessed on the Government-Wide Reporting—Proactive Disclosure website.[20]

The TBC Secretariat publishes an annual Purchasing Activity Report (henceforth, the "Report") that contains statistical information about the purchases made and contracts entered into by federal entities. The Report is meant to be an annual publication but, currently, the latest available report covers the 2013 calendar year. The 2014 report has still not been issued. In any event, the information provided in the Report is of limited use.[21]

The Report is intended to create a picture of the purchasing activities undertaken by the federal government, based on the government's policy framework that was in effect in the year in question, though this is not required by statute. The data in the Report are not audited, and as a result, there are no warranties or legal safeguards that attest to

[18] Available at: <http://stat.wto.org/Home/WSDBHome.aspx?Language=E>(accessed July 23, 2016).

[19] Disclosure of Contracts: Foreign Affairs, available at:<http://w03.international.gc.ca/dc/index_fa-ae.aspx?lang=eng&p=2>(accessed July 23, 2016).

[20] Available at: <http://www.tbs-sct.gc.ca/pd-dp/gr-rg/index-eng.asp> (accessed July 23, 2016).

[21] Available at: <http://www.tbs-sct.gc.ca/pubs_pol/dcgpubs/con_data/siglist-eng.asp>(accessed July 23, 2016).

whether the information is accurate or comprehensive. The Report supplies its readers with concise tables summarizing the total number and value, including net amendments, of contracts above and below $25,000, contracts under $25,000, and contracts of $25,000 and above. It provides further information in detailed summaries that showcase statistical information and value for contracts above $25,000, goods contracts above $25,000, services contracts above $25,000, and construction contracts above $25,000.[22]

The Report should be read in tandem with the contracting statistics information that is posted on the Buyandsell.gc.ca website. Buyandsell.gc.ca is the Public Works and Government Services Canada website that facilitates public access to Government of Canada tenders. Users can review the publishing status, publication date, amendment date, closing date, description, notice type, procurement entity, and region of opportunity for tenders for goods and services. The website also contains information about policy and guidelines, and procurement complaint mechanisms. Where available, since January 2009, all tender notices have been linked to information about contracts awarded by PWGSC and its issued active standing offers and supply arrangements held by prequalified suppliers. Goods and Services Identification Number (GSIN) codes connect all of the procurement data on the site, and the federal government then uses the GSIN codes as a means of identifying generic product descriptions for Government of Canada commodities. If a user has the GSIN code relating to the business they are interested in, they can use it to search for opportunities or past contracts and prequalified suppliers.

Since March 23, 2004, the federal government has mandated that contracts over $10,000 be published. As of October 31 of that year, the PWGSC Disclosure of Contracts website has been updated quarterly to add information about any new contracts awarded.[23] As of June 2008, the policy also requires any contract amendments valued over $10,000 to be disclosed. The quarterly reports include the vendor name, description of work, contract value, and further details of the contract.

While some provinces appear to have adopted policies related to proactive disclosure of data related to public procurement, our research did not identify any databases that would provide meaningful insight into the evolution of public purchasing, such as the penetration over time of foreign suppliers in provincial procurement markets.

11.2.3 PROCUREMENT METHODS USED

PWGSC is the main buyer of goods and services for the Government of Canada, and its primary responsibilities center on helping federal agencies and departments describe

[22] All information in the paragraphs dealing with the Report is taken from <http://www.tbs-sct.gc.ca/pubs_pol/dcgpubs/con_data/par-13-rpa-eng.asp>(accessed July 23, 2016).

[23] See the Public Works and Government Services Canada Reports, available at: <http://www.tpsgc-pwgsc.gc.ca/cgi-bin/proactive/cl.pl?lang=eng&SCR=Q&Sort=0> (accessed July 23, 2016).

their requirements or scope of work, and making acquisitions for the best value. Such procurement activities are largely carried out under a legal framework comprised of statutes and regulations; agreements; policies, directives, procedures, and guidelines; and the challenge process. When a federal department or agency makes a request to PWGSC, the procurement process is initiated and depending on the requirements, the request may be handled by a contracting officer at headquarters or through a regional office.

Procurement is done by way of either a competitive procurement process (which is the most common process) or, in certain special circumstances, a non-competitive procurement process. The key objective of the competitive process is to secure the best value for Canadians while simultaneously improving access, competition, and fairness. The bulk of contracts that are awarded to small and medium-sized enterprises (SMEs) are done on a competitive basis through one of the contracting methods identified below. PWGSC also uses contracts and standing offers and supply arrangements as the methods of supply through which it purchases goods and services.

The three competitive bid solicitation methods are: (a) traditional competitive, (b) electronic bidding, and (c) Advance Contract Award Notice (ACAN). The traditional competitive method of procurement gives public notice of a call for bids of a proposed contract through the use of traditional bidding procedures and in a way that is consistent with broadly accepted trade practices. This is the default method at the federal level.[24]

Electronic bidding encourages supplier access to and transparency in the procurement process and simplifies the federal government's receipt of best value by using a public notice, either through an approved electronic information service of procurement activities (such as buyandsell.gc.ca) or through an electronic information service featuring proposed directed procurements through an ACAN. Electronic bidding can be used in any of the procurement methods approved by the Treasury Board.[25]

An ACAN permits entities to post a notice for at least fifteen calendar days indicating to suppliers that it plans to award a good, service, or construction contract to a pre-identified contractor. As long as no other supplier enters a statement of capabilities that meets the requirements posted in the ACAN during the fifteen-day posting period, the posted contract can be awarded under the electronic bidding authority limits set out by the Treasury Board.[26]

Standing offers are normally carried out by way of open competition, the goal of which is to identify a defined number of qualified suppliers who agree to provide defined goods or services, for a set term (typically two or three years), on set commercial terms and on an "as and when needed" basis, on a call-up (essentially, a purchase order) basis. This procurement device is often used for recurring needs (office supplies, certain types of IT or consulting services, etc.).

[24] See <http://www.tbs-sct.gc.ca/pubs_pol/dcgpubs/con_data/par-13-rpa-eng.asp> (accessed July 23, 2016).
[25] See <http://www.tbs-sct.gc.ca/pubs_pol/dcgpubs/con_data/par-13-rpa-eng.asp> (accessed July 23, 2016).
[26] See <http://www.tbs-sct.gc.ca/pubs_pol/dcgpubs/con_data/par-13-rpa-eng.asp>(accessed July 23, 2016).

Standing offers can provide for call-ups to be competitive (as between suppliers selected in the standing offer process) or simply called upon by the contracting authority without further competition. In the latter scenario, there is normally no further negotiation of terms or price, which are set in the standing offer process. Standing offers sometimes also provide for a rotation between qualified suppliers and may provide for an apportionment of the business between qualified suppliers (e.g., first ranked supplier will get 50 percent of the business, second ranked will get 30 percent, third ranked will get 20 percent).

Table 11.1 presents statistics from the 2013 Report (the latest available) regarding the method of procurement utilized in awarding contracts above the $25,000 threshold.

From Table 11.1, we can observe that competitive procurements by way of electronic bidding or traditional competitive bidding (tenders, requests for proposals, etc.) are by far the most prevalent method of contracting at the federal level, hovering at just over 80 percent of all contracts awarded. Compared to the data in past Reports, this proportion does not appear to have changed materially in the last several years (coming in consistently within two or three percentage points above or below 80 percent). The available

Table 11.1 Method of procurement utilized in awarding contracts above the $25,000 threshold (2013 data)

Solicitation procedure	Number	Percent of total number	Value ($'000)	Percent of total value
Awards pursuant to public notice or invited competitive bids				
Competitive awards				
Electronic bidding	8,311	28.92	4,207,974	31.65
Traditional competitive	14,823	51.58	2,593,938	19.51
Total of competitive awards	23,134	80.50	6,801,912	51.16
Net competitive amendments[27]	N/A	N/A	3,079,065	23.16
Subtotal of competitive awards, including amendments	23,134	80.50	9,880,977	74.32
ACANs	695	2.42	403,715	3.04
Net ACAN amendments	N/A	N/A	581,990	4.38
Subtotal of competitive awards and ACANs, including amendments	23,829	82.92	10,866,682	81.74
Awards not pursuant to public notice or invited competitive bids				
Non-competitive awards	4,910	17.08	1,817,053	13.67
Net amendments	N/A	N/A	610,476	4.59
Non-competitive awards, including amendments	4,910	17.08	2,427,529	18.26
Total of contracts $25,000 and above	28,739	100.00	13,294,211	100.00

[27] "Competitive amendments" refers to contract amendments that affect the value of contracts, negatively or positively. The $3,079,065,000 figure in this table reflects the value of the contract amendments that increased the value minus the value of amendments that decreased the value of contracts in 2013.

data also do not indicate if there is a correlation between the procurement method employed and the level of participation by foreign bidders.

It must be recalled, however, that this information relates only to procurement by federal departments and agencies, which is only a fraction of total public procurement carried out in Canada. None of the provinces provides procurement data in this sort of organized fashion. Generally available statistics in Canada also do not permit meaningful analysis as to the identity and nationality of the winning bidders or the number of tenders received. It remains, therefore, challenging to measure the precise extent to which the trade agreements may have had a meaningful impact on the accessibility of public procurement in Canada.

That said, it should also be recognized that Canada generally has an open procurement system (at all levels of government) and that the nationality of the supplier or Canadian content requirements are not usually relevant selection criteria, except in some specific areas such as national defense and rolling stock for public transit, where there are overt offset or Canadian value content requirements.

From a transparency perspective, it is generally believed that the trade agreements have generally had a salutary effect in Canada. Until the adoption of NAFTA and the GPA, Canada did not publish on a regular basis any of the procurement statistics now available in the Report. While it could be argued that the Report would have been published in any event as part of transparency efforts driven by domestic political forces, it is clear that expanded transparency in procurement has coincided with Canada's adoption of the various trade agreements to which it is a party, and that the transparency commitments in these agreements have provided an added incentive in publishing procurement statistics to demonstrate compliance and assist in furthering Canada's trade agreement negotiating agenda.

Given the prevalence of international companies in the Canadian economy, Canadian subsidiaries of multinational corporations have always played a very important role in public procurement in Canada. Whether the trade agreements have caused a greater proportion of public contacts in Canada to be awarded to foreign-owned suppliers is not possible to confirm through the statistics that are generally made available by the various levels of government in Canada. The data necessary to make such an analysis may be available from the government through available access to information laws, but we are not aware of any basic research published in this regard.

With the implementation of the trade agreements in Canada, it is undeniable that procurement practices have become more open/transparent and that overt forms of discrimination in favor of local suppliers have been largely eliminated (save for the National Defense offsets program,[28] certain other specific Canadian value content

[28] For major defense and security-related projects, Canada applies the Industrial and Regional Benefits Policy which, in simple terms, requires an investment in Canada equal to the value of the contract. For more details on this program, see <http://www.ic.gc.ca/eic/site/042.nsf/eng/home> (accessed July 23, 2016).

requirements such as on rolling stock for public transit,[29] and unique situations such as Ontario's now-cancelled renewable energy program that was the topic of a successful WTO dispute settlement challenge).[30] That said, this development has been most prevalent in relation to federal procurement. The very large provincial and sub-provincial procurement markets have been impacted to a lesser degree by the adoption of trade agreements, and to the extent that greater transparency and fairness has been adopted in procurement, it has been largely in response to domestic forces. For example, Québec's sophisticated procurement integrity regime has been adopted largely in response to very high-profile government contracting scandals rather than to implement any trade agreement commitments.

At the federal level, it is generally acknowledged that the development of the CITT bid challenge process has had a profound and lasting impact on procurement practices, forcing federal departments and agencies to adopt more transparent and less discriminatory procurement practices. The bid challenge process in Canada is explained in greater detail in Section 11.3.

11.3 **Domestic Review Procedures in Canada**

The CITT has the authority to investigate whether federal purchasing entities are complying with the trade agreements, and CITT decisions are subject to judicial review by the Federal Court of Appeal. The federal and provincial courts of record have jurisdiction to hear claims brought by bidders alleging that solicitation processes have been carried out in breach of their common law rights. Additionally, the superior courts of record have general supervisory jurisdiction over government action. Suppliers and potential suppliers may apply for judicial review of procurement decisions made by contracting authorities. However, the courts rarely intervene in the procurement process under the principles of administrative law as applied in Canada. At the federal level, the Office of the Procurement Ombudsman (OPO) can also hear complaints that do not fall

[29] For example, Quebec maintains a Canadian content preference on rolling-stock for public transit. For a description of Quebec's program, see <https://web.archive.org/web/20150508201610/http://www.mtq.gouv.qc.ca/centredocumentation/Documents/Partenaires-prives/Services-ferroviaire-maritime-a%C3%A9rien/Transport-routier/Transport%20collectif/Transport%20collectif%20des%20personnes%20et%20de%20la%20SOFIL/pagtcp.pdf> (available in French only). A similar preference is applied in contracts for public transit rolling-stock in Ontario. The ability to apply these preferences was partly preserved in the Canada Europe Comprehensive Economic and Trade Agreement; see of the *Technical Summary of Final Negotiated Outcomes* (p. 17), Canada, Department of Foreign Affairs and Trade Development, available at: <http://www.international.gc.ca/trade-agreements-accords-commerciaux/assets/pdfs/ceta-aecg/ceta-technicalsummary.pdf>.

[30] Appellate Body Reports, *Canada–Certain Measures Affecting the Renewable Energy Generation Sector/Canada–Measures Relating to the Feed-In Tariff Program*, WT/DS412/AB/R/WT/DS426/AB/R, adopted May 24, 2013, available at: <https://www.wto.org/english/tratop_e/dispu_e/cases_e/ds412_e.htm>.

either within the jurisdiction of the courts or of the CITT. The OPO has the power to investigate and make recommendations, but cannot reverse procurement decisions or order that compensation be paid.

A CITT review normally takes ninety days but this can be extended to 130 days in certain circumstances. Canadian courts usually take between ten and eighteen months to hear and adjudicate on an application for judicial review. Common law claims for damages resulting from the procurement process proceed by way of civil action, and may take anywhere from one and a half to three years to go to trial. The OPO does not have a set time frame, but generally concludes its investigations within a few months.

The CITT jurisdiction is limited to adjudicating on complaints relating to "designated contracts," which means that the purchasing entity is covered by the agreements, the goods or services are not excluded under the applicable trade agreements, and the value of the anticipated procurement meets the value thresholds in the agreements. Additionally, the complainant must be a supplier or potential supplier on such a designated contract, and must be a national of either Canada or another signatory country.

Common law standing principles will apply in actions for damages or applications for judicial review. Normally, it is only the bidder or the prime contractor who has rights; subcontractors generally do not have any rights or standing against the purchasing entity with regard to the contracting process.

Review applications and appeals are subject to specific deadlines. A complaint to the CITT must be filed within ten working days of the date the complainant knew or ought to have known of the grounds for complaint.[31] Under the Federal Courts Act, applications for judicial review must be brought within thirty days from the date of the decision or action under review. At the provincial level, different deadlines may apply. Common law claims for damages are limited by the applicable federal and provincial limitations statutes. For example, under the Ontario Limitations Act, contract claims are subject to a two-year limitation period.

An application for review does not have an automatic suspensive effect that blocks the continuation of the procurement procedure or the conclusion of the contract. The CITT may issue a "stop award order" on request. However, the CITT must lift any such order in the event that the purchasing entity files a certificate with the CITT attesting to the fact that delaying the implementation of the contract would not serve the public interest.

The courts have the power to issue injunctions to stop the award of a contract, though this power is rarely exercised. The established three-part test for issuances of injunctions

[31] See section 6 of the *Canadian International Trade Tribunal Procurement Inquiry Regulations* (SOR/93-602). Under subsection 6(2) of these Regulations, the ten-day deadline can be suspended where the supplier files an objection with the contracting authority. A fresh ten-day deadline then applies from the date the objection is rejected by the contracting authority.

in Canada requires that the claimant demonstrate that there is an arguable case on the merits; that the claimant would suffer irreparable harm if the injunction is not issued; and that the balance of convenience favors the issuance of the injunction.

It is not necessary to notify unsuccessful bidders before the contract with the successful bidder is concluded. There is no particular statutory or regulatory rule governing the timing of notice to an unsuccessful bidder. In many cases, the conclusion of the contract and the award notice to the bidders take place simultaneously.

Federal and provincial access to information legislation provides for the disclosure of documents and information to an applicant. However, in light of the exception dealing with commercially sensitive third-party information where disclosure would likely harm the third party, proposals from competitors are usually not disclosed. When such proposals are disclosed, the disclosure is subject to the redaction of sensitive information. The CITT has the power to issue subpoenas and compel disclosure of records that are in the possession of the relevant purchasing entity. In cases where the bidder claims damages, the Canadian court process has a framework for detailed disclosure of relevant evidence through the discovery process.

It is not customary for disadvantaged bidders to file review applications, and Canadian court litigation concerning procurement is relatively rare. In Canada, there are only a few dozen cases annually that deal with tendering law. Federally, the CITT typically deals with anywhere from sixty to 100 complaints annually. The CITT's bid challenge process is available to local suppliers and suppliers from signatories to the applicable trade agreements. Foreign bidders, however, are not entitled to plead violations of the AIT.[32]

It is possible for a concluded contract to be cancelled or terminated following a review application by an unsuccessful bidder if the procurement procedure that led to its conclusion violated procurement law. In such cases, the Tribunal can recommend that a contract be cancelled, although this rarely happens. It is more common for an award of monetary compensation to be made. Similarly, it is rare for courts to cancel contracts. However, this did occur in the noteworthy case *Alstom Canada Inc. v Société de Transport de Montréal*, 2008 QCCS 8. In that case, Alstom brought a successful action under the Quebec Act Respecting Contracts by Public Bodies in relation to a contract for underground rail cars.

There is legal protection available to parties interested in the contract in the case of an award without any procurement procedure. The CITT has jurisdiction to hear such complaints, and although it is rare, judicial review of the decision to award such a contract is also possible.

If a violation of procurement law is established in an administrative or judicial review proceeding, disadvantaged bidders may claim damages. The CITT has the power to

[32] *Northrop Grumman Overseas Services Corp. v. Canada (Attorney General)*, 2009 SCC 50 [2009] 3 S.C. R. 309.

recommend the payment of compensation where it finds that a supplier's complaint is valid. The compensation most frequently awarded represents the lost profits the supplier would have made had it been awarded the contract. The Procurement Compensation Guidelines[33] published by the CITT explain, among other things, the guiding principles that the CITT applies in determining the appropriate amount of compensation. In short, when determining the amount of compensation to recommend, the Tribunal attempts to place the complainant in the position in which it would have been but for the government's breach of the applicable trade agreement(s). Depending on the circumstances, this may include the supplier's lost profits and lost opportunities. In exceptional cases, the Tribunal may also recommend compensation for damages to the integrity of the procurement system. Generally, such compensation will only be recommended in circumstances where there has been a lack of good faith in conducting the procurement.

Furthermore, depending on the level of complexity, the CITT may award bid preparation costs and order that the unsuccessful party pay the complaint costs of the other party in accordance with a fixed tariff of $1,000, $2,400, or $4,100.[34]

Canada has also developed common law rules relating to competitive contracting that may offer suppliers relief. In accordance with the Supreme Court of Canada case in *R. v. Ron Engineering* and its multiple progeny,[35] when a bidder submits a compliant bid in response to a call for tenders, a contract (termed Contract A) is created between the bidder and the purchaser. The terms of this Contract A include the tender itself, the bid, and certain implied terms of fairness (bidders will be treated equally and fairly, the purchaser will apply the evaluation criteria set out in the call for tenders, mandatory requirements will be adhered to, etc.). Where Contract A is breached by the purchaser, a bidder who is prejudiced by such breach may sue for breach of contract and claim the usual common law remedies (typically damages or specific performance).[36]

Generally, Canada maintains that its bid challenge system, and the CITT process in particular, adequately complies with its obligations under Article XVIII of the revised GPA. We have not identified compelling analysis that suggests that Canada is in breach of its GPA commitments, and we note that there have not been any disputes initiated under the GPA against Canada by any other signatory states.[37]

[33] Available at <http://www.citt.gc.ca/en/Procurement_compensation_guidelines_e>.

[34] See the CITT's "Guidelines for Fixing Costs in Procurement Complaint Proceedings," available at: <www.citt-tcce.gc.ca/publicat/cost04_e.asp>.

[35] *R. (Ont.) v. Ron Engineering,* [1981] 1 S.C.R. 111.

[36] For a good review of the development of Contract A in Canada, see Emanuelli (2012: p. 57 onwards).

[37] The dispute relating to Ontario's Green Energy Act alleged violations of the Subsidies and Countervailing Measures Act, not the GPA. See, footnote 31 (supra).

11.4 The Procurement Chapters in the CETA Agreement

The Canadian Prime Minister, the European Commission President, and the European Council President all signed the Canadian–European Union Comprehensive Economic and Trade Agreement (CETA) on September 26, 2014. CETA is the result of years of negotiations and the scope of CETA is greater than that of NAFTA, which came into effect two decades ago. The text of the CETA agreement is currently subject to a legal review and reformatting process, subsequent to which the complete text will become binding, once Canada and the EU have completed the ratification process.[38]

The major changes that CETA will bring to the international procurement landscape are that Canadian firms will have expanded opportunities to make bids in the EU's government procurement market, while EU companies will have corresponding increased access to Canadian public procurement at both the federal and provincial level. It is the most comprehensive and favorable procurement market access that Canada has ever offered in any of its trade agreements.

With CETA, Canada has made notable concessions to the EU in relation to procurement, which will primarily affect provincial and municipal governments. The federal government in Canada awards approximately $25 billion in contracts annually, while the provinces and municipalities award approximately $130 billion in contracts annually. Prior to CETA, these sub-federal entities have not been within the purview of international disciplines that govern procurement, such as the WTO's GPA or chapter 10 of NAFTA. Despite the fact that the Canada–US GPA does apply to some of the provincial and territorial governing bodies, provincial Crown entities and utilities and the sector of municipal, academic, school boards, and hospitals (MASH) have never been subject to the international disciplines.

Canada's commitments to the EU under CETA include the following unprecedented access: coverage of approximately 75–80 percent of procurement done by major energy utilities throughout Canada, coupled with commitments by any province or territory with major energy production or distribution capacity; coverage of provincial and territorial mass transit, with Quebec and Ontario slated to retain 25 percent of the Canadian value of public transit vehicle procurement and Quebec having the ability to insist that final assembly be in Canada within that 25 percent; and a commitment to create a single electronic access point within five years of the agreement coming into

[38] "Consolidated CETA Text," available at: <http://www.international.gc.ca/trade-agreements-accords-commerciaux/agr-acc/ceta-aecg/text-texte/toc-tdm.aspx?lang=eng> (accessed July 23, 2016).

effect. The last item will theoretically benefit both Canadian and EU entities and promote further transparency in the procurement process.[39]

CETA coverage does not extend to procurements in the following areas in Canada: health care and other public services; ports and airports; procurements of less than $1 million for regional commercial growth in rural areas in the Maritime provinces and the territories; public–private partnerships; shipbuilding and repairs; and procurements made for the purpose of national security. The under $1 million exclusion also applies to procurements meant to support rural employment endeavors in Manitoba, Newfoundland and Labrador, Nova Scotia, Northwest Territories, Nunavut, Prince Edward Island, New Brunswick, and the Yukon.

For Canada, the CETA gains include preferential access to the EU government procurement market, as well as the most comprehensive and favorable market access that the EU has offered to any G20 member outside the EU. It includes such other further commitments as broad coverage for goods and services that will be provided to government entities directly or via EU suppliers that are party to procurement contracts with the following:

- the three primary EU-level institutions, namely the European Commission, the European Parliament, and the European Council;
- the twenty-eight member state legislatures in the EU;
- EU government entities, both local and regional; and
- corporations within the public utilities sector.

Furthermore, the EU has granted more comprehensive coverage than has Canada for areas including energy, bodies governed by public law, cultural industries, and public transit. There are exclusions for ports and airports, broadcasting, the postal sector, and shipbuilding and maintenance. Although Canada has maintained an exclusion for regional economic development, the EU has not. Additionally, it has not provided an exclusion for pre-contractual remedies for the first decade, to ensure that suppliers will be allowed to stop the award of a contract prior to it being signed. If the provinces and territories in Canada refuse to adopt similar remedies under their domestic-review frameworks, the EU will bar access to the pre-contractual remedies to Canada.[40]

Practically speaking, CETA's requirements will force government procuring entities and utilities in the provinces, territories, and municipalities to be cautious when drafting and carrying out procurements and contract awards. This will restrict sole sourcing, which will only be allowed under rare and predetermined conditions. Sub-federal entities

[39] See the CETA "Technical Summary of the Final Negotiated Outcomes (October 2013)," available at: <http://international.gc.ca/trade-agreements-accords-commerciaux/agr-acc/ceta-aecg/understanding-comprendre/technical-technique.aspx?lang=eng#p4> (accessed July 23, 2016).

[40] Footnote 32 (supra).

will also be required to adopt a mechanism of bid protest in some form through which EU suppliers will have the opportunity to challenge procurements and access corrective remedies before the contract is awarded. At the federal level, this will be done by the CITT. CETA also contains a time delay similar to that contained in most treaties, restricting the time within which a supplier can challenge a procurement process or contract award. Usually, the time is limited to ten business days after the supplier is made aware of the substance of the challenge.

11.5 **Impact of the Trade Agreements on Canadian Procurement**

There has been little independent, academic research on the impact of the trade agreements on Canadian procurement practices and on market access opportunities for Canadian companies abroad. That said, there is a high degree of consensus among business organizations that procurement disciplines, such as in NAFTA and CETA, are vital market access accomplishments for Canadian exporters and that procurement commitments should be an important part of Canada's market access objectives in negotiating trade agreements. The federal government and, to a lesser degree, the provinces have also espoused procurement commitments in trade agreements as an important negotiating objective.

At the same time, empirical data on the impact of the trade agreements are difficult to obtain in Canada. We are aware of no statistical analysis of the effect of the trade agreements on the nationality of suppliers on Canadian public contracts, or of any actual increase in procurement successes abroad for Canadian companies that can be causally tied to trade agreement commitments. The collection and publication of such data would be an important tool in demonstrating the openness of the Canadian procurement market and tracking the penetration of foreign suppliers over time. Likewise, there are no statistical data published that allow conclusions to be drawn as to whether the trade agreements materially advantage suppliers from signatories to the GPA (and other agreements containing procurement commitments), or conversely if suppliers from countries that are *not* signatories are materially disadvantaged over time. If the Government of Canada wishes to demonstrate the benefits of procurement-related agreements, it should collect and publish such data.

Whether the trade agreement disciplines have generated more efficiency or better value for contracting authorities is even less clear. At the federal level, the trade agreement disciplines and the fear of CITT review are often blamed for a highly rules- and process-focused approach that may not provide sufficient flexibility to generate the best value. There are reports that the fear of legal challenge by suppliers has resulted in slower procurement processes and an aversion to creative methods of procurement that could generate better results; in other words, that the trade agreements have produced a risk-averse and more costly procurement system.[41]

SME bias is not an overtly prevalent feature of Canadian public procurement. While some federal and other programs do exist to spur SME involvement in government contracting, express weighting of evaluation criteria in favor of SMEs is seldom used by the senior levels of government. Likewise, we are aware of no compelling evidence that covert favoritism is being applied in a systematic fashion to direct competitive contracts to local SMEs. In short, while incidents of improper contracting practices and favoritism emerge from time to time, there are no convincing data available indicating that procurement is increasingly being used to further industrial or regional development objectives.[42] Rather, the trend in Canada appears to be for the opposite effect.

To understand the Canadian procurement landscape, it is also important to appreciate that Canada is a highly trade-dependent, decentralized federation and that the provinces and the federal government have signed a number of agreements that contain procurement-related commitments, including the AIT discussed in the Introduction to this chapter. These agreements contain non-discrimination and transparency commitments that have also had a significant impact on procurement practices, even if they lack effective enforcement mechanisms such as a supplier bid challenge process (except for the CITT in relation to federal procurement). The provinces have largely implemented their commitments by adopting more sophisticated and detailed procurement rules, which have generally reduced buyer discretion in favor of more predictable and standardized procurement processes.

Over the last two decades, the trade agreements have clearly led to tangible reforms in Canada, including the adoption of an effective and active bid challenge authority covering federal procurement. There is a high degree of consensus that the reforms have generally improved the transparency and fairness of the procurement process at the federal level, but they have had more limited impact on provincial and sub-provincial procurement. There is some controversy as to whether the reforms have led to an excessive focus on process and rules, leading to a slower, and more costly and rigid, procurement process. There is also some debate as to whether outcomes are superior in terms of value for money under the new rules. While empirical evidence to settle these controversies is difficult to come by, on balance, the impact of the trade agreements on

[41] See, for example, Government of Canada (2005).

[42] The Ontario renewable energy program, successfully challenged at the WTO (see, footnote 28 (supra)), stands as a prominent exception. There are other notable exceptions relating, for example, to buy-local policies for certain agricultural products and alcoholic beverages, but these would represent a modest fraction of overall public procurement.

federal procurement is generally considered to have been positive in terms of fairness (non-discrimination) and transparency.

Some trade unions and some civil society groups occasionally decry the trade agreements for limiting the ability of governments to impose local content requirements, and advocate for a return to "Buy Canadian" policies in procurement.[43] However, there is no declared appetite in mainstream political or governmental spheres for an expansion of local content requirements or for a return to the higher degrees of contracting authority discretion that existed prior to the implementation of the trade agreements.

ACKNOWLEDGMENTS

While the author wishes to thank Jessie Lamont, Student-at-Law at Dentons Canada LLP, for her assistance in preparing this chapter, he retains full and exclusive responsibility for any errors or omissions.

REFERENCES

Emanuelli, P. 2012. *Government Procurement*, 3rd edn. Toronto: Lexis Canada Inc.

Government of Canada. 2005. "Government-Wide Review of Procurement: Final Report." Presented to the Minister of Public Work and Government Services (available at: <http://www.publications.gc.ca/site/eng/272140/publication.html> (accessed July 23, 2016).

[43] See, for example, "Fact Sheet: Stop Trade Deals That Undermine Local Power," Canadian Union of Public Employees, May 28, 2015 (available at: <http://cupe.ca/fact-sheet-stop-trade-deals-undermine-local-power>).

12 Public Procurement in Mexico

Eduardo Pérez Motta and Paulina Valladares

12.1 **Introduction**

Public procurement plays a major role in the Mexican economy. Government purchases account for a large proportion of the gross domestic product (GDP)—in 2014, the Mexican authorities spent around 8 percent of GDP and 40 percent of the federal budget on goods, works, and services.[1]

As in other nations, public procurement in Mexico is vulnerable to corruption and fraud. According to the Organisation for Economic Co-operation and Development (OECD), corruption in the world amounts US$2.6 trillion, equivalent to more than 5 percent of global GDP, with over US$1 trillion paid in bribes each year. The costs of corruption affecting public procurement in Mexico are significant, reaching between 20 and 25 percent of the contract value, and in some cases 40–50 percent.

Corruption and collusion occur simultaneously. Bid-rigging and collusion in the tendering process take place when bidders agree to eliminate competition in the procurement process, thereby denying the public a fair price. In Mexico, bid-rigging can raise prices up to 20 percent or more. Consequently, and given the economic importance of public procurement, the Mexican federal government has taken major steps to promote market efficiency and competitive tendering in order to ensure the integrity of the entire procurement process.

12.2 **The National Legal Framework for Public Procurement in Mexico**

12.2.1 THE LEGAL FRAMEWORK FOR PUBLIC PROCUREMENT

The legal basis of all government purchasing undertaken in Mexico is contained in Article 134 of the Mexican Political Constitution. This article establishes that all economic resources available for federal, state, and local governments have to be managed

[1] Source: Ministry of Public Administration (its acronym in Spanish is SFP).

with efficiency, transparency, and accountability in order to achieve the best value for money for taxpayers.

It is through this Article 134 of the Constitution that the foundation for a national procurement system—aligned with international standards—is laid. The Constitution sets the fundamental principles for public procurement—efficiency, effectiveness, honesty, austerity, transparency, economy, fairness, and integrity—and the mechanisms to guarantee that the government receives the best available conditions when purchasing goods, works, and services.

Efficiency, as it is intended in the Mexican Constitution, refers to meeting the objectives of the purchase with the most rational use of the available resources, and obtaining the lowest cost possible. *Effectiveness* allows the objectives and goals set to be achieved with the resources available at a given time. *Economy* is seen as the optimal use of spending money and other assets that benefit the whole society. *Transparency* means that the procedures are carried out under the conditions of legality and equal treatment of participants, providing clear and accessible information on procurement procedures and results. *Honesty* refers to the responsible behavior of public officials, that is fulfilling their responsibilities and providing timely service to the public.

To follow these principles, Article 134 establishes that procurement of all types of goods and services, except for some specific cases, has to be conducted through sealed-bid tenders. The objective of such a mechanism is to maximize the efficiency of public procurement using competitive tenders that will result in best prices and lower costs for the contracting authority. In very exceptional cases, public purchasers may use other procedures to public tender: (i) a restricted invitation to at least three suppliers, or (ii) direct award of the public contract.

Two key laws implement and set the rules for public procurement carried out in Mexico: the Law on Procurement, Leases and Services of the Public Sector ("Law on Procurement");[2] and the Law on Public Works and Related Services ("Law on Public Works")[3] (see Figure 12.1). The Ministry of Public Administration is the institution responsible for overseeing public purchases and enforcing the law in case corruption is present.

At the state level, these two laws are observed when it comes to federal procurement resources. But when it comes to local resources, states have local regulations for acquisitions, leases, and public works. These local rules follow the guiding principles for public procurement that are set in the Constitution. However, at the state and local levels, there is a need for better design and implementation of the procurement laws. Doing so will require work on two fronts: (1) fighting bid-rigging and corruption, and

[2] In Spanish, Ley de Adquisiciones, Arrendamientos y Servicios Del Sector Público.

[3] In Spanish, Ley de Obras Públicas y Servicios Relacionados con las mismas.

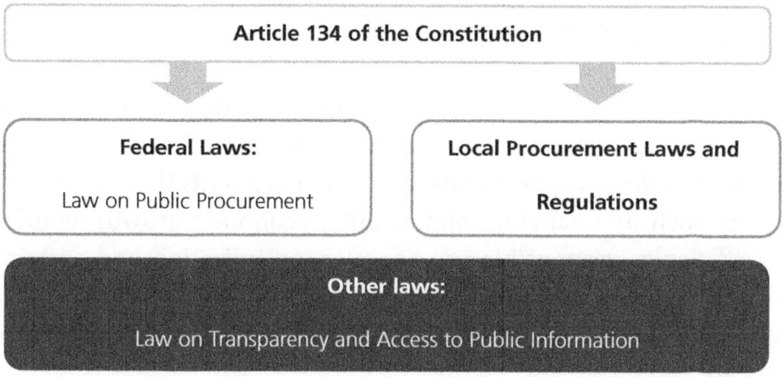

Figure 12.1. National legal framework for public procurement in Mexico

Source: Elaborated by the authors based on current legislation.

(2) promoting reforms to align local laws and regulations with best international standards.

Other laws that regulate public procurement include the Law on Economic Competition and the Law on Transparency and Access to Public Information.

Article 6 of the Constitution establishes that everyone has the right to free access to information. The Law on Transparency and Access to Public Information guarantees access for all citizens to information held by the government. The National Institute for Access to Public Information and Data Protection is responsible for enforcing the Law on Transparency, which establishes a mandatory catalogue of information to be published by the government, including all information regarding public procurement processes.

The Law on Economic Competition prohibits and sanctions bid-rigging in public procurement and collusive practices. The competition authority, the Federal Economic Competition Commission, as provided in Article 28 of the Constitution, is responsible for enforcing this law.

12.3 **The Mexican Procurement Process**

The public procurement process in Mexico has several stages. This section provides a brief description of the steps to be followed by contracting authorities, according to the current legal framework in Mexico, when making public purchases. The main purpose of these stages is to ensure that procurement processes are transparent, objective and competitive, addressing the challenges of collusive tendering and corruption.

12.3.1 PUBLIC TENDERS

Article 26 of the Law on Public Procurement establishes that government purchases, as a rule, should be made through public tenders to guarantee the best available conditions in terms of price and quality. Article 26 sets forth other elements that should be considered when tendering, such as financing, opportunity, economic growth, employment creation, energy efficiency, responsible use of water, optimization and sustainable use of resources, as well as environmental protection.

To achieve these conditions, the following steps for awarding public contracts through public tenders are taken (see also Figure 12.2):

1. pre-tender evaluation/tender design stage
2. tender stage
3. bid evaluation and contract award stage
4. the post-award stage.

12.3.1.1 Pre-Tender Evaluation/Tender Design Stage

The Law on Public Procurement incorporates a planning stage during which the manner in which the procurement process will be conducted is decided. This stage is of paramount importance because it defines what is needed, and when, to meet the

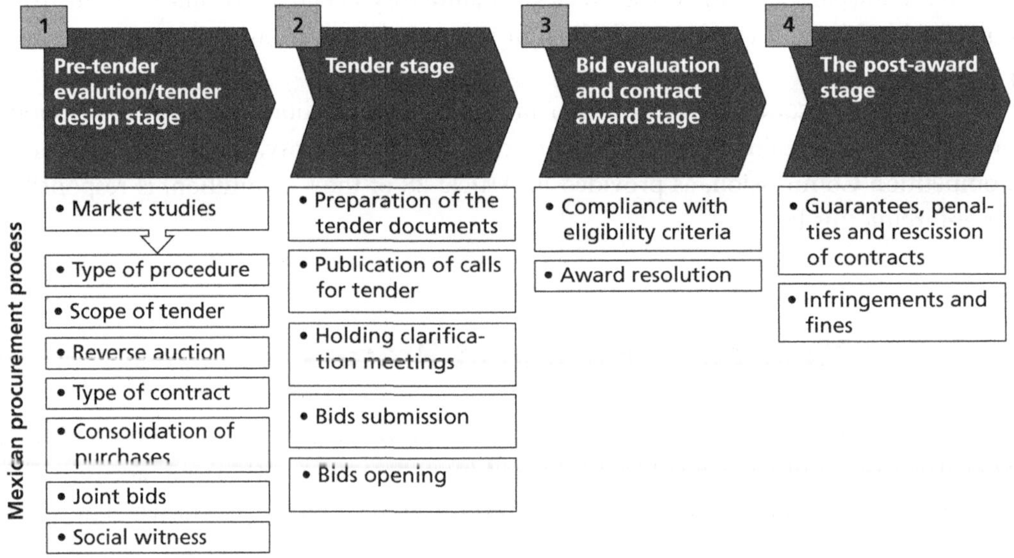

Figure 12.2. Mexico: Steps for awarding public contracts through bidding

Source: The authors.

objectives of the contracting authority. To that end, the law establishes the use of market studies to define the best contractual framework for the public purchase, the best use of procurement tools, and the adequate evaluation criteria. Also, through market studies, the contracting authorities will determine the estimated price to be paid and the availability of the goods and services to be purchased.

This stage considers the following elements of the purchasing process:

- **Type of procedure.** Authorities must select the type of procedure that will provide the best available conditions to the state. As a rule, public purchases have to be conducted through public bidding processes. However, the law provides for exceptions when, for example, there is only one supplier, there is a need to avoid disturbance of public order, or there may be additional costs or significant losses for the state if the purchase is delayed.[4] To address these situations, the contracting authorities may use two alternative procurement procedures: (1) invitation to at least three suppliers, and (2) direct award of the contract.
- **Scope of tender.** The law differentiates between national and international tenders. In this context, authorities have to decide whether the tender will be open only to national businesses, if national and foreign businesses can participate (following the terms of the applicable free trade agreements), or if the tender will be open to all businesses regardless of the nationality of the bidders.
- **Reverse auction.** The contracting authorities should determine the suitability of using reverse auctions in the purchasing process. The Law on Public Procurement allows for reverse auctions only when the characteristics of the goods and services to be purchased are well defined and the legal and technical assessment can be done immediately after the bids are presented. Reverse auctions are an efficient means of obtaining competitive prices, since it is expected that prices go down as bidding continues and bidders offer discounts to improve on the initial price offered.
- **Type of contract.** The law establishes two kinds of contracts: (1) typical contracts, in which the price and quantity to be purchased are fixed; and (2) open contracts, in which contracting authorities acquire goods and services on a regular basis from a supplier that has been selected through a public tender.
- **Consolidated procurement.** Contracting authorities must decide whether a consolidated purchase will be the best option to achieve best terms in respect of price, quality, and convenience. Consolidation of procurement aims at acquiring benefits from economies of scale from suppliers through the use of the enormous buying power of the government, allowing a better use of government resources.

[4] Article 41 of the Law on Public Procurement.

- **Joint bids by multiple suppliers.** This is the case when two or more independent suppliers jointly participate in a tender. When small or new suppliers do not have the capacity to participate in a tender because of its complexity or large scale, the Law on Procurement allows for joint bids. Article 34 provides that joint bids should describe each party's obligations and how these will be fulfilled. It is also stated that joint bidders should comply with the provisions of the Law on Economic Competition. When this option for procurement is used, care must be taken given the possibility that joint bids could facilitate collusive agreements between suppliers, harming competition.
- **Social witnesses.** This a mechanism to increase public participation in the most relevant public procurement procedures, and in particular to guarantee the transparency and legality of the procurement processes. If the amount of public contracts exceeds the equivalent of five million times the minimum daily wage (350 million pesos, or approximately US$21 million), and also in high impact cases, the participation of third parties without any conflict of interest is requested. The Ministry of Public Administration is responsible for the public register of social witnesses, who will participate in all stages of the public procurement procedures.

12.3.1.2 Tender Stage

This stage is about preparing the documents containing the legal, technical, and economic criteria, specifications, requirements, and conditions of participation. The importance of such documents lies in their provision of the guidelines and formal rules governing the tender process.

Article 29 of the Law on Public Procurement sets the requirements that a call for tender should include:

- a detailed description of the goods or services and other aspects deemed necessary to determine the purpose and scope of the procurement;
- the date, time, and venue of the first clarification meeting, of the opening of proposals, and of the awarding of the contract, and whether the tender process will be an electronic tender, a face-to-face tender, or a mixed tender;
- the requirements for those interested in participating in the tender process, which should not limit competition;
- documents that suppliers should provide to confirm their legal status;
- a statement of integrity from bidders stating that they will abstain from bribery, collusion, or other corrupt practices;
- if required, method and approval parameters to ensure specification compliance of the goods and services;

- a statement that indicates whether the procurement covers one or more fiscal years, whether it is an open contract, and the rationale for not accepting joint bids;
- a statement that indicates whether only one contract will be awarded or there will be several contracts to bid for; and
- the evaluation and awarding criteria, preferably using the system of "points and percentages" or, as the case may be, a "cost-benefit analysis."

The Mexican Federal Government publishes calls for tenders in the *Official Journal of the Federation* (DOF, to give its Spanish acronym) and in the Electronic Public Procurement System (CompraNet), which is described in Section 12.3.4.

In addition, Article 33 of the Law on Procurement provides an opportunity for the interested bidders to raise questions or seek explanations of the conditions of a specific tender in a clarification meeting. In these meetings, requiring and contracting areas provide explanations of technical and other requirements of the call for tenders.

Bid proposals will be submitted in separate, sealed envelopes. In the case that the proposals are submitted by the electronic procurement system—CompraNet—envelopes will be generated in a manner that protects the confidentiality of the information. Bid proposals will reveal the price offered and whether the supplier meets the conditions of the call.

To complete this stage, the proposals that have been chosen to participate are opened at a public event to allow bidders to verify the impartiality and integrity of the procurement process.

12.3.1.3 Bid Evaluation and Contract Award Stage

In this stage, procurement officials evaluate the bids to ensure that they comply with the corresponding eligibility criteria. As established in Article 36 bis of the Law on Procurement, the contract is awarded to the bidder that meets the technical, legal, and economic requirements, and thus ensures compliance with the obligations set out in the call for tenders.

Depending on the conditions established in the call for tenders, an evaluation of the proposals could be carried out through one of three mechanisms or systems: (1) points based; (2) cost benefit, or (3) binary. An assessment based on points or percentages would award the contract to the bid that scores the best in a technical and quality assessment. A cost-benefit assessment compares the anticipated benefits of the proposals and the cost involved. This would be measured and verified using concepts such as maintenance, operation, consumables, and performance. The binary system is used for basic goods and services, and awards the contract to the supplier offering the lowest price.

After the winner is awarded the contract, the purchasing authority will make available a document containing the following information:

1. the list of rejected bids, indicating all legal, technical, or economic motives for the decision and the issues that failed to be fulfilled;
2. the list and general description of the solvent bids;
3. the names of the successful bidders, indicating all legal, technical, or economic motives for the decision;
4. the date, time, and place for the signature of the contract;
5. the name, title, and signature of the contracting official and name and signature of the official responsible for assessing the proposals; and
6. in the case of the bid being declared void, the document will state the reasons behind this decision.

12.3.1.4 **Post-Award Stage**

The fulfillment of the contract must be guaranteed by the winning bidders. To that end, the Ministry of Public Administration can sanction bidders/suppliers for not complying with the obligations set forth in the contract.

For infringing the law, Article 59 provides for a fine up to 1,000 times the minimum wage (approximately US$130,000), and for not signing the contract a supplier can be fined up to forty times the minimum wage (approximately US$5,000). The Ministry of Public Administration can also restrict the participation of bidders in public tenders for a period ranging from three months to five years if they breach any provision of the Law on Public Procurement or any other provision relevant to the procurement process in Mexico.

12.3.2 EXCEPTIONS TO TENDERS

As mentioned in Section 12.2, the Mexican Constitution establishes that public procurement has to be conducted through public tenders. However, in exceptional cases, procurement can be carried out through either a restricted invitation to suppliers, or by direct award of the public contract.

These mechanisms are used, for instance, when there are no substitutes to the product or services, there is only one potential supplier in the market, or one supplier has ownership or the exclusive licensing of patents, copyrights, or other exclusive rights. These exceptions also apply when there is a danger of social order being disturbed, public services or provision of health services being disrupted, or when national safety is at risk.

Restricted invitation is commonly used to buy a particular product or service, or to develop a specific public work. In this modality, a call for tender is only sent to certain suppliers. When the contract is awarded directly to one supplier, probably from a list of reliable suppliers, the contracting authority determines the conditions and suppliers that can provide the products or services based on experience, quality, and price.

These mechanisms should be used carefully and only in very exceptional cases as they are highly discretionary and do not ensure the principles of transparency, competitiveness, and competition.

12.3.3 NON-CONFORMITY IN PUBLIC PROCUREMENT

The first chapter of the Title Sixth of the Law on Procurement sets forth the framework for filing claims in case of non-conformity or non-compliance with federal procurement processes. The non-conformities can be raised in the tender stage, the contract award stage, or the post-award stage (for instance, during the call for tenders, clarification meetings, the opening of proposals, or at the award of the contract). Claims should be notified by the complainants to the Ministry of Public Administration or through CompraNet. The final decision may evolve in two different ways: the authority may declare that the complaint is groundless, or it may declare the process null.

Table 12.1 Mexico: Non-conformities in federal public procurement, 2010–14

Year	Non-conformities											Non-conformities resolved				
	Disagreements by type of procurement					Contested decision						Result				
	Total amount	Acquisitions	Leases	Services	Other	Total amount	Call for tenders clarification meetings	Bid opening	Decision	Acts and omissions	Other	Total amount	Justified	No grounds	Not analyzed	Complaint response (working days)
2010	**1,805**	900	10	534	361	**1,805**	311	29	1,405	9	51	**1,785**	449	636	700	43.07
2011	**1,627**	779	13	540	295	**1,627**	263	53	1,198	13	100	**1,538**	419	578	541	60.10
2012	**1,853**	867	23	644	319	**1,853**	283	57	1,409	9	95	**1,699**	458	662	579	63.59
2013	**1,705**	804	13	561	327	**1,705**	283	71	1,286	9	56	**1,567**	410	642	515	80.94
2014	**1,695**	782	8	609	296	**1,695**	251	39	1,333	9	63	**1,637**	393	645	599	84.46

Source: Federal Government of Mexico (2015).

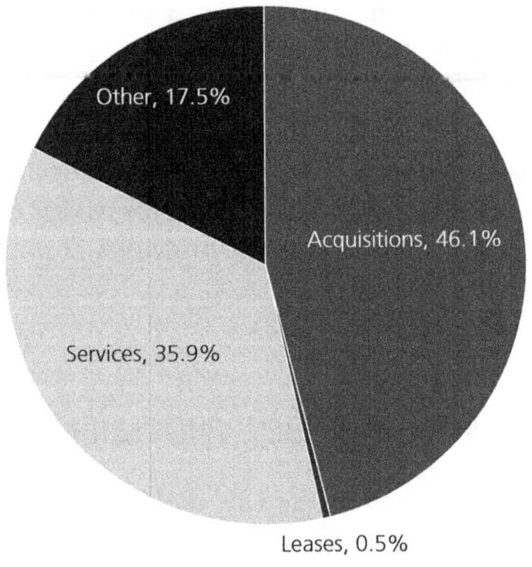

Figure 12.3. Disagreements by type of procurement, 2014

Source: Federal Government of Mexico (2015).

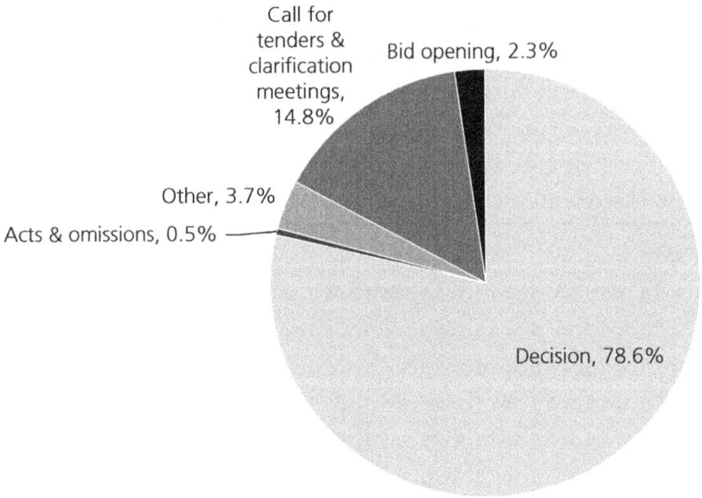

Figure 12.4. Contested decision, 2014

Source: Federal Government of Mexico (2015).

According to the 2014–15 report of the Federal Government of Mexico, the Ministry of Public Administration received 1,695 non-conformities from 1,41,567 contracting procedures carried out in 2014 (Federal Government of Mexico, 2015). Approximately 79 percent of the non-conformities occurred in the decision stage (i.e., the contract award stage). Acquisitions account for the largest share of government procurement, so it is natural that most disagreements (46.1 percent) are concentrated in this type of procurement.

12.3.4 E-PROCUREMENT SYSTEM

The Law on Procurement establishes that all public information regarding government procurement must be available on an electronic procurement system, CompraNet. This tool was developed and is implemented by the Mexican government and has served to further promote and ensure transparency, accountability, and fairness in procurement procedures in the country.

CompraNet sorts, systematizes, and disseminates information on issues relating to the planning, implementation, and results of public procurement. The information collected is provided by federal government purchasing units and by state and local governments (when the latter carry out procurement using CompraNet). When it comes to information about suppliers and contractors, CompraNet shows the data as it has been submitted by them.

The benefits of CompraNet are:

- it systematizes the whole purchasing process;
- the online electronic and automated stages are shorter, less costly, and more transparent;
- it eliminates barriers to participation;
- it eliminates direct and continuous contact between bidders and public purchasers;
- it eliminates discretionary decisions by procurers;
- it makes procurement accountable to society; and
- it contains information accumulated since the 1990s.

CompraNet has five main sections:

1. **Public procurement annual programs.** This section provides estimated total amounts of public purchasing, estimated amounts of purchases from small and medium-sized businesses, and the estimated amounts of purchases not covered by free trade agreements (FTAs) that Mexico has signed. The section also provides planned purchases by government agency, type of business, type of contract, and budget assigned.
2. **Contracting procedures.** This section contains historical data on the amount and number of contracting procedures and whether these were carried out by public tender or by the other two available purchasing mechanisms, as well as data on the nature of the procedure (national or international). The information is classified by

state government, government agency, the number and total amount of public tenders, and by national versus international procedures.

3. **Contracts.** This section discloses the amount and number of contracts, whether they were awarded to micro, small or medium-sized businesses, whether the contracts derived from a process of national or international contracting, and whether they were a procurement contract, leases, or public works contract.
4. **Suppliers and contractors.** This section displays information regarding the suppliers and contractors registered in CompraNet by stratification, nationality, contracts awarded, contracting procedures in which they have participated, and the respective amounts.
5. **Performance indicators of contracting procedures.** There are sixty-six indicators that evaluate different aspects of the procedure, such as the strategies for procurement, analysis of the final outcome, void procedures, number of public tenders compared to other purchasing mechanisms carried out, progress of the contracts in accordance to the program, and time frame analysis.

12.4 **International Legal Framework**

12.4.1 PUBLIC PROCUREMENT IN FTAs

The Law on Public Procurement provides for the opening of public procurement markets to international competition. However, there is still a long way to go in terms of foreign participation in Mexican procurement processes. Article 28 of the Law on Public Procurement establishes that tenders are national in the first instance and that only Mexican nationals may take part in national bids. When the procurement process is declared void, there is no national supplier, or it exceeds certain thresholds specified in a relevant FTA,[5] procurement opportunities are open to international bidders from the signatory countries to the FTA. It is important to highlight that this option is only available after a national tender is declared void. When an international tender subject to an FTA is declared void or, as the law provides, the purchase is funded by an external credit, the tender is open to all international bidders.

Mexico has signed several FTAs that include provisions or chapters on public procurement and which are applicable to federal government entities. The basic principles embodied in FTAs are (1) national treatment and non-discrimination;

[5] The monetary threshold for federal procurement contracts and leases of personal property and services, including those related to public works, by an FTA is approximately US$62,000. Likewise, the threshold for public work contracts is US$8.1 million.

and (2) transparent, effective, and fair procedures. The FTAs signed by Mexico include the following:

- North American Free Trade Agreement (NAFTA)—chapter X
- Free Trade Agreement between Mexico and the State of Israel—chapter VI
- Free Trade Agreement between Mexico and the European Free Trade Association (EFTA)—chapter V
- Economic Partnership, Political Coordination and Cooperation between Mexico and the European Community and its Member States (Mexico—EU)—Title III
- Agreement for the Strengthening of the Economic Partnership between Mexico and Japan—chapter 11
- Free Trade Agreement between Mexico and the Republic of Chile—chapter 15 Bis.

Following the commitments set forth in NAFTA (which served as a basis for subsequent FTAs) on the principles of non-discrimination and national treatment to suppliers of the signatory parties, only federal governments are obligated to provide reciprocal treatment to suppliers under an FTA. In contrast, state and local contracting authorities will accept suppliers from member countries in their procurement processes only if their respective congress so decides.

The above-mentioned FTAs have provisions that allow governments to protect—temporarily or permanently—certain industries that are considered strategic. For instance, NAFTA has a "negative list" of those goods and services that are exempted from the NAFTA procurement provisions. The EU trade agreements, instead, establish a "positive list" that includes goods and services subject to international tenders.

In addition, NAFTA requires purchasing authorities to maintain and adopt a "bid challenge" mechanism in which suppliers are allowed to submit bid challenges concerning any aspect of the procurement processes. The Ministry of Public Administration in Mexico will be responsible for reviewing and making recommendations to resolve such disputes.

Mexico is not a member of the WTO Government Procurement Agreement (GPA). However, provisions on government procurement in the FTAs that Mexico has concluded are closely aligned with the GPA. Mexico has not deemed it necessary to become a member of the GPA because it has signed preferential agreements containing procurement provisions with its major commercial partners. In addition, there are no internal pressures or external requests for Mexico to become part of the GPA.

12.4.2 COMPLIANCE WITH INTERNATIONAL STANDARDS

Mexico is a signatory to the United Nations Convention against Corruption (UNCAC) and, in line with the measures set forth by Article 9 of the UNCAC, the Mexican legal framework for procurement promotes transparency, competition, and criteria for decision-making aiming at preventing corruption in public procurement.

In addition, the Mexican legal framework also complies with the objectives of the United Nations Commission on International Trade Law (UNCITRAL) Model Law. The UNCITRAL Model Law serves as a guiding framework for Mexican authorities to ensure efficiency and transparency in procurement and to promote a pro-competitive procurement framework.

12.5 **Best International Practices**

As mentioned in the Introduction, public procurement is one of the government activities most prone to corruption. Both corruption and collusion distort the functioning of markets. Governments face the risk of corruption and collusion between bidders when trying to obtain the best available conditions for the state. Although these problems are different in nature, their effect is similar when it comes to achieving value for money.

The challenge for the Mexican government is to shield public procurement processes from corruption and collusion through the design and implementation of an institutional and legal framework that ensures that public money is spent ethically, transparently, efficiently, and fairly (see Figure 12.5).

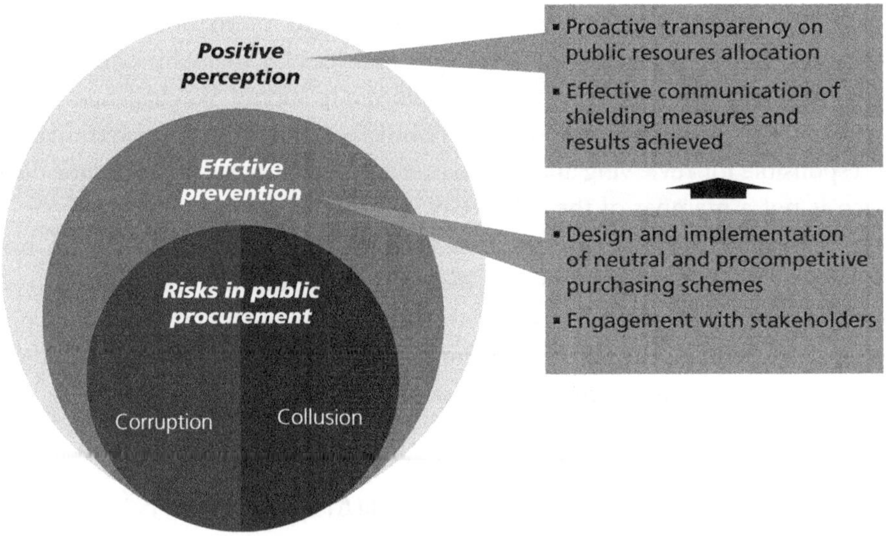

Figure 12.5. Public procurement: Challenges for the Mexican government

Source: The authors.

The Mexican government has taken important steps in this direction, including implementing best international practices developed by the Organization for Economic Cooperation and Development (OECD) on two fronts: integrity and collusion.

12.5.1 INTEGRITY IN PUBLIC PROCUREMENT

Mexican public institutions are working on multiple fronts to promote competition and to combat corruption. The role of the OECD has been instrumental for reviewing, reforming, and implementing sound regulations on public procurement.

The OECD "Recommendation of the Council on Enhancing Integrity in Public Procurement" has served as a benchmark for the Mexican government in conducting public procurement with fairness, transparency, efficiency, and integrity. Following the guiding principles articulated by the OECD, Mexican procurement processes have come closer to best practices in procurement. For instance, in 2012 the OECD, together with the competition authority and the Mexican Institute of Social Security (IMSS),[6] examined the extent to which public procurement regulations in force and IMSS practices were consistent with best practices (OECD, 2012), and areas for improvement were identified.

The recommendations advanced in the report were: removing restrictions to the participation of bidders; promoting a minimum use of exceptions to public tenders; preventing sub-contracting; eliminating mandatory clarification meetings; using remote procurement procedures; introducing a "Certificate of Independent Bid Determination" in addition to the "Integrity Statement"; the overhaul of the IMSS unit for market studies; and strengthening sanctions scheme and training for its procurement staff focused on fighting bid-rigging.

IMSS has built on these efforts by streamlining its procurement processes, working towards a modern, effective, and efficient procurement aligned to world-class standards.

12.5.2 FIGHTING COLLUSION IN PUBLIC PROCUREMENT

In practice, the Mexican procurement legal framework is more focused on achieving transparency and protecting domestic suppliers than on assuring a competitive outcome. In this context, the incentives for collusive agreements or bid-rigging in markets that are highly concentrated are greater, particularly where tenders are restricted to domestic suppliers.

[6] The third largest public purchaser in Mexico and the largest single buyer of pharmaceuticals and medical supplies in Latin America.

For instance, in 2010 the Mexican competition authority found collusive agreements for the supply of two of the largest families of pharmaceutical products—insulin and saline solutions—IMSS. It should be emphasized that the decision of the competition authority was based on sound economic evidence and analysis conducted with information provided by IMSS on the procurement of drugs and medicines. This is a major achievement in prosecuting cartels without direct evidence.

The information provided allowed for the identification of patterns that displayed similar positions and prices in some drugs—indicating collusive behavior between the few suppliers to IMSS. The case was based on collusive bidding patterns, supported by indirect and direct evidence of contact amongst suppliers.

With regard to indirect evidence, applying price and market share screenings, the authority identified medicines for which the lowest bids tended to be identical across auctions regardless of winner, location or contract volume, and for which market shares quickly converged over time. The authority also identified that bids dropped and the above-described pattern disappeared after aggressive entry or when procurement consolidation occurred. These patterns were consistent with the hypothesis of collusion under a dynamic bid-rotation mechanism that requires explicit communication among competitors.

The authority also obtained direct evidence of contact between the firms—both direct and indirect—that supported a finding of concerted action. Direct contact included participation in meetings at the trade association and telephone calls among executives responsible for presenting bids from the involved firms (it was also found that the frequency of such communication increased before major auctions).

In 2010, the authority imposed a fine of US$12.6 million on six pharmaceutical companies for bid-rigging; the decision was upheld in the courts.

The OECD "Guidelines for Fighting Bid Rigging in Public Procurement" are a very useful tool for designing and implementing more competitive procurement processes. The guidelines list the most common strategies for bid-rigging and factors that facilitate collusion between bidders. They also provide two checklists—one on how to design the procurement process to reduce the risk of bid-rigging, and the second on how to detect collusion in public procurement.

In 2011, IMSS committed to adopting and implementing the guidelines with the support of the OECD and the competition authority. The commitments included:

- examining the existing procurement regulation and practices at IMSS and their adherence to the guidelines;
- increasing awareness about bid-rigging among IMSS officials; and
- developing in-house skills to identify and prevent bid-rigging practices.

The adoption of the OECD guidelines by IMSS was a key milestone in Mexico's fight against bid-rigging in public procurement, as it promoted greater competition in the public procurement processes of the most important health institution in Mexico. IMSS calculated that the improvements and efficiencies in its procurement system resulted in savings of approximately US$3.5 billion.

As noted, the Mexican government has undertaken a significant amount of work to enhance procurement processes in the country. Some procurement procedures, however, require further improvement. There is a need for better design and implementation of procurement laws. Doing so will require work on two fronts: (1) fighting bid-rigging and corruption; and (2) promoting reforms to align laws and regulations with best international standards.

These efforts should be carried out jointly by the competition authority, federal and local institutions—in partnership with international organizations such as the OECD—toward achieving the following objectives:

1. raising awareness of the harm to society of corruption and bid-rigging in public procurement;
2. empowering anti-corruption and competition authorities to send a clear signal to the market that engaging in bid-rigging activities and corruption will have a significant cost for the infringers;
3. amending regulations to enhance competitive processes (for instance, allowing greater participation of international bidders in all goods and services, and limiting the use of exceptions to public tenders);
4. reducing the incentives for companies to engage in collusive conducts;
5. reinforcing the capacities of procurement officials to reduce the risk of corruption and increase the detection of bid-rigging; and
6. supporting federal and local public institutions in the adoption of the OECD's guidelines.

12.6 **Conclusions**

The government procurement system in Mexico has the basic elements needed for efficiency and transparency in the procurement decision-making process. Of course, there are always areas that can be improved, for instance, by opening up space for further competition in all stages of the procurement process.

At the local level, a major step would be introducing greater discipline in the decisions of the local and state governments in the procurement process. This could be achieved by progressively aligning their practices and regulations with best practices and international standards.

Another issue worthy of review and consideration to inject additional competition and efficiency into the procurement system is opening up further the process to external operators with which Mexico has not signed preferential agreements. The most efficient way to achieve this could be joining the WTO's Government Procurement Agreement.

REFERENCES

Federal Government of Mexico. 2015. "Tercer Informe de Gobierno 2014–2015".

OECD. 2012. *Public Procurement Review of the Mexican Institute of Social Security. Enhancing Efficiency and Integrity for Better Health Care*. Paris: OECD Publishing.

13 Public Procurement in Brazil

Access for Foreign Suppliers and Compatibility with International Procurement Practices

Cesar Pereira and Rafael Wallbach Schwind

13.1 Introduction

Brazil has a substantial public procurement market. From 2008 through 2013, the Brazilian federal government core agencies' annual expenditure in the procurement of goods and services ranged between US$33.5 billion (2013) and 38 billion (2012).[1] These figures correspond only to purchases made by entities comprised in SISG (a Portuguese acronym for General Services System), a monitoring mechanism that encompasses most civilian federal government agencies. Expenditures made by the Brazilian Ministry of Defense, corporations controlled by the federal government, and all state and local governments are outside SISG and are not covered in such figures.

Arguably, SISG statistics also do not comprise most large-scale infrastructure investments. Federal and local governments pursue infrastructure projects chiefly under concession or public–private partnership (PPP) agreements awarded to private companies. Related purchases and works are therefore not subject to public procurement regulation, but are conducted under purely commercial arrangements. The concessionaires and PPP partners themselves are selected through public tenders.

Finally, another large area of government expenditure not reflected in the SISG statistics is that of procurement by certain government-controlled entities, such as Petrobras (the Brazilian state oil and gas company). They are allowed by statute to adopt distinct systems of procurement rules.[2]

[1] Statistics taken from the July 2014 federal government expenditure report, available at: <http://www.comprasgovernamentais.gov.br/arquivos/estatisticas/01-apresentacao-siasg-dados-gerais-_jan_julho.pdf> (in Portuguese) (accessed July 23, 2016).

[2] At the time of the final revision of this article, no specific act had yet been passed to govern comprehensively procurement by government-controlled entities. Such an act was under discussion and expected soon to be enacted. This enactment may change some of the background discussed here, but any new legislation was then not expected to cause substantial changes in the existing practices for government-controlled entities procurement. In addition, a broad reform of Brazil's public procurement legislation was under discussion at the time of writing, and the Brazilian Senate is expected to pass a bill to that effect by the

Given the current size of Brazil's gross national product (GNP), and regardless of the lower figures from the SISG statistics, an estimate of its public procurement market under international standards amounts to something between $250 and $300 billion.

Still, within the SISG government purchases, two statistics demonstrate the practical relevance of e-procurement and of small and micro-sized enterprise (SME) benefits in the Brazilian government procurement market. In the period January through July 2014, roughly 67 percent of all government purchases were made through *electronic reverse auctions*, in most cases under framework agreements ("indefinite delivery, indefinite quantity," or IDIQ). Approximately 39 percent of the electronic reverse auction market share, or 25 percent of total government purchases, were taken by SMEs under various beneficial arrangements.[3] This corresponded to an increase of 15 percent in the SME market share between 2013 and 2014.

On the other hand, although relevant and controversial in legal theory, the local production benefits ("Buy national" or "Buy Brazilian" benefits) enacted in 2010 and in the following years have not yet resulted in a significant change in the general market. In 2012, only a little over $1 billion in goods were purchased using domestic preferences.[4] This amount corresponds to approximately 2.6 percent of the total purchases in that fiscal year. However, in specific sectors such as oil and gas, the requirement of so-called "local content" for procurement is considered to have had a strong effect in terms of market allocation.[5] Offset obligations have also played an important role, especially in the defense market, as explained below.

The size of the Brazilian public procurement market makes it impossible for the international business community to ignore it.[6] At the same time, Brazil is relatively isolated in terms of internationalization—or lack thereof—of its procurement practices and its refusal to effectively engage in multilateral or bilateral trade agreements.

This chapter focuses on the general features of the Brazilian public procurement regulation and on the current status and future perspectives for its internationalization. The purposes of this analysis is to allow conclusions on four issues: (1) the level of market access given to foreign bidders; (2) the applicability of international

end of 2016. this reform is expected to maintain the basic principles of the current legislation. If passed by the Senate in 2016 and subsequently passed by the House of Representatives, it could be enacted as the new Brazilian public procurement act as early as 2017.

[3] Specific statistics concerning SMEs are available at: <http://www.comprasgovernamentais.gov.br/arquivos/estatisticas/02-informativo-comprasnet-mpe-jan-a-julho.pdf > (in Portuguese) (accessed July 23, 2016).

[4] See the presentation by federal government officials of December 2013 available at: <http://portalapl.ibict.br/export/sites/apl/galerias/6CBAPL/apresentacoes/dia-5-sala-4-Mini_Curso_Oficina_MARGENS_PREFERxNCIA_Julio_Cardoso.pdf> (in Portuguese) (accessed July 23, 2016).

[5] For a discussion about local content in the oil and gas sector, see Prochnik (2011).

[6] A thorough analysis of reasons for international attention to Brazilian public procurement is made by Arrieta (2014: pp. 161–5).

government procurement rules and practices; (3) submission to international conventions and agreements on government procurement; and (4) the level of harmonization between Brazilian domestic government procurement laws and international models.

As much as possible, this chapter also deals with the effects of the current level of internationalization of Brazilian public procurement, especially regarding offset agreements.

13.2 **Legal Framework**

In contrast to the United States and the European Union, the Brazilian government procurement legal framework is based almost entirely on statutes, not regulations. It is also not under any community directive. A government purchases protocol was signed in 2006 in the context of Mercosul, but has not yet been ratified. As a result, Brazil has been relatively free to create its own procurement system to fit its domestic needs. Little attention has been given to international harmonization or to any concerns of making the procurement system more attractive to foreign bidders in practice.

Brazil is a federation of twenty-six states, one federal district (Brasilia) and in excess of 5,000 municipalities, all of which have legislatures entitled to pass laws on public procurement and executive branches that can engage in public procurement. Nonetheless, due to certain distinct features of the Brazilian federation, almost all government procurement legislation is federal, not local. The country's system of government procurement is based on a combination of a series of federal statutes:

- Law no. 8.666, of 1993, is the general government procurement law. It evolved from the classical procurement methodology developed in Brazil since the 1950s, and especially from the more modern procurement laws of 1967 and 1986. It governs the basic procedural framework, competitive sealed bidding, and the cases for single-source or non-competitive awards. It also governs contract administration, including performance, changes, and termination. General contracts law only applies as a source for general principles, since Law 8.666 contains a comprehensive system of rules governing contracts entered into by government entities or departments.
- Law no. 10.520, of 2002, created the reverse auction and allowed for the creation, by regulation, of the electronic reverse auction rules.
- Law no. 12.232, of 2010, governs procurement of public relations and advertisement services.
- Law no. 12.349, of 2010, created benefits for domestic production and technology in public procurement in Brazil. Certain advantages granted to Brazilian-owned

companies by the 1988 Constitution were repealed in the mid-1990s in favor of equal treatment of foreign and domestic bidders. Some of them were re-enacted in 2010.

- Law no. 12.462, of 2011, created the Differential Procurement Regime (RDC). This is a system of rules designed to expedite procurement for works for the 2014 FIFA World Cup and the 2016 Rio Olympics. It was based on propositions made by the Federal Court of Audit (TCU), an agency with similar powers and attributions to the US Government Accountability Office (GAO). Unlike Law no. 8.666, it created a flexible, adaptable procedure which attributes higher risk to the private contractor and, at the same time, makes it easier on the government procuring agency to carry out the bidding procedure. Originally applicable only to the contracts mentioned above, it was later extended to all contracts comprised in the federal government's Growth Acceleration Program (PAC). This extension was first suggested in the Presidential Provisional Measure (PPM) no. 559/2012, which became a bill on June 27, 2012 after being approved at the Senate (Projeto de Lei de Conversão no. 13/2012). The bill was sanctioned by the President of the Republic and became Law no. 12.688/2012. This extension meant in practice that the most important federal government works and projects became subject to the RDC procedure. As pointed out below, the adoption of the RDC procedure is not mandatory, since the procuring agency may in any case opt to apply the general regulation of Law no. 8.666 or Law no. 10.520.[7]
- Law no. 12.598, of 2012, created specific procurement rules for the defense sector, including certain specific types of contracts and protectionist measures designed to generally safeguard the domestic marketplace from foreign suppliers. On the other hand, it favors joint ventures and partnerships of foreign suppliers with domestic partners for local production.
- Law no. 8.987, of 1995, is the general law for public service concessions. It includes a chapter on public procurement for granting the concession, with specific tender evaluation criteria.
- Law no. 11.079, of 2004, is the general PPP law. A PPP under Brazilian law is a concession in which part or all of the concessionaire's financial compensation is paid directly by the government. The selection of a private partner in a PPP requires public bidding, and this law provides for the relevant procedure as well as guidelines on qualification and proposal evaluation criteria.

In addition to such federal statutes, there can be regulations issued by Presidential Executive Orders and relevant case law arising from federal or states courts of audits rulings. The laws are generally detailed and comprehensive, and not much is left to regulation. However, some important exceptions exist. Electronic reverse auction (the

[7] A comprehensive analysis of the RDC can be found in Justen Filho and Pereira (2014).

most important procurement method in Brazil in the 2013/2014 statistics) and framework agreements ("price registration," in the Brazilian law terminology) are governed almost entirely by regulation, based on broad statutory terms.

13.3 **Constitutional Basis**

A distinct feature of the Brazilian procurement system is that it is rooted in the Constitution. Public bidding as a method of selection of contractors is a constitutional requirement. Article 22, XXVII, attributes to the federal Legislature the power to enact general laws applicable to all "methods of bidding and contracting for governmental entities, autonomous government agencies and foundations of the Union, the States, the Federal District, and the Municipalities, in accordance with Article 37, XXI, and, for government-owned corporations and mixed capital companies, pursuant to Article 173, para. 1, III."

General laws enacted by federal legislature are binding on all levels of government. State and local legislatures are allowed to supplement the federal general laws, but not to enact a repeal of legislation or derogate from them. However, some states have enacted their own procurement laws with innovations not provided for in federal law, and the courts have generally upheld such innovations as lawful.

The coverage of the federal general law extends to all forms and levels of government. Its scope of application comprises the so-called "direct administration"—which corresponds to the government departments directly linked to the political entities of the federal, state, and municipal administrations—and the "indirect administration"—which comprises the autonomous government agencies, foundations, government-owned corporations (in which the government holds 100 percent of the shares), mixed-capital companies (in which the government has a controlling stake), the public consortia, and all possible forms of government-controlled entities.

However, the constitutional framework for procurement in government-owned corporations and mixed-capital companies is distinct. Such companies may be tools for the government to compete in the market with other, purely private companies. In that case, public procurement rules must adjust and provide for more flexible procedures. With a few renowned exceptions (Petrobras is the most important, but not the only one), government companies still do not have distinct procurement legislation and are subject to the general laws enacted pursuant to Article 22, XXVII, of the Constitution.[8] However, their transactions are not subject to public procurement when

[8] This was the situation at the time of closing of this article, but new legislation governing procurement by government-controlled entities might be enacted and cause changes to these conclusions and information.

they are freely competing in the market, such as Petrobras selling gas or buying oil under market conditions.

The contents of the general public procurement laws are guided by Article 37, XXI, of the Constitution. Many of the rules subsequently included in the relevant statutes, listed above, stem directly from such constitutional provision, which states as follows:

> Article 37. The direct and indirect public administration of any of the powers of the Union, the states, the Federal District and the Municipalities shall obey the principles of legality, impersonality, morality, publicity and efficiency, and also the following:
>
> XXI—with the exception of the cases specified by law, public works, services, purchases and sales shall be contracted by means of a public bidding procedure that ensures equal conditions to all bidders, with clauses that establish payment obligations, maintaining the actual conditions of the bid, pursuant to the law, which procedure shall only allow the requirements of technical and economic qualifications that are indispensable to guarantee the performance of the obligations.

Article 37 of the Constitution contains what could be dubbed an administrative code for all levels of government in Brazil. In addition to establishing the principles for government conduct and the rules for numerous other aspects of government, the rule sets forth the general outline of the public procurement system:

a. The requirement of a public bidding is the general rule; it may be waived only in the cases specified by law.
b. Public bidding procedures must ensure equal access for all bidders. This principle requires clear and publicized rules in the solicitation, which are binding on the procuring agency and the bidders.
c. The provision regarding *the actual conditions of the bid* is the basis for the protection of the economic and financial equilibrium of the contract, which is the single most important protection for contractors in Brazil in the contract administration phase (from signature to termination, including changes). It gives constitutional status to the contractual allocation of risks. Any supervening change that alters the "actual conditions of the bid" (i.e., that is outside the risks assumed by the contractor, such as formal or constructive change orders) entitles the affected party to compensation.
d. The qualification requirements (technical and economic aspects) must be as unrestrictive as possible. The wording of the Constitution is *indispensable to guaranteeing the performance of the obligations*. If the requirements go beyond, they may pose an undue restriction to the participation of possible bidders, and may be invalid. This provision also serves as a guideline in the interpretation of legal rules and solicitation requirements.

Government-owned corporations and mixed-capital companies that engage in economic activities in the marketplace may be subject to a specific procurement law (Article 173 of the Constitution). Since no such specific law has been enacted, general laws apply to them as well. However, there are two caveats.

First, specific statutes grant the executive branch the power to create by executive order procurement rules for certain government companies, namely Petrobras,[9] Eletrobras,[10] and Empresa Brasil de Comunicação (EBC),[11] in accordance with broad principles provided for in the statutes.[12] This matter is often subject to dispute, since such specific regulation is said to depart from certain essential principles of the general bidding regulation, and is frequently brought to the courts. The Brazilian Supreme Court has numerous appeals pending resolution on this matter. A final decision is expected on the validity of this possible delegation of legislative powers and of separate procurement regulations for certain entities.

Second, when a government company participates in a competitive commercial market, the formalities of public procurement are waived in order to allow the company to effectively pursue its business goals. Therefore, transactions such as the purchase and sale of natural gas by a state-owned natural gas distributor are not subject to public procurement laws (see Pereira, 2013).

This chapter focuses mostly on the tendering phase of Brazilian government procurement. However, it must be noted that many practical difficulties relate to the contract administration phase, especially to provisions allowing the government to unilaterally change or terminate the contract due to reasons of public interest. This contractual instability has, in practice, resulted in increased prices and reduced value for money in Brazilian government purchases.

13.4 **Auditing Bodies: The Importance of TCU**

A peculiar feature of the Brazilian public procurement regulation is the importance placed on the audit bodies rulings. In particular, the Federal Court of Accounts (Tribunal de Contas da União, or TCU) examines in great depth the application of the public procurement regulation with regard to expenditure of federal funds.

The review of procurement action by the Courts of Accounts takes place in auditing procedures, as well as in adversarial procedurals commenced by interested parties. Any citizen has the legal standing to submit to the competent Court of Accounts a complaint concerning compliance with public procurement regulation (Article 113, para. 1, Law no.

[9] Law no. 9.478 and Executive Order no. 2.745.

[10] Law no. 3.890-A, of 1961, as amended by Law no. 11.943, of 2009. No executive order has been issued yet, so Eletrobras does not apply this separate procurement system.

[11] Law no. 11.652, of 2008, and Executive Order no. 6.505, of 2008.

[12] This was the situation at the time of closing of this article, but new legislation governing procurement by government-controlled entities might be enacted and cause changes to these conclusions and information.

8.666). The Courts of Accounts are also available to provide consultation by request of certain high-ranking authorities. The rulings of the Courts of Accounts, particularly the TCU, form an important set of guidelines on the application of public procurement regulation.

13.5 **Coverage**

The general rules of Law no. 8.666 apply to all levels of government. Within the states and municipalities, they apply as general rules and admit additional local rules, provided that these do not contradict the federal general rules.

They also apply to the government-owned corporations and mixed-capital companies mentioned in Article 173, para. 1, item III, of the Constitution due to the omission in the enactment of the specific regulation for such entities, with the two caveats described in Section 13.3 of this chapter.

An interesting case is that of the quasi-governmental entities known as *serviços sociais autônomos* (autonomous social services). These entities are linked to the private sector and are generally involved in welfare and education within a certain economic field (commerce, industry), but they are maintained with revenue from taxation, namely, a charge attached to certain social security taxes. Therefore, they are required to carry out public biddings but pursuant to their own rules, not to the general law.

13.6 **Principles and Purposes**

The original wording of Article 3 of Law no. 8.666 reproduced a traditional notion in Brazilian public procurement law and stated that the purposes of the public bidding were to simultaneously obtain the best offer for the government and ensure equality among bidders as possible contractors or suppliers.

Law no. 12.349, originated from Presidential Provisional Measure (PPM) no. 495, originally issued in July 2010, added a third purpose: the advancement of national development. Therefore, according to the statutory language, a bidding procedure in Brazil has now the pursuit of sustainable national development as one of its purposes. In more precise terms, the purposes of the bidding procedure remain the same: to ensure equal access to government contracting, and to select the most advantageous bid. What Law no. 12.349 created was a new purpose for the future contract whose contractor the public tender aims to select. As the future contract may be used as a means to advance sustainable national development, the corresponding bidding procedure may contain the stipulation of advantages in favor of suppliers who are able to contribute to such sustainable national development. These advantages are not to be granted arbitrarily, but must be reasonable and clearly provided for in the solicitation. Law no. 12.349 contains some specifications, and more detailed regulation is given by Decree no. 7.546.[13] Specific decrees have been issued from time to time stipulating margins of preference that may be granted to products and services in various sectors.

Decree no. 7.767, of June 2012, for example, establishes margins of preference—varying from 8 to 25 percent—in favor of nationally manufactured pharmaceutical and medical products. Decree no. 7.756, also of June 2012, stipulated margins of preference of 20 percent for the federal biddings in relation to acquiring clothing, footwear, and apparel manufactured in Brazil. Another example is Decree no. 7.709, of April 2012, which allowed margins of preference varying between 10 and 18 percent for the acquisition of backhoes and bulldozers.

Article 3 of Law no. 8.666, as amended by Law no. 12.349, reads as follows:

> Article 3. The purposes of the bidding process are to ensure compliance with the constitutional principle of equality and to select the bid that is the most advantageous for the Administration and advance the sustainable national development, and shall be processed and decided in strict accordance with the basic principles of legality, of impersonality, of morality, of equality, of publicity, of administrative probity, of the binding force of the solicitation, of the objective evaluation of bids and related principles.
>
> The principle of legality means that all government action must be based on a legislated statute. The meaning of this principle goes beyond the idea of mere adherence to the texts of law. The government is expected to comply with the law as a whole, comprising especially the Constitution. No government action is allowed in the absence of an authorization by law. Depending on the subject matter, such authorization must be more or less explicit.

The principle of impersonality provides that the mere person of the bidder must be irrelevant or neutral to the procuring agency. Of course, the person of the bidder (as a reference of his capacity and aptitude to perform the contract) will be examined, but the bidder may not be granted or denied the contract based merely on his personal traits and without connection with the contract.

The principle of morality has growing importance in Brazil, since it is expressly listed in Article 37 of the Constitution as a founding principle of the Brazilian government. It requires honesty and integrity, as well as loyalty from the government and its officers. The violation of morality is a defect in itself and is able to cause the government action to become void.

The principle of equality (equal access and treatment) forbids unfounded discrimination. Any public procurement procedure involves a choice between several prospective suppliers or contractors. Therefore, it always involves discrimination. The key aspect is

[13] The effects of Law no. 12.349 with regard to the purposes of public bidding procedures are examined in Justen Filho (2014 and 2015), both available in Portuguese.

that the factor taken into account for the discrimination must not be arbitrary, capricious, or unreasonable. As a general rule, domestic and international bidders had equal treatment under Brazilian bidding law. The introduction of the advancement of sustainable national development as a purpose of the contracts, and as a factor to consider in the bidding, will allow the government to legitimately grant certain advantages to bidders with activities in Brazil, within the parameters of Law no. 12.349.

Publicity requires transparency: it entails that all aspects of the bidding should be public, with the exception of matters relating to certain sensitive areas, such as defense. This principle is reflected in rules such as Article 7, para. 8, and Article 63 of Law no. 8.666.

The idea of "administrative probity" (honesty) is related to Article 37, para. 4, of the Constitution. Cases of fraud and breach of honesty duties are subject to harsh civil prosecution and sanctions pursuant to Law no. 8.429/1992 (the Administrative Improbity Act) and Law no. 12.846/2013 (the Brazilian Anti-Bribery Act). As a principle, administrative probity is one of the aspects of the principle of morality.

The binding force of the solicitation is a specific public procurement principle, reflected in Article 41 of Law no. 8.666. The procuring agency uses its discretion to define the conditions for the contract to be awarded and prepares the solicitation according to such definitions. After the solicitation is made and advertised, it becomes binding on the bidders and the procuring agency, and no further discretion is allowed to the procuring agency. Any change, except if merely clerical, must be followed by new advertising and a postponement of the bidding deadlines. This idea of "binding force" originally led to a formalistic view of the bidding procedure, in which bidders could be disqualified and bids rejected for minor discrepancies. A famous Superior Tribunal de Justiça (STJ) ruling in 1998 (MS no. 5.418/DF) was the starting point for a change in this understanding, and now the standard view in Brazilian public procurement regulation is that minor discrepancies, clerical mistakes, and failures that do not affect the offer may be corrected and should not lead to disqualification or rejection. Certain statutes, such as Law no. 10.520 (reverse auction), Law no. 11.079 (PPP) and Law no. 12.462 (RDC) already expressly provide for the fixing of defects in bidding procedures.

The objective evaluation of bids is a central principle of the Brazilian bidding regulation. It means that the criteria for qualification of bidders and for the evaluation (judgment) of bids must be clear, free from subjective interpretation, and focused on the object to be procured, not on the persons involved. Many rules in Law no. 8.666 relate to this principle. At several points, Law no. 8.666 requires mathematical certainty—for example, Article 31, para. 5, requires that the financial standing of the bidder be evaluated according to economic indexes previously provided for in the solicitation. This premise creates difficulty in certain areas where a subjective judgment is almost inevitable. Law no. 8.666 tries to avoid some of these problems by providing for the method of "contest" as a form to procure technical, artistic, or intellectual specialized work based on an evaluation made (with some subjectivity) by a panel of specialists. Law no. 12.232/2010 has addressed another field of great controversy, consisting of the government advertisement contracts. It is generally difficult to evaluate offers for advertisements (strongly based on creativity and trust) with strictly objective criteria.

13.7 **Methods, Thresholds, and Transparency**

Law no. 8.666 provides for five methods of bidding: sealed competitive bidding (*concorrência*), request for prices (*tomada de preços*), invitation (*convite*), contest (*concurso*), and auction (*leilão*). Law no. 10.520 adds reverse auction (*pregão*) to this list, and its regulation creates the electronic version of reverse auction. As mentioned in Section 13.2, Laws no. 8.987 and no. 11.079 provide for a combination of sealed competitive bidding, auction, and reverse auction that is applicable only to the award of concessions and PPP. Law no. 12.462 creates the RDC, which consists of an entirely different procedure, preferably electronic and assembled by the procuring agency for each case based on general guidelines provided by the RDC legislation. Within the RDC sphere of application, a procuring agency may opt to use RDC or one of the standard methods of procurement.

For tenders carried out under Law no. 8.666, Article 22, para. 8, forbids the procuring agency from combining the methods provided for in Law no. 8.666 or creating additional methods; it must observe one of the typical procedures. The choice of specific method is based on the value of the contract to be awarded and on its subject matter.

A sealed competitive bidding is required for the sale of real property (Article 17, I, with the possible exception of Article 19), international bidding procedures (Article 42), for construction works and engineering services above the threshold of R$1.5 million (Article 23, I, "c"),[14] and for other purchases and services above the threshold of R$650,000 (Article 23, II, "c").

It is important to point out that, after the introduction of the reverse auction, sealed competitive bidding is no longer the mandatory method for all purchases and services above such thresholds. The reverse auction may be used only for the purchase and hiring of so-called "ordinary" goods and services. Provided that the object of the contract falls into this category, there is no maximum value for the contract. Therefore, purchases and services above the threshold for sealed competitive bidding may also be made or hired through a reverse auction when applicable.

Since it is a more complete procedure and is open to all possible bidders, sealed competitive bidding can be used in lieu of any other method.

[14] At the time of the final revision of this chapter, the exchange rate was roughly 4.00 Brazilian reais (R$) to one US dollar.

A request for prices is applicable to construction works and engineering services between R$150,000 and R$1,500,000, and to purchases and services in general between R$80,000 and R$650,000. The invitation is the simplest method and is applicable to contracts below the minimum thresholds for the request for prices. As pointed out with regard to sealed competitive bidding, the request for prices can also be used in lieu of the invitation regardless of the amount of the contract.

Article 23, para. 4, expressly forbids that a certain work or service be divided into portions in order to be procured under a simpler method. All contracts that correspond to one single object must be considered together (i.e., consolidated) for the purpose of method selection. However, Article 23, para. 7, admits that whenever possible, bidders submit a bid for a quantity that is smaller than the total quantity to be procured. This is a form of balancing the requirement of procurement for the whole of the intended contract, not for separable parts. Most purchases are also made under framework agreements (IDIQ), governed by Article 15 of Law 8.666 and related regulation. Such agreements may be tendered through reverse auctions or competitive bidding.

In addition to a decreasing complexity in the procedure, the main difference between sealed competitive bidding, a request for prices, and an invitation relates to eligibility. Competitive bidding is open to any bidder who is able to submit, on the scheduled date, the documentation requested for qualification (Article 22, para. 1). A request for prices is open only to bidders who have been previously enrolled at the supplier's registration provided for by Articles 34 through 37 of Law no. 8.666, or to those who have complied with all requirements for such enrollment by the third day before the date for submission of bids (Article 22, para. 2). An invitation is directed to any supplier—previously enrolled or not, and one of a minimum number of three—but also permits the participation of any enrolled supplier that gives notice of its interest in participating by twenty-four hours before the time scheduled for submission of bids.

The methods of contest and auction are selected not based on the amount involved, but on their subject matter.

An auction is appropriate for the sale of movable things belonging to the government, as well as of apprehended goods and of real property under Article 19. The value of the sale is irrelevant for the choice of this method.

A contest is used for the selection of a technical, artistic, or scientific work, by means of the award of prizes or remuneration to the winners. The specific purpose of the contest is to allow for the use of a panel of specialists for the examination of the proposals. Since the examination of works of this nature always involves some subjectivity, a panel of recognized specialists guarantees the fairness of the examination.

The advertisement requirements vary according to each method. A notice containing a summary of the invitation for bids must be published in the official press (*Federal*

Official Gazette or *State Official Gazette*) and in a regular newspaper (Article 21). The law provides for a minimum delay between the last publication of the notice and the date for submission of bids or proposals. This minimum delay is forty-five days for contests and more complex sealed competitive biddings, thirty days for simpler sealed competitive biddings and more complex requests for prices, fifteen days for all other requests for prices and auctions, and five days for invitations.

13.8 **Single-Source Procurement: Direct Award**

As allowed by Article 37, XXI, of the Constitution, Brazilian law provides for several cases of direct award, in which a contract is entered into without prior bidding. Such form of procurement is regulated by Articles 24 through 26 of Law no. 8.666, as well as by some provisions of Article 17.

There are two basic categories of direct award: waiver (*dispensa*) and non-requirement (*inexigibilidade*) of public tender. This terminology is rather arbitrary, but the actual difference between the two situations is relevant. In the case of waiver, the bidding procedure is possible but it is legally considered inconvenient because of time constraints, costs, confidentiality, or another aspect. In the case of non-requirement, the bidding procedure is unviable because a competition would be incompatible with the nature of the governmental need. An emergency purchase is a case of waiver—the bidding is possible, but it is inconvenient due to time limitations. A purchase from an exclusive supplier (sole source) is a case of non-requirement, because there is no possibility of competition.

The practical difference is that cases of waiver are explicitly provided for in Articles 17 and 24. The latter offers a list of (thirty-three, as of 2014) cases of direct award, ranging from small purchases to emergency works and defense contracts. A direct award based on waiver of bidding will only be possible if the situation falls into one of the cases listed in such provisions.

On the other hand, cases of non-requirement are based on a general clause stating that the bidding is not required when the competition is unviable (Article 25). The listed cases (single supplier, services from manifestly specialized professionals, artists) are simply examples.

As indicated above, direct award is still a method of procurement, and a procedure for this method is set forth in Article 26. The procuring agency is required to justify the existence of the situation of waiver or non-requirement of bidding, to state the reasons for the selection of a certain supplier or contractor, and to demonstrate the justification for the price agreed upon.

The pursuit of direct award procurement in cases not provided for by law is a criminal offense punishable according to Article 89 of Law no. 8.666.

13.9 Types of Bidding: Evaluation Criteria

In addition to different methods of procurement, often referred to as "modalities" in Brazilian public procurement legislation, Law no. 8.666 defines the admissible evaluation criteria, usually referred to as "types" of procurement.

Four types are mentioned in Article 45, para. 1, of Law no. 8.666: lowest price, best technique, technique and price, and highest bid or offer. "Lowest price" is the most common type of bidding for procurement in general.

When technical aspects are involved, the procuring agency can opt for "technique and price" bidding, in which it awards relative grades for the technical and the price proposals. A weighted average (e.g., 70 percent for technique and 30 percent for price) is calculated and the bids are ranked according to their final grades.

Another option is the purely "best technique" type of procurement. This is a very uncommon type in practice, due to its complexity and relative ineffectiveness. In this case, the bids are ranked according to their technical evaluation. However, after this ranking, the procuring agency must negotiate with the highest ranked bidder in order to reduce its price to the amount of the lowest offered price. If this price reduction is not achieved, it will negotiate with the second highest ranked bidder, and so on until an agreement is reached.

The highest bid or offer is appropriate for auctions or for other biddings in which the government agency is the seller, such as sealed competitive biddings for the sale of real property.

Article 45, para. 5, forbids the use of other types of bidding not expressly provided for in Law no. 8.666. However, other statutes relating to reverse auction, concessions, and PPP adopt other evaluation criteria. Law no. 12.462, which provides for the RDC procurement rules, has also created additional criteria and changed the existing ones for those specific biddings.

13.10 Standard Procedure: Sealed Competitive Bidding

The standard bidding procedure is that of sealed competitive bidding.

It starts with studies and assessments prior to the preparation of the solicitation. In this so-called "internal phase," all discretionary choices must be made that will reflect on the contents of the bidding documents.

After the preparation of the solicitation (invitation for bids) by a panel of government officers (a styled bidding committee, or *comissão de licitação*), a notice with the summary must be published (as indicated in Section 13.7) and a certain delay must occur between the publication and the date of submission of bids. If any changes are made to the invitation for bids after the publication, it must be fully advertised and the delay will be restored (Article 21).

Within a certain time (two to five days, depending on the case), counting backwards from the date for submission of bids, any prospective bidder or citizen in general may challenge the invitation for bids and request changes (Article 41). If this challenge is granted, Article 21, para. 4, may become applicable and the restoration of the original delay will be obligatory.

At the date scheduled in the invitation for bids, the procuring agency will receive sealed envelopes with qualification documents and bids, which may be divided into technical proposals in one envelope and bids in another. The envelopes with the qualification documents will be opened, the documents examined, and the non-responsive bidders disqualified.

An appeal phase will follow, unless all bidders waive their right to appeal.

After the appeals are finally resolved, the bidders will be summoned for a public session in which the sealed bids will be opened. The non-responsive bids will be rejected and the others will be ranked according to the type of bidding. Appeals are admissible against acceptance, rejection, or the ranking of bids.

Once the final ranking is reached, the bidding procedure will be submitted by the committee for review by a higher administrative authority. This review may result in the annulment of the bidding if a defect is found, in the revocation of the bidding if the procured object is no longer needed, or in the award of the contract to the winner.

The final phase is that of summoning of the winner (the "awardee," or *adjudicatário*) for execution of the contract.

13.11 **Qualification Phase**

Articles 27 through 31 of Law no. 8.666 govern the qualification phase. The bidder's past performance and present situation are examined with regard to its legal regular standing, technical qualification, economic and financial qualification, and regular fiscal situation, as well as to certain specific labor requirements.[15]

The qualification phase is based on documentary evidence, but additional investigation is admitted pursuant to Article 43, para. 3. As mentioned in Section 13.6, there is a

[15] In addition to some requirements existing since 1999 concerning compliance with the prohibition of underage workers, bidders are required to prove their good standing with regard to the rights of their work force. Law no. 12.440, enacted in July 2011 to enter into force six months later, changed item IV of Art. 27 of Law no. 8.666 to provide for "IV—fiscal and labor good standing." It also included item V of Art. 29 with the following language: "V—proof of the inexistence of unpaid debts before the Labor Court, by means of submission of a clearance certificate, in the terms of Title VII-A of the Consolidation of the Labor Laws approved by the Decree-Law no. 5.542 of May 1st 1943."

growing tendency to permit the fixing of minor defects in the qualification documents, or even in the bids. However, the language of Article 43, para. 3, forbids the bidder from submitting any additional documentation that should have been submitted with the bids. This is often a source of dispute.

The basic principle of the qualification phase is the prohibition of excessive requirements that may hinder competition and cause the early rejection of a bidder. However, it is not uncommon for bidders to be excluded on the basis of minor non-compliances. In such cases, both the courts and the auditing bodies usually recognize the right of the bidder to be reinstated and take part in the subsequent phases of the bidding.

The requirements for economic and financial qualification are based on the examination of the last due financial statements and, if required, the submission of a bid bond. The examination must be pursued according to previously defined criteria and formulae. No subjective judgment is admissible.

There are complex procedures for technical qualification, many of them based on the peculiar Brazilian practice in construction contracts. The bidder is required to submit evidence of being registered with its respective professional supervision entity. Its past experience must be proven by means of certificates issued by its past employers and also registered by the respective professional entity (if any exists).

Technical qualification is examined under two aspects: professional capability and operational (or organizational) capability. Both are based on the submission of prior certificates describing past works.

Professional capability refers to the skills of technical personnel. The invitation to bid is forbidden from requiring a description of past works with minimum quantities; it may only require the bidder to produce evidence that its personnel have experience in the relevant activities. With regard to the operational capability—which relates to the bidder as a company, not to its personnel—minimum quantities are admissible.

There are many disputes concerning technical requirements as hindrances to competition. The courts and auditing bodies (TCU) generally accept as valid the requirements of minimum quantities with regard to technical items that (i) are technically and economically relevant to the future performance of the contract; and (ii) do not exceed a reasonable portion of what is to be performed in the contract (there is no fixed threshold for this portion, but quantities higher than 50 percent of the future undertaking are generally considered excessive).

The fiscal good standing requirement aims at showing that the bidder is in a regular situation and apt for the contract. The taxes relevant to this examination are those relating to the contract to be performed.

With regard to legal regular standing, this encompasses proof of the regular formation of the company submitting the bid. International bidders are admitted in domestic biddings, but they are required to produce evidence of being authorized to operate in Brazil (Article 28, IV, Law no. 8.666).

13.12 Evaluation (Judgment) Phase

The evaluation of the bids must be conducted in accordance with the criteria previously set forth in the solicitation. Article 44, para. 1, expressly forbids the use of any element, criteria, or factor that may be secret, confidential, subjective, or classified and that may directly or indirectly hinder the equality between bidders and the competition.

Naturally, there may be items that need to be procured under classified procedures, but that is a field for direct award under one of the cases provided for in Article 24 (for example, item IX deals with defense purchases, subject to secret or confidential procedures). However, in the absence of a justification for direct award, the bidding procedure must be transparent.

The bids will be judged on their responsiveness to the invitation for bids. The committee will examine the offered object as well as the price. The solicitation may not require products of a specific brand, except with due justification for standardization purposes (Article 7, para. 5, and Article 15, para. 7, I). It also may not require as part of the offer that the bidder arranges funding for the contract (Article 7, para. 3). The requirement of samples is admissible provided that it is as part of the judgment of the bids, not in the qualification phase.

The solicitation must set forth the criteria for admissibility of global and unit prices. According to paras. 2 through 4 of Article 44, the bid will be rejected if it contains global or unit prices that are inconsistent. The language of the provision reads as follows:

> para.2 The procuring agency shall disregard any offer of advantage not provided for in the invitation for bids or in the invitation, including subsidized or no-cost funding, or any price or advantage based on the offers of the other bidders.
>
> para.3 The procuring agency shall not admit a bid that presents global or unit prices that are symbolic, negligible or of zero value, incompatible with the market prices of inputs and salaries, increased of the respective charges, even though the solicitation has set no minimum limits, except when they refer to materials and facilities that belong to the bidder and with regard to which it waives all or part of the remuneration.
>
> para.4 The provision of the preceding paragraph applies also to the bids that include foreign labor or imports of any kind.

Although it is evidently not frequent, the law contains provisions for breaking a possible tie between bidders. The first criteria are those set forth in Article 3, para. 2, as amended by Law no. 12.349. Preference in case of a tie will be given to products (i) made in Brazil; (ii) made or provided by Brazilian companies; or (iii) made or provided by companies that invest in research and technology development in Brazil, in this order. If that does not solve the tie, there will be drawing of lots (Article 45, para. 2).

Article 48 provides for estimated criteria for the evaluation of the unfeasibility of prices that are significantly lower than those of the other bidders and of the procuring agency's own expectations. Such criteria are not absolute, and the bidder is allowed to produce evidence of its capability of performing the contract at the low price contained in its offer. If such evidence is insufficient, unfeasibility is a valid ground for rejection of the bid.

If all bids are rejected, a new time period of eight days may be granted by the committee for the submission of amended bids (Article 48, para. 3). This applies also to the situation in which all bidders are disqualified in the qualification phase.

13.13 Award and Execution of the Contract

The award of the contract is made after the government authority that is superior to the committee has ratified the proceedings and considers that there is still a need for the contract at hand.

The award confers upon the winning bidder (the "awardee") the right to enter into the contract with the procuring agency with precedence over any third party (Article 50). Many specialists understand that this provision does not give the awardee the right to force the agency to enter into the contract (or to compensate the awardee for not doing so), but only the right to have its rank in the bidding duly respected if the agency decides to enter into the contract. This view is coming under growing criticism (e.g., Justen Filho, 2014).

According to Article 43, para. 6, after the qualification phase the bidder may not withdraw its bid. Therefore, the winning bidder has the obligation to execute the contract when summoned pursuant to Article 64. Failure to execute the contract will result in the application of penalties and the loss of the bid bond possibly presented at the outset of the procedure.

13.14 Fraud and Penalties

Articles 81 through 88 address the issue of fraudulent activities with regard to the bidding procedures. Penalties may be applied after an adversarial procedure in which the right to full defense must be ensured. As provided for in Article 87, penalties comprise warnings, fines, suspension, and debarment. The conditions and maximum duration for suspension and debarment are different under Law no. 10.520 (reverse auction) and under Law no. 12.462 (RDC).

Law no. 8.666 also provides for criminal offenses relating to public procurement. The bidding crimes and corresponding minimum and maximum sentences are set forth in Articles 89 through 99.

There are no whistleblower provisions as such, but any citizen is allowed to monitor the bidding proceedings (Article 4), obtain information about the performance of works

(Article 7, para. 8), challenge the registration of prices for future purchases (Article 15, para. 6), challenge the solicitation (Article 41, para. 1), and file a complaint with the Court of Accounts or internal auditing bodies (Article 113, para. 1). Other laws, such as the Administrative Improbity Act (Law no. 8.429/1992) and the Citizens Lawsuit Act (Law no. 4.717/1965), provide the means for any individual to denounce wrongdoings in bidding procedures. Law no. 12.846/2013 (the Anti-Bribery Act) provides for additional penalties, but also for leniency agreements to assist in persecution of wrongdoings.

13.15 **Protests and Dispute Resolution (Including Arbitration)**

Law 8.666 provides for a comprehensive system of bid protests, challenges, and administrative appeals. Under the Brazilian constitutional model, all administrative decisions may be subsequently challenged in court (or in arbitration). The Judicial Branch is unitary, unlike the national systems that are based on the French model of administrative justice. However, there are administrative adjudication bodies, such as the Courts of Audit (Article 70 of the Constitution), which function procedurally in a judicial-like manner. In addition, there is a federal court system (Article 109 of the Constitution) with hundreds of district courts and five circuit courts. In civil matters, the federal courts chiefly hear cases in which certain federal government entities are involved, much like the Court of Federal Claims in the US system.

The same laws governing the procurement proceedings also generally govern protests, challenges, and bid review. In addition, causes of action and standing definitions are also found in legislation governing proceedings at the Courts of Audit and in anti-bribery legislation. In general, such mechanisms are equally available to domestic and foreign bidders, and even to non-bidders up to a certain extent. There is a three-level system.

First, a pre-bid protest against the solicitation documents can be filed with the procuring agency up to between five to two days before the date for submission of the tender, depending on the procurement method. This protest has no automatic staying force.

Second, there is a system of appeals within the bidding procedure. In sealed competitive bidding, a bidder is allowed to appeal at each step (qualification, evaluation of the offers, award); under reverse auction or RDC, there is only one final appeal after the award that must cover all possible challenges to any alleged deviation during the proceedings.

Finally, an interested party (which includes any third party that considers that it has incurred any detriment from the proceedings) may file at any time a complaint at the competent Court of Audit. This administrative adjudicatory body may grant a series of remedies such as a stay and avoidance of the proceedings, sanctions, termination, or debarment.

Since all protests, challenges, or complaints at the three levels are administrative in nature, they can also give rise to civil litigation in national courts. Access to the courts is unlimited and the costs are relatively low, which results in a highly contentious environment for public procurement matters. Many procurement proceedings for large government contracts result in civil litigation.

In addition, Brazil has clear legislation and strong case law favoring arbitration as a form of dispute resolution in contracts involving government entities. Several Supreme Court (STF) and Superior Court of Justice (STJ) rulings have acknowledged that arbitration clauses in government contracts are valid and binding. A few scholars and some government agencies—such as, to some extent, the federal court of audit (TCU)—still object to the general use of arbitration in government contracts. The admissibility of domestic and international arbitration with state parties in Brazil is particularly important, since the country is not a member of the International Centre for Settlement of Investment Dispute (ICSID) and is thus not subject to investment arbitration under the Washington Convention.

A landmark ruling of October 2011 by the STJ increased the opportunities for arbitration in Brazilian government-related contracts. It was rendered in recurso especial no. 904.813-PR, filed by Companhia Paranaense de Gás Natural—Compagás against Consórcio Carioca Passarelli with regard to an arbitral award that granted the consortium compensation for costs overrun in a civil construction contract.

In a way, the ruling in Compagás simply restates and reinforces the arbitration-friendly environment. But it also goes several steps beyond, addressing some of the issues that are still sometimes raised in Brazil regarding arbitration involving the state.

First, it confirms a long-standing tradition in Brazilian courts of upholding arbitration agreements entered into by the government. The opinion expressly refers and adheres to the most known precedents, conveying a clear message that it is part of a strong and well-established case law. Second, it acknowledges that a post-dispute submission agreement is a legitimate means for the government to submit a dispute to arbitration in the absence of a contractual provision for arbitration. Since most government contracts under dispute in Brazil do not contain arbitration provisions, this acknowledgement opens an important opportunity for the parties to resort to arbitration as a speedier means to solve their disputes. Based on this ruling, state parties may feel confident that by entering into submission agreements, they will not be breaching any legal obligations that might arise from the bidding procedure conducted prior to the conclusion of the contract under dispute.

In spite of this, disputes in public procurement, even after the signature of the tendered contract, are generally referred to the courts, not to arbitration. Only in government concessions and PPPs have arbitration clauses become usual and often applied in practice. The enactment in 2015 of Law no. 13.129 with an express authorization for arbitration in any government dispute involving patrimonial, waivable rights may give rise to greater use of arbitration in public procurement in general.

13.16 Purchases and Framework Agreements (IDIQ)

According to Article 15 of Law no. 8.666 and Decree no. 3.931, government purchases must be made preferably through a price registration system (framework agreements, or IDIQ). The price registration is a list of prices offered by bidders for possible future purchases.

A contract is entered into only to govern such future purchases, but the government is not obligated to carry out any purchase. However, the winning bidder, who has the lowest registered price, has a preemptive right to supply in case the procuring agency does decide to make a purchase.

This is an adequate system for frequent purchases, for situations in which the performance of a work (and the corresponding need for materials) is expected to occur in stages, for when various different agencies are interested in purchasing the same item, and for situations in which the precise amount needed of a certain item is not known. In Brazilian practice, framework agreements (IDIQ) are responsible for a large share of federal government purchases and are defined as a preferential procurement method by federal executive orders.

13.17 International Supply of Goods and Services

As a general rule, domestic and international bidders have identical standing in public procurement in Brazil. Constitutional reforms in the 1990s eliminated most legislative discrimination between foreign and national suppliers. This trend was reversed only in 2010 with the "Buy National" program created by Law no. 12.349. Before that, only a few limited instances of domestic preferences subsisted in Brazilian legislation.[16]

However, certain practical difficulties still exist. In many situations, a foreign supplier is required to obtain government authorization to operate in Brazil in order to perform contractual obligations in Brazil. This is required by the Civil Code (Article 1.134) and by specific public procurement legislation. Other requirements regarding technical expertise and financial standing may pose difficulties for international companies.[17]

In substance, the rules regarding the selection of contractors and government contract administration are identical for foreign and domestic bidders and contractors. However, it should be noted since 2014, Brazil has been a contracting state of the CISG—the 1980 United Nations Convention on Contracts for the International Sale of Goods. Except

[16] For a comprehensive analysis of the regime for foreign bidders in Brazil, see Schwind (2013: pp. 44–82).

[17] See Schwind (2013) for a detailed list of instances in which foreign bidders may face difficulties that are not apparent in legislation but create serious practical burdens.

when the CISG is excluded or derogated, it may apply to international purchases made by Brazilian government entities and thus affect foreign suppliers.[18]

13.18 Pre-Qualification (Shortlist Stage)

A variation of the two-stage sequence (qualification and judgment) is admitted by Article 114 of Law no. 8.666. In certain situations, a bidding procedure will be launched exclusively to shortlisted companies that will be allowed to bid in the subsequent second-stage bidding. The requirements for pre-qualification are the same of those for qualification in a two-stage bidding procedure.

13.19 Small Companies (Complementary Law No. 123/2006)

Brazil enacted a Complementary Law in 2006 for the advancement of SMEs. One of the fields in which such advancement is sought is public procurement. This has led to the significant participation of SMEs in the Brazilian marketplace. The SISG statistics show that between 2008 and 2014, domestic SMEs were responsible for between 21 percent and 30 percent (in value) of total annual federal government purchases.

A more favorable treatment of SMEs is provided for in Article 170, IX, of the Constitution. Law no. 123/2006 creates a series of simplified and more favorable criteria with regard to qualification (fiscal good standing), preference in case of a "fictitious tie," and biddings to which only small and micro-size companies may be admitted.

A "fictitious tie" is a situation in which the bid of an SME is considered to be equal to that of another bidder if the difference between them lies within a certain percentage (5–10 percent above the best non-SME offer, depending on the situation). In this case, the SME is granted the opportunity for one additional bid in order to, if possible, lower its offer. If it is unable or unwilling to do so, the contract is awarded to the other bidder. This mechanism amounts to a right of first refusal in favor of the SME.

SMEs are defined chiefly by their gross annual income, according to thresholds provided for in Law no. 123. To benefit from this statute, SMEs must be formed and have their main offices in Brazil (i.e., only domestic SMEs are favored in Brazil's government procurement). In addition to the "fictitious tie," there are numerous other advantages for SMEs under Law no. 123: (a) procedural preferences, with facilitated

[18] See Pereira (2015, 2016).

qualification requirements; (b) small value contracts awarded through SME-only competitive tendering (corresponding to 71 percent of the number of federal government contracts in 2013); (c) preference in direct award for single-source small contracts; (d) mandatory subcontracting of SMEs, which the procuring entity may choose to provide for in the bidding documents or not; and (e) a 25 percent quota to be fulfilled by SMEs in contracts for the purchase of separable goods.

13.20 The Differential Procurement Regime (RDC)

From 2009, there was wide discussion about changes in the Brazilian public procurement law for the works, purchases, and services needed for the 2014 World Cup and the 2016 Rio Olympics. A first attempt to change the current legislation was made in June 2010 by the Presidential Provisional Measures (PPMs) 488 and 489, which lost force without being approved by Congress in November 2010. Only with Law no. 12.462 was a change finally enacted.[19]

Law no. 12.462 contains important procedural and conceptual changes. It was originally intended to be applicable only to certain contracts relating to the Games. Legal scholars soon started criticizing this limitation, arguing that the changes should, if valid and convenient, be extended to all contracts. The success of the new system caused it to be extended by Law no. 12.688/2012 to other contracts, comprised in the federal government's growth acceleration program (PAC). Given the lack of strict criteria for inclusion of projects in the PAC, the federal government has wide discretion to submit contracts and tenders to the system created by Law no. 12.462 (the Differential Public Procurement Regime, or RDC, to to use its Portuguese acronym).

This occurs because, when it was created, the PAC program did not want to narrow down the specific areas to which it would apply. Therefore, the decree that establishes and rules the PAC (no. 6.025, from January 2007), contains a very broad provision stating that a "Steering Committee" will define which contracts may be included in the PAC program. In other words, the decision is political and discretional. This broad provision allows a greater number of projects to be submitted to the RDC system.

The RDC contains a series of profound changes to the Brazilian government purchases regulation. It aims at expediting bidding procedures and allowing for more comprehensive, turnkey contracts.

The RDC is laid out in forty-seven Sections, and many provisions will still be subject to further regulation by executive orders. The new legislation ranges from the basic principles ruling the bidding procedures, to the specificity of administrative sanctions

[19] For a point-by-point analysis of the new legislation, see Justen Filho and Pereira (2014).

applicable, to fraudulent behavior. Some of the changes seem adequate for the purpose of expediting the procedures.

As a general rule of interpretation, one must take into account that the RDC provides for a different procurement system. It does not alter the existing regulation, but creates a new one. The previous system is based on a strict statutory definition of bidding procedures; the RDC creates procedural guidelines and a general framework. Each procuring agency will create its own procedure on a case-by-case basis, using the models and formats offered by the RDC rules. Many of the provisions were clarified or complemented by Decree no. 7.581.

13.21 "Buy National" (Law No. 12.349, of 2010)

Law no. 12.349 introduced a new purpose to public biddings in Brazil: advancing sustainable national development. Law no. 12.349 also inserted paras. 5 through 12 to Article 3 of Law no. 8.666, creating a series of specific preferences for products and services that may be considered more capable of stimulating national development. Other measures, such as new cases of waiver of bidding and extended contractual durations, are designed to favor national development.

The basic mechanism is the definition of price margins for local production and compliance with Brazilian technical standards for goods and services. There is a legal limit of 25 percent for the additional price margin that may be granted to companies that are established in Brazil or that comply with certain minimum nationalization and technological innovation requirements. The maximum margin of preference applicable in each sector is defined for a period of five years by presidential executive orders (decrees). Up to August 2014, nineteen decrees had been enacted.

Law no. 12.349, enacted in July 2010, altered the traditional approach of Brazilian procurement regulation, which was based on rigorous equality between foreign and domestic bidders. Together with other new rules (Law no. 12.462, which created the RDC), Law no. 12.349 promises to draw the attention of foreign companies interested in the Brazilian public procurement market to the advantages of a certain level of direct investment in the country.

Brazil already has legislation favoring small companies (Complementary Law no. 123/2006), but it is generally based on the assumption—and the statutory requirement—that they are located in Brazil. Law no. 12.349 favors national development and products and services made in Brazil, but it does not rule out possible joint ventures or partnerships between foreign and Brazilian companies.

In addition, similar to the 2009 United States stimulus package—expressly mentioned by the Brazilian government, together with the "Buy American" regulation of 1933, as the inspiration for the 2010 "Buy Brazilian" rules—Law no. 12.349 provides that any advantage to Brazilian firms may be extended to the Mercosul member states. This extension is not dependent on reciprocity or on the possible ratification of the Mercosul government purchases protocol.

In order to achieve the results described above, Law no. 12.349 amended the current Brazilian general public procurement law (Law no. 8.666/1993) in several topics.

Article 3 of Law no. 8.666 now provides that the purposes of the bidding process "are to ensure compliance with the constitutional principle of equality, to select the bid that is the most advantageous for the Administration and to advance the national development." This rule is complemented by para. 1, I, of Article 3, which rules out "preferences or distinctions based on the place of birth, principal business office or residence of the bidders or any other circumstance that is impertinent or irrelevant to the specific object of the contract." The rule expressly admits the preferences provided for in paras. 5 through 12 of Article 3 of Law no. 8.666, and in Article 3 of Law no. 8.248/1991.

Article 3, para. 2, of Law no. 8.666 has been changed to include new criteria for breaking ties. Preference in case of a tie will be given to products and services (i) made in Brazil; (ii) made or provided by Brazilian companies; or (iii) made or provided by companies that invest in research and technology development in Brazil, in this order. If that does not solve the tie, lots will be drawn (Article 45, para. 2, Law no. 8.666).

As mentioned above, Law no. 12.349 inserted paras. 5 through 12 in Article 3 of Law no. 8.666. In para. 5, Law no. 12.349 provides that "a margin of preference may be determined for national manufactured products and services that comply with Brazilian technical standards." The specific margin will be defined in a presidential decree, but there is already a provision defining that it is "limited to up to twenty-five percent above the price of the foreign manufactured products and services." The margin of preference must be determined in specific decrees after studies that establish criteria based on "job creation and income generation," "effect on the collection of taxes," and "development and technological innovation made in Brazil." However, para. 9 enables the government to disregard such preferences when "there is no output of manufactured goods or capacity to provide the services in Brazil."

Another topic in which Law no. 12.349 departs from traditional Brazilian public procurement law is para. 11. Law no. 8.666 has for a long time provided that it is "forbidden to include in the scope of a bidding process the obligation to obtain financial resources for the execution of the works or services, regardless of the source of such funds, except in the case of projects executed and exploited under a concession system, in accordance with specific legislation." Now, para. 11 of Article 3 provides for the opposite and includes the possibility for the invitations for bids to require the contractor to "carry out or obtain, in favor of the government or (...), measures of trade, industrial or technological offset or access to advantageous conditions of financing, together or not." Offset has been an important tool for the development of the Brazilian defense sectors and innovation in other areas. Article 3, para. 11, intends to extend this experience to procurement in general.

Article 3, para. 12, provides for the existence of certain biddings in which the competition "may be restricted to goods and services using technology developed in Brazil and produced according to the basic productive process referred to in Law no. 10.176/2001."

Article 6 of Law no. 8.666 contains definitions applicable to government procurement, and Law no. 12.349 has included some new definitions: national manufactured products (Article 6, XVII), national services (Article 6, XVIII), and information technology and strategic communication systems. All of these are instrumental for the application of the "Buy National" preferences.

The new item XXXI of Article 24 provides for a waiver of bidding (direct award) in the acquisitions for compliance with Articles 3, 4, 5 and 20 of Law no. 10.973/2004. This law contains a series of measures to advance Brazilian development by means of a stimulus to highly technological processes.

Article 57 deals with the duration of contracts. The new duration may be of up to 120 months (increased from the original sixty months) in specific cases: defense contracts (Article 24, IX, XIX, and XXVIII), and technology contracts (Article 24, XXXI).

Law no. 12.349 expressly applies to reverse auctions (procurement auctions), pursuant to its Article 2.

Law no. 12.349 makes it more difficult for smaller foreign companies to participate in public procurement projects in Brazil. A possible solution to this concern is the creation of joint ventures or partnerships between foreign small firms and local companies. On the other hand, Law no. 12.349 has the upside of introducing clearer rules on local preferences. Article 42, para. 4, of Law no. 8.666 already states that "[f]or the purpose of judgment of the bidding, the bids submitted by foreign bidders shall be increased by the amount corresponding to the taxes that burden exclusively the Brazilian bidders with regard to the sale operation." This rule has been much criticized and is considered inapplicable due to the lack of a general rule establishing that the bidding procedure could be used as a means to advance national development, even if that caused the procuring agency to enter into a contract at a higher financial cost.[20] This difficulty is now solved with the enactment of Law no. 12.349.

13.22 **Offset Agreements and Practices**

Some contracts entered into by the Brazilian government, notably in the area of defense purchases, have adopted offset provisions. Offsets have been formally provided for since 2010 in Law 12.349, which created the "Buy National" system in Brazil, and regulated for

[20] See Justen Filho (2014), notes on Article 42, paras. 3 and 4; see also Schwind (2013: pp. 74–8).

the defense sector since 2012 by Law 12.598. However, they have been used for decades based on general contracting rules or executive orders relating to specific sectors.

Offset agreements may be defined as any compensatory practice the parties may agree upon as a condition for the import of goods, services, or technology, with the purpose of generating certain industrial, technological, or commercial benefits.[21] The offset may be provided for in the same supply agreement or as a separate agreement named an offset agreement, distinct from the main contract.

In other words, as a retribution for the purchase of a certain product from an international supplier, the Brazilian government, as the purchasing country, may require the supplier or related parties (such as its government or controlling entity) to undertake certain obligations such as the purchase of products or materials from Brazilian companies, the transfer of technology, commitments to invest in certain sectors, provision of technical or commercial support, or many others.

Offset is therefore a practice adopted by the Brazilian government in order to (1) advance the technical and qualitative growth of national manufacture; (2) stimulate national production to enhance its international competitiveness; (3) increase the domestic labor marketplace by creating technologically high-end jobs; (4) obtain direct and indirect foreign resources to increase Brazilian industrial and technological capabilities; and (5) increase national content and reduce dependency on foreign markets. The Brazilian State ultimately uses its "spending power" to negotiate offsetting practices that are useful to foster certain macroeconomic policy objectives.

There are two types of offset: a direct offset and an indirect offset.[22]

Direct offsets relate to goods and services that are directly linked to the subject matter of the import contract. In an indirect offset, there is no such direct relationship between the subject matter of the contract and the goods and services covered by the offset.

Certain cases involve both direct and indirect offsets. An example is what happened with the Submarine Development Program (PROSUB), described in more detail later in this section. In this case, the offset agreement involved a transfer of technology for the construction of conventional and nuclear submarines (a direct offset), as well as technical support for the aircraft carrier, *Sao Paulo* (an indirect offset).

Brazilian law provides that offset may take place under a variety of forms: (1) co-production; (2) production under licensing; (3) production under subcontract; (4) foreign investment in industrial and technological capability; (5) transfer of technology;

[21] This is the definition found in Annex II ("Definitions") of Normative Order [*Portaria Normativa*] no. 764/MD, of December 27, 2002, of Brazil's Minister of Defense.

[22] These categories are mentioned in Annex II ("Definitions") of Normative Order (*Portaria Normativa*) no. 764/MD, of December 27, 2002, of Brazil's Minister of Defense.

(6) procurement of materials and instruments; (7) human resources training; and (8) countertrade.[23]

In co-production, a product originated abroad is produced totally or partly in Brazil, based on technical information supplied by a foreign government or company under an agreement entered into by the Brazilian government and one or more foreign governments.

In production under subcontract, part of a component originating from a foreign supplier is made locally. The subcontract does not necessarily comprise licensing of technical information, and usually there is a direct commercial agreement between the foreign supplier and the domestic manufacturer.

In a financial investment, the foreign supplier uses capital with the objective of forming or expanding a domestic enterprise through a joint venture or a direct investment.

Transfer of technology is the result of an offset agreement that may be performed under a variety of forms, such as research and development, technical support, training, or other activities, always with the purpose of a quality increase in the domestic technological level.

The procurement of materials or instruments is not defined by the applicable rules, but it is generally an exchange for the supply of certain types of materials.

Training of human resources aims to make certain people capable of performing relatively complex activities.

Finally, countertrade is made through commercial agreements that can be required in exchange for the supply agreement. It can include one or more of the following techniques: (1) barter, which is the exchange of selected products or services for others of similar value; (2) counter-purchase, which is the commitment by a foreign seller to purchase or cause a third party to purchase a certain amount in domestic products during a period of time; and (3) subcontracting (buy-back), under which the Brazilian party offers and the foreign supplier accepts to receive payment in products that are directly or indirectly linked to the product originally imported into Brazil.

There are therefore many possible offset practices. The list of possibilities indicated above does not exclude other options, and the parties may create innovative mechanisms.[24]

Offset transactions have been made in Brazil since the 1950s, when the Brazilian Air Force purchased Gloster Meteor TF-7 and F-8 aircraft from England in exchange for the same value in cotton (in a barter transaction). Another large transaction took place in 1998, when the Brazilian Army purchased fifty-two helicopters from the French

[23] These various forms are described in Annex II ("Definitions") of Normative Order (*Portaria Normativa*) no. 764/MD, of December 27, 2002, of Brazil's Minister of Defense. Since it is a logical list of possibilities, it can be extended even to contracts with no relationship with Ministry of Defense contracts. This is confirmed by the enactment in August 2011 of Executive Order (*Decreto*) no. 7.546, which kept essentially the same categories of offset measures (Article 2, III).

[24] The list contained in Article 2, III, of Executive Order no. 7.546, does not exclude other possibilities.

company Eurocopter. The transaction involved an offset agreement that provided for the sale of fifty T-27 Tucano aircraft (manufactured by Embraer, which was then a Brazilian government-controlled company) for the French Air Force, in addition to the export of agricultural equipment, investments to restructure Helibras (a Brazilian private company), training for pilots and flight mechanics, and other measures (Modesto, 2004). The Brazilian Navy has also entered into offset transactions that involved the construction in Brazil of destroyers with foreign technology.

However, for a long time Brazil refrained from conducting new significant offset transactions. Only transactions in the aeronautical sector saw some progress, and they resulted in important advantages for the government-controlled Embraer.

In the early 2000s, it is fair to say that there was a "rebirth" of offset transactions in Brazil, mainly due to a policy of modernization of Brazil's armed forces. Brazil saw the need for new equipment as an opportunity to develop a sound defense industry basis, technologically independent from other countries.

This reappearance of offset measures is confirmed by the constant enactment of rules governing offset since the early 2000s.

In 2002, Normative Order no. 764/MD/2002 of the Ministry of Defense was enacted to systematically regulate offset agreements by defining their purpose, form, and general guidelines. One of the most striking provisions is that of Article 8, which makes it mandatory for an offset agreement to be in place in transactions involving the import of defense products up to a "free on board" (FOB) amount in excess of $5 million. Below this threshold, an offset agreement is optional (Article 9). The Normative Order provided also that the rules for negotiation of offset agreements must contain a certain level of flexibility to account for the characteristics of this type of transaction (Article 17). It also made clear that the offset credits may be established in favor of private enterprises, but this must be provided for in specific instruments to ensure the benefits to the armed forces.

In 2008, Executive Order no. 6.703 was enacted to provide for the National Defense Strategy (END). The END contained the guideline to seek partnerships with other countries to "develop the national technological capacity, in order to progressively reduce the purchase of services and final products from abroad," that is, a clear objective was set to enter into offset agreements for the transfer of technology. A similar guideline was provided for by Order no. 59 of the Brazilian Navy.

In 2010, Law no. 12.349 was enacted, and it introduced a para. 11 to Article 3 of Law no. 8.666 (the General Public Procurement Act). This provision defines that "[t]he invitations for bidding for procurement of goods, services and works may, upon prior justification by the competent authority, require the contractor to carry out or obtain, in favor of a body or entity that is part of the government or of the ones indicated by the government based on a process that ensures equality, measures of trade, industrial or technological offset or access to advantageous conditions of financing, accumulatively or otherwise, pursuant to what may be prescribed by the Federal Executive Power."

In 2011, Executive Order no. 7.546 was issued that defined normatively the offset measures.

In 2012, Brazil enacted Law no. 12.598, with specific rules for purchases, contracts, and the development of defense products and systems. Executive Order no. 7.910, of 2013, was issued based on this legislation and created the Defense Industry Joint Committee (CMID), whose attributions comprise assisting and coordinating the defense products acquisition policy, which includes offset policy.

In light of this legislation and related regulations, and considering offset agreements as measures to foster national development and growth, several large-scale projects are ongoing in Brazil involving the purchase of equipment and systems combined with offset transactions.

One of these is the Navy Submarines Program (PROSUB), which aims to develop the domestic capability to design and build submarines, including nuclear propulsion submarines. PROSUB provides for the construction of four conventional and one nuclear submarine, and the construction of one base and one shipyard dedicated to the maintenance and construction of these assets. The value of the contracts is in excess of $10 billion, and the main contractor is Direction des Constructions Navales Services (DCNS), a company controlled by the French government.[25]

Another relevant program is the Project H-XBR for the development and production, mostly in Brazil, of fifty medium-size helicopters for use by the military and the President's Office. The project involves the transfer of technology for the local production of the aircraft, in addition to the increase in the production capability of Helibras, in Itajubá, Minas Gerais. The main contractor is Eurocopter, through a consortium together with Helibras. The project value is roughly $3 billion.[26]

There is also the contract entered into between the Air Space Control Department (DECEA), linked to the Air Force Command of the Ministry of Defense, with the French company Thales Air Systems for the development of monitoring radars. This contract involves offset measures for the radars to be produced by a Brazilian company (Omnisys), which is controlled by Thales.

All such programs with offset measures are subject to the oversight of the Federal Court of Audit (TCU). In its supervision, TCU acknowledges the benefits of offset measures. However, it also points out certain shortcomings. For instance, there is a deficiency in the Brazilian government departments and agencies in the design and structuring of the

[25] Information taken from "*Transferência de Tecnologia*: Programa de Desenvolvimento de Submarinos (Prosub) e Projeto H-XBR – Sumário Executivo" Tribunal de Contas da União, Brasília, 2014, available at: <http://portal.tcu.gov.br/lumis/portal/file/fileDownload.jsp?inline=1&fileId=8A8182A14EFA53A9014EFA865FCC564A> (in Portuguese).

[26] Information taken from "*Transferência de Tecnologia*: Programa de Desenvolvimento de Submarinos (Prosub) e Projeto H-XBR—Sumário Executivo" Tribunal de Contas da União, Brasília, 2014, available at: <http://www.defesaaereanaval.com.br/wp-content/uploads/2015/02/2657464.pdf> (in Portuguese).

projects. The internal control offices of such departments and agencies also lack efficiency, and there are difficulties in managing contracts of such technical complexity. There are difficulties in certain cases of recognizing what can be considered an actual technological innovation. In addition, even though the TCU does not question the possibility that technology is transferred to Brazilian private companies, it has on occasion examined, with some concern, situations in which the Brazilian beneficiary company in fact belongs to the same group of companies of the foreign company that owns the technology.[27]

In practice, both the conception and the management of offset measures are extremely complex. Nonetheless, in spite of all the possible difficulties, offset transactions have resulted in significant gains in terms of incentives for the domestic industry, and have greatly contributed to Brazil's capability to develop highly technological products, especially in the defense sector.

REFERENCES

Arrieta, L. B. 2014. "Taking the *Jeitinho* Out of Brazilian Procurement: The Impact of Brazil's Anti-Bribery Law." *Public Contract Law Journal* 44(1): 157–78.

Justen Filho, M. 2014. *Comentários à Lei de Licitações e Contratos Administrativos,* 16th edn. São Paulo: RT Thomson Reuters.

Justen Filho, M. 2015. *Curso de direito administrative,* 11th edn. São Paulo: RT Thomson Reuters.

Justen Filho, M. and Pereira, C. A. G. (eds). 2014. *Regime Diferenciado de Contratações—RDC,* 3rd edn. Belo Horizonte: Fórum.

Modesti, A. 2004. "Offset: teoria e prática." In Z. Warwar (ed.), *Panorama da prática do offset no Brasil: uma visão da negociação internacional de acordos de compensação comercial, industrial e tecnológica.* Brasília: Projetco Editorial/Livraria Suspensa, 25–53.

Pereira, C. A. G. 2013. "Dicotomia entre Serviço Público e Atividade Econômica e o Regime licitatório das Empresas Estatais." In A. P. N. Bicalho and M. T. F. Dias (eds), *Contratações Públicas.* Belo Horizonte: Fórum and Del Rey, 431–44.

Pereira, C. A. G. 2015. "Aplicação da CISG a licitações e contratos administrativos de compra internacional de mercadorias." In I. Schwenzer, C. A. G. Pereira, and L. Tripodi (eds), *A CISG e o Brasil.* São Paulo: Marcial Pons, 161–74.

Pereira, C. A. G. 2016. "Application of the CISG to International Government Procurement of Goods." In I. Schwenzer (ed), *35 years CISG and beyond.* The Hague: Eleven, 205–22.

Prochnik, V. 2011. "Brazil's Local Content Industrial Policy for the Oil and Gas Supply Chain: The Case of Equipment Purchase for Process Control." Paper Presented at the 13th Annual Scholarly Conference on Public Administration, Technology & Innovation, May 6–7, 2011, Tallinn, Estonia.

Schwind, R. W. 2013. *Licitações Internacionais.* Belo Horizonte: Fórum.

[27] This issue was analyzed in great detail by TCU in Rulings 2.334/2012-Plenary and 2.952/2013-Plenary.

14 Internationalization of Public Procurement Law and Relevance of International Norms and Frameworks

The Case of China

Cao Fuguo and Zhou Fen

14.1 Introduction

About a decade ago, China started to build up a market-based public procurement system that is line with international norms and frameworks, especially those concerning transparent procedural rules.[1] Over the years, China has developed rich and probably diversified experience of procurement reforms and regulation, which provides a good opportunity to test the strengths and weaknesses of the current system and the relevance of international norms and frameworks. China is now looking into the next generation of regulations. The Ministry of Finance (MOF) has been saying that it is "transforming the system," moving away from procedural oversight toward "value for money."[2] The newly enacted Government Procurement Law Implementing Regulation (GPL-IR), effective March 1, 2015, also substantively improves the current system, notably in contract transparency and procurement cycle management.

In the meantime, the international regimes on public procurement have also been subject to significant reform.[3] This provides promising prospects for a convergence of

[1] For a brief review of the evolution of the bidding system in China, see Cao (2003).

[2] See: <http://gks.mof.gov.cn/zhengfuxinxi/gongzuodongtai/201311/t20131128_1017919.html> (last accessed March 30, 2015).

[3] The WTO, UNCITRAL and the EU all have substantially reformed their systems the recent years. The revised WTO Agreement on Government Procurement was formally adopted in March 2012 and entered into force in April 2014; the UNCITRAL Model Law on Public Procurement (2011) was adopted on July 2011; the Guide to Enactment of UNCITRAL Model Law on Public Procurement was adopted on June 2012;

domestic efforts to transform China's public procurement system, which would in turn contribute to China's internationalization process.

One of the significant moves regarding China's government procurement policy in recent years is the country's submission of an initial offer to the World Trade Organization (WTO) Agreement on Government Procurement (GPA) on December 28, 2007.[4] Currently, China has revised its offer five times.[5]

A number of intriguing issues arise with these developments and in light of global internationalization of public procurement law. What are the main features of the Chinese public procurement legal system and, after more than a decade of operation, are they effective? To what extent are international norms and frameworks relevant to the design and operation of a particular procurement system, such as that of China? What is the current status of public procurement in the international legal agreements to which China is a party, such as free trade agreements (FTAs), and China's accession negotiation process to the GPA? What impact could the interplay of domestic and international developments have on China's future prospect of GPA accession and what could be the possible way forward?

This chapter will explore these issues in the specific case of China, and will shed light on the discussion of the general issues of internationalization of procurement laws and the relevance of international norms, where appropriate.

14.2 **Main Attributes of the Chinese System**

14.2.1 REGULATORY STRUCTURE

The primary laws governing Chinese public procurement are the Bidding Law (the BL)[6] and the Government Procurement Law (the GPL),[7] which are enacted by the national legislature. Both laws are implemented by a State Council implementing regulation—the Bidding Law Implementing Regulation (the BL-IR)[8] and the Government Procurement

the Directive 2014/23/EU (Concession Directive), Directive 2014/24/EU (Public Sector Directive), and Directive 2014/25/EU (Utility Directive) were adopted by the European Council in February 2014, and generally the directives will be transposed into national law by EU member states before April 2016.

[4] See Cao (2006a).

[5] See discussion in Section 14.4.1. For a glimpse of the responses of the parties to this revised offer, see the WTO's news brief at <https://www.wto.org/english/news_e/news15_e/gpro_11feb15_e.htm> (accessed July 23, 2016).

[6] The Bidding Law of the PRC, enacted by the national legislature and effective on January 1, 2000.

[7] The Government Procurement Law of PRC, enacted by the national legislature, and effective on January 1, 2003.

[8] The Bidding Law Implementing Regulation, enacted by the State Council and effective on May 1, 2013.

Law Implementing Regulation (the GPL-IR).[9] In addition, there are a number of ministerial measures signed and issued by the competent ministers to implement certain aspects of the BL or GPL. Occasionally, a circular can also be issued by the Treasury, the department in the MOF charged with the main responsibility for supervision and administration of government procurement policies.

The national procurement laws and policies, including those policies issued by an MOF department such as the Treasury, apply nationally. Provincial legislature and governors may also issue rules governing government procurement and, legally speaking, these rules may have primacy over a rule issued by an MOF department such as the Treasury, but in reality, a Treasury policy circular is well respected.

There is a third stream of laws governing the concession and operation of infrastructure (a function traditionally associated with the National Development and Reform Commission, or NDRC) and utilities (a function traditionally associated with Ministry of Housing and Construction) in China. The currently effective laws in these areas are mostly issued by provincial governments, either by the provincial legislature or by the provincial governor. Most recently, with the sudden revival of PPPs in China, the MOF joins the national ministries to lead the PPPs policy initiatives and a new wave of policy and regulations in this respect seems to be thriving. Section 14.2.8 will review this process.

14.2.2 OBJECTIVES

14.2.2.1 Primary Objectives

The primary purpose of the earlier bidding regulations was to reform the administration of government investment and finance in order to reduce corruption and the inefficiencies created by the non-competitive allocation of projects by government agencies. Therefore, the primary objectives found in modern procurement systems, such as value for money, were not a major concern in earlier bidding regulations.[10] The BL significantly improved the old bidding measures by embracing the objectives of "economy and quality" in procurement (Article 1 of the BL). It further revolutionized the award criteria by abolishing the base price criterion and adopting the market-based criteria found in modern procurement regimes. These improvements, among others,

[9] The Government Procurement Law Implementing Regulation, enacted by the State Council and effective on March 1, 2015.

[10] For example, the award criteria, based on setting base prices, undermined the objectives of economy and effectiveness. Even though the procurer was able to negotiate with the successful bidder before conclusion of the contract (a general practice at that time), this was forbidden under the BL as it deviated from the principle of using market-based bidding mechanisms and increased the opportunity for corruption.

have greatly enhanced the ability of procuring entities to meet the new objectives provided for in the BL.

Under the GPL, the declared primary policy was to "increase the efficiency and effectiveness of government procurement funding" and "promote the construction of a clean government." The purpose of the reforms was closely related to the functions and authority of the MOF, either as a means of budgetary reform or of expenditure reform.

14.2.2.2 Social, Economic, and Environmental Policies

14.2.2.2.1 Social, Economic, and Environment Policies under the BL. Except for in a few cases where the bidding regulations implement a buy national policy by first using competition to test whether a domestic source of supply of a certain product exists,[11] the Chinese BL and related regulations, including the BL-IR, provide few explicit secondary policies. However, the BL does leave room for the procuring entities to stipulate secondary policies in the Bidding Document according to other state regulations;[12] therefore, it is likely that secondary policies are implemented in the real procurement field through the qualification process, technical specifications, or during the award stage. Secondary policies may also be implemented where procurement is excluded from coverage.[13]

14.2.2.2.2 Buy National Policy under the GPL. The GPL implements a buy national policy in Article 10, which provides that:

The government shall procure national goods, works and services except where:

(1) *The goods, works or services to be procured are not available within the territory of P.R.C., or though available, cannot be acquired on reasonable commercial terms and conditions;*

(2) *The items to be procured are for use abroad;*

(3) *Otherwise provided by laws and administrative regulations.*

The GPL leaves the definition of the term "national goods, works and services" to be specified by the State Council. Now the GPL's buy national policy is operated through the implementing MOF Measure on the Administration of Imported Products. The Measure apparently reduces the technical difficulty of defining "national" products by referring to them as "made-in-China" products. By the Measure, purchasers are required to justify their purchase of imported products by referring to the buy national provision

[11] See "Temporary Provisions on Domestic Bidding Management in Applying for Import of Mechanical and Electrical Equipment" (1986) by the Office of State Economic and Trade; see also Jingbin (2001). For a brief review of the development, see Cao (2003).

[12] Articles 18 and 19 of the BL.

[13] For the excluded procurement, see the general discussion in Sections 14.2.3.1 and 14.2.3.2.

under the GPL and submit their procurement decision to the competent finance departments for verification. The GPL's proposed implementing regulation had intended to specify a definition for national products under the GPL, but failed to do so. Therefore, it is likely that the operation of the GPL's buy national policy will continue to rely on the MOF Measure described above. The effect of such an approach is that a foreign-invested enterprise incorporated under Chinese law is legally taken as a Chinese enterprise and it qualifies to supply the Chinese government as a domestic supplier provided that the end product that it supplies to the Chinese government is manufactured in China.

14.2.2.2.3 Other Social and Economic Policies under the GPL. Other secondary policies can be implemented through Article 9, which provides that:

> *Government procurement shall be conducted in such a manner as to facilitate achievement of the economic and social development policy goals of the State, including but not limited to environmental protection, assistance of underdeveloped or ethnic minority regions, and promotion of small and medium-sized enterprises.*

Later, implementing measures were enacted requiring purchasers at all levels to give priority to energy-conserving and environmentally friendly products.[14] Another notable development of the policy is the promotion of small and medium-sized enterprises (SMEs) in government procurement.[15] In 2014, the government procurement policy also began to have links to other targeted groups, such as support for enterprises operated by the prison authorities.[16]

14.2.3 SCOPE AND COVERAGE

14.2.3.1 The Bidding Law: Works and Related Goods and Services?

14.2.3.1.1 A General Law Governing All Bidding Activities in China. The BL applies to "bidding activities within the territory of China" (Article 2). Thus, the scope of the application of the BL is built on the concept of "bidding," irrespective of the procurement entity, be it public or private, or even a purchase or sale through bidding. While the concept of "bidding" was not defined under the BL, it arguably refers to the two formal bidding procedures—open bidding and selective (invited) bidding—recognized by the BL itself, and two-stage bidding newly adopted by the BL-IR (Article 30).

[14] For a review of the development, see Cao and Fen (2014).

[15] For a review of China's buy SMEs policy and its implication for GPA, see Cao (2013).

[16] A Joint Circular by the MOF and Ministry of Justice on Supporting the Development of Prison-operated Enterprise through Government Procurement Treasury No.[2014]68.

The practical implication of this approach is that the BL applies to any procurement covered by the GPL provided that it is conducted through bidding. The BL also arguably applies to the selection of concessionaire, provided that the concession law requires the selection of concessionaire through bidding.

14.2.3.1.2 Compulsory Coverage. Article 3 of the BL requires the procurement made under certain infrastructure and utilities works to be conducted through the formal bidding methods, provided, *inter alia*, that the works concern the public interest or public security, or are invested or financed by the state. This requirement also extends to procurement for work-related goods and services. For the purpose of BL application, the nature of the entity, be it public or private, is irrelevant.

Later regulation specifies the works projects that fall under the compulsory coverage of the BL,[17] which include infrastructure projects such as energy, transportation, telecommunications and post, hydraulics, municipal facilities, ecology, and environment; and utilities projects such as municipal engineering, science, education and culture, sports and tourism, sanitation and social welfare, and commercial housing.

The BL provides in subsection (2) and (3) of Article 3 that "projects invested wholly or partly by state-owned funds or projects funded wholly or partly through state finance" and "projects funded through loans or grant from international organisation or foreign governments" shall be subject to compulsory bidding.

State-owned funds generally refers to state fiscal funds, including budgetary and extra-budgetary funds. The implementing provision stipulates that projects invested by state-owned funds include projects that are financed through (a) budgetary funds of any level of government; (b) various government special construction funds; or (c) funds owned by state-owned enterprises or public institutions and actually controlled by state-asset investors.[18]

The implementing provision further specifies that the scope of projects funded through state finance include projects that are financed through (a) the issuing of state bonds; (b) foreign loans or security by the state; (c) state policy loans; (d) financing arrangements by a state-authorized investment entity; and (e) financing arrangements under state concession.[19]

[17] The Regulation on Bidding Scope and Scale Standards of Construction Project (May 1, 2000) by the State Development and Planning Commission (SDPC), a predecessor of the current National Development and Reform Commission.

[18] Article 4 of The Regulation on Bidding Scope and Scale Standards of Construction Project (May 1, 2000) by SDPC.

[19] Article 5 of The Regulation on Bidding Scope and Scale Standards of Construction Project.

14.2.3.1.3 Thresholds. The thresholds for the value of each individual contract are provided in an implementing provision.[20] Thresholds will be deemed to be exceeded if (a) for individual construction contracts, the estimated contract value is RMB2,000,000 or above; (b) for individual supply contracts for key equipment, material, and so on, the estimated contract value is RMB1,000,000 or above; (c) for individual service contracts for survey, design, supervision, etc., the estimated contract value is RMB500,000 or above; or (d) if each individual contract value is below the threshold under (a), (b), and (c), but the total investment value is above RMB30,000,000.

14.2.3.1.4 Exemptions. Contracts falling within the compulsory scope of coverage but below the thresholds are exempted. It is also provided in Article 66 of the BL that procurement involving special circumstances may be exempted from the bidding obligation according to relevant regulations. The Article also provides for a non-exhaustive list of such special circumstances such as national security, state secrets, emergency rescue, or the use of poverty relief funds as remuneration for poor regions or rural laborers.

It is noteworthy that an implementing regulation has effectively added more procurement to this list.[21] Such exemptions include circumstances where (a) construction projects require special confidentiality arrangements; (b) the survey or design of a construction project requires the use of a specific patent or know-how, or there is a specific requirement for an architectural or artistic model; (c) the number of contractors, suppliers, or service providers is fewer than three and effective competition is unattainable; and (d) other circumstances make bidding inapplicable.

The BL-IR (Article 9) recognizes other justifiable circumstances for such exemptions. These include the circumstance where the procurement entity can satisfy its requirement by itself, where the investors in the case of a concession project can satisfy its requirement provided the concessionaire itself is selected through bidding, or where additional procurement is needed for the purpose of compatibility.

14.2.3.2 Coverage of the GPL

Procurement activities must meet three conditions to fall under the coverage of the Chinese GPL:[22]

[20] Article 7 of The Regulation on Bidding Scope and Scale Standards of Construction Project.

[21] Temporary Provision on Adding Bidding Contents and Approving Bidding Method in the Projects Feasibility Study by SDPC (issuing time), as amended.

[22] Article 2 of the Government Procurement Law.

1. the procurement must be conducted by state organs, public institutions, or social organizations at all levels (it is apparently intended that state-owned enterprises are not subject to the GPL);
2. the procurement must be of goods, works, or services listed in the Centralized Procurement Catalogue (CP Catalogue) or above the officially specified threshold; and
3. the procurement must be conducted with fiscal funds.

In addition, Article 4 of the GPL provides that "[w]hereas works is procured through bidding method the Bidding Law shall apply." This provision has caused some problems as to the actual coverage of both the BL and GPL. One ambiguity is related to the question of the extent to which the BL shall apply to government works procurement. A restrictive explanation would be that only the bidding procedure under the BL applies to government works procurement, and many other important aspects of the GPL will prevail over the BL—for example, the buy national policy, the bid challenge system, and the supervisory authority provided in the GPL. A more expanded explanation would be that the BL as a whole applies to government works procurement. In other words, government works procurement is excluded from the coverage of the GPL. This problem of ambiguity seems to result from the overlapping coverage of the two laws, a problem which in essence is rooted in the allocation of regulatory powers among ministries. The BL-IR and GPL-IR invest a lot of effort in coordinating and interpreting the relationship between the application of the two procurement laws. Under the new regulations, in terms of government works procurement, the BL and its implementing rules shall apply when the work is procured through bidding, and the GPL and its implementing rules shall apply when the works is procured through methods other than bidding (Article 7 of the GPL-IR).

Another issue is related to the exemption of the GPL. Article 85 excludes from the coverage of the GPL urgent procurements such as those warranted by natural disaster and force majeure, and those procurements involving state security and secrecy. Still another article excludes military procurement in general and authorizes the Central Military Commission to enact its own procurement regulations (GPL Article No. 86).

14.2.3.3 The Status of Procurement by State-Owned Enterprises

Procurement by state-owned enterprises (SOEs) is covered by Article 2 of the BL provided such procurement is conducted through bidding, or by Article 3 of the BL provided such procurement satisfies the compulsory coverage tests of the BL. This means at least part of the procurement by SOEs can be covered by the BL. In practice, SOEs choose to use more flexible procurement methods, such as competitive negotiation procedure, provided that such procurement is not caught by the BL's compulsory coverage Article.

The GPL, on the other hand, effectively excludes SOEs from its coverage by the entity test—SOEs do not fall under any of the three categories of entities covered by the GPL. This applies regardless of whether these SOEs are using budgetary funds to conduct their procurement or their own funds, whether these SOEs are operating in a competitive sector or a monopolistic sector, or whether or not these SOEs are utilities operators.

However, the current status of SOEs under the GPL may be challenged by China's negotiations on GPA accession—China's major trading partners are expecting much of the inclusion of the large SOEs sector in its offer, at least some of the SOEs and especially those operating in the unities sectors. Therefore, the issue will almost certainly be revisited in the time to come. If and how SOEs should be brought under modern procurement law will require careful consideration by China's policy-makers.

14.2.4 TRANSPARENT PROCEDURAL RULES

14.2.4.1 Choice of Methods, Conditions for Use, and Approval

14.2.4.1.1 The Bidding Procedures under the BL and its Implementing Regulation. Under the BL, only two procedures—open bidding and selective bidding—are adopted, and the two adopted procedures are similar except that under the selective procedure no public procurement notice is required and bidders are invited directly. Bidding procedures have also been made much more rigid and no negotiation is allowed at any stage of the procurement process. The negotiated bidding, which is by essence a negotiated procedure with or without competition and prevalent in the previous bidding regulations, is dropped off by the BL, arguably as a strengthened measure to prevent corruption.

The consequence of more rigid bidding procedures and the omission of the more flexible negotiated procedure is serious. Given the broad and ambitious coverage of the BL and the fact that it applies mainly to procurement of works, the challenge presented of its application to the situation where more flexible procurement arrangements are commercially justified is huge. One of the ways to tackle this dilemma is to exempt the procurements that require more flexibility and where the BL is unrealistically applicable. Thus Article 66, the only Article dealing with such exemptions, provides that in "special circumstances" a procuring entity may be exempted from the obligation to procure by bidding according to relevant state regulations. The recent Implementing Regulation goes further along this line (Article 9 of the BL-IR).[23] Another way to tackle the dilemma

[23] See discussion in Section 14.2.3.1. When these circumstances are met and bidding requirements are subject to an exemption, no other procedures are provided at all by which to conduct the procurement. Thus the excluded procurement is completely unregulated, except for those caught by the GPL, where alternative procurement methods under the GPA are applicable.

is to provide more relaxed bidding methods. The recent BL-IR (Article 30) indeed adopts a new bidding method—the two-stage bidding procedure—which allows interested bidders to submit technical proposals without price in the first stage, to allow the procurement entity to formulate technical specifications and requirements for the procurement based on which it can initiate a formal bidding procedure in the following second stage.

The Procurement Procedures Under the GPL and its Implementing Regulation. The GPL provides a lengthy menu of methods for government procurement: open tendering, selective tendering, competitive negotiation, single source procurement, request for quotation, and "other methods" authorized by the state supervisory authority for government procurement. Under the GPL, open tendering is the preferred procurement method,[24] and the use of other procurement procedures must follow the conditions specified for their use and requires prior approval from supervising authorities.[25]

Both the BL and the GPL require open bidding as the preferred method for government procurement when the procurement is above a certain threshold, and clearly prohibit the evasion of open bidding through disaggregation (Article 4 of the BL and Article 28 of the GPL). The selective bidding method can only be used when (a) the procurement is special and can only be procured from limited sources; and (b) the cost of the procurement through open bidding would be disproportionate to the overall value of the procurement, a concept which can be found in some of the international government procurement regimes.[26]

The preferred status of opening bidding under GPL is confirmed by the result of a survey, as seen from Figure 14.1.

14.2.4.2 Publication of Information on National Legislation and Procedures and Procurement Opportunities in Designated Media

There is a general requirement to publish the rules governing procurement. The rule on procurement transparency also requires publication of procurement opportunities, as well as the criteria bidders/contractors must meet in order to qualify for the government contract.

When using the open bidding method, the procuring entity must publish a bid notice in the government-designated media as a means to invite interested bidders to bid for the procurement.

[24] Article 26 of the Government Procurement Law of PRC.

[25] Article 27, 29, 30, 31 and 32 of the Government Procurement Law of PRC.

[26] For example, Article 20 of UNCITRAL Model Law on Procurement of Goods, Construction and Services.

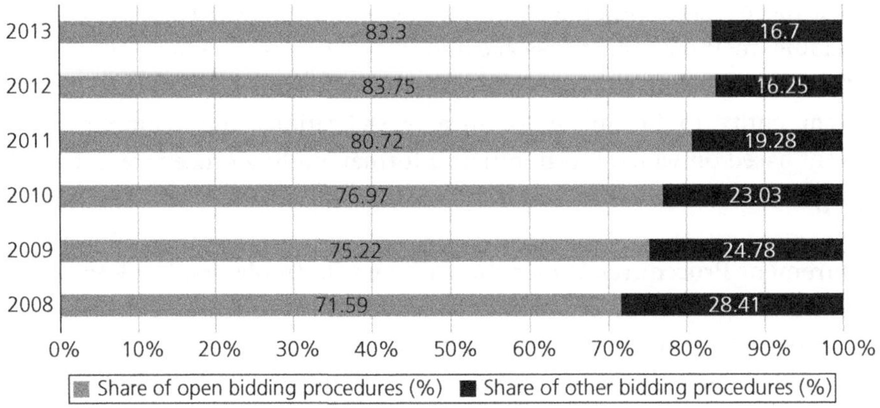

Figure 14.1. The percentage of open bidding procedure in total size of government procurement, 2008–13

Source: Collected data from websites.[1]

For the statistic information on each year, see: http://www.chinanews.com/gn/2014/07-15/6387331.shtml; http://www.zjdpc.gov.cn/art/2013/8/14/art_791_568954.html; http://www.cfen.com.cn/web/cjb/2012-07/04/content_880559.htm; http://www.cgpnews.cn/articles/3432; http://www.mof.gov.cn/zhengwuxinxi/caizhengxinwen/201008/t20100818_333822.html; and http://www.gov.cn/gzdt/2009-08/09/content_1387104.htm (each last visited on 1 March 2015).

When using the selective tendering method, the BL and GPL provide slightly differently. While under the BL there is no requirement for publication of a bid opportunity notice,[27] the GPL seems to prefer the publication of the procurement opportunity even under the selective bidding procedure. The Measure on Administration of Goods and Service Bidding (BM), a ministerial measure from the MOF, provides a definition of selective bidding and further requires in Article 15 that procuring entities publish a pre-qualification notice in designated media and randomly choose three or more bidders from the qualified potential bidders to participate in the biding process.

Under competitive negotiation and request for quotation, suppliers may be invited either through a public notice or selected from a qualified supplier list, on which a supplier is free to register for qualification before a procurement starts.[28] This means that under these two procedures, procurement opportunities are usually openly available to interested suppliers. However, under these two procedures there exists a third possibility—that suppliers can be recommended and invited by a purchaser and a bid evaluation expert, meaning that some of the potential suppliers may be deprived of the procurement opportunities. While the third approach is apparently aimed at more

[27] The selected bidding method is defined under the BL as a bidding procedure under which "the procuring entity invites, through a invitation letter, specified legal persons or other organizations to submit bids" (Article 10 of the BL).

[28] Article 12 of the Measure on the Administration of Procurement Methods other than Bidding, enacted by the MOF.

procurement flexibility and efficiency, it is also likely to open the door to misuse and manipulation. The relevant rule does have some checks and balances to prevent such malpractice by requiring a minimum of three qualified suppliers to be invited, through written recommendation. A purchaser is also required not to recommend more than half of the recommended suppliers.

Under the sole source procurement procedure, it is not clear whether a procurement advertisement should be published. Given the circumstances justified for the use of this procedure, it may not be advisable to place a general public advertisement obligation for this procedure. Rather, the control of such a procedure is placed more on the choice of such a procedure. In addition to submitting for prior approval by the competent authority, a purchaser is required to put a public notice on the designated media disclosing the procurement information and the name of the sole supplier, the GPL-IR (Article 38).

14.2.4.3 Transparent Qualification Procedure

A common doctrine endorsed by both the BL and the GPL regarding the qualification of potential bidders or suppliers is the prohibition of discriminatory or preferential treatment among potential bidders or suppliers based on "unreasonable" terms (Article 18 of the BL and Article 22 of the GPL).

The GPL outlines general qualification criteria for suppliers, which include considerations such as the supplier's commercial reputation, financial and accounting system, professional expertise, possession of equipment required to perform the contract, a clean tax and social security record, as well as a clean legal record for the preceding three years (Article 22).

In addition to the general requirement for fair treatment of suppliers in qualification, the BL-IR specifically addresses the issue of pre-qualification in a number of articles (Articles 15–23). These articles provide transparent rules on pre-qualification, including the requirement for publication of an open notice, selection criteria in advance, time limit, evaluation method, and timely notice of the result of the qualification.

14.2.4.4 Solicitation Document and Specification

Under both the BL and GPL, a procurement entity needs to prepare a solicitation document to conduct the procurement. The eventual solicitation document shall be subject to the test of the general principle of equal treatment for all suppliers, and specifically the solicitation document may not require the reference to particular supplier or its products and contain other provisions that may be preferential to certain suppliers and discriminate among others (Articles 19 and 20 of the BL). This requirement also applies to the preparation for technical specification.

14.2.4.5 Time Limit

The time limit allows suppliers sufficient time to submit bids on procurement opportunities. The BL requires a "reasonable period" for bidders to prepare their bids and for the compulsory procurement projects. A minimum period of twenty days is required (Article 20 of the BL). To ensure transparency and fairness, the BL requires the procuring entity to notify any clarification and amendments to all recipients of the solicitation document in writing at least fifteen days before the deadline for submission of tender (Article 23). The requirement for such a minimum period is intended to ensure that bidders have sufficient time to respond to the clarifications and amendments.

14.2.4.6 Transparency of Decision on Qualification, Contract Award, and Notification Procedures

Whatever the specific qualification for each procurement opportunity, the qualification criteria must be made available to the suppliers in advance. As discussed in Section 14.2.4.3, there is a general requirement for fair treatment of suppliers in qualification. The BL-IR also specifically addresses the issue of pre-qualification in a number of articles (Articles 15–23) that provide transparent rules on pre-qualification, including the requirement for publication of an open notice, selection criteria in advance, time limit, evaluation method, and timely notice of the result of the qualification.

The same can be said in regard to the transparency of contract awards under the BL (Article 41), which provides that the successful tender shall either be:

i. the bid with the lowest price subject to satisfying all substantive requirements provided in the solicitation document (hereafter referred to as the " lowest bid price"). This method should generally be used in the procurement of standard or commoditized goods and common services; or
ii. the bid satisfying all comprehensive evaluation criteria provided in the solicitation document to the greatest degree (hereafter referred to as the " most advantageous method").

For the most advantageous method, the BM provides two variants: the *comprehensive evaluation method* and the *performance/price ratio method*. The *comprehensive evaluation method* (Article 52) allows for comprehensive factors specified in the bidding document to be taken into consideration in the bid evaluation; such factors include "price, technology, financial situation, reputation, experience, after-sales service and the degree of responsiveness to the bidding document," and are quantified and weighted. Price must be accorded a weight of 30–60 percent for goods and 10–30 percent for services. The successful bid shall be the one with the highest evaluated scores subject to satisfying all substantive requirements. Under the *performance/price ratio method*, the non-price or performance factors are evaluated and the score is then compared to the price. The successful bid is the one with the highest ratio between the scores of the performance factors and the bid price (Article 53).

The BL prohibits a bid price that is lower than the product cost (Article 41), while the BM employs the term "abnormally lowest price." When the lowest bid price is considered to be "obviously unreasonable" or lower than the cost, and thus may affect the quality of the goods to be delivered and dishonor a guarantee of good performance, the Tender Evaluation Committee (TEC) shall require the bidder in question to submit a written explanation within a designated period of time with supporting documents (Article 54). Otherwise, the TEC may reject the tender.

Evaluation criteria and method must be provided in the solicitation document in advance and be followed in evaluating and comparing bids.

The proposed award decision shall be published in the government designated media for at least three days before the award can be made (article 54 of the BL-IR).

A much more ambitious contract transparency measure has been effective since March 1, 2015 that requires publication of the full text of government procurement contracts on the designated media within two days after their conclusion, with redactions that only justify the protection of commercial and national confidential interest.[29] In addition, the TEC members and the solicitation documents are also required to be published on the designated media within two days after an award decision has been made.[30]

14.2.5 OTHER MATTERS RELATED TO TRANSPARENCY, SUCH AS MAINTENANCE OF RECORD PROCEEDINGS, INFORMATION TECHNOLOGY, AND THE FIGHT AGAINST BRIBERY AND CORRUPTION

14.2.5.1 Maintenance of Record Proceedings and Collecting and Reporting of Statistics

Under the GPL, purchasers and the procurement agency are obliged to properly maintain all the required procurement documents up to a minimum duration of fifteen years.[31] The required documents include the records of the procurement proceedings,[32] the budget of

[29] Article 50 of the GPL-IR.

[30] Article 43 of the GPL-IR.

[31] Article 42 of the GPL

[32] The record of procurement proceedings should contain the following content at least:

(1) the type and name of the procurement project;
(2) the budget, resources of the fund and the value of the contract;
(3) the procedure of the procurement, if using the procedures other than open bidding, should specify the reasons;
(4) the criteria of inviting the suppliers and the reason of selecting the suppliers;
(5) the criteria of evaluation and the reason of determining the winning bidder;
(6) the reason of cancelling the bidding procedures; and
(7) the record of employing procedures other than open bidding and selective bidding.

the procurement, solicitation documents, bidding documents, the evaluation criteria, the evaluation report, awarding documents, the procurement contract, the certificate of inspection and acceptance, the reply to the complaint, the decision on the challenge, and other relevant documents or materials. In contrast, the BL only requires recording the proceeding of opening the tenders and archiving it for future reference.[33]

There is no specific rule under the GPL and BL relating to reporting statistics, but in recent years, the MOF has collected the government procurement information and published a very brief description of the statistics on its website.[34]

14.2.5.2 Information Technology and Electronic Procurement

Information technology has been reshaping the contracting world and is gradually being embraced in the world of law. The Chinese Contract Law, in broad language, recognizes the validity of contracts consummated in the form of electronic data messages, but does not address a wide range of related issues. The E-signature Law fills some of the gaps by providing legal definitions of the terms "electronic data message" and "electronic signature,"[35] the requirements applicable to the communication and enforceability of electronic data messages, the legal effect and certification of electronic signatures, and the consequences of violating the E-signature Law. These laws generally also govern the world of government procurement through the internet.

With the advancement of IT and the encouragement of e-government, many local governments have been exploring electronic means to conduct business and regulate government procurement through the internet. One such regulation can be found as early as 1999, when Nanning Municipality—the capital of the Guangxi Autonomous Region and a forerunner of Chinese government procurement reform—enacted a regulation governing internet-based government procurement bidding activities.[36] What the regulation describes as "internet-based government procurement bidding" is actually a process of procurement where the government publishes the bidding notice through the internet, receives bids through emails, decides the successful bid, and publishes the successful bid and its bid price

[33] Article 36, para. 3 of the BL.

[34] The published information includes the total size of national government procurement, the percentage of the total size relative to national fiscal expenditure, the respective percentage of goods, service and work procurement in relative to total procurement, the percentage of procurement under open bidding procedure in relative to total procurement, the total size of centralized procurement. Most recently, the MOF has also published information on the size of energy-conserving and environmentally friendly products procured under the GPL. An example of such publication can be found at <http://www.mof.gov.cn/zhengwuxinxi/caijingshidian/jjrb/200805/t20080519_24114.html> (accessed July 23, 2016).

[35] The Electronic Signature Law of the People's Republic of China (E-signature Law) issued by the Standing Committee of the 10th National People's Congress, August 28, 2004, effective April 1, 2005.

[36] Provisional Measure on the Administration of Government Procurement through Bidding on Internet of Nanjing Municipality Guangxi Autonomous Region, issued on June 18, 1999.

on the internet.[37] Many other local governments followed later and enacted their own regulations on internet-based government procurement bidding.[38] Guangdong, one of China's frontier provinces in its open-up policy and economic reform, started to employ electronic ordering, electronic reverse auctions, and electronic quotation for procurements covered under a framework agreement or qualified for the use of a quotation method.[39] Today, many of the governments are following this practice and tend to use electronic procurement for procurement under a framework agreement or qualified for a quotation method, which are in most cases standard items with a smaller value.[40]

Some of the regional governments are more ambitious in introducing ICT into their procurement process whenever possible. For example, since 2013, Shanghai Municipality has incorporated e-procurement into the whole procurement life cycle, including authorization of procurement, solicitation and submission of bid, signature of contract, inspection and acceptance of performance, and supervision and administration of the procurement. It also incorporates ICT into every procurement method, including formal bidding, competitive negotiation, request for quotation, sole source procurement, procurement through e-market, etc.[41] Guangdong province is another region where many local governments are incorporating ICT into the whole procurement life cycle and each procurement method.[42]

Central governments are also experimenting with ICT. For example, in October 2012 the central government's procurement center started to use electronic reverse auctions for procurement covered under the framework agreement.[43] Meanwhile, the center is also

[37] Article 2 of Provisional Measure on the Administration of Government Procurement through Bidding on Internet of Nanjing Municipality Guangxi Autonomous Region, issued on June 18, 1999.

[38] For example, Provisional Measure on the Administration of Government Procurement through Bidding on Internet of Zhejiang Provincial Government, effective on September 1, 2000; Provisional Measure on the Administration of Government Procurement through Bidding on Internet of Hefei Municipality, effective on March 13, 2001; Provisional Measure on the Administration of Government Procurement through Bidding on Internet of Zhuhai Municipality, effective on June 27, 2002; Provisional Measure on the Administration of Internet-based Government Procurement of Shenzhen Municipality, effective on October 15, 2003; Provisional Measure on the Administration of Government Procurement through Bidding on Internet of Shanghai Municipality, effective in December 2004.

[39] The Circular on Promoting Electronic Government Procurement on a Trial Basis, issued by the Department of Finance, Guangdong Province on April 12, 2006.

[40] For instance, the Interim Provisions on Electronic Transaction Platform for Framework Agreement in Chongqing, issued by the Finance Department of Chongqing Municipality; and the Circular on Promoting the Use of Electronic Quotation Method for Some Commonly-used Equipments, issued by Finance Department of Tianjin Municipality.

[41] The Interim Provisions on Administration of Electronic Government Procurement in Shanghai, issued by Finance Department of Shanghai Municipality.

[42] For example, Zhuhai Municipality is one of the leading and earliest governments that is employing ICT in its procurement comprehensively. The Provisional Measure on E-government procurement in Zhuhai Municipality. Foshan Municipality is another local government that piloted its e-procurement practice under a framework agreement as early as 2009, but most recently in 2014 started to employ such technology comprehensively in all aspects of its procurement.

[43] The Circular on Marking Experiments of Developing Electronic Reverse Auction, issued by the Government Procurement Center of Central Governments on September 28, 2012.

operating an e-bid system via which registered and qualified bidders can submit online bids within a designated time period.[44] The central government procurement center has recently begun exploiting the potential benefit of private e-markets for smaller value procurement by incorporating a number of private e-markets into its mall online system.[45]

However, there is no specific national regulation on e-procurement under the regulatory framework of the GPL. The newly enacted GPL-IR seems to recognize the difficulty of providing substantive national regulation, given the diversified developments at different government levels and by different governments. Therefore, while on the one hand it is encouraging the utility of e-procurement, on the other hand it does not seek to provide substantive regulations on e-procurement; it only intends to adopt uniform national standards for the construction of electronic transaction platforms for government procurement (Article 10 of GPL-IR).

Under the regulatory framework of the BL, in contrast, a national rule specifically on electronic bidding under the coverage of the BL has been effective since May 1, 2013.[46] In addition to clarifying the validity of e-transactions as compared to paper-based transactions, the new rule specifically seeks to regulate the e-transaction platform and the electronic bidding process. Under the new rule, both the purchasers and private entity can establish e-transaction platforms freely, provided that they meet with the required standards, and they can compete with each other for e-bid business. The e-transaction platforms are required to be open and inter-connectable, to support co-recognition of e-identification, and to prohibit the practices that discriminate among software tools conforming to the technical standards. The new rule also deals in detail with the particular issues in relation to electronic forms of invitation to bid, submissions of bids, opening of bids, and award of contract.

14.2.5.3 Conflict of Interest and Anti-Corruption

Improving integrity in the government is one of the goals of the GPL. Thus, the parties in government procurement should not collude with each other. It is also forbidden for the supplier or the agency to make bribes in the procurement activities or to take other improper means to seek illegal interest.[47] Otherwise, the parties will be punished severely.[48] Similar provisions can also be found in the BL.[49]

[44] The Operating Rules on E-bidding, issued by the Government Procurement Center of Central Governments, <http://www.zycg.gov.cn/article/show/264973> (last accessed February 1, 2015).

[45] <http://mall.zycg.cn/> (last accessed February 1, 2015).

[46] The Provisions on Electronic Bidding, issued jointly by eight Ministries on February 4, 2013.

[47] According to Article 25 of the GPL, the supplier should not bribe to the procurer, the procurement agency, the members of bid evaluation committee, the members of competitive negotiation panel, or the members of request for quotation panel, or take other improper action for winning the bid or being award the contract. The procurement agency should not bribe to the procurer or take other improper means to seek illegal interest.

[48] According to Articles72 and 77 of the GPL, if the procurer or the procurement agency and its staff maliciously collude with the supplier or procurement agency, or accept bribes or obtain other improper interest in the process of procurement, they should be subject to criminal penalties or administrative sanctions.

[49] See Articles 32, 50, and 53 of the BL.

In addition, significant provisions are provided under both the BL and GPL on the avoidance of conflicts of interest. Purchasers and relevant persons, including those involved in the procurement decision, shall avoid any conflict of interest in their relationship with suppliers that might impair the fairness and impartiality of the procurement. Such relationships may include, but are not limited to, employment with the supplier three years prior to the particular procurement, holding an office as director or supervisor of the supplier three years prior to the particular procurement, or being a controlling shareholder or de facto controller of the supplier three years prior to the particular procurement (Article 12 of GPL and Article 9 of GPL-IR). A supplier shall be prohibited from participating in the procurement where a conflict of interest may arise. For example, a supplier may be excluded from participating in procurement when it has the same officer, direct shareholding, or an administrative relationship with another competing supplier (Article 18 of the GPL-IR). Likewise, a supplier is also prohibited from participating in a procurement where it has provided service under the procurement where conflict of interest may arise (Article 18 of the GPI-IR). Similar provisions can also be found in the BL (Article 37) and BL-IR (Articles 27, 34, 46, and 48).

The BM provides that procuring entities may consult experts or suppliers for advice on the solicitation document "where necessary" (Article 22). While this may be based on the need to specify in further detail aspects of the solicitation document (e.g., technical specifications), safeguards should also be put in place to avoid conflicts of interest, especially where certain suppliers may gain an advantage by participating in the consultation process.

14.2.6 THE REGULATORY AUTHORITIES

14.2.6.1 The NDRC and the Bidding Law

The BL maintains the status quo, which leaves the State Council to provide for detailed rules concerning the allocation of authority. The State Council *Opinions* seem to be based on a compromise between the National Development and Reform Commission (NDRC) and other ministries.[50] On the one hand, it recognizes the key role played by the NDRC in formulating bidding policy, and on the other hand, it allows nine ministries to supervise bidding activities in line with their administrative functions. Under the *Opinions*, the NDRC is delegated authority to guide and supervise key national works procurement (for instance, the Three Gorges Dam), and play a leading role in preparing

[50] The Opinions on Responsibility Division of Administrative Supervision on Bidding Activities by Relevant Departments in State Council (March 4, 2000) by the State Commission Office for Public Sector Reform.

overall policy, implementing regulations. Furthermore, it has the authority to determine the scope of coverage, thresholds, and exemptions for compulsory bidding projects, although this must be done in consultation with the relevant ministries and approved by the State Council. The NDRC also designates official media to publish bid notices. Other agencies are in turn allowed to formulate specific implementing measures in accordance with the BL and other relevant regulations and policies.

A later implementing regulation endorsed the NDRC's supervisory role in relation to its traditional function of approval for construction projects. Under this regulation, the NDRC is responsible for determining the bidding mode (whether to conduct the bidding itself or through a bidding agent) and for decisions relating to the scope of compulsory bidding projects, after which the nine ministries will take over the task of supervision. Throughout the project, the NDRC retains overall authority and reserves the right to suspend execution of the project and withhold funding as the case may be.

14.2.6.2 The Ministry of Finance and the Government Procurement Law

14.2.6.2.1 Separation of Supervision from Procurement Functions. In order to separate supervision and procurement functions, the GPL makes it clear that regulatory agencies, that is the MOF at the central level,[51] shall not set up a centralized procurement agency or be involved in procurement activities (Article 60). This requirement is reiterated in a State Council Notice implementing the GPL at the central level (hereinafter referred to as the Implementation Plan),[52] which establishes the principle of "reasonable separation of functions and check and balance" (*he li fen gong, hu xiang zhi heng)* for the relationships between the regulatory department and the Central Procurement Agency (CPA). That is similar to the Western notion of separation of powers and checks and balances.[53]

14.2.6.2.2 The Regulatory Power of the Finance Departments. There is a general provision in the GPL establishing the MOF and finance departments as the competent authorities to regulate government procurement activity (Article 13). However, the case is not as clear-cut as it may seem. The term "competent regulatory authorities" should be checked against the various substantive provisions in both the GPL and other regulations that define the newly emerging authorities, especially the Implementation Plan. To summarize, the regulatory duties conferred upon the financial departments include the following:

[51] At the local level, the Department of Finance, which is provided in Article 13 of the GPL.

[52] Notice of the State Council Office on Issuing the Implementation Plan to Completely Promote the Government Procurement System across the Central State Organs, No. 53(2002) of the State Council Office (hereinafter referred to as the Implementation Plan).

[53] For example, the separation of the purchaser as the user from the CPA.

i. Government procurement policy and rules. The GPL does not confer any authority on the financial departments to draft new government procurement policy and rules. The GPL makes it clear in Article 87 that "the *specific steps and measures to implement this law shall be provided by the State Council.*" Therefore unless authorized by the State Council, the MOF does not have the power to issue implementing rules on government procurement. However, such authorization can be found in a legal document approved by the State Council Implementation Plan regarding the functions of the MOF in government procurement, though the authorization is only limited to the rules regarding government procurement by central government agencies.[54]

ii. Preparation of the government procurement plan—this is not provided by the GPL but by the State Council Implementation Plan.

iii. Approval of departmental budgets in accordance with the relevant authority and procedures (Article 33 of GPL).

iv. Preparation of the CP Catalogue and the thresholds (for coverage of the GPL and application of open bidding), and submitting to the State Council for the approval.[55]

v. Publication of information.

vi. Approval of new procurement methods by the MOF (Article 26).

vii. Approval of procurement methods and procedures other than open bidding.

viii. Supervision of procurement activities and operation of the CPAs. The measures provided in the GPL for such supervision include checks on the activities of the CPAs (Article 59 and 65), specifying the qualifications of government procurement professionals in the CPAs (Article 62), review of the CPAs' procurement prices and effectiveness of cost-saving, reviewing service quality and supplier reputation, and regular publication of such reviews (Article 66). In addition, the Implementation Plan extends the MOF's function of qualification of procurement professionals to training of government procurement managers.

ix. Regulating contracts—the MOF is the delegated authority to provide for the compulsory articles to be included the government procurement contracts in consultation with other relevant departments (Article 45).

[54] Notice of the State Council Office on Issuing the Implementation Plan to Completely Promote the Government Procurement System across the Central State Organs, No. 53(2002) of the State Council Office.

[55] It is noteworthy that the GPL confers the authority to decide and publish CP Catalogue and the relevant thresholds with the State Council. The Implementation Plan reserves the right of decision for State Council but delegate the preparation work to MOF. It is also noteworthy that the Implementation Plan qualifies such a delegation—it does not include the preparation of threshold for works procurement through opening bidding. Also, According to Article 7, only MOF and the department of finance at provincial level have authority to prepare the CP Catalogue and determine the GP thresholds.

x. Handling bid complaint and review (Articles 55–58).
xi. Other functions. In addition to those provided in the GPL, the financial departments are also conferred with other functions including the management and appropriation of funds for centralized purchase, registration of the bidding agencies, statistics and publicity of government procurement information, and so on.[56]

14.2.6.3 The Inter-Ministerial Coordination Mechanism

The current wording in the primary legislation concerning the allocation of powers leaves substantial room for interpretation. The GPL charges "finance departments at all levels with supervising government procurement and conduct their duties in accordance with law," while also providing that "other departments concerned at various levels shall fulfil their duties of supervision regarding government procurement."[57] Hence, while the GPL establishes the finance departments as the competent regulatory authority, it does not encroach upon the authority of other departments regarding government procurement, especially those whose authority was conferred by the BL.[58]

The result is that each regulator has interpreted the law in its own favor. Therefore, it is advisable that the lines of authority in the two laws are more precisely delineated. The Implementation Plan seems to be following such a more precise approach, defining the scope of the duties of the MOF and reiterating the regulatory power already conferred on the ministries sponsoring the BL.

Implementation of parallel procurement systems requires great coordination efforts. In 2005, the NDRC released measures establishing such a coordination mechanism.[59] The NDRC-led mechanism is comprised of eleven relevant authorities that play either a direct administrative role in bidding supervision or a general role of administrative supervision or regulatory affairs. Inter-ministerial conferences are regularly held and

[56] Notice of the State Council Office on Issuing the Implementation Plan to Completely Promote the Government Procurement System across the Central State Organs, No. 53(2002) of the State Council Office.

[57] These departments include, for example, other departments that are charged with duties of administrative supervision over government procurement conferred by law and administrative regulations, the supervision role of the audit organ of the government, or the supervision role of the discipline organ of the government over public servants.

[58] Whereas the procurement is conducted through a bidding method, the supervision of the bidding activities shall be in accordance with the State Council Notice on Opinions of the Allocation of the Departmental Administrative Supervisory Duties regarding Bidding Activities (No. 34 (2000) of the State Council Office), Notice of the State Council Office on Issuing the Implementation Plan to Completely Promote the Government Procurement System across the Central State Organs, No. 53(2002) of the State Council Office.

[59] Article 2, the Interim Measure on the Inter-Ministries Coordinative Mechanism over Bidding Activities, issued by NDRC, Ministry of Supervision, Ministry of Finance, Ministry of Construction, Ministry of Railway, Ministry of Communications, Ministry of Information Industry, Ministry of Water Resource, Ministry of Commerce, General Administration of Civil Aviation, and Legislative Affairs Office of the State Council on July 14, 2005.

attended by Director-General-level representatives from each ministry, supported by a working-level group of coordinators representing each ministry and an office that deals with the daily operation of the mechanism. Consensus is reached based on the principle of "collective consultation and unanimity" of the ministries and codified in the form of meeting minutes. The mandate of the mechanism is mainly to:

i. analyze the development of national bidding markets and review the implementation of the BL, administrative regulations and ministerial provisions, and discuss work plans and strategies involving multi-sector bidding activities;
ii. resolve contradictions and inconsistencies in the administrative supervision of bidding activities;
iii. exchange information regarding bidding;
iv. strengthen consistency among relevant departments in formulating bidding regulations and model documents; and
v. strengthen communication among relevant departments and local governments in handling bid complaints and enforcement.

The mechanism is encouraging, and its functioning seems effective as far as BL-related activity is concerned. However, it seems to be of little help in harmonizing inconsistencies between the parallel development of the GPL and the BL, since the measure clearly excludes from the mandate any bidding activities relating to procurement of goods and services (Article 4). The MOF is part of the mechanism, but plays a very passive role.

Substantive efforts are made to harmonize the two primary laws in relation to their scope of application and allocation of supervision authorities in the two major implementing regulations, the BL-IR and GPL-IR. As a result of such coordination, with regard to government works procurement covered by both the GPL and the BL, (a) the GPL's social and economic policies shall apply; and (b) when bidding methods are not applicable, the GPL's other procurement procedures shall apply.

14.2.7 THE PROCUREMENT FUNCTIONS

14.2.7.1 The Use of Commercial Bidding Agencies, and Decentralized Procurement under the BL

14.2.7.1.1 The Reliance on Commercial Biding Agencies. Under the BL, a procuring entity may choose to conduct the procurement itself or authorize a bidding agency to conduct the proposed procurement. However, if a procuring entity cannot demonstrate that it has sufficient skills to conduct the procurement, it is obliged to engage a commercial bidding agency. It can be observed that in reality, a large amount of procurement is outsourced and there is a heavy reliance on the use of commercial bidding agencies to conduct procurement. There is, however, little regulation regarding the appointment of these bidding agencies. Ironically, this mechanism of employing commercial biding agencies is designed as a means to prevent corruption, a perceived counterforce to the discretionary purchasing power of the procurement entities. However, there are huge conflict of interest issues associated with this institutional design, and it deprives the public sector of the opportunity to develop its own procurement function and capacity.

14.2.7.1.2 The Bid Evaluation Committee. The Bid Evaluation Committee is charged with the responsibility to evaluate and compare bids and recommend to the procurement entity the successful bidder, a further preventative mechanism, adopted by the BL and followed by the GPL, to limit the purchaser's discretionary purchasing power. The Committee is mainly composed of outside experts drawn randomly from a bank of experts maintained either by the regulatory body or by the commercial bidding agencies. The sentiment around this regulatory design is similar to that of the above design, that is, as there is a risk of corruption, purchasers are not going to evaluate and compare the bids. The mechanism effectively deprives the purchaser of an important decision-making power. However, the weakness associated with this design is also apparent. On the one hand, the public sector is again deprived of building up its own procurement expertise; and on the other hand, as the Committee member depends on the purchaser for their employment, there is also a conflict of interest issue. There is always a shortage in the pool of experts, especially at the local level.

14.2.7.1.3 Decentralized Procurement. As there is a Project Legal Person (PLP) for each individual project and each PLP appoints its own bidding agency (if it cannot afford to maintain its own procurement capacity), mostly without competition, the procurement function is vastly decentralized, presenting a serious issue of scale of economy.

14.2.7.2 Purchasing Functions under the GPL

When procurement reform was initiated, a centralized procurement system was preferred and as a part of common practice, a CP Catalogue was established to define the scope of centralized procurement. The GPL confirms this practice; it requires that government procurement be conducted in a combination of a centralized and decentralized fashion, and the scope of centralized procurement be defined by the CP Catalogue established by central and provincial government, respectively.[60] When the

[60] Article 7 of the Government Procurement Law of PRC.

procurement is covered by the CP Catalogue, a purchaser must engage a central procurement agency, a non-profit-making public institution specially set up to conduct the centralized procurement defined by the CP Catalogue.[61] The law also provides that governments above the provincial level have the freedom to establish a central agency at their own will,[62] but such agencies may not be established by the supervisory authority of government procurement,[63] the finance department. This reflects concern among legislators of a conflict of interest in the event that the supervisory authority gets involved in the procurement process.

In practice, central government and most local governments have set up centralized procurement centers to procure commonly used goods and services for other governments. A few local governments rely wholly on commercial procurement agencies to conduct the procurement.

14.2.8 CONCESSION REGULATION IN UTILITIES AND MUNICIPAL INFRASTRUCTURE SECTORS, AND PUBLIC–PRIVATE PARTNERSHIPS

The development of private sector participation has been gaining momentum following series of policy initiatives at the central level,[64] and along with this development came the third wave of Chinese procurement reform and regulation—the regulatory framework governing the procurement of privately-financed infrastructure projects (PFIP) and the distinctive legislative development of concession regulation in the urban infrastructure and utilities sectors. Beijing Municipality is taking the lead in promulgating the first concession regulation on its municipal infrastructure, and a number of other local governments have enacted concession regulations on municipal utilities.[65]

In recent years, the new administration has adopted a much more market-oriented approach toward public service provision, and the new urbanization initiative and resolution of the debts of provincial and local governments also demand a potentially

[61] Article 16 of the Government Procurement Law of PRC.

[62] Article 16 of the Government Procurement Law of PRC.

[63] Article 61 of the Government Procurement Law of PRC.

[64] For example, the Notice on Publishing the Opinions on Promoting and Guiding Private Investment, issued by the then National Planning Commission on December 11, 2001. Some Opinions On Some Policy Measure To Increase The Development Of Service Sectors In the fifteenth Five-Year Period, issued by the then National Planning Commission in January 2002; Opinion On Promoting The Marketisation Of Urban Public Utilities, issued by Ministry of Construction on December 27, 2003; Measures on Urban Public Utilities Concession, issued by MOC in 2004; State Council Decision Regarding The Investment System Reform, issued by the State Council in July 2004; the Opinions On Encouraging, Supporting And Guiding The Development of Non-State Sector Economies, issued by State Council in 2005.

[65] For a review of the Beijing Municipality regulation, see Cao (2006b); for a review of national development, see Cao (2007).

more important role for private capital. National policy initiatives for public–private partnerships are therefore thriving. The State Council issued a guideline opinion on innovating the investment and financing mechanisms in some key sectors, and public–private partnerships are among one of the most promoted mechanisms.[66] The MOF and NDRC are also rigorously promoting the practice of PPPs,[67] with both formulating new regulations for competitive selection of private capital (partner).[68] Indeed, the MOF and NDRC are said to be competing over issuing PPP policy initiatives and regulations in the wake of PPPs. It can be said that a new legal framework for PPPs is taking shape in China and the regulations as a whole could provide models for future national regulations.[69]

14.2.9 REVIEW MECHANISM: THE ENFORCEMENT AND ACCOUNTABILITY MECHANISMS, INCLUDING ALTERNATIVE DISPUTE INSTRUMENTS/AN ASSESSMENT OF THE USE OF DISPUTE SETTLEMENT MECHANISMS

Both the BL and GPL (with their implementing rules) provide a review mechanism by which a complainant can seek remedy for its allegedly infringed right.[70] The rationale and structures of the parallel provisions are similar except for some differences in particularities. Thus, only the system under the GPL is reviewed here.

The GPL is distinctive in establishing a bid challenge and complaint system. Under this system, the aggrieved bidders may make enquiries (*xun wen*) when they consider the procurement irregular (Article 51). A supplier that believes its legitimate interests have been infringed may file a challenge (*zhi yi*) to the procuring entity for redress (Article 52). When the supplier that initiates the challenge is not satisfied with the reply

66 The Guidance by State Council on Innovating Investment and Finance Mechanisms in Key Sectors and Encouraging Social Investment, issued by State Council on November 26, 2014.

67 The Circular by the MOF on Certain Issues of Promoting the practice of PPPs, issued by the MOF on September 24, 2014; the Circular by the MOF on Guideline of Operating PPPs, issued by the MOF on December 4, 2014; the Guidance by NDRC on Developing PPPs, issued by the NDRC on December 2, 2014, and attached the Guideline on Standard Contract of PPPs (2014 version).

68 The Administration Measures on Government Procurement of PPPs Project, issued by the Treasury of the MOF on December 31, 2014; the Interim Measures on Competitive Consultation Method of Government Procurement, issued by the Treasury of the MOF on December 31, 2014. The NDRC also issued a regulatory proposal of Administration Provisions on Concession in Infrastructure and Utilities attempting to regulate the concession type of PPPs.

69 Cao (2007).

70 Article 65 of the BL; The Measure on Handling the Complaints of Bidding for Construction Projects by NDRC, Ministry of Construction, Ministry of Railway, Ministry of Communications, Ministry of Information Industry, Ministry of Water Resource, and General Administration of Civil Aviation, issued and effective on August 1, 2004 (hereafter referred to as Bid Complaint Measure); the Implementation Regulation of the BL.

concerning its challenge from the procuring entity, or there is simply no timely reply, the supplier may submit a complaint (*tou su*) to the competent government finance department within fifteen working days of the expiry of the challenge period (Article 55). The competent financial department then acts as an administrative adjudicator to settle the dispute between the procuring entity and the complainant (Article 56) through an administrative decision. The administrative decision may be reviewable by a judicial court. Thus, if the complainant supplier is still not satisfied with the administrative decision or the decision is not made in a timely manner, it has the right to apply for administrative review of the decision or to file an administrative suit to the courts (Article 58).

Implementing ministerial provisions provides detailed rules concerning such issues as the standing of *eligible complainants, the scope of permissible complaints, available remedies*, and procedural aspects.

14.3 **The Influence/Relevance of International Norms and Frameworks**

When establishing a market-based procurement system for the first time, China paid fair attention to the recognized international legal norms and frameworks during the legislative process. These include the UNCITRAL Model Law on Procurement, the World Bank's procurement Guideline, the WTO's GPA and the EU's Directives on procurement. A detailed analysis of the influence/relevance of these international norms and frameworks would go beyond the scope of this chapter, but a general observation can still be made here within the limit.

First, there are areas where international norms and frameworks are most relevant; these include, notably, the general principles of the procurement law, the rules on transparency, and the innovative remedies system.

International legal norms generally embrace some basic principles such as openness and transparency, fair competition, non-discrimination, and efficiency in government procurement, and both the BL and GPL adopt similar principles. Furthermore, to some extent the Chinese procurement regulations are based more on principles than on detailed rules. This is possibly because principles are more agreeable than detailed rules among stakeholders, principles provide more flexibility to better accommodate the varied circumstances of a large country, and—as a practical matter—China does not have much experience in formulating detailed rules governing procurement as both procurement and regulation thereof were innovative at that time.

Transparent procedural rule is another area where international norms and frameworks have a better role to play. Transparent procedural rules are guarantees of the attainment of the objectives and principles of an international procurement law, form the majority part of a legal instrument, and are at the heart of a particular international regime.[71] These include rules on the choice of procurement method, advertisement of procurement opportunities, qualification of supplier, formulation of the technical specification, and evaluation and award of bid. Indeed, it is not difficult to observe the resemblances of the Chinese procedural procurement rules to those of the international legal norms, such as those found in the UNCITRAL Model Law on Public Procurement.[72]

A third area where international norms have more relevance is the review and remedy system. Review and remedy mechanisms are important to provide a check against fraud in the contract award process. A remedy system also safeguards the rights of the aggrieved suppliers, and thus is an integrate part of every procurement law.[73] Both the BL and the GPL borrow this innovative system from these international norms. One can also easily observe similar provisions in the Chinese procurement laws to those found in international procurement laws such as the Model Law—that the aggrieved supplier can challenge the alleged breach; that the supplier should approach the purchaser first to seek earlier settlement; that the complaint can be heard preferably by an administrative function; that the administrative decision is subject to judicial review; that there should be a time limit to resolve the dispute in a timely manner; and that interim measures should be in place to protect commercial opportunities. It is thus observed that the relevance of international norms in this respect lies in two aspects: the first is the awareness of the importance of such a system in a particular procurement law, and second is the key policy concerns and main elements of such a system.

[71] As noted in the Guide to Enactment of the UNCITRAL Model Law on Public Procurement (hereinafter referred to as the UNCITRAL Guide), transparency is a tool that allows to monitor, where necessary, challenge the exercise of procuring entities' discretion. It is considered a key element of a procurement system that is designed, in part, to limit the discretion of officials, and to promote accountability for the actions or decision taken. It is thus a critical support for integrity for public confidence in the system.

Transparent Procedure rules are the main part of any international norms. Taking the UNCITRAL Model Law on Public Procurement (hereinafter referred to as UNCITRAL Model Law), for example, transparency procedure rules feature throughout the Model Law. There are in total eight chapters in the Model Law, six of which directly provide the rules for procurement procedures, while the other two chapters also include plenty of rules on transparency requirements. Those rules include, but are not limited to, the following transparency measures: non-discriminatory methods of communication (Article 7); the determination of qualification, examination and evaluation criteria at the outset of the procurement and their public in the solicitation documents (Articles 8–11); and the wide publication of invitation to participate and all conditions of participation (e.g., in Articles 33, 39 and 47–49). For more discussion, see UNCITRAL Guide (p. 45).

[72] For instance, the terminologies of the GPL borrow directly from those provided under chapter II of UNCITRAL Model Law on Procurement of Goods, Construction and Services with Guide to Enactment (1994).

[73] For instance, chapter VI of the UNCITRAL Model Law on Procurement of Goods, Construction and Services with Guide to Enactment (1994); Article XIVIII of the GPA (2012); and EU Directive 2007/66/EC (Remedies Directives).

However, there are certain areas where the international norms and frameworks are less relevant. Take the objectives of a procurement law as an example. It is recognized that international procurement regimes have their own prioritized objectives that may not be in harmony with those of a national procurement law, for example free trade/opening up of the market versus efficiency.[74] Also, as the primary goal of a particular international procurement regime is to open procurement markets, it usually takes a reserved stand towards social and economic policy goals that are usually found in a national regime.[75] The consequential limitation or exclusion of such policy goals in the international regimes means a lack of well-recognized international norms as such, and best practice and guidance of effective implementing mechanism thereof. The intrinsic difficulty of formulating and implementing such a multi-goal system also contributes to the complexities, where the international norms are not a good place to turn to for regulatory reference.[76] Over the past decade, Chinese procurement laws have struggled to come up with a comprehensive understanding of the primary and secondary goals of a sound procurement system, from the emphasis on saving money in the early days, to more emphasis on the macro implications of secondary policies, and most recently value for money. Besides, anti-corruption is occasionally taken as an important—and perhaps the primary—goal of the procurement system, which has a huge impact on both the formulation of the procurement rules (very rigid and high transparent rules at the sacrifice of flexibility and efficiency) and the procurement behavior and culture (procurement for rules, not for value). Another example is the scope and coverage of the international regimes. Both the WTO and EU regimes have unique approaches to defining their scope and coverage which are less relevant to those under the Chinese laws. The UNCITRAL regime does provide a comprehensive list of indicators to decide on the exact scope and coverage of a procurement law, in particular for those entities that are not considered part of the government,[77] but the Chinese procurement laws have

[74] For a discussion of the potential conflicts between the objectives of national and international procurement system, see Arrowsmith (1998) and Arrowsmith, Linarelli, and Wallace (2000: chapters 1 and 2).

[75] The UNCITRAL Model Law is the one international instrument that recognizes the overarching aim of value for money and avoidance of abuse in public procurement. However, the Model Law only provides some discussion in its Guide, but is reluctant to include more provisions on social-economic policies. Many authors have analyzed the positions of such policies under the international laws. See, for example, Arrowsmith (1995); Kunzlik (1999, 2003); Arrowsmith and Kunzlik (2009); Caranta (2010); Arrowsmith and Nicholas (2009); Davies (2011); and Linarelli (2011).

[76] These complexities have been recognized by many authors, for instance, by Arrowsmith and Kunzlik (2009) and Caranta and Trybus (2010).

[77] These include: (a) whether the government provides substantial public funds to the entity, provides a guarantee or other security to secure payment by the entity in connection with its procurement contract, or otherwise supports the obligations of the procuring entity under the contract; (b) whether the entity is managed or controlled by the government or whether the government participates in the management or control of the entity; (c) whether the government grants to the entity an exclusive licence, monopoly or quasi-monopoly for the sale of the goods that the entity sells or the services that it provides; (d) whether the

their own concepts and approach to defining their coverage. The international regimes also provide little guidance on the challenging issue of regulating procurement by SOEs in the Chinese setting.

Still there are areas where international norms and frameworks have little relevance. International regimes tend to focus their regulatory efforts on the awarding phase, and consequentially the pre-award phase (such as planning) and post-award phases (such as contract management) of an effective procurement system are not a prioritized policy concern.[78] However, this inadvertent omission may have a serious negative impact on the effective operation of the procurement system.[79] Both the BL and GPL point their regulatory artilleries towards contract awarding, but the newly enacted GPL-IR has devoted much more effort to the issues of procurement demand assessment and control (Article 11), planning (Article 29) and budget (Article 30), and contact management (Article 45). In addition, the international regimes tend to assume that the operational and supporting infrastructure for the framework procurement laws is already there,[80] but this assumption might be too good to be true for developing countries, especially those that are enacting the laws for the first time, which is the case for China. The need for an operational procurement law has been generally recognized by other international collaborative programs such as the "Country Assessment" program by the World Bank and OECD,[81,82] with indicators that are of importance for the enacting state from an angle of operational procurement law.

entity is accountable to the government or to the public treasury in respect of the profitability of the entity; (e) whether an international agreement or other international obligation of the state applies to procurement engaged in by the entity; (f) whether the entity has been created by special legislative action in order to perform activities in the furtherance of a legally-mandated public purpose and whether the public law applicable to government contracts applies to procurement contracts entered into by the entity; see the UNCITRAL Model Law on Procurement of Goods, Construction and Services with Guide to Enactment.

[78] For instance, as described in the UNCITRAL Guide, the Model Law does not purport to address the procurement planning, contract performance, or implementation phase. Accordingly, issues such as budgeting, needs assessment, market research and consultations, contract administration, resolution of performance disputes or contract termination are not addressed in its provisions (see United Nations, 2014).

[79] "UNCITRAL recognizes the importance of these phases of the procurement process for the overall effective functioning of the procurement system. The enacting State needs to ensure that adequate laws and structures are available to deal with these phases of the procurement phases; otherwise, the objectives of the public procurement law may be frustrated"; see UNCITRAL Guide, para. 83.

[80] For example, "The Model Law is also based on an assumption that the enacting State has in place, or will put into place, the proper institutional and administrative structures and human resources necessary to operate and administer the type of procurement procedures provided for in the Model Law" (United Nations, 2014: p 18).

[81] The World Bank uses the Country Procurement Assessment Report (CPAR) as one instrument for assisting its member countries in analyzing their present procurement policies. For details, see <http://web.worldbank.org/WBSITE/EXTERNAL/PROJECTS/PROCUREMENT/0,contentMDK:20108359~menuPK:84285~pagePK:84269~piPK:60001558~theSitePK:84266,00.html> (accessed July 23, 2016).

[82] In order to provide the basis for formulating capacity development plans to improve the procurement system, the OECD has developed one methodology for assessing the quality of a country procurement

14.4 GPA, FTAs, and Internationalization of Chinese Procurement Law

14.4.1 CHINA'S ACCESSION TO THE WTO's GPA

One of the significant moves regarding China's government procurement policy is China's request to join the WTO's GPA.[83] On accession to the WTO, China made several commitments regarding government procurement, among which is its understanding to become an observer to the GPA upon accession to the WTO Agreement and to "initiate negotiations for membership in the GPA by tabling an Appendix 1 offer as soon as possible."[84] China became an observer of the GPA in 2002 and on December 28, 2007, it finally submitted a formal application (an application for accession into the GPA and Appendix I offer) to become a party to the GPA,[85] meaning the initiation of China's GPA accession process. China later revised its offer in July 2010,[86] November 2011,[87] November 2012,[88] and December 201.[89] The most recent offer is the fifth revised offer, which was submitted to the WTO on December 22, 2014. The new offer covers, for the first time, state-owned universities, state-owned hospitals and state-owned enterprises. It also expands the coverage to include more central and sub-central entities, and new services sectors and construction services. In addition, contract thresholds are reduced to a level comparable to those of the GPA members. It is said that the newly revised offer is in line

system in terms of effectiveness and efficiency. For details, see the OECD Methodology for Assessing Procurement Systems (MAPS), of December 2009.

[83] See also Anderson (2007, 2008) and Wang (2009, 2011).

[84] Para. 341, WT/MIN(01)/3, November 10, 2001, Report of the Working Party in the Accession of China. Other commitments include: (1) before China becomes a party to the GPA "all government entities at the central and sub-national level, as well as any of its public entities other than those engaged in exclusively commercial activities, would conduct their procurement in a transparent manner, and provide all foreign suppliers with equal opportunity to participate in that procurement pursuant to the principle of MFN treatment." See Para. 339, WT/MIN(01)/3, November 10, 2001, Report of the Working Party in the Accession of China.

[85] See GPA/ACC/CHN/1 of January 7, 2008, available at <www.wto.org>. The text in Chinese is available at <http://www.gov.cn/gzdt/2008-05/13/content_971032.htm> (accessed July 23, 2016).

[86] "Accession of the People's Republic of China to the Agreement on Government Procurement," Communication from the People's Republic of China, Revised Offer, GPA/ACC/CHN/16, July 9, 2010 (available at <http://cwto.mofcom.gov.cn/accessory/201007/1279697635138.txt[2011/11/26%200:09:45>) (accessed July 23, 2016). The text in Chinese is available at <http://www.caigou2003.com/perspective/gpa/20110706/gpa_186783.html> (accessed July 23, 2016).

[87] GPA/ACC/CHN/30, November 30, 2011. An English version is available at: <www.caigou2003.com/lib/text/GPA2011.doc.> (accessed April 12, 2012).

[88] See: <http://finance.sina.com.cn/roll/20121217/213214029908.shtml> (last accessed March 15, 2015).

[89] See: <http://www.cgpnews.cn/articles/18948> (last accessed March 15, 2015).

with those of the other GPA members.[90] The GPA parties reviewed China's fifth revised offer at their February 11, 2015 meeting. While the parties expressed due appreciation for the improvements and the efforts China put into preparing the new offer, they also said that a number of significant gaps remain to be filled before China's accession could be concluded. Emphasis was also placed on the need for China to advance work on reform of its procurement legislation. China said it would be difficult for it to make significant further additions to entity coverage, but that it was ready to continue discussions on proposed exceptions.[91]

14.4.2 GOVERNMENT PROCUREMENT UNDER FTAs WHERE CHINA IS A PARTY

China has signed more than ten FTAs and a number of other FTAs are under negotiation.[92,93] It can be observed that government procurement is explicitly excluded from these FTAs. Take the China–New Zealand FTA as an example. Article 6 of the Agreement excludes government procurement from national treatment for trade in goods by reference to Article III provisions under GATT 1994. Article 92 of the Agreement exempts government procurement from the obligation associated with those under chapter 8 on Technical Barriers to Trade. Article 105 exempts government procurement from obligations under chapter 10 on Trade in Services. In addition, Article 137 exempts government procurement from obligations under chapter 11 on Investment. It seems to be clear that those FTAs follow the same approach to dealing with the issue of government procurement under the WTO's multilateral agreements.

Interestingly, however, there seems to be some development in the issue of government procurement under the two most recent FTAs—the China–Iceland FTA and the China–Switzerland FTA. While on the one hand these two FTAs still exempt government procurement from most of its obligations, on the other hand they incorporate a separate and specific article on government procurement. Article 99 of the China–Iceland FTA on Government Procurement specifically addresses the issue of government

[90] See: <http://www.gov.cn/xinwen/2014-12/24/content_2795901.htm> (last accessed March 15, 2015).

[91] See: <https://www.wto.org/english/news_e/news15_e/gpro_11feb15_e.htm> (last accessed March 15, 2015).

[92] These include China–ASEAN FTA, China–Pakistan FTA, China–Chile FTA, China–New Zealand FTA, China–Singapore FTA, China–Peru FTA, Mainland and Hong Kong Closer Economic and Partnership Arrangement, Mainland and Macau Closer Economic and Partnership Arrangement, China–Costa Rica FTA, China–Iceland FTA, and China–Switzerland FTA.

[93] China–GCC (Gulf Cooperation Council) FTA, China–Australia FTA, China–Norway FTA, China–Korea FTA, China–Japan–Korea FTA, Regional Comprehensive Economic Partnership, RCEP, China–ASEAN FTA Upgrade Negotiations, China–Sri Lanka FTA.

procurement. It expresses good will of "co-operation to enhance mutual understanding of their respective government procurement laws and regulations." In addition, it imposes a light transparency obligation on the parties to "publish their laws, or otherwise make publicly available their laws, regulations and administrative rulings of general application." Furthermore, it imposes an obligation to "hold a consultation to consider possible steps to be taken with a view to concluding an agreement on government procurement between the Parties," once China has concluded successfully its accession negotiations to become a party to the GPA. A similar article can be found in the China–Switzerland FTA (Article 13.4). This clear association of the FTAs to the result of China's GPA accession negotiation possibly means a separate chapter under the FTAs in the future, like those under the NFTA. But it is unlikely that China would deviate from its current approach to dealing with government procurement issues under these FTAs, and China is only ready to address the government procurement issue first under the plurilateral framework of the GPA, rather than under the bilateral framework of FTAs.[94] The purpose of more provisions on government procurement under the two most recent FTAs is not to provide substantive obligation in relation to government procurement, but "to achieve further understanding of the government procurement of the Parties and lay the ground for future cooperation in this field," as is indicated in para.2(f) of Article1.1 of the China–Switzerland FTA. It has been declared that China has concluded two more FTAs respectively with Korea and Australia.[95,96] The formal texts of the two FTAs have not been published, but it may be safe to say that China will still want to exclude government procurement from these FTAs.

14.5 **Domestic Reform and Internationalization of Chinese Procurement Law: The Way Forward**

The relationships between the Chinese domestic system and the international system are proactive. On the one hand, as discussed above, international regimes are relevant to the Chinese domestic system, and against the background of China's GPA process, this relevance may be intensified and of special implication. China's GPA accession process has indeed generated stronger political awareness and the political will to further this transformation process. There has also been generated an unprecedented learning process

[94] This may be in contrast with the other states who adopt procurement chapter in their PTAs before they move on to the plurilateral GPA (see Ueno, 2013).

[95] The negotiation process of the China–Korea FTA was finished on February 25, 2015, but the formal text of the agreement has not been published.

[96] The substantial negotiation process of the China–Australia FTA was finished on November 17, 2014, but the formal text of the agreement has not been published.

in connection to both internationalization processes and domestic reform. Never in Chinese history have so many resources and efforts been invested in the study of the issues of public procurement. The effect of the learning process will inform a sound policy-making process and provide a catalyst for further domestic reforms. For example, China has begun to include more service sectors in the coverage of its procurement regulation and has begun to formulate procurement standards. It is indeed only in recent years, when China has stepped up its process of accession to the GPA, that it has begun to conceive of a fundamental transformation of its system. Indeed, China is now on the verge of another reform with the convergence of domestic and international efforts, and some of the newly adopted measures, such as the requirement for disclosure of the full text of government contracts, have indeed led the world in contract transparency.[97] In this, the GPA and other international norms have certainly had a role to play.

On the other hand, a developed Chinese domestic system may contribute to the internationalization of its procurement law. Any major development of the GPA regimes follows the steps of GPA members' internal systems; as one commentator has observed: "it is interesting to note that the successful negotiation of the GATT agreement on procurement and the GPA followed closely on the heels of each of the two major phases of liberalization within the European Union and of the conclusion of CETA and NAFTA," and "[w]ithout this precedent [of European liberalization] it is doubtful that the GATT negotiations would have succeeded in widening the coverage of the GPA."[98] Therefore, it is fair to say that China's future road towards the GPA depends on how well it can manage a comprehensive domestic procurement reform. A developed domestic system will also contribute to the effectiveness of the GPA regime when China becomes a party to the GPA, as the GPA is not intended to replace a domestic system, but rather depends on a developed domestic system to operate effectively.

China's initiative towards the GPA has generated a lot of expectation and speculation, both optimistic and pessimistic. As one of the largest developing and transitional economies with perhaps the largest public sector, China's future accession to the GPA would bring huge market opportunities for international trade. China's accession may also present a benchmark for possible future accession by other similar economies.

Nevertheless, there are also real challenges. One of these challenges is how well China can build up a coordinated procurement system with multiple laws governing different

[97] It is recognized that only a few number of countries, including the UK and Australia, have required a full disclosure of government contracts, while the majority of EU countries and the US do not have such a level of contract transparency.

[98] Woolcock (1993: p. 227), quote from Sue et al. regulating public procurement: international and domestic perspective.

aspects of public procurement. Another challenge is whether China is ready to bring SOEs into the coverage of domestic procurement regulation, and how. Yet another challenge is how China will balance the different policy objectives, especially those between national development and international trade. There are also emerging critical issues for public procurement: the new initiative on contracting out public services, regulation on SOEs procurement, and the initiative towards a national PPP law. The list may be longer and it is fair to observe that until China can manage to handle these domestic challenges, it will be difficult, if not impossible, for it to offer a substantial share of its procurement market comparable to the level of developed members.

The prospect of China's future GPA accession would thus be a long and winding process. However, this may not necessarily be the case, as there is another option that the GPA club accepts China sooner but with a relatively smaller offer, one that leaves behind some of the challenging issues, such as substantive coverage of procurement by SOEs and those in the defense sector. The current members would not lose anything, as the current rules of the GPA are based on reciprocity, but they will gain something as they have engaged China in the first place and may be in a better position to engage China in the future. What is especially valuable in this approach is that it provides Chinese policy-makers with opportunities for more political awareness of the dimensions and rationales for regulating its domestic public procurement markets, and the capacity to launch a comprehensive procurement reform, thus (indirectly) smoothing China's future path towards the GPA. The accession exercise may also prove to be valuable for China to gain technical experience in international regulation, which in turn would enhance China's confidence in future GPA negotiations. Additionally, China's early accession to the GPA would help to accumulate experience in developed nations, thus helping to generate support for future development towards the GPA at home.

Indeed, with China's most recent revised and improved offer, the Chairman of the WTO's Government Procurement Committee has said that "both sides should not lose sight of the benefits at stake in the negotiations" and called on "GPA parties to remain *pragmatic in their expectations and approach to the negotiations*" (emphasis added).[99] If this pragmatic approach becomes true, and the proposed option by the current author is accepted, the way forward for internationalization of the Chinese public procurement law would be quicker, but the future would predominantly depend on more proactive interplay between the Chinese domestic and the international system.

[99] <https://www.wto.org/english/news_e/news15_e/gpro_11feb15_e.htm> (last accessed March 15, 2015).

REFERENCES

Anderson, R. 2007. "China's Accession to the WTO Agreement on Government Procurement: Progress to Date and Ongoing Negotiations." *Public Procurement Law Review* 16: 255–73.

Anderson, R. 2008. "China's Accession to the WTO Agreement on Government Procurement: Procedural Considerations, Potential Benefits and Challenges, and Implementation of the On-Going Re-Negotiation of Agreement." *Public Procurement Law Review* 17: 161–74.

Arrowsmith, S. 1995. "Public Procurement as a Tool of Policy and the Impact of Market Liberalisation." *Law Quarterly Review* 111: 235–84.

Arrowsmith, S. 1998. "National and International Perspectives on the Regulation of Public Procurement: Harmony or Conflict?" In S. Arrowsmith and A. Davies (eds), *Public Procurement Global Revolution*. London: Kluwer Law International, 3–26.

Arrowsmith, S. and Kunzlik, P. 2009. "Public Procurement and Horizontal Policies in EC Law: General Principles." In S. Arrowsmith and P. Kunzlik (eds), *Social and Environmental Policies in EC Procurement Law*. Cambridge: Cambridge University Press, 9–54.

Arrowsmith, S., Linarelli, J., and Wallace, D. 2000. *Regulating Public Procurement: National and International Perspectives*. London: Kluwer Law International.

Arrowsmith, S. and Nicholas, C. 2009. "The UNCITRAL Model Law on Procurement of Goods, Construction and Services: Past, Present and Future." In S. Arrowsmith (ed.), *Public Procurement Regulation in the 21st Century: Reform of the UNCITRAL Model Law on Procurement*. Eagan, MN: West, 6–14.

Cao, F. 2003. "China's Government Procurement Regulation: From the Bidding Law to the Government Procurement Law." In S. Arrowsmith and M. Tybus (eds), *Public Procurement: Global Revolution*. London: Kluwer Law International, 61–84.

Cao, F. 2006a. "Developments in China: The Regulations Implementing the Chinese Government Procurement Law, and Progress Towards GPA Accession," *Public Procurement Law Review* 6, NA205–13.

Cao, F. 2006b. "The Emerging Legal Framework of Private Finance in Infrastructure in China: A Preliminary Review of the Beijing Concession Regulation." *Public Procurement Law Review* 15: 62–9.

Cao, F. 2007. "Regulating Procurement of Privately-Financed Infrastructure in China: A Review of the Recent Legislative Initiatives and the Emerging Regulatory Framework." *Public Procurement Law Review* 3: 147–73.

Cao, F. 2013. "Building up SME Programmes in Government Procurement in China: Legal Structure, Recent Developments and the Way Forward towards the WTO-GPA." *Public Procurement Law Review* 6: 211–24.

Cao, F. and Fen. Z. 2014. "Towards Sustainable Public Procurement in China: Policy and Regulatory Framework, Current Developments and the Case for a Consolidated Green Public Procurement Code." *Journal of Malaysian and Comparative Law* 41(1): 43–68.

Caranta, R. 2010. "Sustainable Public Procurement in the EU." In R. Caranta and M. Trybus (eds), *The Law of Green and Social Procurements in Europe*. Copenhagen: DJØF, 15–51.

Caranta, R. and Trybus, M. (eds). 2010. *The Law of Green and Social Procurements in Europe*. Copenhagen: DJØF.

Davies, A. 2011. "The National Treatment and Exceptions Provisions of the Agreement on Government Procurement and the Pursuits of Horizontal Policies." In S. Arrowsmith and R. D. Anderson (eds), *The WTO Regime on Government Procurement: Challenge and Reform*. Cambridge: Cambridge University Press, 429–43.

Jingbin, T. 2001. "Public Procurement in China: The Way Forward." *Public Procurement Law Review* 10: 208.

Kunzlik, P. 1999. "Environmental Issues in International Procurement." In S. Arrowsmith and A. Davies (eds), *Public Procurement: Global Revolution*. London: Kluwer Law International, 199–217.

Kunzlik, P. (ed.). 2003. *The Environmental Performance of Public Procurement*. Paris: OECD Publications.

Linarelli, J. 2011. "The Limited Case for Permitting SME Procurement Preferences in the Agreement on Government Procurment." In S. Arrowsmith and R. D. Anderson (eds), *The WTO Regime on Government Procurement: Challenge and Reform*. Cambridge: Cambridge University Press, 444–58.

Ueno, A. 2013. "Multilateralising Regionalism on Government Procurement." OECD Trade Policy Papers No. 151, Paris (available at: <http://dx.doi.org/10.1787/5k46l8vvq2np-en> (accessed July 23, 2016)).

United Nations. 2014. "Guide to Enactment of UNCITRAL Model Law on Public Procurement," Paris.

Wang, P. 2009. "China's Accession to the WTO Government Procurement Agreement—Challenges and the Way Forward." *Journal of International Economic Law* 12(3): 663–706.

Wang, P. 2011. "Accession to the Agreement on Government Procurement: The Case of China." In S. Arrowsmith and R. D. Anderson (eds), *The WTO Regime on Government Procurement: Challenge and Reform*. Cambridge: Cambridge University Press, 92–116.

Woolcock, S. 1993. "The European Acquis and Mutilateral Trade Rules: Are They Compatible?" *Journal of Common Market Studies* 31(4): 539–58.

15 Internationalization of Government Procurement Regulation

The Case of India

Anirudh Shingal

15.1 Introduction

India is a federation of states with multiple layers of governance. Understandably, therefore, procurement occurs at various levels of government in India. These include the central government, the state governments, and the three tiers of local government: village, intermediate, and district. Additionally, there are centrally and state-owned enterprises (SOEs). There is no single uniform law governing procurement by all of these public entities; instead a framework of rules, codes, and manuals governs procurement distinctly at the federal level, sub-federal levels, by SOEs, and by entities within the Ministry of Defence and Indian Railways.

Given the diversity and complexity within the country and India's colonial legal legacy, the absence of a single uniform law governing procurement by all of these public entities is not surprising, though the soundness of the procedural framework in place has been noted by the World Bank (2003) in its Country Procurement Assessment Report (CPAR). This said, India would benefit enormously from the harmonization and simplification of these different procedures, leading to improved governance, taxpayers receiving better value for their money, and greater overall efficiency in the economy given the broad range of producer services that governments still deliver within and across the country. Such harmonization and simplification would also make procurement processes more transparent and efficient, improving access for both domestic and foreign suppliers.

In the abstract of its CPAR, the World Bank (2003) also notes that "in the absence of a central lead department or agency in the centre, dedicated to policy and oversight of public procurement, and, in the absence of a central law or state act in public procurement, a 'Public Procurement Law' complemented by a set of Public Procurement Regulations, to replace and consolidate the present fragmented rules, will improve the transparency of the process, and accountability of public officials. Furthermore, the introduction of an independent authority—Public Procurement Tribunal—and a debriefing procedure should be useful steps to improve transparency, as well as simplified review and approval process, and a revamping of blacklisting rules."

Encouragingly, India has already been taking steps in this direction and, significantly, all these reforms have been made unilaterally. For instance, the previous central government was involved in the process of legislating a public procurement bill (Public Procurement Bill, 2012)[1,2] covering procurements undertaken by central government ministries, departments, and SOEs. The Bill incorporates international best practices in this area embedded in the UNCITRAL Model Law on Public Procurement, the World Bank guidelines, and the WTO's GPA, and in some instances even improves upon them.

Several state governments, including Rajasthan, Karnataka and Tamil Nadu, have their own public procurement legislations that are also based on international best practices. In fact, the states of Karnataka and Tamil Nadu were the first in the country to implement end-to-end e-procurement even before the central government, and since 2012 all central, state, and SOE contracts above a certain threshold are mandatorily tendered on an e-portal along with details on contract awards. This e-procurement has not only ushered in greater transparency in the system, but has also led to "better value for money" either in terms of falling tender premiums (ADB, 2011) or improvements in quality (Lewis-Faupel et al., 2014).

Despite these advancements, however, there are many implementation challenges and corruption is rife in the award of public contracts. Besides heterogeneity in performance at the state level, "the quality of the personnel is not as good, and there is much more intervention by politicians, and higher incidence of corruption" (World Bank, 2003: p. 8). Micro and small Enterprises (MSEs) continue to receive purchase and price preferences in procurement by central government ministries/departments/SOEs. Moreover, India does not have a domestic bid challenge procedure, though the Public Procurement Bill, 2012 has provisions for setting up an independent Procurement Redressal Committee. In addition, the Bill itself needs to be re-introduced in the Parliament by the new

[1] The Bill had already been passed by the Lower House of the Indian Parliament before the latter was dissolved in the wake of the newly elected government taking office. It would now need to be re-introduced in the Indian Parliament by the new government.

[2] The draft of the Public Procurement Bill, 2012 is available at: <http://164.100.24.219/BillsTexts/LSBillTexts/asintroduced/58_2012_LS_EN.pdf> (accessed July 23, 2016), and the corrigendum thereto at <http://164.100.24.219/BillsTexts/LSBillTexts/Errata/Cor_EN_58_2012_LS.pdf> (accessed July 23, 2016).

government, subject to review by different committees and the two Houses, and approved by the president of India before it becomes an Act.

Against this background, this chapter provides a case study of the internationalization of procurement regulation in the context of India. Section 15.2 provides some estimates of the size of India's procurement market and access to foreign suppliers. Section 15.3 details various aspects of India's procurement policy, before the influence of international norms on this policy is discussed in Section 15.4. Section 15.5 describes the approach toward transparency and statistical reporting, while Section 15.6 provides an overview of existing procurement impact assessment studies in the context of India. Sections 15.7 and 15.8 assess India's dispute settlement and e-procurement systems and Section 15.9 concludes, discussing *inter alia* the internationalization of India's procurement regulation and the country's position vis-à-vis the WTO's GPA.

15.2 **Data**

Data on public expenditure (current and capital expenses reported in broad economic categories) are available in the budget and finance documents of various central and state government ministries and departments as well as municipal corporations, but information on actual expenses incurred in the purchase of goods and services cannot be retrieved from these data. There is also no single compiling or reporting agency for data on public procurement in India. Moreover, evidence on the contestability of India's procurement markets is at best anecdotal.

This said, the mandatory e-tendering of above-threshold central, state, and SOE contracts since 2012 and details on the award of public contracts is generating a huge information base on procurement in India. An analysis of these central and state e-portals reveals that there is a wealth of procurement information now available for almost all the twenty-nine states and six centrally administered union territories (UTs) and SOEs in the country. This includes information on the value of the contract, the number of bidders, the name and address of the winning supplier, the name and sector of the procuring entity, dates of tender advertisement and award, the tendering method, and the number of days to contract implementation. The information on these e-portals can also be used to examine the extent of foreign procurement by Indian governments by entity, state/UT, and/or sector. While these details can be accessed online easily, a database on these would have to be assembled manually, which is both tedious and time-consuming.

Estimates are also available of the size of procurement markets and foreign involvement in government procurement in India. These estimates involve different methodologies and sets of data, which explains the differences in them. According to Srivastava (2003), for instance, the total value of purchases by the central and state governments and public enterprises, which could in principle be subject to international competitive bidding, varies between 3.4 percent and 5.7 percent of GDP.

The WTO Secretariat's "Trade Policy Review for India" for 2002 states: "In 2000/01 the estimated value of purchases by the central government procurement agency, the Directorate General of Supplies and Disposals (DGS&D) was Rs. 32.8 billion (around USD 0.8 billion); additional procurement by ministries of central and state governments as well as public sector enterprises was estimated at around Rs. 23.1 billion (approximately USD 0.6 billion) for the year 2000/01." These amounts were 0.2 percent and 0.1 percent, respectively, of India's GDP in current US dollars in 2001.

The CPAR of the World Bank (2003) estimated the value of public procurement at all levels of government at about 13 percent of the national budgets (over 20 percent of GDP), while Shingal (2012) estimated the size of the general government procurement market at 7.1 percent of the country's GDP and the value of contestable general government purchases to be in the range of €6.1–18.4 billion in 2007 (0.7–2.1 percent of India's 2007 GDP).

Shingal (2012) developed a methodology to estimate the size of market access in non-GPA countries, including India. This methodology was used to estimate the access of EU firms in India's procurement markets. The EU's disaggregated breakdown across India's procurement markets for the year 2007 from Shingal (2012) is reported in Table 15.1. The findings suggest that EU firms supplied Indian federal and sub-federal entities and SOEs with goods and services worth between €23.8 and €71.4 million in the year 2007, which was 18.6 percent of India's total foreign public procurement in that year. These results also suggest that the bulk of public contracts to EU suppliers were awarded in paper, motor vehicles, electronic equipment, other machinery and equipment, other commercial services (OCS) and other government services (OSG), which together accounted for 83.4 percent of the EU's access in India's public markets.

A recent source of data on general government finance consumption expenditure (GFCE) is the World Input-Output Database (WIOD) (Timmer et al., 2012). The disaggregated breakdown of India's GFCE and public consumption imports for the year 2011 from the WIOD is reported in Table 15.2 (in millions of US dollars). These data suggest that total government final consumption expenditure and total public consumption imports were $209 trillion and $7.1 trillion, respectively, in 2011. While public administration and defense; and education and other community, social, and personal services were the major sectors of governments' consumption spending according to these data, the bulk of public consumption imports were made in miscellaneous manufacturing; electrical and optical equipment; machinery; and chemicals and chemical products.

Figure 15.1 shows the breakdown of India's aggregate public consumption imports by source countries from the WIOD for the year 2011. The figure shows that China, the EU27 and the US were the major suppliers, accounting for more than 50 percent of the

Table 15.1 The EU's access in India's procurement markets, 2007 (€ thousands)

Sector	India[a]	India[b]
Agriculture forests fishery	35.2	105.7
Mining and energy extraction	0.0	0.0
Food beverages tobacco	64.9	194.8
Textiles	266.8	800.3
Wearing apparel	223.0	669.1
Leather products	0.0	0.0
Wood products	0.0	0.0
Paper products, publishing	2988.1	8964.2
Petroleum, coal products	0.1	0.3
Chemical, rubber, plastic products	2050.0	6150.0
Mineral products nec	2.6	7.9
Ferrous metals	0.0	0.0
Metals nec	0.0	0.0
Metal products	165.0	495.0
Motor vehicles and parts	2589.8	7769.5
Transport equipment nec	317.4	952.2
Electronic equipment	4299.0	12897.0
Machinery and equipment nec	3994.2	11982.5
Manufactures nec	86.4	259.2
Electricity	0.0	0.0
Gas manufacture, distribution	18.5	55.6
Transport svs	756.1	2268.3
Other commercial svs (OCS)	3307.2	9921.6
Other govt svs (OSG)	2895.3	8685.9
Total	**24059.8**	**72179.3**
Total contestable market (€ bn)	6.2	18.4
Total FP (€ mn)	129.3	387.9
Coverage, year	Annex1-3, 2007	
Share of EU's market access in:		
Total contestable market (%)	0.39	
Total FP (%)	18.6	

Source: Shingal (2012).

Note: The estimates cover central and state government entities as well as SOEs. "a" and "b" correspond to contestable government expenses being 10 percent and 30 percent, respectively, of adjusted general government expenses. FP = Foreign procurement. For details, see Shingal (2012).

Table 15.2 Disaggregated breakdown of India's GFCE and public imports, 2011 (US$ millions)

Sector	GFCE	Sector share of total (%)	Public imports	Sector share of total (%)
Agriculture, hunting, forestry, and fishing	2,757	1.3	29	0.4
Mining and quarrying	77	0.0	17	0.2
Food, beverages, and tobacco	1,903	0.9	24	0.3
Textiles and textile products	1,899	0.9	156	2.2
Leather, leather, and footwear	21	0.0	6	0.1
Wood and products of wood and cork	9	0.0	34	0.5
Pulp, paper, paper, printing, and publishing	2,150	1.0	43	0.6
Coke, refined petroleum, and nuclear fuel	1,763	0.8	72	1.0
Chemicals and chemical products	1,339	0.6	331	4.6
Rubber and plastics	252	0.1	81	1.1
Other non-metallic mineral	35	0.0	27	0.4
Basic metals and fabricated metal	501	0.2	160	2.2
Machinery-nec	682	0.3	367	5.1
Electrical and optical equipment	429	0.2	838	11.7
Transport equipment	1,515	0.7	132	1.8
Manufacturing, nec; recycling	276	0.1	4,325	60.2
Electricity, gas, and water supply	5,402	2.6	18	0.3
Construction	3,960	1.9	9	0.1
Sales, maintenance, and repair of motor vehicles	145	0.1	13	0.2
Wholesale trade and commission trade	1,125	0.5	66	0.9
Retail trade; repair of household goods	1,837	0.9	32	0.4
Hotels and restaurants	3,777	1.8	86	1.2
Inland transport	3,853	1.8	10	0.1
Water transport	54	0.0	0	0.0
Air transport	158	0.1	0	0.0
Other supporting and auxiliary transport activities	196	0.1	2	0.0
Post and telecommunications	1,918	0.9	23	0.3
Financial intermediation	4,799	2.3	81	1.1
Real estate activities	–	0.0	0	0.0
Renting of M&Eq and other business activities	2,074	1.0	72	1.0
Public admin and defence; compulsory social security	113,309	54.2	15	0.2
Education	30,705	14.7	1	0.0
Health and social work	8,251	3.9	1	0.0
Other community, social, and personal services	11,855	5.7	115	1.6
Total	**209,025**	**100**	**7,188**	**100**

Source: WIOD; Timmer et al. (2012); own calculations.

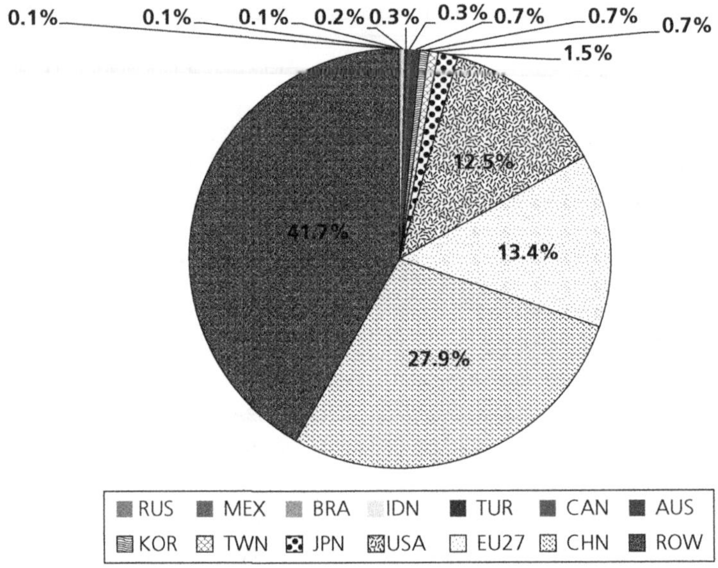

Figure 15.1. Breakdown of India's aggregate public consumption imports by source countries, 2011

Source: WIOD; Timmer et al. (2012); own calculations.

total. Table 15.3, also from the WIOD, reports the disaggregated breakdown of India's public consumption imports by source countries again for the year 2011.

Note, however, that the WIOD data do not include government capital expenses, so the data reported in Tables 15.2 and 15.3 underestimate the value of both public procurement and public imports.

This said, in a regressive development, the data reporting requirements in Article XVI: 4 of the revised GPA (RGPA) are less onerous than those in Article XIX: 5 of the Uruguay Round GPA (URGPA). In particular, unlike the requirements of Article XIX: 5 of URGPA, Article XVI: 4 of RGPA does not require data on awarded public contracts to be reported by nationality of the winning supplier. In the absence of the requirement for actual information on market access to be reported even by GPA contracting parties, the only source of internationally comparable information on market access in both GPA and non-GPA country procurement markets remains the WIOD database or using the methodology in Shingal (2012), both of which can only yield estimates. This also makes it difficult to examine the actual impact of the GPA on market access in GPA contracting parties.

Table 15.3 Disaggregated breakdown of India's public consumption imports by source countries, 2011 (US$ millions)

Sector	AUS	BRA	CAN	CHN	EU27	IDN	JPN	KOR	MEX	RUS	TUR	TWN	USA	ROW
Agriculture, hunting, forestry, and fishing	1	0	3	2	3	0	0	0	0	0	0	0	2	17
Mining and quarrying	0	0	0	12	0	0	0	0	0	0	0	0	0	5
Food, beverages, and tobacco	0	0	0	5	10	0	0	0	0	0	0	0	1	7
Textiles and textile products	1	0	0	49	28	0	1	2	0	0	1	0	7	66
Leather, leather, and footwear	0	0	0	3	0	0	0	0	0	0	0	0	0	2
Wood and products of wood and cork	0	0	0	7	5	0	0	0	0	0	0	0	3	20
Pulp, paper, paper, printing, and publishing	0	0	0	6	11	0	1	0	0	0	1	0	9	13
Coke, refined petroleum, and nuclear fuel	0	0	0	3	11	0	1	7	0	0	0	3	2	44
Chemicals and chemical products	2	1	1	**128**	**93**	3	5	4	1	0	0	3	13	77
Rubber and plastics	0	0	0	38	12	0	2	1	0	0	0	0	4	24
Other non-metallic mineral	0	0	0	10	9	0	0	0	0	0	0	0	1	6
Basic metals and fabricated metal	1	0	0	66	29	0	5	0	0	0	0	0	4	54
Machinery nec	1	0	0	**249**	13	0	5	1	0	0	0	0	5	92
Electrical and optical equipment	0	1	1	**283**	**50**	4	10	**14**	4	0	0	**14**	**231**	**226**
Transport equipment	0	0	0	47	42	0	5	3	0	0	1	0	5	29
Manufacturing nec; recycling	8	3	**9**	**1041**	**362**	**7**	**37**	**15**	1	2	**12**	**29**	**551**	**2247**
Electricity, gas, and water supply	0	0	0	1	16	0	0	0	0	0	0	0	0	1
Construction	0	0	0	0	7	0	0	0	0	0	0	0	0	2
Sales, maintenance, and repair of motor vehicles	0	0	0	0	12	0	0	0	0	0	0	0	0	0
Wholesale trade and commission trade	1	0	0	0	**56**	0	0	0	0	0	0	0	0	10
Retail trade; repair of household goods	0	0	0	0	13	0	0	0	0	0	0	0	0	18
Hotels and restaurants	**27**	0	4	25	27	0	2	0	0	0	0	0	0	1
Inland transport	0	0	0	2	1	0	2	0	0	0	0	0	4	1
Water transport	0	0	0	0	0	0	0	0	0	0	0	0	0	0
Air transport	0	0	0	0	0	0	0	0	0	0	0	0	0	0

(*continued*)

Table 15.3 continued

Sector	AUS	BRA	CAN	CHN	EU27	IDN	JPN	KOR	MEX	RUS	TUR	TWN	USA	ROW
Other supporting and auxiliary transport activities	0	0	0	0	1	0	0	0	0	0	0	0	0	1
Post and telecommunications	0	0	0	13	9	0	0	0	0	0	0	0	0	1
Financial intermediation	0	0	0	0	38	0	1	0	0	0	1	0	29	12
Real estate activities	0	0	0	0	0	0	0	0	0	0	0	0	0	0
Renting of M&Eq and other business activities	3	0	0	7	27	0	0	0	0	0	0	0	19	15
Public admin and defence; compulsory social security	0	0	0	0	14	0	0	0	0	0	0	0	0	1
Education	0	0	0	0	1	0	0	0	0	0	0	0	0	1
Health and social work	0	0	0	0	1	0	0	0	0	0	0	0	0	0
Other community, social, and personal services	1	0	1	12	59	0	31	0	0	0	0	0	3	8
Total	47	6	20	2008	961	15	108	48	6	4	18	51	896	3000

Source: WIOD; Timmer et al. (2012); own calculations.

15.3 **Procurement Policy in India**

15.3.1 THE LEGAL FRAMEWORK FOR GOVERNMENT PROCUREMENT IN INDIA

There is no single uniform law governing procurement by various public entities in India; instead a framework of rules, codes, and manuals governs procurement distinctly at the federal level, sub-federal levels, by SOEs, and by entities within the Ministry of Defence and Indian Railways.

The procurement of goods and services by the central government in India is undertaken pursuant to the General Financial Rules (GFR), 2005 and the Delegation of Financial Powers Rules, 1978, as issued by the Ministry of Finance. The purchase procedures followed by various government departments have evolved in line with these general principles. Where deemed necessary, public procurements are also subject to review by the Central Vigilance Commission (CVC). Procuring entities are required to adhere to the CVC's guidelines in relation to all public procurements.

In addition, there are sector-specific guidelines and regulations on public procurement. For instance, defense procurement is undertaken pursuant to the Manual on the Defence Procurement Procedure (DPP), which is issued by the Ministry of Defence from time to time. Procurement of stores for the central government is undertaken pursuant to the manual of the Directorate General of Supplies & Disposals (DGS&D), which is the relevant authority in respect of such procurements.

DGS&D, under the aegis of the Department of Supply, is the central purchasing organization of the Government of India. Decentralization in the 1970s restricted the role of the DGS&D to finalizing rate contracts for "common use" items. Since then, the role of the DGS&D has declined gradually and, even in nominal terms, purchases by the directorate have fallen over time. Moreover, other ministries and departments and departmental undertakings have been delegated powers, enabling them to make their own purchases.

The procedures followed by state governments are based on the states' financial rules, and a number of states have the equivalent of a central-stores purchasing organization. At the sub-federal level, Rajasthan, Tamil Nadu, and Karnataka were the first states to enact their own public procurement laws, with Himachal Pradesh being the next to publish a draft bill some years later. Recently, the state government of Jharkhand has also come out with a draft procurement policy, the Jharkhand Procurement Policy, 2013.[3]

Interestingly, though, these experiences did not fully inform the draft public procurement bill first published by the Planning Commission in India, which merely included a provision providing price preferences to domestic bidders. Significantly, the nationality of bidders was not listed as a permissible basis for discrimination, making it similar to the UNCITRAL Model Law requiring national treatment in the award of public contracts (Verma, 2014).

The Rajasthan legislation has closely followed the Public Procurement Bill, 2012, besides meeting international benchmarks in public procurement. Two notable aspects of the Rajasthan Public Procurement Rules, 2013, are the extent of institutionalization in undertaking analysis of procurement-related information and the use of a Code of Integrity to reduce corruption.[4] The Karnataka and Tamil Nadu procurement legislations are not as comprehensive as the Public Procurement Bill, 2012, though these states were among the first to implement e-procurement procedures. The draft Jharkhand Procurement Policy, 2013, is the first state procurement policy in India to accord preferential treatment in the award of public contracts to "local" MSEs over enterprises located outside the state.[5]

[3] Available at: <http://jharkhandindustry.gov.in/pdf/JP_Policy_2013.pdf> (accessed July 23, 2016).

[4] The Code of Integrity prohibits anti-competitive practices, bribery, and hampering transparency in the bidding process, besides monitoring conduct in cases of conflict of interest. The bidding documents are required to be free from conditions which could encourage anti-competitive practices.

[5] This preferential treatment should cover at least 20 percent of total annual purchases of goods and a minimum 15 percent of services.

Apart from rules governing procurement at the central and state levels, certain criminal penalties are also prescribed under the Indian Penal Code, 1860, and the Prevention of Corruption Act, 1988, for corrupt and fraudulent practices in the award of public contracts. India also has the Right to Information Act 2005 (RTI Act) giving Indian citizens access to government records.[6]

From 2012, the Government of India was involved in the process of legislating a public procurement bill (the Public Procurement Bill, 2012) covering procurements undertaken by the central government, all bodies owned/controlled by the central government or established by an act of Parliament, or otherwise specified by the central government.[7] The Bill, passed by the Lower House of the Indian Parliament in the previously elected regime, covers procurements of goods, works and services, procurements for purposes of national security and other strategic considerations, public-private partnerships (PPPs), and any other procurements specified by the central government. Significantly, however, the Bill does not contemplate the cessation of the applicability of other legislation in India on this subject but is instead envisaged as operating concurrently with all such legislation, which is a serious lacuna that needs to be addressed.

With the new government, the Bill has lapsed and would need to be re-introduced in the Indian Parliament. The Public Procurement Division within the Ministry of Finance is currently involved in addressing some issues before the Bill can again be put forth for enactment. After this, the minimum time for the Bill to become an Act could still be as much as one year, assuming that all goes well.

15.3.2 REQUIREMENTS FOR FOREIGN PARTICIPATION IN PROCUREMENT PROCESSES

There are no restrictions on foreign participation in procurement processes unless otherwise specified in a particular tender, but foreign investment is prohibited or restricted in certain sectors in accordance with the country's FDI policy.[8] There are also sectors, such as atomic energy and railway transport (except mass rapid transport

[6] Under the terms of the Act, any person may request information from a "public authority" (a body of government or instrumentality of state), which is expected to reply expeditiously or within thirty days. The Act also requires every public authority to computerize their records for wide dissemination and to proactively publish certain categories of information so that the citizens need minimum recourse to request for information formally. This law was passed by Parliament on June 15, 2005 and came into force on October 13, 2005. Information disclosure in India was hitherto restricted by the Official Secrets Act, 1923, and various other special laws, which the new RTI Act overrides.

[7] Subject to these being entities that receive substantial financial assistance from the central government in so far as the utilization of such assistance towards procurement is concerned.

[8] Sections 15.3.2–15.3.4 draw heavily on Lex Mundi Ltd. (2012).

systems), in which private participation is prohibited, which also makes foreign bidders ineligible for participation in the public bids unless specifically permitted by the government.

Foreign companies are, in most cases, not required to set up branches or subsidiaries, or otherwise enter into joint ventures and other commercial arrangements to be eligible for participation in the bidding processes. This said, the terms of certain bids may require that the successful bidder incorporate a special purpose company (SPV) in India to discharge contractual obligations and that the successful bidder also retain specified levels of ownership and control of the SPV so incorporated, typically in the form of shareholding lock-ins and change of control restrictions. To the extent that certain specified portions of public procurement are required to be sourced domestically and/or are subject to offset requirements, foreign bidders would need to meet such requirements.

Finally, apart from bilateral agreements and restrictions on commercial transactions with certain countries,[9,10] there are no general reciprocity requirements for public procurement under Indian law. However, where a procuring entity has prior commercial arrangements with other international entities, the entity may also be subject to requirements of such international entities.[11]

15.3.3 PROCEDURES FOR AWARDING PROCUREMENT CONTRACTS

While there is no centralized bidders registry in India, government agencies may, from time to time, pre-qualify certain bidders for identified categories of projects/assignments on the basis of their technical qualifications. Subsequently, during the validity of these pre-qualifications/evaluations, bid documents for such projects/assignments may only be addressed to these pre-qualified bidders.

15.3.3.1 E-Procurement

Pursuant to the office memorandum issued by the Department of Expenditure in the Ministry of Finance, dated November 30, 2011, and the amendment thereto dated March

[9] The India–Japan Comprehensive Economic Partnership Agreement (CEPA) has a chapter on government procurement.

[10] These include, for instance, restrictions on import of rough diamonds from Cote d'Ivoire and arms and related material from Iraq.

[11] For instance, where any Indian entity has existing loan arrangements with the Export–Import Bank of the United States, such an entity may, due to prior contractual arrangements, be required to not have any dealings with suppliers based in Iran, to the extent that the same is restricted under applicable laws of the United States.

30, 2012, the central government introduced an e-procurement regime. Procurements in respect of tenders of value of Rs. 1 million and above by the central government, central public sector enterprises (CPSEs), and autonomous/statutory bodies constituted by the central government were required to be undertaken through e-procurement. Moreover, to promote e-procurement further and to ensure maximum tendering of central government contracts through this route, the tender limit for mandatory e-procurement was brought down to Rs. 500,000 (effective April 1, 2015) and further to Rs. 200,000 (effective April 1, 2016), following an office memorandum dated January 9, 2014.[12] However, the procuring entity is allowed to opt out of the e-procurement process on grounds of confidentiality requirements, national security, or otherwise to safeguard the interests of the entity.

For participation in bid processes of the central government, bidders are required to register on the e-procurement portal of the central government (<http://eprocure.gov.in>), and also to obtain necessary digital signatures and e-tokens from designated providers. Further, bids are required to be submitted only in identified electronic formats (PDF/.xls/.rar/.dwf), unless otherwise specified by the authority issuing the tender. Additionally, the required bid security and other specified documents may, despite the e-tendering process, also be required to be provided in original hard copy (and not electronically). State governments have similar requirements. The e-procurement process was implemented by states well before the central government, with the states of Karnataka and Tamil Nadu being amongst the first to do so.

15.3.3.2 Other Tendering Procedures

Other prevalent mechanisms for tendering include the following:

i. Procurement via an advertised tender, which in addition to publication on the authority's website/other governmental websites, is also typically published in national newspapers with a wide circulation and in the *Indian Trade Journal* published by the Government of India. In the event of this being a global tender, the bid documents are also required to be circulated to foreign embassies and provided for publication on the websites of these embassies.
ii. Procurement through a limited tender, where the tender is provided to only prequalified bidders.
iii. Procurement via the Swiss challenge method for projects proposed by private parties.

[12] See <http://finmin.nic.in/the_ministry/dept_expenditure/ppcell/eProcurement09012014.pdf> (accessed July 23, 2016).

15.3.3.3 Selection of the Winning Supplier

Commonly adopted mechanisms for the selection of the successful bidder include the following:

i. *Selection of the lowest bidder (L1 method)*, adopted for the selection of the successful bidder, from amongst the technically qualified bidders, for lump-sum and rate contracts.
ii. *Selection of the highest bidder (H1 method)*, adopted for the selection of the successful bidder, *inter-se* technically qualified bidders, for revenue-sharing based contracts and/or contracts that contemplate an upfront premium from the successful bidder and/or provide for a return on equity investment by the procuring entity.
iii. *Selection of the bidder requiring the lowest government grant or the lowest subsidy (evaluated on a net present value basis)*, adopted for projects that have low financial viability.
iv. *Selection of the bidder requiring the shortest concession period*, adopted for projects with a fixed revenue stream.
v. *Selection of the bidder offering the highest extent of capacity creation, investment or quantum of work*, adopted on a case-by-case basis and previously used, for instance, in the bids of production-sharing contracts for oil and gas resources, where the bid parameter is *inter alia* the minimum work program offered to be undertaken by the bidder.

Further selection of the bidder may also be based on the combined scores from the evaluations of their technical bid and financial bid, on the basis of a pre-determined weighting mechanism. In this mechanism, the financial proposals would continue to be evaluated on the basis of the methods listed above, as applicable, given the nature of the bid process.

However, procuring entities are not bound to accept the bid of the highest evaluated bidder and can select other bidders, subject to the procuring entity being able to demonstrate that the selection process was undertaken on a reasonable, fair, transparent, and non-arbitrary basis. Certain procuring entities may also reject bids that are extremely low or otherwise biased in favor of the bidder in financial terms.

15.3.3.4 Criteria for Evaluation and Comparison of Bid Proposals

The criteria for evaluation and comparison of bid proposals are laid down by the procuring entity in its bid documents and *inter alia* include: (i) the satisfaction of technical qualification requirements, which may be specified in terms of the past experience of the bidder (particularly for similar assignments) and availability of qualified personnel (which may also include experience in similar assignments); and

(ii) satisfaction of financial qualification requirements, including net worth and solvency of the bidder, and financial capacity to undertake the proposed assignment under the bid.

15.3.4 REVIEW PROCEDURES

Unlike the requirements of the UNCITRAL Model Law and the GPA, Indian law does not provide for a domestic bid challenge procedure in matters of public procurement. This said, the lapsed Public Procurement Bill, 2012, has provisions to set up a Procurement Redressal Committee, where a bidder aggrieved by the conduct of a procuring entity has recourse to an appeal.

For now, however, the bidding processes of all public entities are subject to limited judicial review in exercise of the writ jurisdiction of the High Courts and the Supreme Court of India. The courts intervene in this process only on the grounds of violation of constitutional or statutory provisions, or on account of a lack of probity, fairness and transparency, or reasonableness, or the presence of arbitrariness. This judicial review mechanism is also applicable to contractual arrangements executed in implementing the procurement bid or in the event of non-compliance with the terms of such contractual arrangements.

The typical dispute resolution mechanisms utilized under contracts in India include:

i. *Dispute resolution through the court process.* This pertains to civil disputes that are subject to the rules of procedure prescribed under the Civil Procedure Code, 1908. Depending on the forum in question (the High Courts or the Supreme Court of India), certain specific rules of procedure may additionally be applicable. Further, decrees of foreign courts, to the extent that the same relate to reciprocating territories identified by the Government of India, can be enforced as such with the assistance of the Indian judicial system, in accordance with the Civil Procedure Code, 1908.

ii. *Dispute through arbitration processes.* Arbitration proceedings in India are governed by the terms of the (Indian) Arbitration and Conciliation Act, 1996 (the Arbitration Act). However, parties have the freedom—subject to the Arbitration Act—to prescribe rules and procedure for such arbitral proceedings under their contractual arrangement, including *inter alia* the number and mode of appointment of the arbitrators. The Arbitration Act recognizes awards issued pursuant to international commercial arbitration (as identified under the Arbitration Act), and such awards are enforceable, in accordance with the provisions of the Arbitration Act.

iii. *Dispute resolution through mutual discussion and conciliation proceedings.* Such dispute resolution mechanisms are undertaken on the basis of the terms and conditions specified under the contractual arrangement between parties. However, given that the Arbitration Act also provides for a statutory framework for conciliation proceedings, it is open to the parties to specify that conciliation proceedings be undertaken pursuant to the terms of the Act. Further, notwithstanding the applicability of the Arbitration Act, any dispute resolution through the means of mutual discussion or conciliation is non-binding, and is typically contemplated as a pre-cursor to other dispute resolution mechanisms.

iv. *Dispute resolution through expert determination.* This dispute resolution mechanism is typically undertaken in the context of technical/financial disputes, wherein the contractual arrangement of the parties stipulates referring disputes relating to certain specified subject matters for determination by an identified expert, in accordance with rules and regulations deemed appropriate by the expert (or otherwise prescribed by the contract).

It may be noted that all non-judicial dispute resolution mechanisms, irrespective of any contractual arrangements to the contrary, are subject to judicial review. However, judicial review of arbitration awards is only available on certain specified grounds, as specifically listed under the Arbitration Act.

Finally, it is also pertinent to note that the Arbitration Act recognizes international arbitration awards in respect of matters identified as related to international commercial arbitration, and such awards can be enforced in accordance with the provision of the Arbitration Act.

However, the scope and possibility of exclusion of the application of the Arbitration Act for international commercial arbitration is presently sub judice before the Supreme Court of India. As per the present judicial precedent, such an exclusion is possible only where (i) the seat and the place of arbitration is outside India; and (ii) the governing law of the contract is not Indian law.

This said, Indian government entities typically prefer the applicability of the provisions of Indian law as the governing law for contracts, and the Arbitration Act as the law governing the arbitration proceedings under the contracts concerned.

15.3.5 PREFERENTIAL POLICIES

Reservations in matters of public procurement still exist for MSEs and for certain products/sectors. Pursuant to the Public Procurement Policy for MSEs, Order 2012,[13] dated March 23, 2012, central government ministries/departments and central public sector enterprises (CPSEs) are expected to procure 20 percent of their total goods and

[13] See <http://eprocure.gov.in/cppp/sites/default/files/ordersandcirculers_contents/ORD_DOC_NO_4/imsme_FinalPressorder.pdf> (accessed July 23, 2016).

services from MSEs over a three-year period, effective April 1, 2012. The minimum 20 percent requirement became mandatory effective April 1, 2015.

The WTO Secretariat, in its *Trade Policy Review for India* (WTO, 2011), notes that "MSEs also receive purchase and price preferences in procurement by central government ministries/departments and CPSEs. Under the purchase-preference system, 358 items have been reserved for exclusive procurement from MSEs and 21 items for exclusive manufacturing in the micro and small sectors. The purchase-preference system offers price preferences of up to 15% to MSEs over the quotations provided by large-scale industries. MSEs are also assisted through the: (i) issue of tender sets free of cost; (ii) exemption from payment of 'earnest money' (deposits); and (iii) waiver of security deposits up to the monetary limit for which the unit is eligible, based on certain 'transparent' criteria. The National Small Industries Commission serves as a single point of negotiation for eligible MSEs for government purchasing preference schemes."

Examples of preferential sectoral policies include the following:

i. The central government has reserved all items of hand-spun and hand-woven textiles (*khadi* goods) for exclusive purchase from the Khadi and Village Industries Commission (KVIC). The central government purchases all items of handloom textiles exclusively from the KVIC and/or the Association of Corporations and Apex Societies of Handloom, and coir products from the Coir Board.

ii. India's National Electronics Policy, 2012,[14] has made it mandatory for all government organizations to give preference to domestically manufactured laptops and tablet PCs. The rules prescribe a "50% preference (in value terms)... to domestically manufactured Laptop PCs and Tablet PCs in Government procurement, subject to the condition that the Laptop PCs and Tablet PCs meet domestic value addition in terms of Bill of Material (BOM) of 25% and 30% respectively in Year 1 to qualify as domestically manufactured."[15] This value addition was increased by 5 percent in March 2014.

iii. In 2007, India issued a five-year drugs policy wherein the central government was required to exclusively purchase certain medicines manufactured by pharma CPSEs and their subsidiaries. The reservation applies to a maximum of 102 medicines notified by the Department of Chemicals and Petrochemicals from time to time. Under this policy, procuring entities, CPSEs, and autonomous bodies may invite limited tenders from pharma CPSEs and their subsidiaries, or purchase directly from them at the National Pharmaceutical Pricing Authority-certified or notified price with a discount of up to 35 percent. However, if no pharma CPSEs can supply these medicines, the procuring entities may purchase

[14] See <http://pib.nic.in/newsite/erelease.aspx?relid=88619> (accessed July 23, 2016).

[15] See <http://pib.nic.in/newsite/erelease.aspx?relid=91915> (accessed July 23, 2016).

from other manufacturers. Pharma CPSEs and their subsidiaries are required to comply with the good manufacturing practices norms stipulated in the Drugs and Cosmetic Rules.

15.4 **Influence/Relevance of International Norms**

The World Bank's (2003) CPAR notes that the procedural framework in place in India to govern and administer public procurement is similar to that of the World Bank-ADB guidelines,[16] the WTO's GPA, and the UNICTRAL Model Law. The frameworks of rules, procedures, codes, manuals, and documents in place are designed to address the key basic guiding principles of public procurement: transparency, economy, efficiency, effectiveness, fairness, and competition amongst prospective suppliers. However, unlike the requirements of the UNCITRAL Model Law and the GPA, there is no independent dispute redressal system, though the lapsed Public Procurement Bill, 2012, has provisions to set up a Procurement Redressal Committee.

In May 2011, India became a party to the United Nations Convention against Corruption (UNCAC).[17] The United Nations Office on Drugs and Crime (UNODC) is the guardian of the UNCAC with the mandate to assist and enhance the capacity of member states to implement the provisions of the UNCAC. In line with this role, UNODC India is implementing two anti-corruption projects, supported by the Siemens Integrity Initiative, to strengthen the country's efforts to effectively implement Article 9 of UNCAC.[18]

[16] The World Bank works to ensure that procurement in projects financed by the International Bank for Reconstruction and Development (IBRD) and/or the International Development Association (IDA) is conducted in accordance with its Articles of Agreement. These Articles require the Bank to make arrangements to ensure that loan proceeds are used only for the purposes for which the loan was granted. They also require proper attention to be paid to economy and efficiency. Political and other non-economic influences or considerations must not influence procurement in Bank projects. Detailed procurement guidelines are available at: <http://siteresources.worldbank.org/INTPROCUREMENT/Resources/Procurement-May-2004.pdf> (accessed July 23, 2016) and the revised World Bank *Guidelines Procurement of Goods, Works and Non-Consulting Services under IBRD Loans and IDA Credits by World Bank Borrowers-Draft March 2010* (2010), available at <http://siteresources.worldbank.org/INTPROCUREMENT/Resources/ProposalRevisionPRGLsMarch2010trackmode.pdf> (accessed July 23, 2016). The procurement guidelines of the ADB can be accessed at <http://www.adb.org/sites/default/files/institutional-document/31482/procurement-guidelines-april-2015.pdf> (accessed August 1, 2016).

[17] Recognizing the importance of strengthening anti-corruption measures in public procurement, the UNCAC, which came into force in 2005, provides for Article 9 ("public procurement and management of public finances") as an important provision in preventing corruption.

[18] The two projects are the Public–Private Partnership for Probity in Public Procurement and Incentives to Corporate Integrity and Cooperation in Accordance with UNCAC. The former seeks to reduce vulnerabilities to corruption in PPP projects, while the latter addresses a larger umbrella of private sector integrity issues, including private sector association with the government under public procurement.

The first project undertook, *inter alia,* an assessment of Indian legislation to assess compliance with the UNCAC, and indicated compliance of the lapsed Public Procurement Bill, 2012, and Draft Rules for Public Private Partnerships, 2011, with the UNCAC. With this legislation, India is well on its way to achieving comprehensive legislative coverage for probity in public procurement.

The Draft Rules for PPP (2011) contain many good practices that strengthen India's compliance with the UNCAC. These rules address bribery, collusion, and, to some extent, money laundering. There is also a separate legislation for money laundering in India. The PPP rules provide for measures against procurement officials who may be originators of corruption, a code of conduct for the private sector, and debarment policies for defaulting bidders. These rules address the procurement stage as well as the contract management and project implementation stages, besides requiring a record of each public purchase to be maintained. The Draft PPP rules also lay down obligations for the government in case the private sector is unable to meet its commitments as per the PPP contract in order to ensure provision of facilities to the public.

Most international legal instruments on the subject of government procurement address either competition/market access or probity issues. For instance, the UNCITRAL Model Law and the Uruguay Round GPA are solely focused on competition and transparency issues, while the UNCAC and the 2008 OECD Guidelines on Public Procurement are more concerned with enhancing integrity in public procurement. In contrast, the lapsed Public Procurement Bill, 2012, addresses both competition and probity issues within the same legal instrument, making it a unique piece of legislation.

Even in the revised GPA, probity and integrity aspects are confined to the Preamble, without any operative clauses to ensure enforcement. The Public Procurement Bill, in contrast, "proposes probity principles by incorporating provisions for a Code of Integrity binding on the procuring entity and bidders, covering bribe-taking and bribe-giving, collusion and bid-rigging, disclosure of conflict of interest/previous transgressions. Breach of the Code excludes bidders from the procurement process, involves forfeitures, recoveries, and debarment from participation in future procurements. Stiff punishment can be invoked for taking or offering gratification in respect of public procurement/abetment of such offences; debarment from bidding can take place in certain circumstances" (CUTS International, 2012).

Moreover, unlike the Prevention of Corruption Act (India's main anti-corruption legislation), the Bill addresses both the supply side and the demand side of corruption, making both the acceptance and the offer of inducement for wrongful advantage in procurement an offense. In this respect, it follows the lead of the UNCAC, which seeks to address corruption in both the public and the private sector.

Thus, the lapsed Public Procurement Bill, 2012, incorporates best international practices reflected in the GPA, the UNCAC, and the UNCITRAL Model Law. In fact, there are instances where the Bill's provisions even improve upon international best practices, such as empowering the government to make electronic procurement mandatory and providing for the setting up of a central e-procurement portal, both of which take the standards of transparency to a higher level than those prescribed in the GPA. It also prescribes e-reverse auction as one of the modes of procurement.

15.5 Approaches toward Transparency and Reporting of Statistics

The lapsed Public Procurement Bill, 2012, seeks to regulate the award of government contracts above Rs. 5 million in order to ensure "transparency, accountability and probity" in public purchases. The Bill provides for a central e-procurement portal for posting and exhibiting matters relating to public procurement, and empowers the central government to declare adoption of e-procurement as compulsory for any stage of procurement. It also requires a procuring entity to maintain a record of procurement proceedings.

However, the provisions of the Bill are restricted to central government purchases only. Moreover, they do not explicitly require data to be compiled on this subject. Data on public expenditure (current and capital expenses reported in broad economic categories) are available in the budget and finance documents of various central and state government ministries and departments, as well as municipal corporations, but information on actual expenses incurred in the purchase of goods and services cannot be retrieved from these data. There is also no single compiling or reporting agency for data on public procurement in India, and evidence on contestability of India's procurement markets is at best anecdotal.

This said, the mandatory e-tendering of above-threshold central, state, and SOE contracts since 2011–12 and details on the award of public contracts is generating a huge information base on procurement in India. An analysis of these central and state e-portals reveals that there is a wealth of procurement information now available for almost all the twenty-nine states and six centrally administered union territories (UTs) and SOEs in the country. This includes information on the value of the contract, the number of bidders, the name and address the of winning supplier, the name and sector of the procuring entity, dates of tender advertisement and award, the tendering method, and the number of days to contract implementation. The information on these e-portals can also be used to examine the extent of foreign procurement by Indian governments by entity, state/UT, and/or sector.

There has been another recent significant development.[19] With support from the World Bank, public procurement observatories are being established by premier

[19] See <http://www.procurementlearning.org/public-procurement-observatories-set-up-in-indian-states/> (accessed July 23, 2016).

management institutions in India with the principal objectives of observing procurement processes and advocating better practices for process improvement. These observatories have been set up at the Indian Institute of Management (IIM) Lucknow, in the state of Uttar Pradesh; IIM Raipur in the state of Chhattisgarh; and Assam Institute of Management (AIM) Guwahati in the state of Assam.

The observatories aim at accomplishing the following objectives:

i. collection and analysis of procurement (including contract implementation) related data in the state;
ii. monitoring and documenting procurement policies and rules in the state and, if possible, the actual contract implementation;
iii. sharing best practices (from other states in India and abroad) in procurement cycle management with state governments through workshops and seminars.

The observatories have begun developing key procurement performance indicators and are in the process of collecting, analyzing, and disseminating procurement data, policies, rules, and so on. Some of the key performance indicators are available on the websites, such as time taken for various activities in e-procurement in Uttar Pradesh in 2011.

The observatories are also serving as vehicles for sharing best practices and capacity-building in the states. Seminars and workshops on procurement processes have already been conducted by the observatories in Uttar Pradesh and Assam, targeting government staff, media, and the general public.

15.6 **Extant Research on the Impact of National Procurement Policies**

In the absence of a national-level procurement policy in the country, there is no research on its impact. In fact, the need for a national public procurement policy is being recognized and advocated more openly now (e.g., CUTS International, 2014). There has been some work assessing the impact of different procurement practices but, given the diversity of procurement regulation in India, research on this subject has been sporadic at best.

In an early paper, Sinha (1994) noted that public procurement practices in the Indian electrical equipment industry failed to incentivize innovation. Indian companies producing power equipment were found to spend only 2 percent of their sales on R&D, compared with foreign companies that entered into joint ventures, technical collaboration agreements, and so on, and spent as much as 12 percent. However, contracting procedures in the industry did not reward innovation, so there was no incentive to improve the product offering. In fact, a product with enhanced facilities was likely to be considered a deviation from contract specifications.

The first substantive paper on India's public procurement policies, including estimates of the size of contestable government procurement, was Srivastava (2003). In its CPAR, the World Bank (2003) carried out an extensive review of India's procurement regime that began in 2000 and covered the central government, four "representative" state governments (Maharashtra, Karnataka, Tamil Nadu, Uttar Pradesh), and CPSEs in three different phases. Gasiorek et al. (2007) provided an analysis of India's procurement policies in the context of a potential EU–India trade agreement, focusing on the barriers confronting EU firms in contesting India's public markets.

There has been more work on this subject recently, in particular by Sandeep Verma, a senior civil servant, who has written extensively in assessing the country's central and state-level procurement policies and their different attributes. In addition to being published in various law and policy journals and print media, his work on this subject is available on SSRN.[20] In fact, the following two sections of this chapter, which assess India's dispute settlement and e-procurement systems, draw heavily on his research.

In other work, the UNODC (undated) has published a report assessing the compliance of Indian legislation with the UNCAC, which was also reviewed in Section 15.4 of this chapter. The ADB (2011) has conducted an assessment of India's e-procurement system, which is also discussed in Section 15.8 of this chapter.

CUTS International (2012), through various projects funded by the UK's Department for International Development (DFID) and the British High Commission, has also carried out extensive research on India's procurement policies and related issues. The projects add value in particular by including analyses of procurement issues in three major sectors: health, IT, and railways. In the health sector, for instance, the CUTS report mentions that "procurement of drugs is often based on the lowest tender price quotations. Many domestic and international pharmaceutical brand suppliers are discouraged by this and cease to participate in the government procurement market resulting in reduced competition and diminished value for money. The 'two-bid' system which has a two rounds of application with both the technical bid and the financial bid may be a step in the right direction."

Finally, in a more contemporaneous paper, Lewis-Faupel et al. (2014) conduct an empirical assessment of e-procurement policies in India and Indonesia. In the case of India, the authors examine procurement practices between 2000 and 2009 for a central government-funded rural road construction program implemented by state road departments, the Pradhan Mantri Gram Sarak Yojana (PMGSY). Under this program, roughly 145 road packages are tendered per state per year.

[20] See <http://papers.ssrn.com/sol3/cf_dev/AbsByAuth.cfm?per_id=1090557> (accessed July 23, 2016).

The authors show that, in both India and Indonesia, e-procurement increases the probability of the winning bidder coming from outside the region where the contract takes place. This is consistent with e-procurement decreasing the costs of submitting bids for those not physically present. However, the authors find no systematic evidence for e-procurement lowering prices paid by the government. Instead, e-procurement was found to lead to quality improvements. In the case of India in particular, they find e-procurement leading to higher quality roads, with the quality grades rising by about 12 percent in e-procurement projects compared to other projects. They also find e-procurement winning contractors in India to have higher quality on average, which suggests that e-procurement in India facilitated the participation of higher quality contractors.

15.7 Assessment of Dispute Settlement Mechanisms

Existing complaint procedures in India generally require proof of criminal behavior on the part of government officials in the award of public contracts.[21] The only other options are either to pursue remedies by complaining to government departments themselves, or to bring litigation before the courts. The first option is not entirely impartial and independent, and the second option suffers from protracted litigation and high costs (Sondhi, 2000), making it an unattractive forum to pursue complaints against contract-award decisions of public entities.

Additionally, there is a lack of procedural clarity and finality in decisions on complaints. These could be made simultaneously to various administrative levels within the procuring entity or to a designated chief vigilance officer (CVO), to the concerned administrative department, or directly to the Ministry of Finance, in addition to other political executives such as the minster concerned. Both in theory and in practice, each of these offices could start independent assessments and reach widely differing conclusions, a situation that is sub-optimal.[22]

External oversight bodies suffer from similar jurisdictional overlaps and an apparent lack of finality. The Central Vigilance Commission (CVC) can make recommendations at best in cases of corruption, the Central Bureau of Investigation (CBI) conducts its own criminal investigations requiring conviction in a court of law, while the office of the Comptroller and Auditor General (CAG) conducts mostly post-hoc audits with non-binding observations that are placed before the Public Accounts Committee of the Indian Parliament.[23]

[21] This section draws heavily on Verma (2010).

[22] See, for instance, Verma (2006a).

[23] An illustrative list of government offices involved in accountability and anti-corruption efforts is provided in ADB/OECD (2008).

A recent and comparatively more focused alternative now available to aggrieved bidders in the context of public procurement in India is the Integrity Pact (IP). IPs, introduced by Transparency International in the 1990s, are a "voluntary" pact between a public buyer and seller to eliminate corrupt practices. IPs were autonomously introduced as an incremental oversight and anti-corruption tool into the Indian public contracting scenario in 2006, with the CVC recommending the adoption and implementation of IPs since 2007, covering all major purchases of PSUs. IPs may "constitute the *first*, if not the most efficient, forum for bidders to bring in complaints regarding agency procurement decisions" (Verma, 2010). A critical analysis of the suitability of IPs as a dispute settlement mechanism in the Indian context is provided in Verma (2010).

Finally, the lapsed Public Procurement Bill, 2012, has provisions to set up a Procurement Redressal Committee, where a bidder aggrieved by the conduct of a procuring entity has recourse to an appeal. However, the grievance redressal mechanism in the Bill is still weak and would need to be adapted along the lines of the GPA and the UNCITRAL Model Law in order to be more effective. For instance, the powers of the independent grievance redressal mechanism are restricted to making recommendations to the procuring entity, hence falling short of ensuring fair play. The procuring entity may reject these recommendations, providing reasons for non-acceptance. The GPA also provides for judicial review in case the review body is a non-judicial entity, like the Procurement Redressal Tribunal under the Bill. However, there is no provision in the Bill for judicial review of the decisions of this proposed tribunal.

15.8 Assessment of E-Procurement Systems

The approach adopted for the implementation of e-procurement systems in India has evolved over time.[24] The concept of e-procurement was new about a decade ago, when IT-savvy resources in individual government departments initiated the implementation of e-tendering in their respective departments using commercial off-the-shelf (COTS) software developed specifically to address government tendering requirements. The adoption of department-specific e-tendering systems gradually increased as the concept became popular.

However, few government agencies initiated implementation of unified e-procurement systems. Institution-driven unified e-procurement system implementations and continued adoption of e-procurement systems in individual departments finally led to the initiative to operationalize the e-procurement Mission Mode Project (MMP) under the National e-Governance Program (NeGP). The Ministry of Commerce and Industry

[24] This section draws heavily on ADB (2011).

(Department of Commerce) was identified as the line department for implementation of the e-procurement MMP in 2007.

The functional scope of e-procurement system referred to in India by e-procurement policy-makers, by application service providers, and in e-procurement implementations is similar to that under definition provided in the multilateral development banks' e-procurement guidelines. Though there is widespread acknowledgement of the end-to-end scope addressed by e-procurement software, not all functional aspects of government procurement are handled electronically in existing e-procurement implementations in India. Even mature e-procurement implementations, such as those in the state governments of Andhra Pradesh and Karnataka and by Indian Railways, do not have a fully integrated end-to-end e-procurement system in full operation.

This said, ADB (2011) notes the following key benefits to government departments of implementing e-procurement systems: (i) a rise in the average number of bidders per tender; (ii) a 15 percent fall in the tender premium; and (iii) a decline in cycle time taken to evaluate tenders.

However, some concerns have been raised regarding possible adverse effects of introducing purely electronic systems on competition levels in public procurement, given the relatively higher cost and skewed regional distribution of ICT access in India.[25] Technical limitations to long-term storage of public key infrastructure (PKI) encrypted electronic records could also lead to problematic situations in the event of public procurement decisions being contested in a court of law.

Moreover, the presence of a large number of websites with little integration, poor organization of information, infrequent updating, and an absence of accurate and up-to-date information, together with largely unprotected sites where digital authentications of downloads is not possible, add to the time and costs involved in accessing information regarding procurement opportunities.

15.9 **Conclusion**

India does not have a national public procurement policy. In its absence, a plethora of rules and procedures govern public purchase practices of federal and sub-federal government entities, including public sector enterprises. While these norms generally follow international best practices, their implementation falls short in providing transparency, accountability, efficiency, and professionalism in the award of public contracts. The system is plagued by delays in procurement decisions leading to additional expenses, delays in payments from procuring entities, collusive practices between authorities and

[25] For instance, see Verma (2006b).

bidders, inadequate enforcement of regulations to check conflict of interests, and the absence of an effective and independent dispute settlement mechanism.

This said, the previous government was in the process of enacting federal-level legislation on procurement that not only addressed several of these concerns, but also provided for compliance with international best practices enshrined in the UNCITRAL Model Law, the GPA, the ADB-World Bank procurement guidelines, and the UNCAC. As of 2012, India has also acquired "Observer status" on the GPA at the WTO. In a first for Indian trade policy, government procurement has been covered in the India–Japan CEPA, though the relevant provisions are limited to the exchange of information in matters of central government procurement. Significantly, there is in-built scope for negotiations leading to a comprehensive chapter on the subject in the CEPA once India declares its intentions to accede to the GPA. In contrast, government procurement has been a sticking point in the ongoing EU–India Bilateral Trade and Investment Agreement negotiations.

The prompt enactment of an improved Public Procurement Bill, 2012, by the new government would go a long way toward the internationalization of procurement regulation in the country. However, since the Bill is only applicable to central government and CPSE purchases, there is a need for other states to develop similar legislation, all of which could come under a single national public procurement policy. This could further lead to the much-needed simplification and harmonization of cumbersome rules and procedures, bringing entities such as the Indian Railways within the ambit of a single national public procurement policy.

Finally, India has come a long way in developing e-procurement systems, but the country needs to find solutions to the implementation challenges discussed earlier. E-procurement is an important measure to enhance transparency in procurement processes. Since procurement in India is decentralized, the emergence of multiple e-procurement systems is inevitable. The implementation of a unified e-procurement system would reduce the number of installations, but multiple e-procurement systems may still exist. The multiple e-procurement systems could be made inter-operable to develop a "national" e-procurement system, in effect by maintaining a national repository of tenders, a national database of registered suppliers, and a national database on supplier performance.

With mandatory e-tendering of central, state government, and PSU contracts already in place, enacting the Public Procurement Bill and integrating states within a national procurement policy would complete the set of procurement reforms needed to usher in transparency and efficiency in public purchases in the country. In fact, to the extent that India has already accomplished some of these reforms unilaterally, the benefits from acceding to the GPA are confined to becoming eligible for reciprocal market access in the procurement markets of the other contracting parties, though even this would largely depend on the actual coverage of Indian central and state government entities and PSEs in this plurilateral agreement. This said, what is arguably as important as unilateral reforms and/or plurilateral/bilateral commitments is a change in mind-set, which must intrinsically reject corruption in every walk of life.

ACKNOWLEDGMENTS

I would like to thank Aris Georgopoulos, Bernard Hoekman, and Petros Mavroidis for their invitation to write this chapter and Robert Anderson and conference participants for their useful comments.

REFERENCES

ADB. 2011. "India: Case Study on e-Government Procurement Development," Asian Development Bank, Manila.

ADB/OECD. 2008. "Implementing the Anti-Corruption Action Plan for Asia-Pacific: Reforms and Anti-Corruption Resources India" (available at: <http://www.oecd.org/dataoecd/8/0/40528776.pdf> (accessed July 23, 2016)).

CUTS International. 2012. *Government Procurement in India: Domestic Regulations & Trade Prospects*, Jaipur, India.

CUTS International. 2014. *Public Procurement: Need for a National Policy in India*, Jaipur, India.

Gasiorek, M., Holmes, P., Robinson, S., Rollo, J., Singhal, A., Mukherjee, C., Nanda, N., Pahariya, N. C., and Simi, T. C. 2007. "Qualitative Analysis of a Potential Free Trade Agreement between the European Union and India." European Commission and CARIS, University of Sussex.

Lewis-Faupel, S., Neggers, Y., Olken, B. A., and Pande, R. 2014. "Can Electronic Procurement Improve Infrastructure Provision? Evidence from Public Works in India and Indonesia." NBER Working Paper No. 20344 (2014).

Lex Mundi Ltd. 2012. "Public Procurement: India," New Delhi.

Shingal, A. 2012. "Estimating Market Access in Non-GPA Countries: A Suggested Methodology." NCCR-Trade Working Paper 2012/06.

Sinha, R. 1994. "Government Procurement and Technological Capability: Case of Indian Electrical Equipment Industry." *Economic and Political Weekly* 29(48): M142–M147.

Sondhi, S. 2000. "Combating Corruption in India: Role of the Civil Society" (available at: <http://unpan1.un.org/intradoc/groups/public/documents/APCITY/UNPAN019103.pdf> (accessed July 23, 2016)).

Srivastava, V. 2003. "India's Accession to the Government Procurement Agreement: Identifying Costs and Benefits." In A. Mattoo and R. Stern (eds), *India and the WTO*, World Bank and OUP.

Timmer, M., Erumban, A., Francois, J., Genty, A., Gouma, R., Los, B., Neuwahl, F., Pindyuk, O., Poeschl, J., and Rueda-Cantuche, J. 2012. "The World Input–Output Database (WIOD): Contents, Sources and Methods." WIOD Background Document (available at: <www.wiod.org> (accessed July 23, 2016)).

UNODC (n.d.). "India: Probity in Public Procurement," New Delhi.

Verma, S. 2006a. "E-Buying: The Works." *The Economic Times*, February 2.

Verma, S. 2006b. "Reforming Implementation of EGP Systems in India." *Express Computers*, October 16.

Verma, S. 2010. "Integrity Pacts and Public Procurement Reform in India: From Incremental Steps to a Rigorous Bid Protest System." HCM RIPA Occasional Paper No. 18.

Verma, S. 2014. "Why Procurement Reform in Indian States Is Tricky" *Business Standard*, February 10.

World Bank. 2003. "Country Procurement Assessment Report for India," Washington, DC.

WTO. 2002. "Trade Policy Review for India." Report by the WTO Secretariat, Geneva.

WTO. 2011. "Trade Policy Review for India." Report by the WTO Secretariat, Geneva.

16 Government Procurement, Preferences, and International Trading Rules

The South African Case

Memory Dube, Liezemarie Johannes, and David Lewis

16.1 Introduction

South African government procurement is, as with many countries, used to advance selected economic and social policy objectives. However, also in common with many countries, the overarching framework also stresses the requirement for fairness, equity, and price competitiveness. A third common feature of government procurement practices is the ubiquity of maladministration and corruption.

This chapter asks whether adherence to international trading instruments and rules, and in particular to the World Trade Organization's Government Procurement Agreement, would, and should, permit the maintenance of national policy criteria in the decision-making matrix for procurement, whilst simultaneously enabling South Africa to realize the efficiency gains of trade liberalization. It also examines the likely impact, if any, that adherence to these rules would have in reducing the procurement system's vulnerability to corruption.

16.2 The Regulatory Framework

Prior to South Africa's transition to democracy in 1994, the procurement system in place was highly centralized. Partly in consequence of this centralization, the procurement of goods and services favored large corporate suppliers, who dominated the market. Price was the overriding formal criterion for the procurement of goods and services by the government, although there is no doubt that public contracts were extensively deployed to support emerging Afrikaner-owned enterprises. However, on the face of it, price determined the outcome of public procurement bids, only overridden when there was clear evidence that the lowest bidder did not have the necessary experience or capacity to undertake the work or was financially unsustainable. That is, only if there was a high risk that the lowest bidder would not complete the contract—the "functionality" criterion—was the tender awarded to another bidder.

As the system of apartheid was dismantled in the 1990s and new fiscal visions were adopted, so too were the forms of fiscal management and administration recast. This vision placed redistribution at the heart of procurement, necessitating decentralization as a framework to support small and medium-sized enterprise. This required a radical shift in the form and content of procurement, which translated into an overhaul of the legislative and regulatory framework governing government procurement and its practical application. Core to this reformulation is the explicit reconceptualization of procurement as a policy tool, allowing government to use its massive spend on goods and services to achieve socio-economic objectives (Uyarra and Flanagan, 2009: p. 2).

Procurement reforms that began in 1995 were directed at two broad focus areas, namely:

- the promotion of principles of good governance; and
- the introduction of a preference system to address certain socio-economic objectives.

These principles and objectives are enshrined in Section 217 of the Constitution of the Republic of South Africa, which reads:

> 217 (1) When an organ of state in the national, provincial or local sphere of government, or any other institution identified in national legislation, contracts for goods or services, it must do so in accordance with a system which is fair, equitable, transparent, competitive and cost-effective.
>
> (2) Subsection (1) does not prevent the organs of state or institutions referred to in that subsection from implementing a procurement policy providing for—
>
> (a) categories of preference in the allocation of contracts; and
>
> (b) the protection or advancement of persons, or categories of persons, disadvantaged by unfair discrimination.
>
> (3) National legislation must prescribe a framework within which the policy referred to in subsection (2) may be implemented.

To give effect to the new policy role of its procurement spend, government embarked upon the process of reforming the procurement system. This was initiated by the formulation of a ten-point plan that provided for interim procurement strategies until the enactment of national legislation consistent with the objectives of the Reconstruction and Development Plan (RDP), government's overarching social and economic plan.

The RDP committed government to the following procurement-related measures:

- improved access to tendering information;
- the development of tender advice centers;

- the broadening of the supplier base for small contracts valued at less than R7,500;
- the waiving of security/sureties on construction contracts with a value less than R100,000;
- the unbundling or unpacking of large projects into smaller projects;
- the promotion of early payment cycles by government;
- the development of a preference system for small, medium-sized and micro-sized enterprises (SMMEs), which are owned by historically disadvantaged individuals (HDIs);
- the simplification of tender submission requirements;
- the appointment of a procurement ombudsman; and
- the classification of building and engineering contracts.[1]

The first thrust of reform was thus born out of a desire to "include emerging small and medium enterprises effectively in government contracts" (Public Affairs Research Institute, 2014: p. 16). These reforms sought to utilize procurement as a device to incorporate previously disadvantaged business owners in the mainstream economy as enacted in the Procurement Act of 2000. That is to say, the initial reform measures appeared to conflate inclusion of previously disadvantaged South Africans with measures to support the inclusion of small and medium-sized enterprises (SMEs).

Ambe and Badenhorst-Weiss (2012: p. 245) note that these reforms were intended to modernize the management of the public sector, in essence to make it more "people-friendly" through decentralization and making the process more accessible to SMEs. This would not only allow government to diversify the supplier base, but it would also allow for more responsive procurement practices sensitive to the variable needs of local communities. However, the manner in which procurement was practically implemented, and the ambitious policy imperatives that underpinned the initial formulation of post-apartheid procurement, meant that procurement did not realize its objectives in relation to growing SMEs. Furthermore, lack of standardization across different government structures led to a review of the system in the early 2000s. Two reviews, the *Report on Opportunities for Reform of Government Procurement in South Africa* (AusAID and South Africa Capacity Building Program, 2000) and the World Bank's *Country Procurement Assessment Review of South Africa* (World Bank, 2003), identified various deficiencies in the system and paved the way for the adoption of legislative and policy reforms that would enable more coherent decentralization, and thus allow public procurement to be used as a redistributive tool.

A plethora of legislation was enacted between 1999 and 2003. This legislative framework is largely created by Section 217 of the Constitution of the Republic of South Africa, Section 112 of the Municipal Finance Management Act No. 56 of 2003 (MFMA),

[1] Bolton (2006: pp. 204–5).

Section 76 (4) (C) of the Public Finance Management Act No. 1 of 1999 (PFMA), the Preferential Procurement Policy Framework Act No. 5 of 2000 (PPPFA), and the Broad-Based Black Economic Empowerment Act 53 of 2003.

In accordance with Section 217(3) of the Constitution, the Preferential Procurement Policy Framework Act (PPPFA) No. 5 of 2000 was enacted to provide the requisite framework for procurement. Section 9(2) of the Constitution also provides for the advancement of black economic empowerment (BEE) policies by organs of state as defined in Section 1 of the PPPFA,[2] which must be pursued within the confines of the framework provided for in the PPPFA. The PPPFA (and the attendant Public Procurement Regulations 2011) is to be read together with the Broad-Based Black Economic Empowerment Act No. 56 of 2003. These are the primary pieces of legislation that set the parameters for the use of public procurement to achieve socio-economic objectives.

The supply chain management (SCM) policy document, published in 2003, sought to address the lack of standardization consequential upon a public procurement process which tasks organs of state in national, provincial, or local government and other public institutions with drafting their own procurement policies, albeit guided by the national regulatory framework (Ambe and Badenhorst-Weiss, 2012). The National Treasury Policy Strategy notes that:

> Supply Chain Management is an integral part of financial management that seeks to introduce internationally accepted best practice principles, whilst at the same time addressing government's preferential procurement policy objectives (National Treasury, 2003).

This document espoused the principle that managers should be given flexibility and discretion to give effect to the constitutional requirements of transparency and accountability. The policy involved the devolution of the SCM function to accounting officers at different tiers of government and aims to ensure "uniformity in bid and contract documentation, and options and bid and procedure standards" which would promote the standardization of SCM practices (National Treasury, 2003: p. 6). These reforms entrenched the decentralization of decision-making in procurement, and gave supply chain managers the discretionary power to determine the form and practices of their SCM units and policies, within a basic requirement framework.

[2] Organs of state are defined in the PPPFA as:

(a) a national or provincial department as defined in the Public Finance Management Act, 1999 (Act No. 1 of 1999);
(b) a municipality as contemplated in the Constitution;
(c) a constitutional institution defined in the Public Finance Management Act, 1999 (Act No. 1 of 1999);
(d) Parliament;
(e) a provincial legislature; or
(f) any other institution or category of institutions included in the definition of "organ of state" in section 239 of the Constitution and recognized by the Minister by notice in the *Government Gazette* as an institution or category of institutions to which this Act applies.

Standardization of decentralized decision-making, combined with an emphasis on economic empowerment of previously disadvantaged groups (as articulated in broad-based black economic empowerment, or B-BBEE, and associated preferential procurement frameworks and policies), are thus essential to understanding procurement in South Africa.

16.2.1 PREFERENTIAL PROCUREMENT

Black economic empowerment has become the critical socio-economic objective that public procurement seeks to promote. Before 2011, the PPPFA, read with the Public Procurement Regulations 2001, provided for the award of preference points for being a "historically disadvantaged individual,"[3] for subcontracting with a historically disadvantaged individual, or for attaining certain specific goals. Contracting authorities or organs of state had the discretion to determine precisely how to award the preference points by selecting the specific social policy objectives to accompany the mandatory promotion of historically disadvantaged ownership (Bolton, 2008). These "specific goals" included, inter alia, the promotion of South African enterprises; the promotion of enterprises in a specific region, municipality or rural area; the promotion of small, medium-sized and micro enterprises; the creation of new jobs; and the improvement of communities.[4] This created a lot of uncertainty in the award of preference points, and had to be done away with in favor of the 2011 Regulations and B-BBEE Codes of Good Practice.

Under the B-BBEE Act, there are various ways in which service providers can attain B-BBEE status level. There is also an innovative option that allows multinational companies to attain B-BBEE status level, in addition to these companies generally being able to acquire B-BBEE points through the various elements created in the Codes of Good Practice. This is in the form of "equity equivalent" contributions that are made in lieu of a direct sale of equity, but which count towards the overall B-BBEE ownership element.[5] A multinational company may thus earn B-BBEE points without any black ownership of the company. Such equity equivalent programs may take the form of enterprise creation programs, programs that promote social advancement, economic development programs, projects aimed at technology diffusion/transfer within the small, medium-sized and macro-enterprise sector of the local economy beyond the multinational's core business activities, programs that promote economic growth and

[3] A historically disadvantaged individual is a South African citizen who had no franchise in national elections before 1994, or is female, or has a disability as per Section 3 (2) of Public Procurement Regulations 2001 (see Bolton, 2008).

[4] S 17 (3).

[5] See B-BBEE Codes of Good Practice, Code 100: Statement 103, issued under Section 9 of the Broad-Based Black Economic Empowerment Amended Act of 2013.

employment through the development of technological innovation beyond the multinational's core business activities, or initiatives that lead to sustainable job creation (Department of Trade and Industry, 2015a).

New B-BBEE Codes of Good Practice were published in the *Government Gazette* on October 11, 2013 and came into effect on October 11, 2014. These codes reduce from seven to five the number of the core elements to be considered for the scorecard from which an entity's B-BBEE status is determined. These are:

- ownership;
- management control;
- skills development;
- new enterprise and supplier development; and
- socio-economic development.

These policies are practically applied using a scoring formula. The Codes set out how each of the elements listed above is to be measured and weighted, and translated into the overall status score. Ownership, skills development, and supplier development are identified as "priority" elements and firms have to attain a prescribed minimum weighting of the total for each element.

However, since price remains a critical criterion in the selection of contracts, the points system created by the Act is "dual-scale" depending on the value of a specific contract. The total number of points that may be awarded to contractors is 100, and to ensure that organs of state still obtain competitively priced goods and services, more preference points are awarded for lower-value contracts. This is evidence of the assumed interplay between the promotion of SMEs, on the one hand, and the promotion of BEE as a means for diversifying the supplier base on the other. For contracts with a value of between R30,000 and R1,000,000, the 80/20 preference system is used where a maximum of eighty points will be awarded for price and a maximum of twenty preference points will then be awarded for the B-BBEE status level of the bidder in accordance with the Preferential Procurement Regulations 2011 as well as the B-BBEE Act and its associated Codes of Good Practice.[6] For contracts with a value of over R1 million, the 90/10 point system applies, where a maximum of ninety points will be awarded for price, and a maximum of ten preference points must be awarded for the B-BBEE status level of bidders as set out in the 2011 Regulations.[7]

[6] Preferential Procurement Policy Framework Act, 2000 (Act No 5 of 2000) s 2 (1) (b) (i) read with Preferential Procurement Regulations 2011, Regulation 5.

[7] Preferential Procurement Policy Framework Act, 2000 (Act No 5 of 2000) s 2 (1) (b) (ii) read with Preferential Procurement Regulations 2011, Regulation 6.

The Preferential Procurement Regulations also provide for exemptions from B-BBEE status level for bidders with an annual total revenue of less than R10 million,[8] who then qualify as exempted micro enterprises (EMEs) in terms of the B-BBEE Act and must submit an affidavit stating their level of black ownership as well as their annual turnover.[9]

Local production and content requirements apply to designated sectors where local production and content is determined to be critical for the award of the tender. Local content is defined as that proportion of the tender price which is not included in the imported content, provided that local manufacturing does take place within the borders of South Africa.[10] Table 16.1 describes the designated sectors and the local production

Table 16.1 Minimum local content thresholds by sector or product

Industry/sector/sub-sector	Minimum threshold for local content
Buses (bus body)	80%
Textile, clothing, leather, and footwear	100%
Steel power pylons	100%
Canned/processed vegetables	80%
Pharmaceutical products:	
• OSD tender	• 70% (volumes)
• Family planning tender	• 50% value
Rail rolling stock	65%
Set top boxes (STB)	30%
Furniture products:	
• Office furniture	• 85%
• School furniture	• 100%
• Base and mattress	• 90%
Solar water heater components	70%
Electrical and telecom cables	90%
Valves products and actuators	70%
Residential electricity meter:	
• Prepaid electricity meters	• 70%
• Post paid electricity meters	• 70%
• SMART meters	• 50%
Working vessels/boats (all types):	60%
• Components	• 10%–100%

[8] The Procurement Regulations of 2011 make provision for R5 million, but this has been raised to Amended B-BBEE Act and the revised scores in the Codes of Good Practice.

[9] This is a change from the previous Codes as well as the provisions of the Preferential Procurement Regulations 2011, whose Regulation 10 required certification from a B-BBEE verification agent.

[10] SABS-approved technical specification SATS 1286:2011.

content requirements identified by the Department of Trade and Industry (2015b). In these cases, an organ of state must advertise the tender with a specific condition which provides that only locally manufactured goods with a stipulated minimum threshold for local production and content will be considered.[11] If it is not a designated sector, then the specific tendering condition on local production and content must be in accordance with the specific directives issued for this purpose by the National Treasury, in consultation with the Department of Trade and Industry.

Where two bidders score an equal total amount of points, then the tender must be awarded to the bidder with the most preference points for B-BBEE. Where functionality is part of the evaluation process and two bidders score the same total amount of points, then the award must go to the bidder who scored the most points for functionality. Where two or more bidders score the same amount of points in all respects, then the tender must be decided by the drawing of lots.[12] It further provides that a bidder must not be awarded BEE points if it is indicated in the tender documents that they intend to sub-contract more than 25 percent of the value of the contract to any other enterprise that does not qualify for at least the same number of points as the bidder qualifies for, unless such enterprise is an exempted micro enterprise.

Additional provision is also made in the PPPFA for the award of a tender to a bidder that does not score the highest points but that meets other objective criteria, in addition to the specific goals[13] set out in the Act, to justify such award. Section 2(1)(f) of the PPPFA provides that:

> the contract must be awarded to the tenderer who scores the highest points, unless objective criteria in addition to those contemplated in paragraphs (d) and (e) justify the award to another tenderer.

The 2011 Preferential Procurement Regulations similarly allow for the award of a contract to a supplier who does not score the highest total number of points, but "only in accordance with section 2(1)(f)" of the Act. A similar provision is contained in Regulation 9 of the 2001 Procurement Regulations, which provide that: "a contract may, on reasonable and justifiable grounds, be awarded to a tender[er] that did not score the highest number of points."

National legislation is mirrored in procurement legislation for the third (municipal) tier of government. The Municipal Finance Management Act of 2003 (MFMA) and its Regulations provide a framework for the procurement of goods and services by a municipality or a municipal entity. Section 111 of the MFMA requires each municipality

[11] Preferential Procurement Regulations 2011, Regulation 9.

[12] Preferential Procurement Regulations 2011, Regulation 11 (5).

[13] The Preferential Procurement Regulations 2011 make no mention of the "specific goals" listed in the PPPFA, but rather make specific reference to B-BBEE status for the award of preference points.

to implement an SCM policy that gives effect to Section 217 of the Constitution. The SCM policy of a municipality or municipal entity must:

- describe in sufficient detail the supply chain management system that is to be implemented by the municipality or municipal entity; and
- describe in sufficient detail effective systems for demand, acquisition, logistics, disposal, risk, and performance management.

Section 113 of the MFMA allows a municipality to consider an uninvited bid outside the normal bidding processes; however, it may only do so within the prescribed rules. If a municipality approves a tender outside of regular processes, the accounting officer must notify the Auditor General, the provincial treasury, and the National Treasury, outlining the reasons why it has deviated from the prescribed procedure. A municipal entity must also notify its parent municipality.

The MFMA Regulations also require any SCM policy to provide measures to combat abuse and corruption in the supply chain management system. Amongst other measures, the SCM policy must enable the accounting officer to consult the Treasury's database prior to awarding any contract to ensure that no bidder is prohibited from doing business with the public sector, as well as to enable the accounting officer to reject the bid of any bidders who have been listed on the Register for Tender Defaulters in terms of Section 29 of the Prevention and Combating of Corrupt Activities Act 12 of 2004.

The MFMA requires the accounting officer of a municipality to implement the SCM policy and to take all reasonable steps to ensure that proper mechanisms are in place to minimize the likelihood of fraud, corruption, favoritism, and unfair and irregular practices. The Regulations further provide that the SCM policy of a municipality or municipal entity must state that the municipality or municipal entity may not make an award to a person who is in the service of the state.

It is clear from the above that in terms of the preferential points awarded, B-BBEE remains the most critical factor. However, despite the social policy dimension afforded by the B-BBEE aspect, price still remains the most important consideration in awarding tenders, and hence value for money and cost-effectiveness are important objectives as well (Bolton and Quinot, 2011: p. 459).[14] Given the complex nature of preferential procurement within this framework, critical to the effectiveness and efficiency of the public procurement system are the mechanisms through which service providers can seek redress in cases where they believe the procurement regulations have been violated by procuring entities or bidding parties.

[14] Courts have also set aside public tenders where the primary consideration for awarding the tender has been anything other than cost; see Cash Paymaster Services (Pty) Ltd v Eastern Cape Province and Others 199 (1) SA 324 (Ck), pp. 351–2, and Lohan Civil-Tebogo Joint Venture v. Mangaung Plaaslike Munisipaliteit (unreported, case no. 508/2009 (O), April 9, 2009), para. 71 (8).

16.2.2 ENFORCEMENT AND DISPUTE RESOLUTION MECHANISMS

Government procurement is subject to the general rules of constitutional and administrative law in South Africa. While there is no specialist adjudicative body in South Africa that deals with procurement matters and reviews alleged non-compliance with legislation, the very act of a government entity awarding a contract constitutes administrative action and is therefore subject to the Promotion of Administrative Justice Act 3 of 2000 (PAJA), which provides recourse for aggrieved persons or parties prejudiced by maladministration. The Constitution provides for the challenge of tender awards or decisions on the grounds of lawfulness, reasonableness, and procedural fairness. Since public procurement is regulated by both public law and private law, service providers have recourse to both public law and private law remedies, including, in private law, delictual remedies in the event that there are damages.

Public law remedies find application mainly in the pre-contractual stage, although they may, in exceptional circumstances, also apply in the contractual and post-contractual stages (Bolton, 2008: p. 781). It is important to note that the South African courts have been very active in clarifying legal issues on judicial remedies for persons or firms affected by procurement decisions. Some of these key findings include the following:[15]

The finding that decisions to invite, evaluate, and award tenders amount to "administrative action" and are therefore subject to judicial review. This was an important decision which stipulates the application of the PAJA in procurement decisions and hence enables the judicial review of procurement decisions, especially as the PAJA provides that judicial review only applies to state actions if such actions are "administrative actions." It is also particularly noteworthy because not every act by an organ of state amounts to "administrative action" under South African law.[16] The above is significant because the right to just administrative action is constitutionally protected.

[15] Where specific case law is given in subsequent paragraphs, the chapter draws from Volmink (2010).

[16] Volmink (2010) notes that the courts have held that a decision by an organ of state to dismiss an employee does not amount to administrative action (Transnet Ltd v Goodman Brothers (Pty) Ltd 2001 (2) BCLR 176 (SCA) at para. 34). The courts have also held that a decision by a public body to cancel a contract that was concluded on equal terms with a major commercial undertaking does not constitute administrative action (Cape Metropolitan Council v Metro Inspection Services (Western Cape) CC 2001 (3) SA 1013 (SCA)). The determining factors in deciding whether state action amounts to "administrative action" include the source of the power exercised, the nature of the power, its subject matter, whether it involves the exercise of a public duty, and how closely it is related on the one hand to policy matters which are not administrative, and on the other to the implementation of legislation, which is construed as administrative (President of the RSA and Others v SARFU and Others 1999 (10) BCLR 1059 (CC) at para 142).

Section 33 of the South African Constitution provides for the right to just administrative action and provides:

1. everyone has the right to administrative action that is lawful, reasonable, and procedurally fair;
2. everyone whose rights have been adversely affected by administrative action has the right to be given written reasons; and
3. national legislation must be enacted to give effect to these rights, and must—
   a. provide for the review of administrative action by a court or, where appropriate, an independent and impartial tribunal;
   b. impose a duty on the state to give effect to the rights in subsections (1) and (2); and
   c. promote an efficient administration.

This right to just administrative action is given effect by the PAJA and the right to access to reasons is given effect by the Promotion of Access to Information Act (PAIA). Section 33 of the Constitution should be read in tandem with Section 195 of the Constitution, which deals with the values and principles that govern public administration.[17] These constitutional provisions, read together with PAJA, are clearly aimed at preventing abuse of power by organs of state in their dealings with the public. They provide that just administrative action is necessary to protect the rights of the individual against organs of state, and that the state has a constitutional duty to achieve and uphold a fair, accountable, honest, and responsive administration which is in the interests of the general public (Beukes, 2004).

South African courts have recognized that a losing bidder in a public procurement tender has had its rights affected by the decision and that such rights merit constitutional protection. While initially unwilling to recognize this right, the courts ultimately declared that the right of a bidder is not the right to be awarded the contract, but rather the right to access information that would enable the bidder to decide whether her right to fair administrative action has been infringed in the procurement process. The

[17] These are:

(a) the promotion and maintenance of a high standard of professional ethics;
(b) the promotion of efficient, economic, and effective use of resources;
(c) a development-oriented public administration;
(d) the provision of services impartially, fairly, equitably, and without bias;
(e) a responsiveness to people's needs and the encouragement of the public to participate in policymaking;
(f) an accountable public administration;
(g) the fostering of transparency by providing the public with timely, accessible and accurate information;
(h) the cultivation of good human resource management and career development practices, to maximize human potential; and
(i) a public administration that is broadly representative of the South African people, with employment and personnel management practices based on ability, objectivity, fairness, and the need to redress the imbalances of the past to achieve such broad representation.

Supreme Court of Appeal has elaborated on this right as being the right to equal treatment before the law.[18] The courts have also held that the right to be furnished with information relating to a tender decision cannot be waived even if the bidder has signed an agreement to that effect with the procuring body.[19]

The courts have also stated that the right to reasons requires that these be quality reasons and not simply standard form reasons where requirements are ticked off against a box. The reasons ought to be specific, detailed, and in clear language that is neither ambiguous nor vague and is not framed in formal legal language.[20]

The courts have also been amenable to awarding punitive costs against the procuring state organ in instances where it has unreasonably refused to furnish the requested information.[21]

Finally, the courts have ruled that organs of state should not use the excuse of "state secrets" in order to circumvent the obligation to provide information to affected bidders.[22]

The PAJA provides that any person may institute proceedings in a court or tribunal for the judicial review of an administrative action and sets out the various instances where a court or tribunal may review an administrative action.[23] Procedures for judicial review must be instituted without unreasonable delay and no later than 180 days after all internal remedies have been concluded (or after the administrative action is concluded if the courts have, in exceptional circumstances, exempted the person from exhausting all internal remedies first).[24] Otherwise, no court shall review an administrative action until all the internal remedies have been exhausted.[25] In terms of remedies for persons whose rights have been infringed by the administrative action, the PAJA states that the court or tribunal may:

- direct the administrator to give reasons;
- direct the administrator to act in a manner required by the court or tribunal;
- prohibit the administrator from taking a particular action;
- set aside the administrative decision or action;
- direct the administrator to reconsider the action;
- substitute or vary the administrative action;
- direct the administrator to pay compensation;
- declare the rights of the parties;

[18] *SA Metal and Machinery Co (Pty) Ltd* v *Transnet Ltd* [1998] JOL 3984 (W). There are four reported judgments involving these parties. To avoid confusion, reference will be made to *SA Metal Machinery Co Ltd v Transnet (1)* to (4) respectively.

[19] *Goodman Brothers (Pty) Ltd v Transnet Ltd 1998* (8) BCLR 1024 (W).

[20] *Nomala v Permanent Secretary, Department of Welfare 2001* (8) BCLR 844 (E).

[21] *Claase v Information Officer of South African Airways (Pty) Ltd* [2006] JOL 18804 (SCA).

[22] *ABBM Printing and Publishing (Pty) Ltd v Transnet Ltd 1997* (10) BCLR 1429 (W) at paragraph 24.3.

[23] Section 6 of the Promotion of Administrative Justice Act 3, 2000.

[24] Section 7 (1) and (2) (c) of the Promotion of Administrative Justice Act 3, 2000.

[25] Section 2 (a) of the Promotion of Administrative Justice Act 3, 2000.

- grant an interdict or other temporary relief;
- award costs.[26]

Bolton argues that the requirements for claiming compensation under the PAJA are controversial and unclear, and essentially require an aggrieved bidder to prove the elements of delict in order to found a compensation claim (Bolton, 2008: p. 781). In some instances, however, he notes that claiming costs under the PAJA may be the best route, such as when contracts are terminated in the public interest or declared invalid because they were concluded without the necessary authority. The PAJA is thus a very useful tool to maintain the integrity of public procurement and ensure that the rights of the public and/or service providers are secure and protected.

Private law remedies for aggrieved bidders are founded in contract law and also in the law of delict. These may include remedies aimed at upholding the contract which could include specific performance and an interdict, cancellation and remedies aimed at compensating the innocent party which could include contractual or delictual damages, or interest on amounts owing (Christie and MacFarlane, 2006). Delictual remedies, as distinct from contractual remedies, could arise for various situations such as:

> fraud on the part of public officials; misleading statements made by an organ of state during the tender process resulting in the conclusion of a more onerous contract than anticipated; the wrongful interference by a third party (an unsuccessful bidder) in the contractual relationship between the successful bidder and the organ of state (Bolton, 2008: p. 781).

Bolton further states that cost-effectiveness is the overriding principle and legislation such as the Public Finance Management Act, the Municipal Finance Management Act, and the Municipal Systems Act give effect to this by encouraging feuding parties to resolve disputes through negotiation and mediation, with litigation being pursued only as a last resort.

However, as Magoro and Brynard (2010) note,

> In practice these [procurement frameworks] are grossly oversimplified, and lead to difficulties and even corrupt practices during the implementation.... These problems occur largely because the principles underlying the procurement system—fairness, equitableness, transparency, competitiveness and cost-effectiveness—often are, or appear to be, in conflict with one another (p. 8).

16.3 A High-Level Assessment of the South African Government Procurement Regime

The depth and breadth of the post-1994 transformation in the procurement regime should not be underestimated. As already elaborated in Section 16.2.1, underpinning this

[26] Section 8 of the Promotion of Administrative Justice Act 3, 2000.

radical transformation was the determination to use government procurement as a key mechanism for redressing the inequities of South Africa's past, in this particular instance racially defined access to business opportunities. Hence from a procurement system that, on the face of it, rested on price and, in practice, on exclusive but otherwise undifferentiated access by white-controlled businesses to government procurement, South Africa moved to a system based partly on price but also on a complex array of preferences largely directed at redressing unequal access, always undergirded by the constitutional requirements of fairness and administrative justice.

A related, and conceivably more disruptive transformation was the comprehensive decentralization—or more accurately described as the "fragmentation"—of procurement. There are a number of reasons for this fragmentation, which is present at both the regulatory and operational levels of the procurement system. One important rationale is the introduction of a quasi-federal system of government with significant powers newly devolved to the second (provincial) and third (municipal) tiers of government. Hence in 2004, the National Treasury made significant changes to the system by introducing a public sector SCM legislative framework that provides for decentralized policy and public sector resource management. In line with the Public Finance Management Act (PFMA) and the Municipal Finance Management Act (MFMA), the aim was to allow managers to manage (National Treasury, 2015: p. 9).

However, decentralization is also related to the introduction of non-price criteria into the procurement decision, because a procurement regime explicitly charged with facilitating the access of small, new entrants provides a further rationale for bringing the procurement decision as close as possible to the only terrain on which producers of this scale could successfully compete, namely, provincial and local government.

The disruption generated by decentralization is experienced across a wide front. Legal or regulatory decentralization introduces significant uncertainty and opacity into decision-making. Operational decentralization requires a massive replication of scarce procurement and SCM skills and renders the exercise of effective oversight significantly more onerous. Both regulatory and operational decentralization provide enhanced opportunities and multiple sites for rent-seeking. Each of these difficulties is compounded by the introduction of multiple and frequently conflicting decision-making criteria.

The data necessary to estimate the price premium, if any, arising from incorporating non-price considerations into the procurement decision and from sacrificing the scale economies of greater centralization of procurement are not available. However, the common sense conclusion that there is a premium to be paid arising both from fragmentation and the imposition of non-price decision-making criteria is widely supported.[27]

[27] "SCM across South Africa is highly fragmented. This makes it difficult for government to obtain maximum value when buying, and making use of, goods and services" (National Treasury, 2015: p. 3).

Balancing the price and non-price considerations in procurement decision-making is inherently complex:

> Finally, there is the challenge of finding the best balance between the two major objectives of procurement. Section 217(2) of the Constitution and the Preferential Procurement Policy Framework (PPPFA) both provide for the use of public procurement as a means of development and transformation. An effective SCM system must also have as an objective to ensure that goods and services are available at the best price, in the right qualities, at the right time and in the right place. Constantly having to make decisions about how to balance these objectives is demanding and difficult. It needs a cohort of SCM specialists with the right skills, experience, social awareness, ethical standards and dedication; and a regulatory and organisational environment that supports and monitors their work in the public interest" (National Treasury, 2015: p. 5).

If hard evidence of the pricing consequences of a regime that is both highly fragmented and requires a balancing of non-price and price considerations is difficult to adduce, then there is little doubt about the extent of non-compliance with the complex array of regulatory requirements. The *National Treasury Review* confirmed findings of the Public Service Commission which put overall compliance with SCM systems in certain departments at as low as 54 percent of all contracts issued (Public Service Commission, 2009: p. ix), with instances of non-compliance ranging over the entire SCM process, from the planning phase to the monitoring phase.

Common findings in the Auditor General's annual reports on SCM non-compliance include:

- appointment of suppliers who are not tax compliant
- failure to use competitive processes for quotations and bids
- incorrect use of the preference points system
- lack of appropriately qualified and skilled bid committees
- use of unqualified suppliers
- passing over of bids for invalid reasons
- use of incorrect procurement processes in relation to threshold values for quotations and competitive bidding
- extension of validity periods
- incorrect use of the limited bidding process
- inadequate controls and procedures for handling bids
- appointment of bid committee members not aligned with policy requirements
- insufficient motivation for deviations from SCM procedures.

This is borne out by the experience of Corruption Watch, a non-governmental organization that receives reports of corruption from the public and which has, in the space of three years, received over 700 reports of alleged irregularities and corruption in public procurement processes (Corruption Watch, 2015: p. 9). The irregularities reported range over contracts awarded when the relevant bid committees have indicated a preference for an alternative supplier, inadequate advertisement of tenders, the alteration of submission dates, contracts rolled over without cause, the appointment of suppliers with scores below those of other bidders, and conflicts of interest between the members of the various bid committees, on the one hand, and bidders on the other.

Responsibility for rampant non-compliance is commonly ascribed to skills and capacity deficits in government, severely exacerbated by the high degree of operational fragmentation of the procurement system. However, with more than eighty different legal instruments that govern public sector SCM, it is probably the high degree of regulatory or legal fragmentation that bears primary responsibility for rendering an already skill-intensive function extremely difficult to operate. The *Review* lists the following as amongst the most serious problems arising from excessive regulatory fragmentation (National Treasury, 2015: p. 11):

- the high degree of uncertainty resulting from significant overlap and duplication among different regulatory instruments relating to infrastructure, construction, public–private partnerships, and SCM policy standards;
- the uncertain legal status of the different regulatory instruments for general and specific procurement regimes, such as the standards for defense procurement and ICT procurement;
- the difficulty of deciding which legal regime applies, given the significant variation in the different legal instruments' scope of coverage; and
- the vast number of standard bidding documents.

These systemic and structural features of the procurement regimes—compounded by and themselves exacerbating severe SCM skill deficits—undoubtedly account for much of the non-compliance that is a feature of government procurement. However they in turn contribute to, and are exacerbated by, a further set of related problems, namely the absence of consequence for non-compliance with the regulatory regime. The *Review* notes:

> There are few, if any consequences for those who, despite support and encouragement, fail to perform at the required level. Repeated negative reports by the Auditor General highlights this lack of accountability. An improved and more dynamic public SCM system should bring out the best in its officials, and there must be consequences for those who are not willing to play their part for the pubic good (National Treasury, 2015: p. 5).

The persistent failure to act upon negative findings of the Auditor General is itself partly a manifestation of the problems that resulted in much of the non-compliance in the first place, namely the absence of the skills required to manage the complex regulatory and operational environment. However non-compliance and the absence of consequences point to another ubiquitous and growing problem, namely, corruption. In short, non-compliance with procurement regulation is not simply a consequence of complexity and human resource constraints; it is frequently the result of a willful attempt to support outcomes that favor a pre-selected winner.

Corruption—and particularly the bribery that characterizes the grand corruption of government procurement—is, by definition, a clandestine conspiracy between a bidder on the one hand, and a public sector official capable of influencing the outcome of the bid on the other. Thus whistleblowers, except in those cases where they are direct participants in the corrupt conduct, rarely witness the exchange of the proverbial brown envelope.

It is, however, significantly more difficult to hide the "irregularities"—the transgressions of the constitutional and other legislative and regulatory provisions that govern the procurement process and that are generally a necessary feature of a corrupted public procurement process. As noted, these irregularities may take a multitude of forms spanning what may appear to be relatively minor bureaucratic transgressions (e.g., permitting a slightly late submission), to more technically complex transgressions (e.g., adjusting key bid specifications in the course of the decision-making process), to transgressions that generate immediate suspicion and, for this very reason, are more carefully concealed (e.g., conflicts of interest between public officials serving on key bid decision-making structures on the one hand, and bidders on the other). As already indicated, the South African government procurement regime regularly experiences the full range of these irregularities.

A recent Constitutional Court judgment found an extremely large government tender awarded by the South African Social Security Agency to be illegal and invalid on the basis of a number of irregularities that were established in the course of hearings before a series of courts. In so doing, it overturned a judgment of a lower court—the Supreme Court of Appeal—that, although it broadly accepted that the tender had been irregularly awarded, nevertheless declined to invalidate the award, reasoning that in its view, even if the bid adjudicators had conscientiously adhered to the prescribed regulations, the result would not have changed. In short, the lower court held that the outcome was not materially affected by the irregularities in the process. In rejecting that argument, the Constitutional Court held:

> deviations from fair process may themselves all too often be symptoms of corruption or malfeasance in the process. In other words, an unfair process may betoken a deliberately skewed process. Hence insistence on compliance with process formalities has a three-fold purpose: (a) it ensures fairness to participants in the bid process; (b) it enhances the likelihood of efficiency and optimality in the outcome; and (c) it serves as a guardian against a process skewed by corrupt influences.[28]

[28] *Allpay Consolidated Investment Holdings (Pty) Ltd and Others v Chief Executive Officer of the South African Social Security Agency and Others.*

In short, the Constitutional Court did not find corruption—it was not asked to do so—but it did find that there were clear irregularities in the awarding process. And it concluded that non-compliance was material, partly on the basis that "compliance with process formalities... serves as a guardian against a process skewed by corrupt influences."

This decision of the Constitutional Court should lead to closer scrutiny by the criminal justice authorities of irregularly awarded government procurement contracts. Indeed, having initially declined to investigate the basis of the irregularities found by a number of lower courts, following the Constitutional Court's ruling the criminal justice authorities did announce that they were opening an investigation into the irregular, and hence inferentially corrupt, bid.

However, notwithstanding this decision of the Constitutional Court, under-enforcement of the robust anti-corruption laws—largely a consequence of poorly resourced and trained enforcement personnel and highly corrupted policing and prosecutorial services—will remain the order of the day for the foreseeable future.

Weak criminal enforcement serves to emphasize that critical to the effectiveness and efficiency of the public procurement system are the mechanisms through which service providers can themselves seek redress in cases where they believe the procurement regulations have been violated by procuring entities or bidding parties.

16.4 **South African Government Procurement: A Multilateral Framework?**

The Government Procurement Agreement (GPA) is a legally binding agreement under the auspices of the WTO. It seeks to "achieve an effective multilateral framework for government procurement, with a view to achieving greater liberalization and expansion of, and improving the framework for, the conduct of international trade."[29] It is, however, a plurilateral agreement, that is, it only binds those WTO member countries that have signed up to it. The first four paragraphs of the preamble affirm the fundamental principles of non-discrimination, predictability, and transparency.

The GPA is an agreement that is intended—consistent with the WTO's general purpose—to promote international trade, in this instance by liberalizing the government procurement markets of member countries. This is bound to generate controversy, not least because government procurement is often thought to be the last redoubt of unfettered industrial policy, the one instrument left with which governments are able

[29] The Amended Government Procurement Agreement, adopted on March 30, 2012 (GPA/113). For detail on the evolution of the GPA, see WTO (2012).

to pursue national social and economic objectives relatively free from the policy constraints imposed by trade liberalization.

On the other hand, most government procurement frameworks explicitly affirm the central importance of price competitiveness in the procurement decision-making matrix, a factor which should give even the most ardent adherents of industrial policy pause for thought before rejecting liberalization of the national government procurement market. Moreover, as is well known, a necessary adjunct to opening a market to international trade is adherence to governance rules that give effect to the new trade regime—rules that potentially constrain the corruption and maladministration that bedevil so many national procurement markets.

The question posed in the title of this section will be examined from two angles. First, the trade and competitiveness implications of signing on to the GPA will be examined. It appears that it is these considerations that underpin the South African government's resistance to the GPA despite the fact that severe data constraints render it impossible to examine this issue with any degree of rigor.

Second, having already described and analyzed the South African government procurement regime in some considerable detail, adherence to the GPA will be assessed by asking whether such adherence would indeed severely constrain the South African government's ability to utilize its procurement budget as an instrument of industrial policy, and whether the rules will lend weight to efforts to combat maladministration and corruption in the country's procurement regime.

The GPA currently has forty-three signatories and covers a market that was estimated at $1.6 trillion in 2008 and $1.7 trillion when the Amended GPA entered into force in April 2014. The eventual accession of the countries currently negotiating accession to the GPA (including China, New Zealand, Montenegro, Albania, Georgia, Jordan, Kyrgyz Republic, Moldova, Oman, Tajikistan, and Ukraine) and those negotiating accession as part of their WTO accession protocols (Macedonia, Mongolia, the Russian Federation, Saudi Arabia, and Seychelles) could potentially increase the size of the liberalized government procurement market by between an estimated $440 billion and $1.127 trillion (Niggli and Osei-Lah, 2014).

In terms of scope and coverage, the GPA agreement applies to the procurement by entities covered under a Party's Annex 1, 2, or 3 to Appendix I of the GPA agreement and procurement whose value is above a specified threshold,[30,31] and in terms of the agreement, procurement is defined as the purchase, lease, and rental or hire purchase of goods and services or any combination thereof.

[30] The Annexes to Appendix 1 identify the specific government and sub-government entities that each signatory has committed to GPA obligations, and thus opened to international competition, as specified by that signatory.

[31] This refers to the minimum threshold values above which the GPA agreement applies.

16.4.1 SOUTH AFRICA AND THE GPA: THE ECONOMIC IMPLICATIONS

The primary consideration when weighing up possible accession to the GPA is centered on the potential national economic consequences of the liberalization of an important market. These are, in turn, measured first by the impact of the enhanced access granted to foreign competitors to the government procurement markets of the nation acceding to the GPA, and second by the reciprocal access granted by incumbent GPA members to their procurement market. Both effects defy easy measurement, effectively relying as they do on an assessment of the responsiveness of national producers to enhanced international competition. Successful penetration on the part of national producers of hitherto closed national procurement markets elsewhere in the world is not guaranteed by greater formal access, just as easing formal access to one's own national government procurement market does not guarantee the ability of international producers to successfully penetrate that market. The price effects of enhanced competition in the domestic procurement are, trite to say, particularly difficult to estimate.

Niggli and Osei-Lah (2014) propose the following steps in determining a country's GPA market access potential, that is, its "offensive" interests:

- identify the GPA Parties that provide coverage in the sectors of interest to it and assess the scope and extent of the said commitments;
- quantify the estimated size or value of market access that has been opened up by these parties;
- determine the competitive strength of its domestic firms to effectively compete in these markets; and
- assess the proximity advantage of regional markets, were several countries in the region to be party to the GPA.

The sectors that provide the clearest basis for South Africa's offensive interests in the GPA are in construction and civil engineering, including the development of large-scale mining projects, as well as in medium technology industrial machinery and transport equipment. Specifics include the repair, maintenance, and upgrading of various kinds of oil and gas marine vessels; and the design, fabrication, and construction of specialized modules or facilities for the oil industry, including storage tanks, processing modules for offshore platform or onshore facilities, docking facilities, tugs/barges, civil structures, and platforms. South Africa is a global leader in coal-based synthesis and gas-to-liquids technologies, and globally competitive in the production of transport and haulage equipment as well as in the mining equipment sector, to mention but a few. That South Africa is competing in medium and high technology sectors also creates the potential for further upgrading in the value chain.

Significant lacunae in government procurement data render the determination of defensive interests extremely difficult. Indeed, given the poor state of procurement data, one can only conclude that the South African government's opposition to liberalizing these markets is based on little more than guess work and a pre-determined opposition to trade liberalization per se. Were serious consideration to be given to GPA accession, policy attention would, as a necessary prior step, have to be accorded to the generation of the data necessary to make an intelligent decision. For a government intent on utilizing industrial policy in order to meet key economic and social objectives, it is clear that one of the most important instruments of this policy—namely, government procurement—is being deployed without the requisite empirical basis.

Nor, it appears, do South African trade officials take much comfort from the fact that, by signing up to the GPA, they are not committing to liberalizing access to the entire government procurement market. Their assessment of power imbalances in the WTO's negotiating framework underpin a fear that the inevitable outcome of negotiated accession will be to concede significantly greater access to the domestic procurement market than is in South Africa's mercantilist interest.

16.4.2 SOUTH AFRICA AND THE GPA: POLICY SOVEREIGNTY

As elaborated in Section 16.2.1, government procurement, as an instrument of industrial policy, is deployed not merely in order to prefer national over non-national producers, but principally to promote the interests of selected classes of national producers over all others.

However the GPA is founded on the principles of transparency and non-discrimination, and its objective is to extend these principles to the signatories' public procurement markets (Alvarez-Fernández and Brandstrup, n.d.). On the face of it then, preferences within the South African government procurement regime would appear to be fundamentally at odds with the principles underpinning the GPA. And yet, in practice, this does not appear to be the case.

Even though the revised GPA is not a drastic departure from the earlier texts, particularly with reference to the fundamental principles of non-discrimination and transparency, it has been significantly simplified and permits greater flexibility for developing country members, designed particularly to make accession to the Agreement easier. South Africa, however, is particularly wary of plurilateral agreements in general, and its default stance has been to exclude any discussion on new plurilateral agreements being introduced to the WTO and certainly to steer clear of existing plurilateral agreements to which the country is not party.

Generally, the governance principles underpinning the GPA are the same as those underpinning government procurement regulation in South Africa, especially regarding considerations of fairness, equity, transparency, competitiveness, and cost-effectiveness.

However, the non-discrimination principle underpinning the GPA may conflict with the social and economic objectives that underpin the South African procurement regime. As already elaborated in Section 16.2, whilst espousing what are essentially principles of non-discrimination in relation to government procurement, the South African Constitution also explicitly provides for the introduction of preferences in the administration of government procurement, preferences which are elaborated in subordinate legislation and regulation. Thus, despite broadly identical high-level principles, the reality of the South African government procurement regime may conflict with unyielding enforcement of the GPA principles.

Of course, jealously guarding national control over government procurement decisions in the name of advancing key social and economic objectives begs the question of whether the stated objectives are actually being advanced by the deployment of the procurement instrument. Once again, hard evidence is strikingly difficult to adduce. However, the National Treasury review of the supply chain mechanism is skeptical of the impact of procurement preferences on the building of sustainable SMEs (National Treasury, 2015: p. 32).

Notwithstanding the lack of evidence supporting government procurement's stated goal of promoting sustainable SMEs and new entrants, South Africa's accession to the GPA will undoubtedly remain conditional upon being able to retain these and other industrial and social policy objectives in its procurement regime. Given that the GPA provisions for special and differential treatment are temporary (through implementation periods) and transitional (through negotiation), South African policymakers will certainly view GPA accession as a potential barrier to SME growth and development, undoubtedly reinforced by the prevailing assessment of its trade officials that holds that power dynamics in the WTO will eventually eliminate its ability to hold its line on the preferential treatment in the procurement regime of selected classes of producers.

A brief survey of South Africa's key bilateral and regional trade agreements is testimony to the country's generalized opposition to any externally imposed disciplines on government procurement. The European Community–South Africa Agreement on Trade, Development and Cooperation (TDCA) of 1999 only provides, as far as government procurement is concerned, that the parties "agree to cooperate to ensure that access to the Parties' procurement contracts is governed by a system which is fair, equitable, and transparent."[32] The Southern African Development Community (SADC)–European Union (EU) Economic Partnership Agreement—whose negotiation was concluded on July 15, 2014 and which, for South Africa, was essentially a renegotiation of the TDCA—also does not include a chapter on government procurement. It appears that negotiations leading to the South Africa–European Free Trade Association (EFTA) Free Trade

[32] What follows draws on McCrudden (2003).

Agreement of 2006 traversed the implications of the black economic empowerment policy for public procurement. However, the text that was ultimately agreed upon simply emphasizes that the countries recognize the importance of cooperation to enhance the mutual understanding of their respective government procurement systems.[33]

Continental trade agreements also confirm this pattern. The Southern African Customs Union (SACU) Agreement does not contain any provisions relating to government procurement, and neither does the Southern African Development Community (SADC) Trade Protocol. South Africa is also currently involved with the negotiations toward the Tri-partite Free Trade Area (TFTA), a preferential trade area that combines SADC, the East African Community (EAC) and the Common Market for Eastern and Southern Africa (COMESA). Again, government procurement is a non-issue in these negotiations, a reflection of South Africa's and other African countries' desire to maintain national policy sovereignty in that area (or possibly a reflection of the level of importance accorded such issues by the relevant countries).

In short, there does not appear to be much support for a multi-country initiative to address issues of government procurement in Africa. Within the TFTA, it is only COMESA that has adopted a regional framework on government procurement. COMESA's Regional Procurement Regulations were adopted in 2012 and were designed to address the weak, inefficient, and uncompetitive government procurement systems in member states.

Other regional configurations would probably benefit from a regional approach to public procurement. This would likely boost intra-regional trade and enable African producers to take advantage of investment and infrastructure development opportunities in Africa. This is particularly so within the context of the TFTA, to which South Africa is party and for which infrastructure development is one of the priority areas. Procurement regimes will play a central role in whether or not South African producers get a share of the market to provide the various goods and services needed to realize the infrastructure development ambitions of the TFTA.

16.4.2.1 **Non-Discrimination and Transparency**

Article IV:1 of the GPA deals with the general principles on non-discrimination and provides for both the most-favored nation as well as the national treatment principle. The South African government procurement regime provides for award criteria that are more concerned with supplier characteristics than with the national origin of the procured goods and services procured being South African. The conditions of competition for both local and foreign firms are, with limited exception, identical in relation to

[33] Article 29 (1) of the South Africa–European Free Trade Association (EFTA) Free Trade Agreement of 2006, as cited in McCrudden (2003).

government procurement criteria; the competing firms are simply required to satisfy the legislated award criteria (Bolton and Quinot, 2011: p. 459). Domestic firms that do not meet the procurement award criteria will be just as disadvantaged as the foreign firms that also fail to meet the criteria. The same conditions and criteria that apply to domestic suppliers with regard to black economic empowerment also apply to foreign suppliers.

Nevertheless, the South African government procurement regime's emphasis on broad-based black economic empowerment effectively puts the South African subsidiaries of foreign-owned firms at a decided disadvantage. In recognition of this, the new preferential procurement regulations allow for differentiated contributions to B-BBEE for local and foreign-owned firms through the use of offsets. In this regard, the Equity Equivalent Programme for multinational companies becomes significant as it does away with the black ownership requirement for B-BBEE status. This approach therefore creates scope for foreign suppliers to compete with local suppliers in the government procurement market.

The use of offsets is expressly prohibited in Article IV:6 of the GPA, which precludes parties from seeking, taking account of, imposing, or enforcing any offsets. At the same time, Article V on special and differential treatment provides for the use of offsets by developing countries on the condition that such requirement is expressly stated in the notice of intended procurement. But this provision is limited in that it is temporary and the transition period would still need to be negotiated with other parties.

Under the non-discrimination principle in the GPA, parties must also not discriminate against the producers of other GPA members for protectionist reasons. However, South Africa does utilize public procurement for the purposes of promoting industrialization, and the Department of Trade and Industry, through its Industrial Policy Action Plan, seeks to support selected sectors in manufacturing. As such, local production and content requirements apply to designated sectors. Again, while this approach is in principle prohibited under the GPA, Article V recognizes that developing countries have different developmental, financial, and trade needs, and allows for special and differential treatment of developing countries.

The non-discrimination provisions of the GPA are supported by the transparency provisions of Article IV:4. This article provides that procuring entities must avoid conflicts of interest and prevent corrupt conduct in their procurement practices. This would speak directly to some of the governance challenges, elaborated in Section 16.3, that South Africa faces in its procurement system.

The GPA would, therefore, provide a potential external constraint on corruption and also facilitate efficiency and cost-effectiveness in government procurement in South Africa. This can be achieved through the transparency and disclosure requirements in Articles XVI through to XVII. Article XVI, in particular, would oblige the government to establish a one-stop portal for procurement information. This would partly address the decentralization problem in procurement. At the same time, it would also limit the discretion of supply chain managers by holding them accountable to publicly available requirements regarding procurement specifications, processes, and award criteria.

Because the GPA requires adherence to principles and practices of transparency, efficiency, procedural fairness, and good governance, accession on the part of South Africa may act to constrain contrary conduct which, as outlined above, increasingly characterizes the government procurement regime. On the other hand, it may be credibly argued that these principles are already enshrined in South African law and that taking on what are effectively identical obligations in the GPA would add little to the domestic provisions already in place. Moreover, the National Treasury review has indicated that it intends making public information pertaining to the demand, acquisition and contract management phases of the procurement process.

16.4.2.2 **Review and Enforcement**

The GPA mandates each Party to establish or designate at least one impartial administrative or judicial authority, which is independent of its procuring entities, to adjudicate the review of procurement cases.

South Africa does not have a review and enforcement mechanism that is dedicated to government procurement issues. As such, determining the effectiveness of the domestic review process requires a judgment of the South African judicial system. While the independence of the South African high courts is generally accepted, the same cannot be said of the National Prosecuting Authority. The upshot is that while judicial reviews—usually initiated by losing bidders—of administrative processes governing the award of public procurement contracts can be relied upon to uphold the principles enshrined in domestic law, the likelihood of criminal investigation and prosecution of allegedly corrupted public procurement awards is relatively remote.

Successful judicial review may result in the setting aside of government procurement contracts. However, the inordinate length of judicial proceedings frequently means that by the time the final appeal court has made its decision, either the disputed contract has run its course or it is at such an advanced stage that termination would result in significant prejudice to the beneficiaries. This conundrum is clearly illustrated in the *All Pay* matter referred to above. At issue was the award of the tender to manage South Africa's massive social security program. In this instance the Constitutional Court, in setting aside the severely flawed tender award, was compelled to craft a remedy that nevertheless enabled the winner of the award to continue servicing the contract so as to ensure that the continued functioning of a complex system was not jeopardized. Given that the decision of the final court was only handed down in the third year of a five-year grant, the outcome effectively permitted the incumbent to complete the contract. One can readily assume that the courts may be similarly constrained when confronted by a half-built dam or football stadium.

The only advantage of the GPA in terms of the domestic review procedures is that it provides the option for Parties to utilize the WTO dispute settlement mechanism where South Africa's laws, regulations, and practices contravene GPA principles. This avenue is not directly open to private foreign bidders but they can lobby their governments to intervene.

16.4.2.3 Special and Differential Treatment for Developing Countries

For developing countries, implementation constraints as well as perceived and actual limitations imposed on policy sovereignty dominate discussion and decision-making surrounding adherence to WTO instruments.

Article V of the GPA, which deals with both the implementation and market access derogations for developing countries, would be considered especially critical by South Africa were the country to consider accession to the GPA. Article V provides that in the accession negotiations, the GPA members shall give special consideration to the developmental, financial, and trade needs and circumstances of developing countries and least developed countries (LDCs). This is the special and differential treatment (S&DT) element of the GPA. S&DT is a basic tenet of the WTO that seeks to level the playing field for both developed and developing countries by relaxing the rules and commitments applied to the latter category of countries.

Through S&DT, developing countries are provided with longer implementation periods for their commitments under the GPA, with the exception of the obligations contained in Article IV:1(b) on non-discrimination of goods, services, or suppliers of any other party. LDCs are given five years in which to achieve implementation, while other developing countries are given three years.[34] These implementation periods may be extended upon request to the GPA Committee, or the Committee may approve new transitional measures if there are special circumstances that were unforeseen during the accession process.[35] Upon a developing country's accession to the GPA, each party is obliged to accord it the most favorable coverage afforded to any other party in the Agreement.[36]

Article V also makes provision for transitional measures for developing countries that cater to both the defensive and offensive interests of developing countries (Niggli and Osei-Lah, 2014). The defensive tools, which give developing countries flexibility as they transition into the open market, include price preference programs, the phased-in addition of specific entities or sectors, and the ability to impose thresholds that are higher than the permanent levels.[37]

[34] Article V: 4 of the GPA.
[35] Article V: 6 of the GPA.
[36] Article V: 2 of the GPA.
[37] Article V: 3 (a), (c), and (d), read with Niggli and Osei-Lah (2014).

With regard to offensive interests, Article V:3 (b) provides for the use of offsets which,[38] in the case of South Africa, would help promote local industry as per the objectives of the Industrial Policy Action Plan. Both the defensive and offensive measures provided for by Article V are designed to give developing countries a temporary reprieve from foreign competition as they transition into the agreement. It must be noted, however, that unlike the longer implementation periods specified for any obligations assumed under the Agreement, the market-related transitionary measures have to be established through negotiation.

There has been increasing discontent among developing countries with the traditional S&DT provisions in WTO agreements. Most of these provisions are deemed ineffective, especially with regard to the capacity-building and technical assistance provisions. The provision in the GPA on the review of Article V provides a unique opportunity for developing countries to strengthen the S&DT provisions. This is especially as there is also a provision for the Committee to review Article V in terms of its operation and effectiveness every five years. In the Trade Facilitation Agreement, agreed to at the December 2013 Bali Ministerial Conference, the implementation of some commitments is contingent on countries receiving capacity-building and technical assistance. Where developing countries have not received the requisite assistance, they shall not be expected to implement the commitments.

Rather than a blanket transition period for developing and least developed countries, the TFA provides for a staggered implementation process that is based on each individual developing country's national trade facilitation needs assessment. This needs assessment is then used to determine the country's capacity and, concomitant to that, the level of assistance needed to implement its commitments under the TFA. Of course, trade facilitation cannot be equated with government procurement in terms of implementation assistance, but the same principle with regard to transition periods and a staggered implementation process could be adopted.

Some programs, such as the black economic empowerment program, could be left open-ended if South Africa were to sign up to the GPA, especially considering the unique circumstances that have created a dual economy in South Africa where the majority of the population was excluded from active participation in the formal economy. Such empowerment policies are needed to effect redress. The major problems with black economic empowerment policies in South Africa are less to do with the policy itself but rather their implementation.

The use of procurement policies for socio-economic objectives itself remains contested, but South Africa seems to have made significant strides in opening up competition in the

[38] "Offset means any condition or undertaking that encourages local development or improves a Party's balance-of-payments accounts, such as the use of domestic content, the licensing of technology, investment, counter-trade and similar action or requirement"(Article 1 (l) GPA).

procurement sector. There appears to be room for South Africa's procurement regime to escape discrimination censure under the GPA, as well as for negotiation of the B-BBEE program as a derogation and exemption.

As elaborated in Section 16.3, there are general challenges to obtaining data on government procurement in South Africa. There is no mechanism in place for data collation, either aggregated or disaggregated, beyond information on how much the National Treasury allocates to government procurement in each year. This creates wastage of resources and inefficiencies in the system, as well as massive loopholes for corrupt practices in government procurement. There is also a lack of data on the total general government procurement, on the number of tender awards and the disaggregation between BEE beneficiaries and non-BEE beneficiaries, and even on the efficacy of the BEE policy itself in government procurement to achieve its objectives.

The National Treasury's Supply Chain Management Review seeks to remedy this and a host of other issues through such measures as a centralized automated government procurement database. A framework is also being put in place to standardize reporting on government contracts and information required will include procurement plans, tenders to be advertised, tenders awarded, supplier company information, the value of each award, and progress in implementing tenders. The information will be made public at varying intervals depending on its nature.

In order to combat the ubiquitous conflicts of interest that beset the award of government contracts, the recently passed (but not yet promulgated) Public Administration Management Act prohibits public servants from doing business with the state. Such reform is in line with the provisions of Article VI and VII, which detail the procedural requirements GPA members have to implement to ensure transparency in the sector. The NGO, Corruption Watch (the local chapter of Transparency International), is participating actively in the latter's global campaign for national public registers of beneficial owners. The campaign, in the first instance, proposes that eligibility for a government procurement contract be conditional upon a prospective bidder being willing to declare, for the public record, the identity of the beneficial owners of its shareholding companies and trusts. This proposal would not only make a significant contribution to detecting money laundering—the principal target of the campaign—but it would also expose, or even better deter, the interest conflicts present in so many government procurement deals.

From a governance perspective, although the South African procurement regime appears consistent with the requirement of GPA membership, there is little doubt that an additional layer of accountability would assist in promoting procurement that is "fair, equitable, transparent, competitive, and cost effective."

However, this consideration will not feature significantly in a decision to accede to the GPA. Of much greater importance will be an assessment, first, of the impact on South Africa's ability to retain national sovereignty over the procurement decision-making framework, and so retain the presence of socio-economic criteria in the purchasing decision; and second, of the extent to which South Africa is able to win a bargain in which it would aspire to access the procurement markets of other countries while defending those parts of its domestic procurement markets in which South African producers will be particularly exposed to foreign competition. Notionally at least, South Africa should be able to hold the line on these objectives. However, it appears that fear of the power dynamics in the WTO negotiating processes—whether well advised or not—seems destined to keep South Africa out of the GPA for the foreseeable future.

REFERENCES

Alvarez-Fernández, A. and Brandstrup, P. (n.d.). "The Access of Third Countries to the European Union's Public Procurement Market." available at: <http://www.maastrichtuniversity.nl/web/file?uuid=62b11268-fbdf-4f38-9f5b-2f60c043d091&owner=44876363-60e5-41e4-a579-da103bb0ec73>.

Ambe, I. and Badenhorst-Weiss, J. 2012. "Procurement Challenges in the South African Public Sector." *Journal of Transport and Supply Chain Management* 6(1): 242–61.

AusAID and South Africa Capacity Building Program. 2000. "Report on Opportunities for Reform of Government Procurement in South Africa." Pretoria: Government Press.

Beukes, M. 2004. "The Constitutional Foundation of the Implementation and Interpretation of the Promotion of Administrative Justice Act 3 of 2000." In C. Lange and J. Wessels (eds), *The Right to Know: South Africa's Promotion of Administrative Justice and Access to Information Acts*. Cape Town: Siber Ink.

Bolton, P. 2006. "Government Procurement as a Policy Tool in South Africa." *Journal of Public Procurement* 6(3): 193–217.

Bolton, P. 2008. "The Public Procurement System in South Africa: Main Characteristics." *Public Contract Law Journal* 37(4): 781–802.

Bolton, P and Quinot, G. 2011. "Social Policies in Procurement and the Government Procurement Agreement: A Perspective from South Africa." In S. Arrowsmith and R. D. Anderson (eds), *The WTO Regime on Government Procurement: Recent Developments and Challenges Ahead*. Cambridge: Cambridge University Press.

Christie R. H. and MacFarlane, V. 2006. *The Law of Contract in South Africa*, 5th edn. Durban: Butterworths.

Corruption Watch. 2015. "Annual Report 2014," Johannesburg (available at: <http://www.corruptionwatch.org.za/wp-content/uploads/2015/05/Corruption-Watch-Annual-Report-2014.pdf> (accessed July 23, 2016)).

Department of Trade and Industry. 2015a. "Guidelines: Equity Equivalents Programme for Multinationals," Pretoria (available at: <https://www.thedti.gov.za/economic_empowerment/equity_programme.jsp> (accessed July 23, 2016)).

Department of Trade and Industry. 2015b. "Industrial Development," Pretoria (available at: <https://www.thedti.gov.za/industrial_development/ip.jsp> (accessed July 23, 2016)).

McCrudden, C. 2003. "Social Policy Choices and the International and National Law of Government Procurement: South Africa as a case study." In H. Corder (ed.), *Global Administrative Law*. Cape Town: Juta and Co.

Magoro, M. J. and Brynard, P. A. 2010. "Difficulties Associated with the Implementation of the Preferential Procurement Policy in Conjunction with a Low-cost Housing Programme: A South African Contextualisation." University of Pretoria Research Article. Available at: <http://repository.up.ac.za/handle/2263/*15953*>.

National Treasury. 2003. "Policy Strategy to Guide Uniformity in Procurement Reform Processes in Government" (available at: <http://www.treasury.gov.za/legislation/pfma/supplychain/Policy%20to%20Guide%20Uniformity%20in%20Procurement%20Reform%20Processes%20in%20Government.pdf> (accessed July 23, 2016)).

Niggli, N. C. and Osei-Lah, K. 2014. "Infrastructure Provision and Africa's Trade and Development Prospects: Potential Role and Relevance of the WTO Agreement on Government Procurement (GPA)." WTO Staff Working Paper No. ERSD-2014–20, Washington, DC.

Public Affairs Research Institute. 2014. "The Contracting State: Outsourcing & Decentralisation in Contemporary South Africa," Johannesburg (available at: <http://www.pari.org.za/wp-content/uploads/PARI-The-Contract-State-01082014.pdf> (accessed July 23, 2016)).

Public Service Commission. 2009. "Evaluation of SCM Practices within the R200000 Threshold," Pretoria (available at: <http://www.psc.gov.za/documents/2009/R200%20000.pdf> (accessed July 23, 2016)).

Uyarra, E. and Flanagan, K. 2009. "Understanding the Innovation Impacts of Public Procurement." Manchester Business School Working Paper No. 574.

Volmink, P. 2010. "Enhancing Transparency within Public sector Procurement: The South African Experience." Paper Presented at the 4th International Public Procurement Conference, Seoul, August 26–28 (available at: <http://www.ippa.org/IPPC4/Proceedings/18TransparencyAccountabil ityinProcurement/Paper18-11.pdf> (accessed July 23, 2016)).

World Bank. 2003. *South Africa—Country Procurement Assessment Report: Refining the Public Procurement System*, vol. 2, Washington, DC (available at: <https://openknowledge.worldbank.org/handle/10986/14764>(accessed July 23, 2016)).

WTO. 2012. "Agreement on Government Procurement," Washington, DC (available at: <https://www.wto.org/english/tratop_e/gproc_e/gp_gpa_e.htm>(accessed July 23, 2016)).

17 Government Procurement Polices across the Tasman

What Role Is Played by (Preferential) Trade Agreements?

Malcolm Bosworth

17.1 Introduction

The government procurement market in both Australia and New Zealand (henceforth, "ANZ") is significant, especially if procurement by sub-central government agencies is included. Procurement covers both goods and increasingly services, including construction. Australian Commonwealth procurement alone amounted to AUD$48.9 billion in 2013–14, up from $39.3 billion in 2012–13, and total state government procurement is about the same. Total state and Commonwealth procurement in 2013–14 amounted to about 6.5 percent of GDP. Such procurement is overwhelmingly sourced from Australia, including within own states. New Zealand government procurement (excluding by local governments) amounts to some NZ$38–40 billion annually, equivalent to currently around 15 percent of gross domestic product (GDP).

ANZ have evolved decentralized systems of government procurement both at the national and sub-central government levels. Purchasing is done by the procuring agency following rules and procedures set by centralized agencies and with their guidance and monitoring.

Due to its importance, the efficiency of government procurement can significantly impact on a country's overall resource-use efficiency, and on government budgets. Thus, reforming government procurement to open the market to overseas competition is likely to help address budgetary concerns and, more importantly, significantly improve economic efficiency. Mindful of this, greater attention is now being devoted globally to negotiating government procurement provisions in trade agreements, whether multilateral, bilateral, or plurilateral/regional. A critical issue is therefore whether these trade agreements have been effective in promoting significant domestic reforms in parties' government procurement systems. Or put another way, have they helped domestic liberalization, had no impact, or even possibly hindered such domestic reforms? These questions have become even more pertinent given the proliferation of discriminatory preferential trade agreements (PTAs), with many more being negotiated or in the pipeline. This PTA explosion stems largely from governments heralding them as big improvements on earlier versions and as modern twenty-first-century agreements by including provisions in new areas, such as government procurement. Government procurement therefore provides an excellent case study of PTAs generally and of their capacity to reform such policies, in order to see whether PTA provisions deliver nothing more in practice than merely expanding negotiations of commitments on "paper."

Consistent with this approach, this chapter examines the impact of trade agreements on ANZ domestic government procurement policies, and not on the extent to which they may have raised export opportunities by opening overseas procurement markets. While the latter commercial opportunities are often seen by governments and trade ministries as the main benefits of trade agreements, this is a misnomer. The main gains from trade openness accrue from self-liberalization, not from others opening their markets to increase export opportunities. This is because replacing domestic production with more efficient imports improves an economy's allocative efficiency by releasing resources to be used more productively, whether in import-competing, exporting, or non-tradable activities. Increasing exports per se, especially of particular goods or services to certain markets, does not necessarily raise GDP or national welfare, while trade creation from imports displacing inefficient activities does so unambiguously. Thus good economic sense is to focus on the impact of trade agreements in increasing an economy's imports, not its exports. This is the primary economic test by which all trade agreements, including PTAs, should be assessed.

It is common for the economic benefits of trade agreements through increased export potential to be exaggerated and oversold by trade ministries and governments (APC, 2009). Market opportunities are only a minor contributor to export success. Opportunities must be realized, and this depends on supply responses and the exporters' competitiveness, which is affected by many factors—mainly their efficiency, which is in turn affected by home economic (including trade-related) policies (e.g., their economy's openness) and exchange rates.

Thus, for trade agreements to be worthwhile economically, they must help promote domestic unilateral reforms—the best and ultimately the only sustainable method of achieving meaningful economic openness and gains. This is where trade agreements, especially PTAs, are failing. PTAs in particular are potentially harmful economically because they promote discriminatory liberalization, usually through tariffs.[1] PTAs rarely change actual non-tariff measures, but where they do they also open up possibilities of

[1] In contrast to the World Trade Organization (WTO), where tariff bindings (caps) are negotiated, such that actual tariffs may not be changed, actual tariffs are negotiated in PTAs. However, changing actual tariffs preferentially brings with it the prospect of generating trade diversion in goods, which—if on balance exceeding trade creation—can reduce the national welfare of PTA parties.

trade diversion. Trade agreements, including PTAs, typically involve negotiating "on paper commitments" that either match existing actual measures, or more likely contain substantial binding overhang by being less open than actual measures, and hence have no impact on actual trade barriers.

Thus, PTAs embrace discriminatory or preferential approaches (conditional MFN treatment) to liberalization, in contrast to normal WTO "unconditional" MFN agreements. More importantly, PTAs contradict unilateral reforms, the most efficient approach since by nature they would be non-discriminatory based on "unconditional" MFN. PTAs undermine unilateralism as governments focus on keeping "negotiation coin" for future PTAs and base their trade policy thinking on flawed mercantilism that national welfare is enhanced mainly by getting other countries to liberalize, and not from self-liberalization. PTAs also erode the WTO multilateral system by weakening its fundamental principle of "unconditional" MFN. In this regard, the WTO Government Procurement Agreement (GPA) is even an exception to the WTO, being an unattractive plurilateral "conditional" MFN or preferential/discriminatory agreement.

Given the mercantilist dynamics of negotiating trade agreements, especially PTAs, overselling their perceived benefits from overseas market access is virtually inevitable. Each party negotiates from the position that "exports are good and imports are bad," and accordingly adopts defensive strategies to get other parties to liberalize while conceding as little reciprocal opening as possible. Governments are not using trade agreements to promote self-liberalization, from which most of the economic gains derive, but more often to entrench current protective arrangements or even to extend them. Thus it is no shock that trade agreements end up being "more gloss than substance," snowed-in window dressing being negotiated for foreign policy and other reasons but sold on dodgy economic gains.

This chapter attempts to shed some light on the domestic policy implications by examining the role played by ANZ PTAs in setting their government procurement policies. Evaluating the effectiveness of trade agreements against each country's actual procurement policies is the only meaningful benchmark to use since it is actual policy changes that matter, not simply negotiating commitments "on paper." ANZ are negotiating a network of bilateral and interlocking plurilateral PTAs, often containing government procurement provisions. New Zealand has also just acceded to the GPA and Australia has announced it is likely to follow. Both countries previously rejected joining the GPA as it was seen to be a bad agreement.

The chapter is structured as follows. Section 17.2 examines the development of Australian government procurement policies at the Commonwealth level and, most importantly, the state level. Section 17.3 briefly looks at the New Zealand central government procurement policies. Section 17.4 examines the approach and commitments made by ANZ in their trade agreements, especially in PTAs (or their equivalent).

Section 17.5 examines Australia's continued use of government procurement as industry policy. Section 17.6 concludes.

17.2 Australia's Government Procurement Policies

An important milestone in Australian government procurement policies was the National Preference Agreement (NPA) signed in 1986 by the Commonwealth and state governments to phase out respective price preferences that favored own-state suppliers. Price margins were calculated using the amount of own-state content, and were also applied against imported content. During the 1980s, the push to remove inter-state price preferences developed as they became increasingly seen as major impediments to Australian growth.

New Zealand joined the NPA in June 1989. This followed a review of the Australian and New Zealand Closer Economic Relations Trade Agreement (ANZCERTA), which entered into force in 1983. ANZCERTA agreed to a single Tasman government procurement market by calling for ANZ to work towards eliminating price preferences favoring domestic procurement (Article 11), and to remove offsets on procurement.

While the NPA removed inter-state price preferences by states agreeing not to apply them against each other, preferences remained against imports.[2] New South Wales (NSW), Victoria (VIC), Queensland (QLD), and South Australia (SA) joined the Commonwealth in applying 20 percent margins, while Western Australia (WA) and Tasmania (TAS) applied 10 percent margins.[3] The Commonwealth and VIC subsequently removed price preferences on imports in 1989. These price margins, together with the zero price margins adopted by New Zealand, VIC, and the Australian Capital Territory (ACT) were subsequently incorporated into the NPA.

Although the ANZCERTA extended the coverage of government procurement reforms to New Zealand suppliers in creating the single Tasman procurement market, the essence for the NPA was the unilateral removal by Australia of inter-state preferences as part of domestic reform. This followed a report by the Australian Industry Assistance Commission, now called the Productivity Commission (PC), that showed preferences were penalizing the efficiency of the heavy engineering industry.

Australia removed inter-state preferences some three years before New Zealand was granted the same treatment as Australian content. New Zealand's accession to the NPA extended simultaneously reciprocal national treatment on price preferences to New Zealand suppliers. Australia therefore effectively extended discriminatory market access

[2] State preferences applied only to goods and related services, not to just services.

[3] The Australian Capital Territory (ACT) never applied preferences to its suppliers against other states or imported content.

treatment to New Zealand via price preferences while New Zealand, which had no price preferences against imported content, committed never to introduce any against Australian content.

In 1991, the NPA was re-named the Australian and New Zealand Government Procurement Agreement (ANZGPA).[4]

17.2.1 THE GOVERNMENT PROCUREMENT AGREEMENT (ANZGPA)

The ANZGPA, like the NPA, encouraged cooperation in government procurement and the elimination of inter-state preference schemes and other forms of discrimination based on origin. ANZ suppliers could compete on an equal footing for government contracts in all states and in New Zealand. The ANZGPA also fostered discussions to promote greater uniformity in procurement policies and practices, such as common contractual, technical, and performance standards and specifications. The ANZGPA and its predecessor, the NPA, as domestic legislation signed by both governments formed the basis of implementing the single Tasman government procurement market.[5] Accession to the ANZGPA, like ANZCERTA, is closed to other governments.

The ANZGPA covered Commonwealth, state or territory bodies, statutory and non-statutory authorities, and government-controlled contracting bodies, but excluded procurement by local governments as well as by government-owned corporations, body corporate, or other legal entities with the power to contract, unless the parties decided otherwise. Exemption from the application of preference margins but not from other provisions of the NPA for specified Commonwealth and state bodies, except VIC and the ACT, were dropped in the ANZGPA; New Zealand had made no such exemptions under the NPA. As per the NPA, certain classes of procurement were also exempt from specific provisions (Box 17.1). ANZ could exempt new developments in purchasing policy, or use that policy to implement other policies, provided there was no discrimination based on origin; and advance purchases to stimulate depressed industries.[6]

The ANZGPA committed ANZ to provide services, products, and suppliers equal opportunity and treatment no less favorable than that accorded to their own domestic products and suppliers, and to ensure no inter-state and trans-Tasman application of preference schemes and other discrimination based on origin. "Origin" is defined using the ANZCERTA rules. Thus, as for ANZCERTA and imports of goods generally, the

[4] Throughout this document to avoid confusion the WTO Government Procurement Agreement is referred to by the abbreviation "GPA" and the Australian Government procurement Agreement as the "AGPA."

[5] The ANZGPA is administered by the Australian Procurement and Construction Council (APCC), in which New Zealand has full participation rights.

[6] These provisions were seemingly never used.

BOX 17.1 SPECIFIC EXEMPTIONS FROM THE ANZGPA

Joint bodies with other governments, bodies funded mainly from special industry levies, community groups, special grants or public donations, and bodies competing substantially with the private sector if significantly commercially disadvantaged by applying the preferences.

Procurement exempt from all provisions is:

- from own departments or authorities if no other supplier asked to tender, unless public tenders called irrespective of whether a government body tenders; and
- in emergencies, for example natural disasters.

Procurement exempt from specified provisions is:

- dual or multiple sourcing based on sound and practical reasons not deemed to breach provisions prohibiting discrimination on origin;
- proprietary items to ensure machinery or equipment integrity, and of proprietary equipment of a work, health, or safety nature specified in industrial agreements (provisions on selective use of specifications), unless available from a number of sources and public tenders called;
- strategic defense and other items affecting national security subject to provisions prohibiting discrimination but not subject to monitoring;
- Australian governments in accordance with Commonwealth non-procurement policies deemed not to contravene the ANZGPA; and
- when a local source is essential to ensure supply in case of a natural disaster or similar circumstances, and preferences are necessary for the viability of the local source, subject to unanimous agreement.

rules of origin act as a non-tariff measure restricting trans-Tasman government procurement. This is because New Zealand goods not meeting these rules of origin are ineligible for receiving Australian state preferences and are hence discriminated against as non-New Zealand content.

The ANZGPA also called for promoting opportunities for ANZ suppliers to compete for government business based on value for money, and to avoid biased purchasing practices. It specifically excluded certain discriminatory or biased procurement practices that denied equal opportunity.[7] Value for money became the primary determinant in procurement—which included quality, price, delivery and service support—using life-cycle or similar costing techniques where appropriate.

Australia, as under the NPA, met the ANZGPA's national treatment obligation by extending state price preferences against imported content to New Zealand suppliers.

[7] For example, designing tender specifications and issuing tender requests to exclude ANZ suppliers; biasing specifications towards or against particular firms' products; the timing of tender opening and closing to prevent interested ANZ manufacturers developing proposals and submitting tenders; specifying quantities and delivery schedules reasonably judged to prevent ANZ firms meeting requirements; and adopting purchasing practices to avoid public scrutiny.

Such price preferences continued not to apply to non-New Zealand imported content, thereby discriminating against it. The national treatment obligation did not require Australia to remove its inter-state price preferences, but rather that they apply also to New Zealand content.

While it would have been preferable economically for Australia to extend such market access unilaterally to all trading partners (not just New Zealand), even without reciprocity, this was never contemplated. Reforming government procurement was seen mainly in the context of removing inter-state price preferences and establishing the single Tasman market.

17.2.2 COMMONWEALTH GOVERNMENT PROCUREMENT

Total Commonwealth procurement of goods and services in 2012–13 was $48.9 billion, comprising over 66,000 contracts. Almost two-thirds were related to services. Of the total Commonwealth procurement, some 11 percent by value and 5.6 percent by number of contracts was contracted overseas in 2013–14, mainly covering goods and services unavailable domestically. Thus, some 89 percent was likely to be procured domestically in 2013–14 (up from 82 percent in 2012–13, when 92 percent of services were likely to have been sourced from Australian suppliers and 70.1 percent of goods).[8] Rather detailed centralized statistics are available on Commonwealth government procurement.

Over the past three years, the Commonwealth has purchased 93 percent of services from Australian suppliers (totaling $60.2 billion) and 60 percent of goods (totaling $28.7 billion). Much of the overseas procurement covered large military contracts for goods not produced domestically. Some half, by value, of Commonwealth procurement covers defense.

Commonwealth procurement was decentralized from the outset by devolving purchasing responsibilities to the procuring entities. Commonwealth procurement guidelines (CPGs) were first issued in 1998 under the Financial Management and Accountability (FMA) Act 1997. These were replaced by Commonwealth procurement rules (CPRs) in December 2008. Commonwealth procurement was always underpinned by the core principles of value for money (on a whole-of-life basis), supported by efficiency and effectiveness; accountability and transparency; ethics; and industry development. Procuring entities have to consider the commercial and practical benefits of

[8] However, classifying Australian-sourced goods and services, especially by the Commonwealth, may be overstated because the only means of identifying local sourcing are the tenderers' Australian Business Taxation Number and their business address. No information is available on the extent to which supplied goods and services is local content. Seeking further information from tenderers to determine local content shares would, the Government believes, add unreasonable complexity and "red tape" to government procurement processes.

buying from competitive ANZ industries in evaluating value for money, and ensure that procurement methods do not discriminate against them, especially SMEs.

Key principles now also cover encouraging competition, risk management, and procurement methods. Value for money remains the core procurement rule, but procuring entities are also to consider the non-financial costs and benefits of procurement. Suppliers must be treated equitably and not be discriminated against irrespective of size, degree of foreign affiliation or ownership, location, or origin of their *goods* and services. Provisions also exist on ethical and non-corrupt behavior and procurement, and to ensure accountable and transparent processes.

The Department of Finance is responsible for the CPRs, which apply to all goods and services as well as to procurement by all agencies falling under the FMA Act 1997 and prescribed bodies under the Commonwealth Authority and Companies Act 1997. The CPRs were last updated in July 2014. They exclude procurement to maintain or restore international peace and security, to protect human health, for essential security, and for national artistic, historic, or archaeological treasures. The new Public Governance, Performance and Accountability Act 2013, applied from July 2014, governs government procurement and includes CPRs as part of its rules.

Commonwealth bodies have always had to source at least 10 percent of purchases from SMEs (ANZ firms with up to 200 full-time employees). Procurement practices should not unfairly discriminate against SMEs and should provide them appropriate opportunities to compete. Determining value for money should include consideration of the benefits of contracting with competitive SMEs; barriers to entry that may prevent SMEs from competing (e.g., costly preparation and submission of documents); SME capabilities and commitments to local or regional markets; and the potential benefits of having a larger, more competitive supplier base.

In 2012–13, overall SME participation in Commonwealth procurement was 31.7 percent by value, well above the 10 percent target, and 60.5 percent based on the number of contracts awarded. Another 12 percent was contracted to small enterprises.

Procurement above $5 million also has to take account of, and the tender documentation must reflect, any industry development criteria and associated evaluation methodology, where appropriate, to extend opportunities for SMEs to participate. Procurement methods are not stipulated, but are decided by the procurement entity on a case-by-case basis. Tenderers for projects exceeding $5 million ($6 million for construction) in significantly populated indigenous areas must consider opportunities for these communities.

The CPGs were substantially revised in 2005 to incorporate additional mandatory procurement and tendering procedures and rules on procurements at or above $80,000 for FMA agencies, and $400,000 for relevant CAC Act Bodies (excluding construction services, where the threshold is $7.5 million). These changes are included in domestic legislation commitments agreed by Australia with the US in their free trade agreement.

BOX 17.2 PROCUREMENT EXEMPT FROM MANDATORY PROCEDURES

Procurement that is exempt from mandatory procedures is:

- real property or accommodation, excluding construction and goods and services procured;
- outside Australia for external consumption (including construction);
- from another government entity if no commercial market exists or when legislation or Commonwealth policy requires using a government provider, for example tied legal services;
- by, or on behalf of, the Defence Intelligence Organisation, the Australian Signals Directorate, or the Defence Imagery and Geospatial Organisation;
- from a business primarily providing services to disabled persons;
- from a business that primarily exists to provide the services of persons with a disability; and
- of goods and services from an SME with at least 50 percent indigenous ownership funded by international grants, loans or other assistance, grants and sponsorship payments from non-Commonwealth entities;
- directly for providing foreign assistance;
- research and development services;
- experts or neutral persons, including barristers, for current or anticipated litigation or dispute;
- fiscal agency or depository services, liquidation and management services for regulated financial institutions, and sale and distribution services for government debt;
- motor vehicles;
- by the Future Fund Management Agency of investment management, investment advisory, or master custody and safekeeping services for the purposes of managing and investing the assets of the Fund;
- blood plasma products, plasma fractionation services, government advertising services and labor hire.

Consistent with this agreement, some specific procurement contracts exceeding the thresholds for FMA agencies and CAC bodies are exempt from these mandatory procedures (Box 17.2). For example, the exemptions for indigenous SMEs or suppliers primarily servicing disabled persons allows for direct contracting.

These mandatory rules relate mainly to procurement processes and procedures, such as a presumption for open tendering, when and under what conditions limited tendering could be used, and minimum time limits for tendering. By including these mandatory procurement procedures for generally non-construction procurements exceeding AUD$80,000 into the CPGs/CPRs, the Commonwealth effectively extended these procedures and processes in AUSFTA provisions to all of Australia's trading partners. Thus, the Commonwealth effectively extends to all suppliers the same treatment that it has committed to under its PTA commitments on government procurement. But of course, PTAs were not needed to achieve this outcome—it could have been better achieved by adopting these changes as part of a broad-based unilateral, non-discriminatory procurement policy at the central government. Moreover, given the complexities of their procurement systems, it is unclear if this is the case for at least some states.

17.2.2.1 Procurement-Connected Policies

These are provided for in the CPGs/CPRs and cover Commonwealth policies where procurement has been identified as a means of delivery. They have proliferated in recent years to number twenty-four, administered among eleven Commonwealth departments (Table 17.1). The relevant policy-owning entity is responsible for administering, reviewing, and providing information on the policy as required. They set special regulations that all suppliers to Commonwealth procurement must meet, including meeting other employment, worker disability, and national codes or principles.

Table 17.1 Selected procurement-connected policies

Procurement-connected policy	Relevant policy agency	Start year	Suppliers affected			Minimum threshold ($ million)
			Small (<20)	SME (<200)	Large (>200)	
Procurement On-Time Payment Policy for Small Business	Finance	2012	X			Up to $1
Competitive Neutrality Guidelines	Treasury	2004	X	X	X	
Legal Services Directions	Attorney General's	2005	X	X	X	$5
Intellectual Property Principles for Australian Government Agencies	Attorney General's	2008	X	X	X	
National Code of Practice for Construction Industry Implementation Guidelines	Employment	2013	X	X	X	
Protective Security Policy Framework	Attorney General's	2013	X	X	X	
Trade Sanctions	Foreign Affairs & Trade	2014	X	X	X	
Information, Communications & Information Systems Security Manual	Signals Directorate, Defence	2005	X	X	X	
Commonwealth Disability Strategy	Social Services	2010	X	X	X	
Fair Work Principles (revoked July 1, 2014)	Employment	2010	X	X	X	
Workplace Gender Equality Procurement Principles and User Guide	Employment	2013	X	X	X	
The National Code of Practice for Construction Industry Implementation Guidelines	Employment	2013	X	X	X	
Australian Government ICT Sustainability Plan	Environment	2010	X	X	X	
ICT SME Participation Procurement Policy	Industry	2010	X	X	X	$20
National Public Private Partnership Policy Framework & Guidelines	Infrastructure, Regional Australia	2008	X	X	X	$50
Indigenous Opportunities Policy	Prime Minister & Cabinet	2011	X	X	X	$5
Australian Industry Participation Plans for Government Procurement	Industry	2010	X	X	X	$20

17.2.2.2 Policies to Assist Industry Participation in Procurement

The Australian Industry Participation (AIP) National Framework was signed by Commonwealth, state and territory Governments in April 2001. They committed to incorporating in their industry development policy the principles of full, fair and reasonable opportunity, free of interstate preferences, regional development, competitive neutrality, value for money, transparency of process, policy consistency, and consistency with Australia's international obligations. In addition to the AIP National Framework, each state has its own industry participation policies aimed at increasing Australian industry participation in public- and private-sector investment projects.

Some industry participation assistance schemes fall under the AIP programs administered by the Department of Industry. They are designed to encourage full, fair, and reasonable opportunities for Australian industry to compete in major public projects. Since 2010, AIP programs have required tenderers for Commonwealth procurement over $20 million to prepare and implement plans outlining proposed actions to provide Australian suppliers, especially SMEs, with opportunities.[9] Requirements apply to all covered entities and have been adopted by some Commonwealth authorities and companies. The ICT SME participation procurement policy works the same for ICT contracts, but requires higher AME participation for SME participation of 20 percent of the contract value for software/services (10 percent for hardware contracts).

Commencing in December 2013, all major projects, both public and private, with a minimum capital expenditure of $500 million must meet mandatory requirements (Australian Jobs Act 2013), which include developing and implementing an AIP.

The Department of Defence's procurement promotes Australian industry participation (Box 17.3).

17.2.3 STATE GOVERNMENT PROCUREMENT

State governments have their own procurement policies. They generally utilize the same principles as the Commonwealth—value for money, competition, non-discrimination, and so on—but do not necessarily implement them in the same way. The availability of detailed statistics on government procurement varies substantially between states. State procurement systems have also evolved to be complex and cumbersome, full of "red tape," largely coinciding with efforts to replace relatively straightforward price preferences favoring local content with more hidden discretionary forms of discriminating against foreign content.

[9] As at end of February 2014, six AIP plans had been approved.

BOX 17.3 DEFENSE MATERIAL PROCUREMENT

Governments prefer directing defense capital expenditure to Australian-based firms to foster long-term, sustainable growth in the domestic defense industry. Hence, the Department of Defence's procurement policies and practices form part of a broader industry policy framework. Offsets or purchasing preferences are no longer used to procure capital equipment, but industry is provided more detailed and timely information on the Department of Defence's future capital investment plans and operational aspects of its procurement policies and practices. Industry assistance is provided through a combination of:

- carefully tailoring and closely monitoring direct grants or subsidies to Australian-based firms, typically in industry skilling, innovation, and export market development;
- adjusting timing of capital projects to assist Australian-based firms bridge gaps in their workload, if achievable at reasonable cost and within operational plans;
- paying price premiums to build or maintain domestic industry capabilities of especially high military-strategic value, in strict accordance with value for money; and
- implementing and progressively strengthening procurement rules so that tenderers can fully explore opportunities for Australian industry participation, and to accept those that are competitive.

These procurement rules are embedded in the Australian Industry Capability (AIC) Program. It differs from the AIP by eschewing the use of quotas or minimum targets to ensure domestic goods and services are properly considered. An AIC plan must be prepared for procurement projects exceeding $20 million. The AIC Program's affects mainly acquisition projects where the comparative advantage of Australian-based firms is generally weakest. On average, capital equipment acquisition projects absorb around 30 percent of the Department of Defence's total in-country equipment spend.

The program also expressly provides that an AIC plan be prepared for all procurement projects involving priority industry capabilities (PICs). These are capabilities for building or supporting defense capital equipment which, if not available in-country, are deemed to place at risk the nation's defense self-reliance and operational needs. The PIC program is to maintain industry capability at the minimum level consistent with identifiable need. PICs are assessed within a value for money framework.

Defense spend is around $10 billion annually on acquiring and sustaining capital equipment; most is in-country (averaging 50–60 percent). Defense expenditure accounts for 60 percent of all shipbuilding and repairs in Australia.

17.2.3.1 New South Wales (NSW)

The NSW procurement system is decentralized—entities manage their own procurement. The Procurement Board administers the framework and associated regulations (Public Works and Procurement Act 1912). It develops and implements a government-wide strategic procurement approach, ensures best value for money (the overarching requirement), improves competition and facilitates access by the private sector (especially SMEs and regional enterprises), reduces administrative costs of procuring agencies, and simplifies procurement processes while ensuring probity and fairness.

Procurement by all agencies and prescribed state-owned corporations is covered. Also covered are goods and services (including construction) procured by or for an agency either to exercise statutory functions or pursuant to statutory procurement powers. Procuring entities must follow the Board's policies and directions, adhere to probity and fairness, and provide requested information on procurement.

The Board has an Agency Accreditation Scheme to assess agencies' capability to undertake different levels and/or types of procurement. They can generally only engage in procurement consistent with their accreditation. When the scheme is extended to construction, accredited agencies will be able to procure services over $1.3 million.

17.2.3.1.1 Price Preference Margins. Until recently, NSW applied price preferences of 20 percent to goods and related services of ANZ origin. Margins applied to the imported content of all tenders claiming local content, and were added to the tendered price used to evaluate tenders. Tenderers had to supply details of imported (non-ANZ) and local content, and substantiate if required.

NSW firms also received additional country location preferences of 2.5 percent or 5 percent under the Country Industries Preference Scheme (CIPS). This preference was added to all other tender prices after applying the 20 percent preference margin against overseas content. If an inter-state or New Zealand supplier was the preferred tenderer after applying the ANZ preference, no country preference was applied. If, for tenders above $100,000, an Australian tenderer was not the lowest but was within 20 percent of the lowest tender (before the application of preference), the responsible minister could provide Australian tenderers an opportunity to reduce prices. Such ministerial discretion could be exercised on significant purchases where the preference margin was insufficient for the Australian tenderer to win on price, or if it was believed the circumstances warranted it. While the preference scheme recognized that the fundamental principle guiding procurement was to achieve best value for money, other factors also needed to be considered, such as technical performance, delivery, maintenance, and the NSW government's wider economic development and social objectives. The Price Preference Scheme applied to all bids exceeding $700,000.[10]

While the ANZ Price Preference Margin and Country Industries Preference Scheme ceased for large enterprises from 2008, it continued for SMEs as permitted under the AUSFTA. NSW also extended other AUSFTA procurement commitments, including on procedures and processes, by extending the minimum AUSFTA thresholds on covered procurement ($7.769 million for construction, and $551,000 for goods and services) so that suppliers from the parties were treated the same as domestic suppliers. NSW had

[10] The 20 percent price discount applied to the ANZ SME content in tenders. The discount was not based on whether the tenderer was an SME, but rather was applied based on ANZ SME content. In addition, the CIP price margin applied as appropriate, but not to services with no manufacturing component. Tender prices adjusted for price discounts were used to evaluate the tender.

also certain exceptions specified in AUSFTA from covered procurement, such as health and welfare services, education services, and motor vehicles.

A new procurement scheme for SMEs called the Local Jobs First Plan was implemented from July 2009.[11] It improved opportunities for SMEs to compete when providing ANZ content.[12] It covered all goods and services, including ICT and consultancies, exceeding $700,000, and all procurement methods.[13] Agencies established specifications and evaluation procedures to provide ANZ SME suppliers with opportunities to compete on value for money, designed tendering procedures to minimize costs to tenderers, and included SME participation as tender criteria. For contracts from $1 million to $4 million, agencies also ensured tenders included SME participation criteria that were weighted in tender evaluation. For tenders above $4 million, tenderers had to submit an SME participation plan (SMEPP) that included SME participation criteria. SMEPPs had a weighting in the tender evaluation of at least 6 percent.[14]

The Local Jobs Plan was replaced in early 2013 by the NSW Government Procurement: Small and Medium Enterprises Policy Framework. This framework is intended to increase government business opportunities, support competition, reduce administrative burdens for SMEs, maximize SME access to government procurement opportunities to win public business, and allow SMEs to deal more easily with government. Agencies must improve SME access to procurement opportunities by taking reasonable steps to obtain at least one written quotation from a prequalified SME supplier for contracts up to $1 million.

Price preferences for ANZ-SME content were removed. However, procuring agencies instead have to develop SME opportunity statements on the impact their procurement has on SMEs. The threshold for having to submit SMEPPs on how tenders will support local industry was also raised from $4 million to $10 million. They are still considered in the tender evaluation and, if successful, become part of the contract.

Open public tenders are no longer legislatively mandated as the default form for procuring goods and services. Procurement processes must be probity rich and transparent, suitable for the particular purchase, and have appropriate regard for policy and trade agreements.

[11] ANZ SMEs are firms employing up to 200 full-time equivalent persons.

[12] ANZ SME content was the value-added content sourced from ANZ-based SMEs. It included ANZ value-added in supply chains by SMEs where it could be shown, but excluded overseas-based value addition and/or imported content. Goods not made in New Zealand but imported via the country and not meeting ANZCERTA rules of origin are not considered ANZ content.

[13] The Plan excluded construction and related services and community service grants, unless purchasing a service from state contracts or other prequalified panels.

[14] SMEPPs have quantitative details on employment, investment and other impacts, and comments on the tenderer's SME involvement in supply chains.

The government supports purchasing opportunities for businesses employing disabled people. Provisions simplify purchasing of some goods and services for directly engaging disability employment organizations, subject to achieving value for money. Agencies can buy goods and services up to $150,000 from a recognized Aboriginal business, provided the suppliers' prices are reasonable and consistent with normal market levels, and at least one written quotation is obtained.

17.2.3.2 Victoria (VIC)

The Victoria Government Purchasing Board (VGPB) was established in 1995 under the Financial Management Act 1994. It develops procurement policy and practice. Since its inception, the VGPB has led government procurement of goods and services to deliver value for money. In particular, it also develops procurement capability, minimizes risk, and enables all businesses to access procurement opportunities. It monitors departmental compliance with procurement policies and ministerial directions, and reports irregularities to the relevant minister.

VGPB policy and practices apply to all government departments, the Victoria Police, and to twelve specified administrative offices. They do not extend to government business enterprises, construction, non-contractual agreements or any form of assistance (including grants, loans, equity infusions, fiscal incentives, subsidies, guarantees, co-operative agreements and sponsorship arrangements), purchasing arrangements associated with a project undertaken in accord with the Partnerships Victoria policy, or property (land) transactions.

Procurement methods include open, selective, and limited tendering as well as quotations for procurement up to and including $150,000. Larger procurement is to be let by open or selective tender unless subject to an exemption. The rules were revised to incorporate the provisions of Australia's PTAs, most notably with the US. For example, exemptions from conducting open or selective tenders to engage by limited tender incorporate the Agreement's provisions as does the list of procurements exempt from VGPA rules, and applying the minimum number of days for an open tender to close, are extended for covered procurement exceeding the agreed value thresholds.

Procurement policies seek to maximize opportunities for local suppliers, that is the achievement of a desired procurement outcome at the best possible—not necessarily the lowest—price based on a balanced judgment of relevant financial and non-financial factors. Competition and contestability are seen as important drivers for achieving value for money. The significant costs of tendering, especially for SMEs, are recognized, and the government is committed to creating government procurement business opportunities for SMEs.

Departments must consider non-metropolitan regional suppliers if they offer at least the same value for money.

17.2.3.2.1 The Victoria Industry Participation Plan (VIPP). The VIPP encourages bidders for government contracts to use local suppliers, including SMEs, in delivering procurements. It is concerned with procurement activity where the goods and services are considered contestable, and competitive international and ANZ markets exist. The VIPP is administered by the Industry Capability Network (ICN) Victoria. The ICN certifies VIPPs prepared by shortlisted bidders, and assists them in preparing VIPP Plans under strict probity arrangements. In 2013–14, the ICN secured orders of $22 million for local industry under the VIPP.

VIPP processes cover procurement wholly or partially funded by government equal to or above $1 million in regional VIC and $3 million in Melbourne. Procurement must be registered on the VIPP Management Centre website when the ICN advises if the activity has contestable items. If so, shortlisted bidders must prepare VIPPs detailing ANZ content.[15]

Since 2013, an introduced "contestability assessment" focuses on procurement of "contestable" goods and services where local suppliers compete with international firms to promote local business opportunities without compromising value for money, but to avoid the costs to bidders of completing VIPP Plans on projects that, by their nature, will be delivered locally.[16]

No VIPPs are required for activities assessed with no or limited contestability procurements (i.e., no competitive international suppliers or local suppliers). The agency must still meet the VIPP objectives and record the estimated local content of shortlisted suppliers. If assessed as a contestable procurement (i.e., competitive local and international suppliers), the standard VIPP process applies and shortlisted suppliers must provide an ICN-certified VIPP. The government can also declare projects and procurement as strategically significant to the VIC economy if valued at $250 million or more, or if they have capital costs of at least $100 million. The government can then set minimum local content requirements and other conditions on the delivery of outcomes for local industry. During 2013–14, the eight projects that were declared strategic exceeded a total value of $11 billion and committed to an average local content of over 84 percent.

[15] VIPPs also contains details on the number of new jobs created and existing jobs retained; the introduction of new technology, opportunities for skills transfer and employee training; and the number of new apprentices/trainees engaged that are retained.

[16] The revised guidelines also enhanced details on suppliers' opportunities by requiring ICN Victoria to provide agencies and shortlisted bidders a list of "contestable" goods and services on specific procurement activities, highlighting opportunities for local firms early in the procurement process by being included in the tender request. A new electronic VIPP with improved assistance features for businesses and agencies was also added, along with more robust monitoring and reporting requirements to demonstrate the local content outcomes achieved through the VIPPs' implementation, including introducing a post-contract verification process.

BOX 17.4 CONTESTABLE PROJECTS

Of the 216 "contestable" contracts requiring VIPPs, 163 (worth $1.68 billion) commenced in 2013–14. Successful bidders committed to using 84.1 percent local content on average, representing $1.41 billion in local orders, creating 1,282 new jobs, and retaining a further 5,103 existing jobs. The contracts are also expected to create 214 new and retain 606 existing apprenticeships/traineeships across Victoria. Activities covered included infrastructure works, purchase of medical equipment, construction of schools, and supply of IT equipment. In 2013–14, 324 SMEs were reported to have prepared VIPPs. During 2013–14, 128 contracts worth $948 million were reported as completed. Most contractors claimed to have at least achieved their local content commitments. Average local content commitment planned was 90.2 percent, and contractors reported an aggregated local content outcome of 90.2 percent. A total of 1,111 new jobs were created in Victoria.

In 2013–14, the contestability of 399 contracts, worth over $5 billion, was assessed, of which 216 contracts (valued over $2.5 billion) were found contestable and required shortlisted bidders to submit VIPPs (Box 17.4). Of the rest that had no or limited contestability, 85 percent were found to be local by nature, that is the items tendered were only available locally with low international competition. The remainder were assessed to be international by nature with products or services being unavailable locally.

17.2.3.3 Queensland (QLD)

QLD's procurement policy focuses on value for money, determined by price, non-price factors (e.g., social and economic objectives, including sustainability, regional development and employment, fitness for purpose, quality, service and support), and cost-related factors (e.g., whole-of-life costs and transaction costs). Procurement policy aims to help regional development and competitive local businesses by encouraging agencies to buy locally. QLD had already removed its 20 percent price preferences on government procurement for ANZ local content.

Goods and services can be procured by several means, including open, selective, and limited tendering. QLD's SME procurement policy, which includes ANZ businesses, aims at providing local industry full, fair, and reasonable opportunities to obtain major work. The QLD procurement market is around $6 billion annually.

17.2.3.3.1 Industry Capability Network Queensland (ICN Queensland). This is a free government-subsidized service to increase local content and industry participation in procurement, working to reduce imports and maximize opportunities for local industry. It identifies Australia's best products, services, capabilities, and capacity to competitively meet private- and public-sector procurement needs. The ICN provides information to support government priorities for QLD jobs and building regions. It evaluates local capability across many industries to assist firms to raise the local content of their tenders.

17.2.3.3.2 ICT SME Participation Scheme. This scheme applies to ICT procurement by all agencies and assists ICT SMEs to gain greater access to public contracts. Following recent revisions, any procurement must have at least one capable SME shortlisted in evaluating tenders, and at least two SME offers for contracts between $150,000 and $250,000.[17] Larger contracts require an SME participation score and a procurement plan. Agencies can also now directly engage SMEs to provide innovative solutions up to $500,000.

17.2.3.3.3 Procurement Transformation Program (PTP). A revised procurement policy, PTP, was released in 2013 that essentially reinforced previous arrangements. In place until end of 2015, it aims to better implement the policy and design whole-of-government better-practice procurement processes. Procurement is still being used to advance the government's economic, environmental, and social objectives.

17.2.3.3.4 Queensland Government Building and Construction Training Policy. This policy replaced the Indigenous Employment Policy for Government Building and Civil Construction Projects (IEP), and the Building and Construction Contracts Structured Training Policy from July 2014.[18] It supports employment and skills development in QLD's building and construction industry, and focuses on increasing the economic independence of indigenous people. All departments and statutory bodies must comply on public building projects of at least $500,000 and civil construction projects of $3 million or over. Eligible projects include those in specified indigenous areas.

For indigenous projects, the 10 percent share of the total labor hours required for training must be met by indigenous apprentices, trainees, and workers. An extra amount, equivalent to 10 percent of the total labor hours (which equates to a minimum of 3 percent of the estimated project value for building projects and a minimum of 1.5 percent of the estimated project value for civil construction projects), must be allocated to an agreed

[17] The SME participation score is used to rank tenders, whereby the score contributes 10 percent to the final tender score. The tenderer with the highest participation level is given a score of ten, with the remaining tenderer's scores being assigned as a proportion of 10. SME participation levels are calculated on the net proportion of the contract that is to be paid to SMEs.

[18] The IEP, introduced in 2001, applied to all civil construction, and building construction projects above $250,000. It required at least 20 percent of total labor hours to be supplied by indigenous workers in nominated indigenous areas, with half of these hours to be accredited training. The Structured Training Policy required a minimum of 10 percent of the total labor hours on any government building or civil construction project (over $250,000 for buildings or $500,000 for civil construction) to be met by indigenous workers, apprentices, trainees, or cadets, or to be used for the up-skilling of existing employees (to a maximum of 25 percent). It covered all QLD areas except the indigenous areas specified in the IEP.

Indigenous Economic Opportunities Plan. This sets minimum agreed outcomes and provides flexibility so that the project's local economic opportunities can be maximized.

Procuring agencies can select building or civil construction projects outside specified indigenous areas as indigenous projects if they are proposed as indigenous projects, are specifically for use and benefit of indigenous people, or are located in a specified priority regional area, or as agreed with the Director-General of DATSIMA.

17.2.3.3.5 Charter for Local Content. This provides all businesses with full, fair, and reasonable opportunities to tender for procurement. It covers all goods and services, including construction, but excludes ICT. It does not mandate agencies to use local suppliers, but provides a mechanism for them to effectively and efficiently consider a wide range of potential suppliers. The Charter supports agencies to embed local content within procurement that is seen to support the objective of value for money by also encouraging greater competition, providing market opportunities for local firms, and demonstrating equivalence with private-sector best practice.

Procurements subject to the Charter include those with a government contribution exceeding $5 million (or $2.5 million in regional QLD), public–private partnerships for projects and capital asset acquisitions exceeding $5 million, strategically significant purchases set by the procuring agency (e.g., in an area of high unemployment or affected adversely by economic or other events such as a natural disaster), and infrastructure projects with Commonwealth funding via the QLD government exceeding $20 million.

17.2.3.4 South Australia (SA)

In 2013–14, the SA government procurement market was about $4 billion, of which about 70 percent was services. Competitive tendering processes covered some 61 percent of contracts (89 percent by value); the rest was let mainly by direct negotiation (limited tendering). Most (96 percent) of all contracts were let to ANZ suppliers (98 percent by value); over two-thirds of total contracts were with SA suppliers (80 percent by value) and only 4 percent (2 percent by value) were let overseas. The share, by value, of contracts with SA suppliers rose from 42 percent in 2011–12 to 51 percent in 2012–13.

The State Procurement Board began overseeing procurement by public authorities in 2005 (State Procurement Act 2004). It facilitates strategic procurement by agencies; reviews policies, principles, and procurement guidelines; develops, issues, and reviews standards for electronic procurement; and investigates and reviews compliance with policies.

Procuring agencies are to obtain value for money, treat participants ethically and fairly, and ensure probity, accountability, and transparency. Value for money involves determining the extent to which proposals will optimally deliver whole-of-life cost and quality (non-cost) factors, and contribute to government priorities.

17.2.3.4.1 The Industry Participation Policy (IPP). A new IPP policy that started in July 2012 was updated in 2014 to make local jobs, investment, and supplier inputs critical to procurement. The government is committed to ensuring that capable state SMEs receive full, fair, and reasonable opportunities to be considered for major public and private works. The IPP is not intended to alter the prime goal of value for money, but to ensure that it is assessed mindful of the contract's broader impact on SA, including on local industry (especially SMEs). This includes the impact on employment, industry capability and capacity via investment, retention of state economic activity and additional value-adding activities, innovation, and supply chain development. The IPP does not mandate local content levels or preferential treatment of ANZ suppliers, such as by price preferences.

The IPP covers all expenditure by public authorities prescribed under the State Procurement Act 2004 exceeding $22,000, including expenditure on infrastructure and construction, public–private partnership projects, federally funded infrastructure and construction projects managed by the SA government, and private-sector projects with significant SA government support (over $2.5 million cash and in-kind).

While no specific requirements exist for tenders under $22,000, agencies are to use local businesses where possible and encourage winning tenderers to use local SMEs. For contracts between $22,000 and $220,000 where a minimum of three quotes are being sourced, at least one must be from SA. For contracts between $220,000 and $4 million ($1 million in regional SA), agencies are to use the Industry Capability Network (ICN) Gateway database.

For contracts of between $4 million and $50 million (or $1 million and above in regional areas), tenderers must submit standard Industry Participation Plans (IPPs). These must identify how they will provide full, fair, and reasonable opportunities for local SMEs to compete for contracts or participate in major public and private-sector projects (or more specifically, consider products and capabilities provided by local SMEs); how they will promote economic contribution to the state, including employment and growth; and how they will monitor and record SME involvement.[19]

For contracts of $50 million and over and projects (regardless of value) declared by the SA government as "strategic" (in accordance with the IPP criteria), tenderers must prepare a tailored IPP. This will include a detailed methodology to identify and consider local SME participation, and information on additional economic benefits for the SA economy. It should also give opportunities to involve local SMEs in value-added research, design work, and advanced services.

The IPP is considered through a weighted evaluation criterion in awarding tenders. The assessment criteria will vary depending on the nature of the procurement, but will

[19] While completing a standard IPP is voluntary on contracts between $4 million and below $10 million, firms not doing so will receive a zero score for the IPP weighted criteria. For contracts above $10 million, an IPP is mandatory.

typically include the number of jobs and the value of investment in SA directly linked to the contract; the approach to consider SME involvement through supply chain opportunities; and the tenderer's record in meeting IPPs. The procuring agency sets the weighting subject to a general minimum 5 percent, and 10 percent for heavy and civil engineering construction, professional, scientific and technical services, non-residential construction, and electrical equipment.

In 2014, an Employment Contribution Test (ECT) was added for procurements between $22,000 and $4 million in Adelaide, and $1 million in regional SA. Agencies must first determine if the procured goods and/or services are available within SA. If so, all tenderers must provide the number of labor hours associated with the primary contract and any sub-contracts. For such procurements in Adelaide, the ECT receives a minimum 5 percent weighting in the tender evaluation. In regional SA, it is intended that at least 15 percent of the jobs from the procurement will go to local people. On specific procurements, a 15 percent weighting will apply, which can be higher in particular areas to provide greater flow-on regional economic benefits.

While the same IPP's weighting apply to procurements above $50 million, a merit assessment is to determine the appropriateness of the minimum weightings. For these contracts, the OIA will advise on the higher weightings (above the minimum levels) for the IPPs, help develop a template for a Tailored IPP, and initiate the identification of SME opportunities.

In all procurements with an ECT or an IPP, the agency or government can raise the mandatory minimum weightings based on the proposal's merit, for example if the potential exists for significant economic and social benefits to SA or to specific regions, including employment, investment, and supply-chain benefits. Factors to be considered in lifting the weighting include whether the activity is in an area or sector of the economy with high unemployment and/or low socioeconomic standing, if a local supplier exists that may replace imports, if it can stimulate a local industry still developing or in decline, it if provides skills transfer or up-skilling of local workers, or if it offers capital investment with long-term benefits for SA.

17.2.3.5 Western Australia (WA)

In 2012–13, Tenders WA recorded 4,760 agency-specific contracts, totaling $7.58 billion (goods, services, and infrastructure). About $5 billion was spent on WA suppliers under the state's Buy Local Policy.

The State Supply Commission (SSC) delegates purchasing and contracting authority to agencies (State Supply Commission Act 1991). Procurement must achieve best value for money. Agencies must align their procurement with government policies, objectives, and strategies, and actively support whole-of-government initiatives. Cost and non-cost factors must be considered. The value for money test may vary in complexity depending on the purchase, from a simple price assessment for low-value highly commoditized goods or services to a detailed assessment.

Direct purchase and verbal quotations are allowed for procurement up to $50,000 ($20,000 before July 2014). Written quotations are needed for contracts up to $250,000 (previously $150,000). For contracts above $250,000 ($150,000 before July 2014), open and effective competition must provide suppliers with fair and equitable access while maintaining transparency and integrity. These minimum requirements may be waived, for example, if buying from an indigenous business up to $250,000 ($150,000 before July 1, 2014) or from businesses primarily providing services for disabled persons.

17.2.3.5.1 Buy Local Policy. Operating since 2001, the Buy Local Policy maximizes opportunities to develop both WA and Australian businesses while gaining value for money. The Policy has initiatives and price preferences to enhance local business opportunities in procurement. Agencies must give priority to indigenous tenderers and consider implementing indigenous employment strategies.

Agencies' requests for quotation or tender must reflect local business capability and recognize local content in evaluating bids. Tenders of $750,000 and above must have a local content evaluation criterion with a minimum 20 percent weighting. Social, economic, environmental, and regional development impacts are also to be considered. Agencies are encouraged to use a similar approach on smaller contracts. The intent is to select contractors supporting local WA businesses offering value-for-money tenders. A minimum local purchasing target of 80 percent applies.

17.2.3.5.2 Price Preferences. There are two price preferences: the Imported Content Impost (ICI), and the Regional Price Preferences (RPP). The ICI requires agencies to apply a 20 percent price impost to non-ANZ goods and related services. Two RPPs apply: the Regional Business Preference (RBP) and the Regional Content Preference (RCP). The RBP applies to eligible regional businesses within a prescribed distance from a regional purchase or contract point of delivery to the total bid value. The RCP applies, under certain circumstances, to all WA tenderers buying services or materials from regional businesses for use in regional contracts. The RCP applies to the cost of services or materials bought from businesses located in the prescribed distance, and used to deliver the contract. Due to the ANZGPA, when bids received from inter-state or New Zealand suppliers are being considered, the RCP and RBP do not apply.

The RBP and RCP price margins are 10 percent for the total cost of goods and services (up to $50,000) and 5 percent (up to $50,000) for "housing and works" purchases. Chief executive officers can raise these caps on individual procurements where further support to regional businesses offers demonstrated economic benefits. In July 2013, RPP caps were raised to $250,000 each, and the total maximum preference claimable was raised to $250,000 for goods and services and to $500,000 for housing and works.

From December 2009, the application of these price preferences was amended to comply with Australia's PTAs, including with the US. Local content weightings for awarding tenders were removed on covered procurements for US and Chilean businesses, that is, such imported content is treated like ANZ content.

17.2.3.5.3 Building Local industry Policy. This Policy maximizes procurement opportunities for local businesses and creates employment opportunities. An Industry Participation Plan (IPP) must be prepared for all public projects over $20 million or where the capital equipment exceeds $1 million.[20] It aims to build a project-wide procurement strategy by providing WA industry with full, fair, and reasonable opportunity.[21] IPPs should describe the project's direct economic impact on WA industry (via employment, skills transfer, strategic alliances, and regional development) and the type, number of, and size of procurement packages and/or eligible goods; and clearly state how the proposal will maximize the use of competitive local business. The Policy applies to all WA government purchasing, including using a local content selection criterion with a minimum 20 percent weighting in evaluating public tenders of $750,000 or more. Special focus is to be given to promoting the local indigenous participation.

The Industry Capability Network WA, a joint industry government initiative, helps enhance global competitiveness of purchasers, while supporting local industry participation. It advises agencies on WA industry capacity and competitiveness. Since implementing the framework in July 2011, contracts worth some $60 billion have been won by local suppliers.

17.2.3.6 Tasmania (TAS)

Procuring agencies must pursue value for money by obtaining the best price after weighing up the purchase's costs and benefits. Value for money factors are to be specifically included in the evaluation criteria, and can include the contribution to government policy objectives of supporting local and regional business by fostering industry development and job creation. Procurement must be impartial and open, and encourage competitive offers using transparent, non-discriminatory processes.

[20] An IPP may be needed on smaller projects, for example if potential exists for low levels of local industry participation due to the firm being new to WA; the supply chain of the lead contractor excludes WA suppliers; it involves skills or knowledge sets prioritized by WA; it is in a region targeted for development; or potential exists for regional employment.

[21] The IPP should try to ensure all project participants gain a greater knowledge of WA capabilities by brokering linkages between project proponents, the contractors involved in the project, domestic and global supply chains and WA industry. It needs to support longer-term industry development objectives by encouraging consortia-building and strategic partnering among local firms, and by facilitating the integration of Australian industry into domestic and global supply chains. In addition, the IPP should also address the economic impact of the project.

Agencies must ensure local businesses can participate in procurement, and adopt the government's Buy Local Policy requirements. They do not provide preferences, but must actively seek local bids and ensure that processes do not unnecessarily preclude local businesses from bidding or disadvantage local suppliers.

Procuring agencies can receive direct quotes to buy goods and services at or below $50,000. They must seek at least three written quotations for larger contracts up to $250,000, unless granted approval for direct/limited tendering for "covered procurement" under Australia's PTAs, or for other procurement if the costs to the agency and suppliers of seeking quotations or calling public tenders would outweigh the value for money benefits, or where exceptional circumstances exist justifying the use of direct/limited tendering. Where local capability exists, at least one quotation must be sought from a TAS business. It is expected that direct/limited sourcing will be rare.

Agencies may directly procure from businesses mainly providing services to disabled people. If activated, the mandatory requirement to seek three written quotations or to call open tenders can be waived.

17.2.3.7 **Buy Local Policy**

This provides mandatory procurement planning requirements, a local benefits test, and Industry Participation Plans (IPPs). For procurements exceeding $50,000, agencies must submit a pre-procurement local impact assessment ensuring local suppliers can participate with success. For smaller contracts, the impact on local suppliers is to be assessed. Agencies must ensure the planning process and procurement specifications do not disadvantage local SME suppliers, and disaggregate all substantial procurement opportunities unless exempted.[22] Exemption may be granted where the benefits of aggregation clearly outweigh the potential negative impact on local SMEs or the local economy.

Suppliers must prepare IPPs for tenders exceeding $5 million, and may be required to for smaller projects over $2 million. The agency must approve IPPs. For private-sector projects over $5 million with government support of $500,000 or more, the funding agency must ensure an IPP is prepared. Executive Summaries of IPPs are published by the Treasury.

Agencies must request that suppliers provide a Local SME Industry Impact Statement for procurements of $2 million or above, or $5 million and over if the agency has decided that no IPP is required.[23] The evaluation criteria for contracts over $50,000 must include the local SME Industry Impact Statement or the IPP. While voluntary, suppliers not

[22] Any combined contract of $250000 or more. Under this level, disaggregation is at the agency's discretion.

[23] Local SMEs are ANZ businesses with below 200 employees.

submitting these plans and IPPs will receive zero weighting. The weighting is set by the agency of at least 10 percent.

17.3 New Zealand Government Procurement Policies

The New Zealand government spends some NZ$38–40 billion annually on goods and services, including infrastructure. Each agency conducts its own procurement. New Zealand started reforming its government procurement in 2009 to achieve cost savings, to build capacity and capability of procurers, to enhance business participation, and to improve governance, oversight, and accountability. Aggregated procurement of selected common-use goods and services through "all-of-government" contracts was developed using Centres of Expertise in designated lead agencies. The Rules of Sourcing replaced the 2006 Mandatory Rules for Procurement by Departments from October 2013, and were reviewed in May 2014. Revised rules are to be released shortly to align with internationally recognized standards of the GPA, to which New Zealand has recently acceded, and commitments on government procurement in recent PTAs. The Rules on Sourcing are the government's standards of good practice for procurement planning, approaching the market, and contracting. Centralized statistics on national government procurement do not appear to be readily available.

The procurement rules are administered by the Ministry of Business, Innovation and Employment (MIBE). They apply to all public service departments, the New Zealand Police, the Defence Force and, from February 2015, all Crown agents including district health boards. The rules cover contracts of at least $100,000 for goods and services ($10 million or more for construction). They promote value for money, which means also considering non-price factors such as total cost of ownership and other direct benefits. Contracts are to be let to the tenderer with either the best value for money over the whole-of-life of the goods, services or works, or with the lowest price if price is the only criterion.

Government is committed to open, transparent, and competitive procurement with no discrimination against suppliers (domestic or international) by origin. The first rule covers the key procurement principles applicable to all contracts, namely to plan and manage procurement, be fair to all suppliers, get the right supplier, obtain the best deal for all, and play by the rules. Fairness means treating all suppliers equally (i.e., non-discrimination), giving New Zealand suppliers a full and fair opportunity to compete, and making it easy for all suppliers (small to large) to bid. Social, environmental, and economic effects must be considered.

Other rules cover procurement integrity, no offsets, non-discrimination among suppliers based on foreign ownership or overseas business affiliations so that foreigners are treated no less favorably than New Zealand suppliers, protecting supplier's information, requirements to openly advertise unless exempted (Box 17.5),[24] and agencies' annual submission to the MBIE of Strategic Procurement Outlooks and Procurement Plans. These rules help provide open and fair competition that supports innovation and helps create a productive New Zealand supply base. Certain opt-out procurements apply from the rules but are still subject to the procurement principles.[25] Open tendering is the default method for procurements over $100,000.

New Zealand maintains procurement measures to accord more favorable treatment to the Maori population, including meeting the government's obligations under the Treaty of Waitangi. It also appears that limited price preferences of between 2 percent and 5 percent were applied by a few local governments to home suppliers on procurement, but it is unknown if they still exist (APEC, 2003). The New Zealand government has no direct control over procurement by local authorities, which varies. Central government departments are directed to obtain from suppliers information on any local content they offer, but this is intended only to enable agencies to consider any commercial and practical value-for-money advantages of local supply. Agencies are still expected to obtain the best value for money supplier, either domestic or international, based on their judgment of all costs and benefits (APEC, 2003).

With the possible exception of some relatively minor local government procurement and preferential schemes for the indigenous population, the New Zealand procurement market has been open without discrimination to foreign suppliers, due to unilateral policy decisions.

This situation contrasts sharply with the less transparent and more restrictive arrangements emerging in recent years in Australia, especially at the state level.

[24] If exempt from open advertising, the agency must use either a closed competitive process (with a limited number of known suppliers) or a direct source process (with a known supplier). Such exemptions cannot be used to avoid competition, protect domestic suppliers, or to discriminate against any domestic or international supplier.

[25] Valid opt-out procurements include procurements between government departments, New Zealand Police or New Zealand Defence Force unless an open tender process is used; overseas for consumption abroad; for overseas offices; non-contractual arrangements; buying land or buildings; under conditional grants; funded by international aid, grant, loan or other assistance or that must comply with an international organization's procedure where that procedure is inconsistent with the rules; certain types of public health, education, and welfare services; government's central financial control functions; and procurement necessary to protect military and essential security and national defense interests as well as maintaining international peace and human health (e.g., arms, ammunition, war materials, peace-keeping deployment, and measures to protect public morals, order or safety); human, animal or plant life or health; intellectual property; or relating to goods, services or works of persons with disabilities, philanthropic or not-for-profit institutions, and prison labor.

BOX 17.5 EXEMPTIONS FROM OPEN ADVERTISING (TENDER)

These cover emergencies and in the following cases:

- after an open tender advertised within the last twelve months where the contract's core requirements are unchanged and no responses compliant with the pre-conditions or requirements (including quantity), or were only from suppliers verified to have colluded;
- only one supplier exists of the goods, services or works, and no reasonable alternative or substitute exists due to technical reasons preventing real competition, or procurement is of (i) intellectual property or associated (including patents or copyrights) or other exclusive rights, or (ii) a work of art;
- goods, services or works are additional to original requirements and necessary for complete delivery where (i) the original contract was openly advertised, or (ii) changing supplier is impossible for economic or technical reasons and would significantly inconvenience or substantially duplicate agency costs;
- buying a prototype for research, experiment, study or original development, including limited production or supply necessary to (i) perform field tests and incorporate the findings, or (ii) prove the good, service or works can be supplied in large numbers to an agreed quality (excluding production or supply to establish commercial viability or to recover research and development costs);
- goods purchased on a commodity market;
- very short-term purchases in exceptionally advantageous conditions but not from regular suppliers;
- contracts awarded to design contest winners where it is organized consistent with the rules and the judges know they will be awarded a contract, and have no conflict of interest;
- the agency does not need to openly advertise contracts awarded by an established panel of suppliers; and
- the agency receives an unsolicited unique proposal for goods, services, or works not otherwise readily available in the market that aligns with government objectives, and is value for money.

17.4 **Role of Trade Agreements**

ANZ belong to an increasing number of discriminatory bilateral and regional PTAs (so-called free trade agreements, or their equivalent) with government procurement commitments. Both have created a network of overlapping or criss-crossing PTAs with themselves and trading partners belonging to several agreements.

Also, while the GPA is a plurilateral agreement within the WTO, it is like a series of PTAs because it is applies "conditional MFN" treatment and discriminates between WTO GPA members and other WTO Members. Moreover, while not a conventional (i.e., binding) trade agreement, the Asia Pacific Economic Cooperation (APEC) can be considered a trade agreement. Most ANZ PTAs are with other APEC economies.

Government procurement commitments in ANZ's trade agreements tend to use a positive list identifying those entities covered by the commitments (subject to minimum threshold values) and a negative list of measures and types of procurement that are excluded from the commitments, including national treatment. With the exception of APEC, they are also discriminatory as they are based on conditional MFN.

17.4.1 ASIA PACIFIC ECONOMIC COOPERATION (APEC)

This is a voluntary trade agreement comprising a large number of Asian and Pacific economies, including the US and China, formed in 1989. APEC was based on the concepts of "open regionalism," namely, non-discrimination and concerted unilateralism. This, however, no longer is the case, especially given the proliferation of PTAs in the region and the widespread support that now exists to negotiate a discriminatory APEC PTA.

APEC's Non-binding Principles on Government Procurement were endorsed in 1999, including by ANZ. These cover key principles of value for money, open and effective competition, accountability and due process, fair dealing, and non-discrimination (see Table 17.2). While conceptually covering all central and sub-central government procuring entities, the principles are non-binding. APEC economies had to choose to unilaterally apply them. Many APEC principles reflected those of the GPA, although usually less prescriptively.

ANZ helped formulate the APEC principles, which generally reflected and supported unilateral reforms implemented by the mid-1980s. Thus, these principles were by and large common elements of their procurement arrangements, at least at the central level. Some Australian states especially and New Zealand local governments still maintained discriminatory price preferences against imported non-ANZ content. This reflected APEC's voluntary nature and the fact that the principles did not formally commit to national treatment or MFN.

17.4.2 WTO GOVERNMENT PROCUREMENT AGREEMENT (GPA)

The GPA is a plurilateral agreement formed among a sub-set of WTO Members in 1996. A revised GPA came into force in April 2014, but the practical value of the revisions would appear limited. Its key principles are conditional non-discrimination (national treatment on covered procurement and conditional MFN treatment—that is only between GPA parties, thus discriminating against non-parties), transparency, value for money, and open and effective competition, including on the use of non-open tendering (see Table 17.3).

Unlike APEC, the GPA is binding on and between those WTO Members that have joined (about to increase from forty-three to forty-five economies). It is thus a discriminatory agreement centered on conditional MFN treatment. Its national treatment obligation that effectively banned price preferences for non-developing countries is

Table 17.2 Summary of APEC non-binding principles on government procurement

Feature	Description
Value for Money (VfM)	Procurement to achieve best VfM on a whole-of-life basis using comparative analysis of all relevant costs & benefits. Lowest price not necessarily best VfM. Must also consider factors like market maturity; performance history of prospective suppliers; relative risk of proposals; financial considerations; & contract options. Market approaches must specify relevant conditions for participation & evaluation criteria to properly identify, assess & compare costs & benefits fairly & equitably over the procurement cycle.
Open & Effective Competition (OEC)	Competition important for due process, fair dealing & VfM. OEC requires conducting an appropriate competitive process open & accessible to all suppliers. Bidding should be predictable & enable new entrants. Procurement procedures to encourage competition & non-discrimination, & to effectively address any limits identified to competition.
Accountability & Due Process	Governments must be accountable for procurement & officials responsible for their actions by being answerable through set lines of accountability & using open & transparent processes. Due process & transparency (e.g., documentation, policy & legislative obligations, disclosure, reporting & complaints processes) important. It is an established government process executed regularly, fairly & according to regulation. It safeguards individual rights, & procurement rules must cover legitimate public interests & not unfairly or arbitrarily treat suppliers. It should safeguard rights of aggrieved suppliers to a fair hearing. Independent scrutiny facilitates accountability & due process.
Fair Dealing (FD)	FD is conducting business openly with full disclosure & no conflicts of interest or self-dealing by officials. Procurement to be fair, reasonable & equitable with integrity. Commercially sensitive information to be secure. Ethical behavior, for example honesty, integrity, probity, diligency.
Non Discrimination (ND)	ND prevents bias for/against businesses or products. Suppliers assessed on ability to meet requirements using legal, commercial, technical & financial capacities, not excluded or denied equitable treatment due to their degree of foreign affiliation or ownership, location or size. Bids awarded on published criteria.
Transparency	Transparency assures procurements processes are appropriate & that policy & legislative obligations are met. It involves taking steps to support appropriate scrutiny of procurements.

also conditional in that it only applies to covered procurement specified by each signatory, that is the purchase of goods and services above the relevant threshold values specified for included procuring entities unless specifically exempted/excluded, of which there are many. Each party nominates the central, sub-central and other agencies along with the goods, services, and construction services covered. Moreover, the offsets prohibition only applies to covered procurement.

As Australia and, until now, New Zealand never joined the GPA, it had little direct impact on reforming their government procurement systems. New Zealand felt that the GPA concessions were discriminatory, and that the regulatory burdens imposed by its procedural requirements placed overly prescriptive rules and guidelines on procuring agencies. Australia argued that the GPA departed from the MFN principle, allowed bilateral agreements between signatories that carved out sensitive sectors, and set

Table 17.3 Summary of key provisions of the GPA

Provision	Details
Coverage & scope	Measures affecting covered procurement, defined as buying goods & services, including construction, specified by each Member for non-commercial sale or resale by any contractual means (e.g., purchase, lease, rental, hire purchase) exceeding the specified threshold values by a non-excluded procurement entity. Members nominate the central, sub-central & other agencies covered (positive list).
Exclusions	Acquisition or rental of immovable property (e.g., land, existing buildings); non-contractual agreements or any form of assistance (e.g., cooperative agreements, grants, loans, equity infusions, guarantees & fiscal incentives); purchases of fiscal agency or depository services, liquidation & management services for regulated financial institutions or services related to the sale, redemption & distribution of public debt, including loans & government bonds, notes & other securities; public employment contracts; procurement specifically for foreign aid & assistance, under an international agreement for stationing troops or to jointly implement by the signatories a project or particular procedures or conditions of an international body, or funded by foreign grants, loans or other assistance.
Security & general exemptions	Action necessary to protect (a) essential national security or defense (e.g., buying arms, ammunition or war materials). Cannot be used to discriminate arbitrarily or unjustifiably between Members where identical conditions prevail or as a disguised trade restriction (b) public morals, order or safety (c) human, animal or plant life or health (d) intellectual property or (e) goods or services of disabled persons, philanthropic institutions or prison labor.
General principles	Non-discrimination (national treatment) & conditional MFN: For covered procurement, each Member to accord immediate and unconditional treatment to goods, services & suppliers to each other (and among each other) no less favorable than the treatment of domestic goods, services & suppliers. Cannot treat local suppliers less favorably based on foreign affiliation or ownership or discriminate against a locally established supplier based on the goods or services offered by that supplier for a particular procurement are goods or services of any other Member. Effectively bans price preferences (except for developing countries as violating national treatment).
Conduct	Transparent & impartial manner; avoid conflicts of interest & prevent corrupt practices.
Rules-of-origin	For covered procurement must apply the same rules-of-origin to goods or services from another Those applied in the normal course of trade with that Member.
Prohibited	Offsets (except for developing countries)
Procurement forms	Open & selective tendering, & limited tendering (cannot be used to avoid competition, discriminate against suppliers of other Members or to protect domestic suppliers) where (i) in the initial open tender no conforming tenders were submitted or suppliers satisfying conditions requested participation, or the tenders colluded (ii) a certain supplier can provide the goods or services & no reasonable alternative or substitute exists due to is for (a) a work of art (b) patents, copyrights or other exclusive rights (c) no competition for technical reasons (iii) for additional deliveries by the original supplier beyond the initial procurement if (a) changing suppliers is impossible for economic or technical reasons eg requirements of interchangeability or interoperability with existing equipment, software, services or installations procured under the initial contract (b) would significantly inconvenience or substantially duplicate costs; (d) only as strictly necessary due to extreme urgencies from events unforeseeable so that goods or services were unavailable in time using open or selective tendering; (e) goods purchased on a commodity market; (f) to procure a prototype or a first good or service developed in the course of, and for, research, experiment, study or original development, including limited production or supply to incorporate field testing results and to show the good or service can be supplied in quantity to acceptable quality standards (excludes production or supply to establish

(continued)

Table 17.3 Continued

Provision	Details
	commercial viability or to recover research and development costs); (g) very short term purchases under exceptionally advantageous conditions for unusual disposals (e.g., liquidation, receivership or bankruptcy); (h) or where contracts are awarded to design contest winners provided it is organized consistently with the GPA's principles (e.g., publication of a notice of intended procurement and judged independently).
Awarding contracts	Unless shown not in the public interest, contracts to be awarded to suppliers assessed capable of fulfilling the contract's terms & that based solely on the documentation's evaluation criteria has submitted the most advantageous tender or the cheapest if price is the sole criterion.

prescriptive procedural requirements at odds with state practices (e.g., preferential price preferences). These criticisms against the GPA remain equally valid today.

17.4.2.1 **Australia**

The Australian Department of Foreign Affairs and Trade (DFAT) announced in June 2015 that Australia would launch negotiations on GPA accession; Australia presented its accession offer to the WTO Committee on Government Procurement in September 2015 and negotiations with GPA parties have commenced (DFAT, 2015). DFAT's view is that current arrangements are substantially compliant with the GPA, so that joining would require only a few changes (e.g., implementing effective, timely, transparent, and non-discriminatory review procedures for suppliers and certain processes for prequalification and limited tendering).

Thus Australia's position on joining the GPA has changed even though it still has the same weaknesses. This possibly reflects an "agreement addiction" that now seems to exist in the Australian trade policy setting which focuses on non-transparent negotiations of non-MFN PTAs, including discriminatory arrangements on procurement.[26] This has made joining a conditional MFN and highly selective plurilateral GPA politically attractive, even though, as with PTAs, in general the real benefits to Australia are debatable. Governments have seemingly changed the onus from one of joining a trade agreement only if there are proven economic benefits to joining a trade agreement regardless. This is despite the Productivity Commission's conclusion that the economic benefits are being oversold and are based on publicly non-contested DFAT-commissioned "dodgy"

[26] A common bureaucratic ploy for avoiding difficult or sensitive decisions is to refer the issue to a committee. This gives the pretence that a decision has been taken when that is not the case—a so-called "Clayton's decision," that is the type of decision made when not actually making a decision. One could easily be excused in thinking that the same motivation undermines many government decisions to rush into negotiating international agreements, including PTAs.

economic modeling results, without any appreciation of the possible adverse impacts PTAs are having on Australia's past unilateral trade policy successes and on the multilateral trading system generally.

Australia's accession is unlikely to significantly change its procurement arrangements. There are many general exemptions allowed in the GPA, and acceding to it will almost certainly see Australia negotiating substantial carve-outs to enable continuation of discriminatory measures on non-covered procurement, including procurement benefiting SMEs and local content generally. Moreover, even for covered procurement the emergence of murky non-transparent measures and procedures in government procurement, especially by the states, are leading to more obscure and distorting forms of discrimination in practice that are very difficult to identify and curb.

The Australian DFAT claim that Australia has a world-class government procurement system, based on the principles of value for money and non-discrimination, that is already open to foreign competition is at best misleading. As this chapter shows, Australian state and Commonwealth procurement has gone backwards in recent years, with less transparent schemes being implemented to raise local content, especially for SMEs. These murky arrangements help hide the extent to which government procurement schemes discriminate in practice against imported content. Such negative outcomes may also reflect the attention given by the GPA and PTAs to banning price preferences as Australia positions itself by introducing other less transparent and more "legally" acceptable measures to discriminate in favor of local suppliers. Of course, this is de-reform. And if Australia is doing this it seems highly likely that other countries will be doing likewise.

Unfortunately, DFAT's misleading claims, which overlook the potential for significant bias towards local content in state and Commonwealth government procurement, indicate that Australia will not be using its GPA membership as a vehicle for significant domestic reform. Most probably, the outcome is for Australia to recycle in its accession negotiations its PTA commitments, especially from AUSFTA, which as shown in Section 17.4.3.3, have also not prompted reform. Again, other countries acceding to the WTO, such as China, will also probably follow the same defensive approach.

DFTA's preoccupation with exports at the expense of domestic reform of Australia's discriminatory government procurement arrangements favoring local content is evident in the material so far released. It discusses only the benefits to Australian exporters of joining the GPA. DFAT states that the Chinese government procurement market is around US $1.5 trillion and that as it is acceding to the GPA, Australia by joining would gain valuable future access to this market. However, based on experience such benefits appear largely illusory and must be kept realistic given what these negotiations are likely to achieve.

Unless Australia is to use its accession to the GPA to reform its increasingly non-transparent restrictive government procurement arrangements, then the economic benefits to Australia are likely to be modest at best.

Decisions to enter into trade agreements, including the GPA, should be based on proper and independent assessments of the economic impact on Australia of negotiated outcomes. This is not done in Australia. Any such purported analysis is based on dodgy studies controlled by DFAT, usually done in advance based on ambitious liberalization outcomes that fall well short of actual negotiated outcomes, especially on market access abroad. By the time the details of negotiated outcomes are released publicly, the negotiations have been concluded and signed.

In deciding to join the GPA (as with PTAs generally), it would have been highly desirable if greater transparency of negotiated positions, including by Australia, occurred throughout the negotiations. A good starting point would have been to have the question of Australia's accession to the GPA referred to a public inquiry by the independent Productivity Commission, the government's main advisor on trade and micro-reform initiatives. While DFAT and the government would argue that such transparency would harm Australia's negotiating positions, this is really a ruse for maintaining rigid domestic control over the negotiations. Their non-transparency (and discrimination) is appealing to governments. It enables them to make unconstrained/unchallenged inflated claims of economic benefits during the negotiations and to help secure a "trophy" that they can boast about achieving. Greater transparency would not only lead to better decision-making in terms of Australian welfare by enhancing public scrutiny throughout the negotiations, but would also help prevent potentially damaging speculation being publicly developed that may be an incorrect understanding of what is happening in the negotiations. It could muster public support for beneficial PTAs, therefore helping rather than hindering the government's negotiations and ensuring that there are no hidden surprises in the final deal.

17.4.2.2 New Zealand

New Zealand formally applied for accession to the GPA in September 2012, which was accepted in October 2014 (Table 17.4). Its offers largely reflect its commitments negotiated in its PTAs.

The areas of possible but relatively minor discrimination against foreign suppliers in government procurement—such as for indigenous populations and by local government—are excluded from coverage. Also, some other types of government procurement have been excluded from coverage. The extent to which this is to provide cover for existing discriminatory or preferential practices in New Zealand, as opposed to simply being included in the negotiations for future "negotiating coin" or to allow some future backsliding in these areas to introduce discriminatory practices, is unknown. Trying to gauge the openness of a country's trade regime based on commitments in trade agreements is dangerous. Such commitments usually do little to improve the transparency of a country's trade regime.

Table 17.4 Summary of New Zealand's commitments under the GPA

Feature	Description
Coverage	
Central	Ministries of/for Primary Industries, Business, Innovation & Employment, Culture & Heritage, Defence, Education, Education Review Office, Environment, Foreign Affairs & Trade, Health, Justice, Māori Development, Pacific Island Affairs, Social Development, Transport, & Women's Affairs; Canterbury Earthquake Recovery Authority; Departments of Conservation, Corrections, Inland Revenue, Internal Affairs & Prime Minister and Cabinet; Crown Law Office, Government Communications Security Bureau; Land Information NZ; NZ Customs Service; Serious Fraud Office; State Services Commission; Statistics NZ; The Treasury; NZ Defence Force. & NZ Police.
Sub-central	District Health Boards of Auckland, Canterbury, Capital & Coast, Counties Manukau, Hutt, Mid-Central, South Canterbury, Waikato, Waitemata, Bay of Plenty, & Southern; City Councils of Auckland, Wellington, & Christchurch;* & Regional Councils of Waikato, Bay of Plenty, Greater Wellington, & Canterbury.* Procurement by the listed District Health Boards through their agent health, Alliance Limited, is covered.
Other	Accident Compensation Corporation, Careers NZ, Civil Aviation Authority, Energy Efficiency & Conservation Authority, Housing NZ Corporation, Maritime NZ, NZ Antarctic Institute, Fire Service Commission, NZ Qualifications Authority, NZ Tourism Board, NZ Trade & Enterprise, NZ Transport Agency, Sport NZ, Tertiary Education Commission, Education NZ, Airways Corporation of NZ Ltd, Meteorological Service of NZ Ltd, KiwiRail Holdings Limited, & Transpower NZ Ltd.
Procurement by covered entities excluded	*Sub-central*: covers only procurement by specified Councils of goods, services & construction for transport projects funded, at least partly, by the NZ Transport Agency. *Other*: This Agreement does not cover procurement by Accident Compensation Corporation of pension fund management, public insurance & fund placements, investments & financial services related to securities or trading on an exchange; by Sport NZ of goods & services containing confidential information related to enhancing competitive sport performance; & by Transpower NZ Ltd of electrical stringing services, tower painting services, & projects funded directly by private sector customers where those projects would not be undertaken except for the funding provided by those customers.
Threshold values	*Central entities*: goods SDR 130,000, services SDR 130,000, construction SDR 5,000,000; *Sub-central entities*: goods SDR 200,000, services SDR 200,000, construction SDR 5,000,000; Other entities: goods SDR 400,000, services SDR 400,000, construction SDR 5,000,000.
Procurement excluded outright	Research & development; public health, education, & welfare services; under contracts for construction, refurbishment or furnishing of chanceries abroad; outside NZ territory for overseas consumption; commercial sponsorship arrangements; a covered entity on behalf of a non-covered entity; a covered entity covered from another covered entity, unless tenders are called; for developing, protecting or preserving national treasures of artistic, historic, archaeological value of cultural heritage; & measures deemed necessary to accord more favorable treatment to Māori to meet obligations under the Treaty of Waitangi, provided measures are not used as a means of arbitrary or unjustified discrimination against other Members or as a disguised trade restriction (the Treaty's interpretation, including as to the nature of the rights and obligations arising under it, are excluded from the Agreement's dispute settlement provisions).

Moreover, while price preferences and other more obvious discriminatory measures appear minimal in New Zealand, it is unknown whether the government's efforts to redress the perceived disadvantages faced by domestic firms, especially SMEs, in submitting competitive tenders and to promote local content provide an advantage over imported content. For example, departments must include in their internal documentation justification, signed off by senior management, for the rejection of any New Zealand tender for contracts of NZ$100,000 and above (WTO, 2009). The Industry Capability Network New Zealand freely helps New Zealand firms, departments, and public bodies identify major procurement opportunities, including supplying goods and services that would otherwise be imported that can be met competitively locally. As the Australian case shows, such schemes can become murky and provide obscure discrimination in procurement against imported content that is difficult to identify.

Nevertheless, subject to these qualifications, the New Zealand government procurement market seems relatively open and non-discriminatory. If so, the main advantage for New Zealand of joining the GPA would be to lock in via international commitments its unilateral liberal procurement policies. This is a positive outcome that could help limit backsliding. However, if there is significant "water" in the commitments or areas of procurement excluded from the GPA, backsliding is facilitated. Also, since New Zealand has not backslid in its procurement policies without these international commitments, the additional real value provided by the GPA would seem overstated. Experience has shown that the enforceability of these commitments in the WTO has been weak, with very few dispute cases mounted. The best insurance against backsliding in procurement policies, as for other trade-related policies, is a firm unilateral commitment by governments to trade openness as good domestic economic policy, irrespective of what protectionist policies other countries may follow.

The MBIE and the Ministry of Foreign Affairs and Trade jointly prepared a National Interest Analysis (NIA) of New Zealand's membership of the GPA (Box 17.6). However, this "analysis" is far too general to be of much use in determining policy, and falls well short of what is needed for good policy analysis. The NIA, better called a "statement," only assumes New Zealand suppliers will be able to access the procurement markets of GPA parties upon accession. It does not examine the actual degree of increased openness in these markets for New Zealand nor the extent to which these opportunities will be realized by New Zealand exporters. Instead, large numbers of the size of procurement markets in GPA members are given and summed, giving the misleading impression that a significant share of these markets will be captured by New Zealand exporters. This is highly unlikely (as evidence repeatedly shows).

Moreover, the flawed mercantilism export bias of the NIS is clear. Benefits are seen entirely as increasing New Zealand exports from greater overseas market access, while liberalizing its own procurement market to overseas exporters is seen as a disadvantage—or cost—of joining the GPA. The NIA also states as a positive economic

BOX 17.6 SUMMARY OF NEW ZEALAND'S NATIONAL INTEREST ANALYSIS ON JOINING THE GPA

New Zealand sees accession to the GPA as contributing to its Business Growth Agenda, specifically to increasing exports to "40 percent of GDP by 2025," which is seen as "necessary to lift economic growth and living standards."

The main benefit to New Zealand identified from membership is to secure for the country's businesses "legally guaranteed binding access to procurement markets of the existing GPA Members," worth an estimated USD $1.7 trillion annually, as well as "access to the government markets of new members without having to increase the access that NZ would have to provide." Other benefits identified include:

- address "some existing barriers overseas for NZ businesses accessing procurement sales, for example some firms wanting to bid for US government contracts cannot always do so directly, being required to substantially transform their product in the US or sell it through a US intermediary";
- put New Zealand in a position to seek "further access to procurement in future free trade negotiations";
- provide "opportunities to participate and influence the evolution of the GPA"; and
- provide a mechanism for new Zealand and its businesses to resolve procurement disputes with GPA parties.
- Disadvantages identified of joining the GPA are:
- *Reduced scope for flexible procurement practices,* by placing "some constraints on NZ's ability to develop policies or apply practices which would be discriminatory in nature, the most obvious of which would be preferential buy local policies for procurement covered by our market access commitments." However, "ability to support local suppliers in other ways than through preferential policy is not constrained by the GPA," for example efforts by the MBIE to "develop the tendering capabilities of businesses so that they can be competitive both domestically and in foreign markets. These and other initiatives to support local businesses, such as through access to research grants or other incentives, are not precluded by GPA accession";
- *Precedent effect:* as New Zealand's GPA offers a broader range of government entities than in its PTAs raises the possibility that negotiating partners in future PTAs may seek similar access. In general, it is in the country's interests to promote liberalization of government procurement markets in order to increase exports, but these will need to be weighed up against the demands of negotiating partners;
- *Less negotiating coin for future PTAs:* GPA accession could "mean that there is less available access that NZ could offer in a future PTA with a GPA party";
- *Disputes:* accession "could give rise to legal proceedings within NZ courts against a covered entity. As New Zealand already provides rights of redress to foreign tenderers through its courts, the risk of any increase in legal proceedings by an aggrieved supplier from a GPA party is considered minimal."

outcome that GPA membership will not constrain New Zealand's ability to support local suppliers using non-preferential measures and other initiatives, such as research grants or other incentives. This highlights the misplaced emphasis on trade negotiation outcomes. Also, as New Zealand has negotiated access on this basis, it is only logical to expect that other GPA parties have done likewise. Thus it is even less likely that GPA accession will open up significantly members' government procurement markets to foreigners generally, including to New Zealand exporters.

Indeed, the New Zealand government's stated objective of increasing exports to 40 percent of GDP by 2025 is economically flimsy. While a business growth agenda based on enhancing the efficiency of the New Zealand economy may well lead to increased export competitiveness and greater export share of GDP, it is a mistake to assume that higher exports per se automatically raise living standards. This depends on many factors, such as whether exports to new markets are diverted from existing markets, and where the resources to produce these exports come from. If, for example, the exporting activity is relatively inefficient and/or such sales are assisted so that resources are attracted from more efficient activities, including possibly other exporting activities, national welfare is likely to be reduced. Moreover, the main determinant of the size of a country's traded sector is its exchange rate and associated (including macro-) economic policies. With floating exchange rates, any efforts to substantially raise exports would significantly appreciate the New Zealand dollar to reduce the competitiveness of exports and import-competing activities and make imports more competitive, thus working against achieving the export target (unless the increased exports are associated with a corresponding rise in imports and/or net capital outflow). Simply put, there is no sacrosanct policy ratio of exports/trade to GDP for any country—the appropriate size should depend on the underlying economic fundamentals, not on government fiat.[27]

Given the inadequacy of the NIA, it would have been better for the government to have referred a study on GPA accession to its Productivity Commission for an independent and transparent evaluation of the real economic costs and benefits. However, as in Australia, it seems the government's main micro-economic reform advisor, which was modeled on the Australian version with statutory independence, is—by government choice—being left out of such decisions and not being given an opportunity to conduct transparent public policy analysis in these trade areas.

Also, as in Australia, the public examination of treaties, including trade agreements, suffers from weaknesses. Their parliamentary examination is left until the treaties have been negotiated, when the details are made public for the first time. This is far too late to have any influence on the negotiations. This evaluation of what has been negotiated is only done when the government has already decided to sign off on the treaty, thus tainting the parliamentary examination and any subsequent government or departmental assessment. It would be almost impossible for any such report to be overly critical of the agreed treaty negotiated, or to conclude that it is a bad agreement not in the country's national economic interests. The NIA was not done until November 2014, after New Zealand's offer was accepted, and was not released publicly until January 2015.

[27] Export targets are sometimes advocated as a means of galvanizing national efforts to achieve a particular goal, such as increasing growth. But experience shows the ever present danger that once set, if they are not achieved through appropriate efficiency-enhancing policies at home (e.g., removing the anti-export bias of protection), governments are pressured by vested interests to implement economically costly policies, such as using trade agreements primarily to achieve foreign market access for exporters rather than promoting self-liberalization to be seen to be meeting the targets.

17.4.3 AUSTRALIAN PREFERENTIAL TRADE AGREEMENTS (PTAs) AND OTHER ARRANGEMENTS

Australia has embarked on an aggressive policy of negotiating PTAs since 2000, both bilaterally and plurilaterally. Some contain government procurement provisions. The general provisions of these agreements include conditional non-discrimination (i.e., national treatment applying only to covered procurement), subject to many exclusions/exemptions and extended only to the PTA parties—so-called "conditional" MFN. Australia's most recent PTA with China, however, contained no specific government procurement provisions.

Australia's offers on covered procurement in PTAs have become very repetitive and stereotyped, and have done little to advance much needed reforms. Indeed, despite these provisions, PTAs have been negotiated to facilitate development of murky measures in state and Commonwealth procurement to discriminate in favor of local content and industrial development, especially of SMEs. Australian procurement, especially by its states, has become more restrictive. Australia unfortunately has not used PTAs to reform its government procurement market, where most economic benefits would accrue.

17.4.3.1 Australian and New Zealand Closer Economic Relations Trade Agreement (ANZCERTA)

ANZCERTA came into force in 1983. It called for ANZ to eliminate price preferences for domestic procurement, and to remove procurement offsets. It also called for a single Tasman procurement market. ANZCERTA provided impetus for including New Zealand in the ANZ Government Procurement Agreement, subsequently negotiated to achieve the Tasman procurement market, and to ensure national treatment. Those states with price preferences for domestic firms extended them to New Zealand suppliers by including their content as local content.

17.4.3.2 Singapore Australia Free Trade Agreement (SAFTA)

Entering into force in July 2003, SAFTA's government procurement provisions reflect some of the GPA rules (Table A1). The key principle of non-discrimination (national treatment) applies to covered procurement, subject to exclusions. No minimum value thresholds apply to procurement by covered entities. Open and limited tendering is allowed. Procurement must achieve value for money.

Substantial procurement excluded from coverage includes procurement to promote industry development (e.g., to assist SMEs) and for Australia to promote regional

Table A1 Summary of key government procurement provisions of SAFTA

Feature	Description
Coverage	Law, regulation, procedure or practice regarding procurement by covered entities, & by contractual means, for example purchase, lease, rental, hire purchase. Entities covered via positive list.
General principles	NT for goods, services, & suppliers, including local foreign-owned/affiliated firms. Cannot discriminate against local firms based on the goods & services supplied from the other Party. No discrimination in favor of corporate bodies with government shareholding. Parties to follow competitive neutrality using reasonable measures to ensure that governments at all levels provide no competitive advantage to businesses based on government ownership.
General exclusions	Goods & services from own entities if no other supplier invited to tender, unless the entity tendered under open tendering; proprietary items ensuring integrity of machinery, equipment or systems or of a work, health or safety nature specified in industrial agreements, unless available from several sources & open tendering used; foreign aid; overseas to consume abroad; asset management & financial advisory services pertaining to government reserves; & to promote industry development, for example to assist SMEs.
General exceptions	Action or not disclosing information necessary to protect essential security interests in procuring arms, ammunition or war materials, or indispensable for national security or defense. Necessary measures to protect public morals, order or safety, or human, animal or plant life or health; intellectual property; of handicapped persons, of philanthropic institutions, or of prison labor; conservation of exhaustible natural resources;
Tendering processes	Open or limited tendering allowed.
Awarding contracts	Ensure tendering procedures provide mechanisms to eliminate conflicts of interest; achieve value for money; conducted fairly & non-discriminatorily.
Rules-of-origin	Those applied in the normal course of trade between the parties.
Thresholds	None
Australia	
General exclusions	Promoting employment & training for indigenous people in such regions (not to arbitrarily or unjustifiably discriminate between Parties or be a disguised trade restriction).
Central entities	A number of Commonwealth Departments, including Defence, and Financial Management & Accountability Act Agencies.
Singapore	
Entities	A number of ministries, departments, Organs of State, & statutory boards.

employment and training for indigenous people. Also excluded is procurement from own entities if no other supplier was invited to tender, unless the entity submitted a tender under open tendering; proprietary items to ensure integrity of machinery, equipment or systems or of a work, health or safety nature specified in industrial agreements, unless items are available from several sources and open tendering used; and for foreign aid. Moreover, the coverage of procurement entities is limited, especially for Australia.

Other exclusions from covered procurement are purchases to protect essential security interests of arms, ammunition or war materials, or that are indispensable for national security or defense; necessary measures to protect public morals, order or safety, or human, animal or plant life or health; intellectual property; those relating to handicapped persons, philanthropic institutions, or prison labor; and conservation of exhaustible natural resources. Rules of origin also restrict government purchases between the two markets, as the GPA does not cover goods imported from each other that do not meet the origin requirements that are applied "in the normal course" of trade between the parties.[28]

SAFTA has had minimal impact on Australia's procurement system, especially at the central level. While it may have had some implications for the price preferences for domestic suppliers run by some states, it still left opportunities for these to be applied on non-covered procurement (e.g., promoting SMEs and indigenous opportunities), and for murky non-price measures to encourage local content to be adopted, including by the Commonwealth, with discrimination becoming hidden in procurement procedures and processes.

17.4.3.3 **Australia United States Free Trade Area (AUSFTA)**

AUSFTA became effective in 2005. Many procurement commitments cover procedures (e.g., on the use of selective and limited tendering, the timing and evaluation of tenders, and review provisions). In other areas, such as on specific measures and coverage of covered procurement, it contains pretty standard provisions in accordance with standard templates used to negotiate PTAs.[29] It lists general principles applying to covered procurement, such as conditional non-discrimination (i.e., national treatment only on covered procurement between the parties, so-called "conditional MFN"). It covers entities at various government levels above minimum thresholds, with many general and specific exceptions. As the coverage has broadened, so have the exclusions (Table A2).

Generally excluded by both parties are necessary measures to protect public morals, order or safety, or human, animal or plant life or health; intellectual property; those relating to goods and services of handicapped persons, of philanthropic or not for profit institutions, or of prison labor. These excluded measures must not arbitrarily or unjustifiably discriminate between parties under the same prevailing conditions, or act as a disguised trade restriction.

Australia specifically excluded procurement benefiting SMEs; measures protecting national treasures of artistic, historic, or archaeological value, for indigenous health/welfare and for their economic and social advancement; plasma fractionation services and government advertising services; and buy national requirements on articles, supplies, or materials used in construction. National treatment is not extended to Australian Industry Involvement programs and its successors; the Australian Reward Investment

[28] This assessment is based on interpreting that the reference to "in the normal course" of trade refers to that occurring under the PTA.

[29] There are essentially two templates. The NAFTA template followed, for example, by the US, and the GATS-based template followed mainly by developing countries.

Table A2 Summary of key government procurement provisions of AUSFTA

Feature	Description
Coverage	Goods & services (including construction,[30] unless excluded) by contractual means (e.g., purchase, rental or lease), build-operate-transfer & public works concession contracts, exceeding the relevant threshold values by an entity not excluded from coverage. Defense procurement is covered by the 1995 memorandum between the two Governments on reciprocal defense procurement.
General principles	NT for goods, services & suppliers, including local foreign-owned/affiliated firms. Cannot discriminate against local firms based on the goods & services supplied from the other Party.
Prohibited	Offsets.[31]
General exclusions	Procurement funded by any assistance, for example grants, loans, equity infusions, fiscal incentives, subsidies; from own entities & by or between procuring entities; foreign aid; research & development; overseas to consume abroad; by fiscal agency or depository services, liquidation & management services for regulated financial institutions, & sale/distribution services for government debt.
General exceptions	Necessary measures to protect public morals, order or safety, or human, animal or plant life or health; intellectual property; of handicapped persons, philanthropic or not for profit institutions, or of prison labor (must not arbitrarily or unjustifiably discriminate between Parties or act as a disguised trade restriction).
Rules-of-origin	Those applied in the normal course of trade between the Parties.
Country exceptions	
Australia	
National	Preferences benefiting SMEs; measures protecting national artistic, historic, or archaeological treasures; indigenous health/welfare & their economic/social advancement; plasma fractionation services; government advertising services; buy national requirements on construction articles, supplies or materials. NT not extended to Industry Involvement Program & successors.
Central entities	Procurement by/of many specified defense-related & other goods by Defence Department & Defence Material Organization seen essential for security, covering design, development, integration, test, evaluation, maintenance, repair, modification, rebuilding & installation of military systems & equipment; Government-owned defense facilities; space services; services supporting military forces overseas; Defence Intelligence Organisation, Defence Signals Directorate, & Defence Imagery and Geospatial Organisation.
Central entities (other)	Australian Reward Investment Alliance of investment management, investment advisory or master custody & safekeeping services for managing & investing assets of Government superannuation funds. Motor vehicles by List A government enterprises & telecom services by the War Memorial.

[30] Australia requires tenderers for construction to meet the National Code of Practice for the Construction Industry and related implementation guidelines of central and regional governments.

[31] Australia to phase-out NSW & QLD non-compliant offset & preference schemes, along with non-compliant parts of the NT's *Building Northern Territory Industry Participation* program, within three years from the date of the Agreement's entry into force. Any QLD measure providing for inclusion of offsets in procurements and non-compliant parts of VIC Industry Participation Policy also to be phased out over the same period.

States	Procurement of health, welfare & education (ACT, NSW, QLD, SA, TAS); utility services (ACT); government advertising (QLD, SA, TAS); motor vehicles (VIC, ACT, NSW, QLD, SA); set-asides for Charles Darwin University under Government Partnership Agreements (NT); by a covered entity for a non-covered entity (NSW, QLD & VIC).
United States	
National	Procurement by/of set asides for small or minority businesses (e.g., any form of preference like exclusive rights to provide goods & services, & price preferences); transportation services as part of, or incidental to, a procurement contract; covered entity on behalf of non-covered entities at a different level of government; specified basic telecommunications network & services, for example public voice & data services; maintenance, repair, modification, rebuilding & installation of goods/equipment as well as of equipment for ships; non-nuclear ship repair; government-owned facilities; facilities of the energy department & the National Aeronautics & Space Administration; research & development facilities; utilities; transportation, travel & relocation services: services supporting military forces overseas; dredging services; buy national requirements on construction articles, supplies or materials.
Central entities	Procurement by/of Defence Department of many specified defense-related & other equipment, for example buses, hand & measuring tools, textiles/clothing/footwear, war materials, ammunition, & other goods & services essential for security; & Defence Department facilities.
Central entities (other)	Procurement by/of energy & national security departments to safeguard nuclear materials or technology (*Atomic Energy Act*), *or* oil bought for the Strategic Petroleum Reserve; agriculture department of goods for agricultural support or human feeding programs; shipbuilding of the National Oceanic & Atmospheric Administration (NOAA); by the Transportation Security Administration, Coast Guard; Federal Aviation Administration; General Services Administration of hand tools, measuring tools, cutlery & flatware; Rural Utilities Service (sole List B government enterprise for federal buy national requirements set as funding conditions for all power generation projects); & excludes all other aspects of its procurement, for example restrictions on financing for telecommunications. Restrictions attached to Federal funds for airport projects by List A & List B government enterprises exempt.
State entities	Procurement by/of Office of Fish & Game, & construction (Arkansas); beef, compost or mulch (Georgia); software & construction (Hawaii); construction, automobiles or aircraft (Kansas); construction (Kentucky); services (Mississippi & Tennessee); public authorities & public benefit corporations with multi-state mandates, transit cars, buses, or related equipment (New York); construction (Oklahoma); boats, automobiles, buses, or related equipment (Rhode Island); beef (South Dakota); preferences for motor vehicles, travel agents, & rubberized asphalt paving made from scrap tires by a state facility (Texas); & fuel, paper products, boats, ships & vessels (Washington); & for those many entities identified with pre-existing restrictions, construction-grade steel, motor vehicles & coal. Preferences or restrictions in programs promoting development of distressed areas or businesses owned by minorities, disabled veterans, or women; restrictions to promote states' environmental quality (provided not a disguised trade barrier); restrictions attached to Federal funds for mass transit and highway projects; & printing.
Tendering Procedures	Open tendering. Selective tendering allowed provided invited as many domestic & other party suppliers consistent with efficient procurement, & used either an appropriate multi-use list of suppliers, or a list of suppliers responding to an invitational notice to apply, or a list of suppliers responding to a notice requesting expressions of interest provided notice published & contains information required & invites all interested suppliers (unless the notice stipulates the number invited may be limited); or a list of all licensed suppliers, or one determined by the appropriate body to comply with specific legal requirements independent of the procurement process, provided that (a) licensing requirements or need to comply with specific legalities is essential (b) appropriate body maintains the full list of such suppliers & it is accessible & (c) all listed suppliers are invited to tender. Limited tendering allowed (provided not used to avoid competition, protect domestic suppliers, or discriminate against other Party suppliers) if no responses received to a prior notice, invitation

(*continued*)

Table A2 Continued

Feature	Description
	to participate or tender or conformed to the essential requirements, or no supplier met the conditions; items only available from a certain supplier & no reasonable alternative or substitute exists due to (a) covers works of art (b) protect patents, copyrights, or other exclusive rights, or proprietary information (c) competition is absent for technical reasons; for additional deliveries by the original supplier to replace parts, extend, or continue services for existing equipment, software, services, or installations, where changing suppliers would compel buying item not interchangeable with existing equipment; commodities; a prototype or an item for limited trial or developed at its request in the course of, and for, a particular research, experiment, study, or original development; as strictly necessary to meet emergencies from unforeseen events; new construction services of repeated similar services initially awarded by open tender, or by selective tender complying with these provisions if the initial procurement notice stated limited tendering may be used; purchases in exceptionally advantageous short-term cases, for example unusual disposal, unsolicited innovative proposals, liquidation, bankruptcy, or receivership; or for contracts awarded winners of a design contest consistent with these provisions & judged independently.
Multiple thresholds	(a) central entities—G&S = A\$80,000 or US\$79 507; construction = A\$7.767,000 or US\$7 864,000 (b) regional government entities—G&S = A\$551,000 or US\$558,000; construction = A\$7 767,000 or US\$7 864,000 (c) government enterprises—G&S = A\$402,000 or US\$397 535 for List A agencies & US\$629,000 for List B agencies;[32] construction = A\$7 767,000 or US\$7 864,000.[33]

Alliance of investment management, investment advisory, or master custody and safekeeping services for managing and investing the assets of government superannuation funds. The purchase of motor vehicles by List A enterprises and telecom services by the War Memorial are also excluded.

Also specifically excluded from covered procurement are certain types of procurement above the minimum thresholds by covered state entities. These include health, welfare and education (ACT, NSW, QLD, SA, TAS); utility services (ACT); QLD, SA, TAS government advertising; motor vehicles (VIC, ACT, NSW, QLD, SA); NT set-asides for Charles Darwin University under Government Partnership Agreements; and procurement by a covered entity for a non-covered entity (NSW, QLD, VIC).

The United States has also followed suit and made many similar exemptions at all government levels from covered procurement.

Given the many exemptions—both general and specifically negotiated by both parties—the extent to which AUSFTA has liberalized respective markets in government procurement is largely illusory. Also, rules of origin mean that covered procurement excludes goods failing these requirements, so that they are a non-tariff measure on government procurement.

[32] Australia listed no List B agencies.

[33] Thresholds adjusted biennially, starting January 1, 2006.

AUSFTA has not significantly impacted on the core elements of Australia's government procurement arrangements, except requiring procedural changes (for example, on non-open tendering). While having some implications for remaining state price preferences favoring domestic suppliers, state governments still had plenty of opportunities to apply them to non-covered procurement (e.g., promoting SMEs and adopting other less transparent non-price measures) to encourage industry development and local content, including by the Commonwealth.

17.4.3.4 Others

AUSFTA's government procurement provisions set the basis for Australia's commitments in subsequent FTAs; these are the Australia–Chile Free Trade Agreement (ACFTA), effective March 2009, the Japan–Australia Economic Partnership Agreement (JAEPA), effective in January 2015, and the Korea–Australia Free Trade Agreement (AKFTA), effective in December 2014.

These agreements essentially repeat the principles for covered procurement negotiated in AUSFTA (Tables A3, A4 and A5, respectively), including on conditional non-discrimination (national treatment only on covered procurement and conditional MFN). However, like AUSFTA, the comprehensive exemptions maintained by the parties to these PTAs, including on rules of origin, mean state governments have had minimal impact on reforming their procurement policies.

17.4.4 NEW ZEALAND FREE TRADE AGREEMENTS (CALLED CLOSER ECONOMIC PARTNERSHIP)

Several of these partnerships (PTAs) negotiated by New Zealand, both bilaterally and plurilaterally, contain provisions on government procurement.

17.4.4.1 Agreement between New Zealand and Singapore on a Closer Economic Partnership (NSCEP)

NSCEP entered into force in 2001. It calls for establishing a single government procurement market to maximize competitive opportunities and reduce costs. Both parties committed to implementing the APEC Non-Binding Principles on Government Procurement on transparency, value for money, open and effective competition, fair dealing, accountability and due process, and conditional non-discrimination, with national treatment subject to exceptions and applied only on covered procurement, and

Table A3 Summary of key government procurement provisions of ACFTA

Feature	Description
Coverage	goods/services (including construction)[34] by any contractual means (e.g., purchase, rental or lease, build-operate-transfer contracts and public works concessions contracts) equal to or above specified value thresholds conducted by specified procuring entity, and subject to the conditions specified in Annex 15-A. Positive list of central & sub-central entities.
General principles	Goods, services and suppliers to receive NT, including for locally established foreign-owned or affiliated suppliers, irrespective of degree of foreign affiliation or ownership. Cannot discriminate against a locally established supplier on the basis that the goods or services it supplies for a particular procurement are from the other Party.
Prohibited	Offsets
General exclusions	(a) under non-contractual agreements or any form of assistance, for example grants, loans, equity infusions, fiscal incentives, subsidies, guarantees, cooperative agreements and sponsorship arrangements (b) by direct foreign aid (c) funded by international grants, loans or other assistance (d) public employment contracts (e) financial service (f) of goods & services procured from another entity or with a regional or local government, where no other supplier has been asked to tender (g) overseas procured goods & services for consumption abroad (h) funded by grants &/or sponsorship payments received from a person other than a procuring entity (i) by fiscal agency or depository services, liquidation & management services for regulated financial institutions, or services related to the sale, redemption and distribution of public debt, including loans and government bonds, notes, derivatives & other securities (j) rental of land, existing buildings or other immovable property or rights thereon where not part of procurement of construction.
General exceptions	If not applied to arbitrarily or unjustifiably discriminate or a disguised trade restriction measures necessary to protect (a) public morals, order or safety; (b) human, animal, or plant life or health;[35] (c) intellectual property; (d) or relating to goods & services of handicapped persons, of philanthropic or not for profit institutions, or of prison labor. Actions considered necessary to protect essential security indispensable to national security or defense.
Multiple thresholds	(a) central entities—goods & services of A$87,000 or CLP$35 911,000, construction of A$9 570,000 or CLP$3 940 806,000 (b) non-central entities—goods & services of A$679,000 or CLP$279 557,000, construction of A$9 570,000 or CLP$3 940 806,000 (c) other—goods & services of A$436,000 or CLP$179 558,000,[36] construction of A$9 570,000 or CLP$3 940 806,000.[37]
Tendering procedures	Only open or selective tendering. To ensure effective competition under selective tendering, largest number of domestic & tenderers from the other Party to be invited consistent with the

[34] Chile has excluded construction services intended for Easter Island. Australia requires as a condition to receiving NT and participating in procurement of building and construction services compliance with the National Code of Practice for the Construction Industry and related implementation guidelines of central and sub-central governments, and their successor policies and guidelines. Buy national requirements on articles, supplies or materials acquired for use in construction services contracts covered by this chapter shall not apply to goods of either Party.

[35] Covers environmental measures.

[36] Australia has excluded procurement of motor vehicles for these specified entities.

[37] Thresholds to be adjusted biannually, starting January 1, 2010, to align with the adjusted thresholds for equivalent procurement categories listed in respective FTA with the US.

	procurement system's efficient operation, & selected in a "fair and non-discriminatory" manner. Limited tendering only allowed (provided not aimed at avoiding competition, protecting domestic suppliers or to discriminate against suppliers of the other Party) if (a) in response to a prior notice, invitation to participate, or invitation to tender (i) no tenders were submitted (or that conformed to the essential documentary requirements) or no suppliers requested participation (ii) no suppliers satisfied participatory conditions (b) where, for works of art, or to protect exclusive rights, for example patents, copyrights, proprietary information, or where competition is absent for technical reasons, goods/services can only come from a certain supplier & no reasonable alternative or substitute exists (c) for additional deliveries by the original supplier (or authorized agent) to replace parts, extensions, or continuing services for existing equipment, software, services or installations, where changing supplier would compel procurement of goods/services not compatible with existing equipment, software, services, or installations (d) for goods purchased on a commodity market (e) to procure a prototype or a first good/service intended for limited trial as part of a particular contract for research, experiment, study, or original development (f) extra construction services not in the initial contract but come within the objectives of the original tender documentation have under unforeseen circumstances become necessary to complete the construction services limited to 50 percent of the total value of the initial contract (g) for new construction services repeating similar services that conform to a basic project of an initial contract awarded using of open or selective tendering, & where the subsequent use of limited tendering for such services has been stated in the notice of intended procurement concerning the initial construction (h) for purchases under exceptionally short-term advantageous conditions, for example from unusual disposals, unsolicited innovative proposals, liquidation, bankruptcy or receivership & not for routine purchases from regular suppliers (i) where a contract is awarded to the winner of a design contest provided (i) the contest has been organized consistently with the Agreement & (ii) judged by an independent jury (j) where essential due to extreme urgency from unforeseen events unforeseen by the procuring entity the goods/services could not be timely procured by open or selective tendering.
Australia National	Any preference benefiting SMEs, and measures to (a) protect national treasures of artistic, historic, or archaeological value (b) for the health & welfare of indigenous people or for their economic and social advancement. NT exception applied to the Australian Industry Involvement Program & its successors. Specifically excluded is procurement by Department of Defence & DMO, Defence Intelligence Organisation, the Defence Signals Directorate or the Defence Imagery & Geospatial Organisation, as well as design and all activities associated with military systems and equipment; operation of Government-owned facilities, space services, & services supporting military forces overseas; the Australian Reward Investment Alliance of investment management, investment; advisory or master custody and safekeeping services for managing and investing the assets of Australian Government superannuation funds; health & welfare services;[38] & of telecom services by the Australian War Memorial; research & development services, plasma fractionation services or government advertising services.

[38] ACT, NSW, SA, VIC have excluded the procurement of health and welfare services, education services, utility services or motor vehicles; NSW, QLD have excluded procurement by a covered entity on behalf of a non-covered entity; NT has excluded set-asides on behalf of the Charles Darwin University pursuant to Partnership Agreements between the NT Government and Charles Darwin University; QLD, SA have also excluded procurement of government advertising; TAS has excluded the procurement of health and welfare services, education services or advertising services. VIC has excluded procurement of motor vehicles.

Table A4 Summary of Key government procurement provisions in JAEPA

Feature	Description
Coverage	Goods/services (including construction, unless noted otherwise) by any contractual means (including purchase, rental, or lease), build-operate-transfer contracts, & public works concessions contracts equal to or exceeding the relevant threshold values by a covered entity not excluded from coverage.
General principles	G&S, & suppliers receive NT, including for locally established foreign-owned or affiliated suppliers irrespective of degree of foreign affiliation or ownership. Cannot discriminate against locally established suppliers on the basis the goods/services supplied are from the other Party.
Prohibited	Cannot seek, take account of, impose or enforce any offset, that is any condition or undertaking that encourages local development or improves a Party's balance-of-payments accounts, for example use of domestic content, technology licensing, investment, counter-trade.
General exclusions	Non-contractual agreements or any form of assistance, for example grants, loans, equity infusions, fiscal incentives, subsidies; goods/services from own entities & by or between procuring entities; directly for foreign aid; research & development; overseas (including construction) to consume abroad; public employment contracts; acquisition or rental of land, existing buildings, or other immovable property or rights thereon; under an international agreement for stationing troops or relating to the joint implementation of a project; fiscal agency or depository services, liquidation & management services for regulated financial institutions, or services related to the sale, redemption & distribution of public debt, including loans & government bonds, notes, derivatives & other securities; under the particular procedure or condition of an international organization, or funded by international grants, loans, or other assistance where the applicable procedure or condition would be inconsistent with these provisions.
General exceptions	Action considered necessary to protect essential security interests indispensable for national security or for national defense purposes. Necessary measures to protect public morals, order or safety, or human, animal or plant life or health;[39] intellectual property; relating to G&S of handicapped persons, of philanthropic or not for profit institutions, or of prison labor must not arbitrarily or unjustifiably discriminate between Parties under the same prevailing conditions, or act as a disguised trade restriction.
Country exceptions	
Australia National	NT & non-discrimination not extended to the Australian industry capability program and its successor programs and policies. Blood &related products, including plasma derived products & plasma fractionation services; government advertising services; health & welfare services; legal services; telecommunications; education services; financial services; & transport services. Excludes any form of preference benefiting SMEs; measures protecting national treasures of artistic, historic, or archaeological value; measures for the health/welfare of Indigenous people, & their economic & social advancement; & financial advisory & asset management services pertaining to reserves held, including for the purposes of funding retirement

[39] Covers essential environmental measures to protect human, animal or plant life or health.

	benefits. Suppliers of construction services must comply with the National Code of Practice for the Construction Industry & related implementation guidelines at all government levels.
Central entity (mainly defense-related)	Many specified defense-related & other goods by Department of Defence & Defence Material Organization judged essential for security; covering the design, development, integration, test, evaluation, maintenance, repair, modification, rebuilding & installation of military systems & equipment; operation of Government-owned defense facilities; space services; services supporting military forces overseas; G&S procured by, or on behalf of, the Defence Intelligence Organisation, the Defence Signals Directorate, the Defence Imagery and Geospatial Organisation.
Central entities (other)	Motor vehicles (including by "other" entities) & telecomm services by the Australian War Memorial.
States	Health & welfare services (ACT); education services & motor vehicles (NSW); by a covered entity on behalf of a non-covered entity (NSW, QLD, VIC); set-asides on behalf of the Charles Darwin University pursuant to Partnership Agreement with state government (NT); by departments, or parts of departments, which deliver health, education, training and/or arts (QLD); health services, education services, training services, arts services, welfare services, government advertising & motor vehicles (QLD); health & welfare services, education services, advertising services, or motor vehicles (SA); health & welfare services, education services, or advertising services (TAS); & motor vehicles (VIC).
Japan	
National	Contracts awarded to co-operatives or associations under laws & regulations existing when the FTA entered into force. A positive list of specified services covered, including of telecomm services, thereby excluding many services.
Central entities (mainly defense-related)	A positive list of goods covered by the Ministry of Defence, thus excluding most defense-related products.
Central entities (other)	Na
"Other" entities	Contracts awarded by Group A entities for purposes of their daily profit-making activities exposed to competitive markets (cannot be used to circumvent GP provisions). Procurement related to operational safety of transportation; could disclose information incompatible with the Treaty on the Non-Proliferation of Nuclear Weapons or with international agreements on intellectual property rights; for safety-related activities aimed at utilizing & managing radioactive materials & responding to emergencies of nuclear installation; related to geological & geophysical survey; advertising services, construction & real estate services; & ships jointly privately owned.
State entities	G&S related to operational safety of transportation; electricity production, transport or distribution; contracts awarded for purposes of their daily profit-making activities where subject to competitive markets cannot be used to circumvent the GP provisions.
Tendering Procedures	To be non-discriminatory & transparent. Open, selective or limited tendering allowed. For selective tendering, to invite as many domestic & other party suppliers consistent with efficient procurement & considering market conditions. Suppliers to participate to be selected in a fair and non-discriminatory manner. For selective tendering, may use a list of qualified suppliers or a multi-use list established under these provisions. Limited tendering allowed (provided not used to avoid maximum competition, protect domestic suppliers, or discriminate against other Party suppliers) if no responses received to a prior notice, invitation to participate or tender or conformed to

(*continued*)

Table A4 Continued

Feature	Description
	the essential requirements, or no supplier met the conditions, or all tenderers colluded; G&S only available from a certain supplier & no reasonable alternative or substitute exists due to (a) covers works of art (b) protect patents, copyrights, or other exclusive rights, or proprietary information (c) competition is absent for technical reasons; for additional deliveries of G&S by the original supplier to replace parts, extend, or continue services for existing equipment, software, services, or installations, where changing suppliers would compel buying G&S not interchangeable/interoperable with existing equipment or would cause significant inconvenience or substantial duplication of costs for the procuring entity; commodities; a prototype or a G&S for limited trial or developed at its request in the course of, and for, a particular research, experiment, study, or original development;[40] as strictly necessary to meet emergencies from unforeseen events; new construction services of repeated similar services initially awarded by open tender, or by selective tender complying with these provisions if the initial procurement notice stated limited tendering may be used; purchases in exceptionally advantageous short-term cases, for example unusual disposal, unsolicited innovative proposals, liquidation, bankruptcy, or receivership; or for contracts awarded winners of a design contest consistent with these provisions & judged independently.
Awarding contracts	Supplier most capable of fulfilling the contractual terms & based solely on the criteria & requirements specified in the notices & tender documents, submitted the most advantageous, best value or overall greatest value tender; or where price is the sole criterion, the lowest price.
Multiple thresholds depending on particular entity:	
Australia	(a) central entities—G&S = 130,000 SDR; construction = 5,000,000 SDR(b) regional government entities—G&S = 355,000 SDR; construction = 5,000,000 SDR (c) government enterprises—G&S = 450,000 SDR; construction = 5,000,000 SDR.[41]
Japan	(a) central entities—Goods = 100,000 SDR; Services, construction = 4 500,000 SDR, architectural, engineering & other technical services = 450,000 SDR, other = 200,000 SDR (b) regional government entities—Goods = 200,000 SDR; Services, construction = 15,000,000 SDR, architectural, engineering & other technical services = 1 500,000 SDR, other = 200,000 SDR (c) other entities—Goods = 130,000 SDR; Services, construction = 4 500,000 SDR or 15,000,000,[42] architectural, engineering & other technical services = 450,000 SDR, other = 130,000 SDR.[43]

[40] May include limited production or supply in order to incorporate the results of field testing and to demonstrate that the G&S is suitable to produce or supply in quantity to acceptable quality standards.

[41] Thresholds to be adjusted biennially, starting January 1, 2016.

[42] 15,000,000 SDR for all Group A entities except 4,500,000 SDR for Japan Post Holdings Company Limited, Japan Post Company Limited, Japan Post Bank Company Limited, Japan Post Insurance Company Limited, and Management Organization for Postal Savings and Postal Life Insurance. All Group B entities 4,500,000 SDR.

[43] Thresholds to be adjusted every even-numbered year.

Table A5 Summary of key government provisions of KAFTA

Feature	Description
Coverage	G&S, including construction (unless noted otherwise)[44] by any contractual means (including purchase, rental, or lease), build-operate-transfer contracts, & public works concessions contracts equal to or exceeding the relevant threshold values by a covered entity not excluded from coverage. Parties affirm the Memorandum of Understanding on Defence Industry Cooperation between respective defence ministries of 2001, including amendments or extensions. They recognize that the benefits & responsibilities established under the MOU will continue.
General principles	G&S, & suppliers receive NT, including for locally established foreign-owned or affiliated suppliers irrespective of degree of foreign affiliation or ownership. Cannot discriminate against locally established suppliers on the basis the goods/services supplied are from the other Party.
Prohibited	Cannot seek, take account of, impose or enforce any offset, that is any condition or undertaking that encourages local development or improves a Party's balance-of-payments accounts, for example use of domestic content, technology licensing, investment, counter-trade.
General exclusions	Non-contractual agreements or any form of assistance, for example grants, loans, equity infusions, fiscal incentives, subsidies; goods/services from own entities & by or between procuring entities; directly for foreign aid; research & development; overseas **(including construction)** to consume abroad; public employment contracts; acquisition or rental of land, existing buildings, or other immovable property or rights thereon; under an international agreement for stationing troops or relating to the joint implementation of a project; fiscal agency or depository services, liquidation & management services for regulated financial institutions, or services related to the sale, redemption & distribution of public debt, including loans & government bonds, notes, derivatives & other securities; under the particular procedure or condition of an international organization, or funded by international grants, loans, or other assistance where the applicable procedure or condition would be inconsistent with these provisions.
General exceptions	Action considered necessary to protect essential security interests indispensable for national security or defense purposes. Necessary measures to protect public morals, order or safety, or human, animal or plant life or health;[45] intellectual property; relating to G&S of handicapped persons, of philanthropic or not for profit institutions, or of prison labor must not arbitrarily or unjustifiably discriminate between Parties under the same prevailing conditions, or act as a disguised trade restriction. The Australian industry capability program & successor programs & policies.
Country exceptions	
Australia	
National	NT & non-discrimination not extended to the Australian industry capability program and its successor programs and policies. Blood &related products,

(*continued*)

[44] Australia may require tenderers for construction to comply with National Code of Practice for the Construction Industry and related implementation guidelines at central and regional government.
[45] Covers essential environmental measures to protect human, animal or plant life or health.

Table A5 Continued

Feature	Description
	including plasma derived products & plasma fractionation services; government advertising services; health & welfare services; legal services; telecommunications; education services; financial services; & transport services. Excludes any form of preference benefiting SMEs; measures protecting national treasures of artistic, historic, or archaeological value; measures for the health/welfare of Indigenous people, & their economic & social advancement. Suppliers of construction services must comply with the National Code of Practice for the Construction Industry & related implementation guidelines at all government levels.
Central entity	Motor vehicles, many specified defense-related & other goods by Department of Defence & Defence Material Organization; covering the design, development, integration, test, evaluation, maintenance, repair, modification, rebuilding & installation of military systems & equipment; operation of Government-owned defence facilities; space services; services supporting military forces overseas; G&S procured by, or on behalf of, the Defence Intelligence Organisation, the Defence Signals Directorate, the Defence Imagery and Geospatial Organisation.
Other entities	Motor vehicles & services (other than construction) excluded.
States	Health & welfare services, education, utility or motor vehicles (ACT); **health, welfare,** education services & motor vehicles (NSW); by a covered entity on behalf of a non-covered entity (NSW, QLD, VIC); set-asides on behalf of the Charles Darwin University pursuant to Partnership Agreement with state government (NT); by departments, or parts of departments, which deliver health, education, training and/or arts (QLD); health services, education services, training services, arts services, welfare services, government advertising & motor vehicles (QLD); health & welfare services, education services, advertising services, or motor vehicles (SA); health & welfare services, education services, or advertising services (TAS); & motor vehicles (VIC).
Korea	
National	Excludes any set-asides for SMEs in accordance with the Act Relating to Contracts to Which the State is a Party and its Presidential Decree, and the procurement of agricultural, fishery and livestock products in accordance with the Grain Management Act, the Act on Distribution and Price Stabilization of Agricultural and Fishery Products, and the Livestock Industry Act. Set-asides for SMEs under the Act on Private Participation in Infrastructure are also excluded. Exempted is procurement to maintain public order, of blood-related products (including plasma-derived), in furtherance of human feeding programs. & for airports. A positive list of specified services covered, thereby excluding many services.
Central entities	A positive list of goods covered by the Ministry of National Defence & Defence Acquisition Program Administration, thus excluding most defense-related products for essential security reasons. Only services, including construction, listed in Section E & F, & procurement by the Public Procurement Service covered. Excludes procurement by the National Police Agency & Korea Coast Guard to maintain public order. Excludes set-asides for SMEs under the Act on the Management of Public Institutions & the Rule on Contract Business of Public Institutions & Quasi-Governmental

	Institutions, the Local Public Enterprises Act and the Enforcement Regulations of the Local Public Enterprise Act.
"Other" entities	Services (other than construction) excluded.
Sub-regional entities	None
Tendering Procedures	Open, selective or limited tendering allowed. For selective tendering, to invite as many domestic & other party suppliers consistent with efficient procurement & considering market conditions. Suppliers to participate to be selected in a fair and non-discriminatory manner. Limited tendering allowed (provided not used to avoid maximum competition, protect domestic suppliers, or discriminate against other Party suppliers) if no responses received to a prior notice, invitation to participate or tender or conformed to the essential requirements, or no supplier met the conditions, or all tenderers colluded; G&S only available from a certain supplier & no reasonable alternative or substitute exists due to (a) covers works of art (b) protect patents, copyrights, or other exclusive rights, or proprietary information (c) competition is absent for technical reasons; for additional deliveries of G&S by the original supplier to replace parts, extend, or continue services for existing equipment, software, services, or installations, where changing suppliers would compel buying G&S not interchangeable with existing equipment or would cause significant inconvenience or substantial duplication of costs for the procuring entity; commodities; a prototype or a G&S for limited trial or developed at its request in the course of, and for, a particular research, experiment, study, or original development;[46] as strictly necessary to meet emergencies from unforeseen events; new construction services of repeated similar services initially awarded by open tender, or by selective tender complying with these provisions if the initial procurement notice stated limited tendering may be used; purchases in exceptionally advantageous short-term cases, for example unusual disposal, unsolicited innovative proposals, liquidation, bankruptcy, or receivership; or for contracts awarded winners of a design contest consistent with these provisions & judged independently.
Awarding contracts	Supplier determined to satisfy participatory conditions & whose tender evaluated the most advantageous or best value for money, in accordance with specified requirements & criteria.
Multiple thresholds depending on particular entity:	
Australia	(a) central entities—G&S = 130,000 SDR; construction = 5,000,000 SDR (b) sub-central government entities—G&S = 355,000 SDR; construction = 5,000,000 SDR (c) other entities—Goods = 450,000 SDR; construction = 15,000,000 SDR.[47]
Korea	(a) central entities—G&S = 130,000 SDR; Services, construction = 5,000,000 SDR (b) sub-central government entities—G&S = 200,000 SDR; Services, construction = 15,000,000 SDR (c) other entities—Goods = 450,000 SDR; Services, construction = 15,000,000 SDR.

[46] May include limited production or supply in order to incorporate the results of field testing and to demonstrate that the goods and services is suitable to produce or supply in quantity to acceptable quality standards.

[47] Thresholds to be adjusted biennially, starting January 1.

Table A6 Summary of key government procurement provisions of NSCEP

Feature	Description
Coverage	Goods & services, including construction. Procurement covers, for example purchase, hire, lease, rental, exchange & competitive tendering & contracting (outsourcing) by government-controlled bodies, for example departments & statutory authorities. Best endeavors, consistent with good commercial practice to apply provisions to regional or local governments or authorities, & to services by non-governmental bodies exercising powers delegated by central, regional or local governments or authorities.
General principles	Establish single procurement market to maximize competitive opportunities & reduce costs of doing business by adopting APEC Non-Binding Principles of transparency, value for money, open & effective competition, fair dealing, accountability & due process, & non-discrimination; ensuring suppliers can compete equally & transparently with no preferential schemes or discrimination based on origin.
General exclusions	May be agreed for covered government bodies.
General exceptions	Procurement of joint bodies with any other State or separate customs territory not in the Agreement; bodies funded primarily from special levies on particular industries, by community groups or from special grants or public donations. No government body is intended to be granted full exemption. When considering applications for partial exemptions, governments are to exercise authority with due diligence. Excludes internal procurement from its own bodies where no other supplier asked to tender, unless tenders are invited, irrespective if the body submits a tender; proprietary items required to ensure machinery or equipment integrity, but only as they relate to biased specifications, unless such items available from a number of sources &/or tenders are invited. All provisions apply except as they relate to biased specifications; urgent procurement of goods & services in emergencies, for example natural disasters, or to meet urgent requirements of UN peacekeeping or humanitarian operations; of proprietary equipment of a work, health or safety nature specified in industrial agreements (only as they relate to biased specifications), unless such items available from a number of sources &/or tenders are invited (all provisions apply except as they relate to biased specifications); defense procurement of a strategic nature & for national security; under development assistance programs.
Prohibited	Offsets
Rules-of-origin	Those applied in the normal course of trade between the Parties.
Awarding contracts	Value for money primary determinant, based on competition & non-discriminating. This is best available outcome for money; test involves comparing the whole-of-life costs & benefits, for example fitness for purpose, quality, performance, price, delivery, accessories & consumables, service support & disposal.
Threshold	Above 50,000 SDR.

conditional MFN.[48] Suppliers in principle are to compete equally and transparently, with no preferential schemes or other forms of discrimination by origin (Table A6). Value for money is the primary determinant, based on competition and non-discrimination, taking into account whole-of-life costs and benefits (e.g., fitness for purpose, quality, performance, and price).

[48] APEC's Non-Binding Principles were formulated on the basis that any exceptions to national treatment would be minimal and that APEC economies would adopt these voluntarily according to "unconditional" MFN, that is no discrimination between APEC and non-APEC economies.

Included is covered procurement by mainly central agencies below 50,000 SDR. Also excluded is procurement funded primarily from special industry levies, community groups or special grants or public donations; generally inter-governmental activities; proprietary items to ensure machinery or equipment integrity; emergencies (e.g., natural disasters) or urgent requirements of UN peacekeeping or humanitarian operations; proprietary equipment of a work, health, or safety nature specified in industrial agreements; defense procurement of a strategic nature and for national security; and under-development assistance programs. Rules of origin applied to covered procurement are also a non-tariff measure.

NSCEP had minimal impact on reforming New Zealand's procurement system. It had already voluntarily adopted and applied the APEC Non-Binding Principles on a non-discriminatory basis to almost all procurement (the main exception being relatively minor local government procurement) for all trading partners under its unilateral reforms to open the economy to foreign competition.

17.4.4.2 New Zealand–Thailand Closer Economic Partnership Agreement (NTCEP)

NTCEP entered into force in July 2005. It has very weak government procurement provisions, simply reaffirming a "desire" to implement, to the extent possible, the APEC Non-Binding Principles on transparency, value for money, open and effective competition, fair dealing, accountability and due process, and non-discrimination, as well as the APEC Transparency Standards for Government procurement on a "conditional" MFN basis (Table A7). It established a working group to meet regularly to, inter alia, review these provisions. It was to report to the CEP Joint Commission within twelve months of the Agreement's entry into force with recommendations on the commencement of bilateral negotiations to expand these provisions. No such provisions on government procurement have been added, and NTCEP has had no impact on New Zealand's government procurement arrangements.

Table A7 Summary of key government procurement provisions of NTCEP

Feature	Description
General principles	Reaffirm desire to promote & implement to the extent possible the APEC Non-Binding Principles on transparency, value for money, open & effective competition, fair dealing, accountability & due process, & non-discrimination; & the APEC Transparency Standards. Working Group established to regularly discuss relevant issues & to review provisions. It was to report to the CEP Joint Commission within twelve months of the Agreement's entry into force recommending the commencement of bilateral negotiations. Procurement disputes do not apply to these provisions unless mandated in by future negotiations.

17.4.4.3 Trans-Pacific Strategic Economic Partnership Agreement (P4)

P4 came into force in 2006 with Brunei, Chile and Singapore. Government procurement provisions cover purchases by a positive list of government entities above thresholds of 50,000 SDR for goods and services and 5,000,000 SDR for construction, subject to substantial general and specific exemptions (Table A8). Its objective is to base procurement on the key principles of transparency, value for money, open and effective competition, fair dealing, accountability and due process, and conditional non-discrimination via a commitment to national treatment but only for non-excluded covered procurement and between the P4 parties ("conditional" MFN).[49] Rules of origin applied to covered procurement also act as a non-tariff measure.

The P4 made no changes to New Zealand's procurement system.

Table A8 Summary of key government procurement provisions of P4

Feature	Description
Coverage	Procurement of goods & services by a positive list of agencies exceeding minimum thresholds.
Objective	Conduct procurement using key principles of transparency, value for money, open and effective competition, fair dealing, accountability and due process, and non-discrimination.
General principles	Goods, services, & suppliers receive national treatment, including for local foreign-owned or affiliated firms. Cannot discriminate against local firms based on the goods/services from the other Party.
Prohibited	Offsets
Rules-of-origin	Those applied in the normal course of trade between the Parties.
General exclusions	Inter-agency procurement, unless tenders are called; non-contractual agreements; any form of assistance to persons or governmental authorities, for example foreign assistance, grants, loans, equity infusions, fiscal incentives, subsidies, guarantees, cooperative agreements, sponsorship arrangements; funded by international grants, loans or other assistance with inconsistent conditions to the Agreement; of goods & services for consumption abroad; acquisition of fiscal agency or depository services, liquidation & management services for regulated financial institutions, & sale & distribution services for government debt; & hiring of government employees or other long-term staff & related employment measures.
General exemptions	Procurement necessary to protect essential security for purchasing arms, ammunition or war materials, or indispensable for national security or defense. Necessary measures to protect public morals, order or safety, or human, animal or plant life or health; intellectual property; relating to goods & services of handicapped persons, of philanthropic or non-profit institutions, or of prison labor (must not arbitrarily or unjustifiably discriminate between Parties or act as a disguised trade restriction).

[49] Brunei was given two years to negotiate its government procurement schedule, and until then is not entitled to the procurement commitments of Chile, Singapore, and New Zealand.

Tendering methods	Open or selective tendering. Limited tendering allowed (cannot be used to avoid competition, protect domestic suppliers) if no responses received to a prior notice, invitation to participate or tender or conformed to the essential requirements, or no supplier met the conditions; goods & services only available from a certain supplier & no reasonable alternative or substitute exists due to covering works of art or protecting patents, copyrights; no competition for technical reasons; further deliveries by the original supplier to replace parts, extend, or continue services for existing equipment, software services, or installations, where changing suppliers would compel buying goods & services not interchangeable with existing equipment; commodities; a prototype or item for limited trial or developed at its request in the course of, and for, a particular research, experiment, study, or original development; as strictly necessary to meet unforeseen emergencies; extra construction services under the original tender's objectives that for unforeseeable circumstances are necessary to finish the construction services (total value not to exceed 50 percent of the main contract); purchases in exceptionally advantageous short-term cases, for example unusual disposal unsolicited innovative proposals, liquidation; commodities; contracts awarded to winners of a design contest consistent with these provisions & judged independently; new construction services of repeated similar services initially awarded by open, or by selective tender complying with these provisions if the initial procurement notice stated limited tendering may be used.
Awarding tenders	Unless determined not to be in the public interest, to the supplier determined fully capable of undertaking the contract and offering best value for money or be the most advantageous in terms of the essential requirements and evaluation criteria set forth in the tender documentation.
Specific exemptions	
New Zealand	
National	Procurement by a covered entity for a non-covered entity; of research & development; construction, refurbishment or furnishing of chanceries abroad; & of public health, education & welfare services.
Chile	
National	Procurement by a covered entity for a non-covered entity; all financial services of covered entities.
Singapore	
National	Procurement by a covered entity for a non-covered entity; of services (including construction) not in a positive list; construction contracts for chanceries abroad and headquarters buildings by the foreign affairs ministry; internal Security & Criminal Investigation Departments, the Security Branch & Central Narcotics Bureau of the home affairs ministry & that has security considerations.
Multiple thresholds	Goods & services = 50,000 SDR; construction = 5,000,000 SDR.

17.4.4.4 New Zealand–Hong Kong, China Closer Economic Partnership Agreement (NHKCEP)

NHKCEP entered into force in 2011. It largely repeated New Zealand's commitments in the P4, including exceptions along with conditional non-discrimination based on national treatment subject to exceptions and applying only to the parties ("conditional" MFN) (Table A9). It had no impact on New Zealand's procurement system.

Table A9 Summary of key government procurement provisions of NZHK

Feature	Description
Coverage	Goods & services, including construction unless indicated otherwise, by contractual means, for example purchase, hire purchase, rental, lease, build-operate-transfer contracts & public work concessions by covered entities exceeding relevant value thresholds. Positive list of central government entities covered & excludes defense-related entities (no sub-regional entities).
General principles	Procurement to accord with the fundamental principles of the APEC *Non-Binding Principles on Government Procurement* of transparency, value for money, open and effective competition, fair dealing, accountability and due process, & non-discrimination, to facilitate competitive opportunities. Goods, services & suppliers receive NT, including for local foreign-owned or affiliated suppliers. Cannot discriminate against locally established suppliers based on goods/services supplied from the other Party.
General exclusions	Procurement from own entities unless tenders are invited; foreign aid; overseas to consume abroad; non-contractual agreements; any form of assistance to persons or governmental authorities, for example cooperative agreements, sponsorship arrangements, grants, loans, subsidies, equity infusions, guarantees, fiscal incentives & governmental provision; international agreement on stationing troops or to jointly implement a project; under an international organization, or funded by international grants, loans, or other assistance; acquisition of fiscal agency or depository services, liquidation & management services for regulated financial institutions, or services related to the sale, redemption & distribution of public debt, for example loans government bonds, notes & other securities; hiring of government employees & related employment measures; by a covered entity for a non-entity.
General exceptions	Action or not disclosing information considered necessary to protect essential security interests for buying arms, ammunition or war materials, or to indispensable for national security or defense. Necessary to protect public morals, order or safety, or human, animal or plant life or health; intellectual property; relating to goods & services of disabled persons, of philanthropic institutions, or of prison labor.
Specific exemptions	
New Zealand	
National	Procurement (including construction) to construct, refurbish, furnish chanceries abroad; for not-profit institutions (cannot arbitrarily or unjustifiably discriminate between Parties or a disguised trade restriction)
Central entity	Research & development; public health, education & welfare services.
Hong Kong	
National	All consultancy & franchise arrangements, for example build-operate-transfer contracts & public works concession contracts; air mail; statutory insurances, for example third party liability for vehicles & vessels, & employer's employee liability insurance; & buying office or residential accommodation by the Government Property Agency.
Central entities	A positive list of covered services, for example certain telecoms & financial services.[50]
Tendering procedures	Open or selective tendering. Limited tendering (cannot be used to avoid competition or protect domestic suppliers) if no responses received to a prior notice, invitation to participate or tender or conformed to the essential requirements, or no supplier met the conditions; items only available from a certain supplier & no reasonable alternative or substitute exists due to covering

[50] Suppliers of telecoms may require licensing under the Telecommunications Ordinance and be established in Hong Kong under the Companies Ordinance.

	works of art or protecting patents, copyrights; competition is absent for technical reasons; further deliveries by the original supplier to replace parts, extend, or continue services for existing equipment, software services, or installations, where changing suppliers would compel buying goods & services not interchangeable with existing equipment; commodities; a prototype or an item for limited trial or developed at its request in the course of, & for, a particular research, experiment, study, or original development; as strictly necessary to meet unforeseen emergencies; extra construction services under the original tender's objectives that due to unforeseeable circumstances are necessary to complete the construction services (total value cannot exceed 50 percent of the main contract); purchases in exceptionally advantageous short-term cases, for example unusual disposal, unsolicited innovative proposals, liquidation; commodities; contracts awarded to design contest winners consistent with these provisions & judged independently; & new construction services of repeated similar services initially awarded by open, or by selective tender complying with these provisions if the initial procurement notice stated limited tendering may be used.
Awarding contracts	Supplier determined fully capable of undertaking the contract & whose tender offers the best value for money; or the lowest price; or is the most advantageous in terms of the essential requirements & evaluation criteria contained in the tender documentation.
Multiple thresholds	
New Zealand	Goods & services = 130,000 SDR; Construction = 5,000,000 SDR
Hong Kong	Goods & services = 130,000 SDR; Construction = 5,000,000 SDR

17.5 **Using Government Procurement as Industry Policy**

The WTO noted in its 2011 "Trade Policy Review of Australia" (WTO, 2011) that:

> *Australia has continued to use government procurement as an instrument of economic policy aimed at fostering industrial development in certain sensitive areas (e.g. real estate property or accommodation, R&D services, and motor vehicles) that are exempt from the mandatory procurement procedures applying to procurement above certain thresholds. The target of sourcing at least 10 percent of purchase value from small and medium-sized enterprises (SMEs), as well as preference margins for local suppliers and local-content requirements by certain state governments have been maintained and, in certain areas, reinforced but applied in line with FTA commitments.* (Italics mine)

That this situation has not changed, or has probably worsened, is confirmed in the latest 2015 WTO "Trade Policy Review" (WTO, 2015), which states:

> *Australia has continued to use government procurement as an instrument of economic policy aimed at fostering industrial development in certain sensitive areas that are exempt from mandatory rules applying to procurement above certain thresholds. Procurement rules were amended, inter alia, to redefine procurement methods and adjust to new legislation's terminology. The target of sourcing at least 10 percent of purchase value from small and medium-sized enterprises (SMEs), as well as preference margins for local suppliers and local-content*

requirements by certain state governments have been maintained and, in certain areas, revised. However they are applied in line with RTA commitments. Foreign participation in the bidding may require the submission of an Australian Industry Participation Plan. (Italics mine)

Despite government procurement commitments in PTAs, Australia still uses Commonwealth and state procurement policies to meet industry policy and other localization objectives, such as regional development, local content—especially for SMEs—and assisting the development and employment opportunities, including for indigenous people. Thus, after reforming government procurement in the 1980s to remove interstate price preferences, reform stalled. Indeed, it has gone backwards by replacing more transparent price preferences with murky and discretionary mechanisms promoting localization. These policies need reforming and PTAs are not contributing; indeed, they are entrenching these negative developments by excluding such measures from commitments. Unfortunately, governments are assessing the economic value of PTAs by the ambiguous extent to which they open foreign markets instead of the degree to which they promote self-liberalization, where most of the gains to Australia are available.

Unlike in Australia, New Zealand procurement has seemingly remained relatively open and non-discriminatory on an "unconditional" MFN basis in practice, and has not been used significantly as an industry policy measure.

17.5.1 PRICE PREFERENCES

The ANZGPA did not end price preferences for Australian content, despite the commitment to non-discrimination and national treatment. Instead, the state price preferences were extended equally to New Zealand suppliers by including them in the Australian content. This made Australia's government procurement system more discriminatory against non-New Zealand suppliers. Thus, the ANZ single procurement market was achieved by adding greater discrimination against other countries, thereby raising the likelihood of diverting government purchases from more efficient non-Tasman suppliers, to Australia's economic cost.

Australian PTAs similarly have not resulted in Australian states removing their price preferences. NSW's response, for example, was to remove them for large enterprises and instead to focus preferences on SMEs, which, with industry policies, are exempt from covered procurement. It subsequently removed these price preferences on SMEs, but not because they had to under PTA commitments. WA—the only state currently with price preferences, including for SMEs—removed their application for businesses located in the United States or Chile for "covered procurements." Thus, the imported content impost is not applied to any portion of a bid that comprises goods or services imported from New Zealand, the US or Chile. Again, rather than removing price discrimination outright,

Australia's procurement regime in WA became more discriminatory against non-PTA parties. To the extent that these price preferences were used to assist SMEs (and possibly industry development), they would have been in any event excluded from Australia's PTA commitments.

National treatment obligations in PTAs only apply to covered procurement, leaving plenty of scope to apply such price preferences. Also, national treatment does not require their removal, but rather that they be extended uniformly to PTA partners. Thus embedding national treatment into PTAs does not necessarily mean the end of price preferences.

17.5.2 WHAT ARE REPLACING PRICE PREFERENCES?

Australia, with the exception of WA, has removed price preferences favoring domestic suppliers. However, the price preferences are being replaced by murkier and more (economically) costly forms of discrimination, representing a step backwards. These non-transparent and discretionary measures may have a greater impact on prices and resource allocation than price preferences. This is similar to the substitution of tariffs with non-tariff measures that has accompanied reduced tariffs under the WTO.[51]

This highlights a general weakness of trade agreements. Governments will always fashion their commitments to provide leeway to assist domestic industries if the political economy at home necessitates providing selective industry assistance. The evidence supporting the argument that trade negotiations can successfully address this problem by mounting pressure from exporters benefiting via enhanced market access abroad to counter the demands by other sectors for import protection has proved thin. Similarly, there is little evidence globally that trade agreements have reduced non-tariff measures "on the ground" rather than simply "on paper." Hence the crucial role of unilateralism in liberalizing trade, including of government procurement policies.

All states and the Commonwealth now operate extensive "buy local" arrangements as integral parts of their procurement. They require tenderers to prepare various plans (e.g., industry participation plans) that must be submitted in the tender outlining proposed actions to provide Australian firms, especially SMEs, with supply opportunities. State and Commonwealth government objectives, such as promoting regional development and local industries (including SMEs), are to be taken into account in determining value for money. In some states—such as SA, WA, and Tasmania—such plans for local content

[51] As the world and trade agreements have focused on reducing transparent tariffs easily cut by negotiations, application of formulae and verification, NTM use rose as governments were encouraged to move out of tariffs—economically the least costly form of protection—into non-transparent and economically more damaging trade restrictions.

use must be given significant minimum weightings in the tender evaluation, with wide discretion to raise them where considered appropriate. While it is claimed that these procurement arrangements are not designed to favor local industries over those from other states and abroad, and are still to meet value for money, the reality is more obscure and dubious.

While value for money is still in principle the overarching goal, it has increasingly been broadened to incorporate government local content and regional development objectives, especially promoting SMEs, which are often contradictory.[52] Increasingly, evaluating contracts is being interpreted in practice as value for money subject to meeting governments' industrial development goals. Thus discrimination persists, but it is now more discretionary and disguised.

Published procurement figures show that almost all Commonwealth and state contracts are still let to local industries, including SEMs, using almost entirely local content. Moreover, this is increasing not falling. In state procurement, almost all contracts are supplied by ANZ firms, including own-state suppliers using own-state local content. For example, most (96 percent) of all SA procurement contracts let in 2012–13 were to ANZ suppliers (98 percent by value); over two-thirds of total contracts were with SA suppliers (80 percent by value), and only 4 percent (2 percent by value) were let overseas. The share, by value, of contracts with SA suppliers rose from 42 percent in 2011–12 to 51 percent in 2012–13.

While this may be partially explained by the natural advantages of dealing with easily accessible local suppliers and in many cases by their efficiency, the extremely high share of local participation and content is suspicious. It adds credence to the argument that a significant contributing factor is the hidden and discretionary discrimination that still abounds, and is worsening, in Australian procurement policies. It would be in Australia's national interest to reform such discrimination at all government levels.

17.5.3 EFFECTIVENESS OF TRADE AGREEMENTS IN OPENING GOVERNMENT PROCUREMENT MARKETS

ANZ's experience with trade agreements not opening their procurement markets to international competition is not unique. Considerable evidence suggests this is also the case internationally. Empirically, it seems that neither the GPA nor PTAs have

[52] For example, SMEs are commonly likely to be at a cost disadvantage compared to large firms because they simply lack economies of scale and hence would be unable to come first on a simple ranking of value for money. Thus one way of discriminating in favor of SMEs would be for the procurement agency to let smaller individual contracts instead of aggregating them into one large contract so as to lessen their cost disadvantage.

substantially reduced governments' propensity to "buy national," highlighting the difficulty of regulating non-transparent areas via international treaties (Rickard and Kono, 2011, 2014). Another study based on Switzerland and Japan found that foreign access in services procurement has not risen since negotiation of the GPA (Shingal, 2011).

This is not surprising, as trade agreements are usually negotiated intentionally to have minimal impact on self-measures, focusing instead on getting other parties to liberalize policies. In such circumstances, it is little wonder that the impact of trade agreements on promoting self-liberalization is minimal, even though this is where the main economic gains would accrue. Trade agreements rarely lead domestic reforms; at best, they can follow unilateral reforms and help lock them in, but even in this role they are imperfect. This certainly seems to be the case for Australian government procurement, and PTAs in general.

Not only is the coverage of commitments inadequate, enforceability is also lacking. The loopholes and ambiguity in government procurement commitments under PTAs and the GPA, together with the non-transparent and discretionary measures often utilized to protect government procurement which make them hard to detect and objectively qualify, undermine enforceability. Thus, it is not surprising that there have been few formal WTO disputes among GPA parties; mounting these challenges is difficult and likely to fail. The same applies to PTAs. Moreover, informal discussions and consultations under the GPA and PTAs, to the extent they occur, are also likely to lead to minimal improvements.

17.5.4 MOTIVATION FOR MAKING COMMITMENTS ON GOVERNMENT PROCUREMENT IN TRADE AGREEMENTS FLAWED ECONOMICALLY

Australia's motivation for making government procurement commitments in trade agreements, including PTAs, is based on the flawed notion that obtaining greater access to overseas procurement markets is what trade policy is primarily about. However, evidence shows clearly that what is of most economic gain to a country is opening its own policies to foreign competition. Australia should use its trade negotiations, including on government procurement, to do this if PTAs are going to be of significant benefit. Otherwise, trade agreements will continue to be more about achieving non-economic factors and will continue to be oversold by governments on their economic benefits.

Since all parties approach trade negotiations, including on government procurement, from a mercantilist perspective, they inevitably under-perform in opening markets. Consequently, broad and misleading statements and estimates of export benefits actually realized are advanced that do not reflect reality and the many exceptions to covered procurement included in PTAs. They rank poorly compared to unilateral reforms as part of a country's domestic micro-economic agenda. Unilateralism must therefore remain the "main game in town" in setting a country's trade measures, which are ultimately domestic policy. The danger is that with greater focus on trade negotiations, governments will lose sight of the far greater benefits that can arise from self-liberalization, and effectively make this conditional on obtaining overseas market access.

Mercantilists, of which there are many among trade officials and politicians, would argue that Australia is benefiting substantially in its government procurement negotiations by getting better access to foreign procurement markets. They would argue that getting market access abroad without self-liberalizing in negotiations is a win-win situation. But mercantilists are never correct economically. They fail to appreciate that the main economic gains to Australia accrue from self-reform, and assume that trading partners with which the country is negotiating PTAs are somehow less successful than Australia in negotiating to retain trade restrictions protecting their procurement markets. The negotiations are based on the mistaken view that outcomes are a zero-sum game, and hence trade negotiators must "outsmart" each other to try and maximize benefits at the expense of trading partners.

Unfortunately, Australia is assessing trade agreements not on the extent to which they promote unambiguous national-welfare enhancing self-liberalization where most gains arise, but on the extent to which they promote ambiguous marketing opening abroad, which is usually largely illusory and/or of uncertain economic benefit.

17.5.5 The Main Restrictions to Government Procurement Often Lie Elsewhere

Often the main restrictions on foreigners accessing a country's government procurement markets have little to do in practice with government procurement arrangements. A major example is with services, which are increasingly being procured by governments.

To tender for government projects, foreign suppliers must first be able to trade their services with the country. For example, if foreign investment barriers restrict them from establishing a commercial presence (mode 3 under the GATS), then they will be unable to access the government procurement market. Similarly, restrictions on foreign suppliers exporting services cross-border (mode 1) or by temporarily moving persons (mode 4) can also hinder their capacity to competitively supply services. Thus, so long as these restrictions to trade in services exist, no amount of government procurement reform will open the market to foreign suppliers.[53] Liberalizing trade in services (especially mode 3) in these cases should be the main priority. Again evidence shows that trade agreements,

[53] While the GATS recognizes this link, its commitments on MFN, national treatment, and market access do not apply to government procurement of services (GATS Article XIII). Multilateral negotiations on government procurement in services under the GATS were to be held by 1997, but these have not occurred.

including PTAs, achieve little actual services liberalization, and that unilateral reforms offer the best way forward.

PTAs also introduce non-tariff measures on government procurement trade via rules-of-origin. Goods not meeting the PTA rules-of-origin set on trade between parties are not covered by commitments on government procurement.

17.5.6 WILL NEW ZEALAND'S ACCESSION TO AND AUSTRALIA'S PROBABLE MEMBERSHIP OF THE GPA HELP?

In terms of promoting self-liberalization of government procurement policies, the answer is highly unlikely. As accession will become no more than a means of exchanging concessions with minimal impact on actual government procurement practices of the parties, realized economic gains to ANZ are likely to be minimal, despite government claims of large benefits via increased exports from opening overseas procurement markets.

For example, the Australian DFAT indicates that joining the GPA would provide meaningful and legally binding market access abroad, especially to China on its accession, even though it also states that Australian firms are not automatically disqualified from participation in GPA member markets. While such market access benefits are tantalizing to governments and industry, in reality such export gains from trade agreements are often illusory at worst, and highly overstated at best. In the case of AUSFTA, for instance, DFAT claimed at the time that it gave Australian suppliers access to the US federal procurement market, worth at least US$535 billion annually, and would open thirty-one state governments to Australia. However, such access was seriously constrained by many exceptions negotiated by the United States (as did Australia). The AUSFTA study commissioned by DFAT to highlight AUSFTA's economic gains to Australia unrealistically assumed that its suppliers would achieve 30 percent as much penetration in the US market as Canadian businesses, thereby providing export benefits to Australia of $200 million annually. However, a more realistic estimate would have been to reduce these benefits to about one-eighth, or about $25 million annually (Dee, 2004). It is even unclear if these more modest amounts have been realized.

Thus, Australia will achieve little in the way of economic benefits from joining the GPA unless it uses these negotiations to reform its worsening government procurement arrangements, where most gains lie. Since it has not done this in its PTAs, largely because it is virtually impossible given the mercantilism approach inherent in trade negotiations, there is no reason to believe it will happen in any GPA negotiations. Australia will almost certainly base its negotiated GPA offers on its PTA commitments, most notably AUSFTA. Thus, the same coverage weaknesses and significant exclusions will continue to allow non-transparent and discretionary Australian government procurement practices to discriminate in favor of industrial development and local content.

Indeed, if joining the GPA, like signing PTAs in general, were subject to a proper benefit cost analysis they would probably fail, at least on economic gains. Many of the advertised benefits—such as market access abroad—would be heavily discounted, and other claimed gains—such as helping Australia adopt liberalizing measures on an unconditional MFN basis because by their nature they cannot be applied discriminatorily—would be ignored completely. Many of the costs—such as failure to enhance self-liberalization—would be magnified.

At least New Zealand's government procurement policies seem relatively open in comparison, so that locking in its unilateral openness may have some benefits. However, to the extent that it used the negotiations to maintain some discriminatory practices, joining the GPA represents a lost opportunity for further reform.

17.5.7 PROLIFERATION OF "RED TAPE"

Many of the disciplines included in PTAs and GPA commitments on government procurement cover methods and procedures to be followed during the tendering cycle. These cover, for example, publication of tender information, minimum time limits when issuing tenders, rules governing the form of tender, and publication of tender awards. While stipulating such procedures and processes and applying some minimum standards may be useful, applying them is not costless. They add significant "red tape" that can make the tendering cycle more cumbersome and costly for governments and bidders. Thus a balance is needed, with the worst of all outcomes possibly occurring. Trade agreements are imposing such costs without much opening of procurement markets to foreign competition.

The complexity and cumbersomeness of Australian procurement systems have also increased, especially at the state level, largely coinciding with the shift from relatively straightforward means of discriminating locally—such as price preferences—to hidden discretionary measures that involve local content plans and weightings to be applied in awarding contracts to still attain, in principle, best value for money but also having to take of account other often contradictory objectives, like promoting regional industry development, especially for SMEs. Such arrangements compound "red tape" and make tendering more costly for suppliers and procurement entities.

17.6 Conclusions

ANZ trade agreements have, by and large, had minimal impact on government procurement policies. Reforms in both countries substantially pre-date their PTAs. These reforms can be traced back to the mid-1980s when, for example, Australia unilaterally removed inter-state price preferences, including for New Zealand, to form a single procurement market, and a few states and the Commonwealth removed them against imported content.

Those states that maintained price preferences extended them to New Zealand content. Thus, the single Tasman market was achieved by Australia extending discriminatory practices to protect New Zealand content, at the expense of non-ANZ suppliers. New Zealand—seemingly having no significant price preferences or other discriminatory practices—continued to practice national treatment with minimal exceptions on an unconditional MFN basis. New Zealand took substantial unilateral steps to reform its government procurement market without using trade agreements and conditional MFN.

These reforms were reflected in the APEC Non-binding Principles on Government Procurement, in which ANZ participated. By the late 1990s, they had adopted government procurement arrangements, at least at the central level, considered consistent with these principles. Price preferences operated by some states remained inconsistent, however, but were permitted owing to APEC's non-binding nature.

While New Zealand has continued to unilaterally maintain this relatively open government procurement market, the opposite is true for Australia. Its procurement system still has major areas needing reform, both at the Commonwealth and state level. One state, WA, still retains price preferences, although not in regard to covered procurements with trading partners under PTAs. The states have ensured their procurement arrangements are consistent with PTA commitments, but in a way that has not reformed procurement policies.

Indeed, Australia's procurement system has gone backwards, especially at the state level. While price preferences have largely been eliminated (not because of PTAs), they have been replaced with murky, less transparent discretionary measures designed to promote industry development and local content, especially involving SMEs. Such open-ended discriminatory measures are difficult to evaluate and are highly likely to be more distortionary and economically inefficient than price preferences that are transparent, work directly through the price system, and cap the assistance potentially provided to domestic suppliers. Accompanying these changes has been also increased complexity and "red tape" in government procurement arrangements, especially at the state level, which has made contracting more costly for tenderers and procuring entities.

Australia's PTAs have not prevented these backward developments. Instead, they have entrenched them by negotiating commitments based on "conditional liberalization" whereby the national treatment obligation only applies to covered procurement, which excludes Australia's use of government procurement policies to promote industry development and local content, especially by SMEs and indigenous businesses.

Australia has unfortunately negotiated its PTAs to minimize their impact on government procurement policies, both centrally and at the state level. PTAs, including in New Zealand, are being incorrectly assessed using a mercantilist approach highlighting the (ambiguous) economic benefits of increased exports due to opening foreign markets, rather than the extent to which they promote self-liberalization, from where most of the gains to Australia would flow. Reforming its government procurement policies, irrespective of what other countries do, would yield most economic benefits to Australia, and hence should be the priority. As evidence repeatedly shows, PTAs achieve little actual liberalization of non-tariff measures in practice, especially when the fine print is read and other restrictions are taken into account. This is because PTAs are negotiated on the basis that offering self-liberalization is a "cost" or "concession" to receive the benefits of increased market access abroad.

Thus, Australia's PTAs have played a minimal role in promoting much needed reform to government procurement. It still uses these policies to achieve industry policy and local content objectives, both at the state and Commonwealth levels, undermining national welfare. Reforming these policies requires unilateral reforms—PTAs will not achieve this.

ANZ's PTA offers are repetitive, which for Australia involves regurgitating wide-ranging general and specific exemptions to benefit SMEs and promote local content generally to allow its murky discretionary discriminatory policies.

ANZ had not joined the GPA because they considered it a bad agreement due to conditional MFN, major exclusions from covered procurement, and overly prescriptive approaches to government procurement. However, while the GPA still suffers from these weaknesses (as do ANZ PTA commitments), New Zealand has just acceded to it with offers closely resembling those in its PTAs. New Zealand's GPA commitments have primarily locked in its unilateral and unconditional MFN openness, although there are still exceptions to national treatment that may accommodate some discretionary policies, especially by local government. If this covers substantial exemptions in practice, then GPA membership—as with its PTAs—represents lost opportunities for New Zealand to further reform its government procurement system.

Australia has commenced negotiations to accede to the GPA. Such membership is highly likely to follow its approach in PTAs of excluding from commitments discretionary discriminatory procurement measures, entrenching policies favoring industrial development and local content, especially for SMEs and the indigenous population. Commitments will almost certainly repeat PTA offers, especially AUSFTA, thus prompting no domestic reform in areas that matter, while increasing "red tape." Australia seems set on erroneously assessing accession based on achieving (dubious) export gains from greater market access to foreign procurement markets, rather than on whether it advances self-liberalization of procurement policies, where most gains unambiguously lie.

The failure of trade agreements to open ANZ procurement markets is reflected internationally. Studies have shown that government procurement commitments in PTAs and the GPA have not opened procurement markets. Hence inflated assessments of the extent to which trade agreements will create exports to foreign procurement markets must largely be discounted to maintain reality.

Given the politicization of PTAs in ANZ and the governments' fetish for negotiating them, which reflects international developments, a serious policy shortcoming in domestic processes is the severe lack of transparency of such negotiations. ANZ experience in negotiating trade agreements highlights the secrecy with which governments and trade ministries conduct such negotiations. Trade ministries holding consultations with interested stakeholders, especially the private sector, achieve little and inadequately address these transparency concerns. By the time the negotiated agreement and its contents, including the country's offers, are released for public scrutiny and assessment, also by parliament, the government has "signed off" on it. There are no sensible reasons why such details, including the government's offers, cannot be released publicly during the negotiations to enable public scrutiny. Such transparency would produce better decision outcomes on national welfare and make governments and trade ministries more accountable for their negotiations. After all, trade policy is domestic economic policy. Their secrecy primarily reflects flawed mercantilism that it will produce better results. This is untrue, and in reality secrecy is kept to allow trade ministries and governments to keep control over the negotiations by avoiding public scrutiny.

As trade ministries have vested interests in negotiating trade agreements, experience shows that they cannot be relied upon to professionally assess their economic assessments on the national welfare implications. Efforts in ANZ, as elsewhere, have highlighted that so-called independent studies commissioned by trade ministries on the gains from trade agreements are flawed and biased towards government views. Once the decision to conduct such a study is made, these are always supportive of the agreement. The public NIA prepared by New Zealand on GPA accession was highly inadequate, as was the study commissioned by DFAT to assess the gains to Australia of AUSFTA, including the export benefits from the perceived government procurement access to the US.

It is therefore disappointing that ANZ governments have not let their primary trade and other micro-economic advisors, including the Productivity Commission, play any role in assessing the national welfare effects of trade agreements, especially PTAs, on their economies. Without this constraint, the ANZ governments are given free rein to exaggerate and oversell the economic benefits of trade agreements, including on government procurement. Hopefully, Australia will enable the Productivity Commission to conduct an independent study of its GPA accession.

If, as appears probable, governments are going to persist in pursuing PTAs, it is vital that these discriminatory arrangements do not come at the expense of the WTO and, more importantly, unilateral trade reforms, both of which are based on the key principle of non-discrimination (unconditional MFN). However, experience suggests achieving this is easier said than done. PTAs tend to displace these other superior approaches to reform, as the example of government procurement in ANZ highlights.

REFERENCES

Dee, P. 2004. "The Australia US Free Trade Agreement, An Assessment." Paper Prepared for the Senate Select Committee on the Free Trade Agreement between Australia and the United States of America, Canberra, June.

Rickard, S. J. and Kono, D. Y. 2011. "Policy Transparency and Preferential Trade Agreements." APSA 2011 Annual Meeting Paper.

Rickard, S. J. and Kono, D. Y. 2014. "Think Globally, Buy Locally: International Agreements and Government Procurement." *The Review of International Organizations* 9(3): 333–52.

Shingal, A. 2011. "Services Procurement under the WTO's Agreement on Government Procurement: Whither Market Access?" *World Trade Review* 10(4): 527–49.

WTO 2009. "Trade Policy review of New Zealand," Geneva.

WTO 2011. "Trade Policy Review of Australia," Geneva.

WTO 2015. "Trade Policy Review of Australia," Geneva.

Part III

Taking Stock and Looking Forward

18 International Public Procurement

From Scant Facts to Hard Data

Lucian Cernat and Zornitsa Kutlina-Dimitrova

18.1 Introduction

Public procurement is a major component of public spending, with a sizable impact on the total demand of any domestic economy. Public procurement expenditures represent about one-third of total government expenditures in Organisation for Economic Co-operation and Development (OECD) countries. In 2013, in GDP terms, government procurement expenditures as measured in national accounts amounted to an average of almost 14 percent of gross domestic product (GDP) in the European Union (EU) and to more than 10 percent of GDP in the United States (US).[1] But actual public procurement spending is in reality higher, as these national accounts aggregates do not include procurement spending of public utilities providers. For example, in the EU the total public procurement spending (including utilities) accounted for €2.4 trillion, corresponding to nearly 19 percent of EU GDP in 2011.[2]

Around the world, public procurement contracts historically have to a large extent benefitted domestic companies, thus ensuring a safe market for local suppliers of goods and services. This preference for domestic producers, the so-called "home bias," raises serious efficiency considerations. It can significantly distort trade flows and international specialization, particularly in sectors characterized by a large share of public consumption in total demand and in sectors affected by monopolistic competition (Trionfetti, 2000). Moreover, domestic preferences in government procurement such as "buy national" provisions may alter international companies' outsourcing choices and significantly affect production decisions along global value chains. Empirical evidence of the presence of this home bias is provided in a series of studies (Brülhart and Trionfetti, 2001; Shingal, 2011, 2015). The combination of a large share of government expenditures

[1] See OECD statistics, available at <http://stats.oecd.org/> (accessed December 5, 2014).

[2] See also the EU official submission to the WTO reported under Article XIX:5 of the GPA agreement, available at <http://www.wto.org/english/tratop_e/gproc_e/notnat_e.htm#statPro> (accessed July 24, 2016).

in GDP and the "home bias" characteristics makes public procurement one of the few fields in which liberalization efforts at the international level have substantial untapped potential, and thus an area of growing importance in international negotiations.

Liberalization efforts in the area of government procurement at the multilateral level started as early as 1979, leading to the adoption of the plurilateral Government Procurement Agreement (GPA) under the aegis of the World Trade Organization (WTO). However, only a small set of countries undertook binding commitments to open their procurement markets for foreign goods and service suppliers. In recent years, the importance of liberalizing public procurement markets has been recognized not only as part of the GPA negotiations, but also in a bilateral/regional context. A growing number of recent free trade agreements (FTAs) contain legally binding public procurement provisions with various degrees of liberalization ambition.

Despite gradual improvements in the openness of public procurement markets for GPA members and many FTA partners, a large number of WTO members are not part of the GPA. It is still fair to say that by and large, public procurement markets around the world are yet to become part of future liberalization rounds.

There are many intrinsic and political economy reasons why public procurement (alongside other economic activities) is less prone to internationalization. However, unlike other negotiating areas where progress is sometimes difficult, public procurement negotiations are fraught with an additional difficulty: the lack of often basic comparable information (e.g., market size, the cross-border share of foreign company participation and geographical breakdown, or a clear taxonomy of barriers and their restrictiveness) that renders the negotiating process even more complex. The lack of such basic statistics also negatively affects the implementation and monitoring efforts of existing agreements.

Given the importance of having hard data on public procurement and a common analytical base, one of the main aims of this chapter is to suggest ways to deal with this lack of a sound analytical framework that is needed for successful procurement negotiations and implementation efforts. The chapter goes further and argues that negotiating partners need to frontload this analytical infrastructure as part of their current and future negotiating agenda. It also puts forward an empirically driven conceptual approach for how to structure and adapt these future data collection efforts in order to identify existing barriers to international public procurement, with a view to addressing them in future negotiations.

The rest of the chapter is organized as follows. Section 18.2 takes account of the importance of government procurement provisions at the multilateral and EU level, inter alia, by reviewing the public procurement disciplines found in the RTAs announced to the WTO. Using national accounts statistics, Section 18.3 describes public procurement patterns in terms of the size of procurement markets, the composition of procurement spending, and the level of government procurement. Section 18.4 puts forward a basic conceptual framework for future data collection on public procurement that would best serve the future negotiating agenda in this area. Finally, Section 18.5 concludes and identifies a straightforward set of priorities for this important policy area.

18.2 **Internationalization of Public Procurement**

18.2.1 THE MULTILATERAL DIMENSION OF PUBLIC PROCUREMENT

At the multilateral level, government procurement is negotiated under the aegis of the WTO. Liberalization efforts in this area started in 1979, when the Tokyo Round Code on Government Procurement was signed. More than a decade later, in 1987, the agreement was amended and in 1994, joint efforts of the negotiating countries led to the Agreement on Government Procurement, which was signed on the same date as the agreement establishing the WTO. Further liberalization efforts in the area of government procurement in a plurilateral context led to the entry into force of the revised GPA on April 6, 2014. The revised GPA is characterized by an extended scope, as a number of additional government entities have now been included. The coverage of the revised GPA has also been enlarged by adding new services and public procurement activities. The gains from the extended GPA are assessed to range from US$80 to $100 billion annually (WTO, 2014a).

The GPA also involves provisions on the collection and submission of statistical data on government procurement by the GPA parties, pursuant to Article XIX:5. This data-reporting requirement is supposed to cover the number of contracts awarded and a breakdown of the award value by government entity and type of contract (i.e., works, services, or supplies).[3] In addition, the GPA data submissions by parties should provide information on cross-border purchases and the country of origin of the purchased goods and services.[4]

Despite these GPA provisions, the process of data collection and submission has not functioned well, as acknowledged by the WTO Secretariat (WTO, 2014b). For instance, there are GPA countries that have never submitted a statistical report (such as Israel and Iceland), and countries for which the latest report submitted dates a few years back (to 2008 in the case of the United States).

[3] This requirement applies only for procurement covered by the GPA. Note that obligations may differ across GPA annexes.

[4] The revised GPA has amended the obligation to provide cross-border statistics to the extent that such statistics are available.

Even more important, in an international context, is the fact that cross-border data are scarce. Looking at the GPA parties who have submitted a statistical report, only two have provided information on cross-border procurement purchases in recent years: Japan and Chinese Taipei. There is information on the cross-border dimension of government procurement submitted by the EU and Korea, but it dates back to 2007 and 2003, respectively. Apart from the fact that information on cross-border procurement expenditure is outdated, even where such information is available it covers in general only a few countries of origin. In the case of Japan, for example, a breakdown is provided for government procurement purchases from five countries and then the rest of the world. The most complete information on the origin of the goods and services purchased by governments abroad is submitted by Korea, which includes cross-border procurement from fourteen countries and the rest of the world in 2003.

The fact that the data on cross-border government procurement are so scarce makes any attempt to analyze the economic impact of liberalization efforts in this area an ambitious challenge. This applies not only to an economic impact assessment of market opening in public procurement at the multilateral level, but also to identifying the economic benefits of public procurement provisions in bilateral FTAs.

The latter is crucial also because there is a trend for increased importance of government procurement provisions in regional trade agreements (RTAs). Analyzing all the RTAs announced to the WTO in terms of stand-alone public procurement provisions (a chapter or an article, for example) shows that, until the year 2000, out of all agreements announced to WTO only seventeen had a separate legal provision on procurement.[5] From 2000 until today, the amount of agreements with a stand-alone procurement article or chapter has almost quadrupled, reaching eighty-eight FTAs. This shows that negotiating countries are aware of the importance and untapped potential of cross-border procurement markets and are willing to increase market opening and/or improve transparency provisions.

18.2.2 GOVERNMENT PROCUREMENT IN THE EUROPEAN UNION'S FTAs

Since 1970, the EU has announced forty FTAs to the WTO, out of which thirty-six have already entered into force.[6,7] An analysis of these FTAs shows that none of the thirteen

[5] For this analysis, the WTO's list of all RTAs was used, available at: <http://rtais.wto.org/UI/PublicAllRTAList.aspx> (accessed December 8, 2014). Of these, the agreements on custom unions were excluded.

[6] As at December 4, 2014. Taken from the WTO's list of RTAs at: <http://rtais.wto.org/UI/PublicAllRTAList.aspx> (accessed December 8, 2014).

[7] The four EU agreements that have been negotiated but are yet to be notified are with Canada, Singapore, SADC, and West Africa. They have been included in the data analysis of this sub-section.

RTAs signed prior to 2000 had a stand-alone chapter or article on public procurement.[8] Of the twenty-four EU FTAs signed since 2000, however, thirteen have a separate public procurement provision (corresponding to a share of 54 percent). Of these thirteen EU FTAs containing separate public procurement provisions, nine have a dedicated a chapter on public procurement and the remaining four contain a stand-alone article on government procurement.[9]

This trend shows that the importance of bilateral negotiations in the area of public procurement has increased substantially and they are still to play a major role in upcoming EU trade negotiations, as this is a key negotiating area in the Transatlantic Trade and Investment Partnership (TTIP) with the US.

18.3 Characteristic of Public Procurement Markets

This section aims at quantifying the size, composition and level of government procurement. The data sources used for this purpose are EUROSTAT and OECD national accounts statistics. The advantage of using national accounts lies in the cross-country comparability of the data, as national statistical authorities follow the same methodology for collecting and reporting the data (OECD, 2013). However, as already mentioned, these public procurement aggregates do not include procurement spending of state-owned corporations, such as state-owned utilities, and therefore the size of the market is underestimated in countries where utilities providers are state-owned. Public procurement, as measured by the OECD and in this section, comprises of intermediate consumption (e.g., government expenditures on IT systems or stationary), social transfers in kind via market producers (e.g., medical expenses ultimately refunded by national social security systems), and gross fixed capital formation (infrastructure expenditures on building new roads for example).[10,11] The data cover the most recent year for which data for almost all OECD and all EU member states is available, which is 2012.

[8] The agreements between the EU and Israel and the EU and Korea were not considered as having a separate public procurement provision, as both parties are members of the GPA and the procurement provision mentioned in the FTA refers to the GPA.

[9] For this analysis "Titles" in RTAs are considered as chapters.

[10] Note that government procurement as accounted for in national accounts may be overestimated, as the above-mentioned categories may include non-procurement government expenditures (OECD, 2011).

[11] The public procurement data analyzed in this section include total procurement spending at all levels: central, state, and local. They do not, however, include expenditures of state-owned corporations, such as state-owned utilities providers.

18.3.1 SIZE OF PROCUREMENT MARKETS BASED ON NATIONAL ACCOUNTS DATA

In 2012 the size of government procurement markets ranged from nearly 23 percent of GDP in the Netherlands to 8 percent in Switzerland (Figure 18.1). Public procurement expenditures in GDP terms are particularly high in Finland (18 percent), Sweden (16 percent), Japan (16 percent), and Denmark and France (15 percent). In the US, government procurement spending accounts for nearly 11 percent, and in Canada for 14 percent of GDP.

In 2012 the average procurement spending in the Eurozone stood at almost 14 percent and for the sample of countries presented in this section it stood at 15 percent (Figure 18.1). This shows the significant importance of public procurement entities as buyers of goods and services in an economy. Converted into absolute values, the size of these public procurement markets in 2012 was nearly €1.8 trillion in the EU, nearly €1.3 trillion in the Eurozone, and $1.7 trillion in the US. If there was any doubt, the magnitude of these figures also shows the importance of achieving cost-efficiency in government spending. For example, in the EU policy measures that would achieve savings on procurement expenditures of 10 percent would result in an efficiency gain of almost 1.4 percent of GDP, the equivalent of around €180 billion.

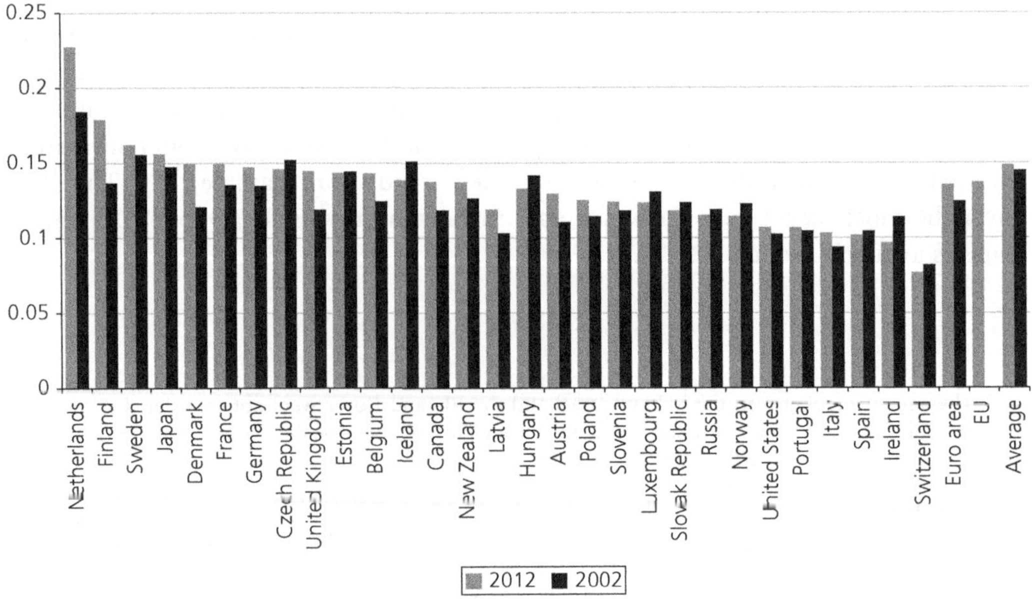

Figure 18.1. Public procurement in percent of GDP, 2012 and 2002

Source: EUROSTAT and OECD National Account Statistics (accessed December 5, 2014), and own calculations. *No complete data on Australia, Chile and Turkey. There are no data for the EU for the year 2002.

In this respect, an interesting analysis shows that the expected procurement cost decreases as the number of bidders for a contract increases, and especially so if the number of bidders reaches five or six (McAfee and McMillan, 1989). Consequently, policy measures which would foster international competition on government procurement markets, increase transparency of tendering procedures, and insure non-discrimination among bidders would induce cost savings with a significant impact on the entire economy.

From 2002 to 2012, procurement spending in relation to GDP increased in the Eurozone by 9 percent, and in respect to the average of the country sample included in Figure 18.1, by 3 percent. Government purchases increased the strongest in Finland (by 31 percent) and in the Netherlands and Denmark (by 24 percent). There are a few countries, however, in which procurement spending decreased in the ten-year period considered here. The strongest decreases took place in Ireland (15 percent) and Iceland (8 percent).

Finally, government procurement purchases account for a considerable amount not only of GDP but also of total government expenditure. In OECD countries, the share of public procurement expenditure in total government expenditure amounts to around 30 percent (OECD, 2013).

18.3.2 COMPOSITION OF PUBLIC PROCUREMENT

Comparable cross-country data on government procurement expenditures for aggregate categories is of great importance for assessing spending by broad categories. Figure 18.2

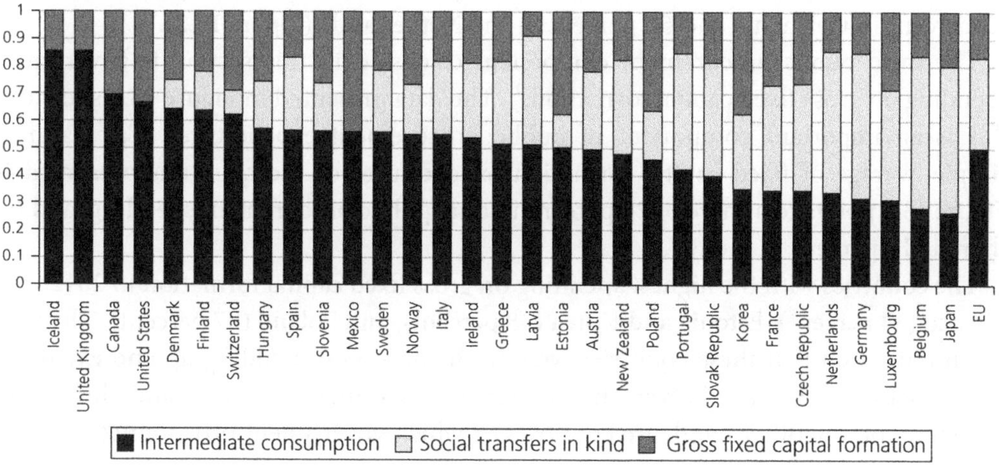

Figure 18.2. Public procurement composition by category, 2012

Source: EUROSTAT and OECD National Account Statistics (2011a, 2011b) (accessed December 5, 2014), and own calculations.

*No complete data on Australia, Chile and Turkey.

provides information on the composition of the three government procurement aggregates: intermediate consumption, gross fixed capital formation, and social transfers in kind among the country sample.

In general, intermediate consumption—that is government purchases of goods and services—is the most important government procurement expenditure. Looking at the average of the countries included in the sample, intermediate consumption accounts for 50 percent of total procurement purchases, and it accounts for 49 percent in the EU. However, intermediate consumption expenditures as a share of total procurement expenditures vary widely across the countries considered here. In Iceland and the UK, procurement of goods and services accounts for 85 percent of total expenditures (Figure 18.2). Canada and the United States are other examples of countries with high intermediate consumption expenditures shares (69 percent and 66 percent, respectively).

At the other end of the spectrum, intermediate consumption accounts for only 26 percent in Japan, 28 percent in Belgium, and 31 percent in Germany and Luxemburg.

The second most important component of public procurement spending is social transfers in kind via market producers. Calculating a simple average of the countries included in Figure 18.2 shows that 26 percent of total procurement is spent on social transfers. For the EU as a whole, the proportion of social transfers is higher and stood at 34 percent in 2012, reflecting the greater weight of the European social system as compared to the average of the countries considered here. There are also substantial differences across countries in this category of procurement expenditures. Spending on social transfers through market producers is practically non-existent in the United Kingdom, Iceland, the US, Canada, and Mexico. At the same time, government purchases of goods and services produced by companies and offered to households (e.g., medical care or special equipment) reaches 56 percent in Belgium, 54 percent in Japan, 53 percent in Germany, and 52 percent in the Netherlands (Figure 18.2).

The third public procurement component discussed in this section is government spending on gross fixed capital formation.[12] The data presented in Figure 18.2 show that this is an important component of public procurement expenditures. Calculating a simple average of fixed capital formation expenditures of the countries presented in Figure 18.2 points to a share of 24 percent in total public procurement spending, and the share is 17 percent in the EU.

The countries with the highest spending on gross fixed capital formation in 2012 were Mexico (44 percent), Estonia and Korea (38 percent), and Poland (37 percent). This may be an indication that these countries were in the process of building up and extending infrastructure capacities. Latvia, the Netherlands, Germany, Iceland, and the United Kingdom, on the other hand, are countries in which government procurement of fixed

[12] Gross fixed capital formation is the annual acquisition of capital less the sales of fixed assets.

assets as a share of total procurement is particularly low, standing at 9 percent in Latvia and 15 percent in the other four countries (Figure 18.2).

18.3.3 PUBLIC PROCUREMENT PATTERNS BY GOVERNMENT LEVEL

Gaining knowledge about public procurement expenditures by level of government is of great importance in the framework of negotiating international commitments in bilateral and multilateral agreements, as this gives an indication of the size of the public procurement market at central, state, and local levels. In this respect, Figure 18.3 depicts the share of central-level procurement in relation to general government (total) procurement and, as a residual, the share of sub-central-level procurement.

The breakdown of public procurement by level of government reveals vast differences between the countries considered here (Figure 18.3). Central-level procurement ranges from 80 percent in New Zealand to just 8 percent in Belgium. Central government expenditures account for 72 percent of the public procurement budget in Portugal, 68 percent in Ireland, and 61 percent in the United Kingdom. On the other hand, sub-central public authorities account for 87 percent of the public procurement expenditures in Germany and Canada, and 86 percent in Japan.

The reason for this immense gap lies to a large extent in the legal and regulatory architecture of the countries considered. Figure 18.3 shows that in general, federal states have significantly larger sub-central-level procurement compared to the rest of the countries. Indeed, local and state procurement of federal states like Belgium, Germany,

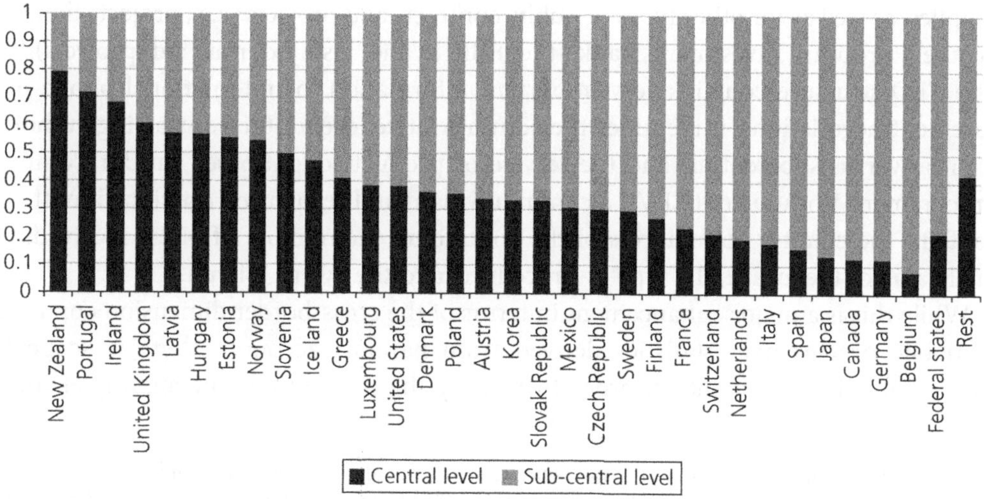

Figure 18.3. Public procurement expenditures by level of government, 2012

Source: EUROSTAT and OECD National Account Statistics (accessed December 5, 2014), and own calculations. *No complete data on Australia, Chile and Turkey.

Canada, Spain, Switzerland, Mexico, and the United States accounts on average for 78 percent of total national public procurement, whereas the average for the rest of the countries is 57 percent. Spending at the central level of non-federal countries is more than twice as high as the central-level spending of federal countries.

Nonetheless, some non-federal states, such as Japan, Italy, and the Netherlands, also have high spending ratios at the sub-central level.

18.4 **International Public Procurement: Modalities of Delivery**

Section 18.3 illustrated the existing statistical information on public procurement that can be derived from national accounts and data on overall public spending, essentially across OECD countries. Based on this standard source of data, one can derive a handful of useful indicators, such as public procurement market size, the distribution of spending between the central and sub-central level, expenditure patterns, and so on.

However, these national account figures do not provide information on cross-border public procurement. The reason for this is that many countries do not systematically make such figures available across various agencies, levels of government, and types of contract. Nevertheless, in a number of economies such information exists. One of the best known examples is the EU Tender Electronics Daily (TED) database. The TED database is part of the e-procurement system across Europe, which allows for the electronic publication of public tenders and awards for services, public works, and supplies, as well as for other types of public contracts and projects (e.g., projects financed by the European Investment Bank, the EBRD, and also external aid projects).[13,14] The TED structure contains very important information for international public procurement negotiations: it identifies the administrative level of the contracting authority (central versus sub-central) and the service or product sought based on the Common Procurement Vocabulary (CPV), a commonly used and recognized classification. It also contains the country and address of the contractor, the number of offers received, the final value of the award, the type of procedure, and the award criteria.[15]

While this is a major enhancement in terms of the cross-border dimension compared to public procurement statistics derived from national accounts, there is scope for considerable improvement. In order to identify the most important missing elements

[13] The TED database covers not only EU member states, but also EEA countries and Switzerland.

[14] A recent paper by Kutlina-Dimitrova and Lakatos (2014) analyzes the determinants of direct cross-border public procurement by using, *inter alia*, TED data.

[15] A growing number of countries, both developed and developing, have started to adopt comprehensive e-procurement systems covering similar types of data (or parts thereof) as the TED system.

that would be needed in an international negotiation on public procurement (and its subsequent monitoring and implementation), one has to consider the complexity of today's global economy and to draw inspiration from the way in which goods and services are delivered across borders in a non-public procurement context.

When looking at international public procurement transactions through this new lens, several important additional elements become apparent if one wants to capture the various ways in which "home bias" and discriminatory policies hamper the internationalization of public procurement.

The first dimension that needs to be taken into account when trying to generate statistics relevant for international public procurement negotiations is the "value-added" dimension, reflecting the existence of global supply chains.[16] The second important element that needs to be considered is the "mode of supply," a concept already widely used in services negotiations.[17] As in the case of services trade, public procurement purchases, irrespective of the type of contract (i.e., works, supplies, etc.), can take place under different modalities. Think of an infrastructure project involving setting up a new 4G mobile telecom network, a new power grid, a railway upgrade, or simply a new building. In all these cases, foreign companies can participate through various channels and ways of bidding, either directly from abroad or through local subsidiaries. In doing so, they will use a combination of domestic and imported goods and services needed for the public project. Alternatively, foreign companies can be subcontractors or merely suppliers of certain parts and/or intermediate services to a domestic company that will carry out the project.

Thus, one can differentiate between three key dimensions that comprise an international component in public procurement: (i) the nationality of the firm; (ii) the location of the bidding firm (located abroad, domestic subsidiary of a foreign firm, etc.); and (iii) the purchase of foreign value added along the supply chain, irrespective of the location and nationality of the companies winning the public tender. Based on these key dimensions, one can distinguish three main modalities of international public procurement of goods and services:

- **Direct cross-border international procurement:** a foreign company submitting a bid and winning "from abroad." This mode is conceptually similar to the traditional mode 1 for services trade.

[16] See, for instance, the EU-sponsored World Input-Output-Database (WIOD), the OECD–WTO Trade in Value Added (TiVA) database, and the associated literature for a comprehensive set of international trade in value-added indicators for both goods and services.

[17] A recent paper (Cernat and Kutlina-Dimitrova, 2014) argues that "modes of supply" also have to be considered in other trade areas (e.g., custom valuation), as there is large amount of services traded embodied into goods.

- **Commercial presence procurement:** a domestic subsidiary of a foreign company wins the public contract "locally." This mode is conceptually similar to mode 3 for services trade.
- **"Value-added" indirect international procurement:** a foreign company participates indirectly with parts and components (goods and services) without necessarily being part of the winning bid. In this case, the foreign company may supply goods and services to a domestic company winning the bid, or to another foreign company that received the public contract.

Equipped with this simple set of international procurement modalities, one can make better sense of the scant data currently available. Take the TED data, for instance, analyzed in Kutlina-Dimitrova and Lakatos (2014). These data only cover the direct cross-border public procurement contracts and do not distinguish specifically international procurement through a commercial presence (e.g., the public contracts won across the EU by domestic subsidiaries of foreign firms in Europe). Neither does the TED database (nor probably any other similar e-procurement platform in other countries) capture "value-added" international procurement, since there is no systematic assessment of the foreign value-added content in the final basket of goods and services purchased by public authorities. Therefore, the very few papers that have tried to quantify the foreign penetration of public procurement markets severely underestimate the actual openness, since they capture essentially one mode of supply and only a part of total international procurement.

The existing anecdotal evidence and the various case studies carried out in the past seem to suggest convincingly that, for a number of reasons, the value of public procurement through a commercial presence would be significantly higher than that of direct cross-border procurement (Ramboll/HTW Huhr, 2011). On the one hand, public procurement through a commercial presence may be less subject to discriminatory restrictions against foreign participation whenever national treatment is granted to foreign affiliates (as in the case of the EU procurement markets). On the other hand, there are good objective reasons why a commercial presence would be the preferred way of bidding, since given the complex technical nature of certain procurement contracts, both contracting authorities and prospective companies value proximity and local presence.

Value-added indirect procurement contracts also have certain specific characteristics. First, the GPA distinguishes clearly between companies and their goods and services provided under public procurement contracts. Therefore, the existing disciplines create a different set of rules when one looks at the products and services delivered, as opposed to a "company-based" approach. Similarly, domestic public procurement legislation subjects such value-added international participation to different rules than the foreign companies themselves. For instance, a particular procurement contract may be only open to domestic companies, but it may put no restrictions on the purchase of key components (such as steel or high-tech equipment) from foreign firms or on minimum local value added. Conversely, government procurement provisions may be very liberal with regards to foreign companies, but at the same time there might be strong discriminatory value-added "buy local" restrictions on imported intermediate goods and services.

Therefore, two clear conclusions come out of this conceptual taxonomy of different modalities of international procurement. First, any statistical indicators capturing openness in public procurement need to reflect the fact that foreign companies, as well as their goods and services, can become part of public contracts abroad under different modalities of international procurement. Incomplete data and definitive conclusions drawn based on only a subset of procurement modalities may lead to wrong political perceptions and policy priorities.

Second, having such a comprehensive and structured approach to public procurement data collection by modality of delivery (both under the new GPA statistical work program and as part of bilateral trade negotiations) would allow a more informed debate about the different nature of restrictions and barriers affecting each procurement mode of supply, and facilitate the implementation of existing rules. Some countries may be more restrictive towards one mode or another. Other countries may have an interest in trying to liberalize one mode or another in a particular negotiation, once more systematic data collection enables identification of the nature of the procurement market restrictions and the value of international procurement flows for each mode of supply.

18.5 **Challenges and Looking Ahead**

The current chapter has tried to argue in favor of a rather straightforward point: the internationalization of public procurement should be a key priority for trade negotiators, given the significant size of public procurement markets and the high level of restrictions that still persist, despite decades of attempts to arrive at binding commitments and less discriminatory policies.

However, this task is made more difficult by the absence of a suitable factual basis for negotiations. In the absence of hard data and clear indicators that measure existing international procurement flows, the "home bias" tendency and pronounced offensive interests may hamper progress on new, more liberal procurement rules, as well as monitoring and implementation of existing procurement provisions.

Comparable and commonly accepted figures based on a solid methodology are also needed to build consensus for new prospective members to understand what the benefits are from participating in future public procurement negotiations.

All these tasks remain daunting, but not impossible. For some modalities of international procurement (e.g., value-added indirect participation), the figures would have to rely on estimates, whereas for other modalities of delivery (e.g., direct cross-border or through a commercial presence) the actual data can be collected during the procurement process.

A first step would be to agree on an international procurement data collection methodology that all WTO members would be ready to apply in their domestic procurement legislation. The methodology could be tested and fine-tuned based on some pilot cases, covering countries with different legal systems and levels of development. The data collection process in developing countries could be supported by donors and other relevant international organizations (e.g., the OECD, the IMF, the World Bank, and UN agencies), with benefits also for a number of other domestic policy objectives. As happened in other trade and investment areas, policy-makers and the academic community could join forces to form the basis for a comparable and consistent data collection process that could eventually put public procurement on the same level of analytical rigor and data availability as the WTO trade negotiations in the goods and services areas.

ACKNOWLEDGMENTS

The opinions expressed in this chapter are the authors' own and do not necessarily reflect the views and opinions of the European Commission. The authors would like to thank Desislava Borisova for data analysis of the WTO list of all RTAs and their colleagues in DG TRADE for comments and fruitful discussions.

REFERENCES

Brülhart, M. and F. Trionfetti. 2001. "Industrial Specialisation and Public Procurement: Theory and Empirical Evidence." *Journal of Economic Integration* 16: 106–27.

Cernat, L. and Kutlina-Dimitrova, Z. 2014. "Thinking in a Box: A 'Mode 5' Approach to Services Trade." *Journal of World Trade* 48(6): 1109–27.

Kutlina-Dimitrova, Z. and Lakatos, C. 2014. "Determinants of Direct Cross-Border Public Procurement in EU Member States." Chief Economist Note 2014-2, Directorate General for Trade, European Commission.

McAfee, R. and McMillan, J. 1989. "Government Procurement and International Trade." *Journal of International Economics* 26: 291–308.

OECD. 2011a. *Government at a Glance 2011*. Paris: OECD Publishing.

OECD. 2011b. *National Accounts at a Glance 2011*. Paris: OECD Publishing.

OECD. 2013. *Government at a Glance 2013*. Paris: OECD Publishing.

Ramboll/HTW Huhr. 2011. "Final Report: Cross-Border Procurement above EU Thresholds," DG Internal Market and Services, European Commission.

Shingal, A. 2011. "The WTO's Agreement on Government Procurement: Whither Market Access?" *World Trade Review* 10(4): 1–23.

Shingal, A. 2015. "Econometric Analysis of Home Bias in Government Procurement." *Review of International Economics* 23(1): 188–219.

Trionfetti, F. 2000. "Discriminatory Public Procurement and International Trade." *The World Economy* 23: 57–76.

WTO. 2014a. "Annual Report 2014," Geneva.

WTO. 2014b. "Statistics Reports under Article XIX:5 of the GPA" (available at: <http://www.wto.org/english/tratop_e/gproc_e/gpstat_e.htm> (accessed December 8, 2014)).

19 How Open Are Public Procurement Markets?

Patrick Messerlin

19.1 Introduction

In recent years there has been a "beauty contest" over which country is the "most" open in terms of public procurement. This debate has been going on in the World Trade Organization (WTO) forum, but has been even fiercer in the negotiation of preferential trade agreements (PTAs). In particular, some European Union (EU) member states and the European Commission have claimed that the EU public procurement markets are more open than those of its main large trading partners. More importantly for the future of the world trade regime, countries that believe they are the most open often hold the view that they are entitled to "reciprocity"—meaning that they have a "right" to increased access to foreign public procurement markets without providing new concessions. In March 2012, for example, the Commission tabled a proposal for a regulation on "the access of third-country goods and services to the Union's internal market in public procurement and procedures supporting negotiations on access of Union goods and services to the public procurement markets of third countries" (COM/2012/124/FINAL). The discussions on this regulation often called for a so-called "reciprocity" clause which would open up the legal possibility for the EU to deny access to its public procurement markets to firms originating from countries with public procurement markets that the EU regards as less open than its own markets.[1]

A basic goal of this chapter is to provide some robust evidence on the relative openness of the public procurement markets of the major trading nations of the world. As the data suggest conclusions that are very different from the EU claims, an effort is made to understand the reasons for such a divergence between discourse and reality, and some lessons are drawn for trade policy initiatives and negotiations on public procurement matters.

[1] According to the Commission's work programme for 2015, the proposal will be amended in line with the priorities of the current Commission; see <http://ec.europa.eu/growth/single-market/public-procurement/international/index_en.htm> (accessed July 24, 2016).

19.2 How Open are the EU Public Procurement Markets? A Brief Review

The study that triggered the claims that the EU was more open than its major trading partners was a background report commissioned by the European Commission in preparation for its 2012 proposal for a regulation on public procurement (Ramboll Management Consulting and HTW Chur, 2012, hereafter the "Ramboll study"). This study was followed by an impact assessment working document (IAWD) that served as the analytical basis of the Directive proposal and that reinforced the Ramboll study's conclusion (European Commission, 2012). For the sake of simplicity, the IAWD is examined in detail in Annex 1.

The Ramboll study tries to provide evidence on the relative openness of the EU public procurement markets compared to those of four large countries (Canada, China, Japan, and the US). It relies on two key variables drawn from the national accounts: (i) the total demand for goods and services, defined as the sum of intermediate consumption plus final consumption expenditures, gross capital formation, and exports for every sector; and (ii) imports of goods and services for every sector. Each of these two variables is split into a private and a public component. For instance, public sector demand (hereafter "public demand") for goods and services is defined as the final consumption expenditure by governments plus the intermediate consumption by the sectors carrying out procurement procedures (for details, see Ramboll Management Consulting and HTW Chur, 2012: pp. 17–18).[2] Public sector imports of goods and services are defined accordingly.

The key data reported in the Ramboll study are summarized in its table 6, which provides the shares of total—extra-EU *plus* intra-EU—public imports in public demand for goods and services for the twenty-one EU member states for which there are data (the UK is the only large missing member state) and the aggregate EU21 in 2005. These shares are reproduced in Table 19.1 under the heading of "Ratio 1."[3] They suggest that the EU is more open than the four other countries. However, comparing the EU Ratio 1 with the Ratio 1 of the four other countries—as the Ramboll study does—strongly overestimates the relative openness of the EU public procurement markets, simply because Ratio 1 includes intra-EU imports. These should be considered "domestic"

[2] These industries are: (i) electricity, gas, and hot water supply; (ii) collection and purification of water; (iii) land transport and transport via pipelines; (iv) post and telecoms; (v) public administration and defense, compulsory social security; (vi) education; (vii) health and social work; and (viii) sewage, sanitation, and similar activities.

[3] There is no available data for six EU member states: Bulgaria, Cyprus, Latvia, Luxembourg, Malta, and the UK.

Table 19.1 Penetration ratios of public procurement markets, selected countries

	Ratio 1 Total public imports to public demand % [a]	Ratio 2 Estimated public intra-EU imports to total imports % [b]	Ratio 3 Extra-EU public imports to public demand % [c]	Ratio 2b Ratio 2 required for EUMS to be as open as Japan [d]	Ratio 4 Intra-EU public imports to public demand % [c]
Austria	9.6	74.1	2.5	51.4	7.1
Belgium	7.0	74.2	1.8	33.1	5.2
Czech Rep.	13.9	81.4	2.6	66.2	11.3
Denmark	5.6	65.1	2.0	16.3	3.6
Estonia	12.5	76.3	3.0	62.6	9.5
Finland	7.0	61.2	2.7	32.8	4.3
France	5.8	61.0	2.3	19.6	3.6
Germany	6.5	58.3	2.7	28.3	3.8
Greece	7.1	58.2	3.0	34.2	4.1
Hungary	12.6	68.4	4.0	62.8	8.6
Ireland	9.3	66.7	3.1	49.9	6.2
Italy	6.0	59.4	2.4	21.8	3.6
Lithuania	12.3	59.3	5.0	62.0	7.3
Netherlands	6.8	49.4	3.4	31.0	3.3
Poland	6.1	65.3	2.1	23.1	4.0
Portugal	8.5	76.6	2.0	44.8	6.5
Romania	18.1	63.0	6.7	74.1	11.4
Slovak Rep.	16.3	77.8	3.6	71.3	12.7
Slovenia	11.1	79.4	2.3	57.9	8.8
Spain	8.3	62.8	3.1	43.8	5.2
Sweden	5.7	70.4	1.7	17.4	4.0
EU21 [e]	9.3	67.1	3.1	49.9	6.3
EU21 [f]	7.0	61.8	2.7	33.4	4.3
Canada	6.9	–	6.9	–	–
China	6.1	–	6.1	–	–
Japan	4.7	–	4.7	–	–
USA	4.6	–	4.6	–	–

Source: Ramboll Management Consulting and HTW Chur (2012).

Notes: "Public imports" means public sector imports. (a) Source is table 6 in Ramboll Management Consulting and HTW Chur (2012). The figures for Canada, China, Japan, and the US are reported in this column because they were (wrongly) judged by the Ramboll study to be comparable with the Ratio 1 for the EU. (b) Shares of public intra-EU imports assuming that these shares are the same as the shares of public and private intra-EU imports (see Section 19.2) based on data drawn from table 6 (EU member states not followed by a star) and from table 8 (EU member states followed by a star) of the Ramboll study. (c) Ratio 3 is derived from Ratios 1 and 2 and constitutes the "penetration" ratio comparable to those for the four non-EU countries. The figures for Canada, China, Japan, and the US are reported in this column because they are comparable with the Ratio 3 for the EU. (d) Ratio 2b is the ratio of intra-EU public imports to EU total imports that are required for the EU member states and the EU21 to be as open as Japan's public procurement markets (4.7 percent). (e) Unweighted average for the twenty-one EU member states with available data. (f) GDP-weighted average for the twenty-one EU member states with available data.

trade. In analyses of trade in goods, the routine procedure is to compare the shares of extra-EU imports alone to GDP with the shares of imports to GDP for the EU partners.

The correct comparison should thus have relied only on the shares of extra-EU public imports in EU public demand for goods and services. However, at the time the Ramboll study was undertaken, this was problematic as there were no systematic specific data on intra-EU or extra-EU public imports. Two alternative methods would have provided an imperfect but acceptable solution to the data problem, and would have suggested a very different conclusion in terms of the relative openness of the EU public procurement markets compared to those of the other countries.

The first alternative method assumes that the shares of public intra-EU imports in total public (intra- and extra-EU) imports are the same as the shares of public and private intra-EU imports in total public and private (intra- and extra-EU) imports. Ratio 2 in Table 19.1 presents these estimated shares of public intra-EU imports (based on the shares reported in tables 6 and 8 of the Ramboll study). Ratio 3, which is defined as Ratio 1*(1-(Ratio 2/100)), provides a measure of EU "penetration ratios" (the shares of *extra-EU* public imports in total demand for public goods and services for each EU member state and for the EU21 as a whole). This is the only indicator that is truly comparable to the penetration ratios of the four non-EU countries. In sharp contrast with Ratio 1, Ratio 3 indicates clearly that the EU public procurement markets are not more open than those of the four non-EU comparator countries.

The second alternative method is to calculate "Ratio 2b," which is defined as the share of intra-EU public imports in EU total imports that would make EU public procurement markets "as open as" those of a non-EU country taken as a reference. In Table 19.1, Japan is used as the reference country because, at the time of the Ramboll study, public procurement issues were at the core of the preliminary discussions on a Japan–EU preferential trade agreement. Using this measure, for instance, France's penetration ratio would be equivalent to Japan's penetration ratio if the share of French intra-EU imports in France's total imports were only 19.6 percent—instead of 61 percent. Such a huge difference is highly unlikely.

The data in Table 19.1 suggest three additional observations. First, Figure 19.1 plots the (logarithmic) correlation between EU member states' Ratio 1 and their GDP. This correlation is much higher for small countries, which makes sense as it seems reasonable that a small country will less easily satisfy its needs for goods and services for public procurement purposes by purchasing domestic goods and services compared to a large country that has a wider, more diverse domestic production base. Second, Figure 19.2 shows that the slope of the correlation using Ratio 3 (based on only extra-EU public imports) is somewhat flatter than in Figure 19.1. This observation seems consistent with the following proposition: for some kinds of public procurement, supplies are systematically less easily available in the EU member states, hence there is a need to have

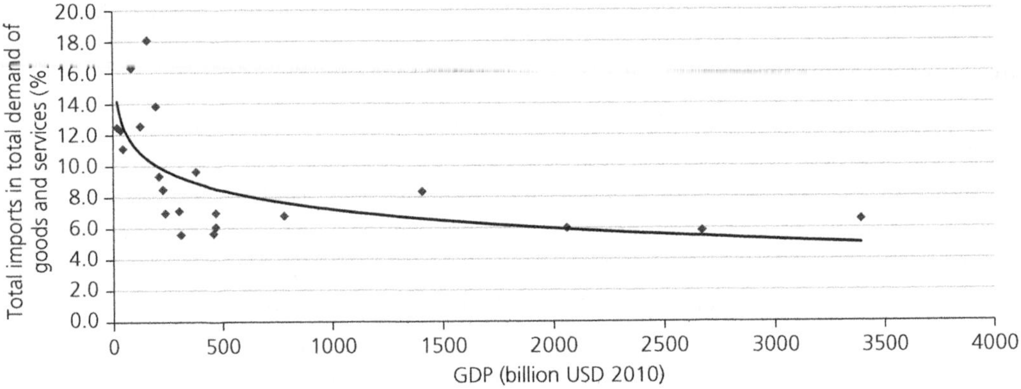

Figure 19.1. GDP and Ratio 1 (share of total public imports in public demand)

Sources: Table 1 and World Bank GDP data; author's calculations.

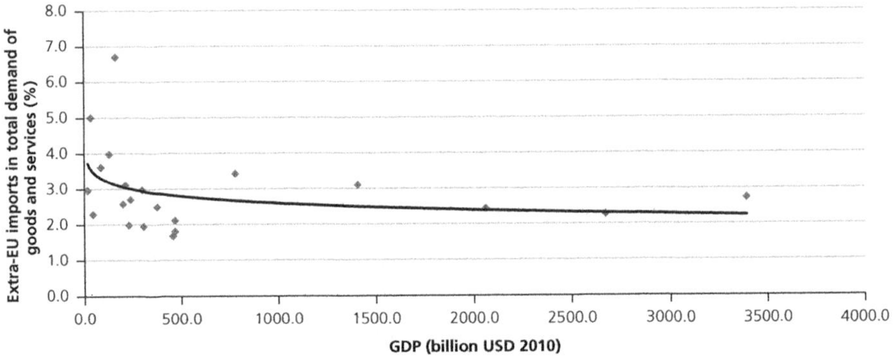

Figure 19.2. GDP and Ratio 3 (share of extra-EU public imports in public demand)

Sources: Table 1 and World Bank GDP data; author's calculations.

recourse to firms originating in the rest of world—whether the member state in question is small or large. This phenomenon explains, as least partly, the fact that the GDP-weighted average ratios for the EU are smaller than the unweighted average ratios (see Table 19.1).

Finally, Ratio 4 reported in Table 19.1 (the difference between Ratios 1 and 3) can be interpreted as the "penetration ratios" *within* the EU internal market. These ratios are often higher than Ratio 3 for the non-EU countries, but not invariably. This last observation suggests that there is still a substantial way to go for the functioning of the EU internal market in terms of public procurement—a point re-examined in Section 19.3.

19.3 Openness of Procurement Markets: More Evidence on Key Countries

The above findings—that EU public procurement markets are less open than those of its main trading partners—differs so much from the views expressed by the EU, and in particular by a few EU member states (notably France and Germany), that it should be backed up by more evidence in order to ensure this is a robust result.

The recent World Input-Output Database (WIOD) (Timmer, 2012; Timmer et al., 2015) is one source of information that can be used to undertake such a robustness test. It has three key advantages: (i) it covers goods and services; (ii) it provides country-specific data for the fourteen largest economies in the world (with the EU counted as one economy), as well as for the individual EU member states; and (iii) it does so on an annual basis starting from 1995 through 2011.[4]

Table 19.2 provides the "penetration" ratios (that is, Ratio 3 in Table 19.1) for the thirteen individual EU trading partners based on WIOD data. It also gives those ratios for the EU27 as a whole as well as for the EU2, a subset of two EU member states (France and Germany), for reasons explained later in this section. Table 19.2 deserves a preliminary observation related to the Great Crisis (since 2008). All the countries show a marked decline in penetration ratios in 2009–10. The fall is quite large in many cases (more than 10 percent) except for two countries: Australia and India. These declines are followed by a bounce of variable magnitude, depending on the country. There is little doubt that this evolution is (at least partly) related to the structure of the stimulus packages implemented after the 2008–9 peak crisis years. These packages are likely to have had a "domestic bias" for different reasons. In particular, they may have focused on public demand in the sectors with relatively low foreign penetration (a composition bias not necessarily driven by protectionist goals) or they may have used procedures discriminating against foreign competitors (a clear protectionist bias).

The Transatlantic Trade and Investment Partnership (TTIP) negotiations make it particularly interesting to focus on the EU27 and US penetration ratios. As illustrated by Figure 19.3, these ratios were relatively similar from 1995 to 2009, but since then the EU27 ratios have been higher than those of the US. It is worth noting that the growth rate of the US penetration ratio is lower than that of the EU from 2003, that is, a few years before the US measures strengthening the restrictions in US public procurement were introduced in the aftermath of the 2008 crisis.

[4] The main difference between the WIOD data and the data used in the Ramboll study is that WIOD provides a balanced set of world input-output tables where national accounts have been fully harmonized across countries. The data are different but more comparable across economies. There are minor differences in the industry classification that do not allow us to replicate exactly the calculations of the Ramboll study but it does not put at risk our robustness test.

Table 19.2 Public procurement markets: Import penetration (WIOD data)

	1995	1996	1997	1998	1999	2000	2001	2002	2003	2004	2005	2006	2007	2008	2009	2010	2011
EU27 Extra	2.6%	2.7%	2.3%	2.7%	2.8%	3.6%	3.7%	3.5%	3.4%	3.7%	4.2%	4.6%	4.5%	5.1%	4.4%	5.1%	5.3%
EU2 Extra	2.2%	2.2%	2.4%	2.3%	2.3%	2.8%	3.1%	2.9%	2.8%	3.0%	3.4%	3.8%	3.9%	4.3%	3.4%	3.8%	3.9%
Australia	5.1%	5.0%	5.4%	5.4%	5.9%	5.9%	5.8%	6.1%	5.5%	5.9%	6.0%	5.9%	6.2%	6.0%	5.4%	5.3%	5.8%
Brazil	2.1%	2.0%	2.1%	2.1%	2.7%	3.1%	3.5%	3.5%	3.3%	3.3%	3.1%	2.9%	3.0%	3.3%	2.9%	3.2%	3.7%
Canada	4.2%	4.3%	4.6%	4.9%	5.1%	5.1%	5.0%	4.9%	4.8%	4.7%	4.9%	4.6%	4.6%	4.8%	4.8%	4.2%	4.3%
China	3.8%	3.1%	3.3%	2.8%	3.0%	3.4%	3.3%	3.6%	4.5%	5.5%	5.6%	5.7%	5.2%	4.9%	3.9%	4.5%	4.7%
India	4.2%	4.4%	4.0%	4.4%	4.5%	4.4%	4.0%	3.5%	3.4%	4.6%	5.8%	6.3%	6.3%	6.4%	5.8%	6.7%	6.2%
Indonesia	7.9%	7.8%	7.9%	13.9%	9.3%	11.4%	11.6%	9.5%	8.2%	9.9%	10.6%	8.9%	8.8%	8.9%	6.1%	6.8%	8.0%
Japan	1.9%	2.2%	2.3%	2.1%	2.0%	2.3%	2.3%	2.4%	2.5%	2.8%	3.2%	3.8%	4.2%	5.2%	3.4%	4.0%	4.8%
Korea	7.5%	7.5%	8.4%	8.1%	7.7%	9.6%	9.3%	8.9%	9.1%	9.7%	9.9%	9.9%	10.2%	14.0%	11.6%	12.0%	14.4%
Mexico	4.8%	4.9%	5.2%	5.1%	4.9%	5.2%	4.9%	4.5%	5.0%	5.6%	5.8%	5.9%	6.3%	6.5%	5.7%	6.5%	7.4%
Russia	3.3%	3.5%	3.6%	4.6%	6.2%	5.3%	4.7%	4.2%	4.4%	3.7%	3.8%	3.3%	3.1%	3.1%	2.4%	2.6%	3.2%
Taiwan	9.9%	10.1%	10.8%	11.9%	10.7%	10.5%	10.2%	11.3%	11.2%	12.4%	11.9%	12.9%	13.5%	16.7%	13.7%	15.7%	17.3%
Turkey	5.4%	7.3%	6.5%	5.2%	4.4%	5.8%	7.2%	8.3%	8.1%	8.8%	9.5%	11.3%	10.9%	5.1%	4.6%	4.8%	6.0%
United States	2.7%	2.8%	2.9%	2.8%	3.0%	3.6%	3.5%	3.3%	3.6%	4.0%	4.4%	4.3%	4.4%	4.9%	3.7%	4.4%	4.8%
Rest of World	6.4%	6.8%	6.9%	6.9%	6.7%	7.1%	7.2%	7.9%	8.4%	8.8%	9.4%	9.1%	9.1%	8.7%	7.3%	7.3%	6.7%
World	4.2%	4.5%	4.6%	4.6%	4.6%	5.1%	5.2%	5.2%	5.5%	6.0%	6.4%	6.7%	6.8%	7.2%	6.0%	6.4%	6.7%

Source: World Output-Input Database (November 2013); author's calculations.

As the discussions on public procurement are very important in the TTIP negotiations, an additional database is used to check the trends suggested by Figure 19.3—the OECD Inter-Country Input-Output (OECD ICIO) tables. These tables were created for analyzing trade flows in value added. While similar to the data compiled by the WIOD project, the OECD ICIO data are different in several respects, and have advantages and disadvantages compared to the WIOD data. Among the disadvantages are the facts that the number of years covered is smaller and the data are reported on an annual basis only since 2008. Among the advantages is the fact that the data for 2010 and 2011 are based on more recent input-output tables released by the countries (as the OECD ICIO data were updated in June 2015). Figure 19.4, which is based on

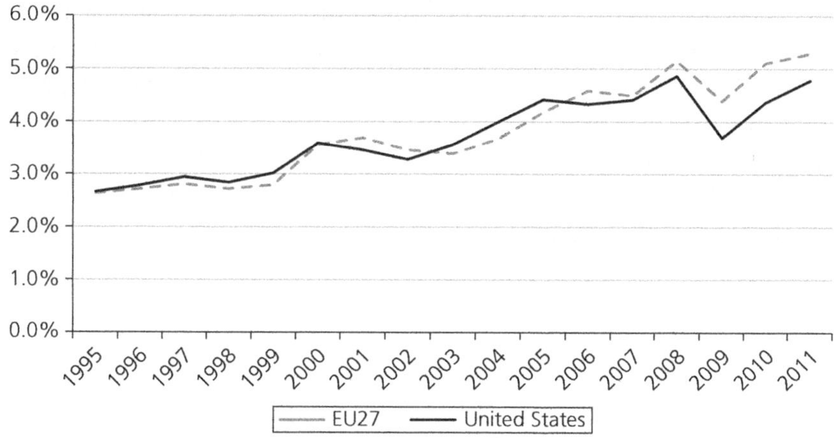

Figure 19.3. EU27 and US penetration ratios, 1995–2011 (based on WIOD)

Source: World Output-Input Database, November 2013; author's calculations.

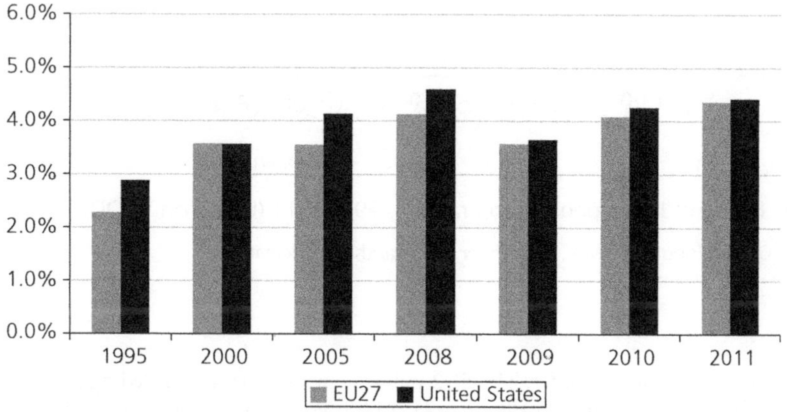

Figure 19.4. EU27 and US penetration ratios, selected years (based on OECD ICIO)

Source: OECD ICIO, June 2015; author's calculations.

the OECD ICIO data, suggests the same catching up of the EU27 compared to the US. However, the sharp decline after 2008 in the US penetration ratios is not confirmed.

Another mega-PTA being negotiated by the EU involves Japan. Here it is preferable to focus on the EU2 (France and Germany) subset for two reasons. First, it allows taking into account the size effect of public demand underlined in Section 19.2—larger countries tend to have smaller penetration ratios. The size of the EU2's combined public demand is very close to the size of Japanese public demand (1.1 to 1.2 times across the whole period), making the EU2 an appropriate set of EU member states for comparison with Japan.[5] Second, it focuses on two member states that have expressed serious reservations over opening PTA negotiations with Japan, and/or have taken an aggressive stance over opening the public procurement markets of key trading partners (Canada, the US).

Figure 19.5, which is based on WIOD data, shows that Japan's penetration ratios have progressively caught up the EU2 ratios since 2003–4. Since 2007, Japan has been more open than the EU2, despite the intrinsic size-related bias of the EU2 data (see the note of caution in footnote 6). Figure 19.6, which uses OECD ICIO data, reinforces Figure 19.5—Japan's penetration ratio becomes higher than that of the EU2 in 2005, and remains higher in subsequent years.

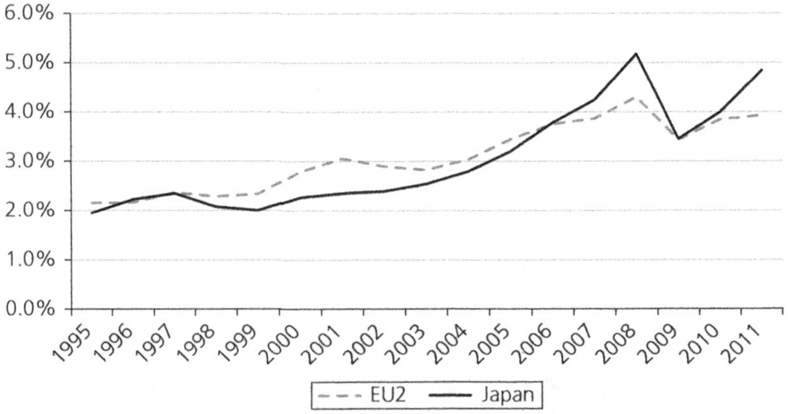

Figure 19.5. EU2 and Japan penetration ratios, 1995–2011 (based on WIOD)

Source: World Output-Input Database, November 2013; author's calculations.

[5] However, some caution is in order. The EU2 public demand is an aggregated figure of two economies which, individually, are significantly smaller than Japan (the economies of Germany and France are 0.6 and 0.5 times the size of Japanese economy, respectively). The EU2 penetration ratios are systematic overestimates of what the penetration ratios of a fully unified EU2 economy would have been, since aggregating these two economies does not eliminate the fact that decisions have been taken in the context of these two notably smaller economies.

Finally, Table 19.3 reports data on the evolution of intra-EU and extra-EU penetration ratios for the EU27 and for the EU2. As illustrated by Figure 19.7, since 2003, the average annual growth of the intra-EU2 penetration ratio has slowed down, and has

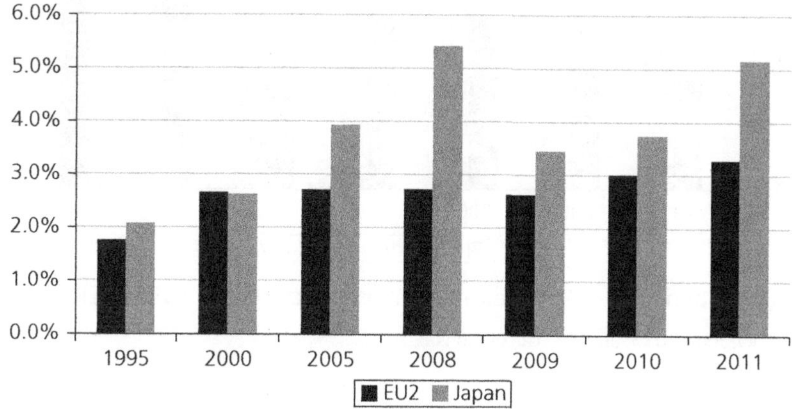

Figure 19.6. EU2 and Japan penetration ratios, selected years (OECD ICIO data)

Source: OECD ICIO, June 2015; author's calculations.

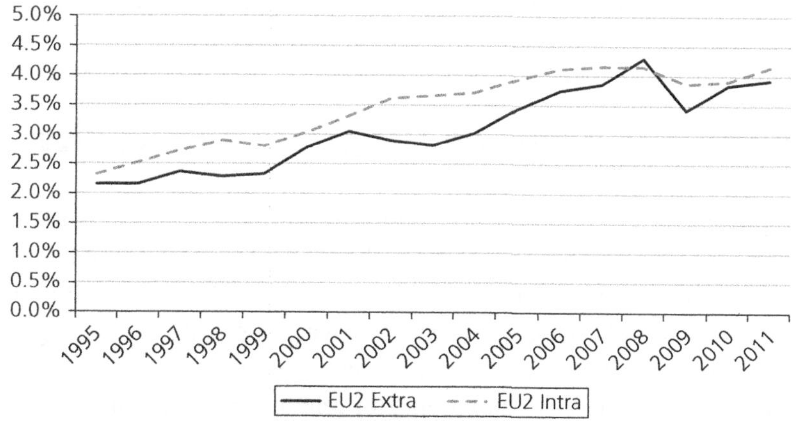

Figure 19.7. Intra- and extra-EU2 penetration ratios, 1995–2011 (based on WIOD)

Source: World Output-Input Database, November 2013; authors' calculations.

Table 19.3 Intra-EU penetration ratios of public procurement markets (based on WIOD)

	1995	1996	1997	1998	1999	2000	2001	2002	2003	2004	2005	2006	2007	2008	2009	2010	2011
EU27 Intra	3.2%	3.3%	3.5%	3.6%	3.6%	3.9%	4.1%	4.2%	4.2%	4.3%	4.3%	4.5%	4.6%	4.8%	4.5%	4.4%	4.7%
EU2 Intra	2.3%	2.5%	2.7%	2.9%	2.8%	3.0%	3.3%	3.6%	3.7%	3.7%	3.9%	4.1%	4.2%	4.2%	3.9%	3.9%	4.2%

Source: World Output-Input Database (November 2013); author's calculations.

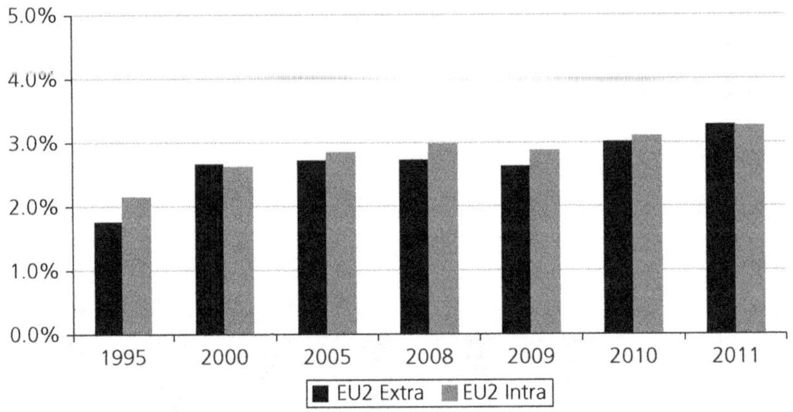

Figure 19.8. Intra- and extra-EU2 penetration ratios, selected years (OECD ICIO)

Source: OECD ICIO, June 2015; authors' calculations.

been smaller than the extra-EU2 ratio since 2008. This evolution may simply reflect more sluggish growth in EU member states, but it may also reflect an internal market in public procurement that is not functioning well, at least to the extent that it involves these two member states. Results using OECD ICIO data (Figure 19.8) highlight the increasing similarity between the extra-EU and intra-EU ratios for the EU2.

19.4 Divergence between Discourse and Reality

The data reported in Table 19.2 permit going beyond bilateral comparisons with the world's largest trading nations. They show that the EU and US public procurement markets are increasingly less open than those of most East Asian economies. These observations raise the following question: How can one explain the huge divergence between the discourse and the reality during the last years?

A first answer is provided by the absence of reliable information in the WTO-GPA forum. All the signatories of the WTO Government Procurement Agreement (GPA) have recognized that a huge effort should be made to collect much better data on the openness of public procurement markets, and to make their notifications much more comparable (Anderson, 2012). The current methodologies used for estimating the GPA-covered public procurements differ so much among the signatories that it is impossible to reconcile them (Anderson et al., 2011: in particular, footnotes 21–23).

These good intentions imply exploring ways to improve on the current measures. The key question is whether it makes sense to continue to rely on the current indicators based on GPA commitments, such as the list of the public procurement markets (entities, sectors) covered. A parallel with trade in goods is useful for shedding some light on this issue. It would not occur to anyone to assess the openness of a country to trade in goods by focusing exclusively on the list of tariff concessions made by the country in question. Rather, assessments of countries' openness routinely take into account the whole universe of goods (the Harmonized System), including the tariffs that a country may enforce without having necessarily negotiated them. This is in sharp contrast with the current way of assessing openness in the GPA context, which focuses only on the lists of products that have been the subject of negotiations for liberalization. Not only is such a method not exhaustive, but it generates variable yardsticks that will reflect the wide differences in the types of goods and services procured and the heterogeneity of the public entities that are listed in national GPA commitments. It does not permit economically sound comparisons among countries.

There is thus a need to use an approach in public procurement similar to that used for trade in goods. Such an approach requires a unique definition of the whole set of economic activities potentially subjected to the universe of "public procurement"—independently from the commitments made by GPA signatories. There are two reasons why national accounts data are the only statistics to offer such a basis. First, public demand is the best common basis for assessing the relative size of the public procurement markets of economies since it takes into account every euro or dollar spent by any public authority, whether central, local, or a specific entity. Second, corresponding public imports benefit from the extensive efforts during the last fifty years of the national accounts authorities in every country in the world to collect comparable data. Last but not least, national accounts provide data over time, independently from GPA commitments related to specific negotiations. In short, the GPA forum should consider adopting a methodology based on that followed in Section 2 to assess levels and trends in openness of procurement markets.

19.5 Lessons for Negotiations on Public Procurement Markets

Four lessons can be drawn from the foregoing measurement exercise. The first two center on improving the preparation of the future negotiations, whereas the remaining two concern ways to improve the negotiating techniques per se.

First, governments should refrain from claiming that their public procurement markets are more open than those of their trading partners without providing robust evidence. There are now enough data to quickly verify such claims. This makes claims that are not well founded costly in terms of reputation for the governments that adopt such a stance, and ultimately weakens their negotiating leverage.

Second, in the case of large economies, "penetration ratios" can be misleading in both an international as well as a domestic context. The EU offers a useful illustration of this.

As shown by Figures 19.1 and 19.2, penetration ratios among the twenty-seven EU member states vary by a factor of almost five. Such a situation is much less likely for trade in goods—once imported in a given "region" of a large economy, goods can circulate freely to the other "regions" of the economy. The fact that tradability is much more limited in public procurement contracts implies that an "average" openness indicator for public procurement in a large economy may well be a meaningless average of "open" and "closed" regions within that economy. As a result, there is a need to start working on data on public procurement openness at the sub-central or sub-federal level for large economies such as the US, India, Canada, and China. It is worth stressing that such efforts are useful in the domestic context as well. As discussed above, in the EU case (the only large economy for which there are data at the "sub-central" level), an average openness indicator reduces the incentives for the most closed EU member states to open up not only vis-à-vis the rest of the world, but also vis-à-vis the other member states.

The two other lessons to be drawn from our measurement exercise center on negotiating techniques. First, the evidence presented in this chapter illustrates an intrinsic weakness of the notion of "reciprocity." To make sense, such a notion requires two conditions: (i) the country stating such a claim should really be more open than its trading partner(s); and (ii) the threat associated with reciprocity—that is, closing the "more open" market if the trading partner does not make its own markets more open without asking for concessions—should be credible. Checking whether this second condition is met is crucial.

For illustrative purposes, Table 19.4 shows that such credibility is unlikely even for a large trading partner—the ratios of EU public demand to the public demand of its three main trading partners are low (in the case of US and Japan) or have recently become low (in the case of China). The implication is that threats could easily result in costly retaliations for the firms of the threatening entity—or worse, could induce other large trading partners to adopt a "reciprocity" tactic. As a result, the threat of a large trading country is meaningful only in case of (much) smaller trading partners. But then, it remains to be seen whether this situation has positive net benefits when one takes into

Table 19.4 Relative size of the public procurement markets, selected countries

	1995	1996	1997	1998	1999	2000	2001	2002	2003	2004	2005	2006	2007	2008	2009	2010	2011
EU27/ USA	1.30	1.29	1.14	1.12	1.04	0.90	0.84	0.91	1.06	1.16	1.16	1.19	1.28	1.32	1.24	1.19	1.28
EU2/ Japan	0.92	1.06	1.03	1.10	0.89	0.73	0.81	0.91	1.03	1.08	1.11	1.23	1.38	1.33	1.10	1.07	1.02
EU2/ China	7.61	6.39	4.67	4.20	3.62	2.85	2.54	2.59	2.78	2.52	2.15	1.95	1.65	1.44	1.25	1.04	0.90

Source: World Output-Input Database (November 2013); author's calculations.

account the substantial political costs that are likely to arise (such as the large country being perceived by the whole trade community as "bullying" the smaller countries).

The last lesson concerns a complex situation that is likely to emerge more and more often as time goes on—the case where goods and services are produced and delivered by state-owned entities ruled by the Government Procurement Agreement in one country, but delivered in another country by privately owned entities under private contract law. A good illustration of this case is provided by the Japan–EU negotiations on a free trade agreement in the rail sector. In both economies, passenger rail services (PRS) operators buy rail equipment. Almost all the PRS operators in the EU are publicly owned, whereas in Japan some 70 percent of PRS are delivered by three privately owned and economically healthy operators (JR–East, JR-Central, and JR-West). Such a situation is frequent in many infrastructure sectors.

Using the Japan–EU rail illustration, what follows explores briefly the option to negotiate a specific chapter on the rail sector that would introduce "parallel" commitments for publicly owned and private operators in a balanced and progressive way. The introduction (*chapeau*) of such a chapter could: (i) state that the FTA's ultimate goal is to improve the welfare of European and Japanese train passengers, and that this goal requires progressively improved market access in the rail supply markets of both partners; (ii) note that coping with prevailing legal differences (private/public operators) requires two sub-chapters, one addressing the issues raised by better access to markets dominated by private PRS operators (whether in Japan or in the EU) and the other addressing the issues raised by better access to markets dominated by publicly owned PRS operators (again, whether in Japan or in the EU); and (iii) spell out the conditions under which a PRS operator would be listed in one or other of these two sub-chapters, and the criteria that need to be met for it to be shifted from one sub-chapter to the other.

The sub-chapter devoted to state-owned operators would state that they should be perfectly consistent with the provisions of the WTO Government Procurement Agreement. The sub-chapter devoted to private operators would state that these operators should have equally transparent purchasing rules, and possibly clarify this statement in the negotiated text or under the form of voluntary codes of conduct to be followed by the private firms (as is indeed done by the three private JR companies in the Japan–EU case). Finally, such provisions could be complemented by measures specifying a progressive liberalization of the covered operators when purchasing equipment. For instance, it could be agreed that the year Y will witness better market access for the purchases of (in this example, rail) equipment by (possibly only a first group of) private operators, and better market access for the public procurement of (again in this example, rail) equipment by (possibly only a first group of) publicly owned operators, with both sets of operators being of roughly the same economic size. Such a progressive and balanced scheduling of improved market access would accommodate the differences in legal situations, while ensuring that benefits accrue to all the consumers in both signatories.

ACKNOWLEDGMENTS

This chapter revisits, expands and updates Messerlin and Miroudot (2012). I thank Sebastien Miroudot very much for continuous discussions on this topic and am grateful to Bernard Hoekman for very helpful comments. All remaining errors are the author's.

REFERENCES

Anderson, R. 2012. "The Conclusion of the Renegotiation of the WTO Agreement on Government Procurement: What It Means for the Agreement and for the World Economy." *Public Procurement Law Review* 3: 83–94.

Anderson, R., Pelletier, P., Osei-lah, K., and Muller, A. 2011. "Assessing the Value of Future Accessions to the WTO Agreement on Public Procurement: Some New Data Sources, Provisional Estimates, and an Evaluative Framework for Individual WTO Members Considering Accession." WTO Staff Working Paper ERSD 2011-15, Geneva.

European Commission. 2012. "Impact Assessment Accompanying a Proposal for a Regulation Establishing Rules on the Access of Third Countries' Goods and Services to the EU Internal Market in Public Procurement." Commission Staff Working Document, COM (2012) 124 final and SWD (2012) 58 final.

Messerlin, P. and Miroudot, S. 2012. "EU Public Procurement Markets: How Open Are They?" GEM Policy Brief, July (available at: <http://gem.sciences-po.fr/content/publications/pdf/Messerlin-Miroudot_EU_public_procurement072012.pdf> (accessed July 24, 2016)).

Ramboll Management Consulting and HTW Chur. 2012. *Cross-Border Procurement above EU Thresholds*. Copenhagen: Ramboll.

Schott, J. and Buurman, J. 1994. *The Uruguay Round*. Washington, DC: Institute for International Economics.

Timmer, M. (ed.). 2012. "The World Input–Output Database (WIOD): Contents, Sources and Methods" (available at: <www.wiod.org> (accessed July 24, 2016)).

Timmer, M., Dietzenbacher, E., Los, B., Stehrer, R., and de Vries, G. 2015. "An Illustrated User Guide to the World Input–Output Database: The Case of Global Automotive Production." *Review of International Economics* 23: 575–605.

Annex 1

The Impact Assessment Working Document (IAWD) is the analytical basis of the Directive proposal (European Commission, 2012). It consists of a cover text and eleven annexes. Annex 3, entitled "Problem analysis," is the key part of the IAWD in terms of market openness since it presents the Commission's estimates of the level of openness of public procurement markets in the EU as a whole (there is no estimate by EU member state) and in twelve major trading partners of the EU.

Table A1 The IAWD's estimates of the openness of public procurement markets

	Size of PP markets covered [a]	de jure commitments (%) [b]	de facto [c] commitments (%)		Preferential trade agreements (PTA) between the EU's trading partners and the EU
			EU % [d]	EU's partners	
	1	2	3	4	5
Parties to the 1995 Government Procurement Agreement					
EU	370	85	–	–	
USA [e]	559	32	46	47	ongoing negotiations
Japan	96	28	70	72	ongoing negotiations
Canada	59	16	10	40	PTA agreement signed
Korea	25	65	82	80	PTA implemented
Israel	2	75	na	75	PTA implemented
Other countries					
Mexico [f]	20	75	na	92	PTA implemented
China	83	0	–	24	no PTA under consideration
Russia	18	0	–	56	no PTA under consideration
India	19	0	–	70	ongoing negotiations
Brazil	42	0	–	38	ongoing negotiations with Mercosur
Turkey	24	0	–	25	Customs Union does not cover public procurement
Australia	20	0	–	63	PTA negotiations to be opened
Total non EU	967	25	18	na	

Source: IAWD Annex 3, tables 3 and 7.

Table A1 recapitulates the figures in Tables 19.3 and 19.7 of the IAWD Annex 3, which summarize the main findings.

- Column 1 presents the size (in billions of euros) of the total public procurement markets above the thresholds as set by the Government Procurement Agreement (GPA) signed at the end of the Uruguay Round (1995).[6]
- Column 2 presents the IAWD Annex 3 estimates of public procurement market openness based on the legal international commitments taken by the EU and twelve countries, either under the 1995 WTO Government Procurement Agreement (GPA) or under existing preferential trade agreements (as best illustrated by Mexico, which is not a party to the GPA). The openness ratios of these so-called *de*

[6] The IAWD presents the potential *de jure* commitments that the EU would take under the new GPA under negotiation in the WTO if these negotiations were successful. This information is not reported in Table 19.1 since the IAWD provides no equivalent estimates for the EU's trading partners.

jure commitments are given by the percentage share of the value of the markets considered as open *de jure* in the total value of public procurement markets above the GPA thresholds.

- Column 3 presents the IAWD Annex 3 estimates of the commitments taken by the EU with respect to its twelve partners when the "general notes or specific derogations" are taken into account. Specific derogations are targeted restrictions imposed by the EU "because of the disparities in commitments" in 1995 GPA (Annex 3, p. 8). For instance, the US has not been granted access to EU public procurement markets in water, airport services, and urban transport (among others), and Japan has not been granted access to EU public procurement markets in electricity and urban transport (General Notes and Derogations from Article III, Appendix I for the EC, Government Procurement Agreement 2003).
- Column 4 presents the IAWD Annex 3 estimates of public procurement market openness for the EU's partners on a *de facto* basis. A market is considered as open *de facto* if "a country does not apply protectionist measures in the public procurement markets that are not open de jure" (IAWD Annex 3, Methodological Box 4). The *de facto* openness ratios are measured by the percentage share of the value of the markets considered as open *de facto* in the total value of public procurement markets above the GPA thresholds.
- For the sake of information, column 6 describes very briefly the current situation in terms of PTAs between the EU and the other countries listed.

The figures in column 2 are those systematically reported by the proponents of the Directive to justify the need for such a Directive. Indeed, these figures deliver a strong impression of asymmetry—the estimated openness of the EU public procurement markets, at 85 percent, is much larger than that of most of the EU's trading partners, which range from 0 to 75 percent.

However, such a comparison does not compare what is comparable. It systematically *over*estimates the EU's level of openness and systematically *under*estimates the level of openness of its trading partners:

- Column 2 systematically *over*estimates EU openness because it does not take into account the "specific derogations" that the EU imposes on a bilateral basis because of the disparities in commitments. These specific derogations are an integral part of the 1995 GPA. As a result, they are the best definition of the "true" EU commitments. Column 3 takes into account those specific derogations and shows a drastic reduction of the level of openness of the EU in all cases except for Korea. For example, the EU's degree of openness drops from 85 percent (column 2) to 46 percent (column 3) in the case of the US and to 70 percent (column 3) in the case of Japan.

- Column 2 systematically *under*estimates the openness of the EU's trading partners because it does not take into account the fact that countries do not apply *de facto* protectionist measures in some public procurement markets. Column 4 shows that taking into account these open market practices dramatically increases the true level of openness of all the EU's partners, which then ranges from 24 to 92 percent.

In short, two important lessons can be drawn from Table A1:

1. The "true" EU level of openness (including specific derogations) and the "true" level of commitments of EU GPA partners (taking into account systematic non-protectionist practices) are generally very similar.
2. The level of openness of non-GPA countries is within the range of the "true" EU level of openness (10–82 percent).

Comparing what is comparable leads to the conclusion that the IAWD on which the Directive proposal relies fails to support the EU claim of public procurement markets that are more open than those of its partners.

To conclude, it is useful to put the "asymmetry" in the level of openness argued by the proponents of the Directive into perspective. Such an asymmetry would imply that the European negotiators (from the Commission and the member states) had negotiated "badly" during the Uruguay Round. This is because, during the Uruguay Round, the GPA was not part of the global trade-off among all issues on the table (industrial tariff cuts, agricultural "tariffication," opening services markets, etc.). Rather, it was a stand-alone negotiation that involved only a limited number of "willing" countries, not all GATT contracting parties (i.e., it was a "plurilateral" agreement). The logic of stand-alone trade negotiations imposes that on the sole issue at stake (in this case, the opening of public procurement markets), every country balances the market access concessions it grants to its partners almost exactly with the market concessions it gets from its partners. The available evidence on the GPA negotiations during the Uruguay Round does not support the hypothesis of a failure by the EU negotiators. The experts who analyzed the 1995 GPA stressed the almost perfect balance of the negotiations between the two largest trading partners in terms of value of the markets opened, with US$103.2 billion opened by the US side and US$103.3 billion opened by the EU (Schott and Buurman, 1994). Indeed, to achieve such a balance, the US negotiators had to bring to the table of negotiations thirty-nine US states (including the five largest) and seven US municipalities (among the twenty-four largest US towns) in addition to federal public procurement markets.[7]

[7] These figures are those related to US commitments with respect to the EU.

Annex 2

As in the Ramboll study, our analysis of import penetration ratios is based on input-output data. Our main results rely on the World Input-Output Database (Timmer et al., 2015), a set of input-output tables that offers two advantages:

- First, it covers all EU economies, as well as thirteen other major countries, over the period 1995–2009. This gives better geographic and time coverage.
- In addition, the dataset provides a global (world) matrix of inter-country and inter-industry transactions. Therefore, it is possible to distinguish between extra-EU and intra-EU imports when it comes to public demand.

The methodology used to construct the WIOD tables is explained in Timmer (2012). The benchmark being national accounts, the data are comparable to those analyzed in the Ramboll study. The figures are not exactly the same, however, because of differences in the way the data are harmonized and balanced in the WIOD and OECD tables used in the Ramboll study.

As a robustness check, the same calculations are done using the OECD Inter-Country Input-Output matrices, which are the underlying data of the OECD–WTO Trade in Value Added (OECD ICIO) database. These tables are also not fully comparable with those used in the Ramboll report, despite also being issued by the OECD. The reason is that they correspond to more recent work (a June 2015 update) and more recently collected input-output information (using the 2010 benchmark input-output tables released by countries in 2013–14).

With both the WIOD and OECD ICIO data, public demand is calculated as the sum of:

- final consumption expenditure by governments; and
- intermediate consumption by industries in public sectors.

The public sectors are defined as: “electricity, gas and water supply” (100 percent), “post and telecommunications” (50 percent), “public administrations and defence, compulsory social security” (100 percent), “education” (100 percent) and “health and social work” (100 percent). There are slight differences between the WIOD and OECD ICIO industry classification of industries, but not for these sectors.

The same classification of public procurement by industry is used as in the Ramboll study (table 2, p. 18), except that “sewage and refuse disposal, sanitation and similar services” is excluded as there are no specific data for these activities in the WIOD and OECD ICIO data (the sector is aggregated with “other community, social and personal services”). As this industry represents a small share of public demand (in terms of imports of intermediate products), our results can be only marginally affected by its omission.

Table A2 is similar to Tables 19.2, 19.3, and 19.4 in the main text, but gives the detailed results of our calculations with the OECD ICIO database (using the June 2015 update).

Table A2 Public procurement penetration ratios, selected countries (OECD ICIO data)

	1995	2000	2005	2008	2009	2010	2011
A. **Penetration ratios (ratios 3 of Table 19.1)**							
EU27 Extra	2.3%	3.6%	3.6%	4.1%	3.6%	4.1%	4.4%
EU2 Extra	1.8%	2.7%	2.7%	2.7%	2.6%	3.0%	3.3%
Australia	4.8%	5.8%	5.3%	5.8%	4.9%	5.0%	5.2%
Brazil	1.4%	2.1%	2.3%	2.1%	2.1%	2.3%	2.4%
Canada	6.1%	5.3%	4.9%	3.8%	4.0%	4.0%	3.8%
China	0.9%	0.8%	1.1%	1.0%	0.9%	0.9%	0.9%
India	3.5%	3.9%	4.2%	6.7%	4.8%	5.2%	6.5%
Indonesia	5.5%	10.3%	9.9%	7.8%	5.6%	6.2%	7.1%
Japan	2.1%	2.6%	3.9%	5.4%	3.5%	3.7%	5.2%
Korea	6.1%	9.2%	10.3%	13.2%	11.6%	12.1%	14.0%
Mexico	3.3%	3.7%	3.0%	4.0%	3.8%	3.8%	3.8%
Russia	4.7%	6.7%	4.9%	4.8%	4.5%	4.6%	4.9%
Taiwan	8.7%	7.7%	10.7%	15.3%	12.7%	14.0%	16.0%
Turkey	8.3%	6.6%	4.7%	5.2%	4.4%	4.7%	4.4%
United States	2.9%	3.6%	4.1%	4.6%	3.6%	4.3%	4.4%
Rest of World	5.7%	5.5%	6.1%	6.2%	5.8%	5.9%	6.0%
World	4.0%	4.6%	5.2%	5.8%	4.9%	5.3%	5.6%
B. **Relative size of the public procurement markets (ratios of EU public demand to trading partner's public demand)**							
EU27/USA	1.32	0.90	1.14	1.31	1.24	1.17	1.23
EU2/Japan	0.93	0.74	1.08	1.31	1.19	1.08	1.04
EU2/China	8.01	2.50	2.00	1.46	1.29	1.10	0.97
C. **Intra-EU ratios (ratios 4 of Table 19.1)**							
EU27 Intra	2.8%	3.1%	3.4%	3.7%	3.5%	3.8%	3.9%
EU2 Intra	2.1%	2.6%	2.9%	3.0%	2.9%	3.1%	3.3%

Source: OECD ICIO (June 2015); author's calculations.

20 International Cooperation on Public Procurement Regulation

Bernard Hoekman

20.1 Introduction

Discriminatory public procurement practices are high on the agenda of recent trade negotiations and agreements. Although a large portion of government expenditures is devoted to social spending and redistribution (e.g., transfer payments), government entities of all types spend considerable sums on a wide range of products—office supplies, equipment, buildings, roads, and so forth. In the United States (US) and the European Union (EU), government entities spend hundreds of billions of dollars/euros a year on goods, services, and works.[1] According to one estimate, some 70 percent of all central government expenditure is associated with a contract of some type. Estimates of the size of contestable public procurement markets across countries are in the range of 5–8 percent of GDP.[2] If many countries pursue discriminatory procurement practices, the end result for the world as a whole is likely to be inferior in welfare terms compared to a situation where governments purchase goods and services from the most efficient suppliers, whatever their origin.

A common goal of most procurement systems is to achieve "value for (taxpayer) money." The mechanisms to attain that goal often center on mimicking the working of the market by requiring procuring entities to seek competitive bids for contracts that exceed a given threshold. In practice, procurement outcomes may not minimize costs because of other policy objectives and constraints that apply to public procurement activities. One common objective is a desire to allocate taxpayer-provided funds to domestic firms, that is, to spend tax revenues at home (Branco, 1994)—in the process generating political support for politicians (Vagstad, 1995). Other reasons to spend at home may include safeguarding national supply capacity in important sectors (such as

[1] While public procurement comprises a huge market, it is less than the 10–15 percent of GDP that is often claimed (by, for example, the WTO—see <https://www.wto.org/english/tratop_e/gproc_e/gproc_e.htm> (accessed July 24, 2016)). This is because much government expenditure comprises items such as the civil service wage bill, social protection, pension payments, interest payments, and debt service. See Audet (2002) for a discussion on the size of public procurement markets.

[2] See <http://archive.transparency.org/global_priorities/public_contracting> (accessed July 24, 2016).

defense equipment) or to achieve social objectives (e.g., to support minorities or disadvantaged communities). Often the pursuit of such objectives results in discrimination against foreign suppliers. Examples include outright prohibitions on foreign sourcing (e.g., civil servants must fly national airlines), threshold criteria for foreign sourcing to be permitted (e.g., minimum cost or price differentials compared to local suppliers), and offset and domestic content requirements.

A prominent example of a country that has made, and continues to make, active use of government procurement to achieve multiple objectives is the US. The US has so-called "Buy America" requirements embedded in federal legislation that apply to public procurement contracts and maintains programs that give formal (legal) preferences to small and minority-owned businesses. Many other countries do the same. Chinese public procurement procedures require that purchasing entities give priority to products developed by domestic firms so as to support the development of innovative capabilities of indigenous firms (OECD, 2010).[3] Reflecting this reality, international development agencies such as the World Bank have for a long time allowed for domestic preferences in their procurement procedures.

Insofar as procurement policies favor domestic firms and products, they can be equivalent to trade barriers.[4] The market access dimension of discriminatory procurement practices is generally the main rationale for negotiating disciplines on government procurement in international trade agreements. Government procurement was excluded from the original General Agreement on Tariffs and Trade (GATT) in 1947. It was not until the completion of the Tokyo Round of multilateral trade negotiations in 1979 that a multilateral Agreement on Government Procurement (GPA) was negotiated. The GPA has changed in important ways since 1981, most notably in a steady expansion in coverage of national commitments. But what has not changed is that participation remains voluntary and is limited to mostly Organisation for Economic Co-operation and Development (OECD) member countries—three-quarters of the WTO membership has not joined the GPA. At the time of writing, there are a total of seventeen parties to the agreement, representing forty-five WTO members. Of these, the EU and its twenty-eight member states account for twenty-nine; European countries together account for 70 percent of the membership.[5] Most of the growth in GPA membership since 1981 has been associated with the gradual expansion of the European Economic Community into the European Union.

[3] The law requires that more than 30 percent of technology and equipment purchased with public funds be for domestic equipment and grants indigenous innovative products a price preference of 8 percent (OECD, 2010).

[4] This need not be the case however, as in some cases the policy may not have any economic effect—see, for example, Evenett and Hoekman (2005).

[5] Other European GPA members are Iceland, Montenegro, Norway, and Switzerland.

In addition to the GPA, preferential trade agreements (PTAs) often include provisions on procurement and, in practice, PTAs have become the main vehicle to extend procurement rules to non-GPA members. Although liberalization occurs on a preferential basis, this is also true for the GPA as GPA signatories may restrict market opening to other GPA members. There are over forty PTAs currently in force that include commitments to open access to procurement contracts on a bilateral or regional basis (Ueno, 2013; Rickard and Kono, 2014).

Export politics are a major factor driving negotiation of market access liberalization for procurement. Domestic constituencies (taxpayers, voters) may prefer to see tax revenues spent on local companies, but national firms and their workers may also have an interest in selling to foreign governments. A quid pro quo exchange of access to markets may allow a government to implement pro-competitive, efficiency-enhancing procurement reforms—as greater participation by foreign firms should in principle lower prices and increase choice and quality—while at the same time generating more economic activity and profits in the export sector. In this respect, the political economy of market access negotiations on procurement is the same as that for negotiations of trade policy more generally. Reciprocity is at the core of efforts to liberalize procurement markets, as the loss of a sheltered home market for domestic firms is offset by an increase in contracts won in trading partners. However, procurement liberalization is more complex than tariff reduction or removal as it involves regulatory regimes—the systems that a government puts in place to allocate contracts and seek to ensure that winning bidders are capable of delivering a product or a project, to reduce the scope for collusion or corruption, and to hold firms and procuring entities accountable for performance. How a government procures goods and services, including the decision to "make or buy," is a regulatory decision in the sense of a conscious act of social (and economic) ordering (Macdonald, 1985).

The regulatory features of procurement regimes are critical in ensuring that public objectives are pursued in an efficient manner. As in any area of regulation, different countries may pursue different approaches and there is no one-size-fits-all optimal procurement mechanism that is appropriate for all situations and all countries. For complex procurement projects involving long-lived infrastructure projects, new technologies, or outsourcing of public services, it may not be clear what the best approach is and there is much to be learned from international experience. Thus, in addition to addressing spillovers generated by *de jure* discrimination and differences in procurement regulation that result in *de facto* discrimination against foreign bidders, the inherent complexity of designing procurement systems to achieve public service objectives efficiently creates incentives for international cooperation.

This chapter briefly discusses prevailing approaches towards international cooperation on government procurement in trade agreements, focusing mostly on the GPA and recent PTAs, and some of the available evidence on the effectiveness of reciprocal negotiations in opening procurement markets to greater foreign competition. A key question for future multilateral cooperation in this policy area is whether mega-regional preferential trade agreements will do more than what has proven possible under the GPA in the last thirty years, and more generally whether PTAs will be a driver for the gradual multilateralization of disciplines on procurement processes. Evidence and experience to date suggests that from an economic welfare and market contestability perspective, what matters more are regulatory cooperation, transparency, and learning as opposed to negotiating market access liberalization commitments. The implication is that trade agreements should do more to promote regulatory cooperation in this policy area.

The chapter is organized as follows. Section 20.2 discusses the state of play in the WTO. Section 20.3 turns to PTAs and compares what has been (and may be) done in PTAs relative to the GPA. Section 20.4 discusses available evidence on the effectiveness of trade agreements in reducing the strong "home bias" that characterizes government purchasing decisions. Section 20.5 argues that international cooperation should center more on learning from the experience obtained on both sides of the Atlantic and in the rest of the world as to what works and why (and why not) in achieving the various objectives that are pursued through procurement. Section 20.6 concludes.

20.2 The WTO Agreement on Government Procurement

Art. III:8 GATT excludes procurement from the national treatment obligation; Art. XIII GATS does the same for services. It was only with the 1979 Tokyo Round Government Procurement Agreement that basic GATT obligations such as non-discrimination and transparency were extended to the purchases of goods by selected government entities. This agreement entered into force in 1981.[6] It bound only those countries willing to sign it—at the time only twelve countries plus the European Communities (EC),[7] which had ten members at the time,[8] for a total of twenty-two countries plus the EC. All signatories were OECD members. The Tokyo Round code was revised once in 1988 to include rental and leasing contracts, to increase the time allowed for submission of bids, and to require publication of information on winning bids (Stern and Hoekman, 1987). It was subse-

[6] See Blank and Marceau (1997) for a discussion of the genesis of the GPA.

[7] Austria, Canada, Finland, Hong Kong, Israel, Japan, Norway, Singapore, Sweden, Switzerland, the United Kingdom, and the United States.

[8] Belgium, Denmark, France, Germany, Greece, Ireland, Italy, Luxembourg, Netherlands, and the United Kingdom.

quently revised in the Uruguay Round of multilateral trade negotiations (1986–93) to expand coverage to include services and additional entities. This second revision of the GPA entered into force in 1996. Negotiations to further revise and expand the GPA commenced in 1997. After more than a decade of talks, the third revision of the GPA was adopted in 2012 and entered into force in April 2014.

20.2.1 COVERAGE

The GPA applies to "any measure regarding covered procurement, whether or not it is conducted exclusively or partially by electronic means" (Art. II:1). The concept of procurement covers all contractual options, including purchase, leasing, rental, and hire purchase, with or without the option to buy.[9] A positive list is used to determine what procurement is covered. The GPA applies *only* to entities and procurement opportunities listed by a signatory in Appendix I of the agreement. There are three "entity annexes" and three "product" annexes. Annex 1 lists covered central government entities; Annex 2 lists sub-central government entities; Annex 3 lists all other entities whose procurement is covered by the GPA;[10] Annexes 4–6 list covered goods, services and construction projects. Annex 3 is a catch-all category that includes entities such as utilities and railways. Entities listed in Annex 3 may be partially or totally privately owned. What constitutes a "government entity" is not defined anywhere in the agreement, reflecting a lack of consensus on what constitutes a public undertaking—more specifically, whether a former state-owned or controlled enterprise that has been privatized or that is subject to competition should be required to follow GPA procurement practices. Instead a pragmatic approach is taken—governments negotiate which entities are listed.[11] The entities listed in the first three annexes are subject to the rules and disciplines of the GPA if the value of the procurement exceeds certain specified thresholds, and the goods or services involved are not exempted from the coverage of the agreement.

[9] The GPA only applies to purchases of goods and services that are not intended for resale. If government entities engage in trade (buying and selling), the WTO disciplines on state-trading (Art. XVII GATT) apply.

[10] Only between a quarter and a third of all outlays are undertaken by central governments (OECD, 2015), highlighting the importance of including sub-national authorities in the GPA.

[11] Attempts by governments to remove a privatized entity from the Annex have been a recurring source of disagreement between GPA members. The Japanese government, for example, has unsuccessfully sought to remove railway companies following their privatization for over a decade (Messerlin, 2014). In the most recent revision of the GPA, an arbitration procedure was agreed to address such disagreements and determine if a privatized entity no longer is controlled by the government and should be removed from the GPA.

The total value of the above-threshold procurement by entities covered by the GPA has been estimated at US$1.6 trillion (European Commission, 2011).[12] This increased by some $80 billion following the expansion in the coverage negotiated in the third revision of the GPA, and will increase further as more countries join. The coverage of the GPA has expanded substantially over time—the value of covered procurement reported by GPA members in 1992 was only $62 billion (Hoekman, 1998).[13] The extent to which commitments made by a WTO member in the GPA apply to other GPA members is a function of whether the former considers that reciprocity has been achieved. Parties to the GPA have made reciprocity a core feature of their cooperation. There are many instances where one member does not apply specific commitments to another. For example, the US applies a higher threshold for construction contracts in the case of Korea because Korea maintains a higher threshold than other GPA members. The US does the same with respect to Japan for procurement by NASA and to Canada for procurement by electric utilities such as the Tennessee Valley Authority. The EU excludes the US from coverage of its services procurement commitments for sub-central governments and contracts issued by many of the utilities that the EU has scheduled. Reciprocity is measured in an apparently straightforward way—as the value of average procurement done by procuring entities. However, there are major differences in views regarding the "real" or effective coverage of GPA commitments that impact on exclusion decisions. These are also influenced by whether a country has specific industry export interests.

The main discipline imposed by the GPA on covered entities is non-discrimination—national and most-favored nation (MFN) treatment (Art. IV). The obligation extends not only to imports but also to subsidiaries of locally established foreign firms. The GPA thus goes beyond the GATT, which does not extend national treatment to foreign affiliates, and the GATS, which does so only if specific commitments to that effect have been made. Under the GPA, all foreign affiliates established in a signatory are to

[12] See also a 2011 WTO briefing note at: <https://www.wto.org/english/thewto_e/minist_e/min11_e/brief_gpa_e.htm> (accessed July 24, 2016). According to the reports by GPA parties (see <https://www.wto.org/english/tratop_e/gproc_e/gpstat_e.htm> (accessed July 24, 2016)), a large share of this reflects procurement by the US states, which adds up to some US$750 billion. Even if US state-level procurement is excluded, the reports to the WTO for the period 2008–10 indicate that the US is the largest GPA procurement market, representing over US$500 billion a year in above-threshold procurement. This compares to US$330 billion reported by the EU. In terms of absolute spending by government, including wages, transfers, and so on, the EU and the US are similar: US government spending in 2015 was some $6.5 trillion (<http://www.usgovernmentspending.com/> (accessed July 24, 2016)) or 36 percent of GDP, while EU governments spent €6.7 trillion in 2015 (48 percent of GDP), two-fifths of which was disbursed on social protection (<http://europa.eu/rapid/press-release_STAT-15-5318_en.htm> (accessed July 24, 2016)); see also OECD (2015).

[13] This figure is almost certainly below the actual above-threshold procurement in the early 1990s by GPA parties. More recent EU reports to the WTO suggests that in 1996 above-threshold procurement in the EU alone was €70.6 billion; see European Union (2013).

be treated the same as national firms. Moreover, signatories may not discriminate against foreign suppliers by applying rules of origin that differ from those they apply in general to MFN-based trade.

20.2.2 PROCUREMENT DISCIPLINES

The GPA does not explicitly require that procurement be competitive or that certain procurement methods be used. The objective of competitive procurement or "value for money" is not mentioned as an objective in the preamble of the agreement. In this regard, the GPA is quite different from the procurement guidelines that international development organizations and national governments apply. Instead, reflecting the market access focus of the WTO more generally, the emphasis is on transparency and on non-discrimination. Regarding the process of procurement, signatories are simply required to "conduct covered procurement in a transparent and impartial manner that is consistent with this Agreement, using methods such as open tendering, selective tendering and limited tendering; avoids conflicts of interest and prevents corrupt practices" (Art. IV:4). Open tendering is any method that allows any supplier to bid (e.g., international competitive bidding). Selective tendering is a method where only suppliers that satisfy specific criteria for participation may bid (usually prequalified suppliers). Limited tendering is non-competitive and usually involves a procuring entity approaching one or more potential suppliers of its choice.

The rules in the GPA regarding selective tendering are basically aimed at ensuring that foreign suppliers can demonstrate that they qualify and are not discriminated against in this regard (a necessary condition for this is that they can obtain the information needed, which explains why the GPA has numerous provisions that aim to ensure transparency, including publication requirements and minimum time periods for bid preparation). Limited tendering may only be used if no tenders were received or they were not responsive, if only one supplier can provide the good or service (e.g., artwork or products protected by intellectual property rights), for additional follow-on deliveries, in situations of extreme urgency, for commodities (the presumption being that there is a world price for standardized, homogenous goods), or for prototypes and winners of design contests (Art. XIII).

There is no explicit hierarchy of the three tendering methods mentioned in Art. IV and governments are free to use others, including negotiation (Art. XII GPA). The preference for competitive procurement methods is implicit in the agreement, reflected in requirements that notices of intended or planned procurement be published (including information on the mode of procurement, its nature and quantity, dates of delivery, economic and technical requirements, and amounts and terms of payment), in the conditions that must be satisfied if governments use limited tendering, and in the disciplines on treatment of tenders and contract awards. Art. XIII on limited tendering makes clear that competition is preferred by requiring that this method not be used to avoid competition among suppliers, to discriminate, or to protect domestic suppliers. Art. XV requires that entities award contracts to the supplier "determined to be fully capable of undertaking the contract" and who is either the lowest tender (if price is the sole criterion) or the tender that is most advantageous (in terms of the evaluation criteria set out in the notices or tender documentation).

The "fuzziness" regarding requirements for competitive bidding may reflect a desire of signatories to see membership of the GPA expand to include developing countries, but it also reflects differences in views among members on what the best approach is for specific types of situations. Until relatively recently, the basic presumption in the procurement literature was that the type of arms-length international competitive bidding procedures that are called for by the GPA and required in the EU (as well as institutions such as the World Bank) would, as a rule of thumb, generate efficient outcomes by awarding contracts to the lowest cost supplier able to meet the technical project requirements (e.g., Bulow and Klemperer, 1996; Bajari and Summers, 2002). However, especially for more complex projects, efficiency may require procuring entities to engage in negotiations and to interact with potential suppliers (see, for example, Estache, Guasch, and Trujillo, 2009; Bajari, McMillan, and Tadelis et al., 2009; Spiller, 2009). This is increasingly the practice in the US and has become one dimension of procurement in which the EU and the US differ, although the EU has also moved towards greater flexibility in procurement policies.

The standard approach in procurement has been to pursue so-called sealed bid auctions or open tendering in the language of the GPA. This contrasts with "competitive negotiations." Recent EU procurement directives make allowance for such negotiations, including "competitive negotiated procedures," where a set of firms is invited to submit tenders and the lowest cost firm is selected, and "competitive dialogue." The latter may be used where an entity knows what outcome it wants to achieve but does not know, and thus cannot specify in a call for tender, the means of satisfying its needs. This may include uncertainty as to the most appropriate legal structure and financing modalities for the project. However, the EU's procurement guidelines state that this approach is only to be used if a project is particularly complex and should be used exceptionally, whereas in the US it is employed much more regularly (Yukins, Chapter 9, this volume).[14] The advantage of competitive dialogue is that it permits companies to engage with procuring entities, allowing the latter to consider alternative solutions and technologies, and to determine what would be most appropriate in addressing their specific needs.

[14] In the EU context, competitive dialogue has tended to be used for public–private partnership infrastructure projects.

Such approaches are premised on there being oversight and accountability mechanisms to prevent collusion and corruption and thus are less appropriate in contexts characterized by weak governance. One reason why open tendering may be used by public entities even if it less efficient than other approaches is because it ensures that they can justify the process through which contracts are awarded. Procurement is subject to both political pressures ex ante and political scrutiny ex post—one motivation for the type of detailed "mechanical" procurement processes such as sealed bid auctions is that officials can protect themselves against ex ante pressures and against ex post criticism if it turns out that a supplier did not deliver a good product. Empirical analysis suggests that such "insurance" dynamics are observed in available procurement data and that they come at a cost to economic efficiency (Chong, Staropoli, and Yvrande-Billon, 2014).[15]

20.2.3 INDUSTRIAL POLICY

Price-preference policies, local content requirements, offsets, and similar discriminatory policies are widely used by governments to achieve equity or industrial policy goals. They are in principle prohibited by the GPA for all covered procurement as a result of the national treatment rule (Art. IV). However, exclusions are possible. Exhibit number one in this regard is the US, which, starting with the 1933 Buy American Act and the 1953 Small Business Act, imposes domestic content requirements. These are both general and specific, including federal procurement preferences for small businesses owned by women, service-disabled veterans, socially disadvantaged businesspeople, and entrepreneurs in historically underutilized business zones. There is an explicit target that almost a quarter of all federal procurement spending be allocated to small business (Yukins, Chapter 9, this volume).

As noted by Weiss and Thurbon (2006), the US pursues an aggressive policy of opening foreign markets while at the same time being very defensive when it comes to maintaining its local preference policies and its ability to use procurement as an industrial policy tool. This creates a problem for countries seeking to improve their access to US procurement opportunities while continuing to be able to use procurement as an instrument to achieve objectives other than "value for money" (Chen, 1995; Kattel and Lember, 2010). Art. V GPA gives developing countries the right to adopt or retain price-preference policies and offset requirements on a transitional basis, and to delay the implementation of any and all provisions other than MFN for up to three years (five years for a least-developed country, or LDC). Moreover, after accession, the GPA

[15] See also Chong, Staropoli, and Yvrande-Billon (2012).

Committee can be asked to extend the transition periods or approve the use of new transitional price preferences or offsets if there are "special circumstances that were unforeseen during the accession process" (Art. V:6). Existing signatories also commit themselves to "give due consideration to any request by a developing country for technical cooperation and capacity building" (Art. V:8). Some scope therefore exists for maintaining a price preference or offset policy—but this is time bound.[16]

There is little empirical research on the effectiveness of procurement discrimination in achieving the industrial and other policy objectives.[17] Tax/subsidy instruments are likely to be more efficient in assisting domestic target groups than procurement favoritism, but not necessarily. Governments may confront fiscal constraints that impede the use of such policies. Moreover, an advantage of procurement that favors specific domestic groups is that it can help the most efficient firms in that group (as they must compete for the contracts), whereas a subsidy to a region or a minority group will be less selective. There are arguments for using procurement to achieve industrial policy goals (e.g., Geroski, 1990; Edler and Georghiou, 2007; McMurtry, 2014). A key feature of procurement is that government is the buyer and thus in principle has greater control over outcomes than when "supply-side" industrial policies are used (e.g., subsidies of varying types). From a policy perspective the question is whether discrimination should be an element of "industrial procurement policy." The prima facie case for discrimination is not compelling, as much knowledge and know-how resides in foreign firms, suggesting that policy should seek to promote inward FDI and support local suppliers and vertical linkages, incentives to transfer knowledge, and so on.

A weakness of the GPA in this regard is the centrality of market access. The procurement process-related rules in the GPA are primarily aimed at supporting the market access goal and not necessarily designed to help governments achieve their

[16] In this respect, the GPA is inconsistent with the procurement guidelines of major development agencies. Thus, the World Bank permits a margin of preference in contracts awarded under international competitive procurement. For locally manufactured goods, the margin is 15 percent; in the case of works, 7.5 percent (the latter are limited to low-income countries). For goods, the determining criterion is not the nationality of the manufacturer but where the manufacturing takes place. In granting the preference, priority is first given to bids where goods have at least 30 percent local content, using domestic production facilities already in place before the bid was submitted, and then to goods that are produced locally as compared to imported goods. For works, bidders must show that they are locally owned to qualify for the preference (see Alexander and Fletcher, 2012). These provisions were maintained in the 2015 revision of the World Bank procurement procedures (World Bank, 2015).

[17] Little is known about the prevalence of price preferences in the allocation of contracts. A study of the use by borrowers from the World Bank of domestic price preferences—permitted under its procurement guidelines—found that during 1998–2009 a total of 153 such contracts were approved, with a value of \$280 million. This compares to a total of 57,000 contracts issued during this period. In only twelve contracts, worth \$4.3 million, did the preference alter the outcome of the bidding process (see Alexander and Fletcher, 2012).

procurement policy objectives.[18] The tension arises because not all countries agree on what type of procurement rules are the right ones for any given type of project—instead, the aim is to minimize the scope for *de jure* and *de facto* discrimination against foreign bidders. In this respect, the GPA differs in several important respects from the new WTO Agreement on Trade Facilitation (TFA). The TFA covers all WTO members, not just a subset, and includes a large number of disciplines that all countries agree make sense for them to implement. All TFA disciplines work towards the realization of one clear goal: to facilitate trade by reducing trade costs. However, it was also recognized that not all rules can be implemented at the same time and that some will require financial and technical assistance to implement. In the GPA context there is no common "positive" goal; instead the goal is "negative"—to abolish discrimination. Arguably the GPA might attract more members if more effort centered on identifying processes and policies that can help governments attain both value for money and industrial policy objectives more efficiently.

20.2.4 TRANSPARENCY AND REVIEW

The nature of procurement is such that unless rapid action can be taken, firms may not have an interest in contesting violations of the rules of the game. Accordingly, the GPA supplements the right of signatories to invoke the WTO dispute settlement mechanism—which is much too slow to be relevant for most real world procurement situations—with a requirement that members establish domestic review procedures. These bid-protest or challenge mechanisms should provide for rapid interim measures to correct breaches of the agreement or a failure of a government entity to comply with GPA commitments (Art. XVIII). Measures to preserve commercial opportunities may involve suspension of the procurement process, or compensation for the loss or damages suffered. This may be limited to the costs for preparing the tender or the costs relating to the challenge, or both.

The GPA members make no effort to monitor or report on the use and effectiveness of these mechanisms. The main focus of the GPA is on ensuring that firms have access to information on bid opportunities on a timely basis and are not placed at a disadvantage relative to local firms. Many provisions of the GPA concern transparency broadly defined. Much attention is given to requiring signatories to specify where information on procurement systems and opportunities will be published (including through

[18] Woolcock (2013) argues that trade agreements have not supported genuine diffusion of liberal procurement regimes because of the central focus on reciprocity (market access) rather than on efficiency considerations, and that this has been one reason why developing countries are not incentivized to join the GPA.

electronic means). These must be listed in Appendices II through IV to the GPA. There are detailed requirements for the publication of notices of intended procurement, the conditions for participation and permitted systems to ascertain that suppliers are qualified, technical specifications and tender documentation, minimum time periods to allow bids to occur, and regular reporting of statistics on procurement activities of covered entities.[19] Arts. IX, XVI and XVII GPA require among other things that GPA members explain why a supplier's application to qualify was rejected or why an existing qualification was terminated, and provide information necessary to determine whether a procurement was conducted in accordance with the GPA, including an explanation why a tender was not selected and the relative advantages of the successful supplier's tender.

The various transparency provisions are potentially the most important elements of the GPA from an economic welfare perspective. There are significant potential gains from disciplines that promote transparent procurement mechanisms, both in encouraging greater participation (competition) and in reducing the scope for corruption and rent-seeking. There is an increasing body of evidence, mostly of a case study nature, that documents the costs of non-transparency. For example, Auriol, Flochel, and Straub (2011) use a database of some 50,000 procurement contracts in Paraguay over a four-year period in the mid-2000s to both document and estimate the effects of rent-seeking in procurement in Paraguay. They show that corruption in procurement generated a far-reaching system of favoritism that inflated costs and created incentives to engage in directly unproductive rent-seeking activity—firms that obtained government contracts were estimated to have an average 35 percent excess rate of return relative to competing firms that sold to private clients (i.e., did not get public contracts). They argue that procurement favoritism and corruption helps explain the bad growth and export performance of the Paraguayan economy.[20] Noteworthy is that discrimination against foreign suppliers was not a prominent feature of procurement favoritism in Paraguay as most goods were imported—what was at stake was the allocation of contracts and the rents generated by inflated mark-ups resulting from bid-rigging and sole tendering (about a quarter of all contracts in 2004–5).

Even if procurement is not collusive or corrupt, a lack of transparency will reduce the number of firms able and willing to bid for public contracts, thus reducing competition and increasing costs. An important technological development in this regard is the

[19] The GPA does not define specific operational procedures such as whether bids should be assessed on price before determining whether bidders can satisfy technical requirements or whether technical selections should precede an assessment of price. In practice, such matters can have an effect on expected procurement costs (see, for example, Blancas et al., 2011).

[20] See also Straub (2014). Other contributions to this literature include Di Tella and Schargrodsky (2003), who assess the effects of reducing corruption in procurement in Argentine hospitals and Hyytinen, Lundberg, and Toivanen (2007), who analyze municipal cleaning contracts in Sweden.

increasing use of e-procurement platforms by government entities. These make it easier for firms to monitor and bid on procurement opportunities. They also facilitate monitoring of procedures used and outcomes of tenders by auditing departments and ministries of finance, as well as civil society organizations (CSOs) and researchers, as long as the data that are generated are compiled and made available.

20.3 Procurement and Preferential Trade Agreements

As mentioned, membership of the GPA is limited to mostly OECD countries. Almost no developing countries have joined in the last thirty years—Armenia being an exception. This has led GPA members to pursue procurement liberalization and policy disciplines in PTAs as an alternative route. There are dozens of PTAs that include chapters on government procurement policies (Bourgeois, Dawar, and Evenett, 2007; Anderson et al., 2011; Rickard and Kono, 2014).[21] Some of these are not far-reaching—they either simply reflect the prevailing status quo as regards procurement policy in signatories or limit commitments to best-endeavor type (non-binding, non-enforceable) language. However, many of the more recent vintage PTAs include extensive coverage commitments that are enforceable—including through domestic bid-challenge type mechanisms. The more ambitious PTAs go beyond commitments to remove discrimination in procurement and include language pertaining to the objectives of procurement policy (e.g., attaining best value for money); the use of new technologies, such as electronic procurement, provisions to create or strengthen national institutions that implement national procurement policies, and associated reforms; how to address likely changes in the scope of transactions falling under the disciplines of the agreement as a result of privatization of government entities; and calls for cooperation on the development of national procurement policies. Noteworthy as well is that some agreements define circumstances under which non-trade objectives of government procurement policy dominate, or are subservient to, market access (national treatment) disciplines (Bourgeois, Dawar, and Evenett, 2007).

The creation of a Single Government Procurement Market in the New Zealand–Singapore Closer Economic Partnership Agreement is an example of a bilateral agreement with very ambitious objectives. Article 46 of this agreement states that the parties agree to establish a single New Zealand/Singapore government procurement market through implementation of the APEC Non-Binding Principles on Government Procurement (relating to transparency, value for money, open and effective competition, fair

[21] Bourgeois, Dawar, and Evenett (2007) discuss government procurement provisions in twenty-seven regional agreements as of the mid-2000s.

dealing, accountability and due process, and non-discrimination), ensuring that suppliers from both countries can compete on an equal and transparent basis for government contracts, and establishing a mechanism to work towards "achieving the greatest possible consistency in contractual, technical and performance standards and specifications, and simplicity and consistency in the application of procurement policies, practices and procedures." Article 49 of this agreement specifies that all government entities are to apply the national treatment rule, promote opportunities for their suppliers to compete for government business on the basis of value for money, and avoid purchasing practices which discriminate or otherwise have the effect of denying equal access or opportunity to contracts.

This example illustrates that greater ambition can be achieved through PTAs than has been possible through the WTO. Of course, this is nothing new—the EU has long been the foremost example of a subset of WTO members agreeing to far-reaching disciplines on discrimination in procurement. What some of the recent PTAs reveal is that it is possible to go beyond the GPA. Deeper integration in some PTAs may be accompanied by complementary measures, including provision of technical and financial assistance to bolster institutional capacity in partner countries. Some PTAs establish timetables for deliberation and review processes. Rather than regard trade agreements such as the GPA as an opportunity to generate one-off reforms, the review provisions that are found in some of the newer PTAs suggest a more dynamic approach that is based on learning and interaction is both feasible and desirable (Evenett and Hoekman, 2013).

A feature of the procurement-PTA landscape is that it mostly involves GPA members and that non-GPA signatories tend to be geographically concentrated. The non-GPA members that are signatories of PTAs with a GPA member—the EU, the US, Japan, Singapore, Korea—tend to be either very open countries or nations that are already deeply integrated into the global economy (Mexico, Chile) or countries that are located in a specific region and that have concluded PTAs with the US (Central America, Colombia, Panama, Peru). Aside from Mexico, there are no procurement agreements with major emerging economies (e.g., Brazil, China, India, Indonesia, South Africa, or Turkey). The US has concluded PTAs with several Arab countries that cover procurement (Bahrain, Jordan, Morocco, and Oman); the CARIFORUM–EU Economic Partnership Agreement (EPA) includes procurement, but other EPAs do not, nor do EU PTAs with non-ACP countries.

The limited coverage of developing countries in recent vintage PTAs is somewhat surprising in that, in principle, a country that has not shown interest in joining the GPA might nonetheless be willing to include procurement in a PTA if this is accompanied by better access to the partner country for exports more generally. A feature of the GPA, and negotiations to accede to the GPA, is that such issue linkages are not possible—trade-offs and reciprocity is constrained to procurement. The fact that a broader set of concessions in other areas is part and parcel of agreeing to a broader PTA may help to explain why some non-GPA countries in Latin America have agreed to include procurement in recent PTAs. Presumably the same applies to countries such as Malaysia and Vietnam in the case of the TPP.

Over time such a process may result in the countries involved in PTAs deciding to join the GPA. One motivation to do so is to reduce potential trade diversion costs, a dynamic that Anderson et al. (2011) argue should over time result in a steady expansion of GPA signatories. In effect, PTAs would then become a path towards increasing GPA membership—helping to overcome a major weakness that is inherent in a "sector-specific" plurilateral agreement that countries are not convinced makes sense to sign onto as such. However, to date this dynamic does not appear to be very strong given that most developing countries do not include procurement in PTAs with the large players. The evidence to date suggests that PTAs are not much more effective in incentivizing developing countries to make international commitments on procurement policy than the GPA.[22] The fact that non-GPA countries made less far-reaching commitments in the TPP on procurement than GPA members is also illustrative in this regard.

Some recent PTAs seem to be used as mechanisms for GPA members to accord each other better treatment than they extend to other GPA members—for example, the bilateral PTAs between Canada, the EU, Korea and the US. This need not involve a broader PTA. The US and Canada concluded a bilateral deal on procurement in 2010 that ensured Canadian firms would be permitted to bid on contracts that they were excluded from under US law—a matter that became a major concern as a result of the large stimulus packages that were put into place by the US government in response to the 2008 financial crisis and that included "Buy American" provisions. The 2010 bilateral agreement involved Canada opening up potential procurement markets worth some C$25 billion to US firms as a quid pro quo for the US making Canadian firms eligible to bid on stimulus-funded projects.[23] The Canada–EU Comprehensive Economic and Trade Agreement (CETA) is noteworthy in for the first time permitting EU firms to participate in Canadian procurement opportunities at the sub-federal level. This includes provinces and territories, as well as contracts issued by provincial Crown Corporations, utilities, mass transit, municipalities, school boards, and publicly funded

[22] As discussed previously, procurement negotiations are driven by reciprocity, and market size considerations tend to determine the sectoral and entity coverage of liberalization commitments. As small countries have little leverage in inducing opening by large countries, it may be that the latter are also less inclined to do so. The US, for example, has limited coverage of procurement disciplines in the TPP context to the central government reflecting such considerations which were stressed by US industries (see, for example, National Foreign Trade Council and others, 2014).

[23] This issue was particularly important for Canadian companies as a result of the deep integration of the two markets. Many of the supply chains that produced the goods and services that were being procured with stimulus funds embodied Canadian content, making them ineligible for projects that used federal funds.

academic, health and social service entities (including corporations or entities owned or controlled by one of the preceding). CETA commitments on opening procurement were unprecedented and exceed those made in other Canadian PTAs.[24]

Canada had long resisted opening access to sub-federal level procurement. Its commitments under the GPA are limited to federal level procurement. As a result the EU, which has made commitments on sub-central procurement in the GPA, excluded Canada from eligibility to bid on such contracts in the EU. The overall package negotiated in CETA allowed the Canadian government to move forward where this was not feasible in the GPA context. This was made possible because of a general understanding that opening of provincial procurement was a key objective for EU participation in the negotiations,[25] in part reflecting the 2010 bilateral agreement between Canada and the US. Absent international trade agreements such as the GPA, CETA, NAFTA, and the 2010 bilateral with the US, foreign participation in procurement is limited through a Canadian Content Policy that is motivated by industrial policy objectives. The Canadian Content Policy applies to procurements carried out by Public Works and Government Services Canada that exceed C$25,000.[26]

In the case of the Trans-Pacific Partnership (TPP), most parties already had agreements with each other. Only three TPP countries are not GPA members or did not have an existing agreement with the US: Brunei, Malaysia, and Vietnam. US procurement commitments in PTAs have tended to be GPA-minus, in that partner countries are offered less than what the US has committed to under the latest iteration of the GPA.[27] The US has found it increasingly difficult to induce its states to participate in the procurement chapters of recent PTAs—only eight states plus Puerto Rico participated in the PTAs with Panama, Peru, and Colombia—and the US opposed including sub-central procurement in the TPP (Grier, 2014).[28] The TPP continues the pattern of being a PTA that is GPA-minus in terms of coverage of products and entities, with a set of process-related rules that are aligned with the GPA. Only five

[24] They may even imply that EU firms will have better access to Canadian procurement opportunities than do Canadian firms, given that there are various barriers to cross-border procurement within Canada. As a result, CETA may be a trigger for revising the existing Agreement on Internal Trade that aims to reduce such internal barriers.

[25] See, for example, <http://www.parl.gc.ca/HousePublications/Publication.aspx?DocId=5431905&File=87> (accessed July 24, 2016) and McMurtry (2014).

[26] Swick (2014); Canadian content is determined by NAFTA rules of origin criteria, with "NAFTA" replaced by "Canada" (see <https://buyandsell.gc.ca/policy-and-guidelines/supply-manual/annex/3/6> (accessed July 24, 2016)).

[27] Thus, the US has scheduled eighty-nine central government entities in the revised GPA, as compared to fifty-three in its early vintage PTAs (e.g., NAFTA and its PTA with Israel) and seventy-eight or seventy-nine in the CAFTA and the PTAs with Chile, Colombia, Korea, Morocco, Panama, and Peru (Anderson et al., 2011); see also Hufbauer and Moran, Chapter 10, this volume.

[28] See Kim (2009) for an analysis of the determinants of US state-level participation in trade agreements.

TPP signatories included sub-central procurement, but only to countries that do so as well. Non-GPA members Malaysia, Mexico, and Vietnam negotiated exceptions to key provisions disciplining the use of offsets and price preferences, and further limited the reach of procurement rules through high thresholds that apply for long transitional periods.

Turning to the TTIP, while it is unclear what will emerge, both the EU and the US are GPA members and both have made substantial commitments to opening access to their procurement markets. However, the EU does not give the US access to procurement of services by sub-central entities or to most procurement by utilities that it has scheduled (with the exception of electricity utilities), reflecting its view that the US needs to provide better access to ensure reciprocity (European Commission, 2013).[29] This view reflects Buy America provisions and the set asides for SMEs, and the fact that the US has only scheduled some of the procurement by thirty-seven of its fifty states, as well as only a very small number of municipalities (Woolcock and Grier, 2015). The discrepancy between EU and US commitments in the GPA reflects the very different institutional contexts. The federal government in the US has little say about what states can do in the area of procurement, and Congress has mandated the Buy American and other domestic content requirements. The EU is in a very different situation in that procurement liberalization is a core part of the objective of creating a single European market for goods and services, with EU legislation requiring that EU member states do not favor domestic firms when allocating public contracts.

A necessary condition for achieving significant further opening of the US procurement market will be an internal agreement among US states, the federal government, and the US Congress that there is enough on the table and that it is in the public interest to refrain from procurement discrimination—as was done in with Canada in the CETA context. It is unlikely that any such agreement will be forthcoming on the basis of a narrow market access calculus and the associated political economy dynamics. There may be better prospects for changing procurement policies gradually over time to reduce the reliance on favoritism and discrimination by pursuing greater joint activities that are centered on regular exchange of information, mutual learning based on experience with alternative approaches towards award of contracts, and the identification of specific practices that are more effective in attaining underlying policy goals. One reason for this view is that it is unclear whether market access-driven exchanges of commitments and the insistence on bilateral reciprocity have done much in practice to reduce "home bias" in procurement—or can do so.

[29] This perception also was an important factor underlying the proposal by the European Commission to permit EU procuring entities to discriminate against bidders from countries that are deemed to not offer reciprocity to EU firms for contracts exceeding €5 million; see European Commission (2012).

20.4 Do Trade Agreements "Work"?

To assess the impact of procurement disciplines in trade agreements—whether the GPA or PTAs—one needs data on procurement awards over time that distinguish between winning bids on the basis of the nationality of ownership of firms. Such data are not reported by most countries. Exceptions among GPA members include the EU, Japan, Korea, and Switzerland. In the absence of detailed statistics on actual awards by entity and type of procurement (goods, services, works), the only source of data that can provide an aggregate indication of government sourcing patterns are the national accounts and associated input–output tables. These data can be used to determine what share of government purchases are sourced from foreign-based suppliers. A measure of home bias can then be derived by comparing the behavior of governments with that of the private sector. The ratio between the public sector's share of imports in total public purchases and that observed for the private sector has been used in the procurement literature since the 1970s for this purpose (see, for example, Francois, Nelson, and Palmeter, 1997; Trionfetti, 2000).

The EU maintains a comprehensive database—the Tenders Electronic Daily (TED)—that includes data on all types of announcements of procurement opportunities in the EU. This database is also used to register the outcomes of calls for tender. TED includes information such as year and date of award, the type of award procedure used, type of product or service procured, the awarding authority, and the geographical location where the contract is performed. There is also information on the nationality of the contract winner. Combining this information permits an assessment of cross-border procurement in the EU as a whole and by EU member state. PricewaterhouseCoopers and Ecorys (2010) find that on average about 3 percent of the value of all procurement contracts in the EU are allocated to foreign companies, including other EU countries. GHK (2010) conclude that cross-border procurement accounts for 1.5 percent of all contracts awarded in the EU, and 3.7 percent of the total value of above-threshold contracts. As is to be expected, smaller countries engage in more cross-border procurement, while local and regional authorities engage less frequently in cross-border transactions than central government entities and public utilities. The latter have the highest share of foreign sourcing of covered entities. SMEs accounted for 60 percent of all above-threshold contracts awarded and around one-third of the value of all contracts during 2006–8 (GHK, 2010).

The picture changes if account is taken of subcontracting and bids that are won by subsidiaries of foreign companies. TED does not identify whether a winning bidder is an affiliate of a foreign firm, but this can be assessed by using other databases on business ownership and cross-holdings. An effort to do so by Ramboll Management Consulting and HTW Chur (2011) concludes that "indirect" cross-border procurement—that is, awards allocated to affiliates of multinational enterprises—is substantially greater than direct cross-border procurement. The study concludes that direct cross-border procurement in 2009 as measured by number of contracts and total value was 1.6 and 3.5 percent, respectively, as compared to 11.4 and 13.4 percent, respectively, for indirect cross-border procurement through foreign subsidiaries. These findings confirm the theoretical prediction that FDI is both a means of responding to (circumventing) discriminatory procurement policies as well as often being a more efficient channel through which to supply foreign governments,[30] for example for services and construction projects (see Evenett and Hoekman, 2005).[31]

Detailed data of the type compiled and reported by the EU are not collected by most countries.[32] As a result, assessments of the share of total government purchases that are allocated to foreign suppliers need to rely on more aggregate sources of information. Messerlin and Miroudot (2012) and Messerlin (2015) use the World Input-Output Database (WIOD) to calculate the public sector import penetration ratio for countries. These data indicate that for the EU27, this ratio averaged 4.5 percent for the 2007–9 period, somewhat higher but quite consistent with what is observed in the TED database. This suggests that WIOD can be used to compare procurement sourcing across countries.

Table 20.1 reports WIOD data for a selection of countries for three time periods, 1995–97, 2007–9, and 2010–11. A number of observations can be made. First, import penetration ratios for the US are very similar to those of the EU. Both of these behemoths import less than the world as a whole. This is to be expected given that large economies will be better able to source domestically from efficient firms. Second, the sample of non-GPA members source more from abroad than the GPA members during the first two periods—4.9 versus 3.9 percent in the mid-1990s, and 6.6 versus 5.7 percent on average during 2007–9. The same is true if the GPA members are compared to the world average. Third, there are large differences across countries, with Brazil only sourcing 3.5 percent from abroad, as compared to Korea at 13.2 percent in 2010–11. Fourth, GPA members see a more rapid increase in foreign sourcing during the 1995–2011 period: over time, there is convergence towards the average level of "openness" of the non-GPA members in the sample and the global average.

30 Note that although supplying foreign governments through affiliates or subsidiaries allows foreign companies to benefit from procurement opportunities, much of the economic activity associated with the contract may occur in the procuring country so that allocating a contract to a foreign investor may be consistent with the pursuit of industrial policy objectives.

31 See European Commission (2011) for an overall evaluation of EU procurement trends.

32 Exceptions include the US and Turkey. Fronk (2014) analyses available US data. Onur, Ozcan, and Tas (2012) analyze 90,000 government procurement tenders held in Turkey during the 2004–6 period. They find that the number of bidders significantly and negatively impacts on the procurement price—that is, greater competition associated with open tendering procedures reduces average prices. Moreover, tenders that are open to foreign participation (i.e., tenders involving international competitive bidding) further reduce prices paid.

Table 20.1 Government purchasing import penetration ratios, selected countries

1.			2.		3.	
	1995–97 simple average	2007–09 simple average	2010–11 simple average	% change 1995–2009 (simple average)	% change, 2008–1009	% change 2007/09–2010/11 (simple average)
Non-GPA-members:	4.	5.	6.	7.	8.	9.
Australia	5.2	5.7	5.6	9.6	−10.0	−1.8
Brazil	2.1	3.0	3.5	42.9	−12.1	16.7
China	3.4	6.4	4.6	88.2	−5.8	−28.1
India	4.2	6.1	6.5	45.2	1.6	6.6
Indonesia	7.9	7.9	7.4	0.0	−31.5	−6.3
Mexico	5.0	6.1	7	22.0	−12.3	14.8
Turkey	6.4	11.1	5.4	73.4	−9.8	−51.4
Average	**4.9**	**6.6**	**5.7**	**34.7**	**−13.4**	**−13.6**
GPA members:	10.	11.	**12.**	13.	14.	15.
Canada	4.4	4.7	4.3	6.8	0.0	−8.5
Extra-EU27	2.7	4.8	5.2	77.8	−13.7	8.3
Japan	2.1	4.3	4.4	104.8	−34.6	2.3
Korea	7.8	11.8	13.2	51.3	−17.1	11.9
US	2.8	4.3	4.6	53.6	−24.5	7.0
Average	**3.9**	**5.7**	**6.3**	**46.2**	**−18.0**	**10.5**
World	***4.4***	***6.9***	***6.6***	***56.8***	***−16.7***	***−5.1***
Memo: Intra-EU27	3.3	4.5	4.6	36	−6.3	2.0

Source: Calculated from data reported in Messerlin (2015), based on WIOD data.

Fifth, and particularly striking, in the post-2008 financial crisis period, the data indicate that for both GPA and non-GPA members import penetration dropped substantially between 2008 and 2009, suggesting a major shift towards domestic sourcing, which may reflect efforts by governments to support domestic economic activity. Import penetration falls *more* for GPA members, suggesting that in times of crisis governments tend to respond in a similar fashion, whether or not constrained by GPA disciplines. Noteworthy, however, is that the decline was much less for intra-EU procurement, which fell by only 6 percent, compared to the −18 percent for GPA members in the sample, and the −13.7 percent for extra-EU sourcing. Moreover, the sourcing ratio bounced back for the GPA members whereas for a number of the non-GPA countries import penetration did not recover. This ratio fell by over 13 percent post 2008 for the non-GPA members—with the greatest declines in Turkey (a drop of over 50 percent) and China

(−28 percent)—while it increased by 10 percent on average for the GPA members covered. Thus, the data are indicative of the GPA potentially playing a role in preventing backsliding and a shift in the allocation of fiscal expenditures towards domestic industries—behavior that governments naturally have stronger incentives to engage in during recessions and times of crisis.

While the sustained growth in foreign sourcing for GPA members is suggestive, these data tell us nothing about the effect of the GPA or PTAs, as they do not distinguish between different bilateral flows.[33] Clearly country-specific effects influence the simple averages reported in Table 20.1—for example, the very large drop in foreign sourcing by China and Turkey post 2009 (Messerlin, 2015)—but the fact that intra-EU public procurement penetration is below extra-EU ratios, below the world average, and shows a relatively low rate of growth suggest that non-discrimination disciplines for procurement may not have had much impact in changing behavior toward greater openness. The divergence in import penetration growth post 2008 suggests that EU and GPA rules may have played a role as a lock-in device. To determine whether this is the case requires more specific empirical analysis.

Signatories to the GPA are required to report data annually on procurement that is covered by their commitments (Art. XVI:4 GPA). Statistics to be provided include data on the number and total value of contracts awarded, broken down by entity and categories of products and services. The revised GPA that entered into force in 2014 differs from the 1994 GPA in an important respect. The 1994 GPA had a provision stating that, "[t]o the extent that such information is available, each Party shall provide statistics on the country of origin of products and services purchased by its entities. With a view to ensuring that such statistics are comparable, the Committee shall provide guidance on methods to be used" (Art. XIX:5(d)). The revised GPA no longer includes this language. Signatories are not encouraged to provide data on country of origin of winning bidders and, indeed, are not even encouraged, let alone required, to report whether a contract went to a foreign supplier. This makes it impossible to assess the effective level of foreign market access in the central government procurement markets of GPA signatories even if they were to comply with reporting requirements. Whether these data are collected is left to national data reporting requirements and the design of national databases. The revised GPA also differs from its 1994 predecessor in that members may—and are encouraged to—post data on procurement contract awards on a national website as opposed to sending specific reports to the WTO Secretariat on an

[33] To evaluate the effects of trade agreement disciplines on procurement behavior, it is necessary to control for general determinants of government purchasing decisions to assess if there is a distinct additional impact that can be attributed to an agreement. This requires, at a minimum, information on the share of all procurement that is awarded to foreign firms. To assess the effects of PTAs, it is necessary in addition to be able to distinguish between foreign firms from PTA partners and other foreign firms.

annual basis. In addition to the weaker reporting requirements, this implies that the role of the Secretariat as an "agent of transparency" is limited at best, as the Secretariat does not monitor implementation of the GPA or analyze the extant data.

Choi (2003), Evenett and Shingal (2006), and Shingal (2011, 2015) have used data reported by the few countries that provide statistics on the national breakdown of winning tenders on contracts that are covered by the GPA, focusing on Korea, Japan, and Switzerland, respectively. Choi (2003) finds that in the period following GPA accession there was no impact on the share of foreign supplied goods—indeed, this share fell between 1993–5 and 1996–8. Evenett and Shingal (2006) conclude that in 1999 in Japan, more contracts fell below the GPA thresholds than in earlier years, and that of the contracts that exceeded the threshold—and thus were covered by the GPA—a smaller share was awarded to foreign suppliers in 1998–9 than in 1990–1. Shingal (2015) undertakes an econometric analysis of the determinants of procurement sourcing over time in Japan and Switzerland, controlling for variables and factors that theoretical considerations suggest could impact on sourcing from foreign firms; these include the state of the business cycle, overall trade policy trends and trade costs, and political economy variables. He finds that GPA membership has no independent effect on sourcing behavior. The same conclusion emerges from an analysis of the extension of the GPA in 1996 to include services procurement. Using data reported by Japan and Switzerland, Shingal (2011) concludes that the share of services contracts awarded to foreigners declined over time for both countries. The import penetration ratio for public purchases of services fell relative to that of the private sector for similar categories of services.

There is even less empirical research on PTAs than there is on the GPA. In part this reflects the absence of bilateral procurement sourcing statistics. Rickard and Kono (2014) assess the effects of forty-three PTAs that include procurement, focusing on overall import penetration. They conclude the PTAs have no impact on the procurement elasticity of trade (the ratio of imports to government demand). Thus, PTAs are no different from the GPA in impacting on procurement behavior. Fronk (2014), focusing only on PTAs that have been negotiated by the US (including the GPA) and on the effects of these agreements on the behavior of US procuring entities, comes to a different conclusion. Using a gravity regression framework, he finds a statistically significant positive effect of procurement trade agreements, generating an increase of 150 percent in the number of contracts won annually by foreign bidders. However, this is only equivalent to an additional 135 contracts—reflecting the fact that the mass of contracts (some 98 percent) is awarded to US firms. Thus, there is an effect, but because the baseline level of foreign awards is small, the magnitude of the impact is also relatively small. Because US data on the nationality of winning bidders only starts in the mid-1990s, this analysis cannot consider the fact that the countries that mostly win procurement bids in the US (Canada, the EU, Japan) are original members of the GPA

(1981) and that much of the procurement that is analyzed has already been subject to disciplines for a long period of time. It is therefore not necessarily the case that the positive sourcing effect attributed to the agreements is in fact due to them as opposed to other factors.[34]

The upshot of available research is that, at least during the 1990s, the GPA seems to have done little to increase market access for foreign suppliers. Moreover, there is also little evidence that PTAs have had an impact on changing procurement sourcing. While the WIOD data discussed previously suggests a trend of greater foreign sourcing in the 2000s, this is observed for both GPA and non-GPA members. The extant analyses suggest that the increase in foreign sourcing observed in the WIOD data up until the 2008–9 crisis is driven by factors other than the market access features of trade agreements. There are many possibilities. One could be technology—a decline in information and search costs through the use of e-procurement and internet platforms. Another is a more general shift in policy toward greater openness to trade and to FDI that is independent of procurement policy. An increase in the global stock of FDI and two-way flows of FDI may result in foreign affiliates winning more bids and relying more on imports than do domestic firms. Yet another possible driver is change in procurement regimes and processes, such as the shift toward greater use of competitive negotiation and dialogue. These may be associated with more intensive scrutiny of government behavior and performance, tighter budget constraints, and greater use of outsourcing and public–private partnerships. A common feature of these possible drivers is that they center on changes in incentives as opposed to top-down international market access liberalization commitments.

There is little research on this question. An exception is Kutlina-Dimitrova and Lakatos (2014), who use statistics for the 2008–12 period reported in the TED database to investigate the determinants of foreign sourcing by EU public entities. They find that the probability of a contract being won by a foreign-based supplier depends positively on the value of the contract awarded and negatively on the number of bids. They also find that GDP per capita (wealth) and a country's overall openness as captured by the trade-to-GDP ratio are positively associated with the probability of cross-border procurement. In addition, they show that measures of the quality of the "behind-the-border" investment climate such as the prevalence of entry-restricting product market regulation, barriers to FDI, and the share of public enterprises in the economy all have a statistically

[34] One potential reason for Fronk's finding is that US PTAs may constrain the use of trade policy more than other agreements do. Cole and Davies (2014) note that governments have different instruments through which to favor domestic firms, including standard trade policies. They find that optimal tariffs can be more protectionist and welfare-reducing than an optimal procurement price preference, suggesting that restricting the latter when countries retain the freedom to use tariffs—most developing countries—may reduce welfare. The implication is that the focus of policy should be on more generally constraining the ability of governments to use trade policy.

significant negative impact on the probability of cross-border procurement. These findings, in conjunction with the empirical analyses that find no effect of trade agreements after controlling for other determinants of government behavior, suggest there may be only a limited payoff from the type of reciprocal procurement market access focus that is central to the GPA and PTAs. Other policies—more general opening towards trade and FDI, pro-competitive regulation of product markets, and the business environment—may have a greater impact.

Where agreements may have a stronger impact is as mechanisms to prevent "backsliding." This is suggested by the trends observed in the WIOD data. Rigorous econometric analysis is required to determine to what extent policy commitments do in fact explain the differences in import penetration trends that are reported in Table 20.1.

20.5 **Procurement Market Access Negotiations versus Regulatory Cooperation**

What does the foregoing suggest regarding the design of international cooperation on procurement? The premise of what follows is threefold: (i) a narrow market access reciprocity focus that is limited to procurement is unlikely to have much of an effect; (ii) the revealed preference of governments to use different types of procurement contracts for industrial policy objectives and to allocate most contracts locally needs to be taken seriously; and (iii) rules of the game matter, including lock-in provisions (policy bindings) and associated intuitional and good governance dimensions of procurement processes.

One reason why market access reciprocity arguably has limited returns is that many contracts that are issued by procuring entities concern products that are difficult to supply on a cross-border basis. Construction and services of many kinds will generally have to be supplied locally, and there may be good reasons for procuring locally even if a good is tradable. If the products procured are intangible (services) or there are problems in monitoring and enforcing contract compliance, discrimination can increase the likelihood of performance by suppliers. The best (economic) case for discrimination revolves around situations where there is asymmetric information—for example, difficulties in monitoring the performance of a contractor if buyer and provider are located far from each other—or there is a need to offer a firm quasi-rents in order to increase the probability of contract compliance through the threat of losing repeat business (Evenett and Hoekman, 2013). Moreover, geographic proximity may be a precondition for effectively contesting procurement markets—making some products, in particular services, in essence non-tradable. Problems of asymmetric information and contract compliance may imply that entities can economize on monitoring costs by choosing suppliers that are located within their jurisdictions. In turn, this will make it more difficult for foreign firms to successfully bid for contracts, even if the goods or services involved are tradable and in the absence of formal discrimination. Such rationales have been explored extensively by Laffont and Tirole (1993), and many of the underlying technical arguments are summarized and synthesized in Breton and Salmon (1995). The policy issue that arises in such situations is whether there are barriers against establishment (FDI) by foreign suppliers, as this is a precondition for them to bid for/supply contracts (Evenett and Hoekman, 2005).

Turning to industrial policy, there are good arguments for why targeted procurement, through which the government creates demand for new or innovative technologies, may be superior to policies that target the supply side, such as R&D subsidies. Geroski (1990) notes that targeted procurement can both stimulate innovation and allow firms to learn by doing. Insofar as governments care about the nationality or ownership of the firms that acquire and control such technologies, discrimination will be a feature of the associated procurement process. However, it is not obvious that this will be optimal in terms of increasing the likelihood that the new desired technologies or products are in fact generated. If control is an objective, then contracts can be structured so as to ensure that the government will be able to determine how the results of what is being financed can be used/made available. If one of the objectives is to utilize and develop local capacity and expertise, then this can be specified as well, implying that firms bidding for the contract need to have a local presence. Discrimination against foreign firms in such "public procurement for innovation" is therefore neither needed nor likely to be desirable in attaining the innovation objective.[35]

The pursuit of non-economic objectives by governments can have very different implications for economic efficiency. In principle, policy should target directly the source of problem at hand: lack of economic opportunities for minority groups, regional economic wealth differentials, market failures, and so forth. For example, take the case where a government awards a tender to an SME instead of to a large company that submitted a lower cost bid because of an SME preference policy. It may be more effective and efficient if, instead, the government were to address the factors that impede the ability of SMEs to compete with larger firms. This can of course be due to different factors, ranging from financial market imperfections to excessively burdensome administrative requirements that are too costly for SMEs to meet. Dealing with these constraints directly as opposed to using an SME preference policy will be more efficient (Evenett and Hoekman, 2013).

These considerations have direct relevance for the design of government procurement policies and international cooperation. Governments may be more inclined to pursue a

[35] For discussions of the use of procurement to achieve innovation objectives, see Edler and Georghiou (2007).

non-discriminatory procurement policy if they understand that other policies are available that are more effective in attaining specific "non-procurement" goals—and that using these will also generate more efficient procurement outcomes. An implication is that the main payoff in terms of creating greater competition may be through other policy reforms. Such other policies include procurement rules, as distinct from removing market access restrictions ("buy national" rules). As is the case with regulation more generally, procurement policy does not lend itself easily to negotiation—for example, seeking to agree that all contracts of type *X* must be procured through process type *Y*. This explains the emphasis in the GPA on transparency and on principles that signatories agree to abide by when engaging in procurement. However, the GPA disciplines are motivated by the market access objective. The goal is not to support learning by regulators, procuring entities, and the public at large (voters) regarding policies and approaches that are effective, efficient in attaining different types of objectives, and generate fewer negative spillovers for trading partners.

International cooperation and fora that support diffusion of knowledge and learning about the effects of alternative procurement approaches have tended to be piecemeal and ad hoc. Woolcock (2013) notes that the Tokyo Round GPA originated in Paris, and was based on a set of principles developed by an OECD working group over the course of a decade of talks (see, for example, Winham, 1986; Blank and Marceau, 1997)[36] and that other innovations in rule-making on procurement, such as incorporating a bid-challenge provision, derived from the Canada–US FTA. Initiatives by the EC were at the source of other changes to the GPA, such as the inclusion of utilities and local government procurement in the GPA, reflecting EU disciplines that were adopted as part of the effort to establish a single European market. However, all such examples of diffusion were very much centered on market access. Starting in the mid-1990s, efforts were made to agree to more general good practices, specifically deliberations on potential disciplines on transparency that were launched at the WTO's Ministerial in Singapore in 1996. These provided a forum for interaction with other entities such as the multilateral development banks, CSOs such as Transparency International, and the UN. These discussions were not successful in generating agreement to initiate negotiations on specific rules, in large part because developing countries were not convinced that

[36] As described in Winham (1986), formal international discussions on government procurement in the OECD started in 1962, when Belgium and the UK brought a formal complaint to the OECD against the US Buy American Act. A working party of the OECD Trade Committee was constituted to hear the complaint, but its report was subsequently deflected by US pressure into a general review of government procurement in member countries. This led to an OECD Secretariat summary of government procurement practices and a short draft text in 1967 on guidelines for government procurement. From then until the matter was transferred to the Tokyo Round in 1976, the issue of government procurement was under discussion in the OECD, but the major trading powers were unable to agree on rules of the game on a stand-alone basis. Adding the subject to the Tokyo Round agenda permitted the issue linkage that made a deal possible.

discussions on transparency would not morph into market access talks. Given that greater transparency is likely to be welfare-improving for a variety of reasons, including by facilitating participation of domestic firms in procurement and reducing scope for corruption and collusion, this was an unfortunate development. It illustrates the challenge confronting efforts to prompt institutions like the WTO, which are designed to promote market access liberalization, to become foci for deliberations on good practices and venues for sharing information and learning from experience.

The last revision of the GPA included agreement to launch work programs and engage in deliberation on several subjects:[37] (i) best practice with respect to measures and policies to support the participation of SMEs in government procurement; (ii) promoting the use of sustainable procurement practices; (iii) safety standards in international procurement; (iv) restrictions and exclusions in parties' coverage commitments under the agreement; and (v) improving procedures to collect and report statistical data relating to the GPA. In addition to these areas, GPA members also agreed to conduct work in the future on public–private partnerships and their relationship to procurement covered by the GPA, and the advantages and disadvantages of developing common nomenclature for goods and services and standardized notices.

A number of these work program areas are focused on procurement practice as opposed to primarily revolving around market access. Their adoption suggests recognition by GPA members that there is value to learning from each other and to identifying good practices. Greater use of the institutional mechanisms that are part of trade agreements to perform a knowledge platform function (Hoekman and Mattoo, 2013; Hoekman, 2015) could increase the value of membership. To be most useful, such deliberation should involve non-parties to the GPA and not be limited to GPA members.

The need/potential payoff of greater effort to identify good practices is substantial. Yukins (Chapter 9, this volume), emphasizes how little the US does to learn from experience elsewhere. He mentions Section 508 of the US Rehabilitation Act, which requires that all information technology bought by the government be accessible to persons with disabilities, and that the EU has been implementing requirements in this area well. No effort was made to coordinate US and EU standards for accessibility; indeed, US regulators explicitly rejected using international technical norms when the Section 508 standards were originally published. More generally, Yukins argues that change in US federal procurement rarely includes consideration of international norms or best practices. Members of Congress, their staff and regulators (e.g., the Federal Acquisitions Regulatory Council) have no ready means or mandate to exchange

[37] See <https://www.wto.org/english/tratop_e/gproc_e/gpa_wk_prog_e.htm> (accessed July 24, 2016).

information with foreign stakeholders or regulators, or to consider international best practices.[38]

The World Bank has at times been a focal point for international dialogue, but as a lending institution it has tended to be more concerned with ensuring that value for money is achieved for its own projects as opposed to focusing on learning from procurement practices around the world and innovations in these practices. Specialized international fora that have focused on procurement policies and practices, such as UNCITRAL, have tended to emphasize legal aspects as opposed to procurement practice, seeking to design legislation rather than exchanges and learning from experience.[39] The type of deliberation that could make a concrete difference in improving procurement practices is illustrated by the Public Procurement Knowledge Exchange Forum, an initiative that was started in early 2000s and that is co-sponsored by multilateral development banks supporting countries in Europe and Central Asia,[40] and the consultative process that was undertaken by the World Bank during 2013–14 and that led to the adoption of a new World Bank Procurement Framework. This new framework moves the World Bank away from a rigid one-size-fits-all approach. Instead, it aims at supporting the delivery of better procurement outcomes by increasing the number of approaches and methods that can be used, reflecting experience and innovations, both technical (e-procurement) and regulatory (mechanism design). A central feature of post-2015 World Bank procurement practice is the Project Procurement Strategy for Development (PPSD). This is an instrument to determine the appropriate procurement process for each project that will be (co-)financed by the Bank, allowing for a significant degree of flexibility—including competitive dialogue, e-procurement, and so on. Moreover, there will be a much stronger emphasis on complementary capacity-building and implementation-related assistance than there has been in the past, including for CSOs and the private sector.

The new World Bank Procurement Framework promotes incremental steps toward greater cooperation with other agencies as well. So-called alternative procurement arrangements by borrowers may be used, for example delegating procurement for investment projects to other development banks, bilateral donor agencies, or UN organizations when it makes sense to do so. Noteworthy is the inclusion of language

[38] Yukins (2015) also points out that while regulators are required to consider the market impact that significant rules may have, in practice the required review is often ignored in rule-making regarding procurement; See also Yukins and Cora (2013).

[39] The work of the OECD on procurement has tended to focus on fighting corruption and improving the integrity of procurement practices.

[40] The aim of the forum is to promote and foster regional cooperation in public procurement, good governance, and anticorruption in the Western Balkans, Central Asia, and neighboring countries. Each year, the Knowledge Exchange Platform participants discuss issues relating to improving public procurement, and report on recent achievements and future plans in each of their countries (see <http://www.worldbank.org/en/events/2015/06/09/11th-public-procurement-knowledge-exchange-forum#4> (accessed July 24, 2016)).

allowing for implementation of procurement under the systems of signatories to the GPA. Given that the GPA disciplines are only a framework, such delegation to the national systems of a GPA member is conditional on an assessment by the Bank of the implementation capacity of the procuring entities concerned. As there are virtually no World Bank borrowing countries that are parties to the GPA, this provision will not have much of an impact in the short run, but it is a significant step toward greater coherence, and may constitute a small additional incentive for developing countries to join the GPA. Much more significant from an operational perspective is the acceptance of procurement regimes of other development banks and agencies, and the emphasis on bolstering implementation capacity. However, while the new World Bank procurement framework now embodies a presumption that the systems of GPA members satisfy its good procurement practice criteria, conditional upon certification by the Bank to that effect, we have yet to see flexibility in the other direction—that is, a willingness of GPA members to embrace what major players in procurement, such as the World Bank, consider reasonable practice, including the open-ended acceptance of domestic local content and price preferences.

Gelderman, Ghijsen, and Schoonen (2010) argue that greater interaction and engagement between stakeholders is needed for improved compliance with procurement rules. Such interaction is important in developing a common view on what constitutes good procurement practice, and should include consideration and discussion of evolving best practices of purchasing in the private sector. There are elements and examples of collaborative interactions among procurement practitioners, including communities of practice such as the one that has been supported by multilateral development banks in Europe and Central Asia. The OECD and APEC have provided opportunities for practitioners to interact, as does the GPA Committee, but there is much more that could be done in this regard, both within and outside of the WTO. This could include a regular global procurement forum, regional knowledge platforms along the lines of those already existing for the Balkans and Central Asia, and greater interaction with the private sector. The work programs that were agreed by the GPA Committee could become building blocks for non-market access-centric deliberations and be opened to participation by any interested WTO Member. Similarly, there is much more that could be done by PTA members to increase dialogue and interaction on procurement practices, and to engage the WTO membership more generally on lessons of experience in cooperating on procurement matters.

20.6 Concluding Remarks

Many countries have yet to commit to procurement disciplines in a trade agreement, whether in a PTA or through membership of the GPA. After more than thirty years, the GPA only applies to one-quarter of the WTO membership. A number of countries that are not GPA members have expanded foreign access to their procurement markets through PTAs, but the extent to which these arrangements will make a difference in country coverage is limited—most of the nations involved in the mega-regionals are members of the GPA or have already made procurement commitments in bilateral PTAs.

Trade agreements are instruments to negotiate market access opening on a reciprocal basis. The objectives of international cooperation on procurement have centered on reducing discrimination against foreign companies as well as identification of better policy (the efficiency and effectiveness of different instruments and practices in achieving specific objectives, approaches that reduce negative international spillovers). The extant research suggests that the market access focus of trade agreements may not achieve much in reducing home bias and de facto discrimination. The available statistics suggest there is not much difference between the sourcing behavior of GPA and PTA members and countries that have not made commitments on procurement in a trade agreement. The data indicate that in recent years, foreign sourcing has increased on average in many countries—for the world as a whole by some 50 percent since the mid-1990s. This suggests that other factors are more important than trade agreements in reducing home bias. These factors may encompass technology, more general improvements in economic governance, greater openness to trade and investment, and learning and innovations in the design of procurement processes and the supply of public goods and services. An implication is that there may be a higher payoff from focusing international cooperation on procurement regulation on identifying good practices and improving economic policies more generally as opposed to what historically has been the dominant focus of trade agreements—namely, market access. That said, the difference in trends in foreign sourcing that are reported by the WIOD database suggests that procurement agreements may play a role as a lock-in mechanism that constrains a shift away from efficient public purchasing in times of economic pressure. This is clearly a subject that deserves further in-depth empirical research.

The focus of trade negotiations on attaining narrowly defined reciprocity in incremental procurement market opening commitments may also detract from using trade agreements as a platform for improving procurement practices. It is the latter that matters for citizens, officials, and economic actors, as the practices through which government entities procure products and works help determine the efficiency with which public goods are supplied. Stakeholders should care about procurement practices in other countries not just because of specific market access concerns, but because market access goals are likely to be better served through cooperation and engagement on procurement policy more generally. Such collaboration will also be beneficial by helping to identify better practices and improve national procurement policy.

It is an open question whether trade agreements can be designed to do more to assist governments and stakeholders to cooperate on identifying good procurement practices. The experience in the WTO with the effort to launch a discussion on transparency in procurement as opposed to market access illustrates that it is difficult to separate the latter from a discussion on the substance of procurement practices. That said, it must be recognized that much of what is in the GPA deals with procurement practice, even if the underlying motivation for most of what is embodied in the GPA is to safeguard and expand market access opportunities for foreign bidders. Transparency in particular is a critical input and precondition for better procurement and may be the most important international regulatory cooperation objective that should be pursued in the context of trade agreements. There is a strong case for enhancing the use of now well-established trade mechanisms for this purpose, including emulation of procedures that have been put in place by WTO Committees dealing with product standards (SPS and TBT), where members can table specific trade concerns that are raised by product regulations of a given country.

Trade agreements more generally may have important indirect impacts on improving procurement outcomes by reducing trade and investment barriers. The more open markets for goods and services are to foreign competition, the less costly discriminatory procurement regimes are likely to be from a welfare perspective, as firms will be operating in a more competitive environment. The importance of FDI as a channel to contest procurement opportunities may imply a high payoff from efforts to use trade agreements to reduce barriers against FDI. The same is true of trade policy more generally, given that governments may seek to use other instruments to favor local firms, including tariffs, which may well be more distorting than procurement discrimination via price preferences (Branco, 1994; Cole and Davies, 2014). Thus, assessing the effects of trade agreements on procurement outcomes must go beyond a narrow consideration of whether procurement per se is included and center on the extent to which agreements promote a pro-competitive environment.

ACKNOWLEDGMENTS

I am grateful to Patrick Messerlin and Robert Wolfe for helpful discussions and comments on an earlier draft.

REFERENCES

Alexander, M. and Fletcher, C. 2012. "The Use and Impact of the Bank's Policy of Domestic Preferences." Review of World Bank Procurement Policies and Procedures, Background Paper.

Anderson, R., Müller, C., Osei-Lah, K., Pardo de Leon, J., and Pelletier, P. 2011. "Government Procurement Provisions in Regional Trade Agreements: A Stepping Stone to GPA Accession?" In S. Arrowsmith and R. Anderson (eds), *The WTO Regime on Government Procurement: Challenge and Reform*. Cambridge: Cambridge University Press, 561–656.

Audet, D. 2002. "Government Procurement: A Synthesis Report." *OECD Journal on Budgeting* 2(3): 149–94.

Auriol, E., Flochel, T., and Straub, S. 2011. "'La Patria Contratista': Public Procurement and Rent-Seeking in Paraguay." CEPR Discussion Paper No. 8282.

Bajari, P., McMillan, R., and Tadelis, S. 2009. "Auctions versus Negotiations in Procurement: An Empirical Analysis." *Journal of Law, Economics and Organization* 25(2): 372–99.

Bajari, P. and Summers, G. 2002. "Detecting Collusion in Procurement Auctions." *Antitrust Law Journal* 70: 143–70.

Blancas, L., Chioda, L., Cordella, T., Oliveira, A., and Várdy, F. 2011. "Do Procurement Rules Impact Infrastructure Investment Efficiency?" World Bank Policy Research Working Paper No. 5528.

Blank, A. and Marceau, G. 1997. "A History of Multilateral Negotiations on Procurement: From ITO to WTO." In B. Hoekman and P. C. Mavroidis (eds), *Law and Policy in Public Purchasing: The WTO Agreement on Government Procurement*. Ann Arbor, MI: University of Michigan Press, 31–55.

Bourgeois, J., Dawar, K., and Evenett, S. 2007. "A Comparative Analysis of Selected Provisions in Free Trade Agreements." Report for DG Trade Chief Economist Office, European Commission.

Branco, F. 1994. "Favoring Domestic Firms in Procurement Contracts." *Journal of International Economics* 37: 65–80.

Breton, A. and Salmon, P. 1995. "Are Discriminatory Procurement Policies Motivated by Protectionism?" *Kyklos* 49: 47–68.

Bulow, J. and Klemperer, P. 1996. "Auctions versus Negotiations." *American Economic Review* 86(1): 180–94.

Chen, X. 1995. "Directing Government Procurement as an Incentive of Production." *Journal of Economic Integration* 10: 130–40.

Choi, I. 2003. "The Long and Winding Road to the Government Procurement Agreement: Korea's Accession Experience." In W. Martin and M. Pangestu (eds), *Options for Global Trade Reform: A View From the Asia-Pacific*. Cambridge: Cambridge University Press, 249–69.

Chong, E., Staropoli, C., and Yvrande-Billon, A. 2012. "Auctions versus Negotiations in Public Procurement: The Role of Public Scrutiny" (available at: <http://www.iese.edu/en/files/1b_Chong_tcm4-80399.pdf> (accessed July 24, 2016)).

Chong, E., Staropoli, C., and Yvrande-Billon, A. 2014. "Auction versus Negotiation in Public Procurement." In E. Brousseau and J. M. Glachant (eds), *The Manufacturing of Markets: Legal, Political and Economic Dynamics*. Cambridge: Cambridge University Press, 120–42.

Cole, M. and Davies, R. 2014. "Foreign Bidders Going Once, Going Twice... Protection in Government Procurement Auctions." Institute for International Integration Studies Discussion Paper No. 441, Trinity College, Dublin.

Di Tella, R. and Schargrodsky, E. 2003. "The Role of Wages and Auditing during a Crackdown on Corruption in Buenos Aires." *Journal of Law and Economics* 46(1): 269–92.

Edler, J. and Georghiou, L. 2007. "Public Procurement and Innovation—Resurrecting the Demand Side." *Research Policy* 36: 949–63.

Estache, A., Guasch, J., and Trujillo, I. 2009. "Multidimensionality and Renegotiation: Evidence from Transport-Sector Public-Private Partnership Transactions in Latin America." *Review of Industrial Organization* 35(1): 41–71.

European Commission. 2011. "Impact and Effectiveness of EU Public Procurement Legislation." Commission Staff Working Paper SEC (2011) 853.

European Commission. 2012. "Proposal for a Regulation of the European Parliament and the Council on Access of Third-country Goods and Services to the Union's Internal Market in Procurement and Procedures Supporting Negotiations on Access of Union goods and Services to the Public Procurement Markets of Third Countries." COM (2012) 124 final, March 21.

European Commission. 2013. "EU–US Transatlantic Trade and Investment Partnership: Public Procurement" (available at: <http://trade.ec.europa.eu/doclib/docs/2013/july/tradoc_151623.pdf> (accessed July 24, 2016)).

European Union. 2013. "Statistics for 2008 Reported Under Art. XIX:5 of the Agreement." GPA/102/Add.7, WTO, Geneva.

Evenett, S. and Hoekman, B. 2005. "Government Procurement: Market Access, Transparency, and Multilateral Trade Rules." *European Journal of Political Economy* 21(1): 163–83.

Evenett, S. and Hoekman, B. 2013. "International Disciplines on Government Procurement." In A. Lukauskas, R. Stern, and G. Zanini (eds), *Handbook of Trade Policy for Development*. Oxford: Oxford University Press, 851–76.

Evenett, S. and Shingal, A. 2006. "Monitoring Implementation: Japan and the WTO Agreement on Government Procurement." In S. Evenett and B. Hoekman (eds), *Economic Development & Multilateral Trade Cooperation*. London: Palgrave Macmillan, 369–93.

Francois, J., Nelson, D., and Palmeter, D. 1997. "Government Procurement in the U.S.: A Post-Uruguay Round Analysis." In B. Hoekman and P. Mavroidis (eds), *Law and Policy in Public Purchasing*. Ann Arbor, MI: University of Michigan Press.

Fronk, J. 2014. "Do Procurement Agreements Work?" Georgetown University, Department of Economics (available at: <http://jaredfronk.wix.com/jobmarket> (accessed July 24, 2016)).

Gelderman, K., Ghijsen, P., and Schoonen, J. 2010. "Explaining Non-Compliance with European Union Procurement Directives: A Multidisciplinary Perspective." *Journal of Common Market Studies* 48(2): 243–64.

Geroski, P. A. 1990. "Procurement Policy as a Tool of Industrial Policy." *International Review of Applied Economics* 4(2): 182–98.

GHK. 2010. "Evaluation of SME Access to Public Procurement Markets in the EU." Report for DG Enterprise and Industry, September.

Grier, J. 2014. "TPP and TTIP Government Procurement Negotiations." *America's Trade Policy*, September 16 (available at: <http://americastradepolicy.com/guest-blog-tpp-and-ttip-government-procurement-negotiations/#.VaC_-fmqpBc> (accessed July 24, 2016)).

Hoekman, B. 1998. "Using International Institutions to Improve Public Procurement." *World Bank Research Observer* 13(2): 249–69.

Hoekman, B. 2015. "Fostering Transatlantic Regulatory Cooperation and Gradual Multilateralization." *Journal of International Economic Law* 18(3): 609–24.

Hoekman, B. and Mattoo, A. 2013. "Liberalizing Trade in Services: Lessons from Regional and WTO Negotiations." *International Negotiation* 18(1): 131–51.

Hyytinen, A., Lundberg, S., and Toivanen, O. 2007. "Politics and Procurement: Evidence from Cleaning Contracts." HECER Discussion Paper No. 196.

Kattel, R. and Lember, V. 2010. "Public Procurement as an Industrial Policy Tool: An Option for Developing Countries?" *Journal of Public Procurement* 10(3): 368–404.

Kim, D. H. 2009. "Local Politics and International Agreement: The Case of Government Procurement in the U.S. States." *State Politics and Policy Quarterly* 9(1): 79–101.

Kutlina-Dimitrova, Z. and Lakatos, C. 2014. "Determinants of Direct Cross-border Public Procurement in EU Member States." Chief Economist Note 2014-2, DG Trade, Brussels.

Laffont, J. and Tirole, J. 1993. *A Theory of Incentives in Procurement and Regulation*. Cambridge, MA: MIT Press.

Macdonald, R. 1985. "Understanding Regulation by Regulations." In I. Bernier and A. Lajoie (eds), *Regulations, Crown Corporations and Administrative Tribunals*. Toronto: University of Toronto Press, 81–154.

McMurtry, J. 2014. "The Political Economy of Procurement." *Canadian Public Policy* 40(1): S26–S38.

Messerlin, P. 2014. "The Japan–EU Negotiations on Railway." ECIPE Policy Brief No.3/2014.

Messerlin, P. 2015. "How Open are Procurement Markets?" EUI Working Paper RSCAS 2015/89, November.

Messerlin, P. and Miroudot, S. 2012. "EU Public Procurement Markets: How Open Are They?" GEM Policy Brief, July.

National Foreign Trade Council and others. 2014. "Letter to USTR Michael Froman on Procurement in TPP," September 14 (available at: <http://www.nftc.org/default/trade/Trade%20Association%20Procurement%20Letter%20090314.pdf> (accessed July 24, 2016)).

OECD. 2010. *OECD Reviews of Innovation Policy: China*. Paris: OECD Publishing.

OECD. 2015. "Size of Public Procurement." In *Government at a Glance 2015*. Paris: OECD Publishing, 136–7 (available at: <http://dx.doi.org/10.1787/gov_glance-2015-42-en> (accessed July 24, 2016)).

Onur, I., Ozcan, R., and Tas, B. 2012. "Public Procurement Auctions and Competition in Turkey." *Review of Industrial Organization* 40: 207–23.

Price-Waterhouse-Coopers and ECORYS. 2010. "Public Procurement in Europe: Cost and Effectiveness."

Ramboll Management Consulting and HTW Chur. 2011. *Cross-Border Procurement above EU Thresholds*. Copenhagen: Ramboll.

Rickard, S. and Kono, D. 2014. "Think Globally, Buy Locally: International Agreements and Government Procurement." *Review of International Organizations* 9(3): 333–52.

Shingal, A. 2011. "Services Procurement under the WTO's Agreement on Government Procurement: Whither Market Access?" *World Trade Review* 10(4): 527–49.

Shingal, A. 2015. "Econometric Analyses of Home Bias in Government Procurement." *Review of International Economics* 23: 188–219.

Spiller, P. 2009. "An Institutional Theory of Public Contracts: Regulatory Implications." In C. Menard and M. Ghertman (eds), *Regulation, Deregulation, Reregulation: Institutional Perspectives*. Cheltenham: Edward Elgar.

Stern, R. and Hoekman, B. 1987. "The Codes Approach." In J. M. Finger and A. Olechowski (eds), *The Uruguay Round: A Handbook for the Multilateral Trade Negotiations*. Washington, DC: The World Bank, 59–66.

Straub, S. 2014. "Political Firms, Public Procurement, and the Democratization Process" (available at: <http://idei.fr/doc/wp/2014/wp_idei_817.pdf> (accessed July 24, 2016)).

Swick, B. 2014. "Public Procurement in Canada." In *Practical Law: Multi-Jurisdictional Guide for Public Procurement*. Thomson-Reuters (available at: <https://www.mccarthy.ca/pubs/Public_procurement_in_Canada_Overview_June_2014.PDF> (accessed July 24, 2016)).

Trionfetti, F. 2000. "Discriminatory Public Procurement and International Trade." *The World Economy* 23(1): 57–76.

Ueno, A. 2013, "Multilateralising Regionalism on Government Procurement." OECD Trade Policy Paper No. 151.

Vagstad, S. 1995. "Promoting Fair Competition in Public Procurement." *Journal of Public Economics* 58(2): 283–307.

Weiss, L. and Thurbon, E. 2006. "The Business of Buying American: Public Procurement as Trade Strategy in the USA." *Review of International Political Economy* 13(5): 701–24.

Winham, G. 1986. *International Trade and the Tokyo Round Negotiation*. Princeton, NJ: Princeton University Press.

Woolcock, S. 2013, "Policy Diffusion in Public Procurement: The Role of Regional Trade Agreements." *International Negotiation* 8(1): 153–73.

Woolcock, S. and Grier, J. 2015. "Public Procurement in the Transatlantic Trade and Investment Partnership Negotiations." CEPS Special Report No. 100. CEPS, Brussels (available at: <http://www.ceps.eu/system/files/SR100PublicProcurementandTTIP.pdf>(accessed July 24, 2016)).

World Bank. 2015. "World Bank Procurement Regulations for Borrowers," Washington, DC (available at: <https://consultations.worldbank.org/consultation/procurement-policy-review-consultations>(accessed July 24, 2016)).

Yukins, C. and Cora, J. 2013. "Considering the Effects of Public Procurement Regulations on Competitive Markets." *Government Contractor* 55(9): 64.

INDEX

Note: Due to space limitations many of the main entries can also be found under particular countries along with entries pertaining specifically to each country. The countries are as follows:- Armenia, Australia, Brazil, Canada, China, European Union, India, Israel, Mexico, New Zealand, South Africa, Turkey, and United States